Henry Wallace's

1948 Presidential Campaign

and

the Future of Postwar

Liberalism

Henry Wallace's 1948 Presidential Campaign and the Future of Postwar Liberalism

THOMAS W. DEVINE

The University of North Carolina Press
Chapel Hill

The paper in this book meets the guidelines for permanence and
durability of the Committee on Production Guidelines for Book Longevity
of the Council on Library Resources. The University of North Carolina Press
has been a member of the Green Press Initiative since 2003.

Library of Congress Cataloging-in-Publication Data
Devine, Thomas W.
Henry Wallace's 1948 presidential campaign and the future of
postwar liberalism / Thomas W. Devine. — First edition.
pages cm
Includes bibliographical references and index.
ISBN 978-1-4696-0203-5 (hardback)
1. Wallace, Henry A. (Henry Agard), 1888–1965. 2. Political campaigns—
United States. 3. Presidents—United States—Election—1948 4. United States—
Politics and government—1945–1953. I. Title.
E748.w23d48 2013
973.918—dc23
2012046984

17 16 15 14 13   5 4 3 2 1

An earlier version of chapter 1 was published as
"The Communists, Henry Wallace, and the Progressive Party of 1948,"
Continuity: A Journal of History, no. 26 (Spring 2003): 33–79.
Used with permission.

To
William E. Leuchtenburg
and
Farzin Avaz

CONTENTS

PREFACE

In the election of 1948, Henry A. Wallace set out to challenge conventional wisdom. At a time when both major parties supported President Harry Truman's foreign policy, Wallace claimed that militarists and international bankers had taken over the government and were deliberately leading the nation down the road to war. Though public opinion polls showed that most Americans viewed the Marshall Plan as a humanitarian aid program that would produce stability and economic recovery in Europe, he denounced it as a reactionary Wall Street plot designed to corner foreign markets, suppress civil liberties, and split the world into two "warring camps." At a time when the vast majority of the population feared the spread of communism and considered the Soviet Union the primary impediment to world peace, Wallace insisted that domestic fascism and American imperialism posed the greater threat. American "monopolists," he maintained, had manufactured the Cold War to divert attention from their global grab for power and profits. As the government took steps to clamp down on the activities of the American Communist Party, Wallace denounced the "Red Scare" and welcomed Communists into his campaign, arguing that it would violate the principles of Jeffersonian democracy to turn them away. And, as southern segregationists split from the Democratic Party rather than accept a platform that supported racial equality for African Americans, Wallace journeyed into the heart of Dixie and proclaimed that segregation was sin.

Inevitably, the Progressive nominee drew criticism for his unorthodox beliefs. Throughout 1948, many journalists and politicians dismissed Wallace as a bitter and confused man, full of contempt for President Truman and easily manipulated by the cynical "agents of the Kremlin" who surrounded him. Cartoonists portrayed him as marionette, mindlessly delivering the latest Moscow line while Stalin pulled the strings. Many of the nation's newspaper editors assailed him as an "appeaser," and even a traitor, who preached the insidious doctrine of "peace at any price." Conservative columnists ridiculed the Iowa native as a "corn-fed mystic," the unbalanced author of the bizarre "Guru letters," and as an eccentric who had a long history of consorting with charlatans and falling hard for their save-the-world schemes. Southerners made Wallace the target of eggs, tomatoes, and a torrent of ugly invective, while many northern liberals considered him the unwitting ally of "reaction."

Less impassioned critics viewed Wallace as a well-intentioned but astonishingly naive figure, a utopian who was more comfortable dreaming about the future than confronting the problems of the present. The 1948 presidential campaign, they believed, had brought out the worst in him. His crusading fervor hardened into dogmatic intolerance; his always emotionally charged oratory grew reckless and strident; his populist suspicion of concentrated economic power devolved into a dubious "devil theory" of Wall Street conspirators plotting to destroy civilization. And, most notably, his tendency to reduce human history into a zero-sum struggle between good and evil kept him from comprehending the moral ambiguities that would characterize international relations in the postwar era—a shortcoming, it should be noted, that Wallace shared with many of the American leaders he criticized.

Wallace's admirers saw an entirely different person. To them, he was the rightful heir to Franklin D. Roosevelt and the New Deal, a man of principle who would have been president if not for the meddling of a small group of "party bosses." Wallace was the people's advocate who would never have heeded the counsel of international financiers and warmongers; the fighting liberal who would have scorned compromise and courageously advanced the march of progressivism; the peacemaker who would have reached an accord with Stalin rather than throwing him on the defensive with "get tough" posturing; the world leader who would have ensured that a "democratic revolution," and not a "Cold War," emerged from the carnage of World War II. In short, Wallace was the symbol of all that might have been had not the "forces of reaction" so cruelly betrayed their postwar dreams.

In 1948, however, Wallace elicited not only wistful regret for the path not taken but also hope for a better future. Progressives found his glittering promises of "peace and abundance" infinitely more attractive than the grim talk of "Soviet aggression" and "communist totalitarianism" emanating from the Truman White House. At the beginning of the campaign, his supporters expressed confidence that regardless of who won the presidency in November, they were building a "people's party" that would eventually achieve the objectives Wallace had laid out. Their self-styled "Gideon's Army," small but determined, would undercut the entrenched power of Wall Street and the military that they believed dominated the two major parties. Once the voters returned progressives to positions of power, the Cold War would thaw and Wallace's heralded "Century of the Common Man" could at last commence.

These men and women had supported the most "advanced" aspects of Roosevelt's New Deal, but they considered themselves independent liberals, not loyal Democrats. Most were well-educated, middle-class professionals who became active in politics to fight on behalf of the "common man." Though many expressed a vague preference for some form of social democracy, they rejected the anticommunism of Norman Thomas's Socialist Party. Indeed, anticommunism of any kind was anathema to them, for they were convinced it undermined progressive unity and thereby strengthened the "reactionaries." Unlike many Popular Front liberals who had also embraced a philosophy of "no enemies to the left" during the 1930s, however, the "Wallaceites" of the postwar period were not uncritical admirers of either the Soviet Union or the American Communists. Their concern was not "revolution" but war. Accordingly, they tended to avoid discussions concerning conditions within the Soviet Union and emphasized instead the need to allay Soviet insecurities by urging Washington to pursue friendly relations with Moscow. Anti-Soviet criticism, they reasoned, could only provoke further insecurity and increase the chances of war. Similarly, they did not esteem the motives and methods of the CPUSA, but neither did they closely scrutinize them. Acknowledging that Communist rhetoric occasionally went too far, postwar Popular Front liberals nonetheless accepted party members as allies so long as the Communists expressed themselves willing to help advance the progressive agenda. Otherwise, these independent liberals preferred not to know exactly what the Communists stood for, how they operated within their own party or within progressive organizations, or even who among the "progressives" were in fact concealed Communists. Pursuing such lines of inquiry amounted to "red-baiting," which was a tool of "reaction." In this sense, Wallace supporters were not "fellow travelers." The latter, though not officially members of the Communist Party, understood and knowingly advanced Communist arguments, submitted themselves to Party "discipline," and kept Party secrets—even if, as some wags put it at the time, they were "cheating the Party of its dues." The Wallaceites deeply resented such a moniker, for it made them creatures of the Party and denied them the political independence on which they prided themselves. In 1946 and 1947, liberals of this persuasion saw in Wallace one of the few remaining progressive politicians who shared their values and spoke out forcefully in their defense. Their initial support for, and in many cases ultimate disillusionment with Henry Wallace the man, constitutes part of postwar liberalism's broader story.

The leaders of the American Communist Party, though they, too, supported Wallace's candidacy, did not see either him or his ideals in such an exalted light. Concerned primarily with halting Washington's move toward implementing an anti-Soviet foreign policy, they seized on Wallace's commitment to pursuing friendlier relations with Moscow and pronounced him the candidate of "peace"—a label Wallace gladly embraced. Likewise, they viewed the third party not as a means for reviving and expanding the New Deal agenda, but as an "anti-monopoly coalition" that would impede what the Communists believed was a conscious "drive" toward war on the part of Wall Street and the U.S. government. The CP's function in this coalition would not be to dominate it—as some charged at the time—but to play a "leading role" in order to ensure that the Party and its priorities were not subordinated to those of the "bourgeois liberals."

Historians' assessments of Wallace's 1948 campaign have acknowledged the Communist presence in the Progressive Party, but they tend either to downplay it or to oversimplify the nature of its influence. In a 1952 letter to Curtis MacDougall, a journalism professor who was beginning work on a history of the Progressive Party, Henry Wallace wrote, "I am convinced that a book on the Party should make its central theme the way the Communists infiltrated the Party."[1] MacDougall did not write that book. His exhaustive, three-volume chronicle of Wallace's 1948 campaign dismisses the role of the Communist Party as insignificant. As a result, it misses the opportunity to explore exactly how the CP came to support a third party; how it influenced Wallace's decision to run as an independent candidate; how it operated within the Progressive Party at the national, state, and local levels; and how non-Communist Progressives grappled with the issue of CP participation in their movement. Most subsequent treatments of the Progressive Party have followed MacDougall's lead. The account that follows instead takes up Wallace's challenge, looking closely at these subjects in an effort to explore the Communists' role within the Progressive Party and to assess how (and how well) a liberal-Communist political alliance actually worked.

Historians sympathetic to Popular Front liberalism have admired such alliances in theory, but they have shied away from examining them too closely in practice. Instead, they lament the fate of Popular Front liberalism in the late 1940s, attribute its eclipse to anticommunist "hysteria," and posit various "opportunities missed" as a result. Some more sophisticated works blame the Popular Front's demise on the unwarranted attacks of anticommunist liberals who allegedly abandoned more radical approaches in favor of gaining legitimacy by embracing the Cold War consensus. Yet such interpretations romanticize Popular Front liberalism, exaggerate its real and potential influence in postwar politics, and largely misunderstand the motives and goals of anticommunist liberals. They also assume that Popular Front liberalism, due to its refusal to exclude the Communists from the "progressive" coalition, was in some way more "left" or "social democratic" than so-called Cold War liberalism. Given the acute hostility toward social democracy expressed in all of the CP literature during this period, this assumption is hard to sustain. Indeed, more broadly, such scholars misrepresent the views of American Communists who stated quite clearly after 1945 that they were abandoning the kinds of liberal-Communist alliances that had characterized the wartime years and that had come to be associated with the discredited leadership of their deposed general secretary, Earl Browder. Enamored with the idea of and sentiments expressed in a "progressive" culture and its alleged potential for producing political outcomes more to their liking, many scholars of Popular Front liberalism fail to assess critically the practical difficulties that made the liberal-Communist alliance so problematic. More persuasive are those historians, including Alonzo Hamby, Robert Zieger, and, more recently, Jennifer Delton and Eric Arnesen, who have argued that liberals' continued alliance with the Communists into the late 1940s was not only a recipe for political disaster but an inherently unstable arrangement because of irreconcilable ideological and ethical differences.[2]

The present account also draws on evidence unavailable to MacDougall and other previous chroniclers of the Progressive Party. These materials, including the National Security Agency's decrypted Venona cables and declassified documents from both U.S. and Soviet archives, provide a clearer picture of the extent and nature of American Communists' influence within the leadership of the Wallace movement and of the Soviet Union's attitude toward the third party. Ironically, though much of the new evidence has demonstrated the close connections between Moscow and the CPUSA, in the case of the Wallace campaign we find two oddities: first, the leadership of the CPUSA did not receive clear orders from Moscow—and likely misinterpreted the signals it did receive; second, the Soviet Union was ambivalent at best about the third party and took only the most perfunctory steps to assist it.

Beyond assessing the efficacy of Popular Front liberalism in the postwar period, this account examines and evaluates the views of Henry A. Wallace and his Progressive Party supporters on the issues of foreign policy and civil rights. Scholars writing in the immediate aftermath of the Vietnam War, convinced that one could draw a straight line from the Truman

Doctrine to the United States' involvement in the Indochinese conflict, hailed what they considered Wallace's prescient critique of containment and regretted his failure to win a fair hearing. Less sympathetic scholars have concluded that Wallace's thinking was imprecise; his speeches full of vague abstractions; his knowledge of foreign affairs surprisingly limited; and his assessment of Soviet behavior and intentions profoundly wrong. Furthermore, they note, in contrast to other Cold War critics like the columnist Walter Lippmann, Wallace did not offer any plausible alternative to the bipartisan foreign policy. The end of the Cold War and the release of new documentation offer an opportunity to take a fresh look at both Wallace's criticisms of U.S. foreign policy and at the political and diplomatic contexts in which he leveled them. Though the record is still incomplete, particularly on the Soviet side, enough new information has come to light to cast serious doubt both on Wallace's benign attitude toward Stalin's intentions and on his dark, conspiratorial view of the Truman administration. Newly available Soviet sources do confirm Wallace's position that Moscow's behavior was not as relentlessly aggressive as many believed at the time, but not his assertion that the Soviet government shared his desire for "One World" in which capitalism and communism would engage in "friendly competition." Regarding the civil rights struggle, Wallace emerges neither as a heroic trailblazer nor as a Communist dupe. Rather, he was a transitional figure who retained the assumptions of the 1930s regarding the class-based nature of racism while embracing the emerging postwar consciousness that characterized segregation in moral terms as "sin." His memorable campaign swing through the South—as well as black and white southerners' responses to it—reveals the shortcomings of arguments that assume racism only masked economic interest and that a civil rights movement based in the pro-Communist left and in the labor movement, rather than in black churches and neighborhood organizations, was a politically viable option in the late 1940s.

In sum, a reexamination of Wallace's 1948 "quixotic crusade" from a post–Cold War perspective paints a far more complicated picture of "Gideon's Army" than historians, both sympathetic and critical, have painted heretofore.

Place Devine in Khr / Haynes vs. Schrecker debate
  - they illustrate the divide + Devine in Khlv/ Haynes
                                                    camp
  - Schrecker not even cited in book
  · Suggest it's time to move beyond this tired paradigm
  - How might Devine's efforts been better spent adding

Henry Wallace's

"bottom up" to his analysis
  - He is just the person to add nuance to this debate

1948 Presidential Campaign

and

the Future of Postwar

Liberalism

Looking @ sources - a "top down" analysis
  - Manuscript collections of SGD, ER, + McCllurm
    prove these were PP well versed in CP foreign policy
    agenda
  - Devine discusses the notion that PP were interested
    in - or perhaps capable of - analyzing CP policy

Not really offering new interpretations, merely
new support for old ideas.
  - Devine: CP responsible for left/ liberal split
    Schrecker: liberals responsible for left/ liberal split
                                        p. 6

1

A FRENCHMAN NAMED
DUCLOS

The Communists and the Origins
of the Progressive Party

The origins of Henry A. Wallace's Progressive Party occasioned heated debate among political partisans throughout the presidential campaign, and they remain a topic of some controversy. Beginning in 1948, critics of the Progressive Party contended that the Communists, on orders from Moscow, had conceived the idea, organized the party according to a "detailed time-table," chosen Wallace as the candidate, and pressured him relentlessly until he accepted his predetermined role. In their view, the Wallace candidacy was an entirely synthetic, top-down venture that the Communists had created with the sole purpose of serving Soviet foreign policy. Accordingly, they portrayed non-Communist Progressives—including Wallace himself—as a motley collection of innocent dupes consciously or unconsciously doing the Kremlin's bidding by dividing and discrediting American liberalism and thus paving the way for the victory of "reaction."[1]

Not surprisingly, Wallace supporters told a different story. In *Gideon's Army,* for some time considered the standard historical account of the Progressive Party, Curtis MacDougall dismissed such an account of the party's origins as a fantastic conspiracy theory. According to MacDougall, the Communists decided to support the third party only after Wallace had committed to run for president and after independent liberals—like MacDougall himself—had laid the groundwork for his candidacy. The New

Party, he maintained, was the inevitable outgrowth of liberals' profound disillusionment with the Truman administration and the only vehicle available for "progressives" to combat the rightward drift of the nation's politics. The Communists might have jumped on the Wallace bandwagon for their own reasons later on, but they had little to do with launching the party.[2]

A close look at the relationship between the evolution of the postwar American Communist Party (CPUSA) line and the origins of Wallace's party offers little support for MacDougall's conclusion. The Communists played a vital role in promoting sentiment for a third party, and, through their influence in Popular Front organizations, saw to it that "independent political action" became the preferred tactic for promoting the "progressive" cause. Their tireless efforts transformed inchoate dissatisfaction into the organized political force that became the Progressive Party. Yet accounts that portray the Communist Party (CP) as painstakingly following a complex blueprint to a preordained conclusion are equally distorting. Much as the American Communists would have liked to have had one, there is no evidence of a Moscow-directed master strategy. Rather, uncertainty, hesitation, internal tensions, and the pursuit of contradictory objectives characterized this period of the Party's history. Major shifts in emphasis came in response to promptings from abroad, but the Party's leaders had no guarantee that they were correctly interpreting these signals. Indeed, individual Communist leaders routinely exploited this uncertainty to advance their own ideological agendas, claiming that they had Moscow's sanction. Moreover, for all the Communists' public bravado about the scientific nature of Marxist-Leninism, their course of action during the immediate postwar years was decidedly ad hoc. Local circumstances and the interplay of personalities often proved determinative in setting day-to-day policy. Even in the development of longer-term strategy, ideological formulations occasionally provided after-the-fact justification for decisions made hastily and amid unfavorable, fluid circumstances. Finally, critics' charges that the Communists' backing of a third party constituted a nefarious plot to produce an electoral triumph for the most reactionary elements in the Republican Party do not stand up to scrutiny. Though the American Communists undoubtedly supported Wallace's candidacy because they believed it served the interests of Soviet foreign policy, Party literature demonstrates that they genuinely feared "Republican reaction" as much as the anticommunist liberals who condemned the third party. This was no replay of 1932, when the German Communists had failed to oppose the rise of Hitler in the hopes that full-blown fascism would pave the way for a Communist revolution. Concern over splitting the "progressive forces" (and thereby isolating the Party) weighed so heavily on Communist leaders that as late as September 1947, they appeared to have abandoned the third party project. In short, the Communists' role in the origins of the Progressive Party was both more extensive than MacDougall acknowledged and more complex than some of the Party's critics have allowed.

■ The April 1945 publication of the so-called Duclos Letter in *Les Cahiers du Communisme*, the theoretical journal of the French Communist Party (PCF), precipitated a major crisis for the American Communists, sending them down the torturous road that would eventually lead to the Progressive Party. The article, which appeared under the byline of Jacques Duclos, a senior PCF functionary, sharply rebuked Earl Browder, the longtime leader of the CPUSA, for presuming that "peaceful coexistence" between Communists and capitalists would continue indefinitely. Duclos maintained that Allied declarations of wartime cooperation, such as the diplomatic agreements reached at the 1943 Teheran Conference, in no way sanctioned a "political platform of class peace" or guaranteed congenial relations between capitalist and socialist nations into the postwar period. He stated flatly that the "achievement of socialism [is] impossible to imagine without a preliminary conquest of power." Here the article took direct aim at Browder's "Teheran thesis," which predicted the "establishment of harmony between labor and capital" and, more significantly, declared that "Europe, west of the Soviet Union, will probably be reconstituted on a bourgeois-democratic basis and not on a fascist-capitalist or Soviet basis." According to Duclos, such a blueprint for the postwar world constituted a "notorious revision of Marxism" and sowed "dangerous opportunist illusions." The French leader also denounced Browder's decision to transform the CPUSA into a Political Association (CPA). In accordance with his Teheran thesis, Browder had envisioned a new role for the Communists in American politics. Rather than continue as a discrete electoral force, the CPA would become an influential participant in a "broad progressive and democratic movement" that would work for realizable reforms within the structure of the two-party system. In rejecting this approach, Duclos accused Browder of dissolving the "independent party of the working class." Browder's "liquidation" of the CPUSA again presupposed an unacceptable degree of "class collaboration" and forfeited the Communists' "leading role" in the struggle against imperialism and monopoly.

Having dispensed with Browder's "erroneous conclusions" about the likelihood of postwar cooperation, Duclos insisted that the American

Communists must emphasize the centrality of the class struggle, and he encouraged his comrades to adopt a combative, confrontational line. Specifically, he backed the more militant position of Browder's long-time rival, William Z. Foster. Duclos quoted favorably from Foster's January 1944 letter to the CPUSA National Committee that rejected the premises of Browder's Teheran thesis and predicted sharpening class divisions, economic crisis, and the resurgence of aggressive American imperialism after the war.[3]

That the French leader had quoted from an internal party document, however, raised some troubling questions concerning the article's origins. So, too, did his public exposure of differences within the American party leadership. Duclos would not have had access to Foster's letter or knowledge of intraparty disputes unless he had been in contact with the Soviet Communists. Finally, it seemed incongruous that an official of the French party would endorse such a confrontational line, given that it directly contradicted the accommodationist position the PCF itself was then taking within the French government. Taking all of this into account, Browder concluded that Duclos's criticisms were a likely message from Moscow.[4]

The opening of Soviet archives has confirmed Browder's suspicions and even called into question whether his Teheran thesis had ever won Moscow's approval in the first place. Beyond adding a brief introduction and an assurance that the PCF had not engaged in any of the CPA's ideological deviations, neither Duclos nor the French Communist Party had anything to do with the article's preparation. It had been composed in the Kremlin and published in Russian in the January 1945 issue of the *Bulletin of the Information Bureau of the CC VKP(b): Issues of Foreign Policy*, a publication distributed only to members of the Communist Party Central Committee and to top Soviet government officials. It had then been translated and sent to Paris for inclusion in *Les Cahiers du Communisme*. Moreover, we now know that Georgi Dimitrov, general secretary of the recently dissolved Comintern, had informed Browder in a March 1944 cable that he was "somewhat disturbed by the new theoretical, political, and tactical positions you are developing." Dimitrov had questioned even then whether Browder was "going too far" in assuming that the Big Three agreements reached in Teheran had allowed for the denial of the "theory and practice of class struggle" and of "the necessity for the working class to have its own independent political party." At the time, Browder had not revealed the contents of Dimitrov's cable to his comrades. Instead, he disregarded its implied criticism and reported to the CPA board that Moscow had endorsed his views.[5]

Confirmation of the wholly Soviet origins of the Duclos Letter has prompted a reexamination of its meaning and significance. Among other things, Soviet authorship resolves the peculiarity of Duclos endorsing a line that his own PCF had rejected, though it does raise the question of whether Moscow had also intended the article as an indirect reprimand to the French party, lest its newfound influence in domestic politics lead to a sense of independence.[6] More important, the letter, written in late 1944 or early 1945, undermines the view that Moscow's belligerent attitude toward the West emerged as an entirely defensive reaction to the dropping of the atomic bomb or to the announcements of the Truman Doctrine and the Marshall Plan. Even before the Yalta Conference, Soviet officials were reconsidering the terms of the Grand Alliance and preparing to take a more confrontational stance. Likewise, the Dimitrov cable to Browder suggests that Moscow had never shared the American leader's conciliatory views. The *Bulletin of the Information Bureau* itself is a revealing source in that its articles from the first half of 1945—intended exclusively for internal consumption—express an open suspicion and hostility toward the Western Allies that did not appear at that time in the Soviet press or in the private exchanges between Soviet and Western diplomats.[7]

Given the Duclos Letter's strident tone and sharp condemnation of Browder's vision for socialist-capitalist cooperation in the postwar world, some historians have considered it a "diplomatic document"—"the first salvo in Stalin's confrontation with the West."[8] At the time, some officials in the State Department shared this view and notified the White House of the letter's potential significance. Indeed, Browder himself later referred to it as "the first *public* declaration of the Cold War."[9] Yet such a view proves too simplistic. New evidence from Soviet and Eastern European archives paints a more complicated picture of Stalin's postwar strategy. That top Soviet officials were envisioning, and indeed preparing for, the possibility of confrontation with the West as early as January 1945—before Roosevelt's death and well before any indication of a "get tough" policy from the United States—should put to rest claims that Stalin's postwar policies were exclusively defensive reactions to American provocations.[10] Nonetheless, Soviet officials were not looking to precipitate a conflict with the West, and in fact hoped to preserve the wartime alliance as long as possible because they believed it suited Moscow's purposes. This is not to say that the Soviets were eager to embrace the kind of "friendly, peaceful competition" with the United States that Wallace and other progressives later claimed would have been possible if not for the Truman administration's allegedly aggressive policies.[11] Rather, it appears that Stalin hoped for continued collaboration with the West, but only if the British and the Americans were willing to accommodate his postwar goals and did not move toward forming an anti-Soviet bloc. As the historian Vladimir O. Pechatnov has maintained, until Winston Churchill's "iron curtain" speech in March 1946—which Stalin interpreted as evidence of an emerging anti-Soviet Anglo-American bloc—"'sharpening of the ideological struggle' remained intertwined with 'peaceful coexistence.'" Similarly, Jonathan Haslam notes that the Duclos Letter reasserted the line "demarcating peaceful coexistence between states and between societies." While the former was acceptable to Moscow, the latter was not, "as it would amount to a denial of Marxism-Leninism in the international sphere."[12]

Yet such subtleties were lost on the American Communists. The leadership read the Duclos Letter as a sharp "left turn" in the international Communist line and hastened to comport with what it believed were that line's new requirements. In practical terms, this meant an end to the Communists' accommodating Popular Front strategy—thereafter reviled as "Browderism"—and the expulsion from the Party of the "great leader" himself. Foster, Browder's longtime rival, moved quickly to dissolve the Communist Political Association and reconstituted the Communist Party, setting down a more classically Leninist line that emphasized the irreconcilable differences between the "imperialist" and "socialist" camps and that favored ideological purity over political pragmatism. "Militant mass action" and "greatly sharpened attacks on monopoly capital" became the order of the day. Though cooperation with certain "progressive" forces remained permissible, the aggressive promotion of the programs of international communism took priority.[13]

The post-Duclos line immediately put strains on the Popular Front coalition that had thrived during the war. Although the CP did not seek to sever relations with sympathetic liberals, the preconditions for a continued alliance became far more stringent. Those reluctant to offer unquestioning support for Communist policies—and more precisely, for Soviet foreign policy—were no longer considered suitable associates. Within Popular Front organizations, the Communists expected their liberal colleagues to accept resolutions predetermined at CP "fraction" meetings without asking embarrassing questions or raising the issue of democratic procedure. Concealed Communists aggressively enforced the Party line while denouncing as "red-baiters" those who criticized their tactics or called attention to their presence. The Communists also cultivated a political atmosphere in which any opinions not in accordance with the Party position became suspect, and those who expressed them traitors to the progressive cause. When intellectual intimidation failed to silence heretical liberals, the latter found themselves publicly branded as "reactionaries," "fascists," and "warmongers." Though many non-Communists intent on preserving progressive unity opted for self-censorship, such intransigence on the part of the CP drove away many of the Party's most valued liberal supporters. Yet rather than run the risk of reverting to "Browderite revisionism," the CPers bid their erstwhile allies good riddance, convinced they were strengthening the progressive forces by cutting their numbers.

Contrary to the later claims of Henry Wallace's political enemies, however, the CP did not immediately commit itself to launching a third party in the aftermath of the Duclos Letter. Indeed, the leadership often appeared unsure exactly how to implement the new line. Tensions soon arose between Foster, a militant hard-liner who seemed willing to sacrifice political success for ideological purity, and the CP's new general secretary, Eugene Dennis, a less dogmatic figure who shared Foster's commitment to Marxist-Leninism but feared that "the old man's" proclivity for "going it alone" would isolate the party and undermine its effectiveness. The tensions between Foster and Dennis were more than a personal rivalry. The struggle between ideological purists and political pragmatists would plague the CPUSA for most of its postwar history, with the former group generally gaining the upper hand, to the overall detriment of the Party's fortunes. Foster and Dennis carefully concealed their differences, however, and most of the Party cadre, much less the rank and file, never learned of such behind-the-scenes disagreements. Still, both men agreed that an independent third party, no matter how desirable, was a long-term goal that the CP should not force on the "masses" prematurely. Two other manifestations of the abrupt change in the Communists' political perspective did appear early on, however. First, the CP and those labor unions and Popular Front organizations in which it exercised strong influence grew stridently critical of the Truman administration's foreign policy; and, second, the CPUSA began trumpeting the need for an "anti-monopoly coalition" to halt the march of "reactionary American imperialism." Both tacks would contribute significantly to the disintegration of Popular Front liberalism in the postwar period.[14]

The war had barely ended when the American Communists unleashed a torrent of invective at the Truman administration. Party publications that in April had hailed the president as "a tireless worker for progress" were discovering "imperialist tendencies" in Truman as early as July 1945. By September, the Party chairman, Foster, was bitterly assailing the president as a "militant imperialist," while the *Daily Worker* discovered that "the center of the reactionary forces in the world today rests in the United States." Even the Soviet press had not yet resorted to such harsh denunciations. As most scholars now agree, the CPUSA overreacted to the Duclos Letter, due in large part to Foster's reading of it as Moscow's endorsement of his own extreme positions on American imperialism and the "war danger." Throughout 1945–47, Foster's views were well to the left of most Western European CP leaders, resembling more those of the ultramilitant Yugoslavian CP under Marshal Josip Broz Tito.[15]

Organizations in which the Communists exercised significant or controlling influence likewise adopted a more critical stance toward the new president, issuing a flurry of sharply worded resolutions denouncing the administration's policies. After V-J Day, the National Citizens Political Action Committee (NCPAC), the Independent Citizens Committee of the Arts, Sciences, and Professions (ICCASP), and Communist-led unions within the Congress of Industrial Organizations (CIO) all shifted their primary focus from issues such as full employment and public housing to foreign policy, particularly to U.S.-Soviet relations. In contrast, liberals who would later renounce Popular Front–style politics continued to concentrate on domestic problems. Indeed, anticommunist liberalism, which would soon find expression in such groups as Americans for Democratic Action, crystallized in large part as a *response* to the growing pro-Sovietism of Popular Front organizations such as NCPAC and ICCASP. In this sense, the Communists within Popular Front groups were largely responsible for precipitating the splits that would plague postwar liberalism.[16]

As the superpowers sparred over Trieste, the Turkish Straits, Eastern Europe, and Iran, the rhetoric emanating from NCPAC, ICCASP, and other Popular Front–oriented groups grew increasingly pro-Soviet. In their public statements, these organizations placed sole blame for the deterioration of relations on the United States and scrupulously avoided any criticism of the USSR, dismissing as "red-baiters" those who did raise objections. In like manner, they cited each infraction of civil liberties in the United States as proof that the nation was spiraling toward fascism, but they ignored (or denied) the human rights violations occurring on a massive scale in Soviet-occupied Europe. When Truman resisted Soviet diplomatic pressure, he was accused of resorting to "Hitlerite tactics," betraying the policies of Franklin Roosevelt, and pursuing a course indistinguishable from that of the "Republican reactionaries." Ghost-written speeches prepared for big "names" to deliver at Popular Front political rallies adopted this same line. Speakers who attempted to alter the content to comport more closely to their own views faced bitter personal attacks and, in one extreme case involving the actress Olivia de Havilland and the screenwriter Dalton Trumbo, the threat of legal action. Trumbo's original draft written for de Havilland compared the United States to Hitler's Third Reich and accused "certain interests" of launching a "drive toward war against the Soviet Union." De Havilland refused to deliver the speech, and with the help of James Roosevelt, the late president's son, and of Ernest Pascal, the treasurer of ICCASP's Hollywood chapter, prepared an edited version that included a line denouncing communism as incompatible with democracy. Trumbo reacted angrily, implying that Pascal and Roosevelt were fascist sympathizers, and threatened legal action if they altered any more of his speeches in the future. The episode angered many of ICCASP's liberals and provoked several resignations in California.[17]

To be sure, organizations like NCPAC and ICCASP were hardly alone in criticizing Truman's foreign policy—most liberals grumbled about the president's awkward handling of international affairs and deplored Washington's part in contributing to the breakdown of "Big Three unity." Nor was anywhere near a majority of these groups' members Communist or even pro-Communist. Yet the concealed CP members who held key paid positions in the national offices and staffed many of the local chapters set the tone. Their single-minded preoccupation with maintaining friendly relations with the Soviet Union and their insistence that accommodating Stalin was the litmus test of a progressive foreign policy distanced their organizations from mainstream liberalism—and indicated the CP's willingness to jettison the wartime Popular Front.[18]

The postwar history of ICCASP's Hollywood chapter, California's most prestigious left-liberal organization, aptly illustrates the Party's role in undermining progressive unity. As early as December 1945, the first fissures had already begun to appear, as even the most sympathetic liberals grew restless at the CP's obstreperousness. "The Communist hard core began to run things openly and to dictate policy," recalled the screenwriter Milton Sperling, an active member of the Hollywood Independent Citizens Committee of Arts, Sciences, and Professions (HICCASP). "They really became obnoxious. They said, 'No, we're not going to do it that way, we're going to do it my way, our way.' And the Party line became very visible. . . . This offended people. It offended them on a personal level, and it offended them on a political level. They drove out the middle road [members], they drove out the liberals, by hewing to a very straight [Party] line and by organizing everything their own way."[19]

Much of this bullying had occurred under the watch of Nemmy Sparks, a veteran commissar who had taken over leadership of the Southern

California Communist Party in 1945. By ham-handedly imposing the TONE post-Duclos line, he systematically decimated the once flourishing Popular Front coalition of Los Angeles. Even his CP comrades considered Sparks unnecessarily intolerant and authoritarian. "He was far too accustomed to simply pounding the table and saying, 'This is the decision and this must be done,'" recalled Dorothy Healey, a prominent California Communist. To make matters worse, Sparks surrounded himself with similarly auto- cratic underlings who soon alienated many of the Party's most influential non-Communist allies.[20] According to Ellenore Hittelman, a concealed Party member who worked for HICCASP, "[Sparks] displayed nearly criminal policies toward other, non-Party organizations. It was the first time I ever saw such direct interference in the affairs of previously allied organizations, so many broken promises, so much rechanneling of funds. His insensitive muscle-flexing gave the Communist Party a bad name in a broader circle than ever before." "The times were bad, no question about that," Hittelman added. "But at the very moment when you should be try- ing to keep every connection that's possible to keep, [we went] around chopping off those connections."[21]

In one of many vexing incidents, Sparks precipitated a schism within the progressive camp during the 1946 primary campaign by demanding that HICCASP and all other organizations under the Party's sway endorse the U.S. senatorial candidacy of the former lieutenant governor and cur- rent congressman Ellis Patterson, a longtime CP ally. Most HICCASP lib- erals preferred Will Rogers Jr., the son of the famous entertainer, who also had the support of many Democratic Party leaders. But, for the sake of internal harmony, they were willing to have the organization remain neutral. The Communists, however, viewed the contest as a struggle for control of the progressive movement in California and as an opportunity to lay the groundwork for a third party. Ignoring pleas not to press the issue, Sparks ordered the Communists on the HICCASP Executive Board to force a vote on the Rogers-Patterson question or face "charges" from the Party. After a "knock-down, drag-out fight," the pro-CP faction won, thus reinforcing what one HICCASP official called "the general feeling that the left was in control." Employing similar tactics, the Communists also se- cured a Patterson endorsement from the Los Angeles CIO Political Action Committee and from the county Democratic Central Committee, both of which were under strong CP influence. Throwing its entire weight into the senatorial primary campaign (to the neglect of Democratic nominee Robert Kenny's gubernatorial race), the left transformed the contest into a bitter intraparty feud and, ultimately, into a litmus test of its own political strength. Pillorying the regular Democrats as fascist-minded reactionaries, the left-wingers set out on their own, determined to demonstrate the efficacy of "independent political action." "When we get through," boasted Philip Connelly, an officer of the Los Angeles CIO-PAC and a concealed Communist Party member, "there won't be any Democratic Party."[22]

The results of this third party "trial run" were hardly encouraging. On June 4, Rogers trounced Patterson, who, in an unexpectedly feeble showing, failed to carry a single county and polled only 37 percent of the vote in the Popular Front stronghold of Los Angeles. Despite conducting a well-financed, high-profile campaign backed by the vaunted Communist Party organization, Patterson drew little support outside of left-wing circles and barely outpolled the Republican candidate, William Knowland, who had cross-filed in the Democratic primary. Postelection analyses noted that the Patterson campaign had neglected state issues, focusing more on ideology, which was of little interest to most voters. The Communists and their allies predictably blamed Patterson's defeat on "Big Business" and on the Democrats' failure to take a more militantly progressive stand on various issues. According to the *Daily People's World*, the dismal primary results actually *confirmed* the need for a third party since the Republicans and Democrats were clearly in the hands of reactionaries.[23] More realistic observers pointed out that the sharp intraparty divisions that Patterson's candidacy had precipitated likely cost Kenny the Democratic gubernatorial nomination, which he lost to Earl Warren, the popular Republican incumbent who had also cross-filed. (Years later Kenny quipped that he had been beaten not by Warren, but "by a Frenchman named Duclos.") The precinct reports of the Kenny vote in the Los Angeles area also revealed that the "progressive base" was not exactly centered in "the toiling masses." Among Democratic voters, the former state attorney general ran well ahead of Warren in Beverly Hills and other "silk stocking" districts, while Warren frequently outpolled him in middle- and working-class precincts. "The California primaries," observed the *Nation* correspondent Carey McWilliams, "clearly indicate what will happen nationally if the third-party question is raised without full consideration of the risks involved. . . . The people are not prepared to join a left-directed political movement." Indeed, even after soundly defeating the left, regular Democrats still fell victim to "guilt by association." Though "progressives" had fiercely attacked the Democratic Party organization throughout the primary campaign, in the general election, the Republicans repeatedly linked Rogers to the Patterson wing of his party, unfairly attacking him as a "Communist sympathizer." Knowland's easy win in November reinforced California Democrats' conviction that the party had to sever all ties with the pro-Soviet left if it expected to remain competitive. Less understandable was the left's view that it could enhance its political strength by abandoning its liberal Democratic allies.[24]

The Patterson debacle drained away what remained of HICCASP's political prestige and prompted many liberals to reconsider their affiliation with the organization. "While most did not dispute the right of Communists to push their own agenda," the journalist Ronald Brownstein has written, "they understood that the alliance with Communists restricted their own political expression. With the Party holding effective control over HICCASP, alliance, in fact, virtually neutered the liberals as an independent political force."[25] In July, the organization's Executive Council failed to pass a mildly worded resolution declaring that the United States and the Soviet Union "could live together in peace and good will," but rejecting communism "as a desirable form of government for the U.S.A." Soon after, disenchanted liberals, including James Roosevelt, streamed out of the organization, leaving the pro-Communist faction to preside over the wreckage. Most had resigned with great reluctance and addressed the Communist issue gingerly, if at all. Appalled by what they perceived as a rightward trend in postwar politics, Roosevelt and other liberals maintained that they had no intention of "joining in the flood of red-baiting which is hitting the country," yet neither would they obediently toe the Communist Party line for the sake of "progressive unity." As the director Philip Dunne later recalled, "We felt we had to deal with our country's problems from within and we certainly were not accepting leadership from any organization outside of the country. It was that simple."[26]

■ If the Communist Party had abandoned the wartime Popular Front, however, in its stead it urged "independent political action" in the form of an "anti-monopoly coalition." Its theoreticians, particularly Foster, had concluded that the "imperialist drive of American monopoly capitalism to dominate the world" was paving the way for "a new blood bath of fascism and war." Terrified by the prospect of the "inevitable" postwar economic collapse, these tycoons had seized control of the U.S. government and were pursuing domestic policies destined to bring the nation to the brink of fascism. It was therefore imperative to assemble an antimonopoly coalition to spearhead the political struggle against these sinister forces—"to pull the teeth of American reaction," as Foster delicately phrased it. This alliance, led by the workers, would also include "poorer farmers, the Negro people, the progressive professionals and middle classes [and] the bulk of the veterans." Realizing that the incorporation of non-working-class elements smacked of "Browderism," Foster insisted that this "Leninist class strategy" was fundamentally different from the heretical "class collaboration" that Browder had espoused. The antimonopoly coalition would remain independent and never subordinate itself to the interests of the "big bourgeoisie" who dominated the "capitalist-controlled" Republican and Democratic parties. The creation of this coalition was also a matter of some urgency, since, Foster insisted, the "democratic forces" were "in a race with time." Adopting a five-minutes-to-midnight tone, Communist speeches and literature emphasized that war, economic catastrophe, and "American fascism" were not only probable but imminent, thus necessitating an immediate, broad-based struggle to alleviate the effects of the coming crisis.[27]

Ironically, the CPUSA's near obsession with the imminence of a U.S.-Soviet war during this period was out of step with Soviet thinking. As evidenced in their public statements and intraparty communications during the late forties, Foster and other CP officials anticipated a direct military conflict between the United States and the Soviet Union in the immediate future, making the need for an "anti-monopoly coalition" to combat the "warmongering" of the American government all the more acute. In contrast, Soviet ideologists, citing Lenin's theory of imperialism, did not foresee such a cataclysm occurring anytime soon. The "major contradiction" that would account for short-term global tensions involved Great Britain and the United States—the two major "imperialist" powers currently competing for foreign markets. Stalin appeared to endorse this view in his oft-quoted address of February 9, 1946, in which he referred to the "inevitability" of war—a reference misinterpreted not only by most U.S. government officials but also by the American Communists. Indeed, Eugene Dennis even cited Stalin's speech as confirmation of the CPUSA's correct position on the "war danger."[28]

Following its own extreme interpretation of the post-Duclos line, however, the CP continued its flirtation with independent political action throughout 1946 and into 1947. A February 1946 special congressional election in New York City gave the Party a chance to gauge the potential strength of the "anti-monopoly" forces. The Communists therefore pressed the American Labor Party (ALP) to run a candidate against the Democratic nominee, Arthur G. Klein, a well-respected New Deal liberal who had served in Congress during the 1930s. The ALP, which played a balance-of-power role in New York politics, would normally have endorsed a proven liberal like Klein. But, reflecting the increasing CP influence within its ranks, it submitted to the wishes of the Communist Party and nominated Johannes Steel, a popular radio commentator whose close ties to the Communists were widely known. (Cables decrypted by the National Security Agency's Venona project would later reveal that Steel had served as a "talent scout" in recruiting American agents for the Soviet Union's People's Commissariat of Internal Affairs, the NKVD.) The Communists then withdrew their own candidate, lined up their liberal and labor allies behind Steel, and secured him the endorsements of the New York CIO Council, NCPAC, and ICCASP. Though Steel lost the election, he ran an impressive race and buoyed Communist hopes for mobilizing progressives by working outside the confines of the two-party system. "We were elated by the outcome of the by-election," the Manhattan County organizer George Charney recalled years later. "[We] believed the Foster line to be fully vindicated, and were persuaded that it was proof of a radical upsurge among the people. To some degree this election contributed to the subsequent formation of the Progressive Party."[29]

Despite such encouraging signs, top Communist leaders hesitated to force the third party issue lest they alienate labor and other groups deemed indispensable to the success of the antimonopoly coalition. "By and large," Dennis acknowledged in mid-1946, "the conditions have not yet matured at this time for crystallizing third parties organizationally on a state or local scale." Though building the CP's "independent political strength" remained a central feature of the post-Duclos line, Dennis—perhaps with one eye on the recent Patterson debacle in California—cautioned against the kind of sectarian behavior and self-isolation that could threaten cooperation among progressives. In particular, he condemned "left-wing forces" within the CIO for jeopardizing labor unity by provoking needless "head-on collisions" with the CIO's president, Philip Murray, the leader of what the Communists liked to call the "Center forces." For the antimonopoly coalition to succeed, Dennis insisted, the center-left alliance must be maintained, even if Murray and others continued to acquiesce in being the progressive "tail" to the Democratic Party dog.[30]

The Communists' reluctance to launch a third party that would present a specific program to mollify the "approaching crisis" reflected not only pragmatic political concerns but also ideological uneasiness. "Practical policy dictated the development of a program to alleviate, offset, or delay the crisis," Joseph Starobin later explained. "Such a program, however, could not be presented in such a way to foster 'illusions' that the 'anarchy of capitalism' could be overcome or that the system could be made to work." In short, "reformism" amounted to "Browderite revisionism." Yet, to achieve its strategic objective of "curbing monopoly capitalism," the Party needed a broad base of allies. As Starobin noted, however, "the Communists could go along with sorely needed allies only in the conviction that even mutually agreed-upon proposals were no more than illusions." This hardly made for a stable coalition of progressive forces.[31]

Still, by the end of 1946, the CPUSA had begun to articulate a strategy for overcoming these seeming contradictions. At a December 5 meeting of the National Committee, Dennis told his comrades that the Communists were to establish or join already existing chapters of such liberal pressure groups as NCPAC and ICCASP (soon to merge into the Progressive Citizens of America) and "talk up" the idea of a third party. Though Dennis did not say as much, Communists would have known to conceal their Party membership and to present themselves to such groups as "independent progressives." Simultaneously, they were to help revitalize the left wing of the Democratic Party without losing their independent political identity. This complicated two-track policy deliberately left open the question of a third presidential ticket in the 1948 election. As Dennis himself readily conceded, such a strategy was "fraught with many difficulties." How could the Party maintain an independent, militant position while spearheading the drive for an antimonopoly third party whose success relied on stable alliances with non-Communist forces? How could Communists strengthen the left wing of the Democratic Party while building a third party movement that would presumably draw left-wingers away from the Democrats?[32]

■ The emergence of Henry A. Wallace as a dissenting figure within the Truman administration gave the Communists yet another factor to consider. Wallace, born in Iowa in 1888, had come to politics relatively late in life. Though he became an influential member of Roosevelt's New Deal, serving eight years as secretary of agriculture and four as vice president, Wallace was never considered an able politician. Still, he held a special attraction for liberals who admired his crusading fervor on behalf of their favorite causes. During the war years in particular, he became a liberal icon, articulating the progressive view of the conflict and reassuring liberals that FDR, despite his numerous political and diplomatic compromises, still shared their values. Wallace's removal from the 1944 ticket and banishment to the Department of Commerce had actually enhanced his standing among liberals who came to see him as a political martyr. Recognizing Wallace's continuing influence within progressive circles, the Communists soon made him the central focus of their discussions regarding a third party. Indeed, Dennis realized that if the "anti-monopoly" coalition was to have any chance of success, a highly regarded and broadly popular non-Communist figure would have to be its public face. Wallace, praised in the Duclos Letter as a committed foe of "monopoly" and considered among left-wing Democrats the "rightful heir" to FDR, seemed to fit the bill. More important, the former vice president retained the political sensibilities of the 1930s, considering fascism, rather than communism, the primary threat to American democracy. He was therefore willing to work with Communists for what he believed were common goals and had demonstrated that he wanted no truck with "red-baiting," which he considered a tactic of the "reactionaries." Wallace, if brought along carefully, could lead either a left-wing insurgency within the Democratic Party or an independent third party, thereby allowing the Communists to postpone a final decision on which track to follow until the "anti-monopoly coalition" had been given more time to develop.[33]

Also recommending Wallace was his growing concern about the issue of peace. Like many Americans, he was horrified by the prospect of another war and had come to believe that the Truman administration's policies were inexorably leading the nation toward military conflict. Accordingly, Wallace considered restoring cordial relations between the United States and the Soviet Union more important than any other issue. He also believed that Washington must take the initiative by making concessions and by offering gestures of goodwill to the Soviets, who were understandably concerned about protecting their security. In taking such positions, he easily found common ground with the Communists, though his motivations differed considerably from theirs.[34]

Wallace's devotion to the cause of peace, however, could lead him to act against his better judgment, though this did not necessarily bother the Communists either. In the fall of 1945, the then secretary of commerce asked to meet with Anatoly B. Gromov, first secretary of the Soviet embassy. Wallace recorded in his diary that at their lunch on October 25, Gromov "did most of the talking," but Gromov, who was also the KGB Washington station chief, indicated in his report to Moscow that Wallace had much to say as well. Wallace recounted for Gromov in some detail the disputes within the Truman administration, claiming that two groups were "fighting for Truman's 'soul,'" but that the anti-Soviet faction currently held the upper hand. Referring to the president as "a petty politico who got his current post by accident," Wallace then suggested that Moscow directly support the efforts of Washington politicians such as himself who were committed to friendlier U.S.-Soviet relations. "You (meaning the USSR) could help this smaller group considerably, and we don't doubt . . .

your willingness to do this," Gromov reported Wallace as saying. If nothing else, such statements constituted an astonishing lack of discretion, and, indeed, had Truman learned of them, it is likely Wallace's dismissal from the cabinet would have occurred a year earlier than it did. Yet for the American Communists, such signs of dissent from Washington's anti-Soviet policies and apparent trust in Soviet officials were both encouraging and to be encouraged. And given that Edwin S. Smith, a close ally of the CPUSA who later became active in the Vermont Progressive Party, witnessed the Wallace-Gromov encounter, it is likely that Foster, Dennis, and others were soon informed of Wallace's views. (For that matter, so was Stalin. On receiving Gromov's memo, Foreign Minister Vyacheslav Molotov instructed that it be immediately sent to the Soviet dictator.)[35]

The CPUSA's embrace of Wallace took a decisive step forward in September 1946, in the wake of his famous foreign policy speech at Madison Square Garden. Initially, the Communists condemned the address since it had featured some mild criticism of the Soviet Union. In fact, local activists who helped organize the rally had excised several anti-Soviet passages from the speech's text even before Wallace took the stage. Wallace himself later recalled that Hannah Dorner, the head of ICCASP's New York City chapter and a concealed Communist, had persuaded him to delete a number of sentences that criticized the Soviet Union.[36] Nonetheless, the left-wing crowd at the venue booed Wallace's chiding of the Russians so lustily that he skipped over several more sentences that might have provoked a similar response, later commenting that he had done so because he believed he had been "booed enough."[37] The next morning, a hostile *Daily Worker* editorial accused Wallace of endorsing "imperialist intervention." "While expounding the peace ideals of the late President Roosevelt," the Communist organ declared, "Henry Wallace defended the policies which are undermining those ideals." Within a few days, however, the Communists changed their tune, acknowledging that "Wallace did say a lot of good things in his speech at Madison Square Garden." Once it became clear that Wallace's remarks had precipitated his dismissal from Truman's cabinet, the CPUSA embraced him completely and set about emphasizing the contrast between the president's "warmongering" and Wallace's devotion to "peace." As the CPUSA functionary George Charney later recalled, "We were persuaded that our judgment of Wallace had to be positive, regardless of his lamentable lapses, since the main edge of his criticism was directed against American foreign policy. And so we came to embrace Wallace as the leader of a new people's movement in America."[38] Thereafter, Wallace found himself quickly drawn into the circle of progressives who welcomed cooperation with the Communists. Various organizations, including ICCASP, NCPAC, and the National Council of American-Soviet Friendship, all made his support for more amicable relations with Moscow a focal point of their press releases and publicity. Increasingly surrounded by admirers who pleaded with him to lead a "crusade for peace," Wallace gladly took up the cause, embarking on a nationwide speaking tour and accepting a position as the editor of the *New Republic*.[39]

The "Wallace movement" as it developed through late 1946 and early 1947, however, was not simply a Communist creation; nor did the CPUSA exercise control over it. At a time when both the international and domestic situations seemed unsettled and potentially threatening, Wallace garnered the support of many Americans who believed the former vice president was trying to carve out a middle ground between pro- and anti-Soviet extremes and in so doing reduce the chances of war. In particular, Wallace won the support of independent liberals and Democrats who believed that only he had the capacity to revive the militant spirit of the New Deal and the goodwill of the Big Three Alliance. Disappointed with what they considered Truman's uninspiring performance in the White House and with the president's apparent inability to beat back the rising tide of "reaction," they hoped Wallace would assume leadership of a resurgent progressivism at home and a worldwide democratic revolution abroad. Playing much the same role he had during World War II, Wallace became the symbol of liberal idealism, the prophet of a progressive future and of the "century of the common man." As other Democratic politicians, the president in particular, seemed engaged in a strategic retreat from the principles of the New Deal, Wallace's uncompromising rhetoric drew a stark contrast. His very presence suggested not only the "path not taken" but the possibility of renewal. Though some acknowledged that Wallace's speeches were short on specifics and his thinking perhaps a bit unclear, they had a ready answer for critics: "Ah, but he *feels* so clearly." For the kind of campaign the Communists wished to wage—one that featured more militancy than programmatic specificity—Wallace promised to be an ideal spokesman.[40]

The matter of whether the campaign would occur within or independent of the Democratic Party, however, remained unresolved. As they had always done, Party leaders looked to Moscow to clarify the issue. While ostensibly covering the foreign ministers' conference in the Soviet capital in March 1947, the *Daily Worker* editor Morris Childs met with B. Vronsky, a section chief of the CPSU Foreign Policy Department. Childs asked Vronsky for the CPSU's opinion on the creation of a third party and on the role the progressive movement in the United States should play in the upcoming presidential campaign. Vronsky forwarded Childs's questions to Alexander Paniushkin, the deputy director of the Foreign Policy Department, who offered some tentative answers. "It seems to us," Paniushkin replied, "that in the U.S. the conditions are not yet in place to create such a party at the present time. One of the main obstacles to this step is that unity of action is lacking in the workers' movement. . . . The CPUSA has little influence in American society to resolve this problem on its own, without making use of these forces. It is perfectly obvious that if such a party were created, it would not receive broad support among workers' and progressive organizations and would not be successful in its struggle against the powerful political parties."[41] According to Philip Jaffe, a left-wing editor who at the time was in close touch with the CPUSA leadership, Childs also met with Solomon Lozovsky, a member of the Central Committee of the CPSU. Lozovsky echoed Paniushkin's concern that a third party ticket without strong labor support was bound to fail. He, too, emphasized that the CPUSA's primary task was to achieve unity of action within the American labor movement. In an apparent rebuke to Foster and his more militant acolytes, Lozovsky also remarked that in determining the proper trade union tactics, "it is not the job of a labor leader to cooperate with more radical political leaders, but it is the job of the radical political leaders to cooperate with the labor leaders"—advice, particularly with regard to the Progressive Party, that the American Communists would have done well to heed.[42]

The tone of the political discussions at the CP's National Committee meeting in June 1947 reflected the cautionary advice Childs had brought back from Moscow. John Gates, who coordinated the Communists' legislative work, delivered a report on the third party issue that reiterated in more precise terms the "two track" strategy that Dennis had laid down earlier. (Bella Dodd, a National Committee member soon to be expelled from the Party, later wrote that Gates's submission was "obviously" not his own work, but "the combined efforts of Eugene Dennis and those Party members with whom he was in close touch through the American Labor Party, the Independent Committee of Artists, Scientists, and Professionals, and the communist forces at Capitol Hill, especially the brilliant Albert Blumberg, . . . a regular courier between Dennis and the communist staff in Washington.") In his report, Gates affirmed that "the movement to build a third party must continue and be accelerated." He did acknowledge, however, its "present narrowness" and emphasized that "much broader forces than are now committed to a New Party will have to join the movement to make it possible for it to come into existence in 1948." A ticket backed only by the Communists and "other Left forces," he observed, "will obviously not be a major third party." In particular, it would be vital to secure labor support *beyond* the Communist-led "Left wing" of the CIO. "Such unions as the United Auto Workers and the Amalgamated Clothing Workers must favor it," Gates advised. As for the immediate future, the "key to defeating the GOP and reaction" was to direct "greater and greater pressure on the Democratic Party" to pursue a progressive course—to hold the threat of a third party over the heads of Democratic politicians as a "sword of Damocles." This approach clearly indicated that even at this late date, the Communists continued to draw distinctions between the two major parties. For the moment, preventing a Republican victory remained the Party's primary objective, since, as Foster warned at the same meeting, a GOP triumph would dramatically increase the danger of war.[43]

In a subsequent address, Dennis built on Gates's analysis. To elect a genuinely progressive presidential ticket in 1948, he declared, there had to be "a coalition candidate, backed by the independent and third-party forces, *running as a Democrat.*" "This," Dennis concluded, "is the *only* way for the third-party and pro-Roosevelt forces to ensure the defeat of the GOP candidate in 1948" (emphasis in the original). To bring this about, he reiterated, the Communists had to avoid "adventurous, desperate, and sectarian actions." Particularly within the labor movement, there could be no "go-it-alone policy"—relations with the "Murray forces" had to be preserved. Dennis held fast to this position in the following months. On September 18, 1947, he declared, "We Communists are not adventurers and irresponsible sectarians. We are not going to isolate ourselves. We never did and do not now favor the launching of premature and unrepresentative third parties or independent tickets." Echoing Dennis in the September issue of *Political Affairs*, Jack Stachel, the Party's longtime expert on labor issues, bluntly declared, "It can be accepted as a fact that the Communists alone, and even with their Left supporters in the labor and people's movement, will not and cannot organize a third party."[44]

■ The CPUSA's "labor influentials" attempted to implement the Gates-Dennis line throughout the summer and early fall of 1947, but the complex—even contradictory—nature of the two-track policy encouraged varying interpretations and emphases. As a result, local figures sought to shape the course of the third party movement to suit their own particular needs. In New York, where the ALP provided progressives an already existing avenue for independent political action, the Communists soft-pedaled agitation for a New Party. They primarily feared jeopardizing their alliance with the powerful Amalgamated Clothing Workers Union, which accounted for a significant bloc of ALP votes and publicly opposed a third presidential ticket. At the ALP's county committee meetings in mid-August, the Communists and their allies agreed to defer the question of a third party, emphasizing instead the need to recruit pro-Wallace candidates to run in the Democratic primaries. Similarly, at a conference shortly before the annual meeting of the New York State CIO, three prominent Communist union leaders assured Louis Hollander, the CIO state chairman, that the "left wing" would not propose any resolutions for a third party, a move that would have precipitated a split with the "Center forces." At the Labor Day weekend convention in Saratoga Springs, they proved true to their word. Indeed, the Party forces were so eager to appear accommodating that they even voted for a resolution criticizing the Soviet Union's frequent use of the veto in the United Nations.[45]

In California, however, some of the CP's "labor influentials" pursued a more aggressive course in agitating for a third party. At the second biennial convention of the Marine Cooks and Stewards Union (MCS) held in San Francisco May 5–9, 1947, Hugh Bryson, the union's outspoken young president, secured passage of a resolution demanding the formation of "a new political party based on the trade union movement and composed of farmers, white collar workers, professional people, veterans, and minority groups." The statement also condemned the Truman administration for abandoning the unity "with other nations and particularly our wartime allies." Bryson directed MCS members who served as delegates to the CIO Industrial Union Councils to fight for the resolution's adoption at their meetings. Those slated to attend the national CIO convention in October received similar instructions. In the ensuing weeks, Bryson moved quickly to advance the third party cause, soliciting the backing of various state and national labor leaders and creating a twenty-three-person joint trade union committee to set up the party's organizational machinery. His activities received extensive positive coverage in the *MCS Voice* and the Communist *Daily People's World*.[46] Though Bryson insisted he was out to create a California version of the ALP rather than a campaign vehicle for Henry Wallace, the former vice president's triumphal speaking tour of the state in mid-May gave the union leader's movement added publicity as rumors flew in the press of a potential third party presidential candidacy.[47]

Such talk concerned many California progressives who, despite their eagerness to unseat Truman, feared that an independent Wallace run would split the liberal vote and ensure a Republican victory. Under the leadership of Robert W. Kenny, they set out to build a Wallace presidential boom *within* the Democratic Party. In their view, pitting Wallace against Truman in the state's 1948 presidential primary would best serve the progressive cause, for if their candidate won, the left would be poised to take control of the state Democratic Party machinery and exercise significant leverage at the national convention. Moreover, even if Wallace failed to secure the nomination, his strong showing would force the Democrats to "dump" Truman in favor of a more liberal candidate.[48]

Shortly after Wallace's appearance in Los Angeles in May 1947, a group of liberal Democrats, labor leaders, and pro-Communist progressives met with Kenny to discuss the implementation of such a strategy. With the more "left" elements taking the lead, the majority urged him to chair a meeting of "Democrats for Wallace" that would initiate the legal process for placing Wallace's name on the primary ballot. Kenny agreed, and called a conference for July 19 in Fresno. Addressing the more than three hundred Democrats in attendance (many of them concealed Communists), he maintained that a Wallace draft would not cause a party split, but restore the unity "destroyed by Mr. Truman's abandonment of the policies of Franklin Roosevelt." The president had already "chloroformed" the independent voters vital to the party's electoral success at the state and local levels, Kenny declared. Truman's nomination would thus ensure defeat for the Democratic ticket from top to bottom. But, he continued, "with Wallace, backed by the Democratic Party and the independent vote he will attract, [we] will get the same kind of majorities that won for Franklin D. Roosevelt in 1932, 1936, 1940, and 1944. . . . In other words, with Truman, we stand to win nothing at all—with Wallace we can win everything." The proper course for progressives was not to launch a third party, Kenny insisted, but to "liberalize" the Democratic Party.[49]

Yet Kenny's left-wing associates had provided him with a skewed impression of the political landscape. Assuming he had the backing of "the people"—and not just of the *Daily People's World*—he had called the Fresno meeting without bothering to gauge the temper of middle-of-the-road Democrats or assessing the depth of support for Wallace among rank-and-file union members. As it happened, his strategy—which was virtually the same as the Gates-Dennis line, accounting for the significant Communist presence at the Democrats for Wallace meeting—held little appeal for his fellow Democrats. Though they acknowledged Wallace's success in turning out enthusiastic crowds, they did not discern the level of broad mass support for the former vice president or for his peace program that their more "progressive" colleagues took as a given. In fact, public opinion surveys told quite a different story. Almost every sampling taken in the state showed Democratic voters backing Truman's foreign policy by nearly four to one. According to a June Gallup poll, Democrats across the country preferred Truman to Wallace as their party's nominee by a 71 to 12 percent margin. When asked their opinion of nine presidential contenders, Democrats gave Truman the highest "favorable" rating and Wallace the highest "unfavorable" rating. Even polls commissioned by Wallace's California backers did not reveal substantial support beyond middle-class and professional voters in Los Angeles. Caught up in its own enthusiasm, however, the Kenny group failed to realize that Los Angeles progressives were hardly representative of the state's electorate. As Ellenore Hittelman, the legislative director of ICCASP's Hollywood branch, later recalled, "Here are the people in Los Angeles who are mad for Henry Wallace, and it's natural that they should be. He was made to order for Los Angeles. He was a very peculiar man."[50]

Understandably, then, Democratic Party regulars in California feared that any association with the "Wallace crowd" was a recipe for disaster. One veteran politician warned Helen Gahagan Douglas, who was up for reelection to Congress in 1948, to stay away from the party's left-wingers. "They're on the wrong track," he said. "Our people were radical when they were hungry. Now they have wrinkles in their stomach from good eating. They don't like this Bolshevik stuff. They like the way Truman has told Stalin to go jump in the Pacific Ocean. You'll stub your pretty toe, my dear, if you line up with . . . Wallace." Douglas and many others heeded this shrewd advice. A week after the Fresno gathering, a special meeting of the state Democratic Central Committee emphatically rejected Kenny's Wallace-for-President movement. By a lopsided 170 to 19, the delegates adopted a statement that endorsed the Marshall Plan and the Truman Doctrine and equated communism with fascism. A Kenny-engineered compromise resolution that would have allowed the anti-Truman faction to save face never reached the floor.[51]

Though the inauspicious showing of Kenny's forces might have given California Communists pause about the prospects for "liberalizing" the Democratic Party—much less launching a viable left-wing third party— they redoubled their efforts on behalf of "independent political action," even at the risk of estranging their non-Communist progressive allies. On August 24, about six hundred delegates turned out at the Odd Fellows Temple in Los Angeles and launched the Independent Progressive Party (IPP), naming Bryson its temporary chairman.[52]

Despite the founding of the IPP, however, the Communists and their allies pledged to continue cooperating with Kenny and his supporters. The New Party's organizers explained that its formation would not undermine Democrats for Wallace. Rather, they claimed, the threat of a third party would strengthen Kenny's cause by increasing the pressure from the left on state Democratic leaders. In part to emphasize its willingness to work in tandem with Kenny, the IPP decided to qualify for the ballot by conducting a petition campaign rather than asking Democratic voters to change their affiliation. The IPP's officials encouraged their supporters to remain in the Democratic Party through the primary so they could vote for pro-Wallace convention delegates.[53]

Regardless of the IPP's stated intentions, Kenny realized that the third party movement would cripple Democrats for Wallace by drawing into the petition campaign the very rank-and-file workers whose services he would need to sustain an intraparty insurgency. Well aware that the Communists were the driving force behind the founding of the IPP, Kenny set up a meeting with the CPUSA's national chairman, William Z. Foster, to express his concern. By severing itself from the Democratic Party, he argued, the left would be committing political suicide at the very moment when he believed it stood a chance to lead a progressive resurgence in state politics. Foster, then on a speaking tour of the West Coast, found Kenny's arguments against a third party compelling. Reflecting the ambivalence of the Party's national leadership, he acknowledged that such an ambitious project, though desirable, might best be postponed until broad mass support could be ensured. Some accounts portray Foster as the ring leader of those Communist officials most eager to launch a third party, but in September 1947 the FBI recorded a conversation that took place in his California hotel room during which Foster revealed his profound skepticism about the venture. He stated that a third party could only succeed if it received wholehearted support from the CIO, which he considered unlikely. "The Communist Party must not make the mistake it made twenty years ago regarding the Third Party movement," Foster warned, " . . . or history will repeat itself and the Communist Party will be no further ahead twenty years from now." Reflecting his syndicalist background, Foster remained dubious about the Communists' involvement in bourgeois electoral politics under any conditions. "Before we were tagging along with the Democrats, and now with Wallace," he complained. In stark contrast, Nemmy Sparks, the Party's combative Los Angeles county chairman also in attendance at the meeting with Kenny, stood by the third party venture. The California CP had already thrown itself into the signature campaign and was not about to reverse course, he declared. So heated did the ensuing exchange between Kenny and Sparks become that the two men almost came to blows. Though Kenny left the meeting convinced he had successfully argued his case, Foster made no effort to call off the local Communists who remained committed to the third party course. "I shook him up," Kenny later recalled, but he "must have gotten unshook afterwards." Ultimately, Kenny's hope of papering over the differences between the Communists and Popular Front liberals like himself was misplaced. His unpleasant confrontation with Sparks epitomized the disheartening experience of many progressives who had tried to sustain a political coalition with the Communists in the wake of the Duclos Letter.[54]

Nonetheless, it does appear that Sparks was out of step with the national leadership. Throughout the summer of 1947, one of the columnists of the *Daily People's World*, Adam Lapin, who kept in close touch with top CP officials in New York, expressed strong doubts about the third party, emphasizing that defeating Robert A. Taft and the Republicans should remain the primary target for progressives. Indeed, by Labor Day 1947, it appeared that the CP, despite its protracted agitation for an independent third party, was cautiously backing away from the idea, at least as far as the 1948 elections were concerned.[55]

■ On October 5, 1947, however, "news from the east" changed everything for the American Communists. A *Pravda* dispatch revealed that at a secret meeting at the Silesian resort of Sklarska Poreba representatives from nine European CPs had founded a new organization, the Information Bureau of the Communist Parties, the Cominform. Andrei Zhdanov, a senior official in the Soviet Politburo, delivered the conference's keynote address, a strident polemic that seemed to represent a sharp veering to the left in the international Communist line. Emphasizing the traditional Marxist-Leninist doctrine of "two camps," Zhdanov declared that the forces of democracy and imperialism were locked in an irrepressible conflict and called on the various parties in attendance to launch an all-out counteroffensive against what he termed the "predatory and expansionist course" of the American imperialist camp. Specifically, he ordered the European Communists to "coordinate their efforts" and attack the recently announced "Truman-Marshall Plan." As the "vanguard of the opposition," they were to "be the leading force in the cause of drawing all anti-fascist, freedom-loving elements into the struggle against the new American expansionist plans for the enslavement of Europe." To accomplish this, the French and Italian Communists in particular were to forge "aggressive united fronts from below," by appealing directly to the "toiling masses" over the heads of their vacillating bourgeois leaders. Since concessions to the imperialists would only make them "still more insolent and aggressive," Zhdanov concluded, "the main danger for the working class at this moment lies in the underestimation of its own strength and overestimation of the forces of the imperialist camp."[56]

The establishment of the Cominform impelled the American Communist Party to carry out yet another of its notorious 180-degree turns. Within a month, all the solemn warnings against "sectarian adventures" and "self-isolating 'go it alone' policies'" had been quietly deposited into the memory hole. Convinced it was following Moscow's will, the CPUSA scrapped its two-track strategy and put the immediate launching of a third party at the top of its agenda, thereby jeopardizing political alliances it had been cultivating for more than a decade. Ironically, there is no conclusive evidence that the Soviets directly "ordered" the CPUSA to switch its position so abruptly. Indeed, Paniushkin had indicated in a memo to his superiors that the American Communists should be instructed to avoid overreacting or reading too much into decrees that did not directly concern them. "We believe," Paniushkin wrote, "that it is absolutely not required that the CPUSA respond to all disputes and dissension that arise from time to time in various parts of the world."[57] As the historian (and former Communist functionary) Joseph Starobin has suggested, however, the American Communists "had misread the meaning of the first meeting of the Cominform, taking the formation of that body to mean that the political polarization taking place in Europe had to be duplicated in the United States."[58] Recent scholarship drawing on newly available Soviet documents supports Starobin's analysis. Despite Zhdanov's universalist rhetoric, the formation of the Cominform had a specific and limited purpose. Rather than marking a profound shift in Soviet policy with global implications, it constituted more a defensive move on Moscow's part, intended in part to coordinate opposition to the Marshall Plan, which Stalin believed threatened Soviet hegemony in Eastern Europe.[59] Accordingly, it did not require any particular reaction from the CPUSA, whose representatives had not even been invited to attend the meeting. Nonetheless, as Starobin notes, the American Communists lived in a "mental Comintern." Their leaders were "so passionately involved with the idea of authoritative leadership from abroad" that they assumed every word from the mouth of Stalin or from his subordinates to have universal significance and to demand an immediate response. "The pull of the Cominform policy," George Charney later concurred, "was irresistible."[60]

In this instance, however, the CPUSA reacted not solely out of blind loyalty to Moscow but also because the confrontational Zhdanov line seemed to sanction the militant inclinations that several Party functionaries and union leaders had long been suppressing. Though they would never say so publicly, not all top CPUSA leaders had approved of Dennis's preoccupation with maintaining close relations with the center forces in the CIO. Some shared Foster's growing frustration with the alliance and longed for a showdown. Convinced that the "coming economic crisis" would undermine the workers' confidence in their "reformist" leaders, they envisioned the emergence of a more "politically advanced" labor federation under Communist leadership. In fact, Foster, who had repeatedly warned against the threat of American imperialism and the increasing war danger, welcomed the Cominform's organization as evidence that the international movement had at last come around to *his* way of thinking. In particular, he cited Zhdanov's call for a "united front from below" as an endorsement of his own plan to precipitate a break with CIO officials. Within this context, abandoning his qualms about a third party proved all too easy for Foster. The Party's rank and file also responded enthusiastically. Members who had been troubled by the "class collaboration" of the war years and felt impatient with the indecisiveness of the immediate postwar line eagerly embraced the opportunity to reassume a "vanguard role" in what many perceived as the approaching (and final) struggle against imperialism. Indeed, several former Communists have observed that the most loyal Party members preferred "left sectarian" policies, even though they knew that pursuing such a course could bring isolation and political failure. Temperamentally, they found ideological certainty and "mass action" more congenial than compromise and negotiation—in part explaining their attraction to the CP rather than to some other, less regimented brand of radicalism. Amid this atmosphere of apocalyptic hysteria, John Gates later recalled, neither he nor his comrades paused to consider that if the international situation was as "thoroughly desperate" as the Party claimed, Communists should have been trying to build broader alliances rather than severing already existing ones.[61]

■ The Communist Party's relationship with organized labor and, specifically, with the CIO's "center forces" was the first casualty of the new line. As far as labor officialdom was concerned, the Communists' decision to abandon the Democrats to launch a third party could not have come at a more inopportune moment. For a time, the notion of a national labor party had attracted a broad and ideologically diverse following, but since

Truman's veto of the Taft-Hartley Bill, such sentiment had nearly vanished. According to Gallup, approval for the idea of a Wallace-led third party peaked at 13 percent in June 1947, just before Truman's veto of Taft-Hartley. This support, which had been heavily concentrated among union members, declined steadily from then on, arguably as a result of the veto. Most union leaders, despite past differences with the administration, now realized that the Republican Party posed a greater threat to organized labor, as the record of the GOP-controlled Eightieth Congress had clearly demonstrated. They therefore concluded that their best bet politically was a continued (albeit officially unacknowledged) alliance with the president and the Democratic Party. Even if Truman could not do things *for* them, at least he could prevent things from happening *to* them. On July 20, in a most dramatic change of heart, A. F. Whitney, the president of the Brotherhood of Railroad Trainmen, warmly praised the president. Only a year before, when Truman had threatened to draft striking railway workers, Whitney had vowed to spend the union's entire treasury (some $47 million) to defeat him. But the president's opposition to Taft-Hartley, Whitney declared, had "vindicated him in the eyes of labor." A third party, he added, was now "out of the question."[62]

Though less sanguine than Whitney about Truman, the CIO's top leadership also opposed a third party, convinced it would dilute labor's political clout just when the times demanded absolute unity. Shaken by the GOP sweep in the 1946 elections, Philip Murray in particular feared that another Republican triumph in 1948 could deal a potentially crippling blow to the industrial union movement. Determined to stem the tide, he and his associates had drawn up an ambitious program of political action to help ensure the election of a pro-labor Congress. For it to succeed, however, the CIO's pro- and anticommunist wings would have to put aside their ideological differences and work in unison. This scenario left no room for any third party adventure. As always, Murray placed loyalty to the CIO and "sound trade union principles" above ideology, and he made it clear that he expected his subordinates to do the same. At a July meeting of the executive board, the CIO president bluntly told his colleagues that he would not tolerate any dual allegiances. "If Communism is an issue in any of your unions," Murray exclaimed, "throw it to hell out . . . and throw its advocates out along with it. When a man accepts paid office in a union . . . to render service to workers, and then delivers service to outside interests, that man is nothing but a damned traitor."[63]

Escalating Cold War tensions and the president's shrewd decision to include labor in the formulation and administration of foreign policy also drew Murray closer to Truman. He welcomed Secretary of State George C. Marshall's June 5 proposal for a European Recovery Program, believing it to be in accord with labor's long-term objectives of increased free trade and U.S. exports. Moreover, Murray had begun to find the CIO Communists' reflexive pro-Sovietism obtuse and disruptive. The disastrous 1946 election results had convinced him that their obeisance to Moscow was earning the CIO an unwarranted "red" reputation that could prove even more costly in 1948. In June 1947 he forced the resignation of Len DeCaux, the CIO's director of publicity and the editor of the *CIO News*. DeCaux, an admitted Communist, had used the paper as a megaphone for Soviet foreign policy, and hostile CIO anticommunists charged that his unpopular political stands were undermining their organizing efforts. Though many assumed that his departure signaled Murray's readiness to move against the pro-Soviet faction, the CIO president still held out hope for preserving unity. According to one of his confidants, Murray was willing to tolerate DeCaux's communism, but fired him because his politics was interfering with CIO business. Even after the pro-Soviet faction stepped up its attacks on the Marshall Plan as a "warmongering Wall Street imperialist plot," the CIO president ignored the pleas of his anticommunist colleagues that he discredit such charges by explicitly endorsing the secretary of state's proposal. Always with one eye on the critical upcoming election, he remained determined to avoid a schism.[64]

On the eve of the CIO's October 1947 national convention in Boston, Murray called together the organization's nine vice presidents to hammer out a compromise resolution on foreign policy that would satisfy all factions and prevent the outbreak of an unwelcome floor fight. The resulting statement—the handiwork of the CIO's General Counsel Lee Pressman, who would soon play a major role in the New Party—was so vaguely worded that each side could interpret it as an affirmation of its own position. As the journalist Murray Kempton later observed, it "managed at once to endorse the Marshall Plan and not mention it by name." The pro-Soviet faction initially considered the compromise a victory, for it had achieved its primary goal of preventing an official CIO endorsement of the Marshall Plan. Some even entertained the illusion that once the convention opened, the rank-and-file delegates would compel the leadership to oppose the plan outright. Murray caught them off guard, however, when he took the unprecedented step of inviting Marshall himself to address the convention.[65]

The secretary of state's appearance on October 15 turned the tide against the pro-Soviet faction. In an obvious slap at the Communist Party line that had characterized Marshall as a "warmonger," Murray introduced him as "one of the world's greatest champions of peace." The delegates, many of them World War II veterans, greeted "the General" with thunderous applause and cheered loudly as he warned them against accepting as "gospel truth" the "welter of ideological generalities and slogans" spread by the "enemies of democracy." Dejected Communists on the auditorium floor quickly abandoned any hope of stampeding the audience into shouting Marshall down and sat in stony silence. Indeed, as one pro-Soviet labor leader explained to his comrades, any such anti-Marshall demonstration would only have revealed just how weak the "left" bloc actually was. The secretary departed the stage to a standing ovation, his tremendous reception leaving little doubt where the majority of the CIO membership stood on the European Recovery Program.[66]

Marshall's address set the tone for the entire convention. Speakers who criticized the Communists and their tactics received enthusiastic approval, while the addresses of pro-Soviet delegates drew laughter and scattered boos. One CIO staffer recalled that immediately after the secretary's speech, Murray signaled the anticommunists that they had "permission [to] launch a slash attack on the Left." They wasted little time. Leather-lunged George Baldanzi of the Textile Workers Union of America (TWUA) taunted those who had denounced President Truman as "another Hitler." "He could not be another Hitler," Baldanzi hollered to the delight of the delegates, "because if he were a Hitler, Russia would work out a pact with him like they did with Hitler." He also dispensed with the rhetorical niceties of the compromise foreign policy statement. "I want America to know that we subscribe to these fundamental ideas that were enunciated by our Secretary of State," he declared, "no matter how in hell we write up those things in this resolution."[67]

The president of the United Auto Workers, Walter Reuther, gave the delegates a brief history lesson. Taking them "back to the Chelsea Hotel in Atlantic City in 1940 . . . [where] one other convention of the CIO discussed foreign policy," Reuther recalled the days of the Nazi-Soviet pact when "those who stood alone against Hitlerism and Fascism were called war mongers." "What was said in that convention?" he asked. "Go back and read it some day and you will find . . . the very people in the CIO convention who were calling Roosevelt a war monger are now calling Truman a warmonger. . . . The Communists were wrong in 1940 when they called Roosevelt a war monger. History proved them to be wrong. Let us hope and let us pray that we don't have to go through another war to prove we are right this time and those same people are wrong."[68]

Uncharacteristically, even Murray entered the fray. As one pro-Soviet delegate declared "when we say we have the right to criticize our foreign policy let us really mean it," the CIO president interjected, "I assume you also believe the heroes of Stalingrad are entitled to take the rostrum and the public platform to expound their views?" Sidestepping the question of whether Soviet citizens enjoyed the right to criticize their government, the delegate responded curtly, "I believe in the American principles of free speech everywhere for everybody." Few heard him over the applause that Murray's barb had provoked. In the midst of a long-winded speech on the Taft-Hartley resolution delivered by James Matles of the pro-Soviet United Electrical Workers, Murray again interrupted, asking him cagily, "Jimmy, are you for or against the resolution?" An embarrassed Matles muttered his reply as the delegates roared with laughter.[69]

Later in the proceedings, however, the CIO president tried to reason with the pro-Soviet delegates, hoping—perhaps naively—that he might persuade them to abandon what he considered their harsh rhetoric and misguided views. Convinced that differences over the Marshall Plan did not warrant jeopardizing labor solidarity, he urged reflection and a commonsense approach. But Murray either underestimated or did not fully comprehend the profound ideological differences between his position and that of the Communists. In essence, he was asking them to give up their worldview so that the CIO would have a better chance of electing a pro-labor Congress in 1948. This made no more sense to the Communists than their esoteric rhetoric made to Murray and others outside the Party's orbit.[70]

The Communists wisely refrained from forcing a showdown in Boston. Indeed, they purposely delayed making public their new line on the third party until the convention had concluded; nonetheless, they remained determined to continue their perilous course. Shortly after the convention, Dennis, John Williamson, the CPUSA's national labor secretary, and Robert Thompson, the New York state director, presided over a series of secret meetings with the so-called labor influentials, reliable Party allies who held leadership positions in the unions. Stung by the CIO convention's rejection of a third party and its unofficial support of the Marshall Plan, these CP leaders nonetheless believed that if they could generate enough rank-and-file opposition, they might yet force Murray to reverse course. According to the president of the Transport Workers Union, Michael Quill, at the first gathering on October 18, Dennis, "in very blunt language," ordered his comrades to disregard everything they had agreed to in Boston and to launch a no-holds-barred attack on the Marshall Plan.

A discussion then ensued on how to put pressure both on the unions and on Congress to defeat the European Recovery Program. The labor influentials were also instructed to ignore the CIO's proscription of any efforts on behalf of a third party. Williamson told Hugh Bryson to press forward with his efforts in California and assigned Ben Gold, the president of the Fur and Leather Workers Union, to raise $5000 and send it to the IPP.[71]

Though the labor leaders followed the Communists' directives, they met with little success. During the following few weeks the Party's position within the CIO further deteriorated. Reuther's overwhelming victory at the convention of the United Auto Workers (UAW) in mid-November drastically shifted the balance of power within the labor federation to the detriment of the pro-Soviet faction. Most commentators believed that with the anticommunist Reuther now in complete control of the UAW's executive board, the Party's sway within the powerful 920,000-member union—and the CIO at large—would not long survive. "The Communists have lost their last chance to dominate or deeply influence an important segment of the American labor movement," wrote the political journalist Stewart Alsop. Moreover, Alsop continued, their defeat had broader political implications, "for without a solid, unassailable base in the labor movement, the Communists are reduced to comparative political impotence." Though hardly accepting Alsop's analysis, Party leaders did acknowledge the setback's significance. In the wake of the UAW convention, they abandoned even their public pretense of preserving the center-left coalition with Murray and shifted their focus toward forging a "united front from below," which aimed to circumvent the CIO leadership and its opposition to their course.[72]

The discussion at the following meeting of the labor influentials, apparently held on December 15, reflected this new outlook. According to Quill's subsequent testimony, Dennis, Williamson, and Thompson informed the union leaders that the CP had "decided to form a Third Party led by Henry Wallace, and that Wallace would come out in the next few weeks and announce that he was a candidate for President of the United States on the Third Party ticket." The CIO Communists would then be expected to "line up endorsements for Wallace as soon as he announced himself on the radio." Quill objected that such a move might splinter the CIO and suggested that the proposal at least be put to a referendum of the rank and file. Thompson responded that this was not a matter for membership to decide and that those in attendance were obliged to follow the orders of the party's central committee, "even if it splits the CIO right down the middle." "To hell with you and your central committee!" Quill shouted, telling Thompson to relay his message to "that crackpot" Foster. "It was a refreshing moment in Party history," the anti-Stalinist writer Dwight Macdonald later quipped. But the Communists remained adamant. Williamson subsequently came up to the TWU president and said, "This is ours; we created it; get busy and support it."[73]

Despite Quill's outburst, the meeting continued along the same line. Thompson declared that the unionists must go all out for Wallace to stop the "rightward trend" in the CIO. As for Wallace himself, the question arose as to whether he was "reliable." In an article that appeared in the *Washington Post*, the veteran journalist Alfred Friendly, drawing on interviews with Quill and other eyewitnesses, reported that Dennis and Thompson acknowledged that "Wallace was not so adhesively consistent as might be desired, but that he could be held as long as the Communists surrounded him and worked on him. The answer was to the effect that 'to the extent that we encircle him, to that extent he'll stick.'" Another account relayed to Friendly, not necessarily inconsistent with the first, held that the CP leadership had decided it did not matter if Wallace should break with the Communists at some future date, as long as he remained a rallying point for the goals of Soviet foreign policy. No longer able to rely on the CIO as an operational base from which to attack the Marshall Plan, the Communists planned to use a Wallace-led third party to fill the void. Indeed, Quill related that when he brought his doubts about the independent party to Gerhart Eisler, the former Comintern agent told him that it was "in the best interests of the Soviet bloc." "[He] made it very clear to me," Quill added, "that that was the only reason why the Third Party ticket was gotten up."[74]

Still, the Communists realized that they could not commit to a third party until they were sure Wallace would agree to head it. As Gates later wrote, "Had he refused to make the decision, the Communists would have been left high and dry. There was no other candidate that could have made a third party even appear to be viable." Therefore, he explained, "Dennis saw to it that Wallace would be for it through our agents around Wallace. . . . The Communists did not merely endorse the decision of Wallace to form a third party. They were also most instrumental in influencing Wallace to make such a decision. . . . The Communist role in shaping that movement was considerable and also conspiratorial." Nor was it a matter of a last-minute push. As Gates observed, concealed Communists operating through Popular Front organizations and even within Wallace's inner circle of advisers had been "working" on the former vice president for more than two years.[75]

To be sure, Wallace himself was not subject to Communist discipline. Though the Party's surreptitious pressure on him undoubtedly contributed to his decision (and misled him regarding the extent of the public support he enjoyed), he continued to follow an independent political trajectory. His primary, even sole concern remained the "fight for peace." Wallace hoped to make the 1948 campaign a referendum on the issue, but he had given little thought as to whether it would be best to do so from within the Democratic Party or as an independent candidate. Such strategic considerations held little interest for him. As he continued to level sharper and more frequent criticisms at the Democratic Party and the Truman administration, however, Wallace was clearly limiting his options. Most mainstream Democratic politicians and activists no longer wanted anything to do with him, whereas the Communists and their allies welcomed him with open arms and gladly provided the organizational infrastructure he needed to ensure that his crusade would continue to garner public attention.

By December 1947, then, it appeared that both Wallace and the Communists had concluded that a third party would best advance their respective agendas. The decision had not come easily, and in the case of the Communists, only what the party read—or, indeed, misread—as a nudge from abroad had overcome the leadership's reluctance to gamble on such a risky course. To the Communists, the antimonopoly coalition would now take the form of a third party; to Wallace, his "crusade for peace" would continue as an independent run for the presidency. The manner in which this awkward alliance would play out became the story of the Progressive Party.

2

I SHALL RUN AS AN
INDEPENDENT CANDIDATE
FOR PRESIDENT

Launching Gideon's Army

After reading a *New York Times* translation of the Zhdanov manifesto in mid-October 1947, Michael Straight, the young publisher of the *New Republic*, grew worried. As he would reveal thirty-five years later, Straight was no stranger to the international communist movement. During the 1930s, he had been involved with Soviet espionage as an associate of the infamous "Cambridge spies," Guy Burgess, Kim Philby, Donald Maclean, and Anthony Blunt. Disillusioned, he quietly broke with the Party in 1940 and thereafter remained wary of any entanglements with the Communists. He now sensed that the establishment of the Cominform would precipitate a major shift in the CPUSA line—one that would directly affect his magazine's editor, Henry Wallace. Straight immediately telephoned Harold Young, Wallace's "cheerful man Friday" and longtime political aide-de-camp. "There's going to be a third party," he informed Young. "You're crazy!" laughed the portly, cigar-chomping Texan. As far as Young was concerned, the third party talk that had been swirling around Wallace in recent months was merely a bluff to catch the attention of the Democratic Party hierarchy. Indeed, Young himself had instigated much of the speculation as part of a calculated strategy to line up support for the former vice president should he choose to challenge Truman for the Democratic nomination. A practical political operative, Young had not hitched himself to Wallace's star merely to pursue some quixotic third party adventure.[1]

Nonetheless, Straight remained uneasy. During the past year, he had watched Wallace come under the influence of a small coterie of new advisers, primarily officers of the Progressive Citizens of America (PCA), some of whom he knew were concealed members of the Communist Party. If the CP decided on a third party, he presumed that these men and women would exert great pressure on Wallace to be its presidential candidate, a move Straight vehemently opposed. "I had bound the *New Republic* to Henry Wallace," he recounted. "He, in turn, had allowed himself to be bound to the PCA. To whom was the PCA bound? I asked myself that question and I feared the answer." When Wallace returned from a national speaking tour in the spring of 1947, Straight tried to alert the former vice president to the Communists' behind-the-scenes maneuvering, urging him not to mistake the noisy demonstrations of a small left-wing minority for an accurate reading of the public mood. The most successful mass rallies, Straight told him, had all been led and organized by the Communists. "Can you prove that?" Wallace asked. "No, I can't," said Straight. "Then you shouldn't say it," Wallace replied. Recalling their exchange years later, Straight reminisced, "We glanced at each other. We were like passengers on passing ships, Henry heading for the land of illusions from which I had come. I knew from my own experience that collaboration with the Communist party would destroy Wallace, but I could not share my experience with him. He looked on collaboration with the Communists, in or out of Russia, as an *idea*. He had traveled on a broad highway from Iowa to Washington, and by daylight. He knew nothing of the back alleys of the political world."[2]

A week after speaking with Young, Straight paid a visit to Calvin Benham "Beanie" Baldwin, the PCA's executive vice president. Baldwin, a native Virginian, had come to Washington in 1933 as an assistant to Wallace who was then serving as the secretary of agriculture. In 1940, President Roosevelt had appointed Baldwin to head the Farm Security Administration, where he proved a staunch defender of the independent farmer and a thorn in the side of big agriculture and its congressional patrons. Harried by the relentless attacks of Capitol Hill conservatives, Baldwin left government service in 1943 to join the staff of the CIO Political Action Committee, founded that year by Sidney Hillman, the president of the Amalgamated Clothing Workers Union. He went on to manage the National Citizens Political Action Committee (NCPAC), the CIO-PAC's middle-class analogue, and was instrumental in bringing about its merger with ICCASP in December 1946 to form the PCA. (Hillman, who died in July 1946, had opposed this combination, fearing it would give the Communists disproportionate influence in any resulting organization.) Throughout this period, Baldwin had worked tirelessly to develop a close relationship with Wallace, and by late 1947 he had replaced Young as Wallace's most valued adviser. Wallace trusted his lieutenant completely, even assigning him to investigate accusations of Communist infiltration into his political circle. (Baldwin reported back that there was nothing to the charges.) Most of Wallace's old associates, however, believed that Baldwin had isolated their colleague from the political mainstream, pulling him much further to the left than he would likely have gone on his own. Others suspected that the Virginian was not being entirely candid with Wallace about his own political commitments. Straight shared their concerns. When he broached the issue of the Zhdanov speech with the PCA executive, Baldwin's response contrasted sharply with Young's and confirmed the publisher's worst fears. "I think that there's going to be a third party," said Straight. "I agree," Baldwin replied.[3]

■ In the coming weeks, events unfolded much as Straight had anticipated, with Baldwin playing a leading role in the effort to launch the third party. He and the full-time staff at the PCA's national office in New York placed mounting pressure on the local chapters to lay the groundwork for a Wallace presidential bid. All other endeavors were to take a backseat to mobilizing pro-Wallace sentiment and to encouraging the former vice president to announce his candidacy at the earliest possible date. Baldwin brought in John Abt, the general counsel of the Amalgamated Clothing Workers Union, to explore the legal possibilities of placing Wallace's name on the various state ballots. Abt, even more than Baldwin, seemed determined to go forward with the third party, regardless of the political risks it might entail. As a longtime though concealed member of the Communist Party, Abt spoke vigorously on behalf of the new CP line at PCA executive committee meetings, grimly insisting that the nation was on the precipice of fascism and war and that a Wallace candidacy represented the last chance to forestall the coming Armageddon. Later, when Baldwin asked Abt to be the New Party's general counsel, Abt explained to Wallace the "political hazards" of his taking the job—his sister, Marion Bachrach, was the public relations director for the CPUSA, and his wife, Jessica Smith, was the editor of *Soviet Russia Today*. Wallace was unconcerned and urged him to accept the position. According to Wallace, Abt claimed to not be a Communist himself, a standard practice for concealed Party members.[4]

Not all rank-and-file members of the PCA shared Abt's and Baldwin's sense of urgency, and they resented the flurry of demands emanating from what they vaguely referred to as "one particular wing" of the organization. Within some chapters, disputes arose over the emphasis on the third party to the exclusion of all other issues. Dissenters feared that the "crisis atmosphere" generated in New York would end up stampeding the organization into a misguided effort that would further weaken the progressive forces. What good was mass action, they wondered, when it was far from certain that the PCA even had the support of the masses? "The 'now or never' approach," the liberal newspaper columnist Albert Deutsch warned Baldwin, "has driven us too often into hasty improvisations that failed and isolated the progressive movement from large potential areas of support." He, for one, was "dead set against the formation of a third party for 1948."[5]

Citing the previous successes of the CIO-PAC at electing liberals and ousting conservatives, other members maintained that political education at the grassroots level remained the best method for influencing votes and strengthening the progressive cause. Rather than pursuing the "daydream" of a national third party, the PCA should focus on community problems and on setting up ward and precinct organizations.[6] Ironically, given that these were the very tasks at which the Communists excelled, concealed Party members within the PCA bitterly opposed such a course. Convinced that *only* an antimonopoly third party could prevent the nation from plunging into fascism, they fervently committed themselves to a Wallace candidacy and expected all "genuine" progressives to fall in line behind them. They berated those who hesitated as "betrayers" and "saboteurs." Occasionally, such disagreements brought to the surface suppressed resentment at the left-wingers' steamroller tactics, but most non-Communists in the PCA made it a matter of principle not to criticize publicly their more "militant" colleagues. Regardless of their misgivings, they remained personally devoted to Wallace; if he chose to lead a third party, they were willing to follow him.[7]

Confident that he had sufficient backing within the PCA, Baldwin turned his attention to Wallace, stepping up his efforts to convince the former vice president that launching a third party was the only viable course for continuing his crusade for peace. On November 21, 1947, Baldwin called a meeting of PCA state directors to report on Wallace's prospects for securing a significant bloc of delegates to the Democratic national convention. Their disheartening findings seemed to underscore the necessity for an independent candidacy—despite extensive efforts, there had been little success in convincing potential delegates to pledge themselves to Wallace.

Furthermore, the California representatives informed the gathering that Wallace's refusal to make a commitment had adversely affected the morale of Independent Progressive Party canvassers. Without an announcement before the first of the year, they feared that the state's ongoing petition campaign would lose momentum and collapse. If denied a place on the ballot in the crucial state of California, the third party stood little chance of catching on as a national political movement. Indeed, the entire effort might have to be aborted.[8] Armed with these arguments, Baldwin believed the moment had come to make his final push. Though several PCA officials held that he should have convened the National Board to review the conclusions of the state directors' meeting, Baldwin feared that time was running short. He chose instead to intensify further his behind-the-scenes lobbying for a third party, quietly lining up various progressive groups and urging them to put pressure on Wallace. Yet this reliance on secretive maneuvering rather than open discussion only fueled suspicions within the PCA that a minority bloc was trying to "railroad" the membership into backing an independent Wallace candidacy. Several individuals active in the organization later recalled that Baldwin seemed to be under intense pressure from the PCA's "left wing" to hasten the founding of the third party. In particular, they cited Abt, Baldwin's so-called left-hand man, as the ring leader of this faction. Straight, too, has recounted that during a conversation in October 1947, Abt expressed determination to "go through with our plan" regardless of whether it had any liberal support.[9]

Frank Kingdon, the PCA's co-chairman and principal fund-raiser, took particular offense at Baldwin's conniving. An ardent Wallace booster, Kingdon at one time was considered the leading advocate for a third party. In recent weeks, however, he had begun to realize that there was no mass support for such a course. At the various Wallace rallies where he served as master of ceremonies, turnout remained impressive, but the level of enthusiasm appeared to be slipping. The chants of "Wallace in '48"—initiated by a PCA staffer from an offstage microphone and taken up by "plants" in the audience—were not catching on as quickly. The left-wing stalwarts remained dependable, cheering on cue at every denunciation of Wall Street and the military, but they hardly constituted a sufficient foundation on which to build a viable "people's movement." Moreover, Wallace's support in public opinion polls, after peaking in the summer of 1947, had been declining steadily since Labor Day. Accordingly, in his column in the *New York Post* on December 4, 1947, Kingdon offered an olive branch to the Democrats, suggesting that he would "like to see Harry Truman and Henry Wallace sit down together to talk over 1948."[10]

Kingdon's column infuriated Baldwin. At a gathering the next evening at the apartment of Jo Davidson, the well-known sculptor and PCA board member, Baldwin took his colleague to task, informing him that the PCA had already decided to back a third party. Kingdon complained bitterly that the decision had been made behind his back. As the co-chairman of the PCA, he resented having such a fundamental change in the organization's political orientation presented to him as a fait accompli. He denounced Baldwin's praetorian manipulations and threatened to withhold his support from Wallace. Even Curtis MacDougall, hardly a critic of the Progressive Party, has allowed that Baldwin's behavior was questionable. "At this stage," MacDougall notes, "Beanie Baldwin was working 'tooth and nail' to get Henry Wallace to commit himself and was taking no chances on his being exposed to any influences which might delay or distract him in making up his mind. The charge that he acted in a highhanded fashion as regards the PCA was, I believe, justified." Baldwin, however, was subject to unseen pressures from other quarters. "The statement by MacDougall that Beanie Baldwin worked tooth and nail to get Wallace to commit himself is accurate," John Gates revealed after his break with the CP. "What MacD[ougall] did not know," Gates added, "was that BB was a Communist and was the chief agent of Dennis and [Albert] Blumberg in influencing Wallace." Baldwin proved up to the task. Indeed, as Kingdon found out for the first time that night, two days earlier, Baldwin had extracted from Wallace what he believed was a binding commitment to run as an independent candidate for the presidency.[11]

■ Yet that Wallace would follow through on his commitment to Baldwin made on December 2, 1947, was by no means certain. Until the day of his official public announcement, it was not entirely clear to even his closest advisers whether he would run as a Democrat with independent support or as the leader of a third party—two very different political conceptions.[12] Contrary to the persistent rumors that he had long intended to head an independent ticket, the Iowan declared repeatedly throughout the year that he preferred to work for reform from within the Democratic Party. On the stump and in his initial *New Republic* editorials, Wallace specifically repudiated efforts to launch a third party, declaring that such a move would split the liberal forces and "guarantee a reactionary victory." To be sure, his demurrals were difficult to hear over supporters' shouts of "Wallace in '48!" and over his own remarks about the need for a "genuine people's party," but through the autumn of 1947, he continued to speak of "saving" the Democratic Party, rather than of setting out on his own. In later years,

Wallace acknowledged that he was trying to put pressure on the Democrats, but added that he was "quite sure" that until December he "wasn't thinking of carrying out the bluff." "Up until that time I was not in favor of running," he recalled. "There must have been something that caused me to think in December that the Democratic Party would not become a genuine peace party. I don't remember what it was, but there must have been something."[13] Lillian Traugott, a PCA field representative who married Baldwin during the 1948 campaign, also testified to the former vice president's hesitancy. "It took a good deal, believe me, to persuade Wallace that this was the way to go," she later remarked. "He didn't like it at first, but finally came around." Available evidence indicates that Traugott, too, was a concealed member of the Communist Party.[14]

Though Wallace may have wished to work within the Democratic Party, his public statements often failed to convey this impression. After the founding of the Cominform, journalists covering his PCA-sponsored speaking tour noted a discernible shift in the phrasing and substance of the speeches that his aides were preparing for him. Where he had previously decried Democratic policies that might produce a "drift toward war," by mid-October he was asserting that Secretary of Defense James Forrestal and others in the Truman administration constituted a "Wall Street war group" that was "out for world domination." Though he conceded that the Soviet Union might also be readying for war, he declared that all Russian preparations were "defensive," while all American preparations were "offensive." Similarly, where Wallace had once maintained that the governments of the United States and of the Soviet Union shared the blame for international tensions, he now claimed that a cabal of Wall Street financiers and military "brass hats" had manufactured the Cold War to enhance their own power and economic standing. Characterizing such men as the real menace to American freedom, he recalled for a Louisiana audience in mid-November Huey Long's statement that "when fascism comes to this country it will be cloaked in the language of Americanism." "Long's prophecy," he exclaimed, "is coming true." The situation in the United States, Wallace declared four days later in Louisville, was "perilously close" to that of Germany in 1932. On December 4, he vowed to do his "small part in stopping the Reactionary express." "That train," he told a meeting in Kings County, New York, "is almost back to the Hoover station now, and the Mussolini and Hitler stations are not far beyond."[15]

Inflammatory charges from left-wing activists of "incipient American fascism" were hardly new. They had first surfaced during the years leading up to World War II as a means of discrediting the arguments of isolationists. Dark tales of fascist "fifth columns" had abounded in progressive circles during the war, and even supposed civil libertarians like the *Nation*'s Freda Kirchwey argued that the "American fascist press" had to be suppressed. "To protect it in the name of democracy," declared Kirchwey, "is an evidence of timidity, not of self-confidence. A self-confident nation takes whatever steps are necessary to secure its existence; it does not allow its institutions to be used by enemies as weapons for its own destruction." Similarly, many on the left assailed politicians like Burton K. Wheeler, an old-line western Progressive, as "Nazi appeasers" and "unwitting aides of the agents of Nazism" for opposing the interventionist position. Prophetically, Wheeler wrote in 1943, "The more internationalists try to smear people now, the more it is going to react against them when this war is over." Indeed, though often overlooked, there are striking parallels between the left's tactics during the so-called Brown Scare of the late thirties and those of the right during the postwar Red Scare.[16]

Wallace himself was a special case. Oddly, he used the same rhetoric of "incipient fascism" to denounce the policies of liberal internationalists in 1948 that he had used against conservative isolationists in 1938, as demonstrated in his evolving assessment of the Marshall Plan. Initially, in June and July of 1947, Wallace had praised the secretary of state's proposal for aid to Europe, expressing only minor reservations. During the following two months he had had little more to add. In October, coinciding with the Soviets' declaration of war on the European Recovery Program (ERP), Wallace began to argue that the ERP was an imperialist plot designed to impose Wall Street control over the economies of the continent. When questioned on his change of heart, he explained that he opposed the ERP "as applied." Since July, he asserted, it had become a "martial" plan. Critics reminded Wallace that the Marshall Plan had not been "applied"; indeed, it did not yet even exist. But rather than offering general support and making specific proposals to influence the course of its development, Wallace rejected the entire undertaking outright and insisted that all aid must be channeled through the United Nations. In so doing, he estranged many of his devoted liberal admirers while reinforcing his identification with the pro-Soviet left, which was already espousing this position. As the historian Norman Markowitz has observed, had Wallace taken a less extreme stand, "he might have carried the PCA rank-and-file with him. After all," Markowitz posits, "he was the group's major asset, and there is little reason to believe that its mass membership did not share his early sympathies for the proposal."[17]

Similarly, with regard to a third party, Wallace appeared to be painting himself into a corner. Though he may not have fully comprehended the political implications of his rhetoric, by late November, the relentless attacks on the Democratic Party that formed the basis of his emotion-charged stump oratory had precluded any realistic chance of reconciliation. Moreover, the "either/or" structure of Wallace's ghostwritten speeches—*either* the Democratic Party proved it was not a "war party" *or* there would be a New Party—closed off all other avenues for continuing his crusade for peace. This formulation, of course, echoed that of Zhdanov who insisted there were only "two camps." Intentionally or not, Wallace had in effect limited himself to the choice of leading a third party or retreating into political oblivion.

During a tour of upstate New York in mid-December, he made his final break with the Democrats. Previously, Wallace had held out hope that "his party" might still be a party of peace, but now he alleged that both the Democrats and the Republicans were "war parties" and that therefore there was no difference between President Truman and the GOP. In fact, he told startled journalists, if given a choice, he preferred the "reactionary" Robert A. Taft for president, since the Ohio senator's commitment to an isolationist foreign policy would be more likely to thwart Wall Street's drive for World War III. Also, he added, "[Taft] is sufficiently honest so that there would be no danger of fascism." After many of his own supporters expressed astonishment at such tortured logic, Wallace sheepishly withdrew his remarks. That an editorial in the Communist *Daily Worker* had presented an identical argument only days earlier made the incident even more embarrassing. Indeed, so closely did the shifts in Wallace's rhetoric parallel the recent changes in the Communist line that many former associates believed that he had become the "captive" of his far-left advisers who, unlike Wallace, made no secret of their determination to launch a third party.[18]

Wallace's defenders then and since have indignantly brushed aside the contention that a small group of Communists posing as "independent progressives" surrounded him and led him down the third party path. As noted, MacDougall dismisses the notion that the Communists and their allies were involved in Wallace's decision to run for president. Likewise, Wallace's most recent biographers also downplay the CP's role in launching the Progressive Party. The charge, however, cannot be so easily dismissed.[19] Indeed, Wallace's heavy reliance on a close circle of advisers was in keeping with his past record. Those who worked with Wallace throughout his career in public service have confirmed that he depended a great deal on the advice and administrative talents of his associates. In 1942, Franklin D. Roosevelt told Harold Smith, the director of the Bureau of the Budget, that he believed Paul Appleby had actually run the Department of Agriculture while Wallace was secretary. Even those like Appleby who benefited from Wallace's free delegation of responsibility worried that he was too easily influenced by subordinates, particularly in political matters. As many an exasperated aide discovered, Wallace had no interest in the mundane but necessary tasks required to transform abstract ideals into a workable program capable of winning public support. He found politicking distasteful and assumed that once he had gotten his message to the "common man," the inherently progressive citizenry would naturally embrace it. "In fact," wrote Robert Kenny, while himself in the midst of trying to engineer a Wallace boom in California, "he places his cause on such a high plane that we who are dedicated to promoting that cause cannot 'sully' it by discussing the crass issues of political strategy with him. When we are able to keep him on the subject a few minutes, he falls asleep." For Wallace, discussions of organization, planning, strategy, and vote gathering were extraneous distractions best left entirely in the hands of others.[20]

Yet for a man who depended so heavily on his lieutenants, Wallace was not particularly discriminating in their selection. Rarely did he inquire into his staff members' backgrounds or political commitments. As secretary of commerce, Wallace had chosen for responsible positions staunchly conservative bankers and businessmen who often held views diametrically opposed to his own. On one occasion, Wallace and a top aide, Alfred Browning, a former army general, announced entirely contradictory policy statements on the same day. The secretary's liberal colleagues frequently intervened to dissuade him from making inappropriate selections. Ironically, Wallace would attack Truman throughout the 1948 campaign for welcoming "reactionaries" into government service, people who were, on the whole, less conservative than his own appointees at the Department of Commerce.[21]

On the other hand, after leaving the cabinet, Wallace did not heed the warnings of close friends and family members who urged him not to surround himself with figures long identified with the pro-Soviet left. The writer William Harlan Hale, who worked under Wallace at the *New Republic*, noticed that by mid-1947, the editor was "seeing more and more of fewer and fewer people." They provided him with carefully screened lines and ideas and soon convinced him that the cause of peace was best served by not writing anything disapproving of Soviet policies. Soon after, Wallace told the *New Republic* staff that all criticism must "stay at home." The journalist Theodore White, who had joined the magazine when Wallace was hired as editor, quit after only six months, disillusioned by the ideological rigidity of the "unpleasant breed of neurotics" who had gained the editor's ear. "There was less freedom to deviate from the line of the *New Republic* than from the line of *Time* magazine," White later wrote. The journalist had taken a pay cut to work at the *New Republic* so he could write for a magazine that shared his liberal views, but to his dismay, White soon found that "'liberalism' in politics does not always extend to personal courtesy or intellectual tolerance." Bruce Bliven, the magazine's managing editor, recalled that he and Michael Straight "promptly told Wallace that some of the people who were moving in on him were undoubtedly Communists or fellow travelers." None of them had ever made any such statements to him, Wallace replied. He informed Bliven that "he had met only one man who admitted being a Communist, a reporter who interviewed him for the *Daily Worker*." Moreover, Wallace argued, it would be improper to question the political beliefs of anyone who was willing to work for peace.[22]

Wallace's embrace of his new left-wing associates reflected an instinctive attraction to those who, like himself, were inspired by utopian visions and grand declarations of principle. As his friend and otherwise admiring biographer Russell Lord has observed, "Wallace had rather too high a tolerance for persons ablaze with intentions, or expressions of intentions, which struck him as vital to the needs of a sick world." More critically, Dwight Macdonald wrote that Wallace habitually mistook "intentions for achievements [and] words for actions," relying on high-sounding rhetoric "to accomplish in fantasy what cannot be accomplished in reality." Those who spoke in similarly idealistic cadences readily won his trust. As other colleagues remembered, Wallace had always been "an easy convert to almost any scheme, provided it was served up with a garnish of broad humanitarianism." In like manner, Wallace esteemed men and women who articulated deeply held political commitments, though often, as in the case of the American Communists, he had only a murky notion of what these commitments entailed. "I admire their utter devotion to a cause they think is just," he once remarked. "I would say that the Communists are the closest things to the early Christian martyrs we have today." Like a later generation of idealists, Wallace was greatly taken by the notion of "authenticity," in which, as one scholar has observed, "the ultimate test of political rectitude becomes the depth of feeling associated with the stand taken."[23]

Wallace's desire to support "great causes" led him to perceive political campaigns as moral crusades in which "good" battled "evil." Opponents who claimed there were legitimate differences over principle were in fact masking base motivations, venality, corruption, and bad faith—the implication being that there was no room for honest disagreement among men of goodwill. In this Manichaean view, one either belonged to the party of "war and depression" or to the party of "peace and abundance." One embraced "good" and stood firm against the temptation to settle for the "lesser evil." Furthermore, criticizing or questioning the motives of those on the side of "good" fostered unnatural divisions and played into the hands of the enemy. This crusading idealism may have been Wallace's greatest source of attraction to his admirers, many of whom had grown frustrated with the unsavory compromises, political backsliding, and breakdown of progressive unity that they believed characterized the immediate postwar period. Yet his uncritical embrace of all who expressed support for a cause he deemed worthy left him vulnerable to the machinations of those with less pristine political ethics. "Anyone who will work for peace is okay with me," Wallace insisted. If the Communists wished to join him, he said, "God bless 'em; let 'em come along."[24]

Perhaps most significant in explaining Wallace's susceptibility to pro-Communist maneuvering was his lack of experience in the political trenches. As the historian David A. Shannon has noted, Wallace, despite his fifteen years of fighting for liberal causes, was still "remarkably innocent of American political realities and . . . astonishingly unknowing about Left Wing politics and methods. . . . [He] was himself so lacking in Machiavellism that he found it difficult to recognize duplicity in others." Wallace, Shannon concluded, presented an inviting target to "political 'con men.'" In a similar analysis, the anti-Stalinist radicals Irving Howe and Lewis Coser characterized the former vice president as a man "anxiously vibrating with good will." He brought together a "home-brewed mysticism, a touch of the Popular Front *Schwärmerei* of the thirties [and] an unbelievable capacity for high-sounding and musty generalization." However, they added, Wallace was "fearful of precise intellectual formulations" and "lacked that shrewdness and decisiveness of mind which had made Franklin Roosevelt so masterful a politician." "In a vague and troubled way," Howe and Coser wrote, "Wallace was an ambitious man, eager for power yet hesitant when it came to him, enveloped in a mist of progressivist rhetoric yet uncertain as to his own ends—exactly the kind of man who lent himself to manipulation by a determined minority group." Indeed, they concluded, "there was something about Wallace that simply yearned to be deluded." Wallace's own statements substantiate their assessment. He had once told a friend, "I am a searcher for methods of bringing the 'inner light' to outward manifestation and raising outward manifestation to the inner light." When the journalist Kenneth Stewart asked him in October 1947, "What would you like to do from now on, above everything else?" Wallace replied, "Fundamentally and eventually the thing I've got to do is the thing that will serve the general welfare in the long run. Whether I like it or not, I've got to do that." It thus fell to Beanie Baldwin and his associates to persuade Wallace that pursuing a third party candidacy would best manifest the "inner light" and serve the "general welfare"—that it was his destiny to save American liberalism.[25]

■ Since most prominent figures in the liberal and labor movements had already gone on record against a third party, Baldwin had to create the impression of a popular uprising to sell Wallace on the feasibility of the venture. The enthusiastic crowds at the various PCA-sponsored rallies had already done much of his work for him, but Baldwin also arranged for Wallace to have direct contact with his supporters. Throughout the late fall of 1947, a procession of callers filed through the offices of the *New Republic*, telling Wallace that regardless of what their leaders said, "the people" were demanding that he run. Often this outpouring of admiration was not entirely spontaneous. "Phil Murray would criticize the Third Party," Straight remembered, "on the following day a 'rank and file' delegation from some painters or auto workers local in New York or New Jersey would troop in to tell Henry that Murray did not speak for the membership." In hindsight, Wallace acknowledged that the opportune timing of such visits had not occurred to him. Earnest emissaries from numerous ethnic, fraternal, religious, and neighborhood groups also made the pilgrimage bearing similar glad tidings. After a while, Bliven complained, it became "like Grand Central Station."[26]

New York City leftists familiar with the CP's synthetic "Potemkin village" rituals scorned the notion that such a farcical cavalcade of pro-Communist flatterers could be mistaken for a genuine people's insurgency. "Populism, indeed!" scoffed the Trotskyist *New International*. "Would William Jennings Bryan—who, whatever his deficiencies, could attract whole counties to his flaming speeches—have been taken in by delegations from such groups as the New York District Council of the CIO Electrical Workers, the Slovenian section of the Passaic IWO, and the Freiheit Mandolin Society?" In fairness to Wallace, it is unlikely that the entreaties of such "people's ambassadors" determined his final decision, but a more politically astute man might have thought twice before launching a campaign based on such flimsy evidence of "grassroots" support. As two of his biographers have noted, "Wallace, a midwesterner, should have realized that New York City was not representative of the rest of the nation."[27]

Instead, Wallace took encouragement from these brushes with the "common man" and ignored more experienced figures on whose counsel he had relied in the past. During the final weeks before his announcement, Helen Fuller, the Washington editor of the *New Republic*, enlisted Eleanor Roosevelt and other old friends from New Deal days in a telephone campaign to disabuse Wallace of the notion that most of the liberals were "with him." Helen Gahagan Douglas, the Railroad Brotherhood president A. F. Whitney, and the southern progressive Aubrey Williams also joined the chorus of those pleading with Wallace to disavow a third party. Even *PM*, the New York left-wing daily that had taken the lead in promoting Wallace as the inheritor of the Roosevelt mantle, announced that it would oppose his independent candidacy. The *PM* columnist Max Lerner warned Wallace that those behind the third party were outside the tradition of independent American progressivism and were using him for their own purposes. Wallace gloomily accepted the argument of his PCA backers that all these well-respected liberals had "lost their nerve" and had succumbed to the anticommunist "hysteria" manufactured by the "warmongers." When Philip Hauser, a personal aide who had helped Wallace draft the Madison Square Garden speech that had led to his dismissal from the cabinet, told him that the Communists had orchestrated the third party movement, Wallace replied sadly, "Phil, now you've become a red-baiter, too."[28]

Ultimately, the combined influences of Wallace's own temperament and the pressure of advisers like Baldwin, Abt, and others persuaded him that continuing the "fight for peace" and launching the third party were synonymous. The historian John Morton Blum has written that the former vice president, "believing that Truman was leading the country and the world toward war, . . . followed his own compulsion to stand political witness to his faith."[29] Undoubtedly, Wallace's decision to oppose the administration's foreign policy was his own. Regardless of whether he had the Communists' support, he would have continued to criticize what he believed to be morally wrong. Yet the channeling of this opposition into a third party movement owed much to the Communists and their allies. Through skillful maneuvering and relentless agitation, they convinced Wallace that this course was his *only* viable option. The impression they created was false. Developments on the domestic political scene had eroded support for a third party among liberals, organized labor, and the non-Communist left—the very groups that had been most critical of the administration's handling of international affairs. By fusing opposition to

Truman's foreign policy with such a clearly unpopular political strategy, the Communist leadership undermined Wallace's crusade for peace and narrowed its appeal.

Following their own sectarian impulses, however, the Communists refused to acknowledge that their determination to create a third party was discrediting the very anti–Cold War insurgency they were hoping to nurture. They and their allies assured Wallace that only through a third party could he get his message to the people. Well aware of his attraction to the role of moral crusader, they convinced him that he alone among America's leaders stood for peace; keen to his religious sensibilities, they told him that his critics were false prophets, but that if he would lead, the people would follow. Oblivious to the political repercussions that a third party would create, and concerned only that the cause of peace be made an issue in the upcoming campaign, Wallace overcame his reluctance to break with the Democrats and followed his advisers' misguided counsel, sincerely believing he was carrying out his duty to the people.

■ After December 2, when Wallace privately conveyed his willingness to run for president, Baldwin began preparations for a publicity blitz to culminate in an announcement before the first of the year. Various student groups and state chapters of the PCA held "Draft Wallace" meetings and forwarded reports of widespread support to the *New Republic* offices. Lew Frank, Wallace's personal aide and primary speechwriter, prepared for publication a variety of campaign leaflets, policy statements, and other materials. As previously noted, on December 15, the Communist Party leadership put out the word that all of its "labor influentials" should begin immediately to line up rank-and-file support for a Wallace candidacy. That same day, Baldwin convened a meeting of the PCA executive committee to draft a statement in which the organization would officially urge Wallace to make the race.[30]

Even within the PCA, however, resistance to the third party juggernaut continued. Co-chairman Robert Kenny, though agreeing that Wallace should announce for president, still viewed his candidacy as a means for independent progressives to gain leverage within the Democratic Party. He insisted that Wallace run in the Democratic primaries wherever possible and even predicted victory over Truman in California and Oregon. Such an impressive showing, Kenny argued, would convince the Democrats to abandon the president in favor of a more "satisfactory" nominee. "If this fight is not made, however," he told Baldwin, "the third party movement will be written off in the public mind as a group of dissidents lacking in any real political strength." Baldwin, Abt, and others were obviously envisioning the Wallace campaign in starkly different terms, but, for the moment, Kenny chose to overlook such discrepancies, so as not to precipitate even further divisions within the progressive ranks. He later said that he could not explain why he had failed to put up more of a fight against the third party advocates in the PCA. Watching with regret as many prominent liberals resigned from Popular Front organizations, Kenny determined that he did not wish to follow suit. Yet he acknowledged that he "had become something of a papier-mâché figure, . . . lending [his] prestige to left causes but unable to influence their course."[31]

Frank Kingdon, the PCA's other co-chair, did not prove as accommodating. After much soul-searching and last-minute hesitation, he abruptly left the Wallace entourage in the midst of the December speaking tour and made no further appearances with the former vice president. Some of Kingdon's detractors within the PCA charged that his desire to win the Democratic nomination for the Senate in New Jersey explained his sudden change of heart. Kingdon himself maintained that he had come to realize he could not work with the Communists who were whipping up progressive sentiment for a third party to serve their own purposes. At an executive committee meeting on December 15, he read a prepared statement that laid out in detail his case against a third party, concluding that if his colleagues put an independent ticket in the field "years of building will be wrecked overnight." If the motion to endorse a third party carried, Kingdon declared, he would resign immediately as co-chairman of the PCA. "In good conscience, I cannot remain a member of any body which launches an adventure which my best judgment tells me will further split the progressives of this country and weaken the whole progressive movement."[32]

Others in attendance also expressed misgivings, echoing Kingdon's concerns about the lack of labor support and about the feasibility of a third party. In a thinly veiled dig at the pro-Communist bloc that made up much of the PCA's full-time New York staff, the *New Republic*'s Helen Fuller, a non-voting board member, told her colleagues, "I rather doubt the ability of New Yorkers to settle the political affairs of the country. . . . I am more interested in what board members have to say. In my own conversations with them around the country, I don't think there's quite the unanimity that's been expressed by the staff." Fuller proposed that the group postpone the decision on supporting a third party until the national board meeting in mid-January, at which time state leaders could add their input. Baldwin maintained, however, that the executive committee's action was actually being taken at the behest of various state boards, citing pro–third party telegrams received from the Maryland and Massachusetts chapters. Others later took issue with such claims. One PCA official suggested in his letter of resignation that the procedural maneuvering to launch the third party had been conducted dishonestly, behind the backs of the local chapter members who were kept in the dark until after the decision had been made. "I have gained the impression that the action of the organization has also not been carried out in an entirely ingenuous manner," he wrote to Baldwin. "Just how this [third party] movement started, I do not know. Surely, I have nothing in my file warning me that such a question was to be made the chief issue in the agenda of the Board Meeting in New York at which the decision was taken. The immediate publication of this decision without prior reference to absent members of the Board, or to State and Local organizations seems to me a somewhat questionable procedure, and I have had the impression, and in this I am not alone, that meetings of Local Boards have been handled in a somewhat similar manner." Yet Baldwin's position was to carry the day. Abt settled the issue by ruling out of order Fuller's motion to postpone the decision. After a lengthy discussion, the third party resolution passed, with Kingdon the sole dissenting vote among those executive committee members present. Unable to stop what he believed was a "mad rush" to "escape from realities," Kingdon tendered his resignation from the PCA.[33]

A handful of other prominent members would soon do the same. The next morning, the well-known San Francisco attorney Bartley Crum, a PCA vice chairman and one of the organization's founding members, announced that he would "never support Wallace for President" and withdrew from the PCA. The liberal newspaper columnist Albert Deutsch followed suit. Though he remained "in general accord with the domestic and foreign policies of PCA," Deutsch wrote, his difference with the organization over strategy was so profound that he could not remain a member. The third party ticket would be "destructive of PCA and ruinous to Wallace," he predicted. The popular radio personality and New York State PCA chairman Raymond Walsh voiced his opposition during his nightly WMCA commentary. Deploring the organization's "political monasticism," Walsh declared that both conservatives and the labor movement would call the third party "a stalking horse for the Communists." "Under present conditions of public opinion," he warned, this would be a "kiss of death." Those PCAers who acknowledged that Wallace could not win but believed that a large vote for him would reassure progressives around the globe that the United States was not "inevitably committed to world reaction" were setting themselves up for disaster. "There is reason to believe that Wallace would get not five million but five hundred thousand votes," Walsh maintained. Such a showing would be a "declaration of bankruptcy. It would kill the chance of progressive politics in America for a long time." On the rival station WLIB, Kingdon presented a similar analysis. "The prevailing consideration," he stated, "is not that [a third party] will elect reaction, but that it will split progressives into fragments and delay any possibility of their coming back in two or four years." Kingdon argued that Wallace should remain a Democrat and fight for the election of a liberal Congress, thus building political support for a 1952 presidential bid. By that time, he posited, the PCA would have grown strong enough to give him a real chance of victory. Though Deutsch's, Walsh's, and Kingdon's presumption that PCA-style progressivism would have a bright future if not for the third party reflected a profound misreading of the public mood, they were indeed more perspicacious than many in foreseeing that the primary effect of the Wallace candidacy would not be to elect a "reactionary" Republican president and Congress, but to destroy the credibility of Popular Front liberalism and thoroughly marginalize the left. Within the PCA, of course, they were traitors, not seers.[34]

As the organization's leaders continued determinedly down the third party path, they encountered some bumps along the road. On December 18, a PCA delegation called on Wallace at the Hotel McAlpin to inform him officially of the executive committee's decision. Though he had privately assured Baldwin of his willingness to run two weeks earlier, as late as December 13, Wallace had hinted to an audience in Albany that he might still support the "entire Democratic ticket in 1948." Lew Frank later recalled that when Wallace heard the outcome of the PCA's December 15 meeting, he expressed surprise at how quickly the organization's position had shifted toward support for a third party. Even at the gathering at the Hotel McAlpin, Wallace indicated that Baldwin might not yet have "secured" him. Looking around the room, he remarked on the lack of any representatives from organized labor. It appeared to him, he said, that the third party movement would be almost exclusively middle class. Indeed, the New York morning papers were reporting that the powerful Amalgamated Clothing Workers Union (ACWU) had reiterated its stance against a third party and would likely withdraw from the American Labor Party (ALP) if it backed Wallace for president. Most commentators believed that the ACWU's departure would cripple the ALP. The wealthy businessman Alfred K. Stern also expressed concern about the lack of labor support and proposed scheduling another meeting to explore the issue. In what must have been an anxious moment, Baldwin agreed to Stern's suggestion. At the conference held the next morning, Stern asked that Wallace delay his announcement until an experienced labor organizer could conduct a nationwide canvass to determine the sentiment of local union leaders. Without waiting for Wallace's response, Baldwin rejected the proposition and upbraided Stern for even raising the matter, thereby ending the discussion.[35]

The exchange between Baldwin and Stern is particularly interesting in that it suggests how the Communist Party's clandestine nature could create unforeseen difficulties. Since most Communists involved in progressive causes concealed their Party membership, it was sometimes unclear, even to other Communists, "who was who." This may have been the case in Stern's near undercutting of Baldwin's efforts to woo Wallace. Stern and his wife, Martha Dodd Stern, the daughter of William Dodd, the former U.S. ambassador to Germany, had been working for the NKVD (the forerunner of the KGB) since the 1930s. Like most Soviet agents in the United States, they were not "card carrying" Party members; but, unlike other operatives, they did travel openly in left-wing political circles, holding positions of influence in organizations such as the PCA. As friends of Henry Wallace and his wife Ilo, the Sterns heartily encouraged the former vice president to lead a third party and were active members after its founding. (Alfred later served on the controversial platform committee at the party's convention in Philadelphia.) Martha's warm relationship with Ilo helped temper some of the deep misgivings she harbored about her husband's independent candidacy and about the constantly hovering presence of, as she called them, "Beanie's boys." As the historians Allen Weinstein and Alexander Vassiliev have observed, however, the Sterns were not privy to the extent of CPUSA involvement or to the identities of secret party members working within the Wallace campaign. The authors note that during a conversation with Valentin Sorokin, their Soviet contact, on March 18, 1948, "Martha and Alfred, apparently unaware of the various Communist links to Wallace's staff and advisers, urged that the Soviet Union become actively involved in supporting the campaign." Ultimately, Moscow authorities made it clear that they did not want Martha or Alfred working for Wallace and specifically objected to their maintaining open relationships with CPUSA officials, some of whom were working undercover in the campaign.[36]

In any event, Baldwin saw to it that labor representatives did put in an appearance before Wallace, lest any lingering doubts remain. Only hours after the meeting at the Hotel McAlpin, a contingent of trade unionists headed by Kenneth Sherbell from Local 65 of the CIO Wholesale and Warehouse Workers Union, and Irving Potash of the New York Furriers Joint Council arrived at Wallace's *New Republic* office with a statement urging him to "give our people an alternative to reaction's bipartisan policy of inflation, depression, fascism, and war." Potash also pledged that his union would contribute $100,000 to the third party. (It never did.) A PCA press release trumpeted that the forty-five member delegation "represented" 263,000 New York workers. At the end of the five-page document, however, a note stated that the union affiliations given with their names were "for identification purposes only," a tacit acknowledgment that the officials were speaking not for their unions or their members but for themselves alone.[37]

The expedition likely brought the third party movement more bad publicity than good. Joseph Curran, the president of the National Maritime Union (NMU), told a *PM* reporter that the three NMU leaders who had signed the pro-Wallace statement had done so "without consulting him" and that "their action was contrary to his own views and those of the national CIO." Other press accounts emphasized that nearly all of the workers involved were from unions under "extreme left wing leadership"—a "red-baiting smear" according to Wallace supporters, but true in point of fact. Potash's presence only added to the controversy, since it was well known in labor circles that the Furriers' Union leader also served on the national committee of the Communist Party.[38]

The effect on Wallace is more difficult to gauge. It is unlikely that he knew of Potash's CP affiliation or would have seen any importance in it. Moreover, he did not realize that the third party was a topic of hot debate within the unions and that it was directly linked to the issue of communism. "I wasn't aware in those days of all the internal divisions in labor," Wallace later recalled. "I didn't know how significant they were as political forces." Wallace's new advisers were decidedly more "aware" and took special care to keep him from speaking with unsympathetic labor leaders— particularly with the CIO president Philip Murray, whom Wallace held in high regard. Surrounded by advisers who saw no need for him to be briefed on union politics, Wallace would enter the race assured of the backing of all "progressive" workers but apparently uninformed of the splits his candidacy would inevitably exacerbate within the labor movement.[39]

■ With the high-profile resignations from the PCA and the mounting criticism from leading liberals and union officials, Baldwin and his staff soon realized that the last two weeks of December would feature more damage control than pro-Wallace build up. In a lengthy response to a hostile editorial by *PM*'s Max Lerner, Baldwin defended the PCA's call for a third party as smart politics. The "millions of Americans who want peace abroad and jobs and freedom at home can be only organized and made vocal around a Wallace candidacy," he maintained. "A Wallace candidacy will provide the stimulus essential to bring out a large vote in 1948—without which progressive Congressmen, particularly those in the nation's many marginal districts, will be defeated." Contrary to Lerner's prediction, Baldwin insisted that liberals and labor would certainly support Wallace. "If you underestimate the rank-and-file feeling among American workers for Henry Wallace," he warned, "you are making a cardinal political error." Nor was the third party an ill-timed "gesture of defiance," as Lerner had claimed. "Let there be no misconception," Baldwin concluded: "This is a *practical* crusade. By asserting ourselves *now* we can give organized, powerful, effective expression to the yearning for peace, jobs, and freedom among our people. . . . We can halt the drift toward war if we let the people of the world know that there are millions of Americans who want peace. . . . By building a functioning people's political machine we can turn America again to the progressive path on which it belongs." A flurry of press releases echoed these points and countered persistent reports of the PCA's internal division by noting that only 4 of 140 national board members had resigned over the third party issue.[40]

Nonetheless, Baldwin's defense of the third party on practical political grounds was, as Lerner observed in his reply, "a fantastic flight from reality." Those who insisted on the "need" for a third party, he maintained, were "immune to events in the world outside their own minds." There was little evidence that Wallace was the only force capable of rallying "millions of Americans" to the progressive banner. In fact, the pro-Wallace or "progressive" wing of the Democratic Party, made up primarily of upper-middle-class Protestants and Jews, had already begun to estrange much of the white ethnic working class that had been a key component of the New Deal coalition. During the immediate postwar period, self-styled "progressives" routinely denounced American Poles, Czechs, and Hungarians who condemned Soviet crackdowns in their native countries as "reactionaries" and as "fascist sympathizers." Their condescending attitude toward all who expressed anticommunist views also irked working-class voters, particularly Catholics, who resented the anti-Catholic edge that often accompanied progressive rhetoric. The polls confirmed the erosion of pro-Wallace sentiment as well—his support in Gallup's presidential "trial heats" had plunged dramatically throughout the fall. In fact, a survey taken shortly after Baldwin's letter had appeared in *PM* showed that Robert A. Taft, the sponsor of the so-called slave labor Taft-Hartley Act, was outpolling Wallace by more than two to one among union members.[41]

Nor did it seem that "millions of Americans" were prepared to rally around a third party that espoused a more conciliatory policy toward the Soviet Union, especially one under left-wing leadership that welcomed Communist support. A poll taken in October 1947 found that 62 percent of the American people thought that the United States was being "too soft" on Russia, while only 6 percent viewed Truman's policies as "too tough." Seventy-six percent believed the Soviet Union was "out to rule the world."[42] The Soviets' angry rejection of the Marshall Plan promised to reduce voters' receptivity to Wallace's peace message even further, particularly among workers of Eastern and Central European descent. As Lew Frank conceded in a memo to Baldwin of November 26, "The foreign policy story must be told in new ways if we are going to broaden rather than narrow our audience." Frank suggested placing opposition to Truman's proposal for Universal Military Training (UMT) at the center of the Wallace attack, but UMT, too, had widespread public support. Indeed, until Wallace, Baldwin, and other PCA leaders recognized that most Americans' fear of war was directly linked to their fear of the spread of Soviet-style communism, the third party had little chance of attracting a substantial following.[43] If anything, Lerner predicted, Wallace's peace crusade would create a backlash. "When the election returns are in," he wrote, "and it is clear that Wallace has not drawn anything like the eight million votes his supporters have been talking of—or even half or a third that number—the victorious party will interpret the results as a mandate from the people to get even tougher with Russia than Truman has been." Lerner's analysis, of course, ultimately proved far more prescient than Baldwin's.[44]

The outcome of a closely watched 1947 congressional race in Washington State offered further evidence that Baldwin and his PCA colleagues had misread public opinion. In the mid-May primary, Charles Savage, who supported Wallace's foreign policy views, had defeated Smith Troy, an avowed "Truman Democrat," in a hotly contested contest. Since Savage had garnered twice as many votes as the victor in the Republican primary, he was expected to be a shoo-in in the June 7 special election. Though the candidate had deliberately avoided any discussion of international affairs and had won the support of several influential anti-Wallace Democrats, many Popular Front liberals nonetheless considered his impressive showing a confirmation of Wallace's growing strength. As election day approached, the local PCA and several out-of-town Communists assumed a high profile in the Savage campaign. They emphasized the candidate's opposition to the Truman Doctrine and brought Wallace into the district to speak on his behalf. More politically savvy than his erstwhile left-wing allies, Savage declined invitations to appear on the same platform as the former vice president. Meanwhile, the local Democratic Party imported several political "big wigs" of impeccable anticommunist credentials to counter the "red" stigma, but the damage had been done. Savage's two-to-one lead evaporated in less than three weeks, and he lost to his Republican opponent by nearly two thousand votes.[45]

Similarly, the Democrats were poised to pick up a House seat in Pennsylvania's Eighth District, which contained the heavily unionized cities of Allentown and Bethlehem. Once again, however, left-wing political activists assumed positions of leadership in the campaign and through their "militant" tactics and rhetoric managed to antagonize almost everyone in the district. When the candidate, Philip Storch, attempted to run an ad in the local newspaper expressing his support for the Marshall Plan and for the vigorous enforcement of all civil liberties as "the best defense" against communism, some of his Popular Front–oriented advisers intercepted it and threatened to pull out of the campaign if he insisted on its publication. They backed down only after an official from the Democratic National Committee threatened to put Storch on a nationwide radio hookup to recount the entire incident. Though polls showed Republicans' support eroding throughout the nation, their nominee beat Storch by more than 17,000 votes. The GOP's most optimistic preelection forecast had predicted a 5,000 vote victory. In short, Both Savage's and Storch's defeats suggested not only that Wallace's foreign policy positions were electoral poison but also that the "stand up and be counted" brand of "fighting progressivism" that Baldwin insisted the people were demanding was completely ineffective when put into practice.[46]

It is difficult to ascertain whether Baldwin actually believed the dubious arguments he made for the political practicality of launching a third party. But whether he was disingenuous or naive hardly mattered, so long as he could secure Wallace as the third party's standard-bearer. Given the temperament of his target, Baldwin wisely chose to set aside talk of "practical politics" in favor of making his case in the loftiest, most idealistic terms.

■ Wallace himself held no illusions about winning the 1948 election, so political calculation played little role in his decision to run. He expressed concern neither for his personal political standing nor for the level of public approval for his stated positions on various domestic issues. These were but distractions from his central purpose—the "fight for peace." "Peace," he assured his colleagues, "is really all our people are interested in right now." Accordingly, Wallace connected his decision to run with the impact he believed it would have on this overriding priority. He explained to those who urged him to enter the race that it would not be worthwhile unless he could be assured of getting three million votes; otherwise, he said, "the cause of peace would be damaged rather than helped."[47]

Once Wallace had accepted that his running for president would serve the cause of peace, however, he endowed his candidacy with a profound spiritual significance and seemingly transformed himself into the self-anointed leader of a holy crusade. As one historian has observed, "Wallace had for many years erected a fire wall between his mysticism and his politics . . . [but] something happened to [him] in 1948 that tore down that wall." Viewing himself as following in the footsteps of the Old Testament's prophets, Wallace was untroubled by evidence of ebbing support. Rather, he welcomed it, proclaiming that it only steeled his resolve. "The defection . . . of all the New Dealers who had once been on his side . . . was so unanimous that it might have shaken another man," the *New York Post* correspondent James Wechsler later wrote, "but Wallace seemed confident that his aloneness was irrefutable proof of his virtue." The columnist Walter Lippmann suggested that since leaving the cabinet, the Iowan had discarded the role of campaigning politician for that of religious martyr. Wallace, Lippmann maintained, had fled from the "laborious give and take of politics and administration to the comforting applause of coteries, to the development of a cult, and to making himself a sacrificial offering for the sins of the world." Characterizing what he believed was the unhealthy relationship between Wallace and his Communist backers, the socialist leader Norman Thomas remarked, "It is the case of a disorganized leader with a Messianic complex who must deal with a well-organized party with a Messianic complex." When Frank Kingdon, an ordained Methodist minister, warned Wallace against running, he appealed to his friend's fondness for biblical references. "Why, Henry," exclaimed Kingdon, "you won't have a Gideon's Army to support you." "That's exactly what we've got," Wallace proudly replied. But, as one student of the Old Testament story has noted, in preparing for his battle against the Midianites, "Gideon himself had done the winnowing down to three hundred men from ten thousand—he had not been deserted."[48]

On December 29, 1947, Wallace ended the speculation surrounding his intentions by declaring his candidacy in a twenty-minute address carried nationally over the Mutual Broadcasting System. Explicitly linking his decision to the issue of "peace," Wallace declared, "The bigger the peace vote in 1948, the more definitely the world will know that the United States is not behind the bi-partisan reactionary war policy which is dividing the world into two armed camps and making inevitable the day when American soldiers will be lying in their Arctic suits in the Russian snow." He called for popular resistance to the "handful of warmongers" and "rich monopolists" who were "willing to sacrifice their sons [and] their money . . . for the sake of world control." A New Party would "fight these war makers," he pledged. "We say that peace is mandatory and that it can be had if we only want it. . . . We can prevent depression and war if we only organize for peace in the same comprehensive way we organize for war." The menace of atomic war could only be overcome by "the organization of a new political party." "To that end," Wallace continued, "I announce tonight that I shall run as an independent candidate for President of the United States in 1948." In an emotional conclusion to his remarks, he reaffirmed in the unmistakable Wallace idiom that "the people are on the march": "We have assembled a Gideon's Army, small in number, powerful in conviction, ready for action. . . . We face the future unfettered—unfettered by any principle but the general welfare. We owe no allegiance to any group which does not serve that welfare. By God's grace, the people's peace will usher in the century of the common man."[49]

Most observers agreed that Wallace's candidacy would more likely usher in a Republican president. "I shouldn't be surprised," declared Lerner, "if in their secret midnight rites, in the fastnesses of their lonely hearts, the Knights of the Elephant make a special votive offering at the shrine of St. Henry." "Yes, Republicans," wrote another political columnist, "there is a Santa Claus. His name is Henry A. Wallace. A day or two late, but he certainly brought a lot of holiday cheer to the GOP." In their immediate reactions to Wallace's announcement, Republican politicians seemed scarcely able to contain their delight. "The Moscow wing of the Democratic Party now has parted company with the Pendergast wing," crowed B. Carroll Reece, the chairman of the Republican National Committee, "and the nation will be the winner when both gangs lose." The "old guard" Republicans especially stood to benefit, it was argued, since the party could now win with "anybody," and, noted one reporter, "'anybody' usually means Taft." Wallace even drew kudos from an old nemesis, Hamilton Fish, the archconservative isolationist, who publicly congratulated him on his candidacy.[50]

Many Democrats, particularly the party's northern liberals, glumly conceded that the Republicans had good reason to celebrate. Wallace would draw the votes of enough "independent progressives" to tip the balance in several key states and thus hand the White House to the GOP. Still worse was the third party's threat to oppose all Democratic candidates for Congress who supported the Marshall Plan. By splitting the progressive vote, pro-Wallace challengers would sabotage the Senate campaigns of such liberals as Hubert Humphrey of Minnesota and Paul Douglas of Illinois and would put out of reach several congressional seats in New York and California that would otherwise have gone to the Democrats. Even in those instances in which the Wallaceites supported a progressive Democrat, liberals argued, the third party's Communist-tainted endorsement would do more harm than good; indeed, it would have to be repudiated if the candidate were to have any hope of victory. Democrats dismissed as "absurd" Baldwin's claim that Wallace's presence in the race would bring out the heavy vote needed to elect a liberal Congress. "Every liberal major-party candidate will be faced with this same problem," wrote one party strategist. "He will necessarily be forced to oppose Mr. Wallace openly and most of the policies on which Mr. Wallace is running, especially in the field of foreign affairs which Wallace is emphasizing in his campaign. Consequently, he could hardly expect to get support from those voters who will vote for Mr. Wallace and his program." Marshall Field's *Chicago Sun,* one of the nation's leading liberal newspapers, acknowledged the validity of Wallace's and the PCA's "broad objectives" but was baffled at the means they chose to achieve them. "This sort of thing just doesn't make sense," the paper commented in a lead editorial. "When progressives find themselves promoting reactionary causes and helping to elect reactionaries, it is time to pause for station identification. The majority of sincere liberals in the Wallace movement owes itself some serious thinking about where it is headed."[51]

President Truman himself made no public comment on the Wallace announcement. Indeed, though Truman's political advisers expressed great anxiety over the potential defection of the Democratic Party's left wing to the Wallace camp, particularly during late 1947 and early 1948, the president himself gave little indication that he shared their concern. Commenting on Wallace in later years, Truman recalled, "I knew the more he talked, the more votes he'd lose." It wasn't so much that Wallace was dishonest, the former president explained; "it was just that half the time and more he just didn't seem to make sense." Contemporary sources confirm that Truman held the same view in 1948. He expressed exasperation at Wallace's "wild statements" and regret at the manner in which he believed the Communists were using the former vice president, but he did not consider him a significant factor in the campaign. Notably, he never bore Wallace any personal animosity despite the latter's almost daily attacks on his character and integrity during the campaign.[52]

Other Democrats also seemed less concerned. Unlike the partisan liberals whose numbers were concentrated in a handful of big cities and who often talked only to each other, the party's full-time politicians and ward heelers were more in tune with the national mood. They were not misled, as were many liberal activists, by the notion that voters supported the Democrats because of the party's identification with the more extreme (or "advanced") policies of the New Deal, commonly associated with Wallace. Removed from the hothouse atmosphere of the liberal "civil war," they were less likely to overestimate the former vice president's potential strength or the electoral clout of the Democratic Party's left wing. They realized that even though Wallace claimed to have the backing of the "common man," his primary base of support had always been limited to a relatively small group of left-leaning intellectuals, middle-class professionals, and CIO labor leaders, many of whom had already broken with him over the third party issue. Some party "regulars" even welcomed Wallace's departure. "Good riddance," cried Frank McHale, the Democratic national committeeman from Indiana. "He is a much confused man and always had his thingamajigs mixed up with his whatchamacallits." Men like McHale even hoped Wallace would take the assorted "crackpots," "screwballs," and "parlor pinks" with him. For every disgruntled New Dealer who might be tempted to follow Wallace out of the party, five more moderate to conservative Democrats who had been alienated by the left-wingers' noisy utopian chatter could be won back. Moreover, with Wallace directing his main fire at Truman and running, in essence, as the Communist Party candidate for president, the Republicans could hardly pin the "red" label on the Democrats, as they had done to such devastating effect during the 1946 elections. In off-the-record remarks, many GOP insiders were already acknowledging as much, conceding that by November Wallace's candidacy might even prove a boon to the Democrats.[53]

In labor circles, the launching of the third party drew a cold shoulder from nearly every national union leader, with the conspicuous exception of those associated with the pro-Soviet faction in the CIO and a handful of AFL locals under Communist control. On January 16, A. F. Whitney, the president of the Brotherhood of Railroad Trainmen and the most prominent union official in the PCA, resigned from the organization and reaffirmed his support for President Truman. The AFL president William Green and A. Philip Randolph, the head of the Brotherhood of Sleeping

Car Porters, likewise repudiated the third party. Philip Murray wired all CIO affiliates that public support of "any party or candidate" before the CIO's executive board meeting in late January would be "contrary to the actions taken by the Boston convention."[54] Even before Wallace's official announcement, the president of the United Auto Workers, Walter P. Reuther, declared that labor would "not go along with the new fellow." At a National Press Club luncheon on December 18, he lamented that Wallace was a "lost soul," the latest in a succession of well-meaning individuals taken for a ride by the Communist Party. "Communists perform the most complete valet service in the world," said Reuther in widely quoted remarks. "They write your speeches, they do your thinking for you, they provide you with applause, and they inflate your ego as often as necessary. I am afraid that's the trouble with Henry Wallace." As expected, Jacob Potofsky, the head of the Amalgamated Clothing Workers, pulled his 300,000-member union out of the ALP, leaving control in the hands of its pro-Wallace left wing, which immediately endorsed the third party.[55]

At an acrimonious meeting of the CIO executive board on January 23, Murray introduced a resolution opposing the third party and explicitly endorsing the Marshall Plan. He encountered vigorous resistance from pro-Soviet board members who were under instructions from the Communist Party to pursue any tactic they could to delay the CIO's outright repudiation of the Wallace candidacy. At one point a bitter exchange erupted between Murray and the president of the International Longshoremen's and Warehousemen's Union (ILWU), Harry Bridges. As they sparred over the Marshall Plan and allegations of Russian atrocities in Eastern Europe, their argument reached an awkward climax when Murray exclaimed that if Bridges were in the Soviet Union denouncing Stalin in the same way he was now criticizing Truman, he would be liquidated. "I am not so sure that's so," Bridges retorted awkwardly.[56] Despite the long and rancorous debate, neither side made any converts and the resolution passed easily, 33 to 11. Even the president of the Transport Workers Union, Michael Quill, who had already expressed his doubts about the third party to Communist officials, voted with the pro-Soviet bloc.[57] In an unprecedented move, Murray released the final breakdown of the board's vote to the press, exposing the pro-Soviet faction as a minority within the CIO, a sign that his patience with its leaders was wearing thin. On February 6, he accepted the resignation of Lee Pressman, the CIO's able general counsel and a longtime Murray protégé, who was identified with the pro-Soviet faction. Soon after, Pressman went to work for the third party campaign.[58]

True to form, the Communist Party welcomed Wallace's "momentous decision" with great fanfare. On the day after the announcement, the *Daily Worker* devoted fourteen columns of pictures and stories to the third party. "Wallace's candidacy . . . is a historic challenge to a vast and sinister conspiracy against the true interests of the United States," the Communist organ proclaimed. "Wallace's candidacy, and the platform on which he makes his fight, sounds the call for a national fight for peace which will show where every progressive really stands—for peace and democracy, or for witch hunts and war." In what sounded more like instructions than observations, George Morris, the *Daily Worker's* labor columnist, remarked, "From what I know of Wallace supporters in CIO ranks, it is a foregone conclusion that they will not obey Murray's injunction [against supporting the third party]." The Communist press in Europe and in the Soviet Union also showered accolades on the New Party, commending its commitment to fight American imperialism and the Marshall Plan.[59]

Such unsolicited praise was political poison, though Wallace was reluctant to say so publicly. At a press conference following his radio address, he told reporters that he supposed Communists would indeed vote for him, "because I'm sincerely in favor of peace." He believed they would support him in the same way as "the Quakers and Methodists who want peace also." "I'd hope, though," he added, "that if the Communists in this country vote for me they didn't come out and say so in formal resolutions." When asked if American Communists were agents of the Soviet Union, Wallace said that he did not know, but that he made it a point to ask every avowed Communist he met "point blank" whether such was the case. "They all answer that they don't seem to have any way of getting in touch with Moscow and that Moscow doesn't seem to want anything to do with them," he remarked. "'They don't invite us to their parties in Washington,' they say, and they sounded kind of pathetic, like poor lonesome souls." As to whether he would disclaim Communist backing, Wallace told reporters, "I will do exactly as Roosevelt would have done and you can look up the record on that." Unhappily, the press took up his challenge and found that Roosevelt had indeed repudiated Communist support, thus keeping alive a question that would plague Wallace throughout the campaign.[60]

Critics maintained that Wallace failed to understand that the real issue was not who *joined* his third party, but who *controlled* it. Freda Kirchwey of the *Nation*, herself often accused of being too uncritical of both foreign and domestic Communists, warned Wallace that by choosing to launch his crusade without first securing broad-based support, he had handed over his movement in advance to "political forces—in this case the Communists—whose decisions are controlled by interests unrelated to the needs and desires of Henry Wallace's 'common man.'" From the opposite end of the political spectrum, the ex-Communist and conservative journalist Eugene Lyons reached a similar conclusion. "While Wallace has the vague support of a large body of dissatisfied people, he does not control directly any single group sufficiently cohesive to provide the things that count in an election: the money, the planned propaganda, the local political machinery. . . . The only solid political base at his disposal," Lyons wrote, "is the pro-Soviet totalitarian left, and that is available strictly on its own terms." After acknowledging that Wallace's appeal had awakened "an unexpectedly large response," Dwight Macdonald suggested that the relationship of the "common man" to the Wallace campaign "was about the same as to the movies: the passive audience; he was not the director, the script writer, or the producer." These roles, Macdonald asserted, were played by the CPUSA, while Wallace, as long as he followed the script, was permitted to star as "The Great Leader." Others emphasized that the Popular Front sensibilities of the third party's non-Communists and Wallace's own detached attitude toward his campaign had made Communist control all but inevitable. The candidate's lack of political acumen and his disinterest in organization and strategy presented a situation ideally suited for the CP. "Anyone who has worked lately in unions or political movements knows that the disciplined Communist minority will take over unless sturdily opposed," declared the Washington columnist Doris Fleeson. With no "right wing" in the third party to resist them, she predicted, "the tireless, zealous core of Communists among the Wallace following" would rush in to fill the vacuum.[61]

For their part, the Communists flatly denied allegations of undue influence in the third party. "We cannot possibly control a movement of such majestic proportions," protested Joseph Starobin, at that time a *Daily Worker* columnist. Yet, significantly, Starobin also defended the post-Duclos line that called for the CPUSA to play the leading role in any "antimonopoly coalition" while retaining its own political independence. In the past, he wrote, "some [progressives] sought our help, at the doorsteps and in the back rooms of their election campaigns, but were the first to turn around and create this system of political castes, of 'untouchables' in American life. 'The Moor has done his work; the Moor must go.' Well, it's time to drop this deformation of American politics. . . . And the man who is frightened at the line of duty because we [Communists] are fighting on that same line could not have had his heart very deep in it to begin with." The CPUSA was never able to reconcile the tension between the requirements of the post-Duclos line and the practical need to mute the Communist presence in the Progressive Party. In retrospect, CPers active in the campaign acknowledged that Wallace's failure to draw more organized liberal support, due in large part to the Communists' own "narrow, possessive, and destructive attitudes," resulted in the CP playing a more obvious and intrusive part in the third party than it had originally intended.[62]

Still, Gideon's Army was not merely "a division of Stalin's foreign legion," as some would later claim. Wallace's assertion that both the Democratic and the Republican parties were in the hands of conspiring "Wall Street monopolists" may have echoed the editorial page of the *Daily Worker*, but it also reiterated one of the oldest themes associated with American populism. Wallace's ability to tap into this political stream undoubtedly accounted for much of his initial support among voters who had no ties to the pro-Soviet left. In the eyes of his non-Communist supporters, observed William Harlan Hale, "[Wallace's] political rise had brought high hope. . . . Fighting militarism, monopoly, and race hatred, he embodied much of what was best in America's progressive tradition." Many who were neither Communists nor fellow travelers shared Wallace's disgust with the two major parties and yearned to cast their vote for a "fighting liberal" committed to "halting the march of reaction." In their angry letters to such liberal publications as *PM*, the *Nation*, and the *Progressive*, Wallace supporters expressed feelings of frustration and betrayal, denouncing the Truman administration for its abandonment of the ideals of FDR and for its alleged complicity with "reactionary" Republicans in thwarting the progressive agenda. Having looked forward to a postwar world of peace and abundance and gotten instead the Cold War and inflation, they were bitterly disappointed and eager for affirmative, idealistic leadership that promised to set things right again. Though most progressives were deeply committed to particular positions on a variety of foreign and domestic issues, their knowledge of these issues did not always match their emotional fervor. They preferred inspirational rhetoric to closely argued analysis, which perhaps explains their attraction to Wallace. "The editorials in the *Nation* and the *New Republic* certainly never inspire any one to anything but different degrees of anger," complained one letter writer. "They are intellectual and truthful, but what is lacking is a sense of hope for the future. . . . Let the *Nation* give us some inspiration along with its wisdom."[63]

Wallace's appeal derived from his ability to spell out in plain, often moralistic terms "what had gone wrong" and from his unbounded optimism that all might yet be well. "Militarists and monopolists," Wallace told his followers, had seized political power and were undermining majority rule by blocking the enactment of the progressive legislation that the people demanded. To enhance their own economic standing, these native fascists had conspired to keep prices high and wages low. To distract attention from their maneuvering, they had manufactured the "Communist threat," which led to anticommunist policies that were subverting civil liberties at home and stemming the tide of "social progress" abroad. In so doing, they had frightened a weak and insecure Soviet Union, forcing the Russians to respond with defensive measures to protect their "social experiment" from the threat of reaction and counterrevolution. Soviet behavior in Eastern Europe was therefore understandable, even if its more brutal aspects might offend Western sensibilities. Unfortunately, American reactionaries had made it the grounds for whipping up even more anti-Soviet "hysteria," which would eventually stampede the country into an unwinnable war. Nevertheless, Wallace promised, if the American people could cast these selfish Wall Street conspirators out of government, progressive men and women could sit down with Stalin and settle all outstanding differences through the auspices of the United Nations. With "the people's peace" secured, the way would be paved for international cooperation and the creation of "One World" in which diplomats would abide by the "doctrines of Christ" instead of "the doctrine of Machiavelli." The communist and capitalist systems would engage in "friendly competition," and the resulting "production for peace" would mean abundance for all. In time, the two conflicting ideologies would converge as the Russians introduced more "political democracy" and the United States embraced "economic democracy." Such a plan for world peace and abundance was not "appeasement" or "Communism," Wallace insisted, but applied Christianity. Indeed, Wallace often cited the Sermon on the Mount as the proper model for American diplomacy.[64]

The former vice president's admirers found his message compelling. The radical journalist I. F. Stone believed Wallace spoke for "the conscience of America—for all that is best in our country, its naive idealism, its irrepressible optimism." "He is saying all the things I have wished to hear some public man say for years," the New Dealer Rexford Tugwell wrote in his journal after attending a Wallace rally in early 1948. Even if he was not always logically right, observed the *New York Post* columnist Samuel Grafton, "Wallace's strength is that he is emotionally right." Supporters claimed for him "an underlying logic which transcends words." But even more important, Wallace spoke out earnestly for peace at a time when most other government leaders appeared to be preparing for war. In June 1947, when

Wallace's popularity was at its peak, a concerned Gael Sullivan, the executive director of the Democratic National Committee, alerted the party that there was "no question that Wallace has captured the imagination of a strong segment of the American public." Though the Communists were stage-managing most of the enthusiasm at Wallace's mass meetings, many in the crowd were not "left wingers," Sullivan reported. "This group feels strongly that the Truman policy means war. They were present honestly to protest against such a policy. There are many veterans who feel the same way. Let's face it," he said, "The veterans of World War II don't relish any thought of another war. They know how tough the Russians are." Three months later, James Loeb of Americans for Democratic Action observed that Wallace's peace message remained enticing, "even among liberals who disagree with much of his thinking."[65]

To those less taken with Wallace, his pleas for peace and a better world, however well intentioned or idealistic, were ultimately meaningless, for, in their view, he offered only eloquently stated objectives rather than workable policies. "As a result," wrote the *Nation*'s Margaret Marshall, "just when you expect him to show you the trail through the underbrush which will get us all to the mountaintop, you find that he is no longer by your side; he has flown on the wings of words to the peak itself and there he stands, against the sky, proclaiming the beauties of peace, security, and abundance." Citing the "rickety framework of half-analysis and distorted analysis" that he believed characterized Wallace's announcement speech, Max Lerner lamented, "His head simply does not keep pace with his heart." Similarly, the *New York Herald Tribune* was struck by the address's "intellectual shallowness." "Mr. Wallace speaks for 'peace and abundance,' which is as relevant, in these complexly difficult times, as coming out against sin and for Santa Claus. Beside his suggestions as to how these ends are to be attained, the bathos of the celebrated 'Cross of Gold' metaphor seems a model of precision, clarity, and the terse translation of a political need into an effective policy."[66]

Wallace's tendency to look past the realities of the moment manifested itself most conspicuously in his discussion of U.S.-Soviet relations. To Wallace, "reaching a complete understanding with Russia" simply required that men of goodwill sit down around a table, discuss their differences, and sign a treaty. Since peace was in everybody's interest, all that was necessary was both sides' genuine desire for it. "How much happier it would be," he mused in July 1947, "if President Truman would take all those things which he believes we want from Russia, and if Stalin would take all those things which he believes Russia wants from us, and at a meeting of the two heads of government, each item was canceled against each other." "And you think Stalin is amenable to this sort of settlement of differences?" a reporter later asked him. "Why, yes," said Wallace. "I am sure he is. He would have to be."[67]

Not all the candidate's old admirers shared his faith in the Russians. One of the most stinging assessments of Wallace's approach to U. S.-Soviet relations came from a rather unexpected source. In a series of "My Day" columns in early 1948, Eleanor Roosevelt directed a barrage of uncharacteristically sharp criticism at the former vice president. "The steady progress of the USSR's political influence over every state which they have taken over shows that they have every intention of spreading Communism wherever they can," she declared. "Are we to be so naive as to believe that, with such a program well under way, a few gentle words from us will change the USSR's policy?" Wallace's incomprehension of the difficulties involved in carrying out policy and his lack of diplomatic experience, she argued, had led him to oversimplify the issues and underestimate the intransigence of Soviet officials. "We live in . . . a much more complicated world than Mr. Wallace seems to understand," she wrote. "I have worked rather more steadily and closely with the representatives of the USSR than has Mr. Wallace. . . . They understand strength, not weakness, and they say many things they know are not true because they think they can make others believe they are true. . . . When Mr. Wallace assumes that by changing certain of our policies until we resemble Mr. Chamberlain, hat in hand, approaching Hitler, we will have the results which he calls 'peace and abundance,' I am afraid he is doing more wishful thinking than realistic facing of facts." "As a leader of a third party," she concluded, "[Wallace] will merely destroy the very things he wishes to achieve. . . . He never has been a good politician, he never has been able to gauge public opinion, and he never has picked his advisers wisely. . . . I am sorry that he has listened to people as inept politically as he is himself." When journalists asked Wallace for a response, he sidestepped the issue, claiming he had not yet gotten a chance to read the comments. Eleanor Roosevelt provides a telling contrast to Wallace, for both had at one time shared a liberal crusading spirit that gave them more in common with each other than either may have had with Franklin Roosevelt. As her biographer Joseph Lash has observed, Eleanor remained a "reluctant cold-warrior," a staunch defender of the United Nations, and a forceful critic of President Truman when it appeared to her that his policies were undermining UN authority. Yet her face-to-face dealings with Soviet officials at the UN proved profoundly disillusioning. Every attempt she made to be conciliatory, she came to believe, her Soviet counterparts perceived as "evidence of weakness rather than as a gesture of good will." "She had begun her career at the United Nations bending over backward to show the Russians she was ready to meet them halfway," Lash writes. "By 1949 she was stating publicly she would 'never again' compromise, 'even on words.'" Wallace, on the other hand, had no firsthand experience negotiating with the Russians and saw U.S.-Soviet relations in largely abstract terms.[68]

■ Amid the political fallout that the launching of the third party had precipitated, the PCA met in Chicago during the weekend of January 17 for its second annual convention. In an embarrassing indication of the fast-changing times, delegates carried folders prominently displaying the photographs of men who had since resigned from the organization. Robert Kenny, the PCA's remaining co-chairman, referred to himself as "the boy on the burning deck, whence all but he had fled." No representatives from organized labor were to be found; also absent were observers from the many other liberal organizations who supposedly supported Wallace. Still, there was no shortage of enthusiasm among the rank-and-file members. "The assembly differed little from an old-fashioned, downstate revival meeting; full of hosannas and good will," observed the *Chicago Sun's* political columnist, Pete Akers. "Now and then, as the mood took hold," he wrote, "one would cast an eye for the sawdust trail, conjecturing, meanwhile, on the likelihood of the congregation breaking forth into the strains of 'Almost Persuaded.'" All around him Akers saw "the Hallelujah boys and girls, delightful lads and lasses who seek utopia with the same zeal my old Macorpia County grandmother sought backsliders."[69]

But there were discordant notes in the hallelujah chorus. In an early indication of the bitterly personal campaign that was to come, the former Minnesota governor Elmer Benson declared that the liberal mayor of Minneapolis, Hubert H. Humphrey, was a "fascist at heart." Benson threatened that if Humphrey received the nomination for the U.S. Senate, the third party would surely run a candidate against him. The Cook County Progressive leader Zalmon Garfield, a concealed Communist, likewise promised opposition to the New Dealer Paul Douglas, whom he denounced as an "open warmonger." "It would be dangerous to have him in the Senate," Garfield asserted. Other angry voices threw into doubt the organization's commitment to democracy. At an afternoon press conference, the entertainer Paul Robeson boldly declared, "I am a violent anti-fascist. I want to destroy fascism, and to do it I'm prepared to accept the opposite form of dictatorship." In addition, as one reporter noted, "the overslick parliamentary procedure that smothered any incipient opposition; the pre-arranged slate of candidates . . . swept into office by acclamation; . . . the brittle sophistry of the official pronouncements that highlighted all the weaknesses of American democracy and ascribed their existence to such subjective villains as 'Wall Street profiteers' and 'warmongers'" combined to give the convention many of the characteristics of a Communist front.[70]

For those who looked closely, there were also the tedious deceits and moral double standards that evidenced the behind-the-scenes presence of the CP. While awaiting Wallace's appearance, the delegates watched a movie that featured the candidate delivering a speech in which he essentially repeated his announcement address of December 29. All of Wallace's references to "Russian extremists," however, had been carefully edited out of the film. The convention resolution on displaced persons heartily endorsed removing U.S. immigration barriers so that "victims of Nazi and Fascist persecution who desire to come to this country may do so," but it made no mention of easing restrictions for the victims of communist oppression, who accounted for a large percentage of Europe's refugees. To those experienced at covering such Popular Front gatherings, the combination of emotional fervor and political sleight of hand was nothing new. "Yes," Akers concluded his column, "the Hallelujah boys and girls raised the rafters, but the Communists too frequently swung the baton."[71]

After the convention, Wallace retreated to his farm in South Salem, New York, to tend his chickens and strawberries. He also began work on what became his foreign policy manifesto, a short book entitled *Toward World Peace* that reiterated the themes of his stump speeches. Michael Straight replaced Wallace as the editor of the *New Republic* and began the gradual process of distancing his magazine from the third party. Bewildered by the rapid turn of events that had produced Wallace's independent candidacy, Harold Young announced his intention to take a "brief vacation" in his hometown of Odessa, Texas. He would not return.[72] Frank Kingdon, having despaired of convincing Wallace that the Communists were using him, continued his futile campaign to capture the U.S. Senate nomination in New Jersey. And, having achieved their goal of securing Wallace, Beanie Baldwin and John Abt returned to Manhattan and set to work on building the New Party organization. Whether it would evolve into a broad people's coalition capable of spearheading the fight for peace, as Wallace had predicted, remained to be seen.

3

ONE ROBIN DOESN'T BRING
NO SPRING

Early Victories and Mounting Attacks

Before February 17, 1948, few people outside of New York City had even heard of Leo Isacson, the American Labor Party (ALP) nominee for Congress who was running in a special election to be held that day in the Bronx. The next morning, however, news of Isacson's astonishing two-to-one victory grabbed front-page headlines across the country. In trouncing "boss" Edward J. Flynn's Democratic organization, Isacson, the candidate backed by Henry Wallace and his third party movement, sent shock waves through the political establishment. Pundits claimed that his victory would have national, even international repercussions, while jubilant Wallace supporters proclaimed that the results amounted to a wholesale repudiation of the Truman administration. As panicked Democrats and independent liberals scrambled to distance themselves from the allegedly "unelectable" Missourian, expectations within Gideon's Army swelled to an all-time high as various state and local organizations sprung up across the country. Speaking at a campaign rally in Florida, Wallace predicted that this early triumph would be the first of many—proof that "the so-called third party can become the first party in 1948." Though few honestly expected a November victory for the former vice president, the Isacson landslide did precipitate a hasty reevaluation of Wallace's political strength. "It is abundantly clear," wrote one New York editor, "that Mr. Wallace, no doubt astonished by what a bit of muscle flexing in the

71

Bronx could start whirling, has only barely begun to make trouble." Within labor and liberal circles, there was no shortage of concern about just how serious this trouble was going to be.[1]

■ The campaign in the Bronx's Twenty-Fourth district had begun on January 14, when the New York Governor Thomas E. Dewey ordered a special election to fill the vacancy left by the Democrat Benjamin J. Rabin's elevation to the state Supreme Court. In an early development, Ed Flynn, the head of the Bronx Democratic Committee, rejected an offer of alliance from the anticommunist Liberal Party. This paved the way for a four-man race consisting of candidates from the Democratic, American Labor, Liberal, and Republican Parties.[2] The Republicans, with no hope of winning in this traditionally Democratic stronghold, did not wage an active campaign. The Liberals, who had withdrawn from the ALP in 1944 to protest the growing Communist influence in the party, nominated the popular Dean Alfange, their top vote-getter. Though party officials conceded that they could not marshal enough support to win the election, they nonetheless planned to wage a vigorous campaign against the Communist-dominated ALP and the "bossism" of Flynn's Democratic machine. Alfange, they declared, was the only genuinely independent liberal in the race. Flynn countered with Karl Propper, a capable attorney and loyal party wheelhorse, but otherwise a man of little distinction. Convinced that a Democratic victory was a given, the boss apparently gave little thought to selecting his candidate. The ALP nominated Isacson, who was soon endorsed by Wallace.[3]

In contrast to his main opponent, the colorless, fifty-five-year-old Propper, Isacson cut a dashing figure. Handsome, athletic, a dynamic speaker, and much younger looking than his thirty-seven years, he was a rising star in the ALP. Raised in the Twenty-Fourth, Isacson graduated from New York University Law School in 1934, opened a small practice, and joined the ALP at its founding two years later. During the 1945 session, he served as the ALP's lone representative in the State Assembly, where he quickly won recognition as a militant champion of labor and veterans' causes. In an unsuccessful run for Bronx borough president the same year, he received the highest vote the ALP had ever polled. After losing his reelection bid to the assembly in the 1946 Republican sweep, he returned to the law, taking on labor and tenant cases. Representing the district's poorer residents in their battles against rent hikes, Isacson became a well-known figure, widely admired for his noble efforts on behalf of "little man." He also established a reputation as an ardent Zionist, serving for a time as the president of the local chapter of the Zionist Organization of America. In a district more than 40 percent Jewish and at a time when the partition of Palestine had stirred passions to a fever pitch, such a credential would serve him well.[4]

The Twenty-Fourth offered fertile ground for a young insurgent like Isacson. Fronting on the filthy East River along the far southeast corner of the Bronx, the district was a bleak area in the midst of a protracted economic decline. Notorious for its lack of quality schools, playgrounds, and health centers, it had the borough's highest rates of juvenile delinquency and disease. Crowded, walk-up tenement houses built at the turn of the century lined the dank, littered streets. Badly heated and inadequately lit, these old-law flats were home to thousands of poor blacks, Puerto Ricans, Italians, Irish, and Jews, many of whom were on relief or barely getting by. "It's a district," one observer remarked, "where tenants' leagues fight every eviction and a nickel rise in grocery prices means a lot." With crime and rents on the rise while wages and living standards remained stagnant, longtime residents were desperate to leave. Yet even those who could afford to do so ran up against the acute housing shortage that plagued the entire city. Frustration was also mounting among the area's newly arrived African Americans and Puerto Ricans. Often scapegoated for causing the neighborhood's deterioration, they were particularly sensitive to racial discrimination and deeply resented the callous indifference of the white "machine" politicians. Indeed, throughout the district, both of the traditional parties had become thoroughly discredited. The mere mention of politics brought bitter comments all around as voters expressed their willingness to embrace any figure who could successfully challenge the status quo.[5]

Isacson and the ALP were well positioned to capitalize on such dissatisfaction. The party had always done well in the Twenty-Fourth, where it polled approximately three times its statewide average. In the previous congressional election, the ALP had finished a respectable second to the Democrats, garnering 27 percent of the vote in a four-way race. More important, in a special election the party could concentrate all of its renowned organizational strength into one district—a technique it had used to great effect in the February 1946 bout involving Johannes Steel. In that contest, the ALP had drawn almost 100 percent of its regular voters to the polls, a remarkable accomplishment since special elections usually attracted less than a 30 percent turnout. As a result, while the actual number of votes cast for the ALP remained constant, the party's percentage of the entire vote jumped from 18 to 38 percent. This exceptional "get out the vote" drive nearly produced an upset victory over the Democrats who thought they had done well to attract 40 percent of their regular voters. If the ALP could even approximate such a performance in the Twenty-Fourth, a district in which it had an even stronger presence, an Isacson victory—though few realized it at the time—was well-nigh assured.[6]

Disregarding the unique advantages the ALP brought to the contest and the mood of discontent among the district's Democratic voters, boss Flynn and the Bronx county leadership chose to portray the election as a gauge of the Wallace movement's strength in New York vis-à-vis the Truman administration. Democrats outside the Empire State followed Flynn's lead and billed the Isacson-Propper showdown as a test case of Wallace's political clout nationally, hoping a poor showing by the ALP would put a quick end to the third party adventure. Picking up on the race's dramatic potential, the press duly reported the politicos' ill-advised preelection analyses, often leaving the impression that Wallace himself was on the ballot. New Party strategists, well aware that their political enemies had handed them a golden opportunity, embraced their opponents' assessment of the election's significance, declaring that it would be nothing less than the American people's referendum on Truman's policies of "depression and war."[7]

The campaign itself was hard fought from the outset. The ALP effort, spark-plugged by the Communists and their allies in the labor movement, relied heavily on house-to-house canvassing. The CP, along with its young people's auxiliary, American Youth for Democracy, recruited its members from throughout the metropolitan area to work for Isacson. Some arrived from as far away as Buffalo or cities and towns in Connecticut and Pennsylvania. The Communist-controlled unions released their staffs of paid employees for two weeks to serve as organizers and doorbell ringers, while the *Daily Worker* urged its subscribers to volunteer in any capacity they could. In all, the campaign drafted well over three thousand men and women who "tramped through the snow" for Isacson. On election day, the ALP had approximately one canvasser for every seventy persons pledged to support the party's nominee. Not only their numbers, but the unwavering political commitment of the ALP and Communist volunteers made them a formidable force. Though the Democrats could muster comparable manpower, many of their recruits simply went through the motions. Their support for Propper never matched the intense feelings of the Isacson partisans. The ALP also far outspent its opposition, blanketing the Twenty-Fourth with car cards, pamphlets, handbills, and giant posters. The image of Isacson's smiling face peered out from hundreds of storefront windows, while party workers in sound trucks plugged for their man in Yiddish, Spanish, and English.[8]

Both the Democrats and the ALP brought their "heavy hitters" to campaign in the district, confirming for many observers the broader significance the parties attributed to the contest. "This will be no pillow fight," declared New York's popular Democratic mayor William O'Dwyer as he announced his intention to go "all out" for Propper. Eleanor Roosevelt, too, agreed to speak on the candidate's behalf.[9] For its part, the ALP, which functioned as the New Party's New York State organization, emphasized repeatedly that Isacson was the "Wallace candidate." Party leaders arranged for the two men to make several joint appearances in the district. To give the campaign some added glitz, they secured the services of various celebrities—the heavyweight champion Joe Louis and the Broadway actors José Ferrer and Canada Lee were among the "names" who entertained the crowds at Isacson rallies. Recognizing the potency of dramatic ethnic appeals, the ALP also relied on the moving oratory of the African American vocalist Paul Robeson to win the black vote and on the legendary histrionics of the East Harlem congressman Vito Marcantonio to mobilize support among Italians and Puerto Ricans. In the district's southwest corner, the president of the Transport Workers Union, Mike Quill, promoted Isacson's candidacy to his predominantly Irish membership in an unmistakable County Kerry brogue.[10]

The ALP's appeal for the Jewish vote, led by Isacson himself, centered on the issue of the Palestine partition. The United Nations had voted in November 1947 to split the British mandate into an Arab and a Jewish state, but during the following few months, difficult questions arose as to how the policy would be implemented. In the meantime, fighting broke out in the region as Arabs opposed to the UN verdict set out to reverse it by force of arms. In hopes of limiting the bloodshed, the UN Security Council requested that all weapons shipments to the area be halted. The U.S. government responded by announcing an arms embargo on December 5, 1947. Zionists and their supporters denounced the administration's action since, in effect, it denied the Jews access to military aid, while the Arabs continued to receive arms from the British under the terms of previous agreements. Some of Truman's more strident critics, including both Isacson and Wallace, took their condemnations even further, accusing the president of "conspiring" with Arab "feudal lords" to deny the Jews a homeland in Palestine.[11] Throughout the special election campaign, ALP literature and spokespersons hammered home that the president's support for Zionism was a ruse and that he was already preparing to "double cross" the Jews in exchange for easy access to Arab oil fields. "Truman spills Jewish blood for Arab oil!" proclaimed one ALP pamphlet printed in Yiddish. In his stump speeches in Jewish neighborhoods, Isacson denounced Washington's vacillating approach and called for an immediate lifting of the arms embargo and for UN enforcement of the partition plan. Though Propper and Alfange endorsed an identical policy, the ALP alleged that they, too, were in league with the Arabs, even spreading a rumor on the final day of the campaign that Alfange, the co-chair of the Committee to Arm the Jewish State, was receiving secret support from King Ibn Saud of Saudi Arabia![12]

Wallace's own opposition to lifting the arms embargo went discreetly unmentioned in his ghostwritten speeches and in all the Isacson literature. Reporters who asked staffers at the New Party's national headquarters to clarify the candidate's position either received the "runaround" or an evasive response that implied Wallace did support lifting the embargo. Only when the press questioned Wallace directly on the issue did it emerge that he took a different position from that disseminated in his own party's literature. This discovery led some of Wallace's political enemies on the non-Communist left to charge that Communists and their allies working for the New Party deliberately "buried" any statements the candidate might make that did not adhere to the Communist position.[13]

Many observers also questioned the sincerity of the ALP's sudden shift to a militantly pro-Zionist position, particularly given the party's close alliance with the Communists. A year earlier, they noted, the CPUSA had been calling for a binational state in Palestine, urging the Jews to reach an accommodation with their Arab neighbors. Only when it developed that the implementation of a UN partition plan might further Soviet strategic interests in the Middle East did the Communists, both in Moscow and in Manhattan, back the establishment of an independent Jewish nation.[14] George Charney, at the time a CP functionary in New York City, later recalled that the new "line" on Palestine baffled even his Communist colleagues, so central had anti-Zionism been to party teachings.[15] Moreover, while the CP and its allies vilified Truman in the Bronx for his "anti-Jewish" policies, the first reports of widespread, state-sponsored anti-Semitism were beginning to emerge from the Soviet Union. Skeptics who pointed out such incongruities received no answer from ALP partisans who denounced them as "red-baiters" and "stooges for the Arab oil sheiks." Isacson, they insisted, was the "only" candidate working for the establishment of a Jewish homeland.[16]

The ALP's rigorous, if something less than honest grassroots campaign soon threw the Democrats on the defensive. But instead of focusing sharply on the local issues—public housing, rent control, the cost of living, and racial discrimination—party stalwarts seemed preoccupied with the national threat Wallace and his New Party supporters continued to pose. Speaking at a rally for Propper on February 12, Mayor O'Dwyer spent the bulk of his address denouncing the third party for dividing the liberal vote and urging the former vice president to return to the Democratic fold. Following O'Dwyer to the podium, Eleanor Roosevelt also expressed her preference for liberals who remained regular Democrats. Such critiques of the third party would later prove effective, but in the Twenty-Fourth, where the Republicans stood no chance of victory, they carried little weight. The fight was between two "progressives"—Isacson and Propper—and in mentioning the latter's campaign only in passing, the mayor and the former first lady failed to make a compelling case for why their man would best represent the district's liberal voters. In fact, New York's left-leaning daily, *PM*, which opposed Wallace's third party, decided to endorse the ALP nominee on these very grounds. Absent the threat of a Republican triumph—in which case the paper would have backed Propper—*PM* chose Isacson "as the man with the most active and militant progressive record."[17]

Two days after the Democrats' gathering, Wallace arrived in New York, making his first appearance as a third party presidential candidate. Led by a squad of motorcycle police with sirens screaming, his fifty-car motorcade toured the district while wildly cheering supporters lined the streets to catch a glimpse of him. At his first stop, the old Hunt's Point Palace, Wallace delivered a rousing speech in support of Isacson, though he, too, focused primarily on national issues. With 3,500 people jammed into the hall and 5,000 more listening outside, Wallace rejected O'Dwyer's plea to rejoin the Democratic Party. The invitation had only come, he declared, "because the Democratic high command in Washington is scared to death." For the remainder of his address, Wallace discussed the Palestine situation, leveling a series of grave accusations against the Truman administration. Behind the present U.S. policy, he told his predominantly Jewish audience, was an "Anglo-American oil conspiracy" that armed "the Arab feudal lords so they can continue the work of Adolph Hitler." The president "talks Jewish but acts Arab," Wallace charged, adding improbably, "[He] could clean up the Palestine situation tomorrow if he wanted to." A vote for Isacson, Wallace concluded, was an opportunity for the average citizen to demand that "we stop perverting our power to support international immorality." Though the speech's rendition of the facts was certainly open to challenge, the partisan crowd roared its approval, sending its hero off with thundering applause.[18]

The fervor Wallace generated at his appearance on the eve of the election impressed even the most incredulous, but few foresaw the coming ALP landslide. Shortly before the polls closed, Propper was still predicting his election by a "comfortable margin." Though sporadic turnout had spurred Democratic workers to halve their earlier estimates of a ten thousand–vote triumph, the front-page headline of William Randolph Hearst's *Journal-American* confidently announced "Propper Certain of Routing Reds." Isacson himself modestly declared that he would be pleased with a 30 percent showing. Less cautious ALPers spoke of a win, perhaps by three thousand if the turnout hit fifty thousand. The final tally, however, gave Isacson 22,697 votes to Propper's 12,578—a 56 to 31 percent victory. The Liberals finished third, while the Republicans ran a dismal fourth, garnering only 3.6 percent of the vote. "I'm still blinking at the figures," exclaimed one delighted Wallace supporter. Even Marcantonio, the party's most popular standard-bearer, had never polled an outright majority on the ALP line. At Isacson's headquarters, the congressman-elect, shocked and on the verge of tears, confessed to his cheering supporters, "Friends, you know, it's almost incredible."[19]

■ The postmortems were not long in coming as spokespersons from across the political spectrum hastened to present their own self-serving interpretations of the surprising results. Republicans were overjoyed, convinced that the Wallace movement's newly demonstrated strength would redound to the GOP's favor in the presidential election. "New York is in the bag," one Republican Party worker crowed gleefully. Conservative supporters of Ohio Senator Robert A. Taft maintained that the upset had worked to their advantage. By their reckoning, it was no longer necessary to nominate the more moderate Thomas Dewey to win the Empire State's forty-seven electoral votes. Kicking the Democrats while they were down, the Republican Senator Owen Brewster of Maine ceremoniously read the official results into the *Congressional Record*, while *Time* magazine gloated that having failed to "prop up Propper," the Democrats were piling up alibis "thicker than mites on a slab of old store cheese."[20]

Meanwhile, Democrats—allegedly "steeped in Stygian gloom"—were wondering what had become of their vote. In 1946, the party's nominee for Congress in the Twenty-Fourth had outpolled his ALP opponent by more than fifteen thousand. Two years later, Propper failed to carry even his own precinct. The ALP had received 50 percent of the vote in neighbor-hoods that usually went Democratic five and six to one. It registered par-ticularly impressive gains among black and Jewish residents. Even in the Irish areas, the traditional stronghold of the Flynn machine, Isacson made significant inroads. As they scrambled for a plausible explanation for their defeat, Democratic leaders blamed a low turnout, but turnout had topped 43 percent—a relatively good showing for a special election. Even some party workers questioned the "official line." In a widely quoted remark, an anonymous Democratic ward heeler lamented, "We got out the voters, but they voted against us." Tally sheets from several precincts confirmed that some Democrats, particularly African Americans, had switched their vote to the ALP. Other observers noted that the Labor Party had received more than six thousand votes in excess of its official enrollment in the district, lending further evidence, they argued, to a "pro-Wallace trend." Yet claims of such mass defections from the Democrats to the ALP were exaggerated. More significant were the thousands of Democratic "stay at homes." Though overall turnout was not particularly low, that among "organization" Democrats was abysmal—less than one-third of the party's 1946 showing. The storied Bronx machine had delivered to Propper only two out of every ten of its registered voters. "If a precinct captain ever turned in the report Flynn did, he wouldn't last overnight," exclaimed one irate Democrat.[21]

In stark contrast to the Flynn machine, the ALP organization had done splendidly, nearly equaling its performance in the 1946 special election. The party had turned out 93 percent of its regular voters. Significantly, the rank and file of the Amalgamated Clothing Workers Union—a power-ful bloc in the Twenty-Fourth district—stuck with the ALP despite their leaders' repudiation of the party for its support of Wallace. As a result, even though the ALP's tally dipped slightly from the previous regular elec-tion, the party's percentage of the vote soared from 27 to 56, thus produc-ing the Isacson landslide. Behind this triumph of political organization, Flynn contended, was the Communist Party. To a certain extent, this was true. The CP could (and did) take credit for its vital contribution to the ALP's victory. Isacson, though not a Communist, had a well-documented record as a reliable spokesman for the "party line" and gladly accepted the Communists' support.[22] But in his postelection statement, the boss clearly overplayed the "red card." "The Communist menace in this country is much greater than most people thought," he intoned. "This is a deplor-able situation. Regimented Communists vote, while those who oppose Communism do not take the trouble to do so." Most commentators rightly dismissed Flynn's overdrawn warnings as a self-serving attempt to divert attention from his own organization's failings. That there were more than twenty-two thousand "regimented Communists" residing in the Twenty-Fourth district seemed preposterous, nor was there any evidence that the Isacson victory revealed a national upsurge in Communist strength. As one Bronx sidewalk philosopher remarked, "One robin doesn't bring no spring. It don't mean the country's going Commo." Even Flynn's longtime admirers like Eleanor Roosevelt dismissed his conjuring of the "red menace." Democrats had better play closer attention to the people's needs, she warned, if they expected to avoid future upsets.[23]

Southern Democrats, furious at Truman's recent civil rights proposals, drew an entirely different conclusion. With the left wing of the party apparently defecting to Wallace, they reasoned, the president would discover a newfound appreciation for their support. Immediately after the special election, the southern governors began to lay down the conditions that the administration would have to meet to ensure their backing. The chairman of the Democratic Party, J. Howard McGrath, did not miss the connection between Isacson's victory and the southerners' increased assertiveness. "They see in the present situation an opportunity to make us bow to their will," he told his publicity chief, Jack Redding. But McGrath, like most political observers, still considered the Wallace movement more threatening than any potential southern bolt. He flatly rejected segregationists' demands that Truman abandon his civil rights program, dismissing such a course as "political suicide." Instead, in a national radio broadcast he nearly begged Wallace to abandon his third party crusade and help the Democrats turn out a large "progressive vote" in November.[24] In sharp contrast, the president himself took the Isacson victory in stride. Aides reported that Truman even seemed pleased with the result. "If we can get the crackpots on one side of the fence, and the fellows who want to look backward on the other," he told one confidant, "honest people ought to be able to do something about the situation in the world and in this country."[25]

Naturally, Wallace supporters sought to assign as broad a significance as possible to their triumph. Downplaying the role of the local ALP organization, New Party leaders insisted that Wallace's name and program had brought victory. Beanie Baldwin, the New Party's campaign manager, hailed the results as having national import. "It is not only evidence of the overwhelming grass roots enthusiasm for Mr. Wallace . . . throughout America," he claimed. "It is a clear-cut people's repudiation of the subservient do-nothing policy of a President and of an administration which has blithely handed the American Government over to Wall Street and the military." Addressing his supporters on election night, Isacson himself asserted, "The people have gone to the polls to say 'No' to the Truman Doctrine [and] the Marshall Plan which plays politics with hunger. . . . They have warned that they will not tolerate the kind of administration which attempts to drag fascism in by the back door."[26]

The Communists, predictably, provided the most spectacular flourishes of political hyperbole. "The outcome of the elections will undoubtedly be a source of encouragement to the peace forces throughout the world," proclaimed Robert Thompson, the chairman of New York State's CP. "They will see in it clear evidence that the mailed fist policy of the Truman Administration in Greece and China does not reflect the aspirations and outlook of the American common man." Indeed, the *Daily Worker* discerned in the results "the voice of the real America that finally got a chance to speak out." On the other hand, Lillian Gates, a Communist Party member who had worked closely with the campaign, conceded that even at the time she considered the outcome "a fluke," though, she added, many of her comrades did see the election as a "litmus test" for the third party's strength throughout the country. Gates, a veteran Communist, recalled that she knew enough to keep her heretical views to herself.[27]

Man-on-the-street interviews with "real Americans" couched the election in far less dramatic terms. In explaining the ALP victory, voters in the district mentioned almost exclusively local factors. "They say it's account of Palestine. That's wrong. It's right here. It's the high cost of living and housing," explained a Bronx merchant who had supported Isacson. Even ALP workers acknowledged that the party's public statements did not tell the real story. "For the record," said one, "we're claiming a victory for opposition to the Marshall Plan." But, he added, "half the voters never heard of the Marshall Plan! They voted against talk without action. They voted against the grim sordidness of the slums." Campaign strategists for the ALP had recognized the most pressing concerns of local voters and had exploited them effectively. Right up to election day, party canvassers circulated unsubstantiated rumors that Propper had represented landlords in eviction cases—a charge that apparently made a deeper impression on the electorate than all of Wallace's extravagant denunciations of the Truman Doctrine. Several voters cited the housing issue as the deciding factor in their vote for Isacson. Said one Bronx housewife, "I didn't vote for [Isacson] because of the third party. I don't think the third party matters. . . . I'm not going to vote for any attorney for the landlords. Many a dispossess I got. Propper probably drew one of them up." The district's recent loss of more than two thousand government jobs, almost all held by African Americans, likewise raised the hackles of many black voters. In response, Isacson canvassers poured into their neighborhoods and distributed thousands of leaflets claiming—falsely—that "the Rankin-Flynn Democratic Gang stole those jobs from us to pay political debts to the lily-white Democratic machine in Missouri!" Judging from the upswing in the ALP vote in fifteen of the district's predominantly black precincts, such tactics paid dividends on election day.[28]

Moreover, as the political analyst Samuel Lubell later reported, the dissatisfaction that helped elect Isacson did not necessarily indicate a groundswell for Wallace. After doing extensive interviewing in the district, Lubell noted that the former vice president's support was quite "soft"—all but one of the likely Wallace voters he surveyed qualified their endorsement by adding, "'if only Eisenhower were running.'" A close look at the ALP numbers also indicates no pronounced trend toward Wallace. Though he was completely identified with the third party standard-bearer in the public mind, Isacson only brought out the normal ALP vote—just as the party's candidate in the Nineteenth district had done in the special election of 1946, before Wallace and the third party had become an issue. Had there been an upsurge of Wallace support, Isacson's final tally would likely have been far higher. As for the claim made by Wallace supporters that the results heralded a national shift toward their way of thinking, Willard Townsend of the *Chicago Defender* expressed humorously a skepticism that panicky Democrats and overjoyed New Party officials would have done well to adopt. "The 'century of the common man' is close at hand," he wrote. "The Bronx has capitulated, Harlem is tottering, Brooklyn is rushing to the barricades; and the only thing that is left is Greenwich Village and the rest of America."[29]

■ Still, there was no denying the psychological boost the Isacson victory brought to the Wallace forces. Around the country, fledgling third party committees reported rapid growth and widespread interest. Groups in several states held well-attended organizational meetings, while the national office launched a media and fundraising blitz. Elmer Benson, the chairman of the Wallace-for-President Committee, boasted that in the aftermath of the Bronx election, 6,000 letters from 1,732 new Wallace clubs had arrived at party headquarters, all requesting instructions on how to "get started immediately." "I have been in politics a long time," said Benson, "but I have never seen a new movement mushroom so fast. The Isacson victory was just a straw in the progressive wind."[30] Their early triumph also gave the New Party an air of permanence. "Many people who were strong for Wallace but did not believe he would get far now see what can be done," declared Beanie Baldwin. Indeed, with this first successful test of vote-getting ability under their belts, party officials were finding it easier to recruit candidates for federal and state offices. Happily quoting a British pundit's remark that "the Democrats should withdraw from the presidential contest so as not to split the Third Party vote," they spurned peace feelers from the administration with buoyant confidence.[31]

News from California offered even more encouragement. On February 18, the Independent Progressive Party (IPP) reported that its petition campaign had secured more than 464,000 signatures. Even allowing for the disqualification of invalid signatures, party leaders calculated that they had more than enough to assure the IPP a place on the ballot. Again, Wallace supporters had confounded the "experts," nearly all of whom had predicted that they would fall far short of their goal. Yet through hard work and effective organization, the Wallaceites proved themselves up to the task. Some twelve thousand people participated in the drive, a remarkable number considering the unglamorous nature of such routine political legwork. They achieved a key victory for the third party, since many progressives throughout the country were awaiting the outcome in California before launching their own Wallace organizations. Those who had hesitated to go forward thus received a reassuring message from the Golden State: "It can be done." Even Robert Kenny, who had opposed the third party movement in the state, acknowledged that with the success of the IPP's petition drive, his "Democrats for Wallace" campaign was now "mostly a state of mind with a small deficit." Coming on the heels of Isacson's victory, the IPP's success seemed to substantiate third party officials' claims that Wallace stood at the head of a "broad people's movement" based on "grass roots" support from millions of "peace loving Americans."[32]

Such a characterization was misleading. The IPP's successful petition campaign, like the Isacson victory, had relied heavily on the efforts of an intensely driven Communist minority. "In every union, in every mass organization, in every area where the Party had influence, support for the Progressive Party became the top priority," recalled Dorothy Healey, a longtime California Communist. According to Healey, the Wallace campaign had become the Party's "single-minded emphasis." Though many non-Communists participated in the day-to-day canvassing, the Communists provided behind-the-scenes leadership, formulated strategy, handled publicity, and supplied the most zealous workers. As Joseph Starobin, another ex-Communist functionary, later maintained, "Only a disciplined group like the California Communist Party, small as it was, could undertake such a drive with any prospect of success."[33] In Los Angeles, the CP's formidable county chairman, Nemmy Sparks, oversaw the local effort in which third party volunteers collected 278,619 signatures—nearly 60 percent of the statewide total. Similarly, Ida Rothstein, the Communists' California district press director, was responsible for the IPP's overall strategy throughout the state, a role that remained publicly unacknowledged.[34] The CP's allies in the Longshoremen's and Marine Cooks and Stewards unions spearheaded the campaign in the San Francisco Bay area, where the fiery pro-Communist labor leaders Harry Bridges, Hugh Bryson, and David Jenkins played leading public roles. Behind closed doors, the political affairs committee of the Alameda County Communist Party, which included officers from the CIO's San Francisco Industrial Union Council and from Bridges's Warehousemen's Local 6, took responsibility for directing the IPP's efforts and for vetting potential candidates.[35] In San Diego, another concealed Communist, Lynn Ackerstein, served as the county director and brought on board many of her comrades to serve in key positions in the local organization. As they had done in the Bronx special election, the leadership of the Wallace campaign either downplayed or denied the CP's disproportionate influence in party affairs, but in so doing the Wallaceites merely postponed confronting their failure to establish a "broad base."[36]

■ A long-awaited announcement from Senator Glen H. Taylor of Idaho also contributed to the rising spirits in the Wallace camp. Six days after the Bronx special election, Taylor declared in a nationwide radio broadcast that he would join the New Party ticket. In explaining his decision, he charged that "Wall Street and the military" had taken over the Democratic Party and betrayed the principles of Franklin D. Roosevelt, leaving him no choice but to throw his support behind Wallace and his third party movement. Later, Taylor told reporters that only Wallace could bring peace with the Soviet Union, since, he claimed, "Russia would believe in Henry Wallace's good intentions." According to Taylor, the Soviets only wanted "peace" and would not be "so severe" with their neighbors if the United States did not pursue such an aggressive policy. "They don't need markets like capitalist countries," Taylor explained. "Nobody gets rich from wars in the Soviet Union. Fascism must spread, dominate, and conquer. But Communism just isn't like that."[37]

The young Idaho senator, a flamboyant character who had led a varied life, had spent most of the 1920s and 1930s performing musical numbers and melodramatic cowboy skits for audiences in countless one-horse towns throughout the west, eventually teaming with his wife, Dora, to form the "Glendora Players." Taylor came to political consciousness during the Depression after reading a tract by the razor blade magnate King Gillette entitled *The People's Corporation*. Gillette proposed that all industry should be held by a giant corporation and every citizen made a stockholder, a somewhat primitive version of the corporate state associated with Italian fascism. Taylor embraced Gillette's views and began to mix political commentary into his "cowboy crooning," telling his audiences that under such a scheme every man, woman, and child in America would get $30,000 a year, while the working day would be reduced to two hours. Playing to many westerners' resentment of controls seemingly imposed from afar, he relentlessly assailed "Wall Street monopolists," "international bankers," and "greedy, soulless corporations," portraying himself as the defender of the "common man" who would do battle with the "stuffed shirts." In 1938, he made an unsuccessful run for Congress, followed by two failed bids for a U.S. Senate seat in 1940 and 1942. An unorthodox campaigner, Taylor, decked out in full cowboy garb, would wheel into town with a sound system mounted on the roof of his car. After parking on the main street, he would strum his guitar and sing "Oh, Susanna!" or "Clementine," while Dora accompanied him on the trombone. Once a crowd had gathered, he would launch into a rabble-rousing speech, generally short on facts and logic but bristling with emotional fervor. In time, he became a virtuoso on the stump, peddling a simplistic evangelical populism to the delight of the state's backcountry voters. Even the Idaho novelist Vardis Fisher, a rock-ribbed Republican, dubbed Taylor "one of the greatest speakers of our time." "I listen to Glen every time I get a chance," Fisher told *Collier's* magazine, "not because he ever says anything, but because he says nothing superbly." Taylor's antics did not win him a Senate seat, however, and to make ends meet during the war, he relocated to California and took a job at a San Francisco defense plant.[38]

Two years later he returned to Idaho to run for the Senate a third time. Convinced by his friends that he had to "tone down" his campaigning style to broaden his appeal, Taylor exchanged his chaps, boots, and wide-brimmed cowboy hat for a business suit and a self-made toupee. Through sheer persistence, he won the Democratic nomination by 216 votes and swept to victory in November, clinging tightly to the coattails of Franklin D. Roosevelt. To the dismay of his Idaho backers, Taylor reverted to form on his arrival in Washington. Unable to find lodging for his family because of the wartime housing crunch, he donned his Stetson, took up his guitar, and appeared before reporters on the steps of the Capitol. To the tune of "Home on the Range," Taylor crooned a musical appeal to the local realtors:

> O, give us a home, near the Capitol Dome,
> With a yard where the children can play.
> Just one room or two—Any old thing will do,
> We can't find a pla-hace to stay.

Official Washington was unimpressed, dismissing the clowning newcomer as an amiable buffoon in search of headlines. As long as he voted the straight New Deal line, however, Taylor won the plaudits of liberal journalists who praised him as a "Cowboy on Our Side."[39]

By late 1947, the Idahoan had grown increasingly strident in his attacks on the Truman administration, particularly with regard to foreign policy. Taylor claimed that "Wall Street's" drive for new markets and higher profits was *the* explanation for the breakdown in U.S.-Soviet relations. He charged that "international bankers" had seized control of the government and were fabricating dangerous "war scares" to reap financial rewards. Failing to account for the role of political, strategic, or ideological considerations in the formulation of policy, he insisted that talk of containing communism simply masked "real" economic motivations. "We have moved into Hitler's shoes and are determined to conduct a war against Russia and then to exploit the world," Taylor informed his skeptical Senate colleagues. "That is part of the scheme to enable our businessmen to infiltrate and gain control of the industries of other countries." According to Taylor, Soviet behavior was a natural defensive reaction to aggressive American imperialism. If the American government could be delivered from the grip of "Wall Street," a lasting peace with the Russians would occur as a matter of course. The responsibility for beginning (and ending) the Cold War therefore fell entirely on Washington. To win support for his position, Taylor embarked on a cross-country horseback ride in late October to preach the cause of peace to the "common man." He was forced to cut short his trip three weeks later when President Truman called Congress into special session. Back in Washington, the singing cowboy, reunited with his trusty sorrel, rode up to the base of the Capitol steps and gladly posed for photographers.[40]

Taylor's warm personality and earthy demeanor contrasted sharply with the more reserved Wallace who, despite his rhetorical celebrations of the "the common man," had trouble connecting with people one on one. The two men did share a single-minded commitment to avoiding another war, however, and from the outset of the third party campaign political observers considered Taylor a likely running mate for the former vice president. Indeed, the Wallace camp approached him early on about joining the ticket. Taylor seemed grateful for the attention, and for two months he conducted a long and very public soul-searching, indicating on several occasions that he would not bolt the Democratic Party yet all the while criticizing the Truman administration in the most derogatory terms. "Whether he would or he wouldn't" became the subject of mounting newspaper speculation. Clearly enjoying his newfound celebrity status, Taylor called journalists into his office almost daily to tell them he had yet to make up his mind. His wife, friends, relatives, and congressional staff repeatedly warned him that joining Wallace would mean political suicide. After a sharp push from Beanie Baldwin, however, Taylor formally committed himself and announced his decision publicly three days later. Convinced that the administration was driving the country straight into World War III, Taylor maintained that "the situation was too desperate" to wait for new leadership to capture the Democratic Party. "I just don't want my sons dying on some Siberian steppe in any war that I can do anything to prevent," he declared.

Though Taylor was sincere in expressing his concerns, his comprehension of international affairs was even more questionable than Wallace's. Even those scholars who have attempted to rehabilitate Taylor's reputation by portraying him as a prescient dissenter from the Cold War consensus acknowledge the senator's proclivity for simplistic analysis and his limited understanding of economics. Contemporary critics were far less generous, dismissing him as an uninformed demagogue. The volatile mixture of Taylor's over-the-top campaigning style and his dark, conspiratorial view of American foreign policy opened him to such charges, but his stump speeches were more embarrassing than menacing; his ideas more half-baked than subversive. What one critic called his "genius for being comical in dignified settings" would give spontaneity to a campaign that often seemed too slick and overly scripted, while Taylor's talent as a showman made up for Wallace's public performances that, despite all the fanfare that surrounded them, were often dull and colorless.[41]

■ While Wallace's supporters celebrated Taylor's addition to their ticket, liberals who opposed the New Party scrambled to head off any further defections to Gideon's Army. In a spirited address at the first annual convention of Americans for Democratic Action (ADA) held February 21–24 in Philadelphia, the president of the United Auto Workers, Walter

P. Reuther, drew a sharp distinction between Wallace's brand of Popular Front liberalism and his own "fighting creed" that had no room for the deception and deceit practiced by the Communists. To combat the comrades' corrosive influence in the liberal movement, Reuther told the delegates, there was a "little job" they had to do. "We have to liberate some of the American liberals," he explained.

> These liberals have become immobilized by the fear of Communist abuse and character assassination on the one hand, and the stupid, vindictive smear campaigns of the Rankins, the Dies, the Thomases, on the other hand. These are the American liberals whose hearts are in the right place, but they haven't got the gumption to fight for the things they believe in. . . . [They] are grievously weakened by that united front psychology; by the fear that to open their eyes and their mouths on the subject of Communist shenanigans is to be guilty of the offense of red-baiting. . . . We must tell them that in the kind of world in which we live they must have the moral courage to . . . dare to take on a fight where the Communists will call them red-baiters and fascists, and the reactionaries will call them Communists.

This could only be done, Reuther contended, "by offering a positive, creative [and] dynamic alternative. . . . If we build that kind of program, we will find that less and less of the liberal mavericks will stray off the range and be victims of Joe Stalin's rustlers."[42]

Just as important to ADA strategy, however, was "unmasking" the Wallace movement as a fraud put over on liberals by American Communists seeking to further the interests of the Soviet Union. "It is an established fact," ADA charged, "that [the New Party] owes its origin and principal organizational support to the Communist party, whose chairman, William Z. Foster, sounded the call for its formation with the purpose of defeating the Marshall Plan." The organization also hit the third party at the point where Popular Front liberalism had always been most vulnerable— its application of a double standard of political morality with regard to the Soviet Union. "The organizers of the Wallace movement," one convention speaker observed, "while proclaiming devotion to civil rights at home, have been strangely tolerant of judicial lynching, slave labor, and the police state abroad." Only the Communists' "prominent and corrupting role" in the third party explained such disingenuousness, and, ADAers believed, there was nothing illiberal about "calling a spade a spade." Energized by the success of their convention, ADA leaders vowed to "take the offensive against Henry Wallace and the third party" and to "answer his specific public statements in every way possible." In the coming months, they would do just that.[43]

Many prominent figures associated with ADA despaired, however, that as long as President Truman remained the likely Democratic nominee, the prospects for advancing an expansive liberal agenda remained bleak. Throughout the spring and early summer, they staged a public campaign to "dump Truman" for a "genuine liberal." "We cannot compete with the Wallace crowd unless and until we have a national Presidential figure to crusade for," declared James Loeb, ADA's executive secretary. Improbably, some, including Loeb, saw in Dwight Eisenhower such a "genuine liberal" and backed the ill-conceived effort to "draft" the general in place of Truman. Like the Popular Front liberals who joined the Wallace movement, ADA liberals expressed frustration with the failure of national politics to move in a more social democratic direction after the war—the unspoken assumption being that such a shift to the left was "natural." (Indeed, ADAers denounced the PCA's pro-Communists for sabotaging the development of social democratic politics in the United States.) Like the PCA, ADA also believed that there was significant public support for a revival and expansion of the New Deal agenda—support that their own "crusading" would awaken. These men and women longed for a dynamic "progressive" leader and assumed that once such a figure emerged, "the people" would surely follow.

Such reasoning reflected a misreading of the public mood. Caught up in the heat of battle with the PCA for leadership of the liberal movement— and initially perceiving themselves as the "underdog"—ADA liberals did not discern that while their brand of social democratic liberalism may have been at the "vital center" in the global ideological struggle, in the more conservative American context it constituted the left wing of politically acceptable opinion. Unlike Democratic Party regulars, ADA liberals failed to recognize that the pro-Communist left was a spent force and that the politically viable alternatives to "Trumanism" came not from the social democratic left but from the right. Not surprisingly, the "dump Truman" campaign failed. Despite all the political sniping, the president never faced a serious challenge for the nomination, while ADA's attempts to unseat him only reinforced Truman's distaste for politically inexperienced liberal intellectuals. Only after the election would ADA come to see the fragility of public support for an aggressive and expansive liberal agenda.[44]

In their analyses of ADA's influence on postwar liberalism, some historians have blamed the organization and its attacks on pro-Wallace progressives during the "liberal civil war" of the late 1940s for "narrowing" the

American political spectrum to the detriment of the left. Ironically, such an interpretation rests on the same assumption that ADA liberals themselves held—that an "advanced" social democratic agenda had widespread, albeit latent backing from the American public. These historians have suggested that liberals' inability to mobilize support for a more "progressive" politics constituted a "missed opportunity" or a "failure of nerve," but their case for the existence of such a deep and untapped wellspring of radical sentiment seems based more on wishful thinking than on evidence.[45] Moreover, in focusing on ADA's anticommunism, and even equating it with "McCarthyism," scholars have mischaracterized the organization's political commitments. As David Plotke and Jennifer Delton have noted, ADA liberalism was not a "watered down" version of the Popular Front simply because it rejected any alliance with the Communists. "Liberals' antipathy to Communists," Delton points out, "was based not on fear or antiradicalism, but rather on a history of disruptive, unpleasant experiences with them." Likewise, writes Plotke, Popular Frontists' claim that liberal anticommunism was a "calculated means of blocking reform relies on a wrong premise—that Democratic leaders aimed to stop reform and betray the New Deal. It was conservative opponents of the Democratic order who tried to stigmatize the regime as Communist-influenced and undermine it." Even the notion of a "liberal civil war," Plotke contends, is something of a misnomer: "Arguments about Popular Frontism did not lead to a real split. . . . Instead, a large majority rejected a small minority and the political isolation of the CPUSA was increased and brightly illustrated." The election returns of 1948 clearly substantiate such a view, but at the time opponents of Popular Front liberalism—lacking the scholar's benefit of hindsight—were genuinely concerned, as evidenced in a letter Dwight Macdonald sent to Loeb shortly after the ADA convention. "I'm worried," Macdonald wrote, "when I see the Commies and Wallace putting on such a vigorous and bold campaign."[46]

Organized labor shared ADA's increasing apprehension over the Wallace candidacy, though its concern was focused less on the possible ascendance of Popular Front liberalism than the more realistic threat of a Republican victory in the fall. Although the AFL, CIO, and Railroad Brotherhoods had issued official statements repudiating the third party earlier in the year, the Wallaceites' recent successes convinced union leaders that more aggressive measures might be necessary. Abandoning their previous reluctance to collaborate with middle-class pressure groups, all three federations sent representatives to ADA's Philadelphia convention. In an unprecedented appearance before a political organization, the

AFL's president, William Green, sharply denounced the New Party. Green proclaimed that shoulder-to-shoulder cooperation between ADA and the AFL's Labor League for Political Education would be "essential" in the upcoming campaign to combat antilabor agitation, on the one hand, and the "ill-timed and ill-conceived political move" of Wallace and his supporters, on the other. Curiously, the role of the AFL in the 1948 presidential election has attracted relatively little scholarly attention, particularly when compared to that of the CIO. Yet the launching of the third party—intended to get labor more politically involved—did provoke the AFL to play an unusually active part in the campaign. To the dismay of third party supporters, however, the extra activity was devoted to *defeating* the Progressive Party. This was especially true in California, where the Wallace challenge spurred the state AFL to go all out for Truman.[47]

The CIO, too, stepped up its efforts against the third party, primarily by targeting Wallace supporters within its own ranks. Though the national organization could not compel its affiliated unions to accept the executive board's decision to repudiate the third party, the CIO president Philip Murray did inform them that they had a "moral obligation" to do so.[48] The real battle, however, occurred within the Industrial Union Councils (IUC). The CIO had created the IUCs in 1937 to carry out its political and legislative policy, but in time the Communists and their allies came to view the councils as an ideal forum for gaining leverage in local politics. By mastering the intricacies of parliamentary procedure and "arriving early and staying late" at the weekly meetings, a small Communist minority soon gained effective control over several of the large, urban IUCs. Insisting that their sole intention was to rally the community behind a "progressive agenda," the councils' Communists also issued a steady stream of pro-Soviet resolutions that embarrassed CIO officials and spurred right-wing efforts to restrict labor's participation in politics.[49] Beginning in late 1947, several IUCs—including those in New York, Los Angeles, and San Francisco—began to agitate against the Marshall Plan and to lobby for a Wallace third party candidacy. When they continued to do so over the expressed objections of the national CIO, council members from unions loyal to Murray found themselves in an awkward position. How, they asked, could workers carry out the CIO program when the leaders of their local councils were campaigning against it?[50]

Murray soon took steps to address the situation. In mid-February, he reminded the IUCs that as subsidiaries of the CIO, set up by and subject to the national organization, they were constitutionally bound to carry out its adopted policies. To ensure there was no confusion, he instructed the councils to issue public statements endorsing the Marshall Plan and opposing Wallace—remaining "neutral" on these central issues was unacceptable. When no such statements were forthcoming from numerous councils, John Brophy, the director of Industrial Union Councils, sent a sharply worded letter to the IUCs reiterating the CIO political position and demanding immediate compliance. Throwing down the gauntlet, Brophy warned that continued intransigence could result in the revocation of an IUC's charter.[51]

Though the matter seemed cut and dried to the national office, pro-Soviet IUC leaders were unwilling to abandon their political views (or their base of power) without a fight. As one Communist official later observed, the IUCs were "the backbone of Popular Front politics"; losing them would leave the Party with no comparable venue for exercising its influence. A showdown, then, was inevitable. The Greater New York CIO Council immediately denounced Brophy's ultimatum as a "distortion of the National CIO constitution, . . . a violation of the principles of fundamental trade union democracy and infringement and abrogation of the democratic and autonomous rights of local unions and their elected representatives." Under Brophy's interpretation of the rules, the council argued, CIO-appointed officers advocating for Truman were violating the constitution no less that those supporting Wallace, since the CIO had not endorsed either candidate. Likewise, in Florida, the state IUC assailed the CIO's attempt at "thought control," while Harry Bridges, the CIO's Northern California regional director and president of the International Longshoremen's and Warehousemen's Union (ILWU), deplored what he termed "an invasion of the autonomy of the councils." Bridges refused to oppose Wallace, and, pointedly defying Brophy and the national office, personally handed out leaflets denouncing the Marshall Plan to the members of his ILWU local.[52]

Brophy answered the dissidents' protests one by one, pointing out that he was merely enforcing rules that they themselves had helped write. Questioning the good faith of the pro-Soviet faction, the national office also suggested that this sudden concern over autonomy was not grounded in principle but arose in response to a change in the Communist Party line. Many of those leveling charges, Brophy maintained, were consciously misrepresenting CIO policy to discredit the national office in the eyes of the membership. He emphasized that the CIO was not denying anyone the right to support and vote for any candidate he or she pleased. Nor did the CIO intend to infringe on local union autonomy. But, he reminded them again, the IUCs did not possess such autonomy. Though under some circumstances the CIO allowed its councils "a wide margin" for variation in policy within the "general framework" of the official position, Brophy declared, "when the National CIO takes a very sharply defined position, rejects compromise, and emphasizes the basic importance of particular issues, as happened in this case," the councils must give "positive aid." An IUC's responsibility was to carry out policy, not to make it. Accordingly, council board members and CIO-appointed regional officers did not speak for themselves or their unions, but for the national CIO. If they could not honestly support CIO policy, they should resign. At issue was the CIO's ability to act as an organization in a concerted and disciplined manner. If it failed to enforce the rules governing the behavior of IUCs, Brophy explained, the CIO "would be simply an aggregate of individuals or local unions, purposeless and powerless to protect the political interests of labor."[53]

Such arguments carried little weight with those in the CIO's pro-Soviet minority. Unionists on both coasts kept up their opposition, accusing the national CIO of resorting to a strategy of "super-legalism" to frustrate the will of the workers. In a democratic organization, they claimed, it was absurd that those elected to IUC offices by constituents opposed to CIO policy would then be compelled to implement that policy. Ultimately, the Greater New York City Industrial Council voted to disregard the Brophy letter, telling the CIO executive to "go jump in a creek." Austin Hogan, one of the IUC's officers, dramatically exclaimed that complying with CIO policy was the equivalent of yielding to the "Hitler-like thought control we fought World War II to abolish." The leadership of Bridges's ILWU local in San Francisco wired Murray: "We . . . pledge ourselves to resist such efforts with all means at our command." If CIO policy was "rammed down anybody's throat," cried Bridges, "there will be trouble and I'll lead some of the trouble." The next day, Murray fired him from his post as the CIO's Northern California regional director.[54]

The Pro-Soviet faction was clearly at a disadvantage. Not only was it a minority—and an increasingly disliked one at that—but the Communists' own history in the CIO revealed that their arguments were disingenuous. In an article explaining the CIO's rules regarding IUCs, Jack Altman, the vice president of the United Retail, Wholesale, and Department Store Employees, pointed out that when the circumstances suited them, those in the pro-Soviet faction could be just as "strongly disciplinarian." "In 1940," Altman recounted, "when the CIO nationally failed to take a stand on a presidential candidate, the New York State CIO endorsed Franklin D. Roosevelt. The left-wing unions walked out on the State Council. Their argument was that, in the absence of national policy, the State Council had no right to take a stand." The election took place during the Nazi-Soviet pact, when the Communist line demanded opposition to Roosevelt and, ironically, to his running mate Henry Wallace. The Communists at that time insisted that the IUCs must not deviate from the policy of the national CIO—precisely the argument they were now condemning. Such were the perils of the constantly shifting party line.[55]

Yet such squabbling within the CIO was but an opening salvo in a larger fight. Throughout the campaign, both sides grew increasingly shrill in their rhetoric and less inhibited in their means of attack. So fundamental did their political disagreement become that each faction ultimately came to view the other as an immediate threat to the survival of the industrial labor movement. But the stakes were higher for the pro-Soviet faction since, as many Communists would eventually acknowledge, in committing itself to the Wallace movement, it had provoked a conflict that would result in its own destruction.

Wallace himself ignored the ongoing disputes within the liberal and labor movements, never comprehending the broader ramifications they would have. Having concluded that peace was the only issue of significance in the campaign, and that he was the only candidate who spoke out on its behalf, he remained confident that once all the political wrangling was done, organized labor and ADA liberals would come to their senses and join Gideon's Army. If they did not, if they, like the bipartisans, were for "war," then it was for the best that the lines of battle be made clear. For his part, Wallace was determined to take his fight directly to the people, regardless of the opposition he encountered from their equivocating leaders. Spurred on by the Isacson victory, he fully expected to spread the "spirit of the Bronx" across the entire nation.

4

WALL STREET IS IN THE SADDLE

Henry Wallace's Critique of Containment

As the New Party's fortunes appeared to be on the upswing, Wallace's views, particularly on foreign policy, came under closer scrutiny. Since late 1947, the former vice president had been denouncing the Marshall Plan in particular as an imperialist plot hatched by Wall Street bankers. Wallace had initially supported Secretary of State George C. Marshall's proposals for European aid, but when the Soviets refused to participate, he concluded that "warlords and moneychangers" had perverted the plan's good intentions and planned to use it to divide Europe. Thereafter, Wallace sharpened his critique of the Truman administration's "bipartisan reactionary war policy" while trying to place Soviet moves in the best possible light. Anything the Soviets did that might appear "aggressive," Wallace maintained, was merely a defensive response to Washington's relentless warmongering. While Truman "fabricated" a war scare and whipped up anticommunist hysteria at the bidding of Wall Street and the military, Wallace insisted that Moscow remained eager to establish peaceful coexistence if only U.S. officials would sit down and negotiate an "understanding."[1] Events during the first half of the new year—particularly the Communist coup in Czechoslovakia and the Soviet blockade of Berlin—undermined Wallace's central argument that ending the Cold War required only a change of leadership in Washington. Regardless of who had initiated the conflict, it was now clear that both sides had a role in escalating it. Even many on the left who had at one time shared Wallace's views on foreign policy grew uncomfortable with his labored justifications for what they considered unacceptable

Soviet behavior. As the historian Karl Schmidt noted, "Potential supporters who never could have been dissuaded by . . . anti-Communist hysteria found these international facts of life persuasive and compelling. Numbers who had already joined now left the third party; many who were previously undecided now stayed away."[2] To most Americans, the image of the New Party had become increasingly pro-Soviet as Wallace failed to make a convincing case for how his positions differed from the Communist Party line. The candidate remained resolute, however, ignoring criticism and bringing his crusade for peace to campaign rallies, congressional hearings, and even to Joseph Stalin himself.

■ Wallace's opposition to the Marshall Plan distinguished him from most liberals who, after some hesitation, had endorsed the administration's program of economic aid to Europe. During a speech in Milwaukee on December 30, Wallace had unveiled his own program for "world peace and prosperity" that would bring about "true cooperation" among all the nations of the world. Thereafter, he spoke frequently on behalf of his proposed alternative that, unlike the Marshall Plan, would operate through the United Nations. When the House Foreign Affairs Committee opened hearings on the European Recovery Program (ERP) in late February, the former vice president asked and was granted the opportunity to testify.[3]

Appearing before a packed room, Wallace delivered a fearsome indictment of the Marshall Plan.[4] Reading excerpts from an eleven thousand–word statement, he warned that the ERP was a "blueprint for war" concocted by militarists and Wall Street monopolists "to suppress the democratic movements in Europe" and to "leave the recipient countries fully as bankrupt as they are today." "The ERP," he claimed, "will not fight hunger but perpetuate it . . . not promote recovery but indefinitely postpone it." According to Wallace, the Marshall Plan "would convert western Europe into a vast military camp, with freedom extinguished." Already, the United States, "in its drive to promote the interests of big business," had frustrated "necessary measures" such as the "widespread nationalization of key industries" in Europe. In but one example, Wallace alleged, administration pressure had forced the British Labour government to postpone indefinitely the steel industry's nationalization. At home, he added, the Marshall Plan "would foist a war economy upon the nation, regiment the people . . . and become the main political and economic weapon of monopoly." Continuing his long litany of charges, he declared that the Marshall Plan would destroy labor unions, raise taxes, hamper foreign trade, abridge civil liberties, become the defense for cutting essential social services, squeeze farmers' commodity prices, necessitate wage freezes and longer weeks for workers, and force the small businessman "to offer up his livelihood and independence upon the altar of Wall Street." The only possible outcome, Wallace insisted, would be depression and war.

He then presented the Wallace Plan, what he claimed was a "realistic alternative" for world recovery that would not be beholden to the "big financial and industrial interests." The plan, modeled on the United Nations Relief and Recovery Administration (UNRRA), would attach no political conditions to loans or grants and would be administered by the United Nations. It would give "priority in the allocation of funds to those nations, including those in Eastern Europe, which suffered most severely from the aggression of the Fascist Axis." As a first step, Wallace suggested the UN establish a "world food granary," an action he had been urging on the U.S. government since early 1942. Farmers of surplus-food-producing nations would harvest to the limit and receive a guaranteed price for their crop, while those countries that needed food could draw from the granary and arrange for payments through the UN.[5] He also advised that "the German industrial heartland in the Ruhr Valley should be placed under international control by the Big Four—the United States, Britain, Soviet Russia, and France—and that all its resources be made available to aid in the reconstruction of all Europe." This proposal in particular raised suspicions about Communist influence over Wallace, since the internationalization of the Ruhr was at the top of the Soviet agenda for a postwar Germany. Immediately after the war, many American liberals had backed such a plan, but during the ensuing three years, the Soviets' behavior in nations where they held significant political and economic influence had narrowed support primarily to those on the pro-Communist left.[6] Wallace calculated that his entire plan would require $50 billion guaranteed in advance over ten years. He expressed confidence that once "Wall Street trusts" had been excluded from the process U.S.-Soviet cooperation on the distribution of foreign aid could easily be achieved. Also, since the United States would only supply half the budget of a plan administered by the UN, his proposal would be much cheaper than the European Recovery Program. The Marshall Plan, according to Wallace, would cost the United States $18 billion in the first twelve months—a number he reached by adding the $5 billion allocated to European recovery, $2 billion earmarked for foreign loans, and the $11 billion defense budget. The third party standard-bearer urged the committee to substitute his proposal for the ERP as soon as possible.

The hostile cross-examination that followed confirmed that Wallace had failed to make any converts. Sol Bloom, a colorful liberal Democrat from New York City, opened the interrogation by asking Wallace how his objections to the Marshall Plan differed from those of the Communists. Wallace replied stiffly that since he was "not familiar with the Communist approach" and since he did not "follow the Communist literature," he was unable to discuss the topic. Responding to Wallace's contention that Marshall Plan aid would threaten the freedom of other countries, the Republican Karl E. Mundt of South Dakota asked if he believed the Soviets were interfering in the internal affairs of Eastern European nations. Wallace retorted that there was no way to ascertain this since "it is impossible to know what the truth is from the American press." Congressman Bartel J. Jonkman of Michigan then questioned Wallace on the financing of his plan. He noted that despite assurances that other countries would offer substantial donations, the United States had ended up providing the lion's share of the aid both to UNRRA and to subsequent relief efforts. "Is there a reasonable anticipation of contribution of other nations based on past experience?" Jonkman inquired. "Past experience" was an unreliable guide, Wallace replied, but he did concede that the U.S. share might reach 60 percent under his plan. Still, he asserted, even if it were 100 percent, "it would turn out to be . . . a much more profitable investment dollar per dollar than the plan under ERP."

As the session progressed, the congressional committee members began to focus more sharply on the details of Wallace's proposals. The South Carolina Democrat James P. Richards wondered why Wallace included the Defense Department budget in the cost of the Marshall Plan but did not count it in the U.S. contribution to his plan. The candidate responded that he added in only "our pro rata share of maintaining a United Nations police force." Such a force would be stronger than the army of any individual nation, he explained, and would therefore do away with the need for a large defense budget. Richards inquired whether Moscow would accept such an international force. If the United States followed "a completely new approach" toward the Soviets, Wallace said, "it could be done." When the Republican Frances P. Bolton of Ohio asked for "an idea of what that approach will have to be," he answered that it was impossible to say specifically. Then, in a formulation he would repeat often during the campaign, Wallace added, "There must be a meeting by the new President and the head of the Russian government, Premier Stalin, and preliminary to that, the various diplomatic and economic experts should assemble in very great detail on both sides, all the pending points at issue. . . . Once the Russians become convinced that we do not intend eventually to invade her, then she will gradually change." The historical record and the tenets of Marxist ideology argued against such an eventuality, Bolton observed. "I am an optimist," Wallace responded. He responded in the same vein when the New York Republican Jacob Javits asked if Wallace could offer any assurance that the Soviets would cooperate with the Western powers in the administration of the Ruhr. "I have absolutely no assurance," Wallace conceded, "but I feel the self-interest on both sides is such that the possibilities are there."

Unconvinced, the committee continued to press Wallace for evidence that the Soviets were eager to engage in international collaboration and would reciprocate a Western show of goodwill. After Wallace remarked that implementing his UN-administered plan might require "rather rapid action on the part of the United States in the Security Council," the Wisconsin Republican Lawrence H. Smith inquired, "What hope have you of accomplishing anything . . . in the Security Council with the Russians exercising the veto as they do constantly?" Under the conditions of his plan, Wallace assured Smith, "The Russians will not exercise the veto." Indeed, he asserted, "[they] would be delighted to come along." When the Republican Donald L. Jackson pointed out that the Soviets adamantly opposed the creation of an international police force, Wallace countered that this was "perfectly understandable," given the aggressive nature of U. S. policies, but, again, things would improve once there was an "understanding" with the Soviets. Such an "understanding," he suggested, did not even require "cooperation." "England had an understanding with Russia in 1907 with regard to the Near East," Wallace noted. "It did not necessarily mean cooperation." "I think we should have the same kind of understanding, covering a somewhat larger geographical area," he declared. Congressman William M. Colmer failed to grasp what good an "understanding" would do if both sides did not cooperate in achieving the common objective of world peace. After Wallace agreed that there should be a "cooperative understanding," the Mississippi Democrat remarked, "[Given] the historical background of events since the cessation of hostilities, upon what do you base your hope for cooperative understanding?" Wallace replied, "I would base it on the fact that Russia and the United States . . . really have no fundamental conflicts that interfere with peace." "Thank you. I do not agree with you," Colmer replied, bringing the session to a close and aptly summing up the view of the committee as a whole.[7]

■ Wallace's appearance provoked widespread reaction. Though few doubted the former vice president's sincerity or humanitarian instincts, most observers found his approach to European recovery utterly utopian.

"We have yet to be convinced that Henry Wallace is a bad fellow at heart," commented the *San Francisco Chronicle*, "but he has a failing that makes him more dangerous than most of the deliberate rascals we have known. The failing is his habit of seeing things as he would like them to be instead of as they are." Wallace's "no strings attached" approach to international aid would be fine, the paper acknowledged, if one assumed that "the motives of all European political groups spring from the loftiest principles. . . . But to condemn all 'political' strings is to assume a degree of Soviet dedication to the principle of brotherhood that simply is not justified on the record." "[Wallace's] entire attack upon the Marshall Plan is based upon a foundation of sand . . . [because] he has never faced up to the problem of why UNRRA failed," wrote Donald Harrington of the *New Leader*. "Through UNRRA, the United States poured relief goods into Southeastern European countries, only to have Russia drain native goods from those same countries to bolster her own economy."[8]

Across the political spectrum, commentators took issue with what appeared to be Wallace's headlong flight from reality. After reading through the specifics of his foreign aid proposal, the syndicated columnist Peter Edson concluded that the candidate was living in a "dream world." "Through page after page of his statement runs this same note of unreality," wrote Edson. "The fact that many of the thirty-two countries supporting UNRRA are now broke and asking for more credit, Mr. Wallace ignores. The fact that the UNRRA idea didn't work out as well as hoped for, he ignores. . . . He wants the German Ruhr run by America, Britain, France, and Russia. . . . The fact that four-power control of Germany and Austria didn't work, Mr. Wallace ignores. . . . The fact that there has been futile conference after futile conference, trying to get an understanding with the Russians, he chose to ignore. . . . What he had to say was completely baffling. The only realities were what he wanted to believe."[9] Margaret Marshall of the *Nation* found Wallace's behavior irresponsible. "What are we to think of a self-styled people's candidate who counters the Marshall Plan . . . with an impossibilist plan which is no more than a gleam in his own eye?" she asked. "A Republican who offered such a program would be accused by liberals of sabotaging aid to Europe, of striking at Europe's morale, and of trifling with Europe's misery." Even the radical journalist I. F. Stone, whose reputation for taking pro-Soviet positions was well established, parted ways with the candidate on the issue of the European Recovery Program. Under ideal circumstances, Stone wrote, Wallace's plan would have the support of all progressives, but, he added, "hunger cannot wait on Utopian conditions."[10]

Modern scholars, too, have dismissed the so-called Wallace Plan. The historian Norman D. Markowitz, generally sympathetic to Wallace and sharply critical of the anticommunist liberals who opposed him, acknowledges that the former vice president's alternative to the Marshall Plan "bordered on the ludicrous" and "added strength to the contention of his enemies that he, and not they, had abandoned the heritage of the New Deal." Similarly, most historians concur that by 1948 a European aid program modeled after UNRRA would have been unworkable, much less politically palatable. Not only had the partition of Europe already proceeded too far but both superpowers had come to believe that this division best served their respective strategic interests.[11]

Dwight Macdonald, an anti-Stalinist radical and perhaps Wallace's most trenchant critic, dubbed the former vice president's approach "Utopian Realpolitik." According to Macdonald, "[Wallace] proposes as immediately practical what could only work if there were a change of Utopian proportions." The Wallace Plan, he scoffed, "was a Utopian proposal masquerading as a practical measure." It had absolutely no chance of passing Congress, and if it did miraculously make its way to the UN, it would die there. "That body is not a united, cooperative parliament of the world," Macdonald maintained. "It is a battleground on which the Soviet bloc and the Western bloc maneuver." The inevitable outcome if Wallace's plan were to replace ERP, he pointed out, would be no aid at all. Indeed, Wallace's personal correspondence from this period indicates that he did prefer no aid at all to the Marshall Plan. "If Congress will not go on a United Nations basis, I would say we should terminate all aid after July 1 of 1949," he wrote to one supporter. "It is better to clarify the issues during the next year than to plant the seeds of inflation, depression, and finally war."[12]

According to Macdonald, Wallace's suggestion that the 1907 "understanding" between Russia and Great Britain provide the archetype for U.S.-Soviet relations represented the other half of the candidate's "Utopian Realpolitik"—"throw[ing] a Utopian veil over proposals that are 'realistic' to the point of being sordid." This notorious Anglo-Russian agreement, which divided Persia—without consulting the Persians—into northern and southern regions with a "neutral belt" in between, essentially extinguished that nation's sovereignty and left the two great powers in complete control of its oil concessions. When the Persians revolted against this partition of their country, Russian and British troops intervened to suppress them. The agreement, a shameful exhibition of old-style imperialism, was denounced even at the time by liberals and socialists, including Lenin. That Wallace, long an ardent "one-world" advocate, would now endorse "the same kind of understanding . . . covering a somewhat larger geographical area" left not only Macdonald but many of Wallace's anti-imperialist followers aghast. It seemed incredible that he, having just assailed the Marshall Plan for dividing Europe and circumventing the UN, would propose—at least by analogy—that the superpowers act unilaterally to partition the world into communist and capitalist blocs. When one congressman queried Wallace on this apparent inconsistency, however, the candidate's response only further muddied the waters. "I am fearful of those approaches which tend to emphasize two-worldliness," he said; "I am for recognizing geographical realities, but I want those recognized within one world."[13]

Wallace's imprecise formulations have continued to baffle historians. As Frank A. Warren has noted, "Not only did [Wallace] make foolish and morally blind comments on the internal conditions and foreign policy of the Soviet Union, but his statements were a jumble of often contradictory elements. Wallace spoke for free trade capitalism and postwar cooperation with the Soviet Union and ignored the fact that the Soviet Union was not anxious for free trade in its sphere of influence. . . . Wallace spoke against imperialism, but urged an expansive capitalism and the penetration of Third World markets, without ever stopping to ask if there might be any conflict between the various positions."[14] Other scholars, citing the famous Madison Square Garden speech of 1946 and subsequent addresses on foreign policy, have attributed to Wallace a prescient understanding that U.S. and Soviet spheres of influence were inevitable and laud him for urging U.S. policymakers to accept this reality. Though Wallace's public statements, particularly in the oft-quoted Madison Square Garden address, certainly lend themselves to a "spheres of influence" reading, Wallace himself rejected such an interpretation, insisting repeatedly that he remained a devotee of "one world" and that commentators who referred to his support for a "spheres of influence" policy had deliberately misrepresented his views. Indeed, a week after his Madison Square Garden speech, Wallace told Truman that he wished to continue speaking about foreign affairs to dispel the impression that he supported spheres of influence rather than a one-world perspective.[15]

European democratic socialists who viewed U.S.-supplied aid as the only realistic hope for economic recovery expressed less concern about Wallace's intellectual consistency than about the propaganda value his continuing critique of the Marshall Plan held for the Communists. On the continent, anxious government officials considered Wallace a "stalking horse for Stalin." They feared that his polemics—featured prominently in Communist propaganda—would give credibility to the party's distortions of the ERP and heighten workers' suspicions of American assistance. Wallace's inflammatory rhetoric was particularly irritating since, like the European Communists, he offered no proof to substantiate his litany of allegations. Journalists on the scene looking for such confirmation usually came up empty. "[Though] the Communists here are charging that the Marshall Plan is a plot to tailor the Italian economy to suit monopoly capitalism," one *New Republic* correspondent reported from Rome, "there is remarkably little evidence to support this contention." The blitz of Communist anti-ERP propaganda did have some effect on European workers, but by mid-1948 the tide appeared to have turned. In June, the American embassy in Paris noted that the Communists had lost support and that the average French worker welcomed Marshall Plan aid.[16]

Animosity toward Wallace was also on the rise in Great Britain. The left-wing press, which had hailed the popular New Dealer as the defender of American progressivism during his visit to England ten months earlier, now attacked him as a "captive" of the Communists. His decision to "oppose ERP root and branch rather than to fight against Congressional attempts to misuse it," declared the *New Statesman and Nation*, "has put him on the wrong side of the fence." *Tribune*, the house organ of the Labour Party's left wing, linked the Communists' enthusiastic support for Wallace with the likely outcome of his third party candidacy—the election of an isolationist Republican who would cancel Marshall Plan aid and leave Western Europe vulnerable to a Communist takeover. In the Wallace campaign, *Tribune* concluded, "Stalin pulls the strings." The *Manchester Guardian*, Britain's renowned liberal daily, brought the attack directly to Wallace. Commenting on his appearance before the House Foreign Affairs Committee, the editors declared that the third party candidate, "long . . . suspected of having lost his political judgment . . . is now losing his respect for truth." In his testimony, the *Guardian* continued, "he invented (the word is not too strong) a series of accusations of American interference in Europe. . . . He never tried to put himself in the place of the Europeans whom he so ostentatiously pities or to consider what they think about Marshall aid."[17]

The Labour MP Jennie Lee, the wife of the left-wing Labourite cabinet minister Aneurin Bevan and a onetime Wallace admirer, had already raised the issue of the candidate's proclivity for leveling false charges. After learning of Wallace's assertion—repeated in his testimony—that "U.S. pressure" had forced the British government to retreat from its nationalization plans for the steel industry, she asked the ADA executive secretary

James Loeb for an explanation. "This is a lie," Lee declared. "Where does Wallace get that sort of story? . . . Maybe he has been misquoted, but if not what can be made of a man of reputedly high moral character deliberately bearing false witness?" She noted that it was a matter of public record that nationalization was proceeding as planned. As it happened, this specific piece of misinformation had come directly from the *Daily Worker* and was apparently passed on to Wallace by the Communist advisers at his elbow. Such a persistent (and precise) echoing of the Communist position ultimately convinced British socialists that the third party candidate had become little more than a sounding board for Soviet propaganda.[18]

The disconcerting similarity of views between Wallace and the Communists, more so than the third party's opposition to the ERP per se, made Wallace's critique an easy target for its political enemies. As early as October 1947, Eleanor Roosevelt had remarked that the Wallaceites' criticisms of the Marshall Plan "follow so closely the arguments put out by the Comintern [that they] do themselves harm, for they offer nothing constructive and thus increase in many less radical but liberal groups the sense of suspicion and uncertainty regarding the influences under which they operate."[19] As anyone could attest who had closely compared Wallace's ghostwritten remarks on the ERP with editorials and signed articles in the *Daily Worker*, there was ample reason to question the third party's political independence. In his appearance before the House Foreign Affairs Committee, Wallace laid out each of the CP's arguments against the Marshall Plan, often using phrasing identical to that in Communist publications. More tellingly, his statement offered nothing further, no line of reasoning that distinguished his position from that of the CP. Even the so-called Wallace Plan repeated—again, almost verbatim—the proposals the Communist Party had submitted to the special session of Congress more than a month before Wallace delivered his Milwaukee address.

Indignant Wallaceites denounced as "red-baiters" those who called attention to such similarities, insisting that any resemblance between their position and the CP's was purely coincidental. That both the Communists and the New Party opposed U.S. foreign policy was certainly no reason for Wallace to refrain from criticism, particularly if he believed the administration was pursuing a dangerous course. Critics like Dwight Macdonald dismissed this argument as disingenuous, observing that the "agreement" between the two parties was "too consistent to be coincidental." As he later commented in *Politics*, "Unless it be maintained the Kremlin takes its cue in foreign policy from Wallace (something which even Henry's well-nourished ego might hesitate to assert), then we must conclude that the influence runs the other way, through the channel of the American comrades." Given Macdonald's jaundiced view of the entire Wallace crusade, he hardly qualified as a dispassionate observer. Yet even those who accepted some of the former vice president's reservations about the Marshall Plan hesitated to support the New Party as long as the real reasons for its opposition to the ERP remained unclear.[20]

As we now know, the resemblance between Wallace's statement before the House Foreign Affairs Committee and the CP line was no coincidence. David Ramsey and Victor Perlo, both of whom were concealed Communists, had written the candidate's testimony. Perlo was subsequently discovered to have been involved in espionage for the Soviet Union. The Progressive Party's "research group," which provided the content for most of Wallace's public addresses, was headed by Tabitha Petran, another concealed Communist. The insistence of the Progressive Party's Communists on producing copy that parroted the *Daily Worker* became a source of contention and embarrassment within the third party, both at the state and national levels.[21]

Many liberals and leftists, of course, opposed Wallace's views on foreign aid not simply because they so closely followed the Communist "line" but because they disagreed with the substance of his arguments. Most well-informed observers believed that the third party critique of administration policy, though occasionally raising valid points, was usually unsubstantiated and often presented a deliberately distorted rendering of the president's motives and actions. "Mr. Wallace makes many criticisms of the Truman Foreign Policy which we would endorse," Norman Thomas wrote in the *Socialist Call*, "but he mars their effect, even when he is right, by his carelessness in the use of facts." Privately, Thomas expressed himself more bluntly. "I am pretty disgusted at the line Wallace is taking on the Marshall Plan," he wrote Senator Arthur Vandenberg. "Isn't it about time we stopped talking about the idealism of a man who, when it suits him, so persistently misrepresents the facts?"[22]

Wallace's penchant for gross oversimplification and the casual dismissal of those with whom he differed as "warmongers" and "Wall Street monopolists" also undermined his credibility—particularly when it emerged that some of those very "Wall Street monopolists" expressed the same views as he did. As the *Nation* pointed out, Ernest T. Weir, the chairman of the National Steel Corporation, declared in his testimony before the House Foreign Affairs Committee that the ERP would precipitate "a depression in the United States more serious and far-reaching than anything we have ever experienced." Yet, the editors inquired facetiously, was not Weir "one of the 'monopolists' who, if Wallace is correct, should be promoting the program with the passion of a zealot?" Most historians, too, have rejected Wallace's overwrought denunciations of his opponents' motivations, though during the late 1960s some Cold War revisionists, particularly Gabriel Kolko, attempted to rehabilitate the former vice president's critique of the Truman administration's foreign policy, and of the Marshall Plan in particular. As Anders Stephanson has observed, however, "It is almost too easy to be critical of Kolko: the apocalyptic tone, the absolute certitude, the often crude determinism are immediately suspect, while the claims are often empirically questionable or one-sided"—a characterization one might readily apply to Wallace's congressional testimony as well.[23]

Though many liberals shared Wallace's concern about the role "big business" would play in implementing the Marshall Plan, most saw no evidence of a plot directed by Wall Street to destroy the sovereignty of Western European nations. Though they were aware that many American companies welcomed the Marshall Plan because it promised additional foreign markets for their goods, they were not convinced that a proto-fascist clique of "international bankers and monopolists" had seized control of the government and was plotting to use the ERP to "suppress democracy at home and abroad." And, although they suspected that much of the altruistic rhetoric emanating from the State Department was just that, they did not accept Wallace's allegation that ruthless American imperialists were out solely to exploit a defenseless Europe.[24]

Even if such a malevolent "Wall Street conspiracy" did exist, that it could somehow "dictate" the economic agenda of an entire continent seemed unlikely. Indeed, historians of the Marshall Plan have emphasized that in evaluating the ERP, one must keep in the mind the distinction between "intent" and "result." Impact studies of the Marshall Plan have demonstrated that regardless of the motives behind U.S. policy, American influence over the beneficiary nations' economic agendas was minimal (often to Washington's dismay). Chiarella Esposito, for example, has shown that the French and Italian governments often used American dollars to pursue national fiscal policies that directly conflicted with U.S. preferences, while neither government adopted New Deal "corporatist" policies. Esposito concludes, however, that the United States was willing to accept this situation since the Marshall Plan was meeting the Americans' principal goal of stabilizing these nations' centrist, non-Communist governments. Without American aid, she argues, "it is difficult to see how those same coalitions could have stayed in power and succeeded. . . . Pouring money into France and Italy (and several other European countries) was seen as a strategically necessary preventive measure." Similarly, Frederico Romero has pointed out that corporatist policies backed by New Deal liberals in the Economic Cooperation Administration were simply not feasible in the Italian context and had to be abandoned. The British scholar Alan S. Milward has also argued that U.S. aid had a minimal impact on achieving Washington's goal of European economic integration and, in fact, hindered this process by supplying the funds governments used to pursue their own nationalist economic policies. Assessing the Marshall Plan in strictly economic terms, he judges it a failure.[25]

In any event, most liberals at the time viewed the Marshall Plan not as an unwanted intrusion but as a welcome initiative that could help diffuse Europe's political and economic crises and improve the lot of millions of people. If this be imperialism, then it was what one historian would later call "empire by invitation."[26] Wallace's demand that the ERP be scrapped in favor of a purist, "one-world" internationalism struck many of his former supporters as misguided idealism at best, and as a callous disregard for human suffering at worst.[27]

■ Growing unrest in Czechoslovakia quickly overshadowed the fallout from Wallace's testimony on the Marshall Plan. A cabinet crisis that had begun in Prague on February 13 culminated in the resignation of several non-Communist ministers. Instead of precipitating a new election, this ill-conceived maneuver opened the door for a Communist takeover. Under pressure from the Soviets, Prime Minister Klement Gottwald mobilized Communist supporters in the labor unions and front organizations who then threatened a general strike and staged "spontaneous" mass demonstrations to intimidate the opposition. Truckloads of well-armed "workers' militia units" poured into the capital city to supplement the Communist-controlled police force. Rapidly organized (and retroactively legalized) "action committees" carried out a ruthless purge of non-Communists from all sectors of public life. With clockwork precision, they seized control of the ministries not yet in Communist hands, silenced the non-Communist press, and crushed all manifestations of dissent. The unprepared democratic parties were powerless to counter the Communists' relentless offensive. By February 25, the ailing Czech president Edvard Beneš, the non-Communist forces' last hope, realized that there was no purpose in holding out any longer. Contemptuous of the Communists but fearful of civil war if he continued to resist, he gave in to Gottwald and accepted his proposal for a new government, reportedly telling the prime minister, "You talk to me the same way Hitler did." The Communists' mop-up operation proceeded at an impressive clip. Within weeks, they had transformed the nation from a pluralist democracy to an authoritarian police state. "I couldn't believe it would be so easy," Gottwald later remarked.[28]

The Czech coup, President Truman observed, "sent a shock throughout the civilized world." Even U.S. policymakers who had expected a Communist crackdown in Czechoslovakia before the May elections marveled at the bewildering speed and brutality of the process. "[It] scared the living bejesus out of everybody," recalled one State Department official. On February 26, the U.S. government joined with the French and British in denouncing the coup as "a crisis artificially and deliberately instigated" to install "a disguised dictatorship."[29] The negligible resistance put up by the majority democratic forces also heightened concern in Washington about the ability of other European nations to stave off similar Communist-inspired putsches. In particular, the Truman administration cast an anxious eye on the unstable political situations in France and Italy, where the Communists might be tempted to follow the Czech precedent. Stalin's ominous invitation to Finland to sign a treaty of "mutual assistance" on February 27 only intensified the crisis atmosphere, as many Americans sensed they might be watching a replay of Munich. Such analogies posed risks, however, for they implied that Stalin was as imminent an aggressor as Hitler had been in 1938, thereby fueling the mounting "war psychosis." Indeed, as fears of war increased, "man-on-the-street" interviews revealed that a growing number of U.S. citizens even supported a preemptive atomic strike against the Soviet Union.[30]

Tensions escalated again on March 10, when news reached Washington of the death of the Czech foreign minister Jan Masaryk. The son of T. G. Masaryk, the nation's founder, and himself now a defiant symbol of Czechoslovakia's lost independence, Masaryk had been one of the most highly regarded diplomatic figures in Europe. The Communists promptly labeled his death a suicide—Masaryk, they claimed, had despaired over Westerners' criticism of him for remaining in the cabinet of the new government—but many, including President Truman, suspected foul play.[31] That same day, the normally restrained Secretary of State George C. Marshall told reporters that Czechoslovakia was in the midst of a "reign of terror" and that the international situation was "very, very serious." Thereafter, anger at the Communists reached a fever pitch. "How can any American even toy with the idea of being a Communist?" exclaimed the New Deal's "Old Curmudgeon," Harold Ickes. "To do so is beyond the conception of any sane, clear thinking, free-living American. . . . It ought to be instinctive on the part of every American, not only to resist communism, but to take his stand firmly and openly against it."[32]

As a full-scale war scare swept the nation, President Truman delivered a dramatic address to a joint session of Congress on March 17. For the first time, he indicted the Soviet Union by name as the primary threat to world peace. Declaring that the United States must act decisively to meet the Russian threat, he urged the swift passage of the Marshall Plan, a temporary restoration of the draft, and the establishment of Universal Military Training. With few exceptions, commentators agreed that the president's firm tone had reassured Americans and helped defuse a potentially explosive situation.[33] Still, as the journalist and historian Robert J. Donovan wrote nearly twenty years later, "No witness to those times in the United States can forget the despair, the rage, and—justified or not—the loathing for Communists behind the Iron Curtain that welled up around the headlines and radio bulletins."[34]

Henry Wallace, however, saw things in an entirely different light. He blamed the Truman administration for the Czech coup. In his first public comment on the situation, Wallace told reporters in Minnesota that the announcement of the Truman Doctrine in March 1947 had predetermined the crisis in Czechoslovakia. Had he been president, Wallace claimed, he would have worked for better relations with Russia and "the unfortunate Czechoslovak situation probably wouldn't have happened." Speaking at the Minneapolis Armory on February 27, Wallace elaborated on his views. "The Czech crisis," he declared, "is evidence that a 'get tough' policy only provokes a 'get tougher' policy. . . . The men in Moscow, from their viewpoint, would be utter morons if they failed to respond with acts of pro-Russian consolidation." Though conceding that "representatives of recognized political groups" had been forced from the Czech government, Wallace reminded his audience that "our own government worked to drive from the governments of France and Italy representatives of those leftist political parties which did not meet with our approval." A week later, during a speech in York, Pennsylvania, he revisited this theme, asserting that one could not say "that the present political situation in Czechoslovakia is less democratic than the situation in France." According to Wallace, the Soviet government's exertion of pressure on the Czechs came in response to—and was no different than—the U.S. government's "eliminating important political parties from the government of France." Thus, he concluded, "at the very minimum, we share responsibility for any restrictions on political liberty in Eastern Europe."[35]

Like many of Wallace's arguments, his explanation of the Czech coup began with a logical premise, but it soon degenerated into a skein of distortion and the misrepresentation of facts. Clearly, the putsch had to be viewed within the larger Cold War context. One could argue plausibly that the Czech Communists' actions—backed by the Soviets—had been a defensive measure to guard against Western penetration of the Russian sphere of influence. Officials of the Truman administration willingly acknowledged as much in their diplomatic correspondence, but, unlike Wallace, they expressed sympathy for the democratic majority.[36] It was far less compelling to insist that the crackdown was *solely* a rejoinder to the allegedly aggressive policies of the U.S. government (and, indeed, as Wallace implied, the *only* logical countermove.) As numerous historians have emphasized, Czech Communists had begun their struggle to secure complete control of the country long before the announcement of the Truman Doctrine or the Marshall Plan. Though acutely aware of increasing East-West tensions, they acted not so much in direct response to Washington's "imperialism" or to Moscow's "orders" than to the political opportunities that presented themselves within Czechoslovakia. Those familiar with Czech politics observed that the Communists' efforts to undermine the democratic parties, though in accordance with the Cominform line, had intensified due to shifting domestic conditions, most prominently, their own loss of popular support in the face of upcoming elections. Moreover—and contrary to Wallace's claims—there was never any evidence that the democratic parties in the National Front intended to exclude the Communists from the government or that the U.S. government was pressuring them to do so. Wallace apparently accepted the Communist argument that all opposition to Communism originated on "Wall Street." He therefore interpreted the Czech Communists' slip in popular support as proof of interference from "U.S. imperialists" out to upset the peace. Ironically, his flawed reasoning mirrors that of many U.S. policymakers who traced all *pro*-Communist agitation directly to the Kremlin.[37]

Wallace was on even shakier ground in equating the political situations in Czechoslovakia and France. In Czechoslovakia, a Communist minority had overthrown the non-Communist majority and established a one-party dictatorship by force and intimidation. Nothing of the sort had happened in France, where the Communists, despite their exclusion from the cabinet, remained a significant presence in French politics. Most French citizens would have been surprised to hear that they lived under a political system no more democratic than that in post-coup Czechoslovakia. Furthermore, to support his contention that both superpowers were equally guilty of intervening in the internal affairs of other nations, Wallace had greatly exaggerated the degree and significance of U.S. pressure on the French government. Though by February 1948 the pro-Communist left had accepted as an article of faith that the Truman administration had "forced" the removal of the Communists from the French cabinet in exchange for a promise of Marshall Plan aid, there was no evidence to substantiate the charge. The cabinet reshuffling of May 1947 had occurred in response to domestic political upheaval, not as the result of direct American pressure.[38] In fact, as one historian has noted, if there was any pressure, it came from the opposite direction—French leaders themselves had hinted to the Americans that loans from Washington would encourage their government to "get rid of the Communists."[39] Even the French Communist Party had not charged Washington with exerting "pressure," though it quickly adjusted its public pronouncements after the first meeting of the Cominform in October 1947. At this point, Communist spokespersons and publications both in the United States and abroad began to insist that Washington had indeed "forced" the Communists out of the French cabinet.[40] Wallace's leveling of this same accusation likely reflected his Communist advisers' insistence that New Party statements adhere to the Communist line of the moment, but it also exposed his own unfamiliarity with what had actually happened in France. In any event, while charges of U.S. meddling in French internal affairs were hard to substantiate, direct Soviet intervention in Czech domestic politics had a long and well-documented history, as seen most notably in Moscow's demand that the Czech cabinet reverse its unanimously approved decision to participate in the Marshall Plan.[41]

Leaving aside specific errors in fact, Wallace's apparent equation of America's offer of Marshall Plan aid with the brutal overthrow of a democratically elected government revealed a deeply flawed moral accounting. Speaking for many on the non-Communist left, the British editor Michael Foot declared, "There is a difference between the offer of dollars to Governments, including Socialist ones, by the United States and the provision of concentration camps and execution squads for victims, including Socialist victims, of Soviet Communism." The refusal of Wallace and his associates to acknowledge this difference lest they undermine the higher cause of "peace" left them increasingly isolated, even from those like Foot who shared their concerns about Truman's foreign policy.[42]

Though Wallace criticized the United States for provoking the Soviets and assigned primary responsibility for the Czech coup to the Truman administration, his assessment of the situation nonetheless irked his supporters in the CPUSA. "Why does Henry Wallace view the advance of the people's democracy against intriguers as 'unfortunate'? Unfortunate in what respect?" asked the *Daily Worker*. "Czechoslovakia is free today, gloriously rid of all Big Money intrigues and conspiracies. Czechoslovakia is a demonstration of the new democracy in action."[43] Even more troubling was Wallace's contention that the Czech Communists had acted in response to Soviet "pressure." There was a "fundamental danger" in such thinking, one *Daily Worker* columnist warned. "To grant for a moment that Czechoslovakia's changes are under Soviet pressure," he declared, "has the effect of robbing each people of their nationality, their specific character, their own inherent right to determine their own affairs." And, though the *Daily Worker* neglected to say as much, it also intimated that Czech Communists were Soviet agents, an intolerable heresy which also raised the specter that American Communists, too, were beholden to the Kremlin.[44]

As far as the Communists were concerned, full credit for the "people's victory" belonged to the Czechs themselves. According to William Z. Foster, the national chairman of the CPUSA, the workers had "smashed a Wall Street plot" masterminded by the U.S. ambassador Laurence A. Steinhardt. "The aim," Foster disclosed, "was to force a reorganization of the government on the basis of excluding the Communists from the cabinet, according to the line followed in France and Italy."[45] This line, apparently scripted in Moscow, would receive heavy play in American Communist publications and speeches in the days following the coup.[46]

It also found its way into Wallace-for-President headquarters. During a March 14 exchange with reporters at his New York office, Wallace abruptly revised his appraisal of the recent happenings in Czechoslovakia. The former vice president said he had been mistaken in his previous comments on the situation because he had spoken before he "knew what Steinhardt had been up to, before the rightists staged their coup." One journalist asked Wallace for more information on this alleged "rightist coup." As Warren Moscow of the *New York Times* reported, "Mr. Wallace assured him that his foreign desk undoubtedly knew about it. Mr. Steinhardt, according to Mr. Wallace, issued a statement designed to aid the 'rightist cause' just 'a day or two before the rightists resigned from the government thereby hoping to precipitate a crisis.'" "The implication Mr. Wallace left," Moscow concluded, "was that the Communists in Czechoslovakia acted in self-defense." Significantly, in this new version of events, Wallace had eliminated any suggestion of Soviet "pressure" on the Czech Communists. Startled reporters immediately pressed him to document his charge, but the candidate announced that he was late for a train and would have to end the press conference. On his way out, he fielded one last question. "What about Masaryk's suicide?" he was asked. "I live in the house that [the former ambassador to Great Britain] John G. Winant lived in," Wallace said, "and I've heard rumors why he committed suicide. One can never tell. Maybe Winant had cancer, maybe Masaryk had cancer. Maybe Winant was unhappy about the fate of the world. Who knows?" Two days earlier, Joseph Starobin had written in the *Daily Worker*, "If Americans find it hard to understand Jan Masaryk, . . . let them remember another suicide—of John Gilbert Winant, a former colleague of Roosevelt's, who found that postwar America was not what he hoped and expected it to be, and could not endure the strain of it." As the journalist James Wechsler later remarked, "I doubt that Wallace read the *Daily Worker*, but undoubtedly others did his reading for him." While longtime associates cringed at the candidate's apparently unwitting regurgitation of the most fantastic Communist assertions, the mainstream press began to speculate openly about Wallace's "clarity of mind."[47]

The allegation that Steinhardt had been fomenting a "rightist coup" was palpably absurd. The ambassador had left Czechoslovakia on November 24, 1947, and did not return to Prague until February 19—two days *after* the cabinet crisis began. Still, Wallace stuck to his story, refusing to grant Steinhardt's demand for an apology. Instead, he cited the ambassador's comments to Czech reporters on February 20 that he believed their country might receive some indirect benefits from the Marshall Plan and hoped that the Czech government "might still join this effort." To Wallace—and to the *Daily Worker*—these pro forma remarks constituted "a clearly provocative statement and a contributing factor to the Czech crisis."[48] Few accepted such tortured logic. "Apparently, Wallace expected Steinhardt to denounce the Marshall Plan," Dwight Macdonald wrote acidly. "But Steinhardt is the American, not the Russian, ambassador." Added Freda Kirchwey of the *Nation*, "If anyone deserves an apology it is those liberals who look to Wallace for a leadership that rises above the level of shabby politics." Even Wallace himself later acknowledged that his failure to denounce the Communist takeover in Czechoslovakia had been his "greatest mistake."[49]

Yet Wallace's obtuse reaction to the Czech coup was not "just politics," as Kirchwey and others implied. His private correspondence reveals that at the time he sincerely believed Steinhardt was to blame for precipitating the crisis.[50] His assessment was thus a symptom of a more serious problem plaguing his campaign throughout 1948, and, more broadly, it called into question the feasibility of any liberal-Communist political alliance.

Indeed, this alliance rendered the range of acceptable opinion unusually narrow within the ranks of the New Party. Some topics, especially if they touched on Soviet foreign policy or on a particularly inflexible aspect of the Communist line, were simply not open for debate. In fact, the preservation of the New Party's fragile liberal-Communist alliance depended on the liberals' a priori acceptance of certain views, regardless of any countervailing position's merits. Employing strictures against "red-baiting" and warnings of "outside forces" attempting to pollute progressive minds, many of the New Party's top officials ensured this unquestioning acceptance. By relying exclusively on a group of like-minded acolytes to supply the content for his public statements, Wallace left himself vulnerable in situations where demonstrable fact and the Communist party line diverged. This had happened in the cases of both the French cabinet shuffle and the Czech coup, when Wallace apparently gleaned his information entirely from men and women he did not realize were concealed Communists. All of this seems to confirm Raymond Aron's sardonic remark that during the late 1940s "progressivism [consisted of] presenting Communist arguments as though they emanated spontaneously from independent speculation." Friends and family members called Wallace's attention to this situation, but to no avail. He had retained a 1930s sensibility that there could be "no enemies to the left," long after most of his colleagues from New Deal days had come to realize this formulation's impracticality. "For the peace and prosperity of the world," Wallace had once remarked, "it is more important for the public to know the liberal truth than the reactionary truth." This he still believed.[51]

Wallace's behavior can also be attributed to his self-image as an Old Testament prophet, completely devoted to his message but besieged by unbelievers who refused to follow the path to utopia that he blazed. "He sees only what he yearns to see," lamented Harold Laski, the renowned British socialist and a longtime Wallace booster, "and he has bitter anger for those who cannot see beyond reality to the visions by which he is haunted."[52] As long as Wallace's staff provided him with "facts" that confirmed his cherished preconceptions and the press persisted in reporting information that undermined them, the candidate, completely convinced of the righteousness of his cause, chose to believe those who stood with him in his crusade for "peace" and ignored all others. This decision would cost Wallace much credibility and associate in the public mind his calls for a more balanced foreign policy with naïveté and misguided utopianism.

Wallace's public statements on the Czech coup damaged his personal reputation, but more important, the Communist takeover in Prague dealt a crippling blow to the fundamental precepts of the Popular Front liberalism that he espoused. Czechoslovakia had been an ideological Garden of Eden for progressives—a nation that had successfully balanced democratic pluralism with economic collectivism. As a "bridge" between East and West, it offered a model for the "new Europe" they hoped would emerge from the carnage of World War II. Moreover, the Czech coalition government had shown that by putting forth a good-faith effort, democrats could achieve peaceful coexistence with Communists—a formula, Wallace's supporters insisted, that if applied on an international scale, would resolve U.S.-Soviet tensions. Czechoslovakia's ability to pursue a foreign policy that allayed Soviet security concerns while preserving individual freedom and national autonomy also demonstrated that adopting a friendlier attitude toward the Russians need not mean appeasement or the abandonment of fundamental principles. In short, Czechoslovakia's experience proved the viability both of the Popular Front and of Wallace's prescription for peace. But the Soviets, with precious little regard for the illusions of Western progressives, unceremoniously blew up the bridge. "The Czech coup," wrote a dejected Max Lerner, "has demonstrated for all except the willfully blind that the Communists use a Popular Front only as long as it is useful to them, and smash it at their first chance to capture power by themselves." The Russians, another disheartened commentator concluded, had no interest in bridges, only in bridgeheads. *Izvestia*, the official organ of the Soviet government, confirmed this analysis, upbraiding those who claimed that Czechoslovakia was a bridge between the East and the West: "They forget that in a vital struggle there can be no middle position." With the new Gottwald government firmly established in Prague, even Popular Front liberals who still had the inclination to do so found it exceedingly difficult to defend Soviet behavior in Eastern Europe.[53]

The putsch in Czechoslovakia also undermined progressives' operating theory that economic stability would ward off totalitarianism. The Czech economy, though still suffering from the effects of the war and from a poor wheat harvest in 1947, appeared to be on the upswing. Living standards, too, were slowly rising. Yet in the end, this offered no guarantee against a Communist takeover. On the contrary, many observers believed the Communists had seized control when they did precisely because the improving economic situation threatened their political position. Counter to the conventional wisdom of Popular Front liberalism, the Czech Communists seemed less concerned with improving the lot of the "common man" than with achieving absolute power over him. The Czech coup had had nothing to do with "saving" socialism or with advancing a "progressive" agenda. The "rightist plotters, saboteurs, and foreign agents" of the majority bloc were all committed to extending socialism. They ran afoul of the Communists only in insisting that this occur within a democratic political culture. The struggle was political and moral, not ideological or economic. "What was at stake in Czechoslovakia," the *New York Times* observed, "was not the ownership of the means of production but freedom, and what has been lost is freedom." In this light, it was difficult to take seriously Wallace's oft-repeated entreaty that capitalism and communism should engage in a "friendly economic competition."[54]

The lessons of Czechoslovakia inevitably carried over into U.S. domestic politics. "If any liberal still has any doubts about the goal of communism or the price of co-operating with it," wrote Frank Kingdon, a former Wallace supporter, "I suggest intensive study of this one week in the life of Czechoslovakia." After the coup, even progressives determined to avoid any hint of "red-baiting" began to view Wallace's close alliance with the American Communists as ill-advised, if not politically dangerous. To many of his onetime supporters, he had become the American Beneš—inspiring and idealistic, but destined to suffer the same degrading fate should he fail to submit to the wishes of his Communist colleagues. Though they still found much to admire in Wallace and were unwilling as yet to support Truman, nagging doubts about the political independence of Gideon's Army kept them from supporting their old hero. The reaction of one young liberal who attended the third party rally at the Minneapolis Armory spotlighted the larger trend. As he listened uneasily to Wallace's awkward justification of the Czech coup, Walter Mondale recalled thinking to himself, "I'm not going to be a part of this." Unfortunately for the New Party, many others were reaching the same conclusion.[55]

■ Yet events abroad scarcely diminished the zeal of Wallace and his tight-knit circle of advisers. The New Party kept up its unsparing attack on the Truman administration, accusing the president of "fabricating" a war scare to railroad the Marshall Plan through Congress and to increase the influence of big business and the military. Outraged by the anti-Soviet tone of Truman's address on March 17, not to mention the president's direct attack on "Henry Wallace and his Communists" made during a dinner appearance later that night, they demanded radio time to answer his "hysteria-breeding speeches." In a nationwide broadcast the following evening, Wallace emphasized the U.S. role in fomenting international tension. Assailing the administration's "program to militarize America," Wallace insisted that there was no evidence of any threat to U.S. national security. "We have come to this world crisis," he declared, "because willful men with private interests are dictating our foreign policy. Their interest is profits, not people. They seek to protect and extend their foreign investments against the democratic actions of people abroad." What these men labeled "Russian aggression," Wallace contended, was in fact "the expression of an inevitable historical trend." In France, Italy, Czechoslovakia, and elsewhere, the "common men and women" were "on the march." They "wanted to try a new approach," he claimed. But, fearing a loss of profits, American "monopolists" stood against the tide of progressive change. To fool the people into accepting policies that would protect the status quo, they were "stirring up hate and fear" by exploiting popular anxieties about communism. Writing two weeks later in the *New Republic*, Wallace reiterated that the "big brass and big gold" had cultivated the current "war hysteria" and were exploiting it to extend their own power. Their design, he claimed, was "to set up an American version of the police state in this country as a necessary part of gaining control of the entire world."[56]

Some historians would later resurrect such claims, contending that Truman and other high administration officials had deliberately deceived the people by exaggerating the danger of war in Europe. The "Communist menace," it was argued, was simply a ruse to line up public opinion behind a militaristic foreign policy that served the interests of large corporations and thwarted the revolutionary, anticapitalist spirit supposedly fermenting in Western Europe and elsewhere around the world. Exploiting the Communist issue also allowed the administration to suppress dissent at home as part of a larger strategy to marginalize the left and to ensure the hegemony of the capitalist class. Such accounts, however, overlook ample documentation that many in the administration, particularly the president himself, were genuinely concerned about the possibility of war.[57] As critics of the "war scare" argument have observed, Truman himself acknowledged taking advantage of Soviet moves abroad to rally congressional support for his containment policies, but it does not follow that the threats to national security the president cited were "fabricated" for ulterior motives. In a more sophisticated analysis of the events of March 1948, Melvyn Leffler notes that although Washington did not expect the Red Army to swarm into Western Europe at any moment, policymakers did fear that "diplomatic risk-taking" by the United States, intended to prevent the Soviets from gaining the upper hand, might result in a Kremlin miscalculation that could erupt into war.[58]

In hindsight, one can appreciate Wallace's strictures against American hubris and against the self-serving agenda of U.S. corporations, yet he once again undermined his message by peppering it with a succession of dubious allegations that sounded more like stale left-wing clichés than serious analyses. His dark tale of Wall Street conspirators plotting to enslave the world had not grown any more credible in the retelling. Moreover, Wallace still appeared unable to face squarely the disturbing realities of the postwar world. His fatuous characterization of the Communist takeover in Czechoslovakia as evidence of the people "on the march" in search of a "new approach" seemed merely a convenient means for avoiding inconvenient facts. It also revealed a moral blind spot that antagonized many liberals who had based their support for Wallace on his humanitarian idealism. As any eyewitness could attest, the only Czechs "on the march" were headed toward the West German border under cover of darkness.[59]

Despite the merit of his basic premise that the United States should share the blame for the escalation of international tensions, Wallace's intemperate oratory during the debate about the Marshall Plan and the March "war scare" did little to bolster support for his point of view. On the contrary, he had squandered much of the political capital the New Party had accrued from the Isacson victory and its successful petition drive in California. By indiscriminately denouncing the program of the "bipartisans" while straining to cast Soviet actions in the most benign light possible, Wallace played into the hands of those who wished to dismiss all liberal critics of U.S. foreign policy as "Communist dupes." He also hurt the New Party's chances for attracting a significant protest vote by associating himself with extreme positions that even many of Truman's harshest critics could not countenance. Indeed, by late March, some Washington politicos had come to believe that Wallace had overplayed his hand and that the president's tough stance against the Soviets was paying political dividends. Off the record, House Minority Leader Sam Rayburn told Frank McNaughton of *Time* magazine that Truman's stock had "gone up to beat hell" on the strength of his stand against further Communist expansion. "More and more people will begin to see the red network around Wallace and take their moderate, sincere liberalism back to the Democratic ticket," Rayburn predicted. "Wallace was whittling at Truman," he acknowledged, but "now the whittling is going both ways." But Rayburn was among an optimistic, if prescient minority. "The consensus among Democrats," McNaughton noted, "is that Wallace has lost ground by his wild and wooly campaign speeches, but that he still represents a serious threat to the Democratic Party."[60]

■ The so-called Smith-Molotov exchange, which appeared to mark a momentary break in the Cold War, brought Wallace back into the foreign policy fray in early May. The episode began on May 4, when the U.S. ambassador to Moscow, Walter Bedell Smith, delivered a confidential note to the Soviet foreign minister, Vyacheslav Molotov. Smith's statement sharply criticized Russian behavior in Eastern Europe and made clear that U.S. policy would remain firm, but in closing it reiterated the United States' desire to "find the road to a decent and reasonable relationship between our two countries" and declared that "the door is always wide open for full discussion and the composing of our differences."[61] Molotov responded on May 9 with a long-winded defense of Soviet policies, but he also expressed Moscow's willingness "to proceed . . . towards a discussion and settlement of the difference existing between us." Smith agreed to forward the seemingly pro forma statement to Washington and left for a fishing trip in Normandy. The following day the Soviet press unexpectedly released carefully edited versions of Smith's note and Molotov's reply. The exchange, in the form the Soviets presented it, suggested that the United States had proposed bilateral negotiations and that Moscow had accepted. As the press spread the word, many people naively concluded that an end to the Cold War was at hand. Hoping to capitalize on the new mood as he addressed a capacity crowd at Madison Square Garden on the night of May 11, Wallace put aside his scheduled speech and read the text of an open letter he had written to Stalin.[62]

The Smith and Molotov notes, Wallace declared, "assume what we have long contended—that the war-time cooperation between the two great powers can be rebuilt and strengthened in time of peace." Then, quoting from his open letter, he advanced six proposals as a starting point for possible negotiations: a "general reduction of armaments—outlawing all methods of mass destruction"; "stopping the export of weapons by any nation to any other nation"; "the resumption of unrestricted trade" between the United States and the Soviet Union; "free movement of citizens, students, and newspapermen between and within the two countries"; "the resumption of free exchange of scientific information and scientific material between the two nations"; and the re-establishment of UNRRA or "the constitution of some other United Nations agency for the distribution of international relief." Wallace also stated that neither nation should "interfere in the internal affairs of other nations," terrorize their citizens through the massing of military forces, or use economic pressure or "secret agents" to achieve political results. Ultimately, he insisted, no American or Russian principle "would have to be sacrificed to end the cold war and open up the Century of Peace which the Century of the Common Man demands." Unlike many of Wallace's ghostwritten speeches, the open letter was more balanced in both substance and tone; indeed, it explicitly acknowledged that both the United States and the Soviet Union bore some responsibility for easing Cold War tensions, a premise rarely expressed in New Party statements throughout the campaign. Nonetheless, it also demonstrated the persistence of Wallace's utopianism for, as even one friendly historian concedes, many of the candidate's proposals "expect[ed] one side or the other to act in a generous manner uncharacteristic of powerful nations."[63]

Wallace's appeal to Stalin would not have received much attention had not the Soviet leader responded to it less than a week later. Despite finding some of Wallace's formulations "in need of improvement," Stalin pronounced the statement "a serious step forward," as it provided a "concrete program for the peaceful settlement of differences." On hearing of Stalin's reply, an emotional Wallace declared himself "overwhelmed." "I am humbled and grateful to be an instrument in this crisis," he told a radio audience in San Francisco. "If I have done anything to further the cause of peace in the world," he added, "I shall have felt my whole campaign a tremendous success." As for the statement itself, Wallace considered it "a real and definitive offer by Russia to sit down and discuss our differences, to find ways and means of ending the 'cold war.'"[64]

The Truman administration saw the Smith-Molotov and Wallace-Stalin exchanges in an entirely different light. Furious at the Soviets for breaching diplomatic protocol by selectively publishing confidential documents, Secretary of State Marshall hastened to reassure Western European ambassadors that Smith had not proposed bilateral negotiations that would circumvent their nations and that his note did not constitute a new departure in U.S. policy. Publicly, the secretary denounced Moscow's "cynical propaganda campaign" as an attempt to mislead world opinion regarding the Soviets' desire to "reach an understanding." Most of the American press concurred with Marshall's assessment. The publication of the Smith-Molotov exchange, wrote the *New York Times* correspondent James Reston, "encouraged that most attractive of all United States illusions: that there was some neat, quick way in which the Russian problem could be solved without danger or expense."[65] Modern scholars, too, agree with J. Samuel Walker that "the widespread euphoria that followed the Soviet initiatives was based on ill-founded hopes," though some historians, including Walker, have criticized the Truman administration for too quickly spurning what might have been a tentative, if unorthodox, Soviet overture to improve relations. Indeed, Walker concludes that the real significance in the Smith-Molotov and Wallace-Stalin exchanges is not that the Soviet overtures might have produced fruitful negotiations if pursued—he concedes that this was unlikely—but that in so hastily rejecting them, American officials displayed a rigidity and self-righteousness that kept them from seeing the world situation in anything but their own terms. As for Stalin's reply to Wallace, the State Department officially described it as "encouraging," but privately, a perturbed Truman snapped, "we aren't dealing with Stalin through Wallace." A closer look at the Soviet leader's response also revealed that despite the conciliatory tone, it had been deliberately selective in its review of Wallace's letter. As a *Newsweek* column noted, Stalin cited approvingly all of Wallace's proposals from which the Soviets stood to gain but omitted any mention of those that might require concessions on Moscow's part.[66] On May 28, Secretary Marshall essentially ended the "peace scare," sternly warning an audience in Portland, Oregon, not to be seduced by Soviet propaganda. Meanwhile, those within the administration who viewed negotiations as pointless seemed to have gained the upper hand. Still, as the historian Robert Divine has observed, in the process of scotching what they considered disingenuous Soviet proposals for negotiations, Truman and Marshall had "weakened already shaky public confidence in their Cold War policies." Moreover, their acknowledgement that they had fallen victim to "a clever Soviet trick" hardly provided reassurance. The president, Divine concludes, "emerged from the episode with his stature diminished as millions of Americans regretted that the bright promise of peace had died so quickly."[67]

The New Party, however, benefited little from public dissatisfaction with Truman's maladroit diplomacy. Wallace's exchange with Stalin did provide a sharp boost in morale among his core supporters, but it also seemed to drive a deeper wedge between the New Party and independent liberals. "No one could expect Mr. Marshall to accept the Wallace formula, which was in fact heavily weighted in favor of Moscow," remarked Freda Kirchwey of the *Nation*. Taking a slap at Wallace's theatrically produced mass rallies, Kirchwey concluded, "Not through staged, flood-lit assemblies but through day-to-day negotiations in a hundred normal contacts, will the reality of the recent peace maneuvers be tested." Likewise, though most Americans remained deeply concerned about the outbreak of another war, they were not receptive to Wallace's approach to U.S.-Soviet relations. A public opinion survey released on May 2 found that 63 percent of respondents considered a meeting between Truman, Stalin, and other world leaders a "good idea," but another poll taken just days earlier had reported that only 10 percent believed the United States should be "more willing to compromise" with Russia, while 61 percent thought it "should be even firmer."[68] When Wallace denounced Truman and Marshall for "turning down an understanding with Russia" and for pursuing policies that "stained the world with blood," he electrified the partisan crowds that attended his rallies, but his attempts to make political hay from Stalin's response to his open letter only fueled suspicions that the Soviets were attempting to interfere in the American presidential election.[69] Both Truman and Marshall had interpreted the events of early May in just such terms, fearing that Moscow had misread Wallace's level of support among the American people. (Ironically, one of the main purposes of the Smith note had been to warn the Soviets that the Wallace campaign would have no effect on the administration's diplomacy.) In fact, although Molotov in particular appears to have overestimated Wallace's political strength, no evidence has surfaced that the Kremlin took any direct steps to aid the New Party campaign, financially or otherwise. Undoubtedly, individual members of the CPUSA donated to the Wallace cause, and some "Moscow gold" directed into CP coffers may have paid Communists who were working for the Progressive Party, but there does not appear to have been any concerted effort by the Soviets to "bankroll" the third party campaign.[70] Arguably, Moscow's heated denunciations of the Marshall Plan, its backing of the Czech coup, and its initiation of the Berlin blockade on June 24 did not help but rather undermined the Wallace campaign at every turn. Nonetheless, in the days following the Smith-Molotov and Wallace-Stalin exchanges, more Americans came to view the New Party not only as pro-Soviet but as in some way *linked* to Soviet diplomacy. As long as this perception continued, Wallace and his partisans had little chance of expanding their base of support.

Yet only in hindsight would the underlying weakness of the New Party stand out so clearly. Democrats watching the polls noted with alarm that Wallace still retained enough support in several key states to deprive them of the White House. As he set off on an exhaustive spring campaign tour that would take him to more than twenty states and culminate at the New Party's founding convention in Philadelphia, Wallace and his Gideon's Army appeared to have the Democratic establishment on its heels, even if the candidate's critique of containment had failed to persuade most voters.

5

LIKE A SILKEN THREAD
RUNNING THROUGH THE
WHOLE THING

Lead-Up to the National Convention and the
Crafting of a Third Party Platform

On the morning of July 23, 1948, Henry Wallace arrived by day coach at Philadelphia's Broad Street Station. Senator Glen Taylor of Idaho, his intended running mate, and a crowd of some fifteen hundred ardent supporters welcomed their standard-bearer with songs, cheers, and waving banners. Acknowledging their adulation, a beaming Wallace declared, "I'm mighty glad to be here in Philadelphia. This convention is going to mark a great turning point not only in the history of the New Party, but also in the history of the world." Wallace came to Philadelphia convinced that the independent liberals who had heretofore withheld their support were now ready to join his crusade. Likewise, he believed that liberal Democrats, having failed to block President Truman's nomination, were now ready to back him and the New Party. The convention, he predicted, would produce a flood of converts and "unleash liberal forces all over the country." Outside campaign headquarters at the plush Bellevue-Stratford Hotel Wallace declared, "After this convention you will be astonished at the rapid turn in events and the great support we will get." Though perhaps caught up in the excitement of the moment, Wallace was surely correct in predicting that his movement's fortunes would hinge on the political extravaganza that was about to unfold in the City of Brotherly Love.[1]

■ In the weeks that preceded the convention, however, Progressive Party officials had found little cause to share their leader's optimism. Serious questions remained about the party's continued viability. Most public opinion polls indicated that Wallace had been steadily losing support since he declared his candidacy in December. The sharpest declines had occurred among those groups that had formerly seemed to be his most enthusiastic followers. Among young voters and union members, Wallace's numbers had dropped by 50 percent between April and July. Publicly, Progressive activists insisted that the polls concealed a huge "hidden" Wallace vote—those who were too intimidated to reveal their support to pollsters. Privately, however, they confessed their disappointment.[2]

Also discouraging was the party's failure to make inroads into the African American community. Wallace took a courageous stand on civil rights throughout the campaign, promising that as president he would launch a direct assault on segregation. Such bold statements initially worried Democratic strategists who feared that the New Party would peel off black votes crucial to President Truman's reelection. After the Dixiecrats walked out of the Democratic convention and the party incorporated a strong civil rights plank into its platform, however, blacks showed little inclination to abandon Truman. On July 24 the *Chicago Defender*, the nation's preeminent African American newspaper, endorsed the president and called on Wallace to withdraw from the race. Ironically, Wallace's candidacy probably helped secure the passage of the Democrats' civil rights plank. Joseph Rauh, an ADA activist and one of the resolution's most effective lobbyists on the convention floor, later recalled that he had presented delegates who feared a massive southern defection with a simple argument: "You want to build a Wallace movement?" The specter of Henry Wallace, Rauh explained, "was our secret weapon in this fight."[3]

To an extent, Rauh was correct, though the evidence suggests that by July Truman's top political advisers were committed to a forthright stance on civil rights and far less concerned than ADA about the Wallace "threat." In general, ADA liberals like Rauh focused far more intently on Wallace during 1948 than did the Truman campaign. Midlevel administration officials who did express concern about Wallace making inroads into the Democratic vote tended to have close ties to ADA. On the other hand, Kenneth M. Birkhead later recalled that shortly after the Research Division of the Democratic Party hired him to prepare "anti-Wallace" materials, he was told, for all intents and purposes, to "forget Wallace," since the administration planned to ignore his candidacy. Nonetheless, on July 26, the president dealt another blow to New Party hopes of attracting African American support when he issued executive orders committing the administration to the desegregation of the military and to equal opportunity in the federal civil service. Though Wallace curtly dismissed the president's announcement as an "empty gesture," it demonstrated how Truman's actions could trump Wallace's rhetoric—an insight not lost on African American voters.[4]

Most analysts agreed, however, that the charge of Communist control remained the primary obstacle impeding the growth of the New Party. In a pre-convention survey, Gallup reported that 51 percent of the nation's voters regarded the Progressives as "Communist controlled." New Party officials repeatedly denied that this was the case and blamed unfavorable press coverage for misleading the public. Still, the fact remained that the Communists were playing a significant and disproportionate role in the party. Fearful of backsliding into "Browderite revisionism," they seemed to be growing ever more sectarian. Not satisfied simply to cooperate with their non-Communist allies, in accordance with the new post-Duclos line, they insisted on playing a "leading role" in the various state organizations and maneuvered to gain control even when their members constituted only a small minority. As a result, their relations with non-Communist progressives in the New Party deteriorated precipitously. Throughout the spring and early summer, protracted conflicts about Communist influence had wracked New Party organizations in Colorado, Nevada, New Mexico, South Dakota, and Wisconsin, alienating non-Communist supporters and chasing away potential recruits.[5]

As the convention approached, a flurry of correspondence ensued among several Wallaceites active at the state and national levels that pressed the issue of the New Party's future course regarding the Communists. Some urged Wallace to ask the CPers to leave the party if they could not work amicably with the liberals, while others insisted that he repudiate the Communists at the convention. During a June visit to Farvue, Wallace's farm in South Salem, New York, the writer Louis Adamic warned the candidate that the Communists were less interested in winning Wallace a big vote than in controlling the New Party after the election, since they feared their own party would be outlawed. Adamic believed that major changes in the management of the New Party were in order. Likewise, Lee Fryer, an official in the National Farmers Union and a longtime Wallace supporter, suggested that Wallace should "clean house in his national organization, removing Beanie [Baldwin] and all the others who seem to form the narrow ideological group." Otherwise, he added, "[the convention] is going to be heavily attended by the CP folks as delegates and leaders." Remarkably, even Earl Browder made a visit to Farvue at Wallace's invitation. Browder told Wallace that he had the potential to win ten million votes, but that he would lose it fast if he did not distance himself from the Communists.[6]

Some of Wallace's public statements suggested that he, too, shared such concerns. Fueling speculation that he would jettison the Communists when he got to Philadelphia, Wallace declared at a press conference in Burlington, Vermont, "If the Communists would run a ticket of their own, the New Party would lose 100,000 votes but gain four million." The following day he made a similar statement at Center Sandwich, New Hampshire. Beanie Baldwin, however, quickly sought to head off such talk. When Wallace took up Adamic's concerns with him, Baldwin hastily dismissed them as "red-baiting," and noted that the Communists were serving a useful purpose in some states. Baldwin seems to have made the desired impression. In a private letter written shortly after the meeting, Wallace lamented that his Center Sandwich remarks could be "interpreted as red-baiting and that the enemy can use them in a way which will lead, sooner or later, to the denial of civil liberties and the declaration of war against Russia." Reviewing these events years later, Earl Browder told the historian David Shannon that although he had known Wallace was "a real innocent," he did not see how it was possible to be "*that* innocent." In time, Wallace himself changed his tune. "My mistake was in not following up again and again my Center Sandwich Declaration," he remarked in 1952.[7]

Nor did international events bode well for the liberal-Communist alliance in the New Party. The Soviet blockade of Berlin that had begun a month before the Convention opened seemed only to confirm the Truman administration's contention that the Cold War was not a dispute between Washington and Moscow but between freedom and tyranny. The U.S.-led humanitarian airlift and West Berliners' dramatic struggle against Soviet intimidation hardly fit the foreign policy narrative the Wallaceites were trying to sell. Indeed, if public opinion polls were to be believed, claims made by Progressive Party officials that Washington was entirely to blame for the crisis had not even convinced likely Wallace voters.[8] Additionally, the recent purges in the Italian, Hungarian, and other European Communist Parties, and particularly the Soviets' denunciation of the Yugoslavian leader Josip Broz Tito for allegedly subordinating the Party to the People's Front, signaled yet another crackdown on all forms of "deviationism" within so-called united front organizations. By early July, political observers were already forecasting that in accordance with Moscow's stricter line regarding coalitions with non-Communist forces, the American Communists would assert themselves even more aggressively within the Wallace campaign. The recent squabbles in the various state organizations seemed to confirm such predictions.[9]

Within this context, New Party leaders realized that if they wanted to expand their political base, the upcoming national convention would have to establish their party as a vigorous, independent political movement. To do so, it would have to draw a large, enthusiastic crowd—one in which the Communist presence could not be overly obvious. Yet a month before the convention's opening day, only a disappointing 535 delegates and alternates had requested credentials. In response, the national office launched a sustained publicity blitz to draw as large a crowd as possible to Philadelphia. Baldwin revised the convention rules to allow for larger delegations, set attendance quotas for various state organizations, and instructed his staff to spread the word that anyone who could get to Philadelphia could come to the convention for free. Reflecting an underlying concern that the presence of too many Communists could prove counterproductive, the campaign's director of publicity, Ralph Shikes, advised state chairs that in assembling their convention delegation, it was best to select a "broadly representative" sample of Wallace supporters. Here lay the conundrum. To avoid the embarrassment of a half-empty hall, party leaders realized they would have to rely heavily on the Communist apparatus to ensure a respectable turnout. Yet too much of a Communist presence—and too many Communists trying to play a "leading role"—would undermine efforts to portray the party as independent and broad-based. This ambivalence manifested itself in various, and occasionally humorous, ways. For instance, *only* the press badges—and not those of the delegates—were red. Still, the dilemma was real and demonstrated the challenge of maintaining a Popular Front given the demands of the post-Duclos line.[10]

The arrest of twelve top Communist officials on July 20 only complicated matters. Concealed Communists within the third party interpreted the arrests as further confirmation that "American fascism" was immanent and wasted no time in broadcasting this view. As their rhetoric grew more heated and their behavior more sectarian, they undermined efforts to portray the New Party as broad-based and ecumenical. Frustrated at this turn of events, Baldwin and other New Party leaders insisted that the timing of the indictments was intended to embarrass the Wallace campaign. Though there was no evidence to sustain such an accusation, questions about the Communist role in the New Party did take on a new urgency as national attention focused sharply on the issue of internal subversion. Much as they tried, party officials simply could not escape the shadow of communism.[11]

Never fully comprehending the complicated dynamics that constituted the Communist-progressive alliance, the New Party's standard-bearers, Wallace and Taylor, did little at their pre-convention press conferences to reassure the public that they could be trusted to keep the Communists at bay. When journalists barraged Taylor with inquiries about a "red infiltration" of the Wallace campaign, he declared that the party was only receiving the support of "pink" Communists—"those who believe in the democratic process of evolution instead of revolution." "Red" Communists, he posited, would back Thomas E. Dewey, since the election of a Republican would be "the best way to get a revolution." Personally, Taylor added, he did not know of any Communists actively engaged in the party. Reporters were hard pressed to say which of these comments was more naive. A quick scan of the convention program revealed the presence of known Communists on almost every committee, while the senator's novel distinction between "red" and "pink" Communists earned him a rare scolding from the *Daily Worker*.[12]

Wallace fared little better with the press the following day. Not only did he fail to put the Communist issue to rest; he also raised serious questions about his judgment and basic knowledge of world affairs. Appearing before nearly four hundred perspiring reporters in the north garden of the Bellevue-Stratford, the former vice president opened his press conference by reading lengthy excerpts from two letters written by George Polk, an American correspondent recently murdered in Greece. In one letter, Polk tendered his resignation from *Newsweek*, accusing the magazine of distorting the facts in its reporting of foreign affairs.[13] Puzzled reporters saw no connection between the Polk tragedy and the business at hand until Wallace began to lecture them on the need for objective reporting. He also hinted that they, as journalists, had not done enough to track down Polk's murderer, "the implication being," one observer surmised, "that they were either too cowardly or too reactionary to care." "Never have I seen . . . such a miracle of tactlessness," commented the British writer Rebecca West who was covering the convention as a guest correspondent for the *New York Herald Tribune*.[14]

Apparently unaware of the hostility he was generating, Wallace then announced that he would not entertain any questions regarding Communist support of the New Party. "No matter how hard you try, I am not going to engage in Red-baiting," he vowed. "No matter how hard you try, you are not going to get me to admit that I am a Communist—so you can save your breath." Instead, he delivered a prepared statement in which he granted that Communist support was a "political liability," but insisted that he would "not repudiate any support which comes to me on the basis of interest in peace." "If you accept the idea that Communists have no right to express their opinions," Wallace said, "then you don't believe in democracy." Though many liberals who embraced Wallace's Popular Front–oriented brand of politics repeated this mantra throughout the campaign, it was largely beside the point. Repudiating the political support of a particular group in no way violated that group's right to free speech.[15]

Having concluded his opening remarks, Wallace opened the floor to questions. Citing the candidate's admonition to collect all the facts, the first questioner asked him bluntly, "Did you write the Guru letters?" The reference was to an alleged correspondence between Wallace and one Nicholas Roerich, the "Guru" of a bizarre mystical cult, who claimed to have pinpointed the site of the Second Coming of the Messiah. The right-wing columnist Westbrook Pegler had unearthed the letters and had been insisting for months that Wallace own up to them. "I never discuss Westbrook Pegler," the candidate retorted sharply. Pegler himself then rose and addressed Wallace. "You twice referred to the subject of letters in your remarks and you have reminded us journalists of the important duty of getting all the available facts. Therefore, I ask you whether you did or did not write certain letters to Nicholas Roerich, addressing him as 'Dear Guru,' and his wife as 'Modra?'" Wallace flushed. "I will never engage in any discussion whatsoever with Westbrook Pegler," he angrily replied. When several other reporters put the same question to him, he labeled them Pegler's "stooges." They resented the characterization and demanded that he answer. Wallace refused. Many reporters snickered at the beleaguered candidate while several Progressive partisans angrily shouted back at them. Finally, the venerable H. L. Mencken pleaded with Wallace to put the whole business behind him by responding to the question. Allowing that the Sage of Baltimore was nobody's stooge, Wallace still declined his request. Mencken later remarked that he could not fathom the candidate's "imbecile handling" of the Guru controversy. "He might have got rid of it once and for all by simply answering yes or no," Mencken wrote, "for no one really cares what foolishness he fell for ten or twelve years ago. He is swallowing much worse doses of hokum at this minute, and no complaint is heard." Wallace never did answer the embarrassing question, but by refusing, to quote the British author Laurence Sterne, he "put upon the reader the odium of the obvious interpretation." Either way, this reminder of Wallace's "mystical" side did little to enhance his credibility. By this point, many of his associates in attendance realized that Wallace had "blown it completely" and, according to Curtis MacDougall, "engaged in stealing out of the room as unostentatiously as possible."[16]

Though the peripheral issue of the "Guru letters" received top billing in the next day's papers, Wallace's remarks on substantive policy issues were even more disconcerting. When asked to comment on the reasons behind the Yugoslav split from the Cominform, Wallace recalled that when he had visited the country in 1929, he had found an impoverished peasantry living in a feudal economy. Tito, he claimed, had been too slow for the Russians in bringing the nation out of feudalism. "How can you talk about objective reporting and make such a statement?" the columnist Dorothy Thompson demanded. There had been no feudalism in Yugoslavia since the fourteenth century. "Yugoslavia before the war was a small home owning economy, with more than ninety percent owning their own farms," she informed him. "Well, I just reported on what I saw," Wallace replied. "This is not a question of your personal sightseeing," the formidable Thompson snapped at him. "This is a matter of facts and statistics."[17] Rebecca West, the author of a well-regarded book on Yugoslavia, *Black Lamb and Grey Falcon*, was astonished by Wallace's lack of basic knowledge of foreign affairs. "What was remarkable," she wrote, "was that he appeared to think that Moscow had been trying to make Tito break up large estates and give the peasants the land, when anybody conversant with the facts knows that Moscow wanted Tito to break up the peasants' properties and form collective farms."[18]

Another heated debate began with a concession from Wallace. "In connection with the agreements at Yalta and Potsdam," he admitted, there had been "some bad faith in connection with the elections." The tension, however, was chiefly the result of "differences about what words mean." Though the Russian pledge of free elections in the liberated territories had not been carried out, Wallace explained, this might have been due to a misunderstanding as to the meaning of the word "free." "Important words like 'free' should be carefully defined before another conference is held," he advised. A reporter who had covered the recent elections in Eastern Europe asked Wallace how he could possibly consider those contests "free" by any definition. Flustered, he shot back, "I'd like to see a free election in this country as far as that goes." "That's no answer!" journalists shouted at him. "I make no pretense that it was a free election in Czechoslovakia," Wallace conceded, but he still added that it all depended on one's viewpoint. "Free," he said, had different meanings for Russians and Americans. The reporters continued to press for a specific answer on how he would bring the two nations to a consensus on the definition of words like "free." "Well," said Wallace, "I'd sit down with the Russians and ask them what they mean by free elections. They would find out what we mean by free elections. And then we'd simply write down our agreement."[19] Given that he had launched his third party primarily on the issue of foreign policy, Wallace's startling lack of knowledge regarding the most pressing issues of the day and his glib insistence that the Cold War could be ended simply by talking things through with the Soviets were in fact stronger indictments against his candidacy than any consorting he might have done with gurus or Communists. In their assessment of Wallace's poor showing, Joseph and Stewart Alsop declared in their syndicated column, "It was somehow painful and embarrassing to see the press conference of a former Vice President of the United States turned into something hardly more edifying than the baiting of a village idiot."[20]

Such uncharitable remarks came all too frequently from journalists covering the Progressive campaign, but Wallace partisans and sympathetic historians have overstated the influence of a hostile press in undermining the Progressives' political fortunes. With a few notable exceptions, most political reporters and columnists were neither "rabid red-baiters" nor the "reactionary lackeys" of giant corporate publishers, as the Progressives sullenly alleged. Doris Fleeson, a liberal columnist who had supported Wallace throughout his political career, estimated that about 70 percent of the reporters at the Bellevue-Stratford news conference were also liberals. In surveying journalists who covered Wallace, the New Dealer Gardner Jackson found that many supported the candidate's specific critiques of the Truman administration's foreign policy—opposition to Universal Military Training, the re-imposition of selective service, and Truman's sidestepping of the United Nations, for example. Yet none of them supported Wallace. "They condemn the provocative exaggeration of Wallace's attacks, his avoidance of direct answers to their questions . . . and the type of martyrdom atmosphere Wallace and his promoters desire," Jackson concluded. The press sharply criticized much of what Wallace said and did, but, as Irwin Ross has noted, "no distortion of the facts was necessary to produce an unflattering portrait."[21]

■ Beyond relying on the personal appeals of Wallace and Taylor, the New Party also sought to win wider support through its platform. In an open letter to every "ordinary American" to "tell us what he wants," Rexford

Tugwell, the chair of the platform committee and one of the few prominent liberal "names" to join the Wallace crusade, invited all "who truly represent the people's interest" to testify at public hearings in Philadelphia the week before the convention.[22] This "people's tribunal" opened on July 18 in the sweltering heat of the Convention Hall ballroom. For three days, Tugwell presided patiently over what one wag dubbed "the stations of the cross of Popular Front liberalism." A long parade of rhetoricians, some claiming to speak for "millions" of voters, others testifying only for themselves, presented an endless litany of demands and complaints. Late into the night, advocates representing organizations ranging from the Provisional World Council of Dominated Nations to the National Council of Women Chiropractors implored the committee to include their particular cause in the platform. Even Dr. Francis E. Townsend emerged from obscurity to peddle his old-age pension scheme. "Enough additional loose timber is lying around Convention Hall for a dozen Wallace-for-President platforms," a tired journalist remarked. The committee finally drew the line when it refused to recognize a spokesman for "Onward Christian Communists" who proposed withdrawing U.S. troops from Germany and turning the country over to the Salvation Army.[23]

Despite the fervor of those who testified, few beyond the Progressive Party circle seemed to pay them any mind. Though the hearings were well advertised and open to the public, the spectators consisted primarily of police officers and journalists, further evidence of the increasingly self-contained nature of the Wallace movement. "Gideon's Army is here, shivering lances and slaughtering dragons amid a strange quiet," observed a correspondent for the *Washington Star*. At times, the ersatz character of the process seemed all too obvious. Late one afternoon, reporters spotted the same man who had already testified for several different organizations running a mimeograph machine in the staff room. The liberal columnist Max Lerner found the atmosphere of the event almost surreal. "As I listened to the platform hearings, with each speaker outdoing the other at militancy," he wrote, "I got a feeling of the pathos of it. There was an expenditure of issues, phrases, dedicated intensities, with no chance of their becoming actualities. It was like one of those fantastic card games between a group of men on a desert island, conducted for fabulous stakes, and carefully recorded on slips of paper which would never be honored."[24] Others wondered at the self-conscious selectivity of the militancy on display. A young Alistair Cooke covering the convention for the *Manchester Guardian* later recalled, "I was shaken by the tremors of passion given off by delegates who—just when the Russians were threatening a European war over Berlin—were exclusively dedicated to liberating Puerto Rico, or drafting a safety code for longshoremen, demanding a Cabinet post for the fine arts or federal funds for dentistry." During this "global search for injustices," another reporter noted, not a single person brought up either Russian behavior in Eastern Europe or the Berlin crisis. If the Popular Front coalition was to be maintained, however, such topics could *not* be mentioned—a trade-off that the non-Communist Progressives were still willing to make.[25]

Conspicuous by their absence were the less exotic interest groups that usually frequented such hearings. Despite the Progressives' resolute wooing of organized labor, the national headquarters of the AFL, CIO, and Railroad Brotherhoods had ignored the party's formal invitation to testify. In fact, the local CIO Industrial Union Council had beaten the Progressives to the punch, providing reporters with anti-Wallace press kits before the New Party's advance men had even arrived in town. Curiously, the Communist Party did not send a representative to testify before the committee, perhaps missing an opportunity to emphasize the distinction between itself and the Wallaceites, a move which might have helped the former vice president in his appeal to independent voters. (The historian James Ryan has noted that the post-1945 leadership of the CPUSA, which lacked the former general secretary Earl Browder's penchant for backroom machinations, was too inept to recognize how such a tactic could be of use.) Ultimately, though, the hearings had little effect on the drafting of the platform, which was essentially completed before the committee even arrived in Philadelphia.[26]

■ Preliminary work on the document had begun in mid-April at the founding meeting of the Wallace-for-President Committee in Chicago. At that time, Tugwell had accepted the position of provisional chairman of the platform committee and Lee Pressman, the former general counsel of the CIO, was appointed secretary. The national campaign headquarters then designated the remaining platform committee members, selecting from lists of names submitted by each of the state organizations. Wallace himself apparently exercised no influence in the committee's composition. After the public announcement that Pressman would act as secretary, the *New York Post*'s James Wechsler asked Wallace what he thought of the selection, given that Pressman's close ties to the Communist Party were well known. Did it concern him, Wechsler asked, that someone so close to the CP would have such a key role in drafting the New Party platform? Taken aback, Wallace replied that he did not know the appointment had occurred, but quickly added that he had seen no "evidence" proving Pressman's political affiliation with the Communists.[27] (In this case, however, Wallace was not as politically naive as he let on. In October 1942, he had written in his diary, "Jim Carey who is secretary of the CIO is being kicked around in the CIO by the communist group, including Lee Pressman, who is still very strong."[28])

The process continued in June when the party's New York–based office staff prepared a tentative outline of the platform and sent it to the state directors for feedback. Meanwhile, both Pressman and Tugwell submitted detailed drafts of their own. The Marxist economists Paul Sweezy and Leo Huberman also penned a full-length platform, a revision of an earlier statement of purpose written late in 1947 under the auspices of the PCA. Finally, Scott Buchanan, a college professor from Richmond, Massachusetts, contributed a three-page preamble modeled after the Declaration of Independence, complete with eighteenth-century-style language.[29]

Though the four documents expressed a similar political outlook, they differed markedly in phrasing and emphasis. The Pressman, or "New York draft," was put together by Tabitha Petran and David Ramsey, concealed Communist Party members who worked in the Progressives' research division. Petran and Ramsey, though not official members of the advisory group or of the platform committee, participated actively in the deliberations of both. In Philadelphia, they also worked with the five-person drafting subcommittee responsible for the actual wording of the platform's resolutions.[30] Their draft, by far the most militant of the submissions, echoed almost word for word the CP's draft platform that had been printed in the *Daily Worker* on May 30. Contending that the two major parties were conspiring to impose fascism and to provoke war to satisfy monopolists, it proclaimed that the New Party "would wage the people's struggle against monopoly, fascism, and war." The draft went on to denounce the Marshall Plan as a scheme to rebuild Nazi Germany as a war base, the Taft-Hartley Act as an attempt to establish a "fascist-like labor front," and the Mundt-Nixon Bill as designed to "impose a police state in America." Though such claims would have sounded preposterous to most voters, the Communists accepted them as irrefutable truths. Indeed, the "*immediate* danger of fascism" in the United States had become a staple of the CPUSA's rhetoric after 1946 and would remain so well into the 1950s. Throughout the succeeding deliberations, the Communist members of the platform committee would prove especially intransigent when their colleagues questioned or tried to tone down such statements.[31]

The Tugwell version, written in collaboration with his colleague Richard T. Watt from the University of Chicago, adopted a more temperate, analytical, and non-doctrinaire approach. Longer and more comprehensive than the New York draft, it avoided inflammatory references to American "fascists," "monopolists," and "conspirators." Rather, its authors concentrated on specific contemporary problems—inflation, international tensions, control of atomic energy, political intolerance—and laid out in systematic terms the New Party's strategies for confronting these issues. Reflecting Tugwell's long-held distrust of big business and his devotion to economic planning, the document concurred with the New York draft that government must play a more active role in regulating the economy. It also condemned the undue influence of private industry in shaping the Truman administration's policies, but it did not characterize the contemporary situation as "fascism." Nor did it ascribe to the theory that big business was deliberately pushing the nation toward war.[32]

Huberman and Sweezy also avoided sectarian language. Primarily emphasizing economic issues, their contribution expressed concern at what the authors considered growing concentrations of private wealth in the United States. They, too, called for extensive economic planning, but argued that the levers of economic power had to be placed in the hands of the government before such a strategy could succeed. More insistently than either the Pressman or Tugwell drafts, their platform called for the immediate nationalization of several major industries. In the realm of international affairs, it warned of possible war, but, unlike the New York draft, it saw the behavior of American capitalists as creating an unintended "drift" toward war, not a conscious "drive."[33]

The Buchanan preamble offered a sweeping statement of political principle. More philosophical than the other drafts, it paid less attention to immediate issues and did not dwell on specific programmatic proposals. In essence, Buchanan argued that the time had come for the New Party because the old parties were no longer responsive to the interests of the people. As had Thomas Jefferson's Declaration of Independence, his preamble enumerated the basic responsibilities entrusted to government and cited the instances in which he believed the U. S. government had failed to live up to them. Buchanan especially lamented what he saw as a steady erosion of civil liberties since the end of the war, singling out the Truman administration's institution of loyalty oaths, the irresponsible tactics of congressional investigating committees, and the FBI's overzealous pursuit of political dissenters. Echoing the other three drafts' indictment of "monopoly," Buchanan's preamble declared, "It is the elementary duty of present government to establish civil authority over economic power." In its tone, however, it was the least acrimonious and seemed most likely to appeal to those not already committed to a far-left perspective.[34]

The weekend before the convention, an advisory group of sixteen members met to combine the four drafts into a single statement that would serve as the starting point for the platform committee in Philadelphia. The task proved more difficult that expected. Though they reached consensus on general principles—opposition to the Truman administration's "get tough" policy toward the Soviet Union, the need to restrain the power of big business and the military, and a concern with the plight of the "common man"—it seemed nearly impossible to agree on specific proposals and on the language that would express these proposals. During the advisory committee meetings, the debate over method and tone grew so heated that the members seriously considered abandoning the attempt to produce a single working draft.[35]

The sharpest disagreement arose over the Buchanan preamble. From the outset, Tugwell and another like-minded New Deal liberal, James Stewart Martin of Maryland, urged its adoption. Considering it an eloquent appeal to reason that avoided the well-worn clichés of the far left, Tugwell held that it best captured the reasons for the founding of the New Party. Pressman, however, denounced Buchanan's approach since, in his opinion, it failed to recognize the economic basis of the current political crisis. Drawing on arguments laid out in the New York draft—arguments that again echoed nearly word for word the official Communist position that General Secretary Eugene Dennis had articulated in *The Third Party and the 1948 Elections*—Pressman insisted that Wall Street monopolists were intent on precipitating a war to guarantee their domination of world markets abroad and high armaments profits at home. To silence those who would interfere with their ignoble designs, they had deliberately set out to curtail civil liberties and to reduce the common man's standard of living. According to Pressman, Buchanan's lofty rhetoric failed to capture this "reality."[36] John Abt, the New Party's general counsel and, along with Pressman, one of the most influential figures in the platform deliberations, now jumped into the fray. He, too, preferred the combative simplicity of the New York draft. The party platform, Abt argued, should appeal to the "specific worries, fears, and concerns of the average working man." It should be short and easy to read "when it's passed out at the factory gates." Whatever literary merit Buchanan's offering might have would be lost on "the workers."[37]

Seasoned veterans of many a contentious negotiation during their years with the CIO, Pressman and Abt made a formidable team. James Carey, the anticommunist secretary-treasurer of the CIO and a frequent political opponent, conceded their proficiency in consistently winning resolutions to their liking. "They were the most skillful pair I have ever seen in splitting people and pitting them against each other," Carey recalled. Though generally soft-spoken and unobtrusive, Abt in particular could be relentless in political debate. When Sweezy commented that he did not believe in "all this drive toward war business" and suggested using instead his more moderate "drift" phrasing, Abt vehemently (and successfully) opposed any such change. "The Drive Toward War" remained as a subsection heading in the advisory group's final draft.

Though such an exchange might seem little more than semantic hairsplitting to the ideologically unlearned, for Abt and other Communists, the exact language *did* matter since "monopoly's *drive* toward war" was a centerpiece of party doctrine—a phrase that appeared regularly in Communist Party literature during this period. On the issue of monopoly's "constructive intent" to foment military conflict, there would be no compromise.[38] Indeed, throughout the two days of deliberations, even the slightest alteration of a particular passage could precipitate a protracted confrontation. According to John Cotton Brown, one of Tugwell's graduate students who witnessed the proceedings, "what would be mere quibbling over words to be settled by pleasant log-rolling in one of the major parties, became in the 1948 Progressive Party the surface manifestation of deep doctrinal clashes." Yet alongside such ideological rigidity on the part of the Communists, an improbable political naïveté seemed to suffuse the proceedings. For instance, given the less than hospitable reception Progressive canvassers received at the hands of blue-collar workers both before and after the convention, Abt's romantic image of the proletariat eagerly reading copies of the party platform "at the factory gates" seemed preposterous. Employing hard-nosed tactics in the service of utopian goals was Abt's and Pressman's stock in trade, however, and they largely succeeded in having their way. Though Tugwell argued vigorously in support of Buchanan's less tendentious approach, at the end of the weekend a majority voted to set the preamble aside entirely and accept the New York draft as a "working skeleton."[39]

■ Though battles over phrasing occupied much of the advisory committee's time, Tugwell also suggested one major substantive change. Hoping to moderate the platform draft's insistently pro-Russian stance on

U.S.-Soviet relations, he pushed for a major reformulation of the planks on foreign policy and the military. Tugwell did not hold the benevolent view of the Soviet Union that many of his colleagues in the New Party accepted uncritically. In particular, he did not share their assumption that unilateral arms reductions and military retreats on the part of the United States without corresponding Soviet guarantees would automatically create a more favorable atmosphere for peaceful negotiations. Unconvinced that the Kremlin would negotiate on the basis of reason and justice rather than of military and strategic potentials, he pleaded with the advisory group to "take cognizance of power politics considerations in evaluating American military requirements." "We have to decide," he declared, "whether the Russians are playing poker or post office, and I don't think they are playing post office."[40]

Tugwell was no Cold Warrior. He expressed strong support for the platform's plank demanding "the repudiation of the Truman Doctrine and the end of military and economic intervention on behalf of reactionary and fascist regimes." He also believed that the New Party was correct to oppose the administration's proposal to reinstitute universal military training, which he characterized as provocative. Nonetheless, Tugwell argued, abandoning policies *after* they had been implemented with no quid pro quo from the Soviets would surely be misinterpreted as appeasement and might even lead to a heightening of tensions. Moreover, incorporating into the platform an unqualified demand for unilateral retreat would be both irresponsible and difficult to justify to the American people. Instead, Tugwell suggested adopting a plank that would declare the United States' willingness to come to terms with the Russians without resorting to provocative measures, "provided there was no shift in the real distribution of power," until both parties reached an agreement with effective guarantees.[41]

Pressman rejected out of hand the chairman's approach to Soviet-American relations, insisting that he could "see no difference between Tugwell's line of reasoning and the Truman Doctrine." Echoing arguments in the Communist press, he insisted that Tugwell's and Truman's positions were identical, since both implied the Soviet Union bore some responsibility for the Cold War. This was impossible because only monopolists wanted war, and the Soviet Union, as a socialist country, had no monopolists. Expressing concern over "appeasing" the Soviet Union was simply a warmongering scare tactic since the USSR, by definition, could not be an aggressive power. Soviet behavior, according to Pressman, was purely a defensive reaction to the assaults of the American imperialists and had nothing to do with power politics. He then preempted any further debate on the matter, declaring that the *only* way to peace was unilateral military and strategic concessions on the part of the United States, which would in turn ease legitimate Soviet security concerns.

In this particular dispute and in subsequent exchanges about foreign policy, Pressman presented the issue of Soviet-American relations as an exclusively "either-or" proposition. "Either the United States and Russia have good relations and peace," he maintained, "or bad relations and war." According to Brown, "he never discussed the possibility of bad relations and an uneasy peace, or the bargaining value of military advantages in negotiating for peace." Pressman grounded his reasoning on the Leninist doctrine of "two camps" that Zhdanov had recently revived at the founding of the Cominform—one either accepted the "progressive" position laid down by the Communists, or consigned oneself to the camp of the reactionaries. This "either-or" formulation proved effective for the Communists in their attempts to influence the "Peace" section of the New Party platform. As long as the debate remained so sharply polarized, any deviation from the CP position could be portrayed as a betrayal of the cause of peace and leave the dissenter susceptible to being branded a "warmonger." Indeed, the Communists had already put such tactics to good use in Eastern Europe. Journalists present at the July convention who had also covered politics behind the Iron Curtain noted the disturbing resemblance between Progressive slogans—"Wallace or War," for example—and those the Communists had used during their bids to consolidate power in Czechoslovakia and Hungary, such as "Gottwald or Fascism" or "Rakosi or Reaction." As one correspondent noted, however, the Wallaceites hardly commanded the political influence of a Klement Gottwald, and as a result their imported techniques and jargon came off sounding "ridiculous rather than alarming."[42]

Still, Pressman was not necessarily "forcing" the minority Communist position on the advisory committee's non-Communist majority. Though they were not identical, both groups' basic worldviews were compatible. The non-Communist committee members continued to see global political alignments much as they had in the 1930s and during the war. Accordingly, they considered the Soviet Union a natural ally in the fight against fascism, and Communism as a more "advanced" variety of progressivism—though perhaps one better suited to "backward" nations than to the United States. Those who drummed up anti-Soviet sentiment undermined antifascist unity, and were therefore (consciously or not) the agents of fascism. In such a Manichaean outlook, anyone who suggested that the Soviet Union be seen as a potential adversary was merely playing into the hands of the fascists.

Not surprisingly, then, Tugwell could find no supporters for a more balanced approach to foreign policy. Though perhaps less ideologically insistent than Pressman, the rest of the group was inclined to agree that the United States bore full responsibility for the current international crisis and should therefore take the initiative in trying to resolve it. Moreover, Pressman's dissertation on the insidious machinations of "monopoly capitalists" comported well with many non-Communist committee members' populist hostility toward big business. As he and other left-wing Progressives repeatedly attacked Tugwell's appeals for a more balanced evaluation of Soviet-American relations, even committee members who Brown believed "on other occasions clearly demonstrated their independence from the Communist party line" consistently opposed any reworking of the "Peace" section of the platform.[43]

Realizing that the extensive changes he had originally suggested had no chance of passing, Tugwell offered a series of successively weaker resolutions. The committee finally accepted a plank stating that in return for the unilateral reduction of American military strength "to adequate levels for national defense . . . the Soviet Union should have no reason for failing to reach a full settlement of existing differences." Even this minor Tugwell victory proved ephemeral—the drafting subcommittee in Philadelphia later eliminated the clause that referred to the USSR.[44]

Frustrated at being voted down on several issues for what he considered "ulterior left-wing political objectives," Tugwell left New York convinced that Pressman, Abt, and others were actively promoting the Communist line to the detriment of the Wallace campaign. Recalling these meetings in October 1948, he acknowledged, "We had a certain number of those who appeared to be more interested when we came to the discussion of the section we labeled 'Peace,' in furthering the foreign policy of the U.S.S.R. than in anything else. . . . They were cohesive and persistent; they had some support. It was not hard to guess that they were there to protect the homeland of Communism." Privately, the veteran New Dealer expressed his disappointment with the rigid formulations in the working draft. He disliked the heated arguments with Pressman and the "smiling impasses" over the wording of specific resolutions, especially when the group refused to discuss openly the fundamental philosophical differences between the Communists and their liberal allies—the "real" issue, as far as Tugwell was concerned.[45] His experience in the advisory group meetings fueled his suspicion that the party's left-wingers had no intention of compromising with "old-fashioned progressives" like himself. Uncomfortable in the role of official spokesperson for a committee many of whose beliefs he did not share, Tugwell decided to resign as chairman. When Brown suggested the possibility of improving the advisory group's draft during the meetings of the platform committee in Philadelphia, his mentor replied dejectedly, "*That* committee will *really* be a hand-picked bunch."[46]

Tugwell's observations were not without merit, but the exasperating situation he confronted was hardly unique. Well organized, ideologically committed factions often exercised disproportionate influence in the process of writing party platforms. The Communists may have been particularly inflexible, but their zealotry did not predetermine the outcome of the debates in New York. The majority of the group's members were neither Communists nor "fellow travelers" consciously committed to a "party line." The planks Tugwell presumed to be Communist-inspired could not have been written into the platform without non-Communist support. No matter how "cohesive or persistent" the Communist minority, the non-Communist majority ultimately bore responsibility for the final product.

The "old-fashioned progressives," however, seemed to regard any expression of dissent on their part as a threat to "unity"—a capitulation to the "red-baiters." As a result, they were not only reluctant to admit that the Communists were acting as a faction—if indeed they recognized them as a faction—but also showed no inclination to question the objectives or methods of their left-wing allies. Given their commitment to cooperating with the Communists, subjecting the CPers to such critical scrutiny or attempting to limit their influence would have been a surrender of principle to the pressures of the Red Scare. The Communists, of course, did all they could to reinforce this line of thinking, which had always worked to their advantage within Popular Front organizations. In addition, the non-Communist liberals did not share Tugwell's concern regarding the pro-Soviet bias of the platform. In fact, they were often the most vocal advocates of pro-Soviet formulations. Their views may have been exceedingly naive, but they reached them of their own accord. As a result, if the platform failed to win broad support from the voters because it resembled too closely the platform of the Communists, it would be due more to the public's rejection of the non-Communists' brand of Popular Front liberalism than to any "dictation" or "committee packing" on the part of the comrades.[47]

■ On Tuesday, July 20, the executive sessions of the platform committee opened in Philadelphia. After a few introductory remarks, Tugwell announced officially that he was stepping down as chairman. Martin Popper, a concealed Communist who later emerged as one of the committee's most vocal members, urged him to reconsider since the press would interpret his resignation as evidence of dissension in the party ranks—again, the plea was for "unity." Popper then nominated Tugwell for permanent chairman. Tugwell demurred, asking that his wishes be respected. When no nominations for a replacement emerged, however, he reluctantly agreed to remain, but only on a temporary basis. The committee then began the process of composing the final platform, adopting the advisory group's draft as the starting point for its work.[48]

According to Brown, Tugwell interpreted Popper's reaction as an indication that the left-wingers might be willing to compromise rather than face the bad publicity that would accompany the resignation of one of the party's most prominent non-Communists. Tugwell reasoned that by staying he might have a chance to shape a platform more to his liking. Appeals to "unity," however, usually worked more to the advantage of the left-wingers. For example, over Tugwell's objections, Pressman shrewdly insisted on releasing the advisory draft to the press *before* the platform committee had finished amending it. As a result, any attempt to significantly alter the draft could be discouraged lest it provide reporters with evidence of a breakdown in party "unity."

The platform committee's deliberations, however, did not go as smoothly has Pressmen had hoped. In what would develop into a motif for the entire convention, the New Party's relationship to the Communists came under immediate scrutiny. After reading the advisory group's draft, some committee members unexpectedly expressed reluctance to endorse a program so close to the Communists' without first renouncing communism. In the afternoon session, Cedric Thomas, a real estate agent from Maine, proposed that the platform's preamble "make it clear that the New Party is non-communist." Adopting a pragmatic view, Thomas maintained that if the party took this step, it would not lose the support of the Communists since the Progressives would still be "closer to them than is either of the two old parties." Charles Rohrer, an Indiana farmer, agreed, arguing that "to the average man, Communism still stinks." To win the "church people" in his state, Rohrer contended, the platform would have to come out "flat-footed against Communism."

Within the Popular Front milieu of the Progressive Party, however, any criticism of communism, even implied or indirect criticism, immediately provoked sharp opposition. Leo Krzycki, a former vice president of the Amalgamated Clothing Workers Union and a longtime ally of the

Communists in the labor movement, added that nothing would be gained by trying to defend the Progressive Party against "smears which are bound to come." Several others warned against inserting any reference to the party's "non-communism," on grounds that such a statement would be "too negative." Hesitant to exacerbate tensions so early in the proceedings, the committee took no action on the proposal and agreed to return to the issue on Friday morning.[49]

As in New York, Communists and fellow travelers did not constitute a majority of the platform committee. The perennial Socialist standard-bearer Norman Thomas, a well-informed observer of left-wing politics who was covering the convention as a syndicated columnist, put their number at about twenty-four of the seventy-four members listed in the program. Thomas defined "fellow travelers" as "men and women, who in the labor movement and in politics, have consciously and consistently followed the Communist party line." In Thomas's definition, "consciously" is the crucial word in distinguishing "fellow travelers" from independent liberals. Though the latter often took positions that paralleled those of the CP, unlike the "fellow travelers," they did not do so *because* a particular stand was in accordance with the "line." Indeed, it is unlikely that most non-Communist committee members were even familiar with the details of the Communist program, let alone with why or how the Communists arrived at their positions. They acted on their own political instincts, giving little consideration to the CPers except as devoted allies in furthering the progressive cause. Still, enough of the non-Communists endorsed *some* Communist views that the left-wingers could secure their formulations by cobbling together a series of shifting majorities. This task simply entailed determining which members accepted which facets of the party line and then rallying them behind the Communist position when the time came to take a vote. Consequently, the CPers' adeptness at operating within a Popular Front coalition allowed them to wield disproportionate influence without raising suspicions that they were trying to impose their views through undemocratic means.[50]

Having witnessed this process unfold in the advisory group meetings and sensing that it was now recurring in Philadelphia, Tugwell grew increasingly anguished. Convinced that Pressman and Abt were manipulating the proceedings, he nonetheless realized he could neither repudiate the committee's Communists nor "unmask" the tactics they were employing without himself being tagged a red-baiter. Nor could he accuse them of violating democratic procedure since they seemed able to win majority support for their positions. Moreover, Tugwell still hoped that the New Party might evolve into the vital progressive force he had initially envisioned, and he therefore did not wish to undermine it by joining the public chorus of its critics. Even so, he feared that unless he acted swiftly, the emerging platform would be precisely the kind of sectarian, pro-Soviet document likely to sabotage the New Party's appeal to non-Communist progressive voters and would reinforce its image as a creature of the Communists.[51]

When the committee opened debate on a motion to change the platform's plank concerning the status of Puerto Rico—from support for "independence" to an endorsement of "self-determination or statehood"—Tugwell sensed an opportunity to stand up to the left-wingers. The working draft of the platform declared that "the New Party will grant independence to Puerto Rico," a position in accordance with the Communist line, but one Tugwell adamantly opposed. The Communists had long demanded "immediate unconditional independence" for Puerto Rico, hoping to call attention to the islanders' "long suffering under the yoke of American imperialism."[52] Tugwell, who had served as governor of Puerto Rico from 1941 to 1946, knew the island and its people well. Realizing that Puerto Ricans would suffer drastic hardship if cut loose from the more than $50 million in American subsidies they received each year, he had pleaded for a modification in New York. "Not five hundred people on the island are for separation from the United States," he declared. Yet the advisory group had voted to retain the wording of the Pressman draft. Given a second chance to make his case, Tugwell was determined not to back down. He knew any change in phrasing would provoke the left-wingers, but he felt confident that he could win the debate on the merits of his arguments. Since he wished to demonstrate that non-Communists like himself could overcome the left's ideological rigidity and play a role in shaping well-reasoned party policy, he almost welcomed their opposition. It was not long in coming.[53]

Pressman and Popper insisted that the Puerto Rico plank remain unchanged. While the committee was still voting on the proposed amendment, but after it became apparent that Tugwell's position would win, Popper hastily stood up to demand further debate. Denouncing any effort at "opposing independence," he coyly reminded the members of the independence plank's special appeal to the half million Puerto Rican voters in New York City. Congressman Vito Marcantonio, himself a leader in the New Party, represented the majority of them, Popper continued, and would surely reject the motion as well. Tugwell pointed out that his phrasing did not "oppose independence," which was included in the possibilities that could result from self-determination. Popper, however, would not relent. Pressman then intervened and calmly suggested postponing consideration of the issue until Friday's session.[54]

On Wednesday evening, Marcantonio appeared at the open hearings of the platform committee to testify in favor of the independence plank. Tugwell purposely absented himself to keep the issue from degenerating into a personal dispute. In his trademark flamboyant style, the fiery New York congressman gave a spirited defense of the cause, shouting at one point that "self-determination is a term of the imperialist demagogues." "Too bad Tugwell couldn't be here to hear this," one committee member remarked facetiously as the harangue finally came to a close. Two others conceded that they had been hard pressed to follow the logic of Marcantonio's arguments. Skeptical reporters speculated that the congressman's knowledge of Puerto Rican affairs did not extend much further than the exact number of Puerto Ricans registered to vote in his East Harlem district. Nonetheless, when the committee took up the issue on Friday, Popper reported that the drafting subcommittee—which he chaired—now recommended that the resolution read, "The New Party demands independence for Puerto Rico."[55]

Tugwell, again not in attendance, relayed through an emissary his continued opposition. Convinced that the Puerto Ricans, if given a choice, would *not* vote for independence, he noted that pledging the Progressive Party to "independence only," actually *contradicted* its support for the principle of self-determination, enunciated in the platform two sentences later. Leo Huberman then announced that Tugwell felt so keenly on the matter that if the committee accepted the independence plank, the chairman would not present the platform to the convention. To head off such a potentially embarrassing situation, the members appealed directly to Henry Wallace to settle the dispute. After conferring separately with Marcantonio and Tugwell, Wallace ruled in the latter's favor. The committee then adopted a compromise resolution that referred to the Puerto Rican's "right" to independence without endorsing such a course.

Tugwell emerged victorious on the specific issue at hand, but he failed to convey his larger point about the need to resist the left-wingers' attempts to control the party's agenda. Unlike Tugwell, the non-Communists—including Wallace—did not view the dispute as one battle in a broader ideological struggle between Marxist-Leninists and reform-minded progressives. Nor did they glean that Tugwell was standing up for reasoned debate backed by evidence against dogmatic adherence to a "party line." Rather, they chose to interpret the fracas as an instance of personal obstinacy. Indeed, by the time Wallace resolved the controversy, Pressman and

Popper had won over a majority of the committee to their position. Without Wallace's intervention, the plank demanding immediate independence for Puerto Rico would have remained. The columnist Max Lerner, more politically sophisticated than the non-Communists on the platform committee, recognized what was going on and appreciated Tugwell's concern. This, he lamented, was the "tragedy about the whole thing"—"the story of the tensions between the Wallace progressives and those members of the New Party who are seeking to use it for the purposes outside American progressivism—of tensions which never developed to the breaking point or even to the breaking out point."[56]

As the convention prepared to convene, Tugwell confided to his wife that he was so heartsick about Communist maneuvering within the party that he was seriously considering disaffiliating from it and had urged Wallace to do the same. Indeed, that very night representatives of the Truman campaign had reached out to Tugwell hoping they could arrange a deal whereby Wallace would withdraw and throw his support behind the president. The same offer had been extended to the Progressive Party's campaign manager, Beanie Baldwin, who, after consulting with Eugene Dennis, the CP's general secretary, flatly rejected it. Informed of these overtures, Wallace, too, dismissed them as "unrealistic" unless the Democrats did an "about-face" on foreign policy. Ironically, in failing to woo him, the Democrats had dodged a bullet. During the next few weeks the special session of Congress heard explosive testimony from Elizabeth Bentley and Whittaker Chambers that put the Communists in government issue front and center and threw the Democrats on the defensive. In such circumstances, a newly forged alliance with the Wallaceites—already seen as "Communist controlled"—would have been an albatross around Truman's neck.[57]

■ In the midst of his standoff with the left over Puerto Rico, Tugwell also faced an attack from his political right. Testifying before the platform committee on Thursday afternoon, James Loeb, the national executive secretary of Americans for Democratic Action (ADA), denounced the New Party as "a dangerous adventure undertaken by cynical men." Loeb pulled no punches, stating flatly that "the presence of Mr. Wallace . . . does not obscure the fact that the Communists and their collaborators guide the major policies and word the major pronouncements of this party." While citing ADA's consistent defense of the Communists' right to maintain their own political party, he sharply condemned any alliances between non-Communist liberals and the CP. The New Party's "so-called united front" structure, he contended, made it "virtually impossible for it to show its independence of Communism." As Tugwell and his colleagues sat in stony silence, Loeb urged them to endorse the Marshall Plan and thereby support "the progressives and socialists of Europe in their heroic struggle for civil liberties and against a ruthless totalitarianism which has extinguished human freedom wherever it has had the power to do so."[58]

Tugwell resented what he perceived as an attempt to bait the committee, though Loeb was hardly revealing anything Tugwell himself did not already know. As soon as Loeb finished speaking, the chairman dismissed him abruptly, foregoing the usual question-and-answer period that had followed the statements of other petitioners. Those assembled booed him loudly and shouted insults. "I was ushered out of the room by four of Philadelphia's finest," Loeb later recalled. "I have always been in favor of an anti-lynching bill, but never so passionately as during those few minutes." As a roomful of Wallace partisans cheered him on, Tugwell denounced Loeb's "intemperate attack" as "insincere, hypocritical, and immaterial."[59] Yet, as Loeb pointed out afterward, Tugwell failed to address any of the substantive issues he had raised or to answer any of his arguments. He questioned how anyone could believe that "the Marshall Plan and other grave issues of the world crisis" did not merit debate. Nor could Loeb understand why non-Communist Progressives refused even to acknowledge the brutality of the Communist regimes in the Soviet Union and Eastern Europe. Though most Progressives were undoubtedly "men and women of good will," he wrote to an ADA colleague, "Mr. Wallace and his friends insist on overlooking . . . the central political fact of the postwar world, namely . . . that thousands of men and women who went to concentration camps and in exile fighting fascism are now once more in concentration camps and in exile."[60]

Overall, Loeb found Tugwell's performance "disgraceful," an indication of how far the New Dealer had strayed from the mainstream of American liberalism. "I can find much more to admire in a guy like Pressman, who makes no bones about his convictions," he commented. "But Tugwell clearly didn't agree with most of what was being done but didn't have the guts to challenge the nonsense."[61] Indeed, Tugwell, who had given speeches in support of the Marshall Plan, had already conceded to reporters that he was "dissatisfied" with the provision that called for its repudiation, but he added improbably that he did not think "it was too important an issue." When asked if Communists held any positions of influence in the party, Tugwell again dodged the question. "I am not close enough to the New Party to know [about] this," he replied.[62] In later years, some of Tugwell's non-Communist colleagues on the platform committee echoed Loeb's remarks, chiding the chairman for being "weak," abdicating his responsibilities, and allowing Pressman to "run the show." Such criticism rings hollow, however, since they, too, had the opportunity to resist Pressman but failed to do so. At the time, the preservation of Popular Front "unity" again took precedence.[63] For his part, Loeb was ultimately more critical of Wallace. "If Wallace gets several million votes, only the tiniest fraction will be Communist or fellow-traveler," he wrote a colleague. "But, when you see the movement in a convention, and especially in a platform committee, you realize how completely and thoroughly this is a Communist operation. You get resentful of Henry Wallace because you realize that without him there would be no Taylor or no Tugwell. And without them this would be [the] same old gang that has been meeting with itself for so many years in a small hotel room."[64]

■ Loeb's dramatic appearance set the context for Friday morning's executive session of the platform committee when attention returned to Cedric Thomas's attempt to clarify the New Party's relationship to the Communists. Rebuffed on Tuesday, Thomas now offered a compromise resolution, suggesting that the platform's preamble include a statement along the lines of one that vice presidential candidate Glen Taylor had made when he had announced his decision to join the New Party. In his February 23 radio address, Taylor had declared that his goal was to make "our economy work so well and our way of life so attractive and our people so contented that Communism will never interest more than the infinitesimal fraction of our citizens who adhere to it now." (Typically, the reprints of this speech, distributed as campaign literature by the Wallace-for-President committee, omit Taylor's reference to communism.)[65] James S. Martin, whose views coincided with Tugwell's, supported Thomas's motion. Though several other committee members also nodded in agreement, they were in the minority. John M. Coe declared that given the indictments of twelve top members of the Communist Party for violation of the Smith Act four days earlier, adopting Thomas's proposal would be tantamount to red-baiting. "Do you mean that a statement which was all right when Senator Taylor said it in February has now become red-baiting?" asked an astonished Tugwell. In response, Popper informed Tugwell that "with these arrests, a qualitatively new change has taken place in the United States." Therefore, Taylor's statement was indeed red-baiting.[66]

Pressman then spoke at length on the perils of red-baiting, resorting once again to the "either/or" line of reasoning he had employed in numerous other disputes. "Either you are going to remain steadfast to our principles or you are not. I understand the temptation of those of us who come from states where there is not a strong mass movement. But when Jefferson was attacked as a foreign agent, he didn't deny it. He went to the grass roots and carried the real issues to the people. It's not easy. It's a fight which determines whether we live or die." The connection between Thomas's innocuous proposal and a life-and-death struggle seemed tenuous. Nonetheless, Pressman's impassioned oratory fortified the committee members' predilection to equate any implied criticism of the Communist Party or Communist positions with the political heresy of red-baiting. They voted down the motion overwhelmingly.[67]

Undaunted, Thomas made one final attempt at the afternoon session to distance the party from the Communists, only to have the tables turned on him. Noting that the "Freedom" section of the advisory group draft contained the sentence, "The Progressive Party will fight for the constitutional rights of Communists and all other political groups to express their views as the first line of defense of liberties of a democratic people," he questioned the political wisdom of giving primary emphasis to the Communists. Thomas moved that the plank should read simply, "the constitutional rights of all political groups." With Pressman's imprimatur, the amendment seemed to gain momentum.[68] Popper, however, angrily denounced any attempt to remove mention of the Communists. Since the Communists were now at the "forefront of the fight for civil liberties," he asserted, the platform would be red-baiting if it did *not* specifically mention Communists in a statement on the rights of political expression. Popper's skillful, if disingenuous, exploitation of his colleagues' antipathy for red-baiting proved effective. The committee voted to retain the resolution's original wording. In fact, Popper's drafting subcommittee recommended that this particular section of the platform *begin* with the party's pledge to fight for the Communists.[69]

With good reason, modern scholars have condemned "red-baiting" as one of the more deplorable aspects of early Cold War political culture. They are less apt to acknowledge the Communists' use of the epithet "red-baiter" to silence potential critics and to stifle substantive debate. Within Popular Front organizations, the Communists denounced as "red-baiters" all who questioned their motivations and methods, and even those who referred to Communist Party members as Communists. As Pressman and Popper clearly demonstrated, such a bullying tactic could prove quite effective, as few progressives were willing to risk being tagged a "red-baiter." Yet such an approach did not strengthen Popular Front organizations;

particularly in the postwar period, it crippled them, reaffirming the arguments of anticommunist liberals that any alliance with the Communists resulted in self-censorship and intellectual dishonesty on the part of the non-Communists.[70]

Similarly, though the Progressives' outspoken defense of the Communists' rights in their platform showed political courage given the prevailing anticommunist sentiment throughout the country, their alliance with the Communists also forced them to accept a highly selective commitment to civil liberties. Standing up for Communists and other progressives was one thing, but upholding the constitutional rights of "reactionaries" was another matter entirely. In an angry speech before the platform committee, Edgar G. Brown, a prominent African American Progressive, demanded that the rebel States Rights Democratic Party be outlawed and the citizenship of its leaders be taken away. The committee failed to incorporate Brown's views into the platform, but its "Freedom" section did declare, "We support the enactment of legislation making it a Federal crime to disseminate anti-Semitic, anti-Negro, and all racist propaganda by mail, radio, motion picture or other means of communication." Though presumably well intended, such statements revealed an authoritarian impulse in the Wallaceites' brand of progressivism. When a group of convention delegates later urged striking this vaguely worded resolution since it obviously violated the First Amendment, the platform committee rejected their initiative without explanation, leaving the impression that "inquisitions" were acceptable so long as they targeted the right groups. Ironically, the same press reports that recounted Brown's call for outlawing the States Rights Democratic Party carried Beanie Baldwin's denunciation of those attempting to outlaw the Communist Party. Critics charged that with the New Party in power, the state of civil liberties would be even more fragile than under the watch of the much maligned "bipartisan reactionaries." This inconsistent commitment to civil liberties, the historian Eric Goldman has argued, was characteristic of Popular Front liberalism. "Henry Wallace and much of his following were inclined to think in a Thirties fashion about civil liberties," Goldman notes. "Economic and social change came first; 'liberty' was a catch phrase of the reactionaries. Besides, the real menace to civil liberties came from the right, not the left." In contrast, by 1948, "most liberals . . . were done with a cavalier attitude toward liberty or with a double standard in judging leftist or rightist dangers to it." This shift boded ill for the Communists, who for obvious reasons preferred the Popular Front conception of civil liberties that the New Party platform embraced.[71]

In yet another instance of the New Party's Popular Front structure shaping the substance of its platform, what did *not* appear in the final draft proved as telling as what did. Nowhere in the 6,500-word document was there any mention of "progressive capitalism." Wallace had long used this phrase in his speeches and writings to describe his essentially Keynesian approach to economic policy—so much so that it had come to be associated with him in the same way that "New Deal" had been synonymous with Franklin D. Roosevelt. The Communists, however, adamantly opposed the former vice president's advocacy of a "mixed" economy. Lest any of the CP faithful be corrupted in the heat of the campaign, in early 1948 the Communist Party press and its theoretical journal, *Political Affairs*, launched a protracted attack on "Keynesian theoretical nonsense." As a result, Communist publications that hailed Wallace as "our great leader" simultaneously lambasted his economic program as "absurd on the face of it," derisively referring to the "illusion of 'progressive capitalism.'"[72] By the late spring, the historian David A. Shannon has noted wryly, "a casual reader of *Political Affairs* might have reasonably wondered if the Communists were for or against Wallace." In overseeing the initial drafting of the platform in New York, Pressman and others had managed to exclude any mention of the offending phrase. Similarly, in Philadelphia, the one attempt to introduce a plank articulating the party's support for "progressive capitalism" failed to win committee approval. In essence, the Communist opposition to Wallace's economic philosophy ensured that no reference to it would appear in the party platform.[73]

The final disagreement within the committee concerned a revision of the platform's "Peace" section. In that it sought a more "balanced" treatment of U.S.-Soviet relations, it came from an unlikely source, Frederick L. Schuman, a professor of political science at Williams College. Schuman's effusive praise for Stalin's domestic and international policies throughout the thirties and forties had earned him the nickname "Red Fred" among his students. At various times, he had vigorously defended Soviet-style "democracy," the Moscow show trials, Stalin's collectivization of agriculture, and the Nazi-Soviet pact. Much as he may have acted like it, Schuman was not a Communist Party member. He admired the Soviet dictator as a ruthless practitioner of power politics, but he held no allegiance to Marxist dogma. Still, Schuman's extravagant vilifications of Truman and members of his administration made him a favorite among progressives. In 1947, he referred to the rather sedate memoirs of the former secretary of state James F. Byrnes as "the most baffling, incredible and terrifying document to come from the pen of a responsible American official in many years." In correspondence with his colleague from Williams College, Max Lerner, Schuman described President Truman as, among other things, "the Devil's disciple" and "that filthy, nauseating, putrid little prototype of the coming American Fascism who wants to build a balcony on the White House." He assured Lerner, apparently in all seriousness, that as a result of Truman's policies, both of them would soon be in "concentration camps." Like many progressives, the historian William L. O'Neill has noted, Schuman failed to realize "how demented this kind of rhetoric seemed to . . . nonbelievers."[74]

Despite his reputation for espousing pro-Soviet positions, as one of the New Party's experts on foreign affairs, Schuman repeatedly emphasized the importance of distinguishing Wallace's program from that of the Communists. In urging that the party give "much greater emphasis" to the idea of a world government, he wrote to Tabitha Petran that such a move "would serve a most useful purpose in differentiating the Progressive Party as a whole from the small group of Communists who are giving it support. The comrades, necessarily echoing the Soviet press, are of course against all projects of World Federation. All the more reason why we should give it the emphasis it deserves. . . . I don't know whether you agree or not," he added, "but I would appreciate your passing this word along." With regard to distinctions between CP and Progressive programs, Schuman told Petran, "I say the more differentiation the better, and the sharper it is the better. . . . The platform must . . . have as little as possible to do with the views and purposes of the comrades." Presumably, Schuman was unaware that Petran herself was a Communist, so it is unlikely that his suggestions made much headway with her. On arriving in Philadelphia, he joined with Scott Buchanan and Rex Tugwell in pushing for a more evenhanded statement on U.S.-Soviet relations.[75]

Sharing Buchanan's and Tugwell's uneasiness with the platform's scathing denunciation of nearly every aspect of American foreign policy, especially when there was no criticism whatsoever of Soviet policy, Schuman composed a lengthy revision of the platform's "American-Soviet Agreement" section. Starting from the premise that the United States and the Soviet Union shared the blame for the current international tensions, he called for a system of world law under which the superpowers could work out their differences. The statement pointedly reproached *both* nations for threatening the world with another war. It also declared that the New Party rejected "the totalitarianism of the Left" no less than "the totalitarianism of the Right," since "both are denials of human dignity and freedom."[76]

Schuman did not finish formulating his amendment until Sunday morning, only hours before the convention was to ratify the final platform. Circumventing the usual channels, he brought the proposal directly to Wallace who approved the new language but balked at the reference to the "totalitarianism of the Left." "This he will not have," Schuman wrote in his diary. "He insists that he and the party must not, cannot, and will not, engage in any form of Russophobia or Red-baiting. I agree in principle. I have doubts in practice, and deem his definition of these terms too broad." Schuman acquiesced, however. He deleted the objectionable phrasing and set off to secure the approval of Glen Taylor. The Idaho senator supported the concept of world government but took exception to any scolding of the Soviet Union. As far as Taylor was concerned, the United States *alone* was responsible for the Cold War, and to say otherwise was to surrender to the "red smear." Wallace himself later cited the world government plank as proof that the platform committee was not subject to Communist influence, but a second look at the carefully worded resolution belies this claim. Since the platform stated that the *prerequisite* for a "world federal legislature" was "the unity of the great powers," a highly unlikely occurrence, the left-wingers had not really conceded anything. Similarly, Pressman and the platform committee rejected an amendment from the convention floor urging the establishment of a United Nations police force—a proposal in full accord with Wallace's desire for a strengthened UN, but in conflict with the Soviet position that any such police force would be beholden to the Western powers.

Schuman was not done making concessions. Baldwin, who had accompanied him to Taylor's hotel suite, told Schuman that if *any* criticism of the Soviet Union, no matter how mild, appeared in the platform, Paul Robeson and others on the floor of the convention would shout it down. Schuman agreed to excise a reference to Soviet "territorial aggrandizement," reworking the resolution to read that "ending the tragic prospect of war is the joint responsibility of the Soviet Union and the United States." By this point, the proposal seemed to fall well short of achieving Schuman's original intent, but Baldwin still feared that the new revision might not pass muster. He finally accepted the phrasing once Schuman called his attention to a sentence in the next paragraph that stated, "Our nation has vastly greater responsibility for peace than Russia because it has vastly greater power for war."[77]

Though any hint that the Soviet Union might bear some responsibility for fueling international tensions was now gone, the amendment's implications still proved too anti-Soviet for some of Schuman's colleagues.

Shortly before the convention began its final review of the platform, he presented his amendment to the platform committee, now convened in the basement of Convention Hall. Martin Popper "blew his top," Schuman later recalled. After nearly an hour, Baldwin put an end to the heated debate, declaring that since Wallace supported Schuman, the changes should be approved. To Popper he added, "You guys have got to make some accommodations." In fact, there had been almost no accommodations; the deliberations of the platform committee had produced a near total victory for the party's extreme left wing.[78]

■ Almost unanimously, contemporary press accounts maintained that the Communists "dominated" the platform committee and "dictated" the document's various planks to Moscow's satisfaction. To emphasize this point, the *New York Times* ran excerpts from the CPUSA and Progressive Party platforms side by side. The similarities in substance, language, tone, and political philosophy are indeed revealing. "It could reasonably be suspected that the same brain trust composed both," wrote William Henry Chamberlin in the *New Leader*.[79]

Such an assessment of the platform writing process tells only part of the story. The Communists and their allies may have established the parameters of what views were "acceptable," but they did not necessarily "dictate" the platform. There was no need for them to do so, since the non-Communists voluntarily accepted these parameters. Although several disputes within the committee pitted individuals who consciously followed the "party line" against those who did not, no two distinguishable factions emerged. This is not to say, as some historians have argued, that no organized Communist clique existed, but rather that no coherent non-Communist bloc developed to oppose the CPers.[80] The non-Communists on the committee would have viewed forming a coalition to combat any disproportionate influence on the part the Communists as the kind of ADA-style "negativism" they were so intent on avoiding. On the few occasions on which individual non-Communists strayed too far afield, Pressman, Abt, and others effectively policed them by repeatedly stressing the need for "unity," implying that dissenters were either "red-baiters" or, more darkly, betraying a concealed allegiance to the camp of the reactionaries.

To the New Party's critics, such tactics might appear transparently duplicitous or heavy-handed, but they did not raise concerns among the Popular Front liberals who gravitated to the Wallace movement. Often subjected to scurrilous smear campaigns in their local communities, they drew inspiration from the Communists who likewise endured persecution for expressing "progressive" views. Many genuinely believed that a combination of reactionary forces—in the press, the government, the business world—was plotting against Wallace and his efforts to improve the lot of the "common man." Likewise, they embraced a simplistic view of foreign policy in which a conspiracy of "interests" misled the "people" into war—more a product of populism and 1930s isolationism than of communism. Indeed, charges of "communism" intended to frighten them away from the New Party standard were, in their view, part and parcel of this conspiracy. The more they heard the cry of "communism," the more resolved they became to ignore it. Though the Communists might make stringent demands on their coalition partners and their methods at times might be too extreme, they nonetheless opposed the forces of reaction and therefore deserved the benefit of the doubt. This line of reasoning, coupled with the liberals' lack of political experience, allowed the CP minority to assume a decisive role in the proceedings almost by default. Arthur F. Stearns, a Nebraska minister who served on the platform committee, aptly expressed the prevailing sentiment among the non-Communists. Though he "didn't know much about the Communists," said Stearns, "they help us and we help them." Stearns then continued with a statement perhaps more telling than he realized: "Mr. Pressman handled everything. He's a smart man. You couldn't tell he was there he was so quiet. Yes sir, he was like a silken thread running through the whole thing."[81]

6

THE WHOLE PLACE HAS GONE
WALLACE WACKY

The Founding Convention of the Progressive Party

On the evening of Friday, July 24, attention shifted from press conferences, platform writing, and other preliminaries to the opening of the convention itself. With great fanfare, some thirty-two hundred delegates and alternates crowded into steaming Convention Hall to baptize their new "people's party." Under blazing television lights—a new attraction in 1948—they shouted out the catchy lyrics of the Wallace campaign songs with an evangelistic fervor. On average, observers noted, the Progressives were twenty years younger and thirty pounds lighter than their Democratic and Republican counterparts. One reporter covering the convention spoke of a "soda parlor atmosphere, not a smoke-filled room." The crowd was also less formal, less wealthy, and less white. Men dressed in polo shirts and the women went hatless. "If you see a man with a necktie," the delegates joked, "he's a reporter"—or an FBI agent, they might have added. Many had hitchhiked to Philadelphia and pitched tents in the parking lot to save on hotel bills. An estimated 150 African American delegates were in attendance, three times the combined total that had participated in the Republican and Democratic conventions. The interracial character of the gathering went well beyond mere tokenism. One black delegate told an observer that it was "the first time his people had walked into a public place where it didn't occur to them to look for their own people or feel self-conscious."[1]

156

Politically, the delegates presented an unusual amalgam. Most were making their first foray into campaign work, hoping to substitute earnestness and zeal for what they lacked in experience and sophistication. To many observers, they seemed wedded to no particular ideology, but rather were "aginners"—against the two old parties, against "Big Business," against "red-baiters," and, most certainly, against war. On the other hand, however, these fresh-faced partisans expressed an almost messianic devotion to Henry Wallace. They dismissed all criticism of their leader as an intolerable heresy unworthy of consideration. For the Progressive delegates, there were no degrees of faith—those who expressed any doubts were the enemies of virtue. Wallace, and *only* Wallace, had the solutions that would bring peace, freedom, and abundance. "I am a very eligible young man to go to war, and I don't want to go," declared Jack Hester, a sixteen-year-old delegate from Omaha. "Wallace is my only hope."[2] But, like Wallace, one reporter remarked, his followers "gave the impression of Orphean good will circumscribed by uncertainty and confusion." Interviewing delegates on the convention floor, the Alsop brothers found that, when pushed to the wall on specific points of fact, "they reveal an astonishing fund of misinformation—that Russia has been disarming completely while America has been building atom bombs; that no one has ever tried to 'get along with Russia;' that the governments of Eastern Europe are what they are because 'the people want it that way'; that the Marshall Plan was 'cooked up in Wall Street,' and so on." Frederick Schuman, certainly a more sympathetic observer, largely concurred. "The dominant qualities of the Convention," he wrote in his private notes, "were enthusiasm, fervor, confusion, and a disposition by many to think, talk, and act in terms of stereotypes (reflecting no particular ideology, save that of traditional American Populism and Progressivism) rather than in terms of concrete problems."[3]

Striking a sharp contrast to these political amateurs were their Popular Front allies, the Communists—"the only group," one newspaper editor asserted, "which really knew what it wanted, and had some notion of how to get it." The syndicated columnist and Socialist Party stalwart Norman Thomas noted wryly that he had no difficulty at the convention distinguishing the CPers from the liberals. "The Communists who saw me nearly spit," he explained, "the non-Communists said: 'Oh, Mr. Thomas, why aren't you with us?'" To the Alsops, the "comrades" were "instantly recognizable—the slick automatic line, the mechanical indignation, the old hackneyed phrases." Their obvious presence greatly troubled those who were otherwise sympathetic to the delegates' youthful idealism and depth of commitment. Indeed, the liberal columnist Thomas Stokes found that the Communists' maneuvering within the Wallace movement gave the entire convention "a deep undertone of tragedy." In newspaper columns and in personal conversations erstwhile admirers warned the Wallace partisans that the Communists were engaging in political misrepresentation and that their disingenuousness would corrupt the ideals for which the third party claimed to be fighting. "No one who has ever known Communists well or worked with them closely takes them at face value or trusts them," wrote one correspondent. "They sour the sweet notes of harmony and peace and abundance and so on, not because a lot of what they say about what's wrong with this country is not true, not because many of their words and ideals are not noble, but because, very simply, there is no security or trust in these people."[4] But the rank and file had been well steeled against such "outside pressure." When talking privately among themselves, some delegates did express concern about "the others." But on the floor of the convention, they insisted to reporters that the Communist presence simply did not matter and that those who raised the issue were red-baiters. Ironically, the press's incessant probing for signs of dissent within Gideon's Army—particularly with regard to the subject of communism—seemed only to solidify its ranks and strengthen its resolve.[5]

After a half hour of singing to commence the festivities, the delegates settled into their seats as a stream of speakers from various walks of life lay out the glowing prospects of the new people's party while castigating the innumerable misdeeds of the old "carbon copy" parties. Though the brief addresses were more remarkable for their inflammatory rhetoric than for their content, reporters nonetheless observed an almost unprecedented spectacle for political conventions. Not only were the delegates actually listening to the speeches but they listened with a rapt intensity that was utterly "mystifying." "These people, intent on saving themselves, the nation, and the world, have no time for the frivolities," wrote Pete Akers, a columnist for the *Chicago Sun-Times*. "They even sit in their seats at Convention Hall with a fixed determination that constitutes, almost in itself, a dare to anyone to object."[6]

At 9:00 P.M. Charles P. Howard, a black newspaper publisher and an attorney from Wallace's home state of Iowa, made his way to the rostrum to deliver the keynote address. Having established the Progressive campaign's major themes—peace, freedom, and abundance—and having taken the obligatory shots at the "red-baiting bipartisan reactionaries," Howard brought down the house with two simple sentences. "The plain fact that I stand here before you tonight defines our party. For the first time in my life," he said, "I am experiencing human dignity." "The roof trembled with applause," wrote Alistair Cooke, "for a confession that one week or four weeks ago would have provoked an embarrassed pause."[7] As the session neared its end, campaign manager, Beanie Baldwin, announced with great fanfare that by unanimous consent, the New Party would henceforth be known as the "Progressive Party." This third resurrection of the Progressive Party, he proclaimed, would not fade away after one election as had Theodore Roosevelt's and Robert La Follette's progressive movements. "This is no Bull Moose convention," Baldwin shouted. "This is no temporary election coalition. This is it! This is the birth of a New Party—soon to be the first party!"[8]

■ The convention's second day opened with the presentation of the newly christened Progressive Party's constitution. Though it was expected to be an uneventful prelude to the nomination of Wallace and Taylor later in the afternoon, the morning session ended up producing the gathering's first public display of dissent. At issue was the adoption of the rules that would determine the permanent organizational structure of the party and the method of choosing representatives for its governing body, the national committee. Though the word "Communist" was never uttered, several delegates indirectly expressed concern that the rules committee had devised a system paving the way for permanent left-wing control of the party.

As had been the case in the drafting of the platform, the majority of the committee's work had been completed before the convention opened. At their April meeting in Chicago, party leaders had agreed that representation on the national committee should be based on population rather than geography. Instead of following the major parties' formula in which each state received two committee members apiece, the Progressives devised a system that awarded the largest states extra representation. Accordingly, New York would receive seven additional seats on the national committee; Pennsylvania would get five extra spots; California would get three, and so on. Delegates to the national convention would then "elect" the states' single list of nominees to the national committee.[9]

This arrangement made representation on the committee more democratic, or so its backers maintained. In theory this was true, but the state organizations slated to receive additional committee members were also those in which the Communists had their greatest strength. It seemed safe to assume that since the Communists voted as a bloc while the non-Communists tended to scatter their support among several potential candidates, such organizations would nominate Communists or reliable pro-Communists to the national committee. As a result, a move ostensibly intended to enhance the party's democratic character actually increased the leverage of a well-organized minority. The most likely result of this "unintended" consequence—Communist control of the national committee—seemed obvious. Yet given the non-Communist Progressives' lack of political savvy and their conviction that raising the issue of party control was tantamount to red-baiting, no complaint was heard.

Additionally, the rules committee proposed creating a smaller "executive committee" to oversee the party's monthly business and a nine-member "administrative committee" that would handle all day-to-day operations. This last group would be elected by the executive committee, which in turn would be elected by the national committee. Though formal authority rested in the decentralized lower tiers of the organization—theoretically, all committees answered to the national convention—in fact, the top policymaking bodies would determine the party's course. Such a pyramidal configuration of authority, in which each successive echelon was chosen by and from the echelon immediately below it, resembled the governmental structures of the newly established "people's democracies" in Eastern Europe. This setup also duplicated the structure that had allowed pro-Communists to gain disproportionate power in the Progressive Citizens of America (PCA), the Popular Front–oriented group that had originally launched Wallace's third party candidacy. Yet these potentially troublesome similarities, too, went unremarked.[10]

The inclusion of so-called functional representatives on the national committee proved more contentious, however. Initially, the leadership considered a plan whereby the "functional divisions" of the party—labor, youth, farmers, professionals, nationalities, veterans, businessmen, and women—would appoint the *entire* national committee. This proposal immediately met opposition from state and local activists who viewed it as an attempt to marginalize the "grassroots" Wallace supporters they had recruited at the ward and precinct levels. Vito Marcantonio, whose American Labor Party (ALP) was probably the most effective Wallace organization in the nation, responded skeptically to the claims of left-wing CIO officials who argued that such an approach would benefit the entire party by reinforcing its "labor base." A shrewd political operative, Marcantonio recognized the contrivance as a thinly veiled power grab by Communist union leaders who were searching for an organizational base to replace the one they were losing in the CIO. Already considered pariahs by Philip Murray, these CPers realized that their support for Wallace was jeopardizing their future in the labor movement. The New Party, if they could secure their influence within it, offered a vehicle for re-establishing themselves as the "vanguard" of the progressive movement.[11]

Though willing to work with the CIO's Communists—and sympathetic to their current predicament—Marcantonio refused to undermine his own position by ceding them control of the Progressive Party. He therefore fashioned a compromise that allowed the functional divisions to appoint national committee members *in addition to* those elected by the state organizations based on population. In Philadelphia, where the discussion about representation continued, Hugh Bryson, the president of the Marine Cooks and Stewards Union, suggested setting aside sixty slots for the functional divisions. By the time Marcantonio presented the rules to the convention, however, the New York congressman had succeeded in having the number reduced to forty. Ultimately, Article 3 of the Progressive Party constitution established a national committee consisting of 180 members, of which 90 members—present in person or by proxy—would constitute a quorum. Even without a quorum, the committee could still transact business provided it received after-the-fact approval from a majority of the members.[12]

Confident that it had reached an arrangement acceptable to all, the rules committee assumed that the convention would approve its final report without debate. Yet as Committee Secretary Bryson read aloud the provisions of the new constitution, a handful of delegates rose in protest. James S. Martin, the co-chair of the Maryland delegation and one of the more politically sophisticated of the non-Communist progressives, was the first to object. Committed to Popular Front liberalism, Martin accepted Communist participation in the Progressive Party, believing that the CPers in the movement were followers, not leaders. Indeed, he had defended the Maryland organization against charges of Communist domination. (He might have moderated his statements had he known that the state party's executive secretary and more than half of Maryland's eighty-eight convention delegates were secret CP members.) Nonetheless, Martin did fear that if liberals like him failed to remain vigilant, the Communists would exert disproportionate influence and gain control of the party. Accordingly, he expressed concern both with the top-heavy representation accorded the larger industrial states and with the addition of the forty members-at-large, which, he noted, were not subject in any way to popular election. Martin objected as well to the rule allowing the national committee to formulate policy without requiring the physical presence of a quorum. He therefore moved that Article 3 be redrafted.

Though, as one journalist reported, the Annapolis attorney restrained his words "to dry technical considerations as if there was nothing involved except some routine details," Martin certainly perceived the provisions of Article 3 as a maneuver of the party's far left to secure control of the national committee. In a subsequent interview he referred to the forty functional members as an "action-committee kind of representation," a reference to the notorious "action committees" that had helped precipitate the Communist coup in Czechoslovakia.[13] Scott Buchanan, another of the party's prominent non-Communists, supported Martin's motion. Already frustrated by his dealings with the left-wingers on the platform committee, Buchanan declared angrily, "This article allows for a minority of this party to conduct the business of the national committee. If we want to do that and spoil the future of the third party, I think there will be some of us walking out of this party!"[14] From the dais, John Abt attempted to allay any concern, promising that each of the functional divisions would "perfect its own democratic organization" for selecting committee members. Addressing Martin's second complaint, Bryson assured him somewhat evasively that there was no reason for a quorum's physical presence. Martin's recommittal motion was then put to a voice vote and shouted down decisively.[15]

The debate did not end there. Others continued to challenge the inclusion of functional representatives on the national committee. Leonard Stein, speaking for a group of University of Chicago graduate students in the Illinois delegation, moved to delete the sentence referring to the extra forty members. Noting that in a quorum of ninety, these members would not only be enough to swing a majority but would almost *be* a majority, he charged that the rule short-circuited the representative process. The convention chairman Albert Fitzgerald, the rotund president of the United Electrical Workers Union, ignored Stein's arguments and abruptly ruled out of order his and several other motions challenging the rules. Stein then insisted on a roll-call vote to appeal the chair's ruling, but Fitzgerald refused to recognize him. As the balconies erupted in protest, the chairman banged his gavel and ordered Stein back to his seat.[16]

Stein had demanded a roll-call vote with good reason. The result of a voice vote or show of hands hardly constituted an accurate representation of the elected delegates' views. Under the official rules, the states could send up to eight delegates for each presidential elector. Depending on how many individuals a state had chosen to send, one hand could represent the entire delegation or as little as one-eighth of a vote. The state organizations in which Communists exercised significant influence sent the largest delegations, allowing the left-wingers to make their voices heard (and their hands seen) to greater effect than those state delegations that did not take advantage of the fractional voting system to pad their ranks.

As an indication of the Progressives' sensitivity on this issue, the Credentials Committee, which deluged the press with reports on the delegates' age, ethnicity, occupation, and gender to illustrate the party's "broad base," failed to release any information on the size of each state delegation. This was done deliberately, one committee member acknowledged, to conceal the lopsided representation of a few large industrial states. The committee even destroyed its working papers to ensure that the state-by-state breakdowns did not become public. Independent observers, however, estimated that New York alone sent more than five hundred delegates and alternates. California, Michigan, and Illinois—whose state Progressive Parties also strongly left-wing—likewise sent disproportionately large contingents. Indeed, about one-third of the delegates and alternates present came from these four states. Entitled to 238 votes in a roll call, their actual strength on voice or hand votes was 1,071.[17] To be sure, fractional representation was an accepted practice at the old parties' political conventions as well, but it was allowed only with the understanding that all contentious issues would be put to a roll call. At the Progressive Party convention, not a single roll-call vote occurred throughout the entire proceedings. Only in hindsight did some delegates express suspicion that the avoidance of such votes had been deliberate on the part of an organized left-wing minority.[18]

Since so few delegates were willing to raise explicitly the issue of left-wing control, however, the phosphorescent revolt over Article 3 quickly fizzled and the convention adopted the rules as originally presented. "The crudity of the performance was slightly staggering," wrote the journalist James Wechsler, who was quite familiar with such tactics from his days in the Young Communist League. Other veteran political observers expressed astonishment that so many of the delegates were not only unwilling to protest but also seemed completely unaware of what was happening right before their eyes. For those few who did understand what was at stake, the entire episode raised doubts they had heretofore kept suppressed. As defenders of the Popular Front, they were committed in principle to working with the Communists. Now, forced to accept the consequences of doing so, they were finding the alliance less and less palatable. Questioned afterward about his current status in the party, Buchanan denied that he was walking out, but he referred vaguely to what "some people" might do if confronted with such tactics again.[19]

Most of the convention press coverage, while dismissing the non-Communist delegates as naive or uninformed "dupes," portrayed the Communists and their fellow travelers as a *monolithic* force committed to a predetermined line. This, too, was an oversimplification. Such accounts overlook or fail to understand the various contending forces *within* the CP orbit. The wrangling over the makeup of the national committee, for example, was primarily a struggle between left-wingers in the labor movement and those like Marcantonio who controlled the local Wallace organizations. Still, as Martin and Buchanan found out, once the two factions had reached an agreement, the non-Communist Progressives—unorganized and unwilling to upset party "unity" by explicitly challenging the orthodox leftists—stood little chance of mounting any opposition.

Having adopted the party's rules and constitution, the convention next turned its attention to the formal nominations of Henry Wallace and Glen Taylor. After several nominating and seconding speeches, the traditional countdown of the states began, occasioning still more speeches. Since Wallace and Taylor were running unopposed, the process itself was hardly spellbinding—there was not even an Eisenhower boom, reporters quipped. Yet at the slightest provocation, the delegates broke into delirious demonstrations, parading jubilantly down the aisles, all the while singing and chanting their slogans with an evangelical fervor more likely to be seen at a tent revival than at a political convention. The mere mention of Wallace's name sent them into ecstatic fits of cheering. When a farmer from Iowa, Fred Stover, mounted the podium to introduce formally his state's native son, the tumult went on for nearly half an hour before he could continue. At the conclusion of the speeches, Wallace and Taylor appeared briefly in the hall, setting off an ear-splitting ovation. The whole place had gone "Wallace wacky," one spectator declared. Barely audible over the cheering, chairman Fitzgerald reminded the delegates of the revels to follow that night at Shibe Park and declared the session adjourned.[20]

Though some journalists dismissed the hoopla as nothing different than the synthetic enthusiasm one saw at political gatherings behind the Iron Curtain, most in attendance found the demonstrations refreshingly genuine, particularly when compared to the staged affairs of the Republican and Democratic conventions.[21] Still, the very fervor of the delegates' devotion to their hero troubled those who had witnessed mass rallies in Nuremberg and Rome during the war. Surrounded by frenzied young delegates, Dorothy Thompson lamented, "How can I convey the sound, taste, smell and haunting sense of having seen it all before . . . in other places—in one place in particular." Others drew back as they watched "the emotionally aroused and automatically responsive followers singing and shouting and instantly accepting whatever was said or proposed." Unlike the "automatons" of the older parties who were merely "singing for their supper," Alistair Cooke wrote, "the New Party . . . has the keener greed of spiritual pride. Its cues are abstract nouns—imperialism, freedom, Israel, red-baiting, the common people—and some are cues to righteous indignation, but most are cues to hatred. I can recall no previous convention whose keynote has been so utterly humourless about its rivals, so solidly a theme of hate. . . . Apart from the raw evangelism of this convention, its vitality in action is seething anger." Remarked another British correspondent, "I shudder to think what a man more politically adept and less honest than Wallace could do with a crowd like this." Such a reaction was understandable, given the totalitarian theatrics these journalists had seen at Communist and Nazi rallies in Europe, but the Progressives in Convention Hall were hardly potential "storm troopers." Their overwrought rhetoric and demonizing of the opposition did resemble the ritual vilification associated with Stalinism, but, viewed less darkly, it was also in the grand tradition of political hyperbole long associated with American democratic politics. Still, the Progressives' grim earnestness and inflated sense of their own significance ultimately proved more off-putting than inspiring to the nonconverted.[22]

■ On Saturday night, the Progressive faithful prepared for the convention's climactic event—a huge open-air rally at Shibe Park, home of the Philadelphia Athletics. Thousands of loyal followers from up and down the East Coast had poured into Philadelphia all afternoon to witness the spectacle. The largest contingent had come from New York City aboard seven special trains provided by the Pennsylvania Railroad. A notice in the *Daily Worker* on July 23 may have accounted for their number. Calling for "all members on vacation to return immediately, and all planning vacations to temporarily cancel them," the Communist organ declared, "Our new and urgent tasks require the fullest mobilization of all our party members." By 4:00 P.M., hundreds lined the streets outside the ballpark waiting to begin their celebration. Inside, wrote H. L. Mencken, the hometown Athletics "picked up so much animal magnetism from the impending orgies that they walloped the Detroit Tigers and went to first place in the league." By the time the field lights came on at 7:50 P.M., nearly thirty thousand people had filed through the turnstiles, paying anywhere from sixty-five cents to $2.60 for their seats. A band featuring Pete Seeger on banjo entertained the spectators, many of whom sang and danced to the music. The Broadway actor Sam Wanamaker served as the master of ceremonies, while Joseph H. Rainey, a local magistrate and NAACP official running for Congress on the Progressive ticket, began the formal program with words of welcome to the visiting delegates.[23]

Vito Marcantonio followed Rainey on the stage. In contrast to the relatively subdued judge, the wiry New York firebrand ignited the crowd with his renowned nails-on-the-blackboard loquacity. Shouting at the top of his lungs and wildly flailing his arms in acrobatic contortions, Marcantonio delivered a scorching attack on the Truman administration and everything it stood for. He called for a march on Washington to protest against the president's "imposition of fascism" and attempts "to put over a program of war and of depression." Confronting the "red issue" head on, the Harlem congressman reviled the recent Communist indictments, proclaiming, "Once the Communist party becomes outlawed in any country . . . the boundary between fascism and democracy has disappeared." "If the people of Germany and the people of Italy had successfully defended the rights of the Communist party," he thundered, "there would have been no successful Mussolini, there would have been no successful Hitler, and there would have been no World War II." Marcantonio's erratic delivery combined with the stadium's poor acoustics rendered most of his address unintelligible, but the crowd cheered him on all the same.[24] Paul Robeson, the next speaker, took over where Marcantonio had left off, continuing the blistering attack on the now familiar targets of Wall Street, monopolists, red-baiters, and particularly President Truman. In an abrupt change of tone, the renowned baritone then delighted the assembly with moving renditions of "This Is America to Me," "Marching on with Henry Wallace," and other favorite campaign songs. Following Robeson, "pitch man" William Gailmore launched into his familiar solicitation for campaign contributions.[25]

Though Marcantonio and Robeson were well received, the decision to feature them prominently undercut the party's objective of using the convention to broaden its electoral base. In the public mind, both men were archetypes of fellow-traveling orthodoxy closely associated with the Communists. Their confrontational style alienated the very voters the Wallaceites were trying to attract, and their presence on the platform plastered the "red" label on the entire event. Even some delegates acknowledged being put off by Marcantonio's ability to whip up the left-wingers in the New York delegation. Particularly those from the South and the Midwest felt uncomfortable watching young zealots jabbing their fists in the air as they gave their leader the Communist salute. Ralph Shikes, the party's director of publicity, had hoped that national radio and television coverage of the Shibe Park rally would give the Progressives a chance to reach the "peaceful minded in Iowa," as well as other potentially sympathetic constituencies. To succeed in such an effort, he believed, the convention would need to downplay the "left atmosphere" that surrounded the party. He threw up his arms in frustration when Abt and Baldwin informed him that they had asked Marcantonio and Robeson to speak. They had no idea what a terrible impression this would make, Shikes later recalled. Instead of taking steps to mute the Communist issue, the convention managers, their judgment impaired by their own sectarianism, seemed to be inflaming it.[26]

After Gailmore had solicited some $50,000 from the crowd, the vice presidential nominee Glen Taylor strode onto the stage to deliver his acceptance speech. His lips heavily made up for the television cameras, Taylor's ludicrous appearance precipitated a wave of laughter through the press box as reporters joked about this latest manifestation of the "red smear."[27] After engaging in friendly banter with the crowd for a few minutes, the Idaho senator began his prepared address. Incongruously shifting from lighthearted pleasantries to a deadly serious tone, he assailed various officials in the Truman administration as "agents of greed," even accusing them of harboring pro-Nazi sympathies. These forces, Taylor shouted, "have embarked America on a policy of preparing for a war of extinction." Continuing in the same vein, he commenced a relentless assault on the Marshall Plan, at various points characterizing it as "the greatest fraud, the greatest steal ever perpetrated in all history." It was, he claimed, "a futile effort to bribe whole nations into becoming our mercenaries in a senseless struggle for world domination" and "a cynical scheme to enable our cartelists and exploiters to filch billions of dollars from the pockets of American taxpayers . . . and send free samples around the world."[28] Though at times articulated in a quasi-Leninist argot that echoed the Communist line, Taylor's opposition to the Marshall Plan derived more from the isolationist tradition embraced by many populists of his native mountain West. Journalists who interviewed convention delegates found that some of them, like Taylor, opposed the Marshall Plan not out of any pro-Soviet sympathies but on "liberal isolationist" grounds.[29]

Regardless of what had motivated it, however, Taylor's attack on the Marshall Plan was entirely out of proportion—even allowing for the usual hyperbole of a partisan political address. "It was a shocking speech," declared the liberal columnist Marquis Childs, "resorting to the most obvious demagogy and prejudice." Norman Thomas denounced the senator's "outrageously distorted" description of the Marshall Plan and his "jingoistic indifference to the plight of the needy peoples of Europe." Reviewing Taylor's address in the *Nation*, Freda Kirchwey wrote, "Many progressives must admit that the [Marshall Plan] may well be used by big business as a source of profit, [but] only a handful will accept the thesis that it is nothing more than a 'capitalist conspiracy' to enslave the world and force it to buy American goods." Indeed, the candidate's assertions ran counter to the views of many in his own party. A recent Gallup poll had reported that 47 percent of likely Wallace voters *supported* the Marshall Plan. In sum, the speech did little to change the public perception of Taylor as a buffoon given to irresponsible and inflammatory rhetoric.[30]

The highlight of the evening's revelry, of course, was the appearance of Henry Wallace. By the time Wanamaker introduced the Progressive standard-bearer, it was nearly 11:00 P.M. Though many in the crowd had been clapping, singing, and cheering for more than twelve hours, they managed to whip up yet another torrent of enthusiasm for their hero. Driven in an open car à la Franklin Roosevelt, Wallace circled the outfield waving to his adoring supporters. As two bright spotlights followed the candidate, a long line of youngsters performed a snake dance in his wake, while the rest of the throng burst into a thunderous round of applause. Stepping to the speaker's platform, he pleaded with his still frenzied audience to take their seats so he could begin his acceptance speech.[31]

Starting off in a bitterly wistful tone, Wallace described what he called "the great betrayal" that followed the death of Franklin Roosevelt. Denouncing President Truman for welcoming into government service "the banking house boys and the oil-well diplomats," he accused him of scuttling Roosevelt's "vision of peace" and siding with "the ghosts who plan for destruction." "Instead of the dream," Wallace declared, "we have inherited disillusion. Instead of the promised years of harvest, the years of the locust are upon us. In Hyde Park they buried our President—and in Washington they buried our dreams."

Undoubtedly, Wallace articulated the frustrations of many Americans who longed for a lasting peace and felt cheated when the postwar world did not live up to their expectations. For those hoping to establish a connection between defending moral values and working for political causes, Wallace offered unapologetically idealistic rhetoric and what sounded like an uncompromising commitment to noble principles. Moreover, he provided a reassuring figure in which they could place their faith. The former vice president's emotion-charged oratory affected many in the crowd who wept openly as he laid out his vision of an American future of peace and abundance.

Yet for all his heralding of an abundant future, the candidate's primary focus remained foreign policy. At the heart of his address, Wallace took up the issue of the U.S.-Soviet conflict over Berlin. Placing full responsibility for the standoff on the United States, he declared, "If I were president, there would be no crisis in Berlin today. I assure you that without sacrificing a single American principle or public interest, we would have found agreement long before now with the Soviet Government." Our whole German policy, Wallace charged, "has been this, and only this: namely to revive the power of the industrialists and cartelists who heiled Hitler and financed fascism." By remaining in Berlin, the United States risked war only to further the interests of international bankers and Wall Street. Striking an uncharacteristically isolationist chord, he declared, "I have yet to meet an American who wants to give up his life to defend Dillon, Read or to obtain the privilege of feeding 2,000,000 people in Berlin." Reaching the climax of his indictment, Wallace cried, "Our prestige in Germany went sinking when we divided Germany and established the western sector as an American and British Puerto Rico—as a colony. When we did that, we gave up Berlin politically and we can't lose anything by giving it up militarily in a search for peace."[32]

It was an argument few would find compelling. Even more striking was what Wallace left unsaid. He scrupulously avoided any mention of the Soviet role in the crisis or of the unhappy fate that awaited the residents of West Berlin if the U.S. troops were to withdraw. At a time when the beleaguered city had come to symbolize democracy's resistance to dictatorship, Wallace appeared to advocate craven capitulation, further enhancing his pro-Soviet image in the public mind. Many sensed a whiff of desperation in his astonishing proposal for unilateral withdrawal from Berlin. Unable to set out any specific, practical alternative to administration policy, Wallace simply advocated retreat cloaked in high-sounding rhetoric. Tellingly, "The Future Is Ours," a condensed version of Wallace's acceptance speech later distributed in pamphlet form by the Progressive Party's national office, omitted all references to Berlin. Public opinion polls confirmed the unpopularity of Wallace's Berlin stance. Even among likely Wallace voters, Gallup found that nearly half said the United States should not withdraw from Berlin. Overall, 90 percent supported the government's decision to stand firm in there, while 80 percent believed that the United States and its allies should stay in Berlin "even if it meant war with Russia." Likewise, a Roper poll taken in late July reported that only 4 percent of those surveyed believed that current U.S. policy toward the Soviet Union was "too tough," while 76 percent believed that U.S. military strength should be increased.[33]

The rest of the speech covered familiar ground. Wallace roundly attacked the usual catalog of villains—Wall Street, the "Big Brass," "red-baiters," "the kings of privilege," John Foster Dulles, the banking house of Dillon, Read and its "distinguished alumni," Secretary of Defense James Forrestal, and General William H. Draper—and described the idyllic world that would emerge once the conspiratorial plotting of these evil forces had been thwarted. He also raised a few eyebrows with his revelation that the Cold War had "already brought death to millions of Americans," explaining improbably that had it not been for the "get tough" policies of President Truman, a cure might have been found for "cancer, tuberculosis, pellagra, heart disease, and polio." At the conclusion of his address, Wallace departed from his prepared text and adopted the idiom of an old-time gospel preacher, referring to "the dream of the prophets of old . . . [when] all the nations of the world shall flow up to the mountains of the Lord." Ending on an almost messianic note, Wallace proclaimed, "All you who are within the sound of my voice tonight have been called to serve, and to serve mightily, in fulfilling the dream of the prophets and the founders of the American system."[34]

Wallace received a respectable send-off at the conclusion of his address, but, overall, his performance proved disappointing. The speech, one aide later confessed, was far too long and the candidate's delivery soporific. Wallace's call for U.S. withdrawal from Berlin, obviously intended as an applause line, elicited no reaction at all. Journalists remarked with surprise that the candidate seemed unable to hold the interest of his audience. Long before he had finished, the Shibe Park crowd, so supportive all night, grew restless and began to filter toward the exits, leaving Wallace to face rows of empty seats.[35]

■ Predictably, a hostile press denounced the address as a faithful echo of the Communist Party line.[36] Many of the positions Wallace endorsed did seem so perfectly synchronized with those of the Communists that some speculation arose about the literary origins of the address. Indeed, six years after the convention, the radio script writer Allan E. Sloane testified before the House Committee on Un-American Activities that he and a colleague, Millard Lampell, had written the Wallace acceptance speech. Sloane identified himself as a former Communist Party member. Lampell, he testified, had recruited him into the party in 1943 and was also a Communist. In June 1948, Hannah Dorner, the former executive director of ICCASP, had told them that the draft Wallace had written was "terrible—it spoke of a dedicated man of Gideon, and that sort of thing." Dorner then asked them to write another version. As he and Lampell sat down to work, Sloane recalled, "without there being a word spoken about 'let us see that this adheres properly and correctly to a preconceived party line' there was an understanding existing in that room . . . [that] I, known to them as a fellow traveler, if not an outright Communist, was enlisted with another fellow traveler, to channel the convention's major speeches."[37]

Wallace may have been reading words the Communists had ghost-written for him, but, for the most part, he concurred with the sentiments they expressed. No behind-the-scenes intrigue or "Communist plot" had tricked him into saying things he had not already come to believe. Indeed, Wallace's suspicion of conspiring bankers and Eastern elites owed more to the midwestern populism of William Jennings Bryan than to the Stalinism of William Z. Foster.

More thoughtful commentators went beyond simply dismissing Wallace as a "red dupe" and took issue with his reasoning, which, like Taylor's, they found simplistic and unconvincing. The candidate's crude conspiracy theory that "Wall Street" had precipitated the current international crisis in hopes of provoking a war proved an especially easy target. "If Henry has to conjure up the fear of mythical monsters to rouse the faithful to a fighting frenzy," wrote Ralph Page, a columnist for the *Philadelphia Bulletin*, "'Wall Street warmongers' are a natural. . . . [But] if the new Progressive Party would read the financial press instead of dreaming and inventing it would discover that far from enjoying the prospect of war, Wall Street trembles at every suggestion of hostilities. The reason is that with each scare, its precious market goes down, and it anticipates a renewal of hated price controls, a revival of wartime excess profit taxes, and other horrors of 'bureaucratic regimentation.'"[38] Wallace's vituperative attacks on the Republican advisor John Foster Dulles and on Truman's foreign policy team also proved ill founded. The *New Republic* noted that Dulles, portrayed at the convention as the epitome of "Wall Street warmongering," was in fact "a chief moderating influence in the Berlin crisis." Likewise, Forrestal and Draper, the very figures Wallace's speech had identified as the most dangerous of militarists, were the least belligerent of the president's advisers on the issue of Berlin. Coming from someone who deeply resented simple-minded analyses of his own motivations, Wallace's unsubstantiated charge that both men were doing the bidding of Dillon, Read seemed particularly disturbing. As James Wechsler later wrote, "He acted like a man who was perfectly certain that anyone who was against him had been bribed, which was probably a measure of the extent to which he had absorbed the outlook of the Communists around him without knowing where he got it."[39]

Others questioned the candidate's approach to international relations, particularly its lack of specificity and practicality. The former interior secretary Harold Ickes, no apologist for the Truman administration's foreign policy, concurred with Wallace that the president and his advisors had "dimmed the hope of peace." "But," he added, "peace is not a negative thing. I for one would like to have Mr. Wallace explain definitely what his blueprint for world peace is. Lacking a convincing blueprint, the frenzied shouting of a political dervish will become less impressive as election time draws near." Those who scrutinized the speech for practicable alternatives to the Truman policies came away with only musty progressive platitudes and a solemn guarantee that somehow things would be different if Henry Wallace were in the White House. Wallace's enticing portrayal of a better world might have captured the imagination of his loyal supporters, but it was hardly a foundation on which to build viable policy. Perhaps the most perceptive observation, however, came from the Sage of Baltimore, H. L. Mencken. "[Wallace's] speech of acceptance in Philadelphia," he wrote his friend Philip Cleator, "was the snarling and defiant harangue of a badly scarred man. The more he whooped and hollered, the more manifest it was that he was fighting with his back to the wall."[40]

■ The convention reconvened at 12:45 P.M. on Sunday to approve the party platform. After Gailmore read the twenty-two-page document to the assembly, Rex Tugwell stepped to the podium to present the report of the platform committee to the delegates. In a voice tinged with regret, Tugwell conceded that he was not entirely pleased with the final product, noting that it represented "compromises and disappointments." Still frustrated with the Communists' rigidity, he had urged Wallace to repudiate them late the night before. Having failed to persuade him, Tugwell now made a final plea to the party's left-wingers, reminding them that it was "better to fight the enemy than to fight your friends." Turning his attention to the non-Communists who remained in the party, Tugwell counseled assertiveness, imploring them to stand up for their beliefs. His speech, one journalist remarked, was "easily the most restrained of the three-day convention," but, as Tugwell himself surmised, it was not as well received as many others "because of my anti-communism." Interestingly, once out of the spotlight, Tugwell chose to disregard his own call to arms. On July 26, he wrote in his journal, "I was dropped by the nominating committee from the list of national officers, so I am now out and through—and glad of it."[41]

Few expected any floor fights over the adoption of the platform. Indeed, various circumstances militated against the development of any organized opposition. Convention rules did not offer any incentive for group discussion, requiring that amendments be submitted by individual delegates.

Similarly, the schedule allowed little time for delegations to caucus and, as it turned out, only a few were able to discuss the platform as a group. Many delegates did not even receive a copy of the platform until the deadline for presenting amendments had already passed. Those who did propose amendments found they had no time to enlist the support of other delegations.[42] Nonetheless, charges of "railroading" sparked by Fitzgerald's brusque handling of dissent during Saturday's discussion of the rules committee report had prompted concern over party "unity" among the convention managers. As discussion of the platform began, they appeared to go out of their way to be obsequious. "Full and ample discussion not only will be permitted, but will be distinctly encouraged," Lee Pressman declared.[43]

Delegates took full advantage of the invitation, introducing scores of esoteric modifications that had not been cleared through proper channels. One of the most memorable requests came from an irate Marylander who demanded that the platform include an official censure of H. L. Mencken and his "Hitlerite references to the people of this convention." Delighted, the irascible Mencken voiced his hearty approval of the resolution and lobbied actively for its passage. Sadly, he wrote in his diary, "the Communist presidium refused to entertain it." A similar fate befell most such amendments. Still, observers agreed that the delegates were allowed to talk freely, albeit to little effect.[44]

The real fireworks began, however, when discussion turned to the platform's foreign policy section. James Hayford, a soft-spoken, bespectacled farmer from Vermont, stirred up a hornet's nest when he proposed that the following statement be added to the plank on U.S.-Soviet relations: "Although we are critical of the present foreign policy of the United States, it is not our intention to give blanket endorsement of the foreign policy of any nation." "The platform as it now stands," Hayford told his fellow delegates, "lays us open to the charge of condemning the American foreign policy practically *in toto*, while saying nothing critical of the foreign policy of any other nation." Anticipating opposition, he added, "It is not the intention of this resolution to Red-bait or introduce any red herrings. The wording of it, I think, amply takes care of any such danger." "Judging by the applause," the *New York Herald Tribune* reported, Hayford's proposal "had substantial backing in other state groups."[45]

Hugh De Lacy, a former congressman from Washington State, immediately opposed including such language and initiated a spirited attack on the so-called Vermont Resolution. In doing so, he employed the same arguments to stifle any implied criticism of the Soviet Union as Pressman had used during the platform committee meetings. Hayford's statement, he shouted, marked a "retreat" from principle, a surrender to "pressure from outside," and a threat to "unity" in the ranks. "If there is any great virtue in this platform," De Lacy exclaimed, "it is . . . to come out fighting for a sound, solid basis for friendship between the United States and the Soviet Union." Adopting the amendment would undercut that position and thereby discredit the entire Progressive Party crusade. Such reflexive pro-Soviet views may have seemed odd coming from a former congressman, but, as John Gates, the onetime editor of the *Daily Worker*, later told Joseph Starobin, "De Lacy was a Communist so his opposition to the Vermont amendment [was] not surprising."[46]

Hayford persisted, however: "It seems to me that anybody reading this platform is perfectly justified in drawing the conclusion that we endorse Soviet foreign policy one hundred percent. . . . I don't support Soviet policy one hundred percent . . . [and] I think we ought to go on record clearly on that." Other delegates rose to support him. Answering De Lacy's remarks, Rev. Schubert Frye of New York stated that he, too, was in favor of peace and friendship with the Soviet Union. But, he continued, "objectivity and honesty does not infringe on friendship in any respect [and] I believe that this convention should be objective." Albert Hartunian, a delegate from Pennsylvania, concurred. "I am one hundred percent in favor of friendship with Russia, but not blind friendship. . . . Let us for once understand that we are not Communists or that we don't endorse everything that Russia does." Genevieve Steefel of Minnesota reminded the delegates that if there was to be a "sincere discussion of differences with Russia," as Wallace wanted, "we must assume . . . that they will let maturity and good judgment enable them to accept from us the same criticisms, where they are deserved, that we address to ourselves." Steefel, the chair of the Credentials Committee and a member of the party's national committee, was the only high-ranking Progressive to speak in favor of the resolution. The opposition persisted in denouncing the Vermont Resolution as a "compromise with the smear campaign." The cry against red-baiting reverberated down the aisles. Carl Edding of Indiana pleaded with his colleagues to "realize the terrific import" of Hayford's seemingly harmless amendment. Perhaps forgetting that earlier in the platform the party had denounced Great Britain for its partition of Ireland, Edding warned gravely, "If this amendment appears in the platform, it will be an insinuation against a wartime ally of the United States."[47]

From the podium, Pressman contended that the amendment was unnecessary since the matter was adequately covered elsewhere in the platform. When a delegate from Michigan asked to know *where* it was covered,

Pressman read him the sentence on the two countries' "joint responsibility" for avoiding war, inserted just that morning at Frederick Schuman's insistence. He did not read the subsequent sentence: "Our nation has vastly greater responsibility for peace than Russia because it has vastly greater power for war."

After a half hour of debate, Fitzgerald announced from the podium that discussion was over and called for a voice vote on the motion. The Vermont Resolution mustered a considerable number of "ayes," but the "noes" clearly won. Its defeat proved a devastating, self-inflicted wound for the Progressive Party. "Their enemies could hardly have done it a greater disservice," the journalist Irwin Ross has concluded. Many committed Progressives cited the outcome of the debate as the catalyst for their breaking ties with the party. "I was with the Vermont delegation on their fight to hold the Third Party down to the base resemblance of a democratic movement. I have walked out," one party member wrote to the *New York Post*; "it is no longer the organization I joined a year and a half ago." Particularly damaging was the impression made on the independent voters the Progressives were so desperate to attract. "Many had come to the convention determined not to be caught up in the Red hysteria," reported the political columnist Pete Akers. "Previously, they had given the Wallaceites every benefit of the doubt. They had not believed that so many persons of good will—most of whom were not, and are not, Communists—could be so easily manipulated by the party's Communist element. But action on the Vermont amendment changed the minds of many." As Wallace's biographers Edward and Frederick Schapsmeier have observed, "When this rather innocuous proposal was defeated, the hammer and sickle was for all intent and purposes unfurled before an amazed gallery of onlookers." The radio audience as well was left to conclude that the Progressive platform *did* give blanket endorsement to the foreign policy of another nation.[48] As he witnessed the bewildering spectacle "in mingled disbelief and awe," Wechsler of the *New York Post* recalled the theologian Reinhold Niebuhr's remark that "it was always a pity to see a man proclaiming 'my country right or wrong,' especially when it wasn't his own country."[49]

Observers who had canvassed the delegates were surprised that the floor vote against the resolution was so large. Though the party leadership seemed peculiarly apprehensive about giving offense to the Soviet Union, Helen Fuller, a correspondent for the *New Republic*, reported, "all signs indicated that the average delegate did not share [their] preoccupation . . . with the Russian question." In fact, John Cotton Brown noted that many delegates he interviewed believed the amendment offered a welcome opportunity to register their discomfort with the platform's apparent pro-Soviet bias. One Alabama delegate who voted "aye" wrote to a friend, "After a plank on 'Peace' which roundly condemned the Marshall Plan, Truman Doctrine, 'anti-Soviet hysteria' *etc. etc.* but said nothing about Czechoslovakia *etc.*, . . . this seemed to be *the* issue & the chance to speak out. I couldn't see anything in the literal wording that even the CP boys could object to & thought they would have been wise to accept it." Yet the resolution went down to defeat on the strength of the *non*-Communists' votes, leaving many wondering how to explain such an outcome.[50]

As had occurred in the closed platform discussions, the pervasive fear of red-baiting played a key role. Once those in opposition had equated the resolution with red-baiting, few appeared willing to challenge them. The majority accepted De Lacy's spurious logic that those who would support such a motion were either "outsiders" bent on sabotage or weak-kneed compromisers who would betray principle by succumbing to "reactionary" pressures. Once the issue was put in such stark terms, many delegates found themselves in the unenviable position of endorsing the amendment's sentiment but fearing the reaction of their colleagues if they publicly expressed their support. Even the more politically sophisticated non-Communists chose to remain silent rather than run the risk of being labeled red-baiters. Josiah Gitt, a newspaper publisher from Pennsylvania and a longtime champion of liberal causes, recalled after the election that he had sat on the platform throughout the discussion hoping that the amendment would pass. "But I did nothing," he confessed. "I guess I lost my nerve." Even James Hayford quickly came to regret his moment of dissent. "I wouldn't have offered this amendment if I had thought at the time how the press will probably treat it," he said apologetically. Later, he changed his mind. "Without our amendment," Hayford told Curtis MacDougall in 1952, "the foreign policy plank committed non-Communists to an unacceptable position. The 'joint responsibility' plank did not overcome this objection, though it was a step in the right direction. There needed to be a showdown as to whether the Progressive Party was really a coalition or a one-sided affair." In 1948, however, Hayford and others were not willing to precipitate that showdown.[51]

Yet the pro-Communists' deft manipulation of their colleagues' sensitivity about "red-baiting" does not entirely explain the convention's reaction to the Vermont Resolution. Many delegates, though themselves not Communists—a charge they deeply resented—agreed with the CPers that the initiation *and* escalation of the Cold War were *exclusively* the responsibility of the "Wall Street controlled, bi-partisan reactionaries" in

Washington. Denouncing Soviet behavior only diverted attention from the primary task of bringing about a change in American foreign policy. Any criticism of Moscow, regardless of merit, was, as stated in the platform, "a mask for monopoly, militarism, and reaction." Those who embraced this position therefore saw little significance in the defeat of the Vermont amendment. They were inclined to interpret it—again, to quote De Lacy—as "a phony declaration that doesn't mean anything." Basing their understanding of the international crisis on a completely different set of assumptions than most Americans, these non-Communist Wallace supporters gave little consideration to how rejecting the Vermont Resolution might appear to those who did not share their viewpoint. Indeed, many were bewildered that the press devoted so much attention to the amendment's fate.

Progressives who assessed the Cold War in these terms were not "proSoviet" in the same sense that many "progressives" had been during the 1930s. They did not admire the USSR as the herald of the future, but they refrained from criticizing it because, in their eyes, such criticism was beside the point and would undermine the fight for peace. Regardless of the "flaws" or "excesses" of the Soviet system, the United States still remained responsible for ending the Cold War. Calling attention to Soviet misbehavior was simply a way of shirking this responsibility. As the historian William O'Neill notes in his study of such progressives, they never came to terms with the double standard of political morality that such a view required them to maintain.[52]

Though the outcome of the Vermont dispute may have had less to do with Communist "steamrollering" than initially reported, the next outbreak of dissent did provide ample evidence of the CP's sectarian impulses run amok. No sooner had Fitzgerald, Pressman, and company quieted the Vermont furor than a new challenge presented itself, concerning, of all things, Macedonian independence. Support for the nationalist aspirations of the Macedonians had long been a Communist war cry aimed at discrediting the anticommunist government of Greece. A standard item in CP policy statements, it had also found its way into the Progressive Party platform. Yet the Macedonian issue had taken on new meaning in the wake of the Tito-Stalin split. Banished from the Cominform a month earlier, Tito persisted in his defiance of Moscow by continuing to champion Macedonian independence as part of his Balkan Federation scheme. With Tito as the arch-heretic of the moment, supporting the Macedonians'—now "imperialist"—cause would have allied the Progressives with Yugoslavia against the Russians. At the eleventh hour someone had averted this impasse by unceremoniously deleting the Macedonians from the platform's list of "oppressed and dispersed people." At the beginning of the Sunday session, Pressman read the "correction" along with several other modifications the platform committee had approved.

Surely nothing would have come of this had not a lone pro-Macedonian delegate from Connecticut demanded an explanation. Though a befuddled Fitzgerald immediately ruled him out of order, reporters' suspicions had been aroused. One asked Tugwell if this sudden loss of interest in the Macedonians had anything to do with their siding with the Stalinist bête noire, Tito. Visibly embarrassed, Tugwell responded grimly, "This is all a surprise to me. Ask Pressman." But for once, Wechsler quipped, even the "belligerent barrister" seemed "suddenly stricken mute."[53]

Soon after the vote on the Vermont amendment, the same delegate again raised the Macedonian issue with the chair. "Why was Macedonia eliminated?" he asked. Fitzgerald, a genial union boss but not very well versed in Balkan affairs, turned to the writer Louis Adamic, the party's resident expert, to render the official explanation. The exasperated Adamic prefaced his remarks by stating curtly that he "[did] not care one way or the other about Macedonia." He then proceeded to deliver an impenetrable obfuscation that, observers noted, would have been no less illuminating had he given it in his native Serbo-Croatian tongue. Dismissing Adamic's ramblings as "gibberish," Wechsler joked: "If Michael Barnaby Wechsler (approaching the age of six) were guilty of an equivalent degree of what we call 'goofy nonsense,' he would be deprived of his supper in even these libertarian precincts." The dissenting delegate, too, was unconvinced. "Since the question has been raised," he said, "and since Mr. Adamic doesn't care one way or the other, I move that we put Macedonia back in the platform." "We will now go on to the next order of business," interrupted Fitzgerald, ending the Macedonian imbroglio with a bang of his gavel. Denied a vote on his motion, the disappointed delegate retreated to his seat, but not before adding incredulously, "There is some significance in this issue of that Macedonian elision."[54]

The sudden "correcting" of the Macedonians out of the platform reflected the extent to which the Progressive Party had submitted itself to the ideological bossism of the Communist minority. Informed political observers could not fathom such obtuse behavior. "What in God's name are these Wallace people trying to do—hang themselves?" asked the veteran *New York Times* correspondent William Lawrence. Such episodes made Progressives' indignant denials of undue Communist influence within their party sound all the more incredible.[55]

The discussion of the platform continued all day. After seven hours of debate, the few remaining delegates unanimously approved it at 7:45 P.M. Half an hour later, the former Minnesota governor and newly elected Progressive Party chairman Elmer Benson closed the convention with an admonition. "This has been a great experience for all of us," he declared. "But the job isn't done. It has just commenced. Our job now is to go home to our precincts, into our townships, into our counties and villages . . . and do a real job of organizing a genuine people's movement."[56] As the delegates streamed out of Convention Hall, they vowed to carry the enthusiasm of Philadelphia back to their state and local communities. Yet whether this fervor would prove contagious was quite another matter. The house lights had barely gone down before the first assessments of the third party "show" began to appear. And for the Progressives, the reviews were not at all good.

7

ROLLING DOWNHILL

Post-Convention Fallout and Dropouts

"It was a great convention," Frederick Schuman wrote to Beanie Baldwin three days after leaving Philadelphia. "You did a magnificent job. It's a good platform. The extent of the smear campaign encourages me. The boys are afraid we are going places. Let's go!" Henry Wallace shared Schuman's unbridled optimism. Referring to the third party's previous high point—the Isacson victory in February—Wallace told supporters, "I was going on faith in those days. But since this convention I'm not going on faith. I know we've just begun to roll. . . . We're getting rolling now and they simply can't stop us." "If the people's movement continues to spread as rapidly as it is at present," one exuberant North Carolina delegate predicted, "Wallace will carry at least forty states in the November elections." As the summer progressed, however, emotional fervor gave way to political reality. By Labor Day, the official opening of the 1948 presidential campaign, few Progressives would venture such hopeful forecasts.[1]

■ Undoubtedly, the three-day gala proved an invigorating morale-builder for many Wallace partisans who had been languishing in the political wilderness. On their arrival in Philadelphia, those who had been ridiculed as "crackpots" or denounced as "commies" in their hometowns happily discovered that they had thousands of like-minded colleagues. On the floor of Convention Hall, a movement culture began to coalesce as the delegates recounted their common experiences and exchanged tales from the trenches. They reveled in this newfound spirit of community, confidently reassuring each other of the righteousness of their cause and of the campaign's growing strength and widespread appeal. "For the first time in all my life," declared the novelist Howard Fast, one of the many well-known writers drawn to the Progressive cause, "I began to understand the deep reaching implications of people's democracy."[2]

The convention, planned more as a well-scripted pep rally than a forum for debate, encouraged this infectious enthusiasm. At the height of the Shibe Park celebration, the columnist Dorothy Thompson reported, young delegates dancing among the newspaper correspondents had turned to her and announced ecstatically, "Don't you see now that we are going to sweep the country? It's dynamic; it's invincible." "They certainly, I thought, believed it," Thompson remarked.[3] The lively shouting of party slogans and group sing-alongs also forged a common bond among the delegates, a bond the leadership effectively reinforced with constant admonitions to maintain party unity in the face of "outside" pressure. Indeed, as one observer noted, at a convention teeming with political dissenters of every stripe, the unanimity of opinion was strikingly anomalous.[4]

Those who had witnessed such left-wing enthusiasm at previous mass gatherings cautioned against overestimating its significance. According to the Associated Press correspondent Hal Boyle, the convention's strategic location in Philadelphia—one of the nation's largest cities and easily accessible from New York, Baltimore, and Washington—made it difficult to determine if the unexpectedly large crowd was the result of "an all-out effort by Communist and Communist-front organizations, or whether it was a spontaneous outpouring of people dissatisfied with the two major political parties." Such a turnout in Cleveland, St. Louis, or Kansas City would have more clearly demonstrated "a powerful cross-section of American discontent," he maintained. Though the emotional demonstrations in Convention Hall and Shibe Park had made for a "good show," the attendance at Wallace rallies during the upcoming campaign, Boyle predicted, would provide a more reliable gauge as to "whether the Progressive Party has astonishing popular strength—or merely was born in a town where all the relatives could get there in time for the baptism." Confirming Boyle's analysis, Sally Turpin, a Philadelphia Communist who went to the Shibe Park rally, observed that most of the faithful seemed to have been bused in from New York City. Discerning the first signs of a coming defeat, she worried about the Progressives' failure to attract enough Philadelphians and about the need to rely on the "comrades" from New York to fill the stadium's seats.[5]

Ironically, the heightened sense of camaraderie on display at Philadelphia may have further contributed to the Wallaceites' political isolation.

"The Progressive Party convention," the columnist Edwin Lahey wrote from the perspective of the mid-1960s, "was a sectarian orgy that would make an anti-Vietnam rally of the 'new Left' today seem rather well-behaved." In the heat of the moment, however, the delegates mistook their echoing self-applause for an accurate barometer of the public mood. "When you're singing very loudly and having a good time," one convention performer later commented, "you imagine everybody else is also singing just as loudly and having just as good a time. It's hard to hear all the people not singing." The *Denver Post* put matters less gently: "The boastful confidence of the Wallace leaders is self-delusion, for the embarrassing fact, which cannot be masked, is that the Progressive Party has no real mass base among the people."[6]

Indeed, in their assessments of the convention's impact, the Wallace and his supporters seemed further removed than ever from political reality. In what almost every observer outside party circles saw as a public relations disaster, Progressives beheld an unqualified triumph. Hailing the work of the party's publicity department in his report to the national committee, Beanie Baldwin declared, "The convention itself cost us $70,000 to run, but the effect it produced on the many millions who heard it on the air, saw it in television, and read of it even in the twisted press reports, was worth vastly more than that to us." Even those who acknowledged that most media coverage had been hostile insisted that this was of no account. In fact, such bad press testified to the convention's success in alarming the forces of reaction. Wall Street and the military, it was argued, so dreaded the prospect of a genuine "people's party" that they had enlisted the press to put down the Progressive challenge. Reporters bought off by "the interests" were naturally out to bury Wallace, not to praise him. "They filed what they were paid to file," Howard Fast claimed. "They were under no specific duress—but what whore is?" "The columnists are beside themselves with fear," Joseph Starobin exclaimed in the *Daily Worker*. "They were scared stiff by the Wallace convention. . . . The men behind them, the owners of the country, the wielders of power . . . are all in a panic today, because, to use Henry Wallace's really profound remark, what happened at Philadelphia was a 'turning point in the history of the world.'" Ultimately, Progressives contended, even the men and women of the "controlled press" could not slow the momentum of the third party crusade. "The magnitude of this convention has taken the edge off what they hoped to do to us," Wallace told a meeting of state directors on July 26.[7]

Not unexpectedly, the "controlled press" saw things differently. The issue was not what the press hoped to do to the Progressives, but what the Progressives had done to themselves. "The proceedings of the New Party convention at Philadelphia can only be regarded as one of the costliest expenditures of goodwill ever billed against an American nominee," James Wechsler declared. The party faithful's fury at convention coverage was hardly surprising, he granted, "for the barest truth was intrinsically uncharitable." Raymond Brandt, a veteran Washington correspondent for the *St. Louis Post-Dispatch*, concurred. "The [third party] campaign thus far," he observed, "has been mainly based on emotions and distortions of fact." "The 'old' [La Follette] Progressives prided themselves on being well-informed and articulate on all issues. . . . Intellectual honesty was an integral part of the 1924 campaign." In contrast, Brandt observed, "the 'new' Progressives were vague when not evasive, and belligerent when not trying to force over their own favorite ideas." At their respective news conferences, "neither candidate made an impression of forthright honesty in opening statements or in replies to questions." "The new Progressives have complained about the 'hostile' press," he concluded, but "they have only themselves to blame."[8]

■ Regardless of who was responsible for the poor coverage, if the convention's aims had been to allay concerns about Communist domination and to broaden the party's base of support, it had failed dismally. "Despite every effort either to evade, compromise or shout down the issue," the *Philadelphia Inquirer* reported, "the precise role of the Communist minority in party policies played the part of Banquo's ghost at the Convention." Rather than repudiating the Communists, the Progressives appeared to be marching in lockstep with them, alienating those few remaining liberals who had been disposed to give Gideon's Army the benefit of the doubt. "The New Party's platform and the speeches of Mr. Wallace and Senator Taylor echoed the party line closely enough to dispel any idea that a break with the Communists is likely," the editors of the *Nation* lamented. "Mr. Wallace himself said that the support of the Communists would be a liability. If he really believed this," they noted with exasperation, "he could, one would think, have established the difference between his views and theirs."[9]

Instead, the candidate had played only a relatively minor role at his own convention, refusing to take an active part in the drafting of party policy on the grounds that he did not wish to "boss" the delegates. As many of Wallace's supporters would later concede, this abdication of leadership proved a costly error, for the Communists felt no such compunctions and moved in quickly to fill the vacuum. Such complaints extended beyond

Wallace's passivity at the convention. "Mr. Wallace never gave any personal leadership to the campaign," recalled Marjorie Lansing, who headed the Massachusetts Progressive Party. "In national committee meetings, at the national convention, in local areas—he always behaved as a sheep who was being led around. That was all right when FDR was leading the party, but it certainly was not all right when John Abt, a rigid, pie-in-the-sky operator, was calling the tunes in the national office. Where was Mr. Wallace when the Vermont resolution was proposed on the floor of the convention? He was waiting for Beanie Baldwin to take him by the hand and lead him to a gathering where he would read Lew Frank's speech." Lansing raised a valid point. Despite being the face of the Progressive Party, Wallace remained an elusive personality and oddly disconnected from his own campaign. He paid scant attention to its day-to-day workings, fell asleep at strategy sessions if he attended them at all, and kept largely to himself while on the road. More troubling, he often seemed unaware of the political positions his national office was attributing to him and grew irritated at reporters when they pointed out that his unscripted statements contradicted party press releases.[10]

Yet not only Wallace's acquiescence in the face of Communist maneuvering disturbed liberals. The CPers' manifest hostility toward unfettered debate and the free exchange of ideas frustrated those Progressives who were not satisfied with simply singing folk songs and voting "yes." For all the talk of open discussion and commitment to democratic procedure, any comments that directly challenged the views of the far-left minority were quickly shouted down with cries of "red-baiting" and "sabotage." The columnist Earl Brown reported that he saw "Communists and their allies and stooges running the Third Party convention as ruthlessly as any dictator ever ran a political show." Such inflexibility threatened to deprive the Progressives of the dynamism they needed to sustain their movement. As one New Yorker who had recently abandoned the party remarked, "By its growing rigidity and intolerance, it stunts its own growth and renders itself politically sterile. There was a great deal of generous, constructive optimism in the movement, but this has tended to degenerate into fanatic blindness. . . . Good will and faith are necessary, but they are not adequate substitutes for critical, open-minded thought." Another supporter who had attended the convention was "appalled . . . to see how thoroughly populated the place was with Communists." "Instead of broadening the party, they have narrowed it," he said. "Looking forward, as I did, for a great Wallace vote as heartening the fight for democratic rights, to create a new anti-fascist coalition, to assert the strong anti-war attitudes on behalf of the American people, I am plainly heartsick at the mendacious sectarianism of the Communists and what they have done to destroy the New Party." Significantly, however, he added, "It's easy to blame the Communists for their cynical exploitation of decent emotions, but those who let themselves be exploited are equally to blame."[11]

Others anticipated similar cracks in the liberal-Communist alliance. Independents who had gone along with the CP militants in the heady atmosphere of the convention, the columnist Carlton Kent suggested, were now suffering an "ideological hangover" and "promising themselves to lay off the strong stuff in the future." In the coming weeks, "fade-outs" more so than "walk-outs" would be the norm among the ranks of the disenchanted, another reporter forecast. "Party unity," he added, "is more a fetish than a fact among Progressives." The novelist James T. Farrell urged his friend Norman Thomas to seize the moment and woo "the non-Commy contingents of Gideon's Army" into the Socialist camp. "The Wallace-Commy propaganda is based on accepting (a) false certitudes and (b) gods and devils—Truman has become Trotsky, as it were. One has to hammer outside this," Farrell advised. Confronting third party supporters face to face in debates and in informal discussions could overcome the manufactured excitement on display in Philadelphia. "The hysteria of the convention is something that [party leaders] must repeat over and over again," Farrell told Thomas. "Hysterics and totalitarianism go together. The Wallaceites are doing what [the] CP does—inoculation against truth by saying that the press lies, that so and so lies, etc. With this, they are keeping their people under pressure. Whatever we can do to put moral and intellectual pressure on them is to the good. They break one by one, not in toto." *Labor Action*, the organ of Max Shachtman's anti-Stalinist Socialist Workers' Party, seemed to relish the prospect of a coming breach. "The liberals will not fight for control of the Progressive Party from the inside," the paper prophesied. "When they feel the hot breath of the Stalinists on their necks, they will fold their tents and steal away with varying degrees of silence."[12]

The Communists themselves did little to repair the damage done to the "united front" coalition they had entered into with the Progressives. At their National Convention on August 3–6, they noisily re-endorsed Wallace and insisted that the precipitous decline of the Progressive Party was a "wrong theory" rather than a demonstrable fact. In essence, the CP faced a dilemma. "The more it threw its own forces in to compensate for the weakness of the Progressives," Joseph Starobin has noted, "the greater the problems within the Progressive Party as its hesitant supporters withdrew in proportion as the Communists came in." The CP, however, would not—or could not—recognize the toxic effect it was having. The Party's chairman, William Z. Foster, vigorously defended the "fundamentally correct line" that insisted the Communists play a "leading role" in any "anti-monopoly coalition." By all accounts, he and other party functionaries remained convinced that the tide was turning their way and that "the people" would ultimately turn away from the "misleaders" in the mainstream liberal and labor movements. In their utopianism, the Communists rivaled Wallace himself.[13]

Not surprisingly, then, the Communists rejected any suggestion that they field a candidate of their own, so as to improve the Progressive Party's prospects. General Secretary Eugene Dennis even chided Wallace for raising the issue, referencing the candidate's remarks in Burlington, Vermont, and Center Sandwich, New Hampshire. To be sure, pursuing such a strategy would not have been unprecedented for the Communists. In 1936, while supporting Franklin D. Roosevelt's reelection, the CP had put forward its own nominee to draw off the "Communist" charges against the president. Twelve years later, however, such a self-effacing strategy smacked of "Browderism," and, Starobin explains, "Having decided that Browder had been guilty of hiding the Party's light under a bushel . . . the post-Browder leadership was hardly able to mount a Browder-type campaign in 1948 even though this might have been most helpful."[14] Indeed, though many in the New Party may have believed that sustaining the wartime Popular Front was the best strategy to advance a progressive agenda, in the wake of the Duclos Letter, the Communists made it clear that they rejected such an approach. Such political alliances, David Plotke has pointed out, "were considered purely as instruments, rather than as joint ventures, much less as forms of cooperation that might entail learning and change on all sides." The Party had dedicated itself to establishing "a government led by the working class," by which it meant a government of the Communist Party. Therefore, while its platform urged support for Wallace and the Progressive Party, it denounced the central concept of Wallace's political philosophy—a reformed or "progressive" capitalism.[15] In doing so, Starobin observes, the Party drew a distinction between itself and the Progressives, and yet, in failing to nominate its own candidate, it refused to make "the concrete and simple gesture that would have been more persuasive to millions of Americans than all the abstract doctrinal distinctions."[16]

■ Events at the state level confirmed the decline in the Progressive Party's fortunes. In California, widely considered a Progressive stronghold, support for Wallace eroded rapidly after the convention. In the spring, some political experts had claimed Wallace would outpoll Truman in the Golden State. Likewise, Elinor Kahn, the director of California's Independent Progressive Party (IPP), boasted in Philadelphia that the New Party ticket would garner between 1.5 million and 1.8 million votes out of an estimated 4 million to be cast. Less partisan observers put the figure at about 400,000, but conceded that the successful petition campaign to place Wallace's name on the ballot had demonstrated the IPP's widespread grassroots support.[17] When canvassers went door to door in early August, however, they found that many previously sympathetic voters were beginning to question the Wallace movement. In particular, they wanted to know why the convention had failed to pass the Vermont Resolution or some similar statement that would differentiate the Progressive Party's program from that of the Communists. One Stanford student reported that he had not visited a single person who had signed an IPP petition who now intended to vote for Wallace. Upton Sinclair, whose 1936 End Poverty in California gubernatorial campaign had made him the state's most revered progressive, wired Wallace urging him to abandon his crusade and return to the Democrats.[18]

Officials from the IPP blamed the Tenney Committee, California's "little HUAC," for undermining the party's efforts. During the late summer and early fall, Chairman Jack B. Tenney, a former radical union leader turned conservative state senator, conducted hearings that touched on Communist influence within the IPP. The press gave extensive coverage to Tenney's investigation, helping publicize the committee's contention that the IPP was "merely a continuation of the Communist Party." Throughout the proceedings, Tenney added to his reputation as an unsavory character seemingly obsessed with the Communist issue. A professional piano player and the onetime president of Local 47 of the American Federation of Musicians in Los Angeles, Tenney had begun his career in the California legislature as a Popular Front liberal, sympathetic to the agenda of the Communist Party. But after witnessing the CP's machinations within the musicians' union, which ultimately undermined his own position, Tenney turned on the Party and commenced an extended crusade to eradicate what he considered its menacing influence on public life. His personal bitterness toward the Communists undoubtedly clouded his judgment, and he frequently leveled baseless allegations in the midst of heated committee hearings. Over the years, his committee had become notorious for its irresponsible behavior and legally questionable procedures. Still, in this instance, the substance of Tenney's allegations was difficult to refute—many of the IPP leaders he targeted *were* concealed Communist Party members. The third party responded to Tenney's charges the best it could while continuing its effort to recruit more members. Canvassers distributed thousands of leaflets urging voters not to be intimidated. Nonetheless, the IPP found it slow going. An all-out drive launched after the June primary produced only meager results.[19]

Intraparty tensions proved just as damaging as attacks from the Tenney Committee. Non-Communist members found it increasingly humiliating to bring their friends to local IPP club meetings only to have them barraged with ill-tempered "party line" harangues and solicitations for Communist literature. These visitors also saw firsthand the difficulties of working with the CP in a united front. Since the Communists did not tolerate any deviation from their party line, the liberals in the organization inevitably did most of the compromising, usually after hours of procedural wrangling about trivial matters. Though not anticommunist per se, most potential recruits had no desire to censor their political expression merely to placate a sectarian minority. Accordingly, they declined to join the IPP. When party spokespersons addressed outside audiences, the results could be equally embarrassing. At a meeting of senior citizen pension-plan activists in Long Beach, Progressive firebrands' "radical statements flavored with profanity" quickly dispatched any third party sentiment among the area's older residents. As it became clear that the Communists were chasing away far more people than they were attracting, non-Communist leaders found it difficult to suppress their frustration. Disheartened, the director John Huston, a prominent Wallace activist in Los Angeles, remarked to his friend and fellow director Philip Dunne, "Phil, why don't we charter a boat, invite all our Communist friends out for a cruise, and, about fifty miles out, gently and lovingly push them overboard."[20]

These animosities surfaced at the IPP state convention the weekend of August 7 when a delegate from San Mateo offered a resolution declaring that "in accepting the National Platform of the Progressive Party, we wish to state clearly that we construe nothing in this National Platform as giving blanket endorsement to the foreign or domestic policy of any other government." In what amounted to a replay of the debate over the Vermont Resolution, a number of IPP delegates vigorously denounced the proposal as the work of "agents of outside forces" who were attempting to "wreck" the party by forcing it into red-baiting. Employing the same strategy that had worked in Philadelphia, they managed to bring their colleagues into line. The convention voted the motion down overwhelmingly, with only two delegates expressing support.[21]

On the resolution's defeat, one of its backers, Paul Taylor, brother to Glen and himself an IPP nominee for Congress from the Eighth district, stormed out of the hall. Taylor had discussed the amendment ahead of time with all the groups from his district who were represented at the convention, and they had unanimously supported it. Convinced that the convention delegates were defending the CP line rather than representing the views of those who had elected them, he contemplated quitting the movement then and there. "I didn't want to be a slave candidate for a slave party," he told friends afterward. In the end, Taylor decided not to leave, taking the view that liberals should remain in the IPP and fight the Communists for control of the organization. The lopsided outcome of the vote, however, did not bode well for any such challenge. Indeed, given the majority position that any implied criticism of the Communists or of their pro-Soviet views was unacceptable red-baiting, it is difficult to imagine how the non-Communists would have waged a successful struggle for control.[22]

If the makeup of the San Diego delegation to the convention is any indication, Taylor's suspicions of the delegates' political affiliations were justified, while his hopes of successfully challenging the CP for control of the IPP were in vain. According to the testimony of Lloyd Hamlin, an undercover FBI agent who operated within the San Diego CP, five of the seven delegates and alternates sent to the state convention were members of the Communist Party. Hamlin himself was elected to the State Central Committee of the IPP and paid in cash by the CP to do organizational work for the third party. He reported that ten of the nineteen members of the IPP County Committee and eleven of the eighteen San Diego representatives on the State Central Committee were Communist Party functionaries. According to Hamlin, the CP "completely dominated" the San Diego IPP from its inception. All matters concerning the operation of the IPP, he testified, were determined in closed meetings of the Communist Party before being brought to the non-Communist members. In an ironic twist, Hamlin took the Fifth Amendment when the Tenney Committee questioned him on his alleged Communist affiliations in early September 1948, so as not to blow his cover.[23]

A challenge to a quorum provision for the forty-member State Executive Committee meetings also got nowhere at the IPP convention when the leadership insisted that ten, rather than twenty-one, was sufficient. "We are just throwing our democratic rights out the window," protested one of the proposal's backers. He and eleven colleagues left the IPP shortly thereafter. Robert C. North, one of those who resigned, remarked that the whole episode convinced him that non-Communist progressives could not participate in a movement with "persons who sounded like Communists" and who answered all criticism with the assertion that "we can get along without the liberals." As was the case with many who left the Progressives' ranks, the Californians agreed with Wallace on the issues but refused to tolerate the heavy-handed tactics of the CP working within the Progressive Party organization.[24]

Similar well-publicized defections took place in New Mexico. Six prominent leaders in the state organization severed ties with the party on July 31. This brought to a close a month-long struggle for control between independent liberals who had organized the party and a pro-Communist fraction. Again, the Communists' so-called rule-or-ruin strategy precipitated the clash. "Enthusiasm for Wallace continued to boom," one sympathetic observer later recalled, "until the organizing machinery experienced the influx of scheming Leftist minorities who engaged in a variety of undemocratic, power-grabbing maneuvers." This "motley crew of self-anointed 'leaders of the masses,'" he reported, "were so politically ignorant that they adopted reactionary tactics of subterfuge and slander against all in the PP who questioned their wisdom."[25]

On July 5, five of the six who ultimately withdrew threatened to quit the party unless Wallace repudiated Communist support. Rose Segure, a regional organizer from the national office (and a concealed Communist), persuaded them to stay on the condition that they could discuss their concerns with Wallace at the convention. In Philadelphia, however, Baldwin and Abt barred them from seeing the candidate, sending the delegation away with the warning that there could be no red-baiting in the New Party. For the six New Mexicans, the subsequent defeat of the Vermont Resolution proved "the last straw." They announced their resignation in a public statement released the following week. The Communists' influence in the Progressive Party, they declared, was "leading toward goals we cannot accept. . . . The platform adopted at Philadelphia demonstrated a refusal to treat objectively the policies of Soviet Russia and showed extreme care in avoiding anything that might be interpreted as slightly critical of the Communist party or Russia." Four days later, three of the top leaders in Santa Fe resigned, citing the presence in the party of a "small but powerful clique intent on stifling independent thought." With elements of the far left now in control, the movement in New Mexico shriveled to a small core of hard-liners incapable of attracting new recruits to the Wallace banner.[26]

The situation in Colorado proved much the same. "The Wallace party in Colorado is being blown to pieces by the stupidity of the commies," the ADA organizer William Leuchtenburg reported in early August. Indeed, the fractional strife that had plagued the organization since May had already chased away many non-Communist supporters. Earlier in the year, Lee Fryer, a political activist in the state, had taken a group of community leaders to a Progressive Party organizational meeting in Denver, hoping that they would join the party and assume leadership positions. "The meeting convened at 8 P.M., and the chairman regained control at 9:30 P.M.," Fryer later recounted. "All of the intervening time was consumed in the row between the CP group and the status quo group on trivial quarrels concerning control. This kind of incident drove away responsible people of broader community connections. It surely drove away many people I knew."[27] Those who remained hoped to dispel rumors of disunity. In Philadelphia, Emil Berkowitz, the chair of the Colorado delegation, told reporters, "There is no party rift as far as we're concerned, and we don't expect any." One week after participating in the deliberations of the platform committee, however, he, too, abandoned Gideon's Army. "I cannot be a member of a party which welcomes Communists," Berkowitz declared. Back in Colorado, support for the Progressives continued to evaporate as the Communists tightened their grip on the state organization. Fryer later wrote that he regarded the "Colorado fiasco" as "only another instance of the same low grade political happening that occurred in New Mexico, Wyoming, Montana, Mississippi, California, [and] Washington." "The CP leaders were pulling an obvious fast one," Fryer recalled. "The whole thing was very clumsy. . . . It was pitiful." On August 8, only two hundred people attended a meeting of the Denver central committee, many of them open Communist Party members. "The convention looked more like a wake than a rally," Leuchtenburg observed.[28]

In New England, departures from the Progressive Party received less publicity but nonetheless signaled liberals' increasing frustration with their Communist allies. "I still believe that Communists have a perfect right to join and work with others in the Progressive Party," Alan MacNeil from Vermont declared in his letter of resignation, "[but] I am very wary of a party that is dominated by them—as I have come to believe the Progressive Party is. . . . If and when there is a change within the Progressive Party itself—if the reins pass to other hands, I and millions like me would like to be part of it. At present, in all conscience, I cannot." Three weeks later his wife resigned. "God knows I hate . . . red-baiting," she wrote, but the Progressive Party "is declining except in N. Y. because the Communists are determined to guide and use it and people just don't like what they feel is a Communist-front political organization." Vermont party officials curtly dismissed the views of the MacNeils and of others who departed, asserting that they had done so not out of principle but for fear of losing financial and social status within their communities.[29] In Connecticut, the Democratic candidate for governor and former New Dealer Chester Bowles observed that the Communists' high profile at the convention had unnerved local Wallaceites. Writing to his ADA colleague James Loeb, Bowles remarked, "There are some signs that a great many of the Third Party people here in this State were rather unhappy about the whole thing as they had believed sincerely that they were right and we were wrong when they said it was possible to work with Communists without being gobbled up by them."[30]

Tensions arose even in the Massachusetts party, where the liberals had tried to make a determined effort to keep the Communists in check. Well-known figures including the literary historian F. O. Matthiessen and the publisher Angus Cameron found themselves constantly quarreling with the party's national office, which they believed to be in the hands of pro-Communists with "fixed attitudes." Their frustration is telling, since in years past both men had been closely allied with the Party and had staunchly supported Communist participation in Popular Front organizations. After the convention, Frederick Schuman, too, became more circumspect in his dealings with the full-time staff in New York. Having completed a lengthy pamphlet outlining the party's positions on foreign policy, he forwarded the manuscript to party headquarters and implied that he did not wish to see it altered to meet the requirements of the CP line. "There are . . . comments here and there about Soviet foreign policy and Communism which I strongly feel need to be made—if not in the platform, then at least in a campaign pamphlet," Schuman wrote. "They state truth, as I see it—and I am convinced that loyalty to truth, at all costs, is the first duty of Progressives. I would not want this published under my name if these were omitted or changed." In his sensationalistic exposé, *I Led Three Lives*, Herbert Philbrick, an FBI informant who posed as a Communist and worked on the Wallace campaign in Massachusetts, claimed that the CP had taken over the state's third party organization and secretly determined its policies and tactics. According to the party's state chair, Marjorie Lansing, Philbrick did not have a complete picture of the balance of power between liberals and Communists in the Massachusetts party. Nonetheless, his description of CP manipulation so closely matches the pattern reported in many other locales that his account should not be dismissed. Lansing herself later claimed that by early August the sectarian behavior of several of the party's senior officials had sealed the fate of

Gideon's Army. "I personally think John Abt lost us several million votes," she asserted. "We slid down-hill daily from the time of the Philadelphia convention."[31]

One Bay State voter lost was the distinguished Harvard historian H. Stuart Hughes. Hughes's experience in the Progressive Party epitomized that of many middle-class men and women initially attracted to Wallace because of his willingness to challenge the rapidly congealing orthodoxies of the Cold War. In retrospect, Hughes characterized himself as "typical of a perplexed minority that stood somewhere between the anti-Communists and those commonly called fellow travelers." He had worked for the State Department for eighteen months in 1946 and 1947. During this tumultuous period, he and several other middle-level "apostates" had grown increasingly concerned about the self-righteous rhetoric and "apocalyptic outlook" of the department's top officials. Though they accepted the Cold War as "a fact of life," they remained hopeful that a spheres-of-influence agreement with Moscow could at least reduce or attenuate the conflict. "In the early months of 1948," Hughes later recalled, "Wallace seemed exactly what people like myself were looking for. . . . He had been forced to resign from Truman's cabinet for much the sort of Cold War 'heresies' of which we were guilty. No member of the left-liberal opposition had his prestige or influence; no other was so qualified to weld together the bits and pieces of dissent on foreign policy." Hughes therefore joined the third party with great enthusiasm, but, he later wrote, "After a four month absence in Europe, I found on returning home that the Communists—whose influence in the Progressive Party had always worried me—had virtually taken over the Wallace movement." He tried to express his apprehension about the party's course during a rally for a local congressional candidate, but when his criticisms were ignored, he decided to resign. Looking back, Hughes lamented, "Perhaps I should have anticipated that it would be impossible for Wallace to voice before a mass audience the nuanced attitude my friends and I had earlier expressed in private conferences and memoranda. We certainly did not expect that his speeches would offer so bizarre a blend of our kind of thinking and undiluted Communist party line. . . . In the end, for me—as for so many others—the Wallace movement was to prove the most ambiguous and painful of my ideological involvements."[32]

A group of politically sophisticated Progressives in Minnesota expressed similar concerns about the Communists' role in the party and at the national convention. A list of questions they drew up showed that not all non-Communist Wallace supporters failed to recognize the CP's maneuvering in Philadelphia. "How were delegates selected—elected by

State organizations or appointed by State Campaign Chairmen?" they asked Baldwin and Abt. "Who determined representation on the Committees? When was Lee Pressman elected Secretary of the Platform Committee and by whom? How did Martin Popper become Chairman of the drafting subcommittee? Who wrote the temporary convention rules that made roll-calls impossible?" All were thorny issues that most non-Communists preferred not to raise, but given the "resignations and loss of interest and support in general since the convention," they maintained, "full and open discussion . . . among the membership [is necessary] to reestablish general political health in the Party." "Taking the long view," they concluded, "the only people that can be hurt by full and open discussion on the question of communist-control are the Communists." Though Baldwin and Abt attempted to assuage the group's misgivings, Genevieve Steefel, its spokesperson, remained skeptical. Non-Communists would have to remain on guard, she believed. "Abt and probably Beanie need a firm rein and we a solid ground for our position," she scrawled on Abt's evasive response to the Minnesotans' questions. "If we *drift*, they provide the current."[33]

On August 6, nine leaders of the Minnesota Progressive Party wrote Wallace urging him to address the Communist issue. At the convention, they maintained, he had failed to distinguish Progressive Party policies from those of the CP and it was imperative that he do so soon. "Mere statements that we stand for settling international differences at the conference table, and denials of communist domination are not enough," they informed him. "Forces opposed to the Progressive Party have now picked up on the failure of the convention to pass [the Vermont Resolution] as specific proof that the Progressive Party is communist dominated, and that it is more pro-Soviet than pro-American. And frankly, we are at a loss for answers. We have no wish to 'red-bait.' We have always, and will continue to fight for the civil rights of all groups. But to sell the Progressive Party to the voters, we must be able to assure them, by concrete statements, that democracy functions within our party at all levels." Wallace's response—a brief, pro forma defense of his previously stated position—failed to convince the Minnesotans that he realized the gravity of the issue. Indeed, Wallace remained reluctant to confront directly the issue of Communist maneuvering within the Progressive Party. In a draft of his response to the Minnesotans dated August 14, 1948, he included the sentence, "Reading between the lines I would say that you have been having trouble with communists in Minnesota. Who are they and what have they done that is wrong?" He crossed out this passage, however, and handwrote in the margin the following: "Now is the time to stand up stiff and strong against the warmongers whose stock in trade is selling red-baiting." This sentence appeared in the final letter sent on August 17.[34]

Non-Communist Progressives in Minnesota and elsewhere faced a troubling dilemma as the campaign wore on. Still deeply committed to Popular Front liberalism, they did not oppose Communist participation in the Progressive Party. Yet they deplored the CPers' manipulative attempts to dominate the party machinery, their routine use of deception, and their resort to personal vilification to discredit those who disagreed with them. These liberals searched, often in vain, for a way to rid themselves of individuals who employed such self-destructive tactics without embracing an openly anticommunist position. "To apply a purge technique is, practically speaking, to identify with the ADA approach. That is unacceptable to me," Steefel wrote to Elinor Gimbel, the chair of Women for Wallace. "To state our position, however, frankly and openly, and put it to the test democratically within the rank and file of the party is not a purge technique. If Communists in the Progressive Party cannot act like progressives, they can withdraw to their own party." "I will work with Communists," Steefel told Gimbel, but "I will not work for them or under their domination. To do that is to betray democracy. That is the problem I face and I have not yet found its solution."[35] It was a tough nut to crack, for Steefel had hit on the quandary that lay at the heart of Popular Front liberalism. The alliance between Communists and progressive liberals could only be sustained if the liberals accepted the Communists' terms.

■ At the national level, Rexford Tugwell struggled with the same dilemma. Firsthand experience had convinced him that it was nearly impossible to work with Communists while remaining faithful to "old-fashioned progressivism." Yet he shared Wallace's conviction that a third party was the only viable alternative to combat what he considered the reactionary policies of the two major parties. In his view, the Progressive Party had to endure if only to provide a foundation on which to build a stronger, non-Communist Progressive Party in the future. At the convention, Tugwell came to believe that the Communist presence was threatening to destroy the party before it ever got off the ground. In private, he urged Wallace to repudiate the Communists around him. To further his case, he showed him a clipping describing Robert M. La Follette's rejection of Communist backing in the Progressive movement of 1924. La Follette, Tugwell argued, had taken "the true liberal position." Wallace held firm. He would have no red-baiting. "If they want to support me I can't stop them," he said gloomily. Publicly, Wallace continued to turn aside questions about Communist control of the New Party. "I can truthfully say that the Communists have not come to me as such," he told reporters shortly after the convention. "I saw one hurriedly in a railroad station not long ago. I don't recall his name. I told him I believe in progressive capitalism. That stopped him and I haven't heard from the Communists since."[36]

On August 20, the *Baltimore Sun* reported that Tugwell had announced himself "an uneasy member of the Progressive Party." In a telephone conversation the day before, Tugwell had told the paper's correspondent Howard Norton that there had been a "big row" in Philadelphia and that he was no longer "officially" connected with the party. He was keeping an "open mind" on whether he would vote for Wallace, but he would not take an active part in the campaign. The struggle between "a certain group" and "those of us who are simply progressives" was still going on, Tugwell confirmed. In what seemed another veiled appeal to Wallace to take decisive action on the matter, he added that "if the wrong people get control," "old-fashioned progressives" like him would leave the party. "By 'the wrong people' do you mean the Communists?" Norton asked Tugwell. "I certainly don't know whether they are Communists," Tugwell replied, "but they act as though they are." The interview received widespread publicity. Though miffed that comments he had intended as "off the record" appeared in print, Tugwell concluded that "it may, nevertheless, do good if it forces H. A. to do what he knows he should do."[37]

The following day, Wallace called to reassure Tugwell, reading him a statement he planned to issue announcing his lack of sympathy with communism. Tugwell was not placated. During their private conversation, he conveyed his displeasure even more bluntly than he had in the interview with Norton. Reviewing his experiences in drafting the platform, he told Wallace that there were Communists on the committee "intent on forwarding Russian imperialist interests." He, for one, would not acquiesce in toeing the CP line on international affairs. "I have been against an aggressive foreign policy on our part," Tugwell declared, "and I am certainly not going to support one for Russia." "In fact," he added, "I will not be put in the position of working for known Communists. And since there are certainly a number in the headquarters organization, I will not work at all under such circumstances." After discussing "a few personalities," Tugwell noted, "I urged him to consider not only cleaning them out, but to think also of moving the headquarters to Chicago." Tugwell was to be disappointed again. Wallace did not act on any of his recommendations. The New Dealer wrote in his journal that the candidate's official reply, delivered a few days later at an appearance in Cincinnati, "was nothing new—a repetition of the Communist line."[38]

Wallace's latest attempt to tackle the Communist issue proved no more successful than his previous endeavors. Reading from prepared notes, he denied that he was a Communist and pledged that "neither the Communists nor the Fascists nor any other group will control my policies or me." "The Progressive Party is not controlled by Communists," Wallace continued, "nor was its convention or program dictated by them." He spurned the support of those who owed their "allegiance to some foreign capital first—whether it is Moscow or any other place." When asked specifically if this meant the Communists, Wallace replied, "There may be some Communists who owe first allegiance to Moscow rather than to Washington, but I don't think it's a majority." Resurrecting Glen Taylor's distinction between the American Communists who favored revolution (whose support he rejected) and those who did not, he asserted that "there is as much variation in the beliefs of Communists as in the beliefs of Democrats and Republicans." In fact, he added, "I doubt if any Marxists today are as violent as Lincoln and Jefferson were in their day."[39]

Wallace's equivocating remarks spotlighted an unattractive blend of disingenuousness and self-righteous innocence that, according to the editors of the *Nation*, had become "at once the despair of his friends and the jest of his enemies."[40] At the very time when Communists throughout Europe were scrambling to expose all manifestations of "deviationism" and decrying in the harshest terms Tito's failure to follow Moscow's lead, Wallace was insisting that there was no direct link between commitment to Communism and allegiance to the Kremlin. Such a hypothesis found few takers, even among those normally reluctant to criticize. "If Mr. Wallace has not yet heard of the Communists' famous 'democratic centralism,' which makes political differences within the party unthinkable, it is time he looked in to the matter," declared the *Nation*. More colorfully, the *Washington Post* concluded, "If Mr. Wallace had suddenly dropped from another planet, he could scarcely have spoken with more naïveté as to what is happening in the world today. . . . [He] does not recognize the policy of violence and the adherence to Moscow when the evidence is plainly before his eyes. . . . In order to justify the course he has taken, he is insulating himself in a dream world."[41] The anti-Stalinist writer Dwight Macdonald, who delighted in pointing out the recurring inconsistencies in Wallace's public statements, noted mischievously that after months of insisting that there was no real difference between the two major parties, it was odd that the candidate would now defend his acceptance of "some"

Communists' support on the grounds that CPers' views varied as widely as those of Democrats and Republicans.[42]

In later years, some historians, citing remarks such as those Wallace delivered in Cincinnati, heralded his foresight in recognizing that communism was not a monolithic movement directed from the Kremlin. To be sure, Wallace was at times more astute than some U.S. policymakers in questioning the monolithic nature of world communism. Yet, in this instance, his contemporary critics were correct to dismiss his claim that the political views of American Communists varied widely and that "the majority" had no allegiance to Moscow. The entire history of the CPUSA argues to the contrary. Moreover, in 1948, the response of the European Communist Parties to the Stalin-Tito split left little doubt as to the firm hand Moscow exercised over their leaders, particularly on matters of foreign policy. Though some have exaggerated the totality of this control, to maintain, as Wallace did, that Communists' allegiance was only to a "system of thought," rather than to Moscow's particular interpretation of this "system of thought," presents an equally distorted picture of the dynamics of communism in Europe and the United States at the time.

Wallace's comparison of the Communists to Jefferson and Lincoln was equally obtuse. In a letter to Tugwell urging him to break publicly with Wallace, Norman Thomas asked, "How can you trust a man capable . . . of such a misunderstanding, a man guilty of comparing by inference Jefferson and Lincoln with a dictator who, on coming to power, liquidated all his original associates in the Central Committee of the Communist Party who survived?" Wallace, he told Tugwell, showed "an extremely poor understanding not only of Communism but of Democracy." Yet the Cincinnati statement did clarify one matter. The remaining non-Communist Progressives who were uncomfortable with the CP's modus operandi within the third party would receive no support from their standard-bearer. In effect, Gideon had once again winnowed his ranks.[43]

The experiences of the non-Communist Progressives highlight the fundamental problem with a liberal-Communist alliance. These primarily middle-class men and women—lacking political experience but closely following current events and genuinely concerned about the outbreak of another war—had gravitated to Wallace hoping that his deep commitment to peace would allow him to win the Soviets' trust, as Franklin Roosevelt had done. Idealistic, perhaps to a fault, they also admired Wallace's refusal to participate in the seamier side of politics, convinced he would never compromise the ideals of the New Deal for political gain (as, some acknowledged, even FDR had done.) Having witnessed the Communists' mendacity, underhanded tactics, and proclivity for manipulation both in Philadelphia and within the various state organizations, however, their confidence had begun to erode. As they waited in vain for Wallace to condemn such behavior and distance the Progressive Party from the Communists, they gradually came to see their hero both as less idealistic and as less independent. Wallace's refusal to take such steps undoubtedly weakened his party, though the Communists themselves played an even more significant role. For all their self-deluding rhetoric regarding the "great people's movement," the Communists undermined at every turn any chance that the Progressives would become the kind of "third force" that Wallace, Tugwell, and others envisioned. Their sectarian behavior destroyed the fledgling Progressive Party at the local, state, and national levels, leaving those who expressed views that dissented from the Cold War consensus with no organized forum to do so. Such men and women found themselves silenced and marginalized—not only by "red-baiters," as many scholarly accounts have emphasized, but by the Communists who paid them little respect, caused them endless anguish, and cost them their credibility.

TOO DAMNED LONG
IN THE WOODS TO BE FOOLED
BY WEASELS

Youth, Labor, Spies, and the Post-Convention Campaign

Though the quarrels within state and local party organizations raised some concern, the national leaders of the Progressive Party focused primarily on mobilizing two core constituencies—youth and organized labor—as they prepared for the fall campaign. From the outset, the Wallace crusade had demonstrated a special appeal to young people. Not surprisingly, the candidate's outspoken plea for peace resonated with those who would be called on to fight the next war. College campuses provided fertile ground for recruiting supporters and often served as the launching point for establishing new local Wallace organizations. By late spring, "Students for Wallace" claimed five hundred members at the University of Chicago, six hundred at the University of California, Berkeley, and active chapters at Harvard, the University of Michigan, and the University of North Carolina.[1] Winning over the next generation of liberals, Progressives realized, would be crucial to securing the party's long-term fortunes.

Similarly, Wallace's supporters concurred with most political analysts that any sustainable third party movement would have to be built on the foundation of organized labor. That the leadership of the nation's largest labor federations—the AFL, the CIO, and the Railroad Brotherhoods—had officially repudiated the third party was regrettable, but no reason to despair. The rank-and-file workers, Progressives convinced themselves, were "ready" for their own party, and, when given the choice, they would abandon their leaders and cast their lot with Henry Wallace. The makeup of the convention delegations indicated the importance the party assigned to youth and labor—60 percent of those in attendance were under forty while 35 percent belonged to a union.[2] Both groups also held special caucuses in Philadelphia to plan strategy and rally the troops. Yet as they dispersed amid great fanfare, serious doubts remained as to whether Wallace's support within these voting blocs was as strong as Progressive partisans claimed.

■ To coordinate the efforts of Wallace supporters under the age of thirty-five, national headquarters authorized the creation of the Young Progressives of America (YPA). Though closely affiliated with the third party campaign, the YPA remained an independent entity, ostensibly to ensure that its members would not be relegated to menial roles in the larger operation— the fate that usually befell the "youth divisions" of the major parties. Instead, YPAers would have their own vehicle with their own leaders and committees to run as they saw fit. Some critics of the third party claimed that the YPA's technical autonomy from the Progressive Party gave the Communists a freer hand in using the organization as a "transmission belt" for enlisting young people into the CP. They noted that no sooner had *Political Affairs*, the Communist Party's theoretical organ, called for the formation of a "non-Party center for the Marxist training and education of the anti-fascist democratic youth of America" than the Progressive Party headquarters in New York initiated the organization of a pro-Wallace youth movement. Fueling such suspicions was the appointment of Seymour Linfield, a longtime CP member, as head of the new group.[3]

The inaugural convention of the Young Progressives of America opened immediately after the Progressive national convention had adjourned. More than two thousand delegates and observers met at the Broadwood Hotel to elect officers, adopt a program, and discuss the issues of greatest concern to young voters.[4] The proceedings began on a theatrical note. As the delegates sat in total darkness in the main ballroom, an offstage voice spoke dramatically to the assembly about the need for a new youth organization. Suddenly, a spotlight focused on a woman in the crowd who stepped to the stage microphone and began to read the official call to the convention. When she had finished, the lights came on and a man appeared on the platform to ask for nominations for chair of the opening session. Someone already standing at the floor microphone proposed

Christine Walker. The man asked for further nominations, but those who shouted out other names were unable to make themselves heard. "I am going to close nominations," he said. "All those in favor of Christine Walker please signify by saying 'aye.'" Duly elected over a few scattered "nays," Walker appeared before the delegates. As it happened, she was the same woman who had read the convention call. Such "scripted spontaneity" would set the tone for the rest of the gathering.[5]

The new chair, a national vice president of the United Office and Professional Workers Association, moved rapidly through the agenda. The group unanimously adopted the name "Young Progressives of America" and accepted without discussion convention rules suggested by the resident committee that had handled all the preliminary planning. The committee's chair was Seymour Linfield. Turning to the appointment of the convention's working committees, Linfield announced that certain (unnamed) "industrial" states would have three members per committee, while all other states would have two. So far, however, only the industrial states had chosen their nominees. Those states that had not picked representatives were to submit the names to a designated staff person within the hour. Linfield then read aloud the list of committee members already appointed—most of whom hailed from New York, Philadelphia, Chicago, and Los Angeles—and moved for approval of the guidelines as proposed.

For some, the proceedings already seemed a bit too slick, and, unlike in the main convention, the non-Communist delegates seemed better organized. Before a vote could be taken, an angry Minnesotan rose to decry the underrepresentation of rural youth. He inquired why some states had received extra slots and who had made the decision to apportion them in such a manner. Moreover, he pointed out, his state delegation had never been told to select committee nominees and the deadline would pass before it would have time to caucus. "Making changes now would be very inadvisable," Linfield informed him, offering no further explanation. Walker then recognized a Bronx high school student who complained that there were no teenagers on any of the committees. "We're not going to be treated like a lot of stepsisters," he exclaimed.[6] The youngster received a considerable round of applause—but no response to his objection. By this time, the aisles were overflowing with shouting delegates demanding recognition. Amid the clamor, a man away from the floor microphone moved that no further discussion be permitted. The chair quickly called for a vote on the motion, despite cries of protest and "point of order" from the floor. Relenting, Walker granted a point of information to a member of the Massachusetts contingent. When, he asked sharply, had the state caucuses that selected the various committee representatives been held? No one had consulted him. Would it be possible to substitute the state's nominees that Linfield had proposed with "more desirable" personnel? Again, no answer was forthcoming, as the chair bypassed the vote to end debate and simply put Linfield's proposal to a voice vote.

The outcome was not decisive; nor was the follow-up hand vote. Nonetheless, Walker declared that the original system of representation had been approved. "All hell broke loose on the floor," reported an observer. "One group began to chant 'roll call,' 'roll call,' while another chanted 'We want Wallace,' 'We want Wallace.'" Cries of "railroading" resounded throughout the ballroom. From the stage, the chair declared that the point had been decided and that Henry Wallace and Glen Taylor were waiting in the wings to address the assembly. "Let them wait!" several delegates shouted, "We want to speak!" Walker, who was proving a skilled parliamentarian, abruptly set aside a compromise motion to continue the debate after the candidates had finished their speeches. As the delegates persisted in their demand, someone switched off the lights and the aisles were ordered cleared. In the darkness, an off-stage voice introduced Taylor, while the ushers escorted from the building twenty delegates whom convention officials characterized as "outsiders only here to cause trouble."[7]

With the lights back on, the Idaho senator launched into one of his signature vaudevillian productions, which immediately diffused the lingering tension in the room. "It's awfully nice to be in a respectable company where everyone bows to you," he said, bowing to his hosts, "instead of giving you this," whereupon he put his thumb to his nose and wiggled his fingers. The crowd howled its approval. Before giving way to Wallace, Taylor took up his guitar and serenaded the audience with a stirring version of "The Isle of Capri," a bawdy number about a man who went swimming with a naked woman, and, after meeting up unexpectedly with her irate husband, "left my teeth on the Isle of Capri." The performance brought down the house.[8]

Wallace took the stage to even more frenetic applause. "How you people can keep this up, I don't know," he declared, smiling broadly. "I'm reveling in your spirit. It means so much to me, this contagious, mounting enthusiasm."[9] While delivering his brief, impromptu remarks, Wallace appeared nearly overcome by the adulation he was receiving. "As he spoke to the youth group he seemed more joyous and self-confident that at any other time in the New Party convention," one reporter observed. Claiming that polls showed that the "bulk" of the nation's youth supported the Progressive Party, Wallace assured his audience, "the party really belongs to the future." As he departed the ballroom, few who witnessed the candidate's performance questioned his sincere belief that he was presiding over the birth of a mass movement.[10]

The next day, the Young Progressives reassembled at Convention Hall to establish the rules of their new organization, elect officers, and adopt a program. Only five hundred of the original two thousand delegates were present. After a morning of panel sessions, the passage of several resolutions, and an address by the New York congressman Leo Isacson— introduced by the chair as "comrade Isacson" in a curious slip of the tongue—discussion of the rules began almost three hours behind schedule.[11] Once again, the conclave got bogged down in parliamentary confusion as various delegates offered conflicting motions to continue and limit debate. Some grew suspicious of the reliance on voice votes, insisting that the "observers" be seated separately from the delegates and proposing— unsuccessfully—that all questions be decided by a show of hands. Ultimately, however, the chair shut down debate and the convention adopted the originally proposed rules. Walker then presented a preselected single slate of candidates for the members to "elect" as officers of the organization. Questions about how the officers had been chosen and who had done so went unanswered. By the time the delegates had approved the list and turned their attention to discussing the proposed YPA platform, however, Walker announced that the rental agreement had expired and that the meeting would have to adjourn, or the YPA would have to begin paying an hourly fee of nearly $2,000 for use of the hall. Without hearing the report of the platform committee, or even voting on a platform, the convention agreed to allow the national board to act as its surrogate and left to it all unfinished business.[12]

As the delegates dispersed, even sympathetic observers acknowledged that the YPA convention "left an impression far from inspiring." More critically, Lewis Coser and Irving Howe later characterized the meeting as a "curious blend of techniques from Madison Avenue, Nuremberg party congresses, Stalinist machine politics, and American hill-billy." "No impartial observer could walk away from the meeting and say that the group was not dominated by a Communist minority," a Students for Democratic Action (SDA) report concluded. The anti-Wallace SDA hardly qualified as "an impartial observer," but its assessment could not easily be dismissed. Other observers familiar with the individuals in the YPA leadership identified numerous key members as known or concealed Communists. Even more so than the national convention, this young people's postscript had been run by a small group of self-appointed "leaders" from the Progressive

Party's far left wing, nearly all of whom were veterans of either the Young Communist League or its wartime reincarnation, American Youth for Democracy. Reprising the strategy of deception they had pursued to gain control of the American Student Union and the American Youth Congress (AYC) during the 1930s, the CPers misrepresented their ideological commitments and concealed their political affiliations to attract non-Communist liberals who would help create the impression of a "broad people's movement."[13]

The masquerade did not work as well this time. Eleanor Roosevelt, who had been taken in by such methods ten years before, wrote in "My Day," her newspaper column, that "Mr. Wallace should really take a good look at those who controlled his convention, both in his own age group and among the younger ones." "By working with the youth movement in the early days of the depression," the former first lady told a colleague, "I learned to understand Communist tactics and what their discipline is. . . . I wish Mr. Wallace had had some of the same experiences." Mrs. Roosevelt renewed her warning to Wallace in a later column when she noted that the American Labor Party, Wallace's political organization in New York, had just hired Joseph Cadden as the executive director of the Bronx County party. While working closely with the first lady in the American Youth Congress, Cadden, a concealed Communist, had repeatedly denied to her any affiliation with the CP. Unaware that she had been misled, Roosevelt told the *New York Times* in 1939 that she was "well acquainted" with Cadden and that he had no ties to the Communist Party. Only later did she discover that Cadden (and many other AYC leaders) had lied to her. Ironically, Cadden's appointment came one day before Wallace's attempt to distance himself from the Communists at a post-convention press conference in Cincinnati.[14]

■ Most young liberal activists shared the former first lady's skepticism. The YPA, despite launching a vigorous drive for new members, never gained a significant following outside of New York City and a few other urban areas where the Communists had pockets of support. Among working-class youth, the group made little headway, despite its focus on local, "bread and butter" issues. One activist spent the last six weeks of the campaign in Chicago trying to organize "trade union youth" into the Wallace movement. "Our success in this field was very limited," she recalled. "In Chicago, as throughout the country, we could not make any significant breakthrough." The Young Progressives' bold stands against segregation in parks, swimming pools, and other recreational areas did win them scattered support from African Americans in Baltimore, Pittsburgh, and Chicago, some of whom would later make a name for themselves in mainstream politics. Among YPA members in Chicago were students from Roosevelt College such as Gus Savage, a future congressman, and the future Chicago mayor Harold Washington. Despite the Young Progressives' courage and sincerity, however, they at times chose their battles unwisely, thereby undermining other liberal youth groups' efforts to fight discrimination. Often their confrontational tactics lost them potential allies, and, accordingly, their attempts to increase their community influence fell far short of expectations. Ultimately, the YPA's appeal—beyond that to young members of the Communist Party—remained limited to a small segment of left-leaning college students.[15]

The temperament of these "campus radicals" may partially explain the organization's failure to broaden its base. Dorothy Thompson described the young Wallace partisans as "the 'intellectual' type of know-it-all which manages to get itself heartily disliked by its contemporary comrades, and thus [is] pushed off into an isolated clique." Though uncharitable, Thompson's characterization was not as far off the mark as indignant YPAers claimed.[16] On the increasingly conservative postwar campus, the young Progressives did sound a discordant note. Karl Schmidt, a YPA leader at Colgate University, found among the student body "general apathy over the possibility of future war or depression and a much greater concern over immediate job prospects." Campus Progressives, on the other hand, set their sights on abolishing global injustice. "These young folks want to remake the world entirely, and in a hurry," observed Tom O'Connor of the *New York Star*. "Strike up a conversation and you get a lecture . . . on what's wrong with the world and what ought to be done about it, right away."[17] Grimly determined in political style and sentiment, these earnest crusaders often found that their own lack of humor made them the butt of their fellow students' jokes. Frequently, Wallace rallies on campus deteriorated into raucous shouting matches in which a small group of Progressives fended off the jeers of their classmates. In one of the more elaborate anti-Wallace demonstrations, several students from the University of Pittsburgh decided to "ridicule the ridiculous." Amid shouts of "Comrades! On to Helsinki!" a group of young men—one sporting a paint-on "Stalin-style" mustache and clad in red underwear and a red-and-white blazer—handed out leaflets urging their colleagues to attend that day's Young Progressives meeting and give the Wallaceites "the royal razzberry."[18]

The YPAers' fervor often proved alienating as well as entertaining. Their dedication to Wallace seemed almost fanatical to outsiders, more an emotional outburst than a reasoned political position. Not particularly skilled in the art of diplomacy, the Young Progressives demonstrated little tolerance for those who did not share their devotion. Their politics slipped into what the historian Richard J. Ellis has called "the prophetic mode"—"awakening people to an a priori truth, rather than a process of mutual persuasion and accommodation during which both sides adjust their views and learn from rival arguments."[19] Much like Wallace himself, many young Progressives were quick to charge venality. "They are animated by a refusal to admit the possibility of honest disagreement," lamented the liberal writer Vincent Sheean, who had tried to engage some of them in honest debate. "They . . . assert that anybody who holds opposing views is evil and corrupt, 'bought by the interests.'" This frame of mind, Sheean feared, did not bode well for democracy. By charging all who worked for the government with "crimes of malfeasance and corruption," and insisting that "those who disagree are scoundrels," this small section of American youth—a minority of a minority—could easily draw the conclusion that "the general will has no merit at all, but is a mere fabrication on the part of sinister and secret wills which control the electorate." When a citizen comes to this conviction, Sheean asked, "Does he not develop an ill-will toward the majority, since he cannot even concede its right to be a majority?" Editors of newspapers and magazines reported receiving a torrent of letters from young Wallace partisans who took exception to their criticism of the Progressive Party. Left-liberal publications including the *Nation*, *Progressive*, *PM*, and, later, the *New York Star* bore the brunt of this attack. "I have seen nothing like it in my eight years of editing the *Progressive*," Morris Rubin wrote to a colleague. "Too many of the letters, and especially the anonymous ones, are explosively bitter and almost morbidly vindictive. The word 'traitor' seems to turn up more often than any other." In responding to one irate correspondent, Rubin recounted, "I tried to suggest in my amiable way that it was possible that there might be an honest difference of opinion among sincere men without either side being guilty of intellectual, political, or religious treason, but this got me nowhere. I was either for Wallace, I was told off, or for Satan (who runs on all the other tickets under different names). What throws me into a bit of a tantrum about three times a week," he added, "is the cool refusal of the letter-writers to argue the issues." When Rubin penned another lengthy reply to a disgruntled Wallace supporter explaining point by point where and why he differed with the third party, he received back a scrawled note declaring only, "Jesus was misunderstood and crucified too." As the journalist Murray Kempton would remark in describing an earlier generation of radicals, many YPAers were "so full of faith and hope as to leave small room for charity."[20]

Not all young Progressives, of course, fit the mold of headstrong zealot. Particularly in its early days, before it developed into a third party, the Wallace movement attracted a wide assortment of idealistic students from across the political spectrum. To a far greater extent than the other party organizations, those around Wallace recognized youth as an untapped resource. Progressive Party leaders offered young people the chance to participate in the electoral process on equal terms with their elders. Many students drawn to politics eagerly accepted the opportunity. "Oh, the Democrats or Republicans won't let you do anything," one Missouri college student explained. "We've got a part in this. The other parties don't want us. [The Wallace group] came out to the University and asked us." Indeed, at its height, the YPA claimed more than ten thousand members, making it the largest left-wing campus group in the nation.[21] The party also tailored its message to appeal to youth. Wallace's promise to restore world peace reassured young people frightened by the constant talk of war and by the prospect of being on the front lines of the battlefield. The draft, YPA literature emphasized repeatedly, was at the heart of the "bipartisan war plans," so young men had a personal stake in opposing the administration's "get tough" foreign policy. Similarly, the candidate's commitment to sweeping domestic reforms fired the imaginations of a new cohort of would-be liberal crusaders. Wallace himself was held up as a hero to the young. The Progressives' public relations machine carefully crafted an image of the former vice president as a selfless maverick devoted to principle and moral righteousness, portraying Wallace as a savior to young people frustrated by the "pork chop" politics of the traditional parties. For some young people, the Wallace "cause," vaguely defined but passionately defended, took on far more significance than simply another political campaign. In a sense, the Progressive Party was out to win souls, not votes. If at times YPA members expressed uncertainty about their more militant colleagues' unorthodox tactics and long-term objectives, many non-Communist YPAers nonetheless remained loyal to the Progressive Party as their only hope for the future.[22]

In the end, however, the Young Progressives did not succeed in launching a new mass movement. Their unpopularity even among student activists testified to this failure. At a meeting of the National Student Association (NSA) in late August, YPAers distributing Wallace literature received a cold shoulder from the delegates who resented their injection of partisan politics into an explicitly nonpartisan organization. The Progressives' protracted campaign for NSA affiliation with the Prague-based International Union of Students (IUS) also raised suspicions that the YPA was out to use the organization as a forum for disseminating Communist propaganda. The NSA had dropped its attempt to join the IUS when that organization failed to protest the Czech government's use of force against student demonstrators during the Communist Party's consolidation of power in late February. Most non-Communists in the NSA considered this reopening of the issue an unwanted intrusion. "We had a lot of trouble with this bunch last year," said NSA president William Welsh. "We expect more now because they have professional advice and organization from the Wallaceites. . . . If the Progressive want a showdown we're ready to give them one," he declared. Rising to the challenge, YPAers at the meeting focused almost exclusively on securing approval for an affiliation with the Communist-backed IUS, which most delegates considered a tangential matter at best. Such sectarian behavior, accompanied by obviously disingenuous accusations of "red-baiting" when other delegates questioned their motives, won the young Progressives few friends. During the five-day congress, the NSA rejected the YPA position on every issue, including affiliation with the IUS.[23]

Though their obtuse insistence on toeing the Communist Party line undoubtedly hurt the Young Progressives in this instance, they remained on the political fringes more so because most young people simply did not share their views. On the key issue of universal military training, 80 percent of twenty-one to twenty-nine-year-olds favored a year of mandatory service in the armed forces, while the YPA put the defeat of such a proposal at the top of its agenda. Similarly, polls showed widespread support for the draft and the Marshall Plan, in stark contrast to the YPA's ardent opposition.[24] Moreover, few young Americans endorsed the Progressives' fundamental premise that the United States was solely responsible for current Cold War tensions. Even radicals like the socialist Sidney Lens rejected such an extreme formulation, maintaining that it gave the Progressive Party "the image . . . of being an unquestioning parrot for the foreign policy of the Soviet Union."

The dogmatic "vanguardism" of the party's Communist minority also took its toll. Initially, Lens and his friend Charles Chiakulas, a young organizer for the United Auto Workers in Chicago, considered joining the Progressive Party. Both believed in the need for a new, independent labor party. After a lengthy discussion, Lens recalled, "we concluded that it would be useless. The communists, who dominated the Progressive Party, would never allow anyone to play a role without controlling them, and neither Charlie nor I would submit to being manipulated like puppets." Lawrence Scott, a well-known peace activist during the 1950s and 1960s, also abandoned the Progressives when he witnessed firsthand the inflexibility of the Communists at the July convention. His experience in Philadelphia, Scott later wrote, led him to search for a less absolutist form of political action. Unable to attract the support of young Americans in the political mainstream and unwilling to accommodate the independent-mindedness of potentially receptive radicals, the YPA did not long survive the November election—another clear indication that the Popular Front strategy had played itself out.[25]

■ The Progressives launched an even more intense effort to establish a presence within organized labor. To do this, they realized that the party would have to bypass union leadership and appeal directly to the rank and file. Russell Nixon, a Harvard Ph.D. "on loan" to the campaign from the United Electrical Workers union, spearheaded this effort as the executive secretary of the National Labor for Wallace Committee. Working with lower-level union officials sympathetic to the third party, Nixon set out in April to establish a network of shop-floor committees, hoping to bypass the international union leadership and to lay the foundation for what the Communists called a "united front from below." At a pre-convention meeting in Philadelphia's Convention Hall, nearly one thousand Wallace supporters from the labor movement gathered to report on their progress.

Albert J. Fitzgerald, the president of the United Electrical Workers union and the chairman of the Progressive Party's National Labor committee, opened the gathering with a dramatic announcement: "I have been reliably informed that a secret meeting was held last night for the express purpose of organizing certain labor groups in this city to enter this hall and disrupt this rank and file labor meeting. We have informed the police and have been provided with ample protection against any contemplated violence." The alleged "secret meeting" was in fact an open meeting of CIO steelworkers who had gathered to discuss whether they should send a representative to the Wallace labor rally to present the views of their union president, Philip Murray. The following evening, the assigned spokesperson arrived at Convention Hall shortly after Fitzgerald had issued his warning. Though the labor group was holding an open meeting, the sergeant at arms refused to admit him as an observer and asked that three police officers be stationed at the door to keep the lone "disrupter" from entering. "I guess I'm the riot threat," the lone steelworker told reporters. "This is typical of left-wing tactics," he complained. "Fitzgerald will probably announce that there are 1000 men out in the halls waiting to break up the meeting." He then added defiantly, "It would not have been any trouble to do just that."[26]

Safe inside, the delegates heard a series of speakers hail the "broad rank and file character" of the party's labor support and condemn such anti-Wallace union leaders as Philip Murray, AFL president William Green, and A. Philip Randolph, head of the Pullman porters union. Observers noted that the boos and hisses that greeted the mention of such names were even more intense than those directed at the National Association of Manufacturers and Republican nominee Thomas Dewey. In his report, Nixon told the assembly that more than three thousand shop committees for Wallace were already up and running. The labor committee itself had more than one thousand members representing nearly one hundred unions from the AFL, CIO, and Railroad Brotherhoods. He asserted that this "grass roots" support extended beyond pro-Soviet unions such as the United Electrical Workers to include a considerable presence within the powerful United Auto Workers and Murray's own United Steelworkers. Before adjourning, the group passed a resolution urging all unionists not to "waste" their vote on the "imaginary lesser evil . . . of one of the Wall Street parties," but to "join with us in building labor's own party."[27]

Despite such public bravado, union members supporting the Progressive Party understood that they faced an uphill battle. Though many workers expressed little enthusiasm for President Truman, particularly in the months before the Democratic convention, this inchoate dissatisfaction had not evolved into pro-Wallace sentiment, let alone the radical awakening the Communists and their allies confidently predicted. Indeed, as Michael Quill, the head of the Transport Workers Union (TWU) had discovered during his visits to various locals throughout the country, even workers in unions affiliated with the CIO's pro-Soviet faction balked at supporting Wallace, often demanding the removal from their districts of those officials who personally endorsed him. In late July, eleven hundred TWU American Airlines workers in Tulsa voted unanimously to renounce the Progressive Party. Only at Quill's insistence did they agree to retain their pro-Wallace International representative. When several Communist organizers in Miami tried to commit the TWU's Local 500 to the Wallace campaign without consulting the membership, only Quill's timely mediation staved off a rank-and-file rebellion. Similarly, in Omaha, Jack Cassidy, a member of the TWU's International Executive Board, resigned his position as chairman of the Nebraska Wallace-for-President Committee under pressure from the anti-Wallace rank and file. Overall, Quill estimated that

85 percent of the TWU membership opposed Wallace's presidential bid.[28] When the union's International Executive Board convened in early September, it intended to bypass the Wallace issue, but Quill mischievously introduced a resolution to endorse the third party candidate to "smoke out" the board's pro-Soviet members. "I wanted to put the boys on the spot," he explained with a grin. "They sang for Wallace for three days in Philadelphia and I wanted to see if they would vote for him. They're afraid to do so because they know the membership would cut their throats." Though the board defiantly repudiated Quill's support for Truman, it wisely tabled his resolution and made no move to endorse Wallace.[29]

Likewise, James Matles, the director of organization for the United Electrical Workers (UE), reported that UE's members "weren't so much pro-Truman as they were anti-Wallace." When he, Albert Fitzgerald, and the union's secretary-treasurer Julius Emspak embarked on a twenty-city tour to gauge support for the leadership's position on Wallace and other issues, they often found their reception to be less than warm. Workers in St. Louis, Erie, and Bridgeport flatly rejected the trio's pitch for the Progressive Party. Even Fitzgerald's own local in Lynn, Massachusetts, would not stand by his personal endorsement of Wallace.[30] The Wallaceites' often overbearing behavior also angered the UE rank and file. When third party activists set up shop in the union hall of Local 768 in Dayton, Ohio, irate members took matters into their own hands. "We had to bodily throw them out," recalled "Oakie" Wornstaff, the local's president. "We were paying their telephone bills, advertising bills, and everything else. So three of us laid off from work one day and bodily threw them out of our local union."[31] In East Pittsburgh, UE officers stumped actively for Wallace, only to provoke a record turnout for Truman among the heavily Catholic workers. In this center of UE strength, the president bettered Roosevelt's 1944 total by 25 percent.[32]

Communists and their allies in other pro-Soviet unions faced similar hostility when they encouraged support for the Progressives. As the Wallace campaign shifted into high gear, many workers complained that political activities had taken undue precedence over more pressing economic issues. In Alabama, the Mine, Mill, and Smelters Union rank and file accused their leadership of neglecting union business and failing to settle grievances. The Wage Policy Committee, they claimed, did nothing in 1948 besides endorse Wallace. Polls showing the Wallace-Taylor ticket garnering barely 10 percent of the CIO vote also confirmed the third party's scant support among members of what was considered the most progressive of the nation's labor federations.[33]

■ Throughout the summer, as the national CIO stepped up its efforts to discredit the Progressive Party, pro-Wallace unionists faced one setback after another. The United Packinghouse Workers of America (UPWA), vocal advocates for a third party since mid-1947, abruptly backed away from this position at their June convention. Wallace's public support of the UPWA during its strike in Chicago during the spring of 1948 had gained him many admirers in the union, and Progressives expected to receive a substantial vote from the rank and file in November. Nonetheless, UPWA leaders feared that direct defiance of Murray's orders to oppose Wallace would strengthen the hand of its increasingly aggressive anticommunist faction and perhaps lead to the ouster of President Ralph Helstein and the union's Communists. The convention's resolutions committee therefore withdrew a motion that would "neither endorse nor condemn the Third Party" and instead advised the delegates to accept the national CIO policy. The International made no attempt at enforcement, allowing those who were active in the third party campaign to continue their work for the Progressives, but, to the Wallace camp's dismay, the union did nothing to aid or encourage these workers' efforts. Unlike in other unions, however, the UPWA membership did not repudiate the Communists and their allies in the union's leadership. The anticommunist faction failed in its attempt to win control of the union because the majority of the workers—many of them African American—expressed satisfaction with the leadership's defense of their interests on the shop floor and its dedication to civil rights, even though they expressed little interest in left-wing political ideology. Still, even though they retained control, the UPWA Communists had to face the grim reality that they did so only by downplaying the CP agenda— a tactic that closely resembled the "Browderite" heresy they were supposed to be struggling against.[34]

On July 25, Joseph Curran's sweeping victory in the National Maritime Union (NMU) elections ended any Progressive hopes for an NMU endorsement. In a record turnout, Curran outpolled a pro-Communist opponent by more than three to one, a better showing that even his most ardent supporters had expected. His slate won all thirty-two posts in the NMU national council, as even the port of New York, a Communist stronghold, shifted to anticommunist control. A longtime ally of the CP, Curran had initially turned against the Communists for reasons unrelated to the third party campaign. After his defection, he had joined the CIO majority in opposing Wallace. With Curran's anticommunist faction now in control of the union bureaucracy, the Progressives could expect little organized support from workers on the waterfront.[35] Harry Bridges's longshoremen's union, whose political machine had provided crucial support for Wallace during California's petition drive, also played only a desultory role in the subsequent campaign. Preoccupied by a lengthy strike at the port of San Francisco during the fall, Bridges delivered but one speech on Wallace's behalf and made no attempt to secure an ILWU endorsement for the Progressive Party.[36]

Progressive activists working through CIO Industrial Union Councils (IUC) and local Political Action Committees also made little headway with union members.[37] In Wallace's home state of Iowa, delegates to the state IUC convention changed their constitution to allow for annual elections and then voted out their pro-Wallace officers. In a second referendum, they rejected the Progressive Party and pledged support to the national policy of the CIO-PAC. The same month, 2,800 steelworkers withdrew from the Duluth IUC because of that council's pro-Wallace stance, while at a meeting in Wisconsin, the state CIO-PAC expelled seven of its executive board members for "misinforming union members about the Progressive Party." The 232 assembled delegates then unanimously passed resolutions condemning the third party and the "so-called labor leaders" in Wisconsin who supported its "rule or ruin program." By early August, CIO headquarters reported that more than 93 percent of its four hundred IUCs were following national policy.[38]

Even in the IUCs where the Communists and their allies were firmly entrenched, securing a Wallace endorsement proved nearly impossible. Generally, a statement of political neutrality was the best the pro-Soviet leadership could manage. And, given the intensity with which the national CIO was enforcing compliance with its anti-Wallace position, even this carried risks. When the Greater Detroit and Wayne County Council passed such a resolution, Michigan CIO leaders immediately pressured the IUC to reverse itself and repudiate the third party. When the IUC officers refused to do so, a group headed by Walter Reuther, the president of the United Auto Workers, urged the national CIO to remove the council's pro-Soviet leadership. Philip Murray sent former Michigan CIO president Adolph Germer to investigate the situation, but Germer concluded that there was not enough dissatisfaction among the IUC's membership to justify such an extreme action. Instead, he proposed a compromise whereby unions that had disaffiliated from the council in protest against its pro-Soviet leadership would be readmitted after paying three months of back per capita taxes (rather than a year's worth of taxes, as the IUC's constitution stipulated). They would then be eligible to vote at the IUC's upcoming convention. Though the Wayne County Council officers had requested an identical arrangement from the national CIO the year before—when it served the interests of the pro-Soviet faction—they rejected Germer's formula. Their intransigence was easily explained, for if the unions in question sent delegates to the convention, there would be more than enough votes to toss out the pro-Soviet leadership.[39]

Determined to settle the dispute, the national CIO compelled the Wayne County officers to accept the compromise by threatening to take over the council if they refused to go along. At the September convention, the harried leadership employed every conceivable tactic to retain control of the IUC—including "hiding" the members of the committee charged with counting the votes so they could not present the report that would confirm the pro-Soviet group's minority status. After two days of heated factional squabbling, Germer announced that he was taking over the organization in the name of the CIO, as was his right. Defeated, the pro-Soviet leadership blasted Germer's "bureaucratic interference" but had little choice but to accept the authority of a newly constituted council that immediately passed resolutions supporting national policy.[40]

In retrospect, two of the ousted Wayne County IUC leaders, Tracy Doll and Samuel Sage, claimed that their CP allies had maneuvered them into an untenable position. Neither was a Communist—as late as 1945, Doll had been identified with the staunchly anticommunist Association of Catholic Trade Unionists—but both owed their council positions to the Communist Party. If they repudiated the CPers and followed national CIO policy, they would lose their primary base of support; but if they toed the Communist line, they risked being removed by Murray. Doll and Sage supported Wallace early in his campaign, but they later grew disillusioned when they saw "ideologists" seize control of the third party. "I could not support him under the circumstances," Sage recalled, "because I could not see splitting our forces and winning, and I felt that that was an election that we had to win and I thought we should go along with Truman." A third leader, Coleman Young, the future mayor of Detroit, stuck with the Progressives, serving as the labor director of the Auto Workers National Committee for Wallace and Taylor. Young's committee recruited several lower-echelon UAW officials, primarily those previously associated with the anti-Reuther caucus, but this backing never translated into rank-and-file support.[41]

The experience of Robert Wishart, the head of the Hennepin County (Minneapolis) IUC, also demonstrates the near impossibility of steering a middle course between the bitterly antagonistic pro-Soviet and anticommunist factions in the CIO. Wishart, a concealed Communist and a prominent figure in the Minnesota labor movement, had broken with the CP when it adopted a more militant line during the immediate postwar period. Yet he did not defect to the anticommunist bloc and hoped to play the role of unifier within the IUC. Throughout the first half of 1948, Wishart took every possible step to isolate his organization from the factional strife that plagued other CIO councils, keeping the IUC neutral or inactive on all contentious political issues. By August 1948, however, he abandoned his efforts, concluding that the political platform of the pro-Soviet camp posed a greater threat to the CIO than disunity. The smear tactics of the Communists and their allies disgusted him, and the embarrassing spectacle of the Progressive convention in Philadelphia proved the straw that broke the camel's back. Wishart sided with the national CIO and procured a council endorsement for the Senate candidacy of Democrat Hubert H. Humphrey, the bête noire of the Minnesota Progressives.[42]

Equally rancorous disputes took place in the California CIO where the pro-Soviet faction controlled the state IUC as well as four county councils in the Los Angeles and San Francisco Bay areas. In response to the IUCs' refusal to follow national CIO policy, Murray decided not to revoke their charters (as was his right under the CIO constitution) but to authorize the creation of parallel organizations to mobilize California's labor vote for the Democrats. The pro-Soviet IUCs remained neutral in the presidential campaign, realizing that an outright endorsement of Wallace would likely cost them their charters.[43]

Pro-Wallace union leaders understandably emerged embittered from such confrontations. They deeply resented the national leadership's unwelcome efforts to impose political orthodoxy and portrayed themselves as the valiant guardians of autonomy and union democracy. Their critique of the national CIO's heavy-handed tactics and bureaucratic approach was not without merit, and it would win a sympathetic hearing from a later generation of historians.[44] Yet to contemporaries, their indignant protests rang hollow, particularly given that these same pro-Soviet leaders had been ardent proponents for *strengthening* the national CIO's authority only three years earlier. Again, the fluctuations of the Communist Party line, rather than trade union considerations, appeared to determine the pro-Soviet faction's position of the moment. Moreover, their desperate attempts to cling to power scarcely seemed manifestations of flourishing democracy. In most instances, the majority of the membership opposed the pro-Soviet faction's political action and foreign policy agenda, and, when given the chance, voted to reject it. Leaders retained their offices through skillful manipulations of the electoral machinery or by exploiting the indifference of less ideologically zealous members. One observer at the Wayne County IUC convention, though sharply critical of the behavior both of the national CIO representatives and of the pro-Soviet faction leaders, nonetheless concluded, "The issue in reality was just the opposite of that claimed by the Stalinists. . . . It was a case of a discredited minority, the Stalinists, seeking to keep bureaucratic control of an organization they had no political, organizational, or any other kind of right to keep, because neither their policies nor leadership were acceptable to the majority of the delegates."[45]

■ Despite such circumstances, the leadership of both the Communist and Progressive Parties still expected that pro-Soviet union leaders would launch an all-out effort to line up their members behind the third party. At first glance, it appeared likely that the Communists' "labor influentials" would deliver. They agreed with the CP's bleak assessment of the two major parties and considered independent political action the only way to revive the progressive movement and to avert a Wall Street–inspired war. They therefore accepted the necessity for a third party. Like the Communist Party theoreticians, they alleged that Truman's mistreatment of American labor—particularly his response to the railroad and coal mine strikes—was inextricably linked to the administration's "anti-Soviet" foreign policy. As Communist "internationalists," they believed that guarding the interests of the Soviet Union was synonymous with advancing the interests of workers. Any "anti-Soviet" move abroad therefore jeopardized the security of workers at home and brought the country one step closer to fascism. Since the Marshall Plan posed a threat to the USSR, it also menaced American workers; since Truman supported the Marshall Plan, he could not possibly be pro-labor and therefore had to be opposed. Such an ideologically rigid view allowed the Communists to distinguish themselves from democratic socialists and other elements on the non-Communist left that they held in contempt, but it was unlikely to get much of a hearing in the CIO, where the majority of the leadership—much less the rank and file—saw no such connection between defending the Soviet Union and the welfare of the American labor movement.[46]

In determining their position on the third party, then, CIO Communists had to choose between an ideologically "correct" and a politically practical course. Their experience in the unions had taught them the value of a pragmatic approach. Though personally committed to communism, the CP's "labor influentials" had routinely downplayed ideology within their locals in favor of economic and organizational issues. Such was the case even within the United Electrical Workers, the largest and most powerful union headed by pro-Soviet leadership. "Since the [Communist] party insisted that socialism was not an issue to be raised beyond its ranks or those of its close followers," James Weinstein has noted, "and since Communists in the CIO . . . accepted the condition that their commitment to socialism remain a private belief, the ideology of UE's leaders had little effect on the politics of the union's rank and file." The members were no more "politically conscious" than workers in other unions and therefore no more receptive to Marxist-Leninist analyses and prescriptions. As the pro-Soviet union leaders readily acknowledged, they retained their members' support only as long as they "brought home the bacon."[47] Since most members had little affinity for communist ideological formulations and political commitments, if, indeed, they even understood them, the "historical necessity" for a Wallace third party candidacy eluded workers on the shop floor. When pro-Soviet leaders tried to explain to the rank and file why they must back Wallace (if they tried at all), the membership did not accept (or follow) their leaders' sectarian logic. As one historian aptly summarized the situation, "CIO members were not convinced that their failure to secure wage increases was a consequence of a plot between Truman and Churchill to destroy the Soviet Union."[48]

Communist union leaders, then, understood the risks involved in supporting Wallace and the difficult position in which they now found themselves. A poor Progressive showing in November could undermine both the Communist Party's and their own position within the labor movement by revealing the weakness of the CIO's pro-Soviet faction. On the other hand, if Wallace did demonstrate some strength and attracted enough votes to ensure Truman's defeat, Philip Murray would surely exact retribution from the Communists for their part in electing an anti-labor Republican president—perhaps even going so far as to expel them from the CIO. Though William Z. Foster, Eugene Dennis, and other commissars from the "ninth floor" may have been ready to cut all ties with the "reactionary Wall Street–Murray forces" in favor of a new CP-led "anti-monopoly coalition," CIO Communists were not as eager to burn their bridges. Indeed, Jack Stachel, the CP's longtime authority on trade union matters, even suggested at a meeting of the National Board that the CP soften its position on Wallace to avoid a "head-on collision" with Murray and the CIO hierarchy. But such efforts proved futile. As his fellow board member Steve Nelson later recalled, "It was as if the heavens had fallen upon him. . . . Foster jumped on him, charging him with revisionism and calling him a 'Browderite.' By the end of the discussion, Stachel was in tears." Yet the "labor influentials" did not abandon pragmatic consid-erations altogether. Under intense pressure from Foster and others to produce official union endorsements for Wallace and from the national CIO to denounce him, they backed the third party personally but did not insist that their members do the same. As a result, the $1 million the Progressives anticipated from official union contributions amounted to only $9,025.[49]

The dilemma of the Communist union leaders highlighted the broader issue of whether it was possible to submit to Party discipline while still representing the interests of the non-Communist rank and file. Taking issue with an earlier generation of scholars who claimed Communist union officials could not be genuine labor leaders because they answered to the party and not to the workers, some historians have argued that party membership did not preclude anyone from being a bona fide trade union-ist and that, in fact, many of the most capable ones were Communists. Ef-fective Communist labor leaders, they maintain, could balance ideological commitment with their responsibilities as a trade unionists. Even if the two appeared in conflict, they would not sacrifice the welfare of the mem-bership for the sake of doctrinal purity. Indeed, throughout the immediate postwar period, many of the more politically sophisticated Communists in the labor movement made every attempt to apply the post-Duclos line in such a way that it served (or at least did not undermine) what they believed were the best interests of the workers. Yet it is difficult to deny that in supporting the Progressive Party, the "labor influentials" did put the CP's political agenda ahead of the welfare of their unions, just as their critics had predicted they would.[50] Bert Cochran, a longtime labor activist and critic of the Communist Party from the social democratic left, offers a thoughtful assessment of the CP labor leaders' worldview and their rea-sons for supporting Wallace. According to Cochran, "they were in the grip of the same apocalyptic specter as the party commissars, that a war crisis was at hand, and that a stand had to be made at Armageddon if all was not to be lost; that they could not compromise further if they were not to be-tray the workers' historic interest." "The tension between the Party and its union officials was a real thing," he notes, "but the international character of the Communist movement, and the reality of state power in the Soviet Union and the East European states—considered by the [CP] faction to be bastions of workers' rule and achievement—acted as a cement to hold together the faction under the hammer blows of the enemy and the weight of the social environment." Ultimately, then, "Party discipline" triumphed, and in spite of their well-founded reservations, Communist union leaders obeyed instructions and lined up behind Wallace. Those who refused to do so—most notably Michael Quill—quit the Party, concluding that devotion to the international Communist movement and devotion to their union were not necessarily one and the same.[51]

Given the combination of rank-and-file hostility and tepid support from pro-Wallace union leaders, the "tens of thousands of labor committees" that had been the subject of such swelling rhetoric simply failed to materialize. Isolated pockets of pro-Wallace feeling did exist, particularly among some African Americans in the auto, tobacco, and maritime unions, but a coordinated effort to mobilize this support on a national level never took place.[52] Nor did the workers themselves launch any spontaneous revolt against their leadership. The "united front from below," one Progressive activist lamented, had been a "pipe dream." Even Hugh Bryson, an early and ardent proponent of the Communists' third party strategy, later conceded that appealing to workers over their union leaders' heads "just couldn't be done," and that the strategy had only "further isolated the progressive people." Ultimately, Curtis MacDougall has concluded, "most of the avowed Progressives among union officials at all levels merely sat on their hands, doing little or nothing to line up their mass memberships as participants in the movement." After the July national convention, he noted, few Wallace rallies featured any significant labor participation.[53]

Those union members who did remain may also bear part of the responsibility for Wallace's waning support among labor's rank and file. As was the case with the Young Progressives, pro-Wallace unionists' penchant for inflammatory rhetoric did little to help their cause. Observers at the Philadelphia labor rally noted that the speakers not only pledged to work for the Progressive Party but also to use the Wallace labor committees as a base for regaining control of unions they had lost to anticommunist elements. "We're going to rebuild this union!" proclaimed one delegate, boldly referring to CIO president Philip Murray's own United Steelworkers. At the YPA convention, another steelworker proudly announced that many of his fellow members were rejecting Murray's counsel and supporting Wallace. Union leaders who failed to oppose "the present war program . . . must be exposed," shouted another delegate.[54] The *Daily Worker* featured various firsthand reports from union members who sharply criticized the CIO president and claimed widespread rank-and-file defections to the Wallace camp. Progressive Party leaflets even attacked Murray personally, citing his alleged "lack of fight" on behalf of the steelworkers.[55] The denunciations of Murray grew so bitter that they became an issue in Lee Pressman's congressional race in Brooklyn. The

CP functionaries running his campaign repeatedly urged Pressman to denounce Murray and his leadership of the CIO. Pressman, however, came to believe that the Communists were "just using him" to get at Murray. He refused to criticize his old boss or the CIO. This experience, Pressman later recalled, marked another step in his "ideological separation" from the Communists. Wallace appeared to have no such qualms. Speaking to a rally in Bridgeport, Connecticut shortly after the national convention, he denounced the labor leaders who supported Truman's foreign policy, declaring, "This kind of leadership means labor's destruction just as certainly as Robert Ley's leadership destroyed organized labor in Nazi Germany." Murray and others threatened to "lead the United States down the long and easy road to American fascism," he exclaimed. Given that there was no evidence of any significant rank-and-file defection from the national CIO position, such overheated rhetoric ultimately came off as more silly than threatening. "The Common Man," one reporter remarked, "apparently faced greater danger from such sinister citizens as Phil Murray and Walter Reuther than from the robber barons."[56]

For their part, pro-Wallace unionists remained blissfully unaware of the damage they were doing to themselves, savoring the opportunity to engage in colorful rhetorical flourishes and to demonstrate their militancy. Indeed, the CIO leadership was beginning to lose patience with such antics. Though it had long been subjected to savage vituperation from the Communists whenever its policies diverged from the international Soviet line, maintaining unity had remained the priority. By the fall of 1948, however, the Communists' political program so directly undermined that of the CIO that Murray concluded the pro-Soviet faction was no longer worth placating. In launching intemperate attacks on Murray and his associates, the CIO Communists were only ensuring an extremely bitter and devastating counterattack by the national CIO once the election was over.

■ Signs of trouble for the pro-Soviet faction became clear when the CIO's executive board met on August 31 to plot its political strategy for the upcoming campaign. President Murray wasted little time in denouncing the Wallaceites' attempts to sow division within labor's ranks. Just as he had predicted in January, differences over the third party had created "splits, hatreds, and prejudices" that had flowed from the highest levels down to the shop floors and now, he believed, threatened the very existence of the CIO.[57] Citing the establishment of Wallace labor committees within the various unions, Murray charged that the Progressives, and not those who opposed them, were to blame for undermining CIO unity. Notwithstanding the pro-Soviet leaders' bombastic assertions, the rank and file did not support Wallace and resented the activities of Progressive partisans who claimed to represent union members' "true sentiments." Many of these self-appointed spokesmen, Murray noted, did not even hold membership in a labor union. In the past month, he had received more than a thousand resolutions from steelworkers condemning those who had organized Wallace committees for participating in "dual activities." Across the country, workers were threatening to jump to other unions unless he took action against the pro-Wallace factions in their locals.[58] "Why be like the proverbial ostrich, and stick your heads in the sand and blind yourself to these facts?" he asked his dissenting colleagues. "The membership of the CIO unions do not want this stuff and that is reflected in the various types of division that are taking place within many of our International Unions." What other purpose could these Wallace "clubs" serve, Murray wondered, than to create "disruption and confusion?"[59]

Donald Henderson, the president of the Food and Tobacco Workers, spoke for the minority. He, too, addressed the need to preserve unity, but added that "the basis of this unity . . . must be the complete political freedom of CIO unions, units, and members to make their own election choices." "Our ranks are honestly divided on major questions of political choice, [but] such divisions must not be allowed to weaken the unity and thereby the effectiveness of the entire CIO in its collective bargaining struggle to protect and advance the welfare of [its] members," he declared. Henderson then assailed "the ever widening terror and intimidation that goes on within the ranks of labor because individuals choose to exercise their political choice." "I am very disturbed," he said, "because . . . the organized hoodlumism and organized vigilantism beginning to spread in our ranks . . . is only a hop and a skip from what . . . happened in Germany."[60]

Murray retorted that Henderson's assessment of the situation was "far-fetched" and "not altogether true." Though acknowledging that the political struggle within the CIO had produced excesses on both sides, Murray said that he had no choice but to crack down on those whom he believed were deliberately acting against the membership's best interests. It was about time, he advised, that pro-Wallace unionists abandoned their "widespread campaign of slander mongering" and recognized "the facts of life." Continued agitation for the Progressive Party would help produce a Republican victory, foreclose any chance of repealing the hated Taft-Hartley Act, and put labor at the mercy of its enemies. The CIO, he warned, could ill afford to "lose its sense of balance in a wild, unreasonable, foolhardy scramble that can only lead to inevitable defeat."[61]

On the central issue facing the board—the approval of a resolution endorsing Truman for president—nothing had changed since January. If possible, the animosities of the intervening months had left the conflicting camps even less prone to compromise. The pro-Soviet board members remained adamantly opposed to any expression of support for Truman or the Democratic Party and considered all efforts by the majority to force an endorsement a violation of union autonomy. The majority countered that supporting Truman and the Democrats offered the only realistic avenue for furthering the CIO's political program.

In a lengthy, emotionally charged exchange with Murray, Ben Gold, the head of the International Fur Workers Union and an avowed Communist, urged the CIO president not to associate himself with the president. To endorse Truman and the "bankrupt" Democratic Party, he maintained, would compromise the good name of the CIO. "The more intelligent workers . . . won't swallow it," he said. "We cannot [give] the better elements in the unions the chance to begin to doubt the CIO." Truman was a reactionary strikebreaker responsible for supporting fascist regimes in Greece, Turkey, China, and Spain. Gold pleaded with Murray to reject Truman and join with the Progressive Party in backing liberal congressmen with pro-labor records. This was the only way to achieve CIO unity at this "late hour," and Murray was the only figure with enough power and influence to rally the entire membership behind such a course.[62]

Unmoved by Gold's appeal or by his attempts at flattery, Murray quickly cut to the chase. As he saw it, despite the "supercilious proclamations" of the pro-Soviet minority, Truman's labor record was not the issue at all. Between 1938 and his death, Roosevelt, too, "was unable to get a single solitary little bit of labor legislation out of Congress." "I can remember distinctly even his discouraging any effort that might be made by the National CIO to promote legislation," Murray added. "President Roosevelt during the last few years of his life, despite his great friendship for us . . . met with exactly the same reverses. He fought; his vetoes were overridden. Truman has done the same under a more severe handicap," he concluded.

The real issue, Murray insisted, was foreign policy and the CIO Communists' fealty to the Soviet Union, and everyone in the room knew it. "Were it not for these international complications," Murray declared, "Truman would be receiving the wholehearted support of this International Board." To Murray, the situation was no different than it had been in 1940 when the Communist line had demanded opposition to Roosevelt. "There are some men sitting in this room," he continued, "who took me on . . . at that time, telling me . . . that I should not become involved in the European

War, and that I should fight Roosevelt. . . . And it might not be remiss for me to remind this Executive Board that in that year of 1940—not so very far back—some of the boys in this room who are espousing the cause of Wallace were fighting him and referring to him as a Wall Street warmonger, because his views happened to correspond with those of Roosevelt's."

Now the attacks had begun again, and, Murray confessed to Gold, he was at a loss for what to do. "You see, Ben," he said, "there just isn't any way under God's sun that I know of anyhow that that aspect of the situation can be composed, when men are so firm and so resolute either in their convictions or in their state of mind that whatever a particular foreign power has to say with respect to international situations it must forever be right, it is never wrong, and anyone who dares to voice an opinion contrary to their convictions about those matters is a Wall Streeter, a warmonger and a traitor." For his part, Murray declared, he would continue to state his convictions regardless of those who "cuss, condemn, castigate, vilify, and refer to [me] as a 'misleader of labor.'" The Communists' ritual denunciations of him in the *Daily Worker* made no difference, he claimed, "because down within the innermost recesses of my own soul I believe they are wrong, and I believe that many of them know they are wrong, but the sense of obligation to the Party is such that they cannot by any stretch of the imagination permit themselves to move one single solitary inch away from that Party line, it makes no difference whether it is for good or for evil, that conviction runs right straight down the middle of that road, and they preach it and they practice it, and through the instrumentality of their Party they seek to impose that will upon the membership of our unions."[63]

The CIO president appealed personally to Gold, his old friend, to break the impasse. "Ben, you and I can't kid each other; you know that. You and I have been too damned long in the woods to be fooled by weasels—you know what I mean. You do a little heavy thinking in this matter, too, see. There is no man on this Board for whom I have greater respect. . . . But say, Ben, move over just an inch or two, you know what I mean. I am an elastic, flexible sort of an individual. . . . I can change my mind, you know; but damn it, my difficulty with you boys, Ben, I can't get you to do that, you see, on certain of these situations, and that is the thing that runs beyond me, see, that inflexibility, that complete inflexibility of position." Gold replied that he wanted to work with Murray, but that he would not support CIO policy if it meant endorsing Truman. The final vote showed no shifts of position since January other than that of TWU head Michael Quill who had broken with the Communist Party during the spring. Indeed, the Murray-Gold exchange confirmed for CIO executives of all political stripes that the usefulness, or even the possibility, of a Popular Front in the labor movement had reached an end. Maintaining the coalition would require concessions from both sides that neither was prepared to make. The board split thirty-six to twelve and announced the CIO's support for Truman the next morning.[64]

The endorsement came as no surprise; it merely stated formally the CIO majority's assumption about how best to channel its political power. Murray and his associates in the CIO saw no other logical course. In their view, union leaders who backed the third party were deliberately sabotaging organized labor's efforts to protect itself from the onslaught of reaction. Despite the Progressives' insistence that the programs of the major parties were identical, Murray remained convinced that a Democratic victory would be in labor's best interests and therefore the CIO must coordinate all its available resources to help achieve that end. The Republican nominee Thomas Dewey's enthusiastic endorsement of the Taft-Hartley Act soon after the CIO executive board meeting only reinforced that view. That trade unionists would work, at least indirectly, to elect a party openly hostile to labor's agenda mystified Murray. He had long tolerated the exotic political beliefs of his pro-Soviet colleagues for the sake of CIO unity, but when their allegiance to such abstract doctrines threatened labor's position, he found it hard to disagree with his more vocally anticommunist colleagues—through the guise of the Progressive Party, the CIO Communists were in fact putting the interests of the Party before those of the union. "I believe the inevitable road to complete disintegration lies in a continued support of the Progressive Party," Murray told the board. Having reached that conclusion, he made it clear that it was only a matter of time before he would move against the Communists.[65]

The Progressives took the CIO endorsement in stride—further proof, they claimed, that labor officialdom had turned against the workers. They could hardly fathom Murray's behavior. Had he not been excoriating Truman on the same issues and in much the same language that they were only a year before? The president's token veto of Taft-Hartley and an outpouring of "soft speeches" seemed no grounds for a complete reversal of opinion. Murray's loyalty to the Democratic Party was misplaced, while his "sell out" to the Wall Street warmongers who had concocted the imperialist Marshall Plan was unforgivable. Those who genuinely supported the interest of the workers were obligated to lay bare such hypocrisy. Progressives held no affection for Dewey and the Republican Party, but Truman with his false promises and empty rhetoric was an even worse alternative. A vote for Wallace, they maintained, offered the only way to resist the drive toward war and fascism. Those who opposed the Progressive Party chose consciously to aid that drive.[66]

■ The weeks after the Progressive national convention also brought a series of events that further tarnished Wallace's public image and cast doubt on his benevolent view of the Soviet Union and the American Communist Party. Only five days after the convention had adjourned, the House Committee on Un-American Activities (HUAC) began its sensational "spy hearings," charging that during the Roosevelt years various government officials—most notably Alger Hiss—had been concealed Communists who betrayed their country by engaging in espionage for the Soviet Union. Citing the revelations of former agents Whittaker Chambers and Elizabeth Bentley—a decidedly unglamorous brunette the press dubbed the "blonde spy queen"—the Republican-led committee launched a bitterly partisan attack on the Truman administration for "coddling" Communists and advancing the careers of known security risks. The president, who suspected that the hearings had more to do with election-year politics than with espionage, dismissed the proceedings—ill-advisedly, as it turned out—as a "red herring."[67]

As historians now know, in 1948 the FBI did have corroborating evidence for Chambers's and Bentley's testimony in the form of decrypted Soviet intelligence cables, part of the top-secret "Venona" project initiated during World War II. Since U.S. Army intelligence officials did not wish to reveal that they had deciphered the allegedly "unbreakable" Soviet code, the evidence could not be used in court. Indeed, security around the project was so tight that it appears that President Truman himself did not have direct knowledge of Venona. The FBI forwarded to the president information contained in the cables without revealing its source. As the historians John Earl Haynes and Harvey Klehr have written, "this omission is important because Truman was mistrustful of J. Edgar Hoover, the head of the FBI, and suspected that the reports of Soviet espionage were exaggerated for political purposes. Had he been aware of Venona, and known that Soviet cables confirmed the testimony of Elizabeth Bentley and Whittaker Chambers, it is unlikely that his aides would have considered undertaking a campaign to discredit Bentley and indict Chambers for perjury. . . . There were sensible reasons for the decision to keep Venona a highly compartmentalized secret within the government. In retrospect, however, the negative consequences of this policy are glaring."[68]

For their part, the Progressives readily concurred with Truman's dismissal of the hearings, but they took their denunciations much further, again positing a conspiracy between the government and powerful financial interests to suppress civil liberties and impose fascism. "There is more involved here than the circus or sideshow," Wallace declared. "There is a whole pattern of terror and fear-making . . . [for] which the leaders of both old parties including Mr. Truman bear full responsibility. . . . The pattern is the same as that which developed in Germany in the Nineteen-Thirties." Subjecting the New Deal's most "progressive" figures to a baseless smear campaign, he insisted, marked yet another step down the road to American fascism.[69] Other Progressive spokespersons built on his analysis. False charges of spying, they argued, only masked the hearings' real objective of suppressing dissent and covering up Congress's own shameful complicity in the "acceleration of monopoly power in the United States." The House Committee on Un-American Activities, according to Carey McWilliams, a pro-Wallace journalist, was "deliberately functioning as a decoy for its real masters, the American opposite numbers for fascists Krupp and I. G. Farben."[70]

The investigation also posed more immediate problems for the Wallace campaign. Three of its prominent figures, Lee Pressman, John Abt, and speechwriter Charles Kramer, all received subpoenas to testify before HUAC. In later years, Pressman told the FBI that he had wanted to cooperate with the committee and was willing to disclose his membership during the mid-thirties in what he termed a Communist "study group." Abt and Nathan Witt, Pressman's law partner who had also been called, vigorously opposed any admissions on his part, however. Both had belonged to the same Communist group centered in the Agricultural Adjustment Administration, but they did not wish to say so publicly. Because of "things that had happened" after Pressman left Washington, they could not answer the committee's questions without putting themselves in jeopardy. They told Pressman that if he broke ranks and testified, they could end up in "a great deal of trouble if they refused to answer." "[The] discussion ended in a lengthy argument, but in the end Witt and Abt won out," Pressman recounted to the FBI.[71] All three men took the Fifth Amendment when summoned before an executive session of the Committee on August 20. A week earlier, Charles Kramer had also taken the Fifth.[72] Years later, decrypted cables from the National Security Agency's Venona project and documents found in the archives of the former Soviet Union confirmed that Abt and Kramer, both concealed Communists, had passed information to NKVD agents, and that Pressman, though he had not stolen any documents, had assisted the espionage network.[73]

Predictably, the "Progressive connection" to the spy hearings brought the party more bad publicity. Some HUAC members used the hearings to spotlight the close ties between the Wallaceites and the Communist Party, portraying the former vice president as a front man for subversives. In one such instance, Representative John Rankin of Mississippi reminded his colleagues that Pressman and Abt served on the Progressive Party staff and that Hiss had worked for Wallace in the Department of Agriculture. Rankin even urged the committee to subpoena the Progressive standard-bearer. "I suggest Henry A. Wallace . . . come before the committee and tell us why these Communists who were plotting the overthrow of the government were placed in key positions in his Department at a time when our young men were fighting and dying on every battle front in the world for the protection of this country," he intoned. Not for the first time, Rankin had garbled his facts. Wallace was not secretary of agriculture during World War II, and the individuals in question had left the department long before the United States entered the war.[74] Others recalled Wallace's earlier remarks to reporters that if he were elected president he would choose the New Dealer Harry Dexter White as his secretary of the treasury. White himself now stood accused of espionage, Wallace's critics were quick to point out.[75] In response, Progressives charged political sabotage. Claiming that the congressional investigations were explicitly designed to "frighten the people," Elmer Benson, the national chairman of the Progressive Party, asserted that "if they hadn't revived that campaign, Wallace and Taylor would have been as good as elected by now." "If it wasn't for the great campaign Wallace has put on here and abroad," he added, "we might very well be at war."[76]

Despite all the political posturing and demagoguery surrounding the hearings on all sides, public opinion polls still showed that a large majority of Americans rejected the view espoused by both Wallace and Truman that the investigations were nothing more than a "smoke screen." Seventy-nine percent of those who had followed the proceedings believed they should continue, while 74 percent agreed that "there was something to these spy investigations." Only 17 percent responded that the committee was simply "playing politics." Even among independent voters, 63 percent stated that they did not believe the inquiries were political. Such numbers suggested that the politicians had not necessarily created public concern; they were merely reflecting—and, arguably, exploiting—it. Nonetheless, Progressives countered that the polls only proved the effectiveness of widespread fear-mongering and intimidation.[77]

Wallace in particular failed to see how anyone could take the committee's accusations seriously, at times allowing his strongly held views to cloud his political judgment. Abt later recalled that after taking the Fifth

Amendment he had offered to resign as the Progressives' general counsel to save the party any further embarrassment. Wallace "would hear nothing of it," he recounted, "and dismissed the hearings with barely a shrug of his shoulders." "Looking back," Abt added, "it seems one further illustration of Wallace's impracticality as a politician. . . . Any politically sensitive and sensible political party wouldn't have retained me as a general counsel, certainly not after my HUAC appearance."[78] When Harry Dexter White died of a heart attack shortly after testifying before the committee, Wallace unleashed a blistering attack on his interrogators. White, he declared, was "killed by the House Committee on Un-American Activities . . . [with] poisonous slander, venomous rumors, with the vicious gossip of self-confessed spies." Such overwrought language rivaled that of the committee members themselves and reflected poorly on Wallace, who, at least until he began his third party campaign, had tried to cultivate the image of a man who preferred civil discussion to name-calling and invective. In later years Wallace did change his tune, observing to Glen Taylor in 1956 that "no fair minded person can laugh off the testimony of Bentley."[79]

In the midst of the spy hearings, another scandal erupted. Oksana Stepanova Kasenkina, a teacher for the children of Soviet diplomats in New York City, fled the consulate in late July and sought asylum at Reed Farm, a refuge for displaced persons run by Countess Alexandria Tolstoy. On August 5, Kasenkina wrote Yakov Lomakin, the Soviet consul general in New York, informing him that she was renouncing her Soviet citizenship and intended to stay in the United States. Unfortunately for Kasenkina, the letter revealed her hiding place. Lomakin hastened to Reed Farm to "rescue" the schoolteacher from the clutches of a gang of "White Russian bandits" and returned her safely to New York. He then staged a preposterous press conference during which he detailed Kasenkina's "kidnapping" and read carefully selected excerpts from her letter that expressed her love for her people and loyalty to her country. He also claimed the schoolteacher had urged him to "come down and take her, to help her be free." The obviously distraught woman, sitting next to Lomakin, declared that she had been "drugged" and taken against her will to Reed Farm. An angry missive from the Soviet foreign minister V. M. Molotov soon followed, charging the U.S. government with complicity in the "kidnapping" operation. Molotov's note was poorly timed, however, for by the time it reached American officials, Kasenkina had leaped from the third floor window of the Soviet consulate. "I was like a bird in a cage," she later told reporters, "I had to get out."[80]

While Kasenkina was recovering from her injuries in a local hospital—her room heavily guarded lest there be another "rescue" attempt—her dramatic story, eventually told in her own words, captivated the nation. Her husband had been liquidated during the purge of 1937 and her teenage son, in disfavor with the government because he was not active in politics, had been conscripted to serve as a storm trooper during the siege of Leningrad in 1942. He never returned from battle, but Kasenkina still hoped she might locate him through displaced person agencies in the United States, which was part of her reason for wishing to stay in America. Though the immediate circumstances differed, the Soviet teacher's desperate jump brought to mind for many the suspicious defenestration of the Czech foreign minister Jan Masaryk only six months earlier. "Masaryk died because he could not live in an enslaved land where the noble ideals of his father had become a lie and a mockery," wrote the columnist William Henry Chamberlin. "Kosenkina [sic] preferred death to returning to a land that is one vast barbed-wire concentration camp."[81]

Throughout the affair, the Soviet consulate and the *Daily Worker* continued to bluster about the growing menace of "White Guard gangsters" seeking to kidnap and brainwash Soviet citizens living abroad.[82] Yet such fanciful diversions failed to draw attention from the Soviets' use of Gestapo-like tactics on American soil. On August 20, the U.S. government charged that Lomakin had "abused" his position and "grossly violated" the proper standards of official conduct when he seized Kasenkina at Reed Farm and compelled her to lie to the American press. President Truman revoked the consul general's credentials and ordered him to leave the country. Several commentators, only half in jest, advised Lomakin to check in to Reed Farm himself, since his clumsy handling of the Kasenkina incident would doubtless result in his own liquidation on his return to Moscow.[83]

This charade-like spectacle combined with the decision of several Eastern bloc athletes to remain in London after the summer Olympics, seriously undermined Progressives' efforts to dismiss all criticism of the Soviet Union as "reactionary scare tactics." As the columnist Robert Ruark contended, the growth of anti-Russia sentiment was not a product of irrational hysteria but rooted in events. The Kasenkina affair and the athletes' defection, even more than the confusing HUAC investigations and the anticommunist riots in Berlin, offered "a poor man's rebuttal of the apologists who say the Soviets aren't so bad." He continued: "The bewildered American . . . may not know whether the pudgy spy queen, Liz Bentley, is a real menace or a neurotic fool. He may not savvy the ins or outs of the Berlin business or who said what to whom at Yalta, but all of a sudden a Russian woman . . . risks death in a dive in order to get into the hands of our police and to avoid being sent home to Papa Joe. . . . Some muscular heroes, once sprung, won't go back home. . . . This, he can believe. This is incontrovertible sense."

Kasenkina's "leap to freedom" did indeed resonate with the public. End-of-the-year news reviews listed it as one the top ten stories of 1948. One scholar has even proposed it as "a different kind of starting point for the cold war: the point at which that phenomenon became emotionally resonant for 'ordinary Americans.'" To the editors of *Time* magazine, Kasenkina's defection "nakedly revealed the bitter despair behind the glowing promises in Communism's workers' paradise" and helped dissolve "the last trace of doubt about the nature of the enemy." Rather than being "on the march," one New England journalist remarked, "it would appear that the common people in the happy lands ruled by the Communists are on the sneak, whenever they get the chance, into the regions controlled by 'monopoly capitalism.'"[84]

Wallace's close alliance with the Communists made it difficult to respond to the galvanizing events of mid-August. In several post-convention addresses he tried to stress the Progressives' independence from the CP, but his evasive language led most observers to question his grasp of the issue.[85] His muted reaction to the Kasenkina story also seemed callous, fueling speculation that the Communists were exercising editorial control over his public remarks: in one speech he awkwardly implied that the incident was yet another diversion from the real evils being perpetrated by the Truman administration.[86] Wallace's failure to protest the wholesale suppression of civil liberties in the Soviet bloc with the same fervor with which he denounced the "police-state methods" of the House Committee on Un-American Activities gave some weight to his critics' charges that the Communists were simply using him as a sounding board for Russian propaganda. Indeed, those non-Communists in the third party who did express "anti-Soviet" views were quickly called to task by their CP allies. When the chair of Women for Wallace, Elinor Gimbel, publicly condemned the Soviets' behavior toward Kasenkina—the only high-ranking Progressive to do so—she was subjected to a withering personal attack in the *Daily Worker*. The author of the piece was Elizabeth Gurley Flynn, a founding member of the American Civil Liberties Union.[87]

Yet Wallace was less a captive of the CP than of his own, increasingly rigid worldview. Perhaps more resolutely than even the Communists, he insisted that the Truman administration, if not the president himself, was deliberately leading the country toward war and fascism. Accordingly, he interpreted every event through the prism of that fundamental premise.

Conflating contingency with conspiracy, he seemed to see in each of the president's often fumbling attempts to deal with foreign and domestic problems another manifestation of the carefully laid plans of Wall Street, the "big brass," and other nefarious forces. Ironically, Wallace's nightmare scenario offered the mirror image of that advanced by his right-wing adversaries who perceived in each step taken by the Communists a diabolical plot to undermine the "American way of life." As the fall campaign opened, Wallace continued to alert his audiences to the grim fate being prepared for them. Fortified by the enthusiasm and fervor he witnessed in Philadelphia, he remained confident that his message would eventually be accepted. Though the "lukewarm liberals" may have surrendered to the sin of "lesser evilism" and backed Truman, Wallace insisted, the "common man" would not be deceived by the machinations of the "bipartisan reactionaries."

Wallace's ebullient rhetoric notwithstanding, the Progressives' fortunes were clearly on the decline by late August. The convention had effectively ended any chance for broadening the party's base, while Communist intransigence was tearing it apart at the state and local levels. The Communists had clumsily taken over the YPA at its founding, undermining the initial enthusiasm the Wallace campaign had generated among young people. Allies in the labor movement had already begun to distance themselves from Wallace, while prominent non-Communists like Rex Tugwell were also entertaining second thoughts. The Soviets had done little to live up to the benign image Wallace had painted of them, making his conciliatory approach to foreign relations appear hopelessly naive. The Progressive Party, in short, sorely needed a boost, if only to ensure that Wallace's message would continue to receive attention. The upcoming campaign swing through the Deep South offered the opportunity for just such a renaissance.

9

THIRTY YEARS TOO SOON

Gideon's Army Invades Dixie

On August 29, 1948, Henry A. Wallace boarded a plane to Norfolk, Virginia, thereby launching a weeklong, seven-state southern tour that would provide his third party crusade with many of its most dramatic moments. Wallace's decision to challenge segregation in the heart of the Jim Crow South grabbed front-page headlines throughout the country, winning the Progressive Party the most sustained media coverage it would receive during the campaign. Had it not been for President Truman's dramatic comeback, one veteran reporter later recalled, the Wallace tour would have been the biggest political story of the year.[1] Expectant Progressives' hopes ran high. Many believed that Wallace's trip would focus nationwide attention on the injustice of segregation, and, more important, unite southern working-class blacks and whites against those who exploited racial divisions to preserve their own special privilege. In the short term, they hoped that Wallace's courageous stance would win him the votes of white liberals and African Americans in the North and inspire a major voter registration drive among blacks in the South, giving the party the shot in the arm it so badly needed.

Convinced that the southern "masses" of both races constituted a natural alliance, the Wallaceites offered their party to the South as a vehicle through which the "common man" could challenge and ultimately overcome the bourbon elite that had long prevented the development of genuine democracy in Dixie. Especially in the one-party South, Progressives argued, the only realistic strategy to combat the wealthy white reactionaries' monopoly of political power was to build a New Party to represent the interests of farmers and working people. In building such a political force, they maintained, southerners of both races would come to understand that they needed each other's help to succeed. For years, segregation and the fanning of racial animosities had obstructed the progress of blacks and whites alike. But the specious barrier of racism that blocked majority rule could be overcome. Integrated political activity, using the Progressive Party as an electoral forum, could be the catalyst for sweeping change.[2] "The Wallace candidacy," Clark Foreman, the Progressive Party treasurer and a native Georgian, declared, "offers the South the greatest chance it has ever had to escape from the feudalism that has been such a curse to its people and to the rest of the country." John Coe, the state chairman of the Florida Progressive Party concurred. "We are in a movement which immeasurably transcends in importance a mere political campaign," he wrote a colleague. "We are in line with the historical development of democracy."[3] For well-born white southern liberals like Foreman and Coe, the Progressive Party was no mere protest movement; rather, it provided the instrument that allowed them to play a leading role in reshaping the South's political and economic landscape. Henry Wallace's "invasion" of Dixie, they hoped, might finally unleash the potential progressivism they were convinced existed in their region.

Several historians have taken up the theme of "latent progressivism" in the South during the immediate postwar period. They portray the failure to cultivate this force—particularly on the part of the CIO—as a "lost opportunity" to bring fundamental change to the region. Indeed, some scholars have sharply criticized the CIO leadership's reluctance to work closely with Communists in the labor unions to pursue a militant civil rights agenda. To varying degrees, they have also blamed anticommunist southern liberals for betraying the progressive ecumenism of the New Deal and for thwarting the emergence of a labor- and left-led civil rights movement.[4]

This line of reasoning has not gone unchallenged, however. Alan Draper, for one, contends that historians of the "lost opportunity" persuasion who blame union leaders for failing to build on alleged rank-and-file militancy are "blinded by romanticism" and fail to appreciate "the depth of and commitment to white supremacy" on the part of the southern white working class. Moreover, they ignore the disproportionate power of the white southern elite, a factor Robert Norrell has emphasized in his study of racial politics in Alabama. "The civil rights activism of the early 1940s," Norrell notes, "worked to reinforce the concerted effort of

Birmingham's upper class to make all whites think in racial or sectional ways—indeed, in any terms *except* class." It is therefore difficult to imagine how a militant campaign for civil rights on the part of the CIO would have improved its chances of organizing the South, especially as segregationists began to embrace popular anticommunist arguments after the war. Norrell concludes that to expect class-based politics in Alabama in the 1940s—what other scholars imply would have been possible throughout the South had the CIO pursued the correct strategy—"is perhaps to look for what could not be."[5] Indeed, rather than illustrating the potential for a left-liberal, biracial coalition in the region, Wallace's tumultuous tour through Dixie instead reveals the fragility of southern progressivism and the formidable obstacles that remained before the walls of segregation could be breached.

■ Wallace's southern expedition began in Virginia, where state law prohibited nonsegregated public meetings. The Progressives had announced at the outset of their campaign that the party's candidates would not address segregated audiences. At brief appearances before crowds in Norfolk, Suffolk, and Richmond, Wallace held true to this pledge, speaking to integrated assemblies without incident. Encouraged by his successful challenge to segregation, he remarked to reporters, "If what I saw in Virginia today . . . is any criterion of what we'll get further on, then I'll be satisfied."[6] Wallace was unaware, however, that the state Progressive committee, hoping to avoid controversy, had issued invitations to these events, thus making them "private gatherings" not subject to the law. Meeting the Progressives halfway, the local police departments had agreed not to interfere. Moreover, Wallace spoke to only relatively small and predominantly black crowds. The white "progressive masses" the party expected to attract were nowhere in sight.[7] "By comparison with the noisy cheering that generally greets Presidential candidates on tour," one reporter noted, "Mr. Wallace's movements in Virginia had something of the eerie quality of an old-fashioned silent movie in a theatre without a piano player."[8] Still, as their plane departed for traditionally "liberal" North Carolina, Wallace and his supporters assured themselves that the success of the day's planned events spoke well for the vitality of southern progressivism. "The situation is very much better than I thought it would be a month ago," Wallace commented on leaving Richmond.[9]

Unlike Virginia, the Tar Heel State had no laws forbidding integrated gatherings. Proud of their reputation for tolerance and moderation, especially on the race issue, white North Carolinians were not immune to charges that they "looked down their noses" at their presumably more "backward" neighbors in the rest of Dixie.[10] During Wallace's visit to Raleigh in June 1947, town officials upheld his right to address a nonsegregated meeting. Likewise, when the all-white Durham City Council voted on August 12 to allow a Progressive rally at the Armory, the probability of a mixed audience was not an issue.[11] As the day of Wallace's arrival approached, Mary Price, the Progressive Party's state chair proudly announced that the candidate had decided to spend an extra day in North Carolina because he was convinced that "the most progressive state in the South" could "go Progressive in November."[12]

Such high expectations, though overstated, were perhaps understandable. North Carolina boasted the South's most active Progressive organization, drawing support from a variety of sources. Members of the state chapter of the Southern Conference for Human Welfare, labor union officials, and influential figures in the African American community all held leadership positions in the party.[13] In the early days of the campaign, college students in particular rallied to the Wallace cause. Even before the formation of the third party, a small group at the University of North Carolina had established a Wallace-for-President Committee. In February, the organizers brought together more than 130 students from throughout the state for a two-day rally in Chapel Hill.[14] On August 3, the party defied expectations—and a good deal of white hostility—by successfully concluding a petition campaign to get Wallace on the ballot, collecting almost thirty thousand signatures. In the process, party canvassers registered blacks to vote in at least six counties where no African American had been on the rolls in fifty years.[15] By doing so, Progressives noted, they had taken an initial step toward building the kind of broad electoral base needed to overthrow the old political elite and its dual commitment to segregation and economic deprivation of the workers. The young black and white volunteers who sparkplugged the effort won accolades from Palmer Weber, the co-director of the Progressives' southern campaign. Their achievement, he argued, demonstrated that a biracial grassroots movement had the potential to succeed in the South.[16]

Most Tar Heel Progressive activists shared Weber's positive outlook. As they prepared for Wallace's visit, many were still basking in the glow of their hard-fought victory. In mid-August, Mary Price declared that the signing of the Wallace petition by "30,000 working men and women" would cause the "reactionary interests to shake in their shoes."[17] Party officials also anticipated that the tour would bring them even more African American support, as black voters witnessed for themselves Wallace's sincerity on the issue of civil rights and his determined opposition to seg-regation. This support, they hoped, would be both electoral and financial. In a pre-tour memo, the Progressive campaign manager, Beanie Baldwin, reminded his staff that as the "center of considerable Negro wealth," Dur-ham promised to be a promising field for fund-raising. Among Progres-sives, then, morale was high and optimism the order of the day.[18]

A closer look at the dynamics of the campaign in North Carolina, how-ever, raises doubt about how broad based it was. Years later, Junius Scales, an active participant and at the time a Communist Party member, agreed that the effort had uncovered "a marvelous wealth of radical populists" throughout the state. Still, he noted, a disproportionate amount of this work was done by concealed Communists, many of whom Palmer Weber had imported from New York and instructed to keep their Party affiliation secret. Though there were "a great many other people supporting the cam-paign in one way or another," Scales acknowledged, "the Communists were the shock troops." When canvassers encountered hostility, usually from poor whites, many of the maverick populists would fade away, leaving a small cadre of Communists and their allies to fill the vacuum. The initial presence of the native radicals, Scales believed, gave the whole campaign "a much broader appearance than it really had."[19] Nor did the success of the petition drive necessarily indicate widespread support for the Progres-sives. Party headquarters in Greensboro had advised canvassers to avoid discussion of election-related issues and to base their appeal for signatures on Wallace's right to be on the ballot.[20]

As for the ardent left-wingers from the North, another local activist recalled, "They acted somewhat like occupying troops in a foreign coun-try." Idealistic but insufferably arrogant, they posed as "deliverers" and expected to be honored as such. "It took a pretty sturdy liberal," Junius Scales later remarked, "to put up with some of the things . . . [that] the Progressive Party leaders had to take from the [Communist] Party." In-deed, at one point, exasperated locals lost their patience and persuaded many of the New York "volunteers" to go further south to "help" with the petition campaign in Georgia. Preferring their politics with a sharp ideo-logical edge and unwilling to adjust to southern mores, these zealous par-tisans likely did more to alienate prospective Progressive converts than to broaden the party's base among the small community of independent liberal voters.[21]

The biracial nature of the Progressive coalition likewise remained more a goal than a reality during the campaign. Blacks and whites worked to-gether in gathering teams and solicited signatures from both races, but they generally received a cool response from whites. The condescending attitude many of the more militant volunteers took toward white textile mill workers no doubt contributed to the antagonism they encountered. "We were like missionaries with all the faults that missionaries have," one canvasser later recalled. "It's a wonder we weren't all lynched." Although party leaders emphasized the importance of establishing a presence in white working-class areas, most volunteers preferred working in black neighborhoods, where they ran less risk of having doors slammed in their faces.[22] As a result, by early summer the Progressives had become known as "the Negro party." An internal postelection memo analyzing the party's performance concluded that "this narrowed our appeal not only among whites, but also with Negroes who feared the Progressive Party lacked enough white support to fight effectively for Negro rights."[23] In particular, the middle-class leadership of the black community remained wary of Wallace's crusade. The Durham Committee on Negro Affairs, perhaps the state's most influential African American political organization, endorsed President Truman.[24] Similarly, the president of the state NAACP, though abiding by the organization's nonpartisan policy, declared that voting for Wallace was no way to solve "the Negro problem."[25]

Organized labor in North Carolina also proved unreceptive to Progressive efforts at coalition building. In an editorial commenting on Wallace's southern tour, the *Durham Labor Journal*, a liberal and well-respected AFL weekly, maintained that "thinking men and women of organized labor cannot see hitching their wagon to the erratic star of Henry Wallace and the Progressive Party." Anthony Valentine, the president of the Textile Workers Union, accused the Progressive candidate of making promises he could not possibly fulfill. "Wallace agrees to give everything to everybody," said Valentine; "if he were elected it would only be necessary to stay home and collect your wages."[26] The state CIO leadership even accused the Progressives of undermining efforts to elect liberal, pro-labor candidates. A case in point occurred in the Democratic primary of the fifth congressional district, where the CIO-PAC backed Bob Duncan against millionaire Thurmond Chatham, the latter considered an "arch foe of labor." The Progressive Party refused to support Duncan or to work for Chatham's defeat, urging liberal voters to stay home on primary day. Progressives defended their decision by pointing out that anyone who voted in the primary would be ineligible to sign their petition to get Wallace on the ballot. Even so, union officials saw little sense in refusing to support a sympathetic candidate who had a chance of winning to back a third party that faced certain defeat and divided the liberal vote in the process. The primary results revealed that Progressive support would have made little difference. The CIO-PAC's prediction of a close contest proved overly optimistic—Duncan lost by more than two to one— revealing that the Progressives were not the only group to overestimate the "essential liberalism" of North Carolina voters. Nonetheless, labor's resentment at the Progressives' tactics did not subside. As a result, the party found itself even more isolated from those it considered its logical constituency.[27]

An unexpected bombshell from Washington also undercut the party's popularity. On July 30, Elizabeth Bentley, testifying before the House Committee on Un-American Activities, charged that during World War II Mary Price had served as a courier for the Soviet NKVD. She also noted that Price had been introduced to her as a member of the American Communist Party. Decrypted Venona cables corroborate Bentley's testimony and indicate that Price continued her underground activities until at least mid-1944, when Earl Browder informed the Soviets that he was transferring her to "political work." At the time, however, Price dismissed Bentley's allegations as "fantastic." Such sensational accusations sounded far fetched to North Carolinians who knew Price, and the local press expressed skepticism as well. Nevertheless, Bentley's testimony fueled public suspicions concerning Communist influence in the Progressive Party, and, for some, it made attacks on the party—rhetorical and otherwise—more justifiable.[28]

In the wake of the HUAC hearings Progressives not only found their recruiting efforts undermined but also saw many of their erstwhile Tar Heel supporters drift away. Some party leaders reacted angrily, claiming that "timid" liberals were simply using the spy charges against Price as an excuse for distancing themselves from the unpopular cause of civil rights. Equating refusal to support Wallace's candidacy with timidity on the issue of civil rights was a spurious argument, but one that Progressive leaders often made. Indeed, years later some former Progressives would repeat this trope, claiming that liberals who would not participate in the third party because they did not wish to work with Communists were obsessed with "red-baiting" and not sincerely committed to such issues as civil rights. Ironically, such self-righteousness may account in part for why the pro-Communist left had such difficulty winning allies in the first place. In the South of the 1940s, anyone who expressed even vaguely liberal views on the issue of race was denounced as a "red"—even if he or she explicitly denounced communism and the Communists. Southern liberals' refusal to work with the Communists is thus more easily explained by fundamental disagreements about means and ends, to say nothing of the constant sniping and vilification the Party directed at those who expressed any doubts about its "correct" course.[29]

Price herself typified the committed Communist's proclivity to lash out against an array of conspiring enemies, as her reaction to Bentley's testimony demonstrates. Declaring to reporters that the allegations against her were part of a Wall Street conspiracy, she characterized the whole episode as an "obvious effort to discredit the great new Progressive Party." "Big business has so long controlled the state and had our political life in its vest pocket," Price exclaimed, "that it will apparently go to any length to maintain that control." Targeting her was merely a ploy to "divide the liberal forces by smearing tactics, just as the people of Europe were divided to make way for Hitler's coming to power."[30] Price's insistence that nefarious "reactionary forces" were trying to silence Wallace and his supporters out of fear also revealed local Progressives' tendency to overestimate the "threat" their party posed to the established order. This rhetorical combination of arrogance and naïveté may have fortified the already converted, but it only alienated or amused everyone else. "There is no 'great new Progressive Party,'" a local columnist reminded Price, "and nobody cares enough about it or fears it enough to try and smear it." The *Greensboro Daily News* noted that she would get no help from them in foiling "a conspiracy . . . that does not exist." "Big business, which does not have 'our political life in its vest pocket,' has so far, in our judgment, gone to no length whatever to do anything about her management of the Progressive Party in these parts."[31]

Still, charges and countercharges concerning Communist influence proved less detrimental to the party than its confrontational—and at times disingenuous—approach to opposing segregation. On August 27 Price abruptly canceled the Wallace party's reservations at the Washington Duke Hotel on the grounds that it would not accommodate the black members of the entourage. At a hastily arranged press conference, she announced to reporters that the candidate would stay at the home of a well-to-do black Durham businessman. Others in the traveling party would be lodged at the Biltmore, a black hotel. This principled refusal to submit to Jim Crow was, in itself, admirable, but even some Progressive supporters believed that Price's public announcement two days before the candidate's arrival had been calculated to provoke, particularly when it came to light that she had known about the hotel's policy on segregation for some time. Southern papers also noted that on previous speaking tours, Wallace had stayed in numerous *northern* hotels that imposed the same restriction. To bring up the issue in the South, Clark Foreman later acknowledged, "made us carpetbaggers."[32]

The disagreement between Foreman and Price about travel arrangements reflected a deeper division among southern progressives. Though Foreman had long opposed segregation, he believed that reform in the South would more likely be achieved by emphasizing economic and political empowerment rather than social equality. This paralleled the beliefs of most Popular Front liberals active in the Southern Conference for Human Welfare, the organization that provided the core of Wallace's middle-class support in the South. In contrast, Price's insistence on highlighting the social issue, as well as her proclivity for dramatic gestures, seemed calculated to stir resentment at the risk of alienating potential sympathizers—an approach that comported more closely with the style of the Communists. After the election, North Carolina Progressives conceded the riskiness of such a strategy. "The weakness of our campaign on [civil rights]," an internal report suggested, "was that we allowed the issue to be placed in the form which Southern white workers find hardest to understand, that of social equality, rather than placing the main stress on economic opportunity and political rights."[33]

If Price was out for publicity, it was not long in coming. Unhappily for the Progressives, the publicity she generated was almost entirely negative. Moreover, Price's announcement enabled the southern press, inevitably hostile to any attack on segregation, to divert public attention away from Wallace's economic message to the divisive, and potentially explosive, issue of social equality. As the local papers splashed across their front pages the news that Wallace would be staying in the home of a black man, any goodwill white North Carolinians might have felt for him quickly evaporated.[34] "The manner in which . . . [Wallace's] local sponsors have managed his Durham appearance is not conducive to harmony and unity," the *Sun* warned. "Durham is being gratuitously offended on the one side and being placed on the defiant defensive on the other." Residents told northern newspaper reporters that the tobacco town was "seething with turmoil in anticipation of Mr. Wallace's arrival." "In 'Rome,'" one Durham editor observed, "Henry Wallace deliberately outraged the Romans."[35] Indeed, since the Progressives staked their fortunes in Dixie on winning support for a political and economic program based on biracial working-class unity, exacerbating racial tensions should have been the last thing they wished to do; and yet their tactics often seemed to undercut their strategy. Rather than stirring the "latent progressivism" of the common people, Wallace's widely publicized, head-on assault against segregation precipitated a backlash that mobilized the opposition.[36]

■ The first indication of this came at the Durham Armory on the night of August 29. About half an hour before Wallace's scheduled arrival, fifteen hundred people packed the house to capacity. Almost evenly divided racially and completely integrated, the crowd—minus about a hundred hecklers—seemed to be pro-Wallace. Observers found the predominantly middle-class audience "well-dressed and well-mannered." They joined the guitarist Pete Seeger in singing campaign folk songs, a staple at Progressive rallies since the July national convention. Several hundred more people, curious but less sympathetic to the Progressives, milled around outside. Among them were about thirty or so young "Dixiecrats," supporters of South Carolina governor Strom Thurmond's "fourth party," which, the *Nation*'s Robert Bendiner noted wryly, had been founded to oppose "the president's tyrannical effort to impose civil rights on a free people."[37] A free-for-all erupted when they determined to storm the building. Leading a charge down the side aisle, one picket brought his sign down on the head of a Wallace supporter. In retaliation, a young Progressive crowned a second picket with a folding chair, knocking him out cold. Another Wallaceite was stabbed five times and left bleeding on the stairs outside. In the back of the hall, fists flew wildly for twenty minutes as police and members of the National Guard drew their pistols and unslung their rifles. In the midst of the mayhem, a warning shot rang out as authorities struggled to regain control. Curiously, those not in the immediate vicinity of the near riot continued singing. The "colored" persons in particular, the *Baltimore Afro-American* reported, "seemed to be contented in sitting back and letting the 'white folks fight it out among themselves.'"[38]

Police had barely restored order when two doors flung open and a National Guardsman holding a drawn .45 caliber revolver rushed in, "looking to the right and left with the mannerisms of a trained soldier entering a building held by the enemy." Behind him was Henry Wallace, smiling broadly and apparently unfazed by the tumult. Greeted with equally loud cheers and jeers, Wallace approached the microphone and addressed the boisterous assembly. "This is the most unique introduction I have ever experienced," he began, as a chant of "We Want Thurmond!" rose from the back of the auditorium and an errant egg sailed in through an open door. Spurred by the opposition, Wallace partisans "shouted, clapped, cheered, whistled, and stamped their feet with mighty vigor," adding to the catcalls and rebel yells of their adversaries.[39]

Wallace's remarks, which forthrightly condemned segregation and proposed a federally funded grant of $4 billion to aid the South's economic development, were barely audible to those beyond the first few rows. Determined to get his message to the people, Wallace cried, "What do we want for the South?" "We Want Thurmond!" the hecklers roared back. Amid these pleasantries, a chain of firecrackers went off, terrifying the already nervous crowd, some of whose members dashed for the exits. Mary Price ran to Wallace's side, but he calmly urged the assembly to be seated. Inspired by their leader's courage, the Progressive faithful immediately erupted into a high-spirited chant of "We Want Wallace!" At the conclusion of his speech, Wallace joined the gathering in a well-earned moment of silence followed by a short prayer. Even after he departed, reports of violence continued. Local white hooligans allegedly beat several Progressives with clubs and stones as the Durham police looked on.[40] It had been a rough night. Only hours into a seven-day junket, one journalist reported, it was already apparent that the former vice president's journey was to be "no leisurely meander through the land of cotton."[41]

Reaction to the Armory incident tended to break down along regional lines. The national press unanimously condemned Wallace's treatment in Durham. Most editorials defended his right to free speech, insisting that no one in America should be denied the opportunity to express his views. Political quarrels, editors lectured their readers, should be settled in open debate rather than with eggs and insults. In contrast, Wallace's attack on Jim Crow elicited little substantive comment. The merits of his views on segregation, the *New York Times* remarked, were "beside the point."[42] In the South, however, segregation most definitely *was* "the point." Local papers, though also upholding Wallace's First Amendment rights, did not believe the issue was primarily one of political disagreement. The *Durham Morning Herald* maintained that the hecklers "knew nothing about Wallace's stands, political theories or practices," but booed him "because he flaunted southern social custom." A *Raleigh News and Observer* columnist concurred, contending that most of the tormentors "had scarcely heard of Wallace twenty-four hours before." Those who harassed Mary Price about Elizabeth Bentley's charges, he continued, did not even know who Bentley was. Some papers even implied that Wallace had gotten what he deserved for violating "accepted" racial mores, ignoring the fact that blacks had warmly received the candidate and invited his entourage into their homes. "The conflict was social, not political," the *Durham Sun* concluded. "There is no great tide of feeling moving with the Progressive Party in Durham. The Friendly City seems somewhat short of ready for the revolution." In hindsight, the southern-born journalist John Popham saw the incident in a similar light. "Many middle class people just didn't believe that this could happen, that their way of life should not be changed by outsiders. Not normally violent, [they] were perfectly willing to express themselves in loud and strong language."[43]

Progressive partisans interpreted the events differently. Immediately following his address, Wallace told a correspondent from the *Pittsburgh Courier* that the crowd's reaction was "a planned attack as reprisal for his long and bitter fight against tobacco trusts." Other Progressives on the scene implied that reactionary businessmen and politicos—"absentee industrial emperors," as Wallace called them—had organized and paid the demonstrators. Whispers of incipient American fascism circulated among the Wallace party.[44] In short, Progressives continued to interpret tensions in the South through the lenses of economic exploitation and political ideology rather than acknowledge the depth of white racism. On returning from his last trip through the region, Wallace had written that he was "convinced that the real purpose of maintaining Jim Crow and racial segregation in public meetings is not hatred of the Negro so much as it is the desire to prevent the expression of progressive sentiment by the underprivileged." To him, the "common man" remained inherently progressive, kept from manifesting his true nature by economic royalists.[45] The veteran New Dealer remained confident that white racism would dissipate once the Progressives implemented their program to eliminate economic deprivation and restore prosperity. His encounters in the South with deeply entrenched social conservatism made little impression. "I have not lost faith in the essential liberalism of the South," he told an audience in Chapel Hill the morning after his appearance in Durham.[46] Other Progressives, including James D. Harris, the young man who had been stabbed outside the Armory, were not so sure. "What hurts me," Harris said, "is that most of those pickets appeared to be from the poor classes that we are trying to help."[47]

Liberals during the 1930s had largely accepted the view that racial tensions in the South were primarily a product of economic scarcity. As the region's standard of living rose during and after the war, however, some began to question whether prosperity would automatically ameliorate racism. For Wallace and those of like mind, this proved a troubling dilemma, since it called into question the inherent progressivism of white southerners—a central assumption on which they based their vision of a new South.[48] Rather than confront this quandary, Progressives attributed Wallace's rough treatment in North Carolina to a cabal of powerful "reactionaries" bent on keeping the candidate from speaking in the South lest workers hearing his message be inspired to mobilize politically. To be sure, the demonstration in Durham was planned, as evidenced by the premade placards. Members of the Wallace traveling party also reported that the same small group of demonstrators followed them from town to town in North Carolina. Even so, Progressives overstated the orchestrated nature of the hostility directed at them. The *Durham Sun*, though hardly an unbiased source, likely came closer to the truth: "The placards may have been a put up job, but, as the wayward youth said of a quarrel with his antagonist, 'Knocking him down may have been the devil's prompting, but kicking him in the face was my own idea.'"[49]

In the wake of the Durham incident, two Progressive congressional candidates from North Carolina withdrew their names from nomination. Both expressed their continued support for Wallace and his opposition to the Cold War, but they objected to the party's defiant stance on segregation. "I cannot support the stupid reasoning of gaining disfavor with the Southern people by deliberately throwing the race issue in their faces. . . . You are allowing the race issue to kill the Progressive Party in North Carolina," Harold Murray wrote Price. "The present strategy of the Progressive Party," L. G. Smith added, "will not achieve the worthy goal which they have honestly hoped to obtain." Facing divisions even within their own camp, Progressives nonetheless vowed to continue their fight. As the rest of the southern tour would amply demonstrate, however, building a broad-based political movement while directly confronting the race issue was exceedingly difficult in the South of the 1940s.[50]

■ The second day of Wallace's trek along Tobacco Road brought still more raucous heckling and the threat of further violence.[51] At a stop in Burlington, a crowd of white textile workers barraged Wallace with eggs and tomatoes. Young "hoodlums" pounded on the car windows, hurling insults at Wallace's African American secretary and the other frightened passengers. When a fistfight broke out between a Progressive Party worker and a man who tried to hit Wallace with a rock, the few police officers on hand moved to break it up, leaving the candidate unprotected. Visibly shaken, with splattered egg pouring down his face, Wallace was unable to make himself heard above the shouts of "nigger lover!" and "Communist!" Fearing for his safety, his aides guided him through the screaming mob and back to the car. The crowd quickly broke past the police and rushed the motorcade, blocking its path. A patrolman brandishing his pistol before him cleared the way, and the party pulled out of Burlington only fifteen minutes after it had arrived.[52]

The next two stops brought more of the same. In the textile town of Greensboro, Wallace climbed the courthouse stairs to address another angry audience determined to prevent him from speaking. He shouted over the jeers and catcalls of the crowd that the South was "the stooge of outside corporations." To those who heckled him, he expressed "profound compassion," for, he declared, "most of them have not had enough to eat." This remark brought only derisive laughter from the apparently well-fed audience. Soaked with perspiration, his gray hair caked with hardening yolk, Wallace exclaimed, "I am sure that when I meet the real vote of the South, I will meet with a real welcome."[53] Stepping away from the podium, he hurried back to his car as another volley of eggs and tomatoes splashed on the hood and windshield. "I wish people had listened," one black woman told another as they walked away from the rally. "I think he's just thirty years too soon," another white man commented to a reporter from the *Greensboro Daily News*.[54] In High Point, one of the state's furniture manufacturing centers, another throng of unfriendly locals—produce at the ready, some waving Confederate flags—lay in wait in front of the county building. Despite the shouts and jeers, Wallace managed to make himself heard. In response to a strained chant of "We Want Wallace," he expressed his confidence in the "fundamental liberalism" of the South, but then quickly retreated to the safety of his automobile.[55]

Despite the intensity of such experiences, Wallace's comments to the crowds that heckled him suggest a curious detachment from his surroundings. The local press quickly picked up on this. "Is it possible that Wallace actually believes that the scatterbrained few who threw things at him— including college students, according to one report—or anybody else in the several crowds were actually hungry?" asked one editor.[56] Indeed, Wallace seemed unaware that references to those "who have not had enough to eat" were more a reflection of his own preconceptions about the South than an accurate assessment of the crowds in front of him. Nor did it occur to him that such patronizing remarks would only further alienate his audiences. Even in the midst of such turmoil, Wallace continued to deal in abstractions, seeing only the oppressed masses subject to the whims of greedy corporations as he wistfully anticipated the embrace of the "real South" that was "fundamentally liberal."

On the outskirts of Winston-Salem, the last stop of the day, a caravan of enthusiastic African American supporters tooting their horns and shouting encouragement greeted the Wallace entourage, marking a stark contrast from the earlier welcomes it had received.[57] If Progressives were discouraged by the persistence and intensity of the white working-class racism they encountered in the Piedmont, party officials remained hopeful that they would garner the support of southern blacks. In Winston-Salem, they were anxious to see firsthand the extent of this support.

Many in the welcoming party belonged to Local 22 of the Food, Tobacco, Agricultural, and Allied Workers Union (FTA), one of the few unions in the South to endorse Wallace's candidacy.[58] The FTA had compiled an impressive record in organizing African Americans in Winston-Salem. Its influence also extended into local politics, where union leaders helped forge an alliance between tobacco workers and the black middle class—an effort that culminated in 1947 with the election of the first African American to the city council.[59] Yet the passage of the Taft-Hartley Act in June 1947 had put the FTA on the defensive. Its international leadership refused to sign the non-Communist pledge, thus depriving the union of the right to appeal to the National Labor Relations Board (NLRB) during contract negotiations with management. Without government intervention through the NLRB, the union would have little chance in collective bargaining with the powerful tobacco companies. In fact, R. J. Reynolds moved quickly to take advantage of the FTA's predicament, announcing that it would neither recognize nor negotiate with Local 22 once its contract expired at the end of April. Faced with this potentially crippling blow, the union directed its energies into the Progressive Party campaign as a means of sustaining morale. Unlike the rank and file in most other pro-Soviet unions, Local 22's African American membership initially accepted its leaders' political guidance and rallied to the Wallace cause. Yet pursuing such a course at a time when the local's very existence was in jeopardy only heightened suspicions that the pro-Soviet leadership was placing the party line ahead of "sound trade union principles." Furthermore, the union's activity on behalf of Wallace alienated middle-class blacks and broke down the very cross-class alliances that FTA activists had worked so assiduously to build.

Arguably, however, the Communist issue was less central in explaining Local 22's eventual decline than was its long record of racial militancy. As a result of Local 22's principled stance on race, the union managed to recruit only 50 to 150 of Reynolds's 5,000 white employees. Though it enjoyed full support from African Americans—about 5,300 workers—Local 22 remained in a vulnerable position as long as it represented only half of the rank and file. When the leadership called a strike in 1947, white workers' refusal to support the union exposed its weakness, which management quickly exploited. As the historian Alan Draper has noted, Local 22's uncompromising position on race meant that the union would "reflect the racial divide within the work force at Reynolds rather than overcome it." The experience of the FTA did not bode well for the North Carolina Progressive Party, which likewise sought to achieve Local 22's goal of working-class biracial solidarity while pursuing a similarly militant civil rights agenda.[60]

At Wallace's appearance in the Southside Baseball Park on the evening of August 30, black unionists from Local 22 turned out in force. African Americans made up about 60 percent of the crowd of two thousand. Though seating at the rally was nonsegregated, blacks and whites voluntarily separated themselves. This made for a football game atmosphere in which many on the black side cheered "We Want Wallace!" while several hundred whites hollered back, "Down With Wallace!" The audience swarmed with uniformed and plainclothes police, but observers found that even the white teenage hecklers seemed more interested in having a good time than in causing trouble. "A lot of the folks were out for a big evening," a local correspondent reported. "They were wearing their best clothes and had their hair slicked up and when the rally took on the aspects of a camp meeting they yelled and yelled."[61] After arriving in the midst of a driving rainstorm, Wallace was able to deliver his address in full and even received a round of applause when he finished.[62]

Cheers and applause from Winston-Salem blacks did not translate into votes for the Progressive ticket, however. Karl Korstad, an FTA organizer, later explained that although southern black workers admired Wallace personally and agreed with his views on civil rights, they did not want to "waste" their vote. Most of those who cheered Wallace that night, Korstad noted, cast their ballot for Truman in November.[63] In fact, as the election neared, leaders in Winston-Salem's black community launched a concerted effort to wean away remaining supporters of the Progressive Party. In an open letter to the leaders of Local 22, J. H. R. Gleaves, the president of the newly organized Negro Democratic Club, denounced their "very poor judgment" in supporting the Progressive Party. This political strategy, he argued, led union members to a "dead-end destination." Gleaves pointed out that supporting Progressive candidates for state and national office who had no chance of winning squandered what little political leverage blacks wielded. Rather than pursuing the Wallace chimera, he urged the union to work for the election of those who could provide more tangible benefits for African Americans. As an indication of the extent to which the political tide had turned, Kenneth Williams, the black alderman elected with FTA support, and Jason Hawkins, the former PAC chair of Local 22, were among the Negro Democratic Club's founders.[64]

Wallace may not have rounded up many votes, but his travails in North Carolina did generate a widespread public outcry. Statements from the Republican and Dixiecrat campaigns sharply denounced his egg-throwing assailants. So, too, did President Truman who called for a stop to this "highly un-American business."[65] Contradicting his earlier remarks that referred to "hired stooges" of northern corporations, the candidate himself tried to downplay the significance of the heckling as "mostly the work of high school kids . . . apparently unorganized and in the spirit of fun."[66] His advisors, however, sought to disseminate a different message. Clark Foreman charged that the Dixiecrats had instigated the egg-tossing and booing to silence Wallace and to "institute a Fascist situation in the South."[67] From New York, Beanie Baldwin issued a blistering press release that berated the "vicious hoodlums in the South who dared to stone the only Presidential candidate who speaks for the people." Baldwin's bluster drew only cringes from southern Progressive leaders who saw little purpose in further escalating such fiery exchanges of oratory—after all, they were in greater proximity to the stone throwers than was Baldwin.[68]

Despite the universal condemnations of Wallace's poor treatment, demonstrations in Charlotte and Hickory followed the previous day's script. If anything, the *New York Herald Tribune* reported, they were "bigger and uglier."[69] Progressive Party workers at the scene in Hickory recalled that they had never been so frightened in their lives. The shower of rotten eggs, fruit, and tomatoes became so thick that Wallace quit his speech mid-sentence to seek shelter. Several bystanders retched at the rising stench. The haggard candidate, with flecks of egg shell still on his wrinkled white shirt, arrived an hour later in the mountain resort town of Asheville, his final destination in North Carolina. There, a heavy police presence ensured Wallace could deliver his address unmolested.[70] As the campaign special pulled out of Asheville's Southern Railway station on Tuesday evening, the traveling party's contingent of New York and Washington reporters were singing, "Nothing could be finer than to get out of Carolina."[71] James Wechsler, a correspondent for the *New York Post*, was more ambivalent. Wallace's upcoming foray into Alabama and Mississippi, he speculated, could well "restore North Carolina's prestige as a health resort and center of enlightenment."[72]

■ After a riotous forty-eight hours in the long-heralded "homeland of southern liberalism," weary Progressives hardly knew what to expect as their train sped toward the "shrine of the Dixiecrat movement." Rumors circulated that the Ku Klux Klan was quietly mobilizing along Wallace's route, allegedly to dynamite his Pullman railroad car before it reached Alabama.[73] During a stop in Knoxville, where Palmer Weber briefed reporters on the next day's schedule, the co-director of the southern campaign offered his own impression of the situation: "Alabama," said Weber, "is a very rugged state."[74]

Just after 7 A.M. the train arrived in Decatur, a small town just south of the Tennessee border. Several officials from the Mine, Mill and Smelters Union—whose members made up the core of Wallace's Alabama supporters—escorted the party to the Morgan County Courthouse, the site of the Scottsboro Boys' notorious trial fifteen years earlier. One thoughtful entrepreneur had parked a truckload of tomatoes near the speaker's stand, causing some initial concern, but the predominantly white crowd of five hundred received Wallace politely. Likewise at Huntsville and Guntersville, the situation remained calm.[75]

Warming to the crowds in these rural communities, Wallace abandoned his prepared text and switched to a more folksy style. He rhapsodized about Alabama's "lovely, rolling hills," fine athletes, and liberal native sons, the Supreme Court Justice Hugo Black and Senator Claude Pepper. Despite his best efforts, however, he failed to establish any connection with his audiences. Striving for "the homeliness of the red-necked demagogues," the southern-born columnist Robert Ruark noted, "Wallace managed to sound like a YMCA counselor lecturing on the evils of sex." His play for the support of local farmers fell flat. While he "promised a bale of cotton per acre under the guidance of the Progressive Party," Ruark observed, "sun baked, hard-hewed men just stared and spat. Henry was talking in a region which habitually yields two to three bales per acre."[76] Nevertheless, in light of the previous night's grim forecasts, indifference was preferable to hostility.

The relatively serene excursion through the cotton lands of northern Alabama ended abruptly in Gadsden. Once a dangerous place for union organizers to show their faces, by 1948 the town was one of the South's labor strongholds, after its steel, textile, and rubber workers had all been brought under the CIO umbrella during the mid-1940s. Nonetheless, the crowd gathered at the Etowah County Courthouse proved one of the most hostile of the week, with white steelworkers leading the anti-Wallace demonstrators. As the men surrounded the approaching motorcade, shouts of "Kill Wallace!" mixed ominously with the customary taunts and jeers.[77] The candidate was not to leave his automobile. J. P. Mooney, a local union official, announced that Wallace would not address a segregated crowd. This infuriated the white protesters who grew even more agitated as the

Wallace party hastily sped out of town. "Now I have seen the eyes of fascism," Wallace declared to his associates.[78] Gadsden, however, provided only a small-scale preview of the theatrics to come in Birmingham. After eight months of murders, bombings, and Klan intimidation, one observer reported, the racial climate in the steel city was "red hot and boiling."[79] Presiding over this cauldron—and making his own contribution to stirring it up—was the notorious Theophilus Eugene "Bull" Connor, the commissioner of public safety.

Bull Connor had first received national media attention in 1938 when he halted the integrated meetings of the newly organized Southern Conference for Human Welfare (SCHW). Eloquently summing up his position, he declared, "I ain't gonna let no darkies and white folk segregate together in this town."[80] The intervening years had done nothing to change his views. In fact, Connor shrewdly continued to exploit the race issue to further his political career. Though willing to collaborate with the city's powerful corporate interests, he also appealed to white trade unionists who resented black agitation for civil rights and admired the commissioner's strong racial stand.[81] In 1945 both the "big mules" and Alabama's CIO leadership backed his successful bid for reelection. The CIO endorsement of Connor drew immediate fire from the Alabama branch of the SCHW. When the local committee threatened to disavow the union, James Dombrowski, the conference's director, warned his colleagues that the CIO's financial support of the SCHW was too important to risk a break between the two organizations. Though the rift was papered over, it revealed the fundamental weakness of the Popular Front–oriented SCHW, as well as the increasing tension between organized labor and civil rights advocates.[82]

When the Progressive vice presidential nominee Glen Taylor appeared in Birmingham to address the left-wing Southern Negro Youth Congress (SNYC) in May 1948, Connor—then a candidate for delegate at large to the Democratic National Convention—sensed an ideal opportunity to score further political points. With the election only a few days away, he resolved to force a public showdown with SNYC, dramatically proclaiming that there was "not enough room in town for Bull and the Commies."[83] Yet despite his heavy-handed attempts to scuttle the conference by intimidating all potential hosts, SNYC leaders eventually secured a meeting site at a small black church. Undeterred, Connor announced that the Birmingham police would enforce segregated seating and require blacks and whites to enter from separate doors. Informed of the situation when he arrived, Taylor, himself no stranger to the dramatic political gesture, attempted to use the "Colored" entrance. Several officers grabbed him, and after a brief scuffle, they hustled the senator off to the station house, charging him with resisting arrest, assault and battery, and disorderly conduct.[84]

As Connor had predicted, the incident prompted "a big splurge in the Eastern newspapers." Liberal commentators deplored the brutish behavior of the police, while Taylor, whose southern campaign swing had gone almost unnoticed until his arrival in Alabama, now made front-page headlines. In the wake of the incident, SNYC publicly thanked Connor for providing "a spark of spirit and purpose" to the gathering. "Had he not done what he did," one member remarked, "then this meeting would have been a dull, routine conference without much spirit." Indeed, SNYC, a civil rights group that shared the SCHW's Popular Front orientation, was already on its last legs in 1948. Its close association with the Progressive Party further discredited the organization, and it folded the following year.[85] As far as Connor was concerned, however, his race-baiting had served its purpose. Bull coasted to an easy first primary victory in a contest that, before the SNYC incident, many had expected to be a tough fight. Accordingly, "with one sharp eye pinned on the governor's mansion," Connor eagerly anticipated Wallace's arrival. Rumors circulated that he had already reserved a freshly swept cell at the Birmingham jail just for the former vice president.[86]

As they paused on the outskirts of town to plan their strategy, the Wallaceites thus had good reason to be wary. Despite Connor's repeated admonitions in the local press that Wallace was to be treated with respect, Palmer Weber never doubted that the commissioner was anxious for an incident. Determined to avoid violence, Weber informed reporters that since segregation was to be enforced, J. P. Mooney would repeat the statement he had read in Gadsden after which the motorcade would slowly circle the Jefferson County Courthouse and move on. Wallace would remain in his car and out of harm's way.[87]

The hostile assembly was hardly pleased with this turn of events. As Mooney spoke, angry shouts of "Where's Henry?" erupted from across the plaza. A large portion of the crowd closed in on Wallace's car. Many took turns pressing their faces against the window, shouting obscenities and taunting the candidate. Others pounded their fists on the sedan and appeared ready to overturn it. After some difficulty, the police cleared a traffic lane and the caravan hastily withdrew. In nearby Bessemer, the afternoon's final stop, local officials again enforced segregation. Indeed, the municipal ordinance specifically prohibiting unsegregated meetings was passed the day before Wallace arrived, giving further indication that the southern tour was mobilizing the enemies of civil rights.[88]

That night, Wallace returned to Birmingham to deliver a radio address. Basing his appeal on a moral rather than a political level, he presented the Progressive program as a blueprint for achieving the highest Christian principles and denounced segregation as "sin." Arrayed against the Progressive Party, he contended, were the Wall Street bankers and a handful of rich and powerful men who kept the southern people divided so as to multiply their own profits. Wallace claimed that these men considered him a "dangerous enemy" who must be silenced and that they were therefore out to destroy the Progressive Party. Citing the hostility he had met in the industrial towns of Gadsden, Birmingham, and Bessemer, Wallace implied that the northern industrialists who "dominated" these communities had incited the violence against him. "With deliberate falsehoods and lies" they had inflamed the passions of the "wonderful, proud, and courageous people of the South who believe in Christianity and democracy," causing them "to act against their deepest Christian principles." Wallace pledged that as president, he would appropriate $4 billion to facilitate the planned development of southern industry and agriculture. This initiative, he predicted, would free the region from Wall Street domination, double the purchasing value of the average southern family's income, and put the South "on the road to a prosperity unsurpassed in any section of the nation."[89]

Wallace partisans hailed the speech as an "oratorical masterpiece." Clark Foreman credited the candidate with forcing white southerners for the first time to view the division of the races as the primary impediment to their economic well-being. Moreover, others noted, Wallace conveyed his populist message using the kind of religious imagery sure to appeal to his churchgoing audience.[90] Writing in the southern edition of the *Worker*, the Communist union organizer Sam Hall declared, "Today throughout the South there are thousands of whites who, as a result of Wallace's challenge to segregation, are beginning to ask themselves, 'What kind of damn foolishness is this?'" "Southern reactionaries know that the people are interested in Wallace's message," Hall insisted. "The Wall Street men and their plantation allies are more afraid of the Southern people than they have been since Reconstruction. And the tremendous turnout at Alabama . . . [has] made it no easier for these frantic reactionaries to sleep at night."[91]

Though few would share Hall's flights of fancy regarding white southerners' response to Wallace, there was some basis for believing that Alabamans would prove receptive to the Progressives' attacks on Wall Street and the moneyed interests. By pursuing just this strategy, James Folsom, the state's popular governor and a longtime Wallace admirer, had scored an upset victory over the handpicked candidate of the "big mules" in the 1946 Democratic primary. Once in office, Folsom echoed many of Wallace's criticisms of the Truman administration, both on domestic and foreign policy. He also shared Wallace's commitment to liberalizing southern politics through the creation of a class-based biracial coalition.[92] Folsom's sudden rise to power invigorated those who had long anticipated the emergence of such a coalition. Reflecting on this unexpected triumph, liberals heralded a "new awakening" in the state, discovering in Alabama an "oasis of enlightenment" where, they claimed, the people had long been ahead of their leadership.[93]

By the time Wallace arrived, however, Folsom and his political faction were in eclipse, due in large part to his opponents' success in refocusing popular attention on race. Discussion of Truman's civil rights proposals had dominated the May 1948 primary campaign in Alabama. Folsom tried to ignore the issue, but his initial refusal to condemn pro–civil rights measures only stiffened opposition to his candidacy for delegate at large to the Democratic convention. In the June runoff, he finished eleventh, an embarrassing repudiation for an incumbent governor. Likewise, every Folsom-supported candidate went down to defeat, while those candidates who attacked Truman's civil rights program the loudest polled the largest number of votes.[94] By the time the Dixiecrat movement emerged later in the summer, it seemed clear that economic liberalism had once again proven no match for social conservatism. Not unaware of the shifting political winds, Folsom severed his relationship with Wallace and publicly repudiated the Progressive Party, embittering longtime allies such as J. P. Mooney. Disappointed liberals immediately blamed the "divide and conquer" tactics of the "big mules," but few paused to consider why appeals to white racial solidarity consistently received a receptive audience while pleas for class-based unity that transcended race fell on deaf ears.[95] One exception among liberals was the southern-born writer Lillian Smith who viewed whites' commitment to racial supremacy as a fundamental element of their self-image, something more than an artificial construct that would evaporate with the arrival of prosperity. "You can't snatch the bone of white supremacy from a starving man until you give him some real food to eat," Smith argued, "and this food can't be just money—not in Dixie."[96]

In attributing his rough treatment throughout his southern tour to the sinister manipulations of nameless northern elites, Wallace indicated that he, too, had not come to terms with the deeply embedded, homegrown commitment to white supremacy that characterized well-nigh every stratum of white southern society. The "rich and powerful men" he castigated may have exploited the race issue when it suited their interests, but they alone were not responsible for sustaining the system of segregation. As union organizers across the South well knew, white working-class southerners adamantly opposed any dismantling of the racial status quo, which, they believed, preserved their interests as well. Their hostility to the CIO stemmed in part from their perception of the organization as a threat to segregation. Indeed, one of the primary impediments to the CIO's making good on its rhetorical commitment to civil rights was the desire of white workers to ensure that certain jobs remained reserved for whites. As the historian Bruce Nelson has noted, CIO leaders faced a dilemma. Though they cautiously tried to implement antidiscrimination policies—usually in conjunction with employers and government— "[they] could not let these concerns jeopardize the institutional survival of their organizations, which were dependent upon the allegiance of white workers and generally reflected their consciousness." Even in unions whose Communist leadership emphasized a militant commitment to civil rights, institutional survival took precedence over the "Negro Question." The Communist leaders of Mine Mill locals in Birmingham, for example, began actively promoting antidiscrimination policies and civil rights only *after* they believed the union's continued existence was assured.[97] Contrary to Wallace's assumption, class consciousness did not act as a solvent for racial divisions. Rather, racial identity played a central role in developing class identity. Caste consciousness and class consciousness were not polar opposites, but overlapping influences that interacted to produce workers' attitudes and behavior. Those who turned out to jeer and egg Wallace did so not because they had been misled about his message, but because they perceived him exactly as he wished to be perceived—as posing a direct challenge to segregation and the racial barrier they wanted maintained.[98]

Journalists on the scene confirmed this. Wallace's unequivocal denunciation of segregation, Edwin Lahey of the *Chicago Daily News* observed, left "race-hysterical" southerners "as inflamed today as their grandfathers were in 1850." Even southern Progressives who deplored the behavior of their fellow citizens told Lahey that they feared the trip had been a "tragic error," akin to yelling "fire" in a crowded movie theater. Lahey believed Wallace's insistence that Wall Street exploited the South by pitting race against race made little impression. "Whatever effect such an argument might have upon workers and small farmers in normal times certainly was lost in the atmosphere of racial tension in which Wallace spoke," he concluded.[99] According to Edward Folliard of the *Washington Post*, the candidate's insistence on "equality for Negroes . . . was unquestionably the overriding reason for the South's violent dislike of Wallace." In conversations with white southerners, he reported, nearly everyone told him that Wallace had "betrayed" his race.[100]

Still, Wallace retained what one historian has called "an almost mystical solicitude for the common man." He remained convinced, despite ample evidence to the contrary, that the majority of white southerners shared his views on racial equality. Commenting on this, one journalist declared that Wallace's "common man" was ultimately "a figment of his imagination . . . something he had created in his own image . . . with the same features, ideas, ideals and mental processes" as his own. "The common man that Henry Wallace is encountering in the South does not conform to Henry's abstract conception. . . . He may be 'common' but he has little in common with Henry Wallace." In an insightful portrait of Wallace, published before he declared his candidacy for president, David T. Bazelon critically assessed the former vice president's "populist faith" in the "common man." Even if "common man" was a figure of speech rather than a concept, Bazelon concluded, it was a "dangerous substitute for analysis."[101]

■ As his southern swing progressed, Wallace's unfamiliarity with the actual conditions in the South grew increasingly pronounced, particularly as he explained his views on the reasons for and solutions to regional underdevelopment. During a radio address in Mississippi, he revisited the same themes he had outlined in Birmingham. "There is a long chain that links unknown young hoodlums in a North Carolina or Alabama mill town with men in cutaways and finely tailored business suits—men who are found in the great financial centers of New York and Boston—men who make a dollar and cents profit by setting race against race in the faraway South," Wallace declared. Wherever one found racial injustice in the South, he insisted, "there look for the long string of dividends that lead to Wall Street." The state of affairs would improve for both blacks and whites only when native southerners owned and controlled the South's industries. To erase the economic and social disparities between the regions, he contended, government should levy heavy taxes on northern corporations that invested in Dixie and then pour this revenue back into local firms.[102]

As in so many of his speeches, however, Wallace offered little specific evidence to support his assertions or to demonstrate the feasibility of his proposals. Critics inquired how taxing northern investors would promote southern prosperity, especially when the most likely result of such a policy would be the withdrawal of badly needed capital from the region. The candidate also failed to explain the connection between an infusion of federal funds into southern-owned companies and the end of discriminatory practices in the workplace, apparently assuming that one would lead inevitably to the other. Indeed, Wallace made no mention of the promised aid being contingent on a formal commitment to racial egalitarianism, stating instead that he had no desire to establish further federal interference in southern affairs.[103] His premise that native ownership of industry was inherently preferable to absenteeism was also disputable. Employees at southern-owned firms did not always enjoy better wages and working conditions. Officials in the CIO often found that northern-owned companies in the South, though hardly receptive to unions, proved more willing to negotiate in good faith and less likely to ignore rulings by the National Labor Relations Board than their southern counterparts.[104] Yet rather than acknowledge these complicating factors, Wallace merely affirmed that "all things are possible when we practice Christianity and democratic principles."[105]

The nation's newspapers were quick to point out the flaws in Wallace's arguments. Angry Progressives accused the press of "red-baiting," but editorials condemned Wallace's economic plan for the South not on grounds that it was "Communistic," but because it was impractical and had no chance of winning congressional support. Editors argued that a candidate who promised what he knew to be undeliverable was simply engaging in demagoguery.[106] To an extent, Wallace's overheated language opened him to such charges, but to follow his line of reasoning, one must appreciate his understanding of economic conflict. Throughout his political career, Wallace seemed to judge economic policy by moral standards, viewing the representatives of major corporations as "bad men"—and not as the hired agents of stockholders who expected maximum return on investment. Accordingly, he believed that appeals to the individual civic responsibility of business leaders could change their behavior and thereby reform the system. The weaknesses of capitalism were thus attitudinal, not structural.[107] George N. Peek, who worked under Wallace in the Agriculture Department during the 1930s, wrote in 1936, "Henry had a mystical, religious side to him. . . . He was apt to view clashes of economic forces as struggles between good men and bad men, and not as between groups, all of whom believed that right was with them. Since Henry was always with the good men, he never quite got the whole of any picture. He believed in low tariffs, for instance, as a moral issue."[108] Wallace's "progressive capitalism" would thus come about when "good men" controlled the flow and distribution of economic resources. Ironically, this was the very point on which he and the

Communists differed most sharply. Yet as long as Wallace limited himself to outlining goals without discussing in precise terms the means of attaining them, Communist Party members—both inside and outside the Progressive Party—could tolerate his ideological heresies. Indeed, such conceptual vagueness fused with emotionally charged populist rhetoric had always been the glue that held the Popular Front together.

Dismissing their critics in the press, Progressives insisted that Wallace's impassioned oratory would stir the emotions of the South's poorer classes, inspiring them to unite against their oppressors. But the sense of outrage needed to catalyze a populist mass movement did not materialize. The candidate's strictures against "Big Business," so tied to the politics of the Depression, elicited only a tepid response from postwar southerners, many of whom had come to view outside investment as the route to prosperity, rather than as the source of hard times.[109] Similarly, the Progressives' caricatures of southern industrialists did not always comport with workers' experiences. For example, Charles Cannon, the owner of a huge textile mill in Kannapolis, North Carolina, was well regarded by his workers. The CIO found that it was almost impossible to convince them that they needed a union. "Cannon employees actually feel that they have a superior deal, and they may have," one dejected organizer reported. Another noted that Cannon's wages were higher and working conditions better than what the union was winning in organized plants. "The only issue we have is freedom from Cannon domination," he lamented, "and Cannon is very popular." In fact, wages and conditions at various Piedmont mills had improved substantially during the late 1940s. Still, Wallace's depiction of southern labor did contain an element of truth. Compared to northern workers, southerners remained worse off. Nonetheless, their standard of living had risen more than northerners' during the war, contributing to the optimistic spirit of the immediate postwar period. White workers in particular perceived their situation as improving at a rate faster than they had previously dreamed possible. In this context, the Progressives' bemoaning of a destitute and benighted South rang hollow. Party leaders' militant rhetoric, which might have won a receptive audience in the thirties, failed to rouse people who believed their lives were getting better, not worse. In covering Wallace's visit to Louisville on August 25, the *Courier-Journal*, considered liberal by southern standards, referred to the candidate as "a strange sad echo of years gone by." Wallace and his supporters spoke and acted like it was 1932, not 1948, one reporter observed. Changing conditions, even more than a rising tide of anticommunism, help explain the eclipse of Wallace's brand of Popular Front liberalism.[110]

Yet conditions in the South had not improved for African Americans. In a statement Wallace sharply condemned while visiting Mississippi, Governor Fielding Wright had warned the blacks of his state the previous May, "If any of you have become so deluded as to want to enter our white schools, patronize our hotels and cafes, [or] enjoy racial equality with the white, then true kindness and true sympathy requires me to advise you to make your home in some state other than Mississippi." Politics in particular remained strictly a "white man's business." In 1947, only five thousand black Mississippians were registered to vote, less than 1 percent of those eligible.[111] Progressives thus harbored few illusions about their chances for electoral success in the Magnolia State. Nonetheless, Palmer Weber and other southern leaders hoped Wallace's militantly pro–civil rights stance would win the party substantial moral support among blacks, and, even more important, precipitate an increase in African American voter registration.

Such was not to be the case. Though they admired Wallace for advocating racial equality, most blacks avoided the Progressive Party. In African American communities, leaders emphasized indigenous grassroots organization as the bedrock for achieving long-range progress. Local activists therefore hesitated to rely on symbolic gestures or onetime rallies to bring about change. The Progressive Party did not have enough time, money, or political clout to offer much more. Nowhere in Dixie, let alone in Mississippi, could the party be characterized as a "mass movement" with widespread grassroots support. The Mississippi Progressive Party was little more than a paper organization; it ran no candidates for state or county office and held no public meetings. The Wallace movement had shown some promise initially, but national headquarters' decision to assign a Communist organizer from the North to drum up support in the state proved disastrous. His sectarian behavior quickly chased away potential recruits and aroused the suspicion of local authorities. In the end, given the unrelentingly hostile climate in which black Mississippians had to live, the potential payoff simply did not justify the risk one incurred by publicly supporting a party as unpopular the Progressives—a problem Wallace and his party faced throughout the South in recruiting blacks.[112]

■ After the initial excitement in North Carolina and Alabama, news of Wallace's southern tour slipped off the front pages of the nation's papers. The entourage soldiered on through Louisiana, Arkansas, and Tennessee, and though it faced hostile crowds and an occasional shower of eggs, there were no further outbreaks of violence. Along the route through the heart of Tennessee Valley Authority territory, the motorcade even passed through several small towns where unexpectedly friendly groups turned out to voice their support.[113] At every stop, Wallace continued to speak out against segregation and denounced injustices that many less courageous politicians would have refrained from tackling while touring the Old Confederacy. If he at times became bogged down in confusion and wishful thinking, the former vice president nonetheless sounded a clarion call against the bigotry and hatred so often camouflaged by the euphemism of "southern tradition." As the seven-day tour came to an end in Knoxville, Tennessee, the time had come to take stock.

Reporters accompanying Wallace on his Dixie journey estimated that he had been the target of seventy-seven eggs, thirty-seven tomatoes, six peaches, two lemons, one orange, an ice cream cone, and a bun. As Edwin Lahey reported from the field, however, "the stink of garbage can be eradicated, but not so the corrosive hatred that you encounter . . . the memory of the horrid faces of baggy, middle-aged women, of red-necked, tobacco-spitting hillbillies who have hurled epithets all along the route." Just as often, though, Wallace met apathy. His audiences totaled only about twenty-five thousand, an average of less than one thousand per speech—a record low for a well-known presidential candidate on tour. Of this number, no more than fifteen thousand actually heard the candidate's prepared remarks over the incessant heckling.[114] As the party flew back to New York, many reflected on the trip's significance and effect. What, if anything, had been achieved?

The Progressive faithful heralded the tour as an unqualified success, a catalyst that would precipitate even more positive results in the long term. An ebullient Clark Foreman declared Wallace's expedition into Dixie "the greatest blow against slavery since the emancipation proclamation." "As the direct result of Henry Wallace's trip through the South," Foreman wrote in the *New York Star*, "millions of Americans who were not aware of the meaning of discrimination in the South have suddenly been jolted. Segregation is no work of fiction, but a brutal fact. The conflict between American democracy and segregation hit home to millions." Later, in the wake of the landmark *Brown v. Board of Education* case, Palmer Weber claimed that without the Wallace tour, there would have been "no 9–0 Supreme Court decision." George Murphy, the Progressives' assistant campaign manager, believed that "thousands of Negro and white Southerners have gotten inspiration and courage to reach across the color-line and grasp hands and join together in this New Party of the common man." Louis Burnham, the co-director of the southern campaign, predicted that the Progressive Party would be "the major party in the South . . . this year, next year, and succeeding years to 1952." Even in North Carolina, the scene of the most vehemently anti-Wallace demonstrations, party officials contended that white workers were "frightened, not hostile" and vowed to redouble efforts to recruit their support.[115]

Wallace himself expressed confidence that the tour had strengthened the party in the South but refused to speculate as to how many votes he would win in Dixie. He continued to present his crusade less as an electoral contest than as a moral struggle against injustice, telling one Tennessee audience that he had "a pretty good idea of what it must have felt like to have been an early Christian martyr."[116] Embracing the role of prophet— literally one who "tells forth"—he insisted that his principal objective was to hold up his vision before the people "with all the fire at my command." On these grounds, Wallace believed, he had scored a major triumph.[117]

Many of his erstwhile critics agreed. "There is no question that the trip has been a victory for the Progressive candidate," declared Newbold Noyes of the *Washington Star*. "He has been able to dramatize the issue of race segregation as a million words could not have dramatized it. . . . Undoubtedly, he put the segregated South in a position where, for better or worse, it will have to think through its problem once again." The *Nation*, too, commended Wallace's refusal to submit to segregation, adding that "a taboo violated with such fanfare can never again be quite as potent." In the midst of hostile, angry mobs, James Wechsler observed, Wallace proved himself "a truly distinguished figure." Beyond establishing in at least a dozen settings that "unsegregated meetings could be held without civil war," Wechsler noted, "he may even have jolted the complacency of a few citizens who had never doubted that the Lord preferred them to those born with darker skins."[118]

By publicizing the injustices inherent in the system, Wallace helped put segregation on the table as a topic that demanded discussion. In a conversation often driven by white reaction to racial atrocities such as lynching, interracial violence, and intimidation, Wallace shifted the boundaries of debate, making the case that segregation itself was an atrocity. Even the Southern Conference for Human Welfare, generally perceived as the most racially "advanced" of the South's liberal organizations, had not directly attacked segregation, focusing instead on the economic issues that exacerbated racial tensions. By 1948, however, many liberals in Dixie and throughout the nation realized they could no longer subordinate segregation to other problems. The Wallace tour and southern campaign reinforced this perception.[119]

This shift in strategy for combating racial injustice, however, occurred within a broader context. Many liberals' understanding of racism had changed during the 1940s, reflecting the emergence of what the historian Peter Kellogg has called a new "racial consciousness." Profoundly influenced by "the racial issues that emerged in the struggle against Nazi racism," liberals came to see racial oppression "as a test of white morality, a matter of individual conscience," rather than as "one extreme instance of class oppression," as they had during the thirties.[120] Accordingly, segregation was not simply a product of economic deprivation, it was a "sin." This new racial consciousness had implications for those who participated in the struggle for civil rights, but also for those who have chronicled and assessed that struggle. Some historians have argued that the rise of domestic anticommunism and the narrowing of political discourse during the postwar period precipitated a shift from a class- and organized labor–based strategy for overcoming racial inequality generally associated with Popular Front liberalism to a church- and community-based approach embraced by the civil rights movement in the 1950s and 1960s. Implicit in their work is the assumption that so-called Cold War liberals abandoned (or even sabotaged) a more "militant" Popular Front strategy to avoid being "red-baited."[121] Kellogg's argument, however, suggests that the new approach was not simply a tactical response to the dawning of the Cold War, but the result of a change in attitude about race and racism that predated the rise of postwar anticommunism. Ironically, then, Wallace, the ostensible leader of the last Popular Front mass movement, played a key role in framing racism as a moral issue and in setting the stage for others who took a similar approach.

Ultimately, however, the legacy of Wallace's brief foray into the South proved more symbolic than substantive. His flaunting of Jim Crow may have inspired some local supporters to step up their struggle against discrimination, but such fleeting moments of defiance did not establish segregation as the nation's most pressing racial issue, let alone initiate the process of dismantling it. Among whites, the shift in "racial consciousness" that Kellogg and other historians have documented did not extend far beyond civil rights activists. Though Gallup polls indicated that white Americans did seem receptive to specific reforms, including the repeal of the poll tax, there was no sign of national moral outrage against segregation in 1948. In March, a Gallup poll surveying opinion of President Truman's civil rights program found that 45 percent of whites outside the South had never even heard of it. Nationally, only 6 percent believed Truman's program should be passed as a whole.[122]

Among African Americans, Wallace's southern tour did not prove the "pivotal moment" Progressives had hoped it would be. Commenting on Wallace's southern swing, *Crisis*, the official organ of the NAACP, expressed respect for the candidate's zeal, but reminded readers that his was not the first frontal attack on segregation—the association had been holding unsegregated meetings in the South since 1934. Moreover, despite all the fanfare, "no new information was uncovered. No new techniques were demonstrated for coping with the problem."[123]

Nor did the Progressives succeed in winning the electoral support of southern blacks, though certainly not for lack of trying. Throughout their campaign in Dixie, they offered what they believed were compelling reasons for African Americans to join their crusade. Unlike their northern brethren, one argument ran, blacks in the South were not institutionally tied to the Democrats—there was no patronage to be lost if they bolted to a third party. Other strategists maintained that even if Wallace could not win, a substantial black turnout for him would compel the Democrats and Republicans to take a more forthright stance on civil rights after the election. According to Earl Conrad, a columnist for the *Chicago Defender* and a Progressive Party supporter, "A large vote for Wallace will be the means of creating a new political apparatus in America that will constantly advance Negro individuals and issues." Earlier in the year, however, the *Norfolk Journal and Guide* had taken issue with such an argument. "If the Negro vote swings in a bloc of decisive proportions to Wallace," its editor, P. D. Young, argued, "neither of the major parties will have any sense of obligation to fight for a better deal for us."[124]

Concerned that they had lost ground after the Democrats adopted a liberal civil rights plank in their platform, Progressives intensified their appeals to black voters as the campaign wore on. Third party literature repeatedly contrasted Wallace's genuine commitment to racial equality with Truman's alleged insincerity.[125] The southern tour, Wallaceites believed, would demonstrate this commitment, providing dramatic evidence of the candidate's unwavering opposition to Jim Crow. Jennings Perry, a former editorial writer for the *Nashville Tennessean* and one of the few nationally syndicated columnists to endorse Wallace, even predicted at the outset of the tour that the Progressive candidate would outpoll the Dixiecrat Strom Thurmond in the South. "The little people who really believe in democracy," Perry declared, "will come out from under the rocks in surprising numbers to support the man whose concern for civil rights is most above suspicion of expediency." As late as October, Earl Conrad predicted that Wallace would poll more black votes than Truman or Dewey. Third party leaders cited the moving words of encouragement Wallace had received from individual blacks along his route as proof that their arguments had taken root. Years later, Virginia Durr, the state chair of the Virginia Progressive Party, acknowledged being "surprised and shocked" at the party's poor showing among African Americans. "We were absolutely sure that we were going to get the Negro vote," she recalled. After the election, Wallace himself lamented that blacks had rejected his candidacy, telling associates that he had given the Negroes "their chance" but that they had "let him down."[126]

As the November returns amply demonstrated, Wallace partisans had mistaken emotional fervor for electoral support. Following the election, C. O. Pearson, an African American lawyer from Durham who ran on the Progressive ticket for attorney general of North Carolina, expressed the disappointment many of his colleagues must have shared. Conceding to his victorious Democratic opponent, Pearson observed dejectedly, "I have been completely repudiated at the polls of Durham County in the precincts that are overwhelmingly Negro."[127]

Caught up in their own grand designs for remaking the South, Progressives misconstrued the temper of the African American population whose interests they claimed to represent. Preoccupied with the more expansive task of launching a new political party, they underestimated the priority southern blacks placed on securing immediately tangible improvements. In stirring tones, Wallace offered his southern audiences abstract promises of equality, justice, and prosperity—the "century of the common man." But when party activists campaigned door to door, they found that local blacks expressed greater concern about more mundane matters. One canvasser recalled that African Americans in the Carolinas and in Georgia frequently told her that Wallace should run for sheriff of their town. That way, they explained, he could do something about their "most important problems—how to get their sons out of jail, obtain street lights, remove potholes in the roads, get more and better schools and colored policemen." Some Progressives at the local level made valiant efforts to address such issues, but the party never established sufficient grassroots support to make it a force in southern communities. Explaining to Virginia Durr why he could not back her party, a black preacher aptly expressed the prevailing sentiment, "You folks can't do nothin' for us, and we got to live some way."[128]

Ultimately, the Progressives' outspoken stance on racial equality did not entice black voters away from Harry Truman and the Democratic Party. Typical was the experience of a party worker in Arkansas who tried to convert a group of African American ministers to the Wallace cause. Arguing that Truman's commitment to an aggressive civil rights agenda was merely a political ploy, he urged them not to be taken in by false promises. Though the ministers listened sympathetically, none offered any firm commitment. "You may not believe Truman," one said at last, "but the Dixiecrats believe him; and that's enough for me." He and his colleagues would vote for the president. The Dixiecrat revolt undoubtedly helped Truman secure the support of blacks around the nation. "After the Dixiecrats walked out of the Democratic convention," one Harlem editor explained after the election, "there was no question how Negroes would vote. Negroes felt if they didn't support Truman no other politician would ever defy the Southerners again." The Dixiecrats' insistence on personalizing the issue of civil rights by denouncing the president's "betrayal" of his race further enhanced Truman's stature among southern blacks. When an African American reporter asked Thurmond what distinguished Truman's civil rights rhetoric from that of Franklin Roosevelt, who also promised justice and equal opportunity to blacks, the South Carolina governor candidly responded, "Truman really means it." Few African Americans failed to take notice of this revealing remark. Despite the Progressives' persistent accusations around Truman's insincerity, the majority of African Americans were willing to take the president at his word. His actions—particularly the executive orders abolishing segregation in the military and establishing the enforcement of fair employment practices in the executive branch—carried even more weight. Indeed, after conducting extensive interviews with African American voters during the campaign, Henry L. Moon concluded that as far as the black electorate was concerned, on the issue of civil rights, "whether or not the candidate's gestures have been motivated by political considerations is of little moment. What is important is the record of performance and the prospect for implementing his promises."[129]

Other African American activists reacted skeptically to the Progressives' eagerness for direct confrontation over the civil rights issue. Impatient for change themselves, but wary of a white backlash, these leaders' concern centered less on the Progressives' militant approach than on their ability to see it through. Recognizing that militancy only succeeded when there was real power to back it up, they remained unconvinced the young party was up to the task. Many concluded that the "Wallace way" meant suicide. The Democratic Party, despite its flaws, offered a more realistic vehicle for continuing their struggle.[130] As a front-page editorial of the *Chicago Defender* declared, "The Wallace tour proved beyond the shadow of a doubt that the civil rights program of President Truman is urgently needed now. . . . The time has come for all Negro Americans to close ranks and support President Truman. We have got to make the South safe for democracy."[131]

The enthusiastic endorsement Wallace received from the Communist Party also played a part in the Progressives' difficulties in the South, though not a large one. The CP's close association with the Progressives provided white southerners with further "proof" that communism and agitation for civil rights were one and the same. Wallace's unorthodox views on racial matters, combined with his demand for a more conciliatory stance toward the Soviet Union, fit popular notions of the "nigger-loving Communist" to a tee, giving the candidate's defiance of segregation the air of "treason." White southerners who might have been uncomfortable voicing overtly racist sentiments found they could justify their condemnation of Wallace and his civil rights agenda on patriotic grounds.[132] As a result, anticommunist rhetoric figured prominently in the verbal assaults the former vice president endured during his southern tour.[133]

Taking note of such rhetoric, many Wallace loyalists claimed that the rising tide of domestic anticommunism sabotaged their efforts, scaring away otherwise sympathetic voters.[134] Yet such an assessment overestimates the significance of the "red issue" in depleting the Progressives' strength. Though denunciations of Wallace as a "red" may have added to the din of criticism against him, race, not fear of communism, was at the heart of the white South's opposition to the third party. Officials in the CIO had already learned this lesson during Operation Dixie, labor's coordinated effort to organize the South. As the historian George M. Fredrickson has concluded, "The effort to create a unified black-and-white labor movement in the South was doomed from the start, and anticommunism was simply a convenient vehicle for the expression of the deeply rooted white supremacist convictions that white workers shared with their employers." Bill Evans, a CP member and organizer at a Durham textile mill during Operation Dixie, corroborates this view. "There were workers in Erwin Mills who didn't know the difference between Communism and rheumatism," he recalled. "All [the owners] had to do was raise the race issue; it would create much more interest and excitement among workers than the Communist issue." "Around here," an Alabama farmer once told John Dos Passos, "communism's anything we don't like," and in 1948, the overwhelming majority of white southerners did not like the Progressive stance on racial equality. Historians who have blamed Cold War anticommunism for impeding the growth of a labor- and left-led civil rights movement have been slow to acknowledge as much.[135]

Finally, the Progressives' quest to recast southern politics along class lines proved impracticable. In viewing the so-called Negro problem as an artificial construct that masked more fundamental class antagonisms, the Wallaceites failed to confront the significance of existing racial attitudes and the formidable impediment they posed to reform. Convinced that race was merely a peripheral issue in the larger struggle between liberals and reactionaries, Progressives underestimated the extent to which caste consciousness permeated nearly every facet of life in the South, overwhelming any vague sense of shared class interests. Frustrated by the persistence of white hostility toward blacks, yet unwilling to explore its political implications, they assumed such animosity resulted from the "divide and conquer" tactics of liberalism's traditional enemies—"Wall Street," "red-baiters," the "big mules." In response, they launched a spirited rhetorical attack against such forces, presuming the southern "masses" would fall in behind them. Once they had enlightened the people to the devious machinations of their oppressors, Progressives reasoned, a more ideologically coherent, class-based political party would naturally coalesce. Rather than reassessing their own reading of the public mood when this failed to happen, Progressives again laid the blame at the feet of their adversaries. The reactionaries had not only distorted the New Party's message, but, fearing its liberating effect on the people, employed any means necessary to keep them from hearing it. Progressives insisted that if only Wallace were permitted to bring his case directly to the people, the "real South" would eagerly embrace the candidate and his vision of a truly democratic Dixie.

This "real South," however, was a myth—a comforting social construct that confirmed Progressives' own ideological and political preconceptions. The southern historian George B. Tindall has written that when myths become "a ground for belief," there arises "a danger that in ordering one's vision of reality, the myth may predetermine the categories of perception, rendering one blind to things that do not fit into the mental image."[136] Wallace did speak directly to the people during the southern tour, yet they did not flock to the Progressive banner. Many irate white southerners threw things at him or shouted him down. Most, however, either ignored him or wished he would go away. On the tour's last day, one reporter remarked that although they expressed regret at Wallace's poor treatment, defended his right to have his say, and respected his fortitude in the face of adversity, "Southern whites don't like him any more now than they did before." "If anything," he concluded, "they probably like him less."[137] Most white southerners still saw blacks as a threat rather than as potential allies. Wallace's memorable trip had done little to convince them otherwise.

For their part, southern blacks also showed relatively little interest in the plans Progressives had laid out for them. Though they marveled at Wallace's resolve and appreciated his willingness to take a stand against the cruelty of segregation, most African Americans never saw in Wallace an effective leader who could follow through on his inspiring rhetoric. Moreover, class divisions within the African American community itself suggested that an alliance between blacks and the white working class would not be as "natural" as Wallace and his supporters assumed. Progressives failed to consider that many blacks might be reluctant either to embrace those whose racism had traditionally been most virulent or to join a coalition in which they would in all likelihood remain junior partners. In their hesitancy to accept the Progressives' Popular Front alternative, African Americans recognized, as the historian Bruce Nelson has noted, that if they "were to achieve full citizenship, they could not allow whites to dictate the movement's program, strategy, and timetable."[138]

At a time when such formidable, broad-based forces as the CIO and the NAACP were struggling to keep their heads above water in Dixie, an openly integrationist, underfunded, and middle-class political organization well to the left of the average southerner—black or white—was not going to attract the kind of support required to launch a successful mass movement. Indeed, the disappointing results of the CIO's Operation Dixie, inaugurated two years earlier, provided sobering evidence that the potential for creating the kind of grand progressive coalition Wallace loyalists envisioned had been exaggerated.[139] Yet as the campaign headed into its final weeks, Wallace and his associates preferred to see their experiences in the South as an affirmation of their basic assumptions rather than as a challenge to them, revealing the strength of the political culture that held them together as a party but also ensuring that they would remain isolated from the American mainstream.

10

TRUMAN DEFEATS WALLACE

Denouement

As he made the long walk from the Yankee Stadium home-team dugout to the podium erected at second base, the deafening cheers and shouts from the throng of nearly fifty thousand people struck a stark contrast to the less welcoming salutations Henry Wallace had received throughout most of Dixie. If nowhere else, the Progressive Party's standard-bearer could still get a standing ovation in the Bronx. His devoted disciples, at least two-thirds of them teenagers and young men and women in their early twenties, had turned out in great force and full voice to welcome their hero returned. As with most large Progressive rallies, the atmosphere at this gathering on September 10 was one of an open-air revival meeting, complete with singing, "pass the hat" fund-raising, and an audience seemingly borne along on its own fervor. With the bright floodlights beating down on him, Wallace stood for ten minutes in the misty night air, smiling broadly and waving his arms to quiet the crowd.[1]

Half an hour before midnight he began his address, recounting with great emotion the dramatic events of his weeklong visit to the South and reiterating his conviction that racism was merely the by-product of economic exploitation. "To me," Wallace declared, "fascism is no longer a second-hand experience. . . . No, fascism has become an ugly reality—a reality which I have tasted. . . . [I saw] how hate and prejudice can warp good men and women; turn Christian gentlemen into raving beasts; turn good mothers and wives into jezebels." Yet the unfortunate people of the South were not to blame, he insisted; they were only the "victims" of "the catchwords of prejudice" that more sinister forces employed. According to Wallace, "Northern-owned steel corporations" were responsible for enforcing segregation in Alabama. "The profits of the men who own the South are multiplied by keeping the people divided," he told the crowd. "But," Wallace added with characteristic optimism, "their days are numbered [for] the good people of the South have learned their scriptures. . . . Just as surely as men everywhere, they want the Kingdom of Heaven here on earth; and they are not going to be stopped any longer by those who spew hate." Returning to another favorite theme, he asserted that the "farmers and workers" of the South were more progressive in their views than Dixie's tepid reformers. Having rejected prejudice and segregation, Wallace claimed, "they are turning from the false leadership of those who have been styled 'Southern liberals.' . . . They are learning that such men are only slightly to the left of Hitler and Rankin." The speech, like many of Wallace's impassioned orations, had an almost otherworldly feel. Even after his many firsthand encounters with white southerners, the line between what he hoped for and what was real remained difficult for Wallace to discern.

In the remainder of his speech, he directed his wrath at the "self-styled liberals" and "Pied Pipers of labor" who had failed to rally to his cause, attacking them as "shameful, immoral, and corrupt" for supporting President Truman and "the Wall Street gang in Washington." He branded them "fearful men" who were "bargaining with corruption." Wallace asserted that the Progressive Party would never back down to the "cheap political tricksters who have joined with those who all their lives have practiced black reaction." Rather, he maintained, "We must work—we will work, so that on November 2, Americans can clearly choose."[2]

The speech, which received a thunderous ovation from his fiercely partisan audience, was one of the bitterest Wallace delivered throughout the entire campaign. Unlike many of his other addresses, this one he had written himself.[3] His righteous contempt for all who opposed him emanated from almost every line, reflecting his deeply held belief that one's choice of presidential candidate was moral, not political. As Wallace saw it, because he was on the side of the Lord, those who did not support him were "immoral and corrupt," and therefore deserved to have their sin exposed. His followers seemed to view things in much the same terms. As they moved slowly toward the exits at the conclusion of the rally, one reporter observed, "their faces disclos[ed] a complacency that comes only with the conviction they had been 'saved.'" Their triumphant voices could still be heard long after they had filed through the stadium gates. To the tune of the "Battle Hymn of the Republic," they sang:

> From the village, from the city, all the nation's voices roared.
> Down the rivers, 'cross the prairies, like a torrent it has poured.
> We will march like Gideon's Army.
> We will fight with Gideon's sword,
> For the people's march is on—Glory, Glory Hallelujah.

Across the prairies in Nebraska, however, only 283 people attended the Progressive Party state convention, held that same evening. Since at least 750 had to be present to qualify the party for the ballot, the Progressives had apparently failed in their attempt. The Nebraska secretary of state, an obliging Republican who was eager to have the third party recognized, opted for a "loose interpretation" of the statute and allowed the Wallaceites to try again the following day, when he would consider their convention still "officially" in session. The next morning, only ten persons showed up.[4]

■ Sadly for Wallace's supporters, by mid-September, the political situation in Omaha was far more typical than that in the Bronx. In "the vast doubt-ful area beyond the five boroughs," the *New York Post* observed, the march of Gideon's Army appeared to be coming to a slow halt.[5] Even the United Electrical Workers (UE), considered at one time to be the keystone of the third party's labor support, failed to endorse Wallace after he spoke at the union's annual convention on September 6. The UE's pro-Soviet leaders acknowledged that such a move would have "split the organization wide open," and, as the director of organization James Matles later recalled, despite relentless pressure from the CP hierarchy, he and his colleagues were determined to avoid "reckless militancy."[6] Most independent liberals who felt uneasy with the anticommunism of such groups as Americans for Democratic Action (ADA) had also fallen away. Those who remained, including the journalist I. F. Stone, viewed the third party not as a na-scent political force destined for future greatness, but merely as a conve-nient means for casting a protest vote. "In thirty minutes, cross-legged, saying 'Oom' with alternative exhalations, I can conjure up a better third party movement than Wallace's," Stone remarked. Acknowledging that the Communists were doing "a major part of the work . . . from ringing door-bells to framing platforms," he nonetheless decided to stick with the third party. "I'm just a poor dupe who can't take Dewey or Truman," he declared. Though the Progressives gladly accepted his support, such remarks typi-fied the dwindling enthusiasm in the ranks of Gideon's Army.[7]

The contention that the Progressives were deliberately splitting the liberal vote to ensure the election of a "reactionary" Congress had also taken its toll. For months, organized labor and ADA had been hammering the third party for opposing candidates who, in their view, had impeccable liberal credentials. They intensified their attacks as the "inevitability" of a Dewey presidency raised the stakes in the battle for control of Capitol Hill. On September 5, the Textile Workers Union of America released a pamphlet provocatively entitled "Third Party: Red Ally of Reaction," which purported to tell "the shocking story of an evil scheme to divide and confuse American liberals." It analyzed eighty-three congressional races to corroborate the union's charge that the Progressives were carrying out a Communist-conceived plan to guarantee the "triumph of reaction." A Wallace spokesperson immediately denounced the broadside as "a complete and vicious distortion of the facts," noting that in many districts, particularly in the South, the Progressive nominee offered the only challenge to a "reactionary" victory.[8] In hindsight, more objective observers concurred that the allegation of a "red plot," though effective propaganda, was wide of the mark. As one study concluded, "When [the] particularly aggressive, non-compromising personalities of 'militant' local Progressive leaders got out of hand, tactical decisions appeared to result more from emotion than from cold calculations of strategy."[9]

Regardless of whether it was the third party's objective to elect conservative candidates, the fact remained that in many close races their presence would do just that. The Progressives found it especially difficult to justify their opposition to liberals in several districts in Southern California. Jack Berman, who ran against Chet Holifield, a popular pro–New Deal congressman from Los Angeles, later conceded that his third party candidacy had been a mistake. "We couldn't even explain it to our own people, let alone the community at large," Berman recalled. Still, as late as August 8, Beanie Baldwin told reporters that the party had no intention of withdrawing its opposition to Holifield, Helen Gahagan Douglas, Franck R. Havenner, and other Golden State Democrats. "We're trying to get a progressive Congress," Baldwin maintained, but Holifield, Douglas, and the others had refused to cross-file on the IPP ticket. The party had no choice but to enter its own candidates to "protect" its line on the ballot.[10]

By the end of the month, however, pressure began to mount from within the party to pull Progressive candidates who were running against liberal Democrats. Particularly influential was the input of pro-Wallace trade union officials who were already looking past election day. Having witnessed their membership's flat rejection of the third party, the leaders of the CIO's pro-Soviet faction had concluded that the CP's proposed "antimonopoly coalition" would never replace the CIO as an alternative power base from which to advance the Communist cause. Already deep into Philip Murray's dog house, they feared the consequences if they had to shoulder the blame for the defeat of pro-labor Democrats without the compensation of a strong Progressive showing. In the first indication of a developing trend, Thomas Fitzpatrick, a concealed Communist and the Progressive candidate for Congress in western Pennsylvania's Thirty-Third district, declared on August 29 the he was withdrawing from the race. Fitzpatrick, the president of UE Local 601, threw his support to Frank Buchanan, the Democratic incumbent, who was considered one of the CIO's most reliable advocates in the House of Representatives. During the next few weeks, a handful of Progressive candidates throughout the country made similar announcements.[11]

In his after-dinner remarks at a Businessmen for Wallace fund-raiser in New York City on September 21, Baldwin formally acknowledged the party's change in tack and promised to issue a "comprehensive statement" on the matter in the seven to ten days. Conceding nothing to his critics, however, he sharply denounced the charges of "vote splitting." Baldwin insisted that the party would "never collaborate with reactionaries" and would "work in unity with any group to help progressive candidates." He pointed out that the Progressives had already withdrawn from the governor's race in Connecticut and had offered to support the Democratic nominee, Chester Bowles, a former New Dealer. Yet Bowles had repudiated the party's endorsement and reiterated his support for the Marshall Plan. Nonetheless, Baldwin explained, the party would not re-enter the contest since Connecticut Progressives believed that "pressure . . . was applied on Bowles to get him to make that decision."

Baldwin went on to report that the party was planning to drop its opposition to liberal Democrats running for Congress in California, despite these candidates' refusal to cross-file in the IPP and their continued support for the Truman foreign policy. Baldwin then asserted that the state Democratic machine had pressured liberals like Douglas not to seek the IPP nomination because it knew that "the Progressive Party in California is destined to be the majority party in that state." Still, he added, "I hope, and I think, that the IPP in California will be supporting Helen Douglas." Baldwin's comments regarding Douglas were false. The congresswoman had always opposed the third party and had even resisted pressure from California Democratic officials who thought she *should* cross-file in the IPP to avoid a three-way contest. Baldwin concluded by implying that further withdrawals in other states should be expected, but emphasized that in every case the national office would leave the final decision to the local organization.[12]

This shift in policy clearly caught Wallace by surprise, resulting in an awkward public exchange between the candidate and his campaign manager that offered further evidence that the third party was beginning to unravel. Taking the podium after Baldwin had sat down, Wallace exclaimed, "But, Beanie, what do you do with our party, with all this talk here—supporting Chester Bowles? Maybe it's the thing to do. Maybe you want to get these scared liberals off our backs. . . . [But] some day you will have to build a party. I got into this campaign because I thought peace was really important. If Bowles doesn't think much of peace, or enough of it to stand up, I wonder how good he will be for peace." Continuing extemporaneously, Wallace declared, "I still don't know how Helen Gahagan Dulles [*sic*] stands on the Truman Doctrine." It would be hard to endorse her, he continued, "when she doesn't want our support." Drawing back, Wallace reassured his audience that there wasn't "any split between Beanie and me," and then he moved on to other topics. Yet in his windup, he returned to the subject, predicting that by 1952 the Democratic Party would be even more reactionary and that politicians like Bowles and Douglas would be forced to go along with it. Accordingly, Wallace maintained, Progressives interested in building a New Party could not afford to support them in 1948. After the morning papers reported what seemed to be a fundamental disagreement within the party's top ranks, Wallace hastily released a statement claiming that he had been misunderstood. He said he believed Baldwin's strategy was the "proper approach" and had only been "discussing the undertones of his remarks." "The bewilderment of outsiders at the tactics of the Progressive Party seems hardly greater than the confusion within the governing circles of that organization," the *Nation* concluded, in one of the more generous assessments of this curious episode.[13]

Indeed, the Wallace-Baldwin exchange only refocused attention on the central issue of who was calling the shots in the Progressive Party. Regardless of how one took Wallace's belated profession of agreement with his campaign manager, it was evident that party officials had not bothered to consult with him before implementing a significant modification in strategy. Wallace had insisted repeatedly both in his public statements and in private correspondence that he could not support under any circumstances candidates who endorsed the Truman foreign policy, since, in his eyes, this meant that they "opposed peace." His off-the-cuff remarks on September 21, not to mention his Yankee Stadium speech, gave no indication that he had abandoned this position. Yet the party that he ostensibly led had now endorsed men and women whose views on the paramount issue of "peace" were fundamentally in conflict with his own.

Similarly, subsequent events belied Baldwin's claim that the local organizations always had the final say on the selection and endorsement of candidates. While announcing the Progressive Party's support of Hubert H. Humphrey's bid for the U.S. Senate, Baldwin explained that the decision had been made on the home grounds in Minnesota and that he had not yet received a "full report" on the deliberations. His statement brought a quick denial from Orville Olson, the Minnesota chairman of the Wallace-for-President Committee. "At no meeting of Progressive leaders in Minnesota has it been suggested that we support Humphrey," said Olson. "Progressives cannot and will not indorse Humphrey on the basis of his program which includes the peacetime draft and support for the Truman-Dewey war program." "Decisions on local candidates will be made by people in Minnesota," he added defiantly. In other states, too, there was no record of any rank-and-file discussion or of public meetings devoted to the subject of withdrawing Progressive candidates. Nonetheless, the new policy went forward. By September 30, the Progressives had dropped out of thirteen congressional races, and in the following weeks they would pull their nominees from several more.[14]

The change in course failed to revive the Progressives' diminishing political fortunes. Rather than inviting a reassessment of the party as its leaders had anticipated, the new policy was widely viewed as a belated acknowledgment that the CIO and ADA had leveled valid charges. Instead of applauding what the Progressives considered a gesture of good faith, political commentators pointed out that the Wallaceites' latest action merely begged the larger question: Why had the candidates been entered in the first place? Others suspected, with some justification, that having failed to prevent congressional approval of the Marshall Plan, the Communists within the Progressive Party had decided that the time had come to stage a tactical retreat. The Communist press never published any criticism of the candidate withdrawals, indicating that the CP had acceded to the Progressives' "right opportunist" strategy, if indeed its agents within the Progressive Party had not initiated the strategy themselves. Ironically, however, the third party's concession to political expedience produced the opposite of its intended effect. While the move failed to win Wallace any new support from independent voters, it demoralized many of the non-Communists who had stuck by the third party precisely because it had refused to back any candidate who endorsed the Truman Doctrine and the Marshall Plan. By capitulating on the issue of foreign policy, these stalwarts argued, the Progressive Party had nullified its very raison d'être.[15]

Most outside observers placed less significance on the change in policy, interpreting it merely as a confession of weakness. Indeed, by the time many of the candidates officially withdrew, the polls showed that they were no longer a factor in determining the outcome of their races. The third party, its critics argued, was simply trying to avoid the embarrassment of a feeble showing on election day. If the liberal Democrat won, they predicted, Progressives would claim that their support had made the difference, but if he or she lost, party spokespeople would attribute the result to the candidate's failure to embrace the Wallace program. For their part, the Democratic beneficiaries of the Progressive withdrawals wanted nothing to do with the Wallace and his partisans. Realizing that any association with the third party would be a "kiss of death," none accepted the endorsements offered them, and most went out of their way to repudiate Progressive support.[16] To veteran observers of Popular Front tactics, it seemed that in order to conceal their own political impotence, the left-wingers were once again trying to envelop themselves in the warm embrace of mainstream liberalism. Though plausible, such an argument assumes that the remaining Progressives recognized the degree to which the voters had rejected them. The most remarkable aspect of the Wallace campaign, however, was its supporters' unshakable faith—even in the face of overwhelming evidence to the contrary—that they spoke for, and had the full backing of, "the people."[17]

■ On September 23, Wallace set off on his final national speaking tour. Everywhere he went the crowds were smaller and less enthusiastic; the "gates" at the evening meetings fell off considerably. "The chill winds of apathy have begun at last to affect Henry A. Wallace's public," observed the veteran *New York Times* correspondent Cabell Phillips. "The members of this group have developed an observable tendency to shuffle their feet and to sit on their hands." In the locales where Wallace was making his second or third appearance, his novelty value had clearly worn off. The formula of slick stage production that had attracted many curious spectators to his earlier rallies had grown stale, while Wallace himself, after campaigning nearly nonstop for almost two years, was hardly an unknown quantity. Outside of the nightly gatherings that attracted the same small circle of supporters in every community, his presence in numerous towns went virtually unnoticed. Even the hostility he had previously aroused petered out into indifference. After officially declaring the Wallace candidacy a "bust," the syndicated columnist Frank Kent observed, "Looking back, it seems remarkable that there ever should have been real apprehension about it."[18]

Wallace's reception in California, where at one time Progressives had believed they would poll more than a million votes, was especially disappointing. Expecting to find enthusiastic crowds in the Central Valley, where striking farm and oil workers were considered natural IPP constituencies, the candidate instead got the cold shoulder. In Bakersfield, only 372 people showed up to hear Wallace speak in a baseball stadium that held 3,000. When Fresno State College withdrew its invitation to Wallace to address an afternoon convocation, local party officials sought to capitalize on the issue of "academic freedom" by inviting students to attend his evening rally free of charge. More than 2,000 took them up on the offer and proceeded to boo, jeer, and ridicule Wallace as he delivered a soporific discourse on extending government price supports for the local raisin crop. In perennially reliable Los Angeles, Wallace spoke to 19,000 paying customers at a mass meeting in Gilmore Stadium, but even this respectable total was down from the 31,000 that had turned out the previous May. Still, IPP officials proudly pointed out that their candidate had attracted 6,000 more people than President Truman when he had appeared at Gilmore Stadium a fortnight before.[19] Yet Wallace's ability to outdraw Truman was hardly a barometer of popular sentiment or an index of the votes to be cast on election day. Though Progressives assumed that there were "thousands more" for every one supporter who attended their rallies, the final results on November 2 plainly indicated they were mistaken. "Those people in that stadium represented only themselves," the Hollywood Ten screenwriter Dalton Trumbo later observed. "They were busy as hell organizing each other and making noise, but when you counted noses at a Progressive rally you were actually counting the full Progressive vote of the district."[20]

A poignant demonstration of the hard times that had befallen the Progressives occurred on September 28 at a campaign luncheon in St. Louis. As Wallace looked on, the chairman of the event, the Reverend Charles G. Wilson, an Episcopal pastor and veteran Missouri liberal, addressed the unexpectedly small audience. "I see a lot of faces that aren't here," he began, "faces of good people who were with us a year ago." "I'm not happy," he declared, "I ask, why are the remaining ones of us here?" As the hardcore partisans in the audience fidgeted self-consciously, Wilson went on to condemn the "oversimplification of the revolutionary utopians—their easy, doctrinaire answers." In a calm but deliberate tone he denounced "the forces of destruction identified with the New Party." There could be little doubt he was referring to the Communists. Citing what he termed "the impossible choice" between Truman and Dewey, Wilson said he would go along with the Progressive Party, but only reluctantly, and solely because of Wallace's association with it. This kind of public soul-searching put the crowd on edge. Such unseemly comments were to be expected from the Progressives' enemies in the anticommunist press, but the elderly minister was one of their own, and less easily dismissed as an "agent of Wall Street." A series of speakers immediately leaped up to chide Wilson for his lack of faith, adamantly declaring that they had no misgivings, doubts, or second thoughts.[21]

In his response to his host, Wallace acknowledged that many of his former supporters had abandoned him. "I can't help feeling that their chief governing motive is that they hate Henry Wallace," he exclaimed plaintively. "I don't know why they hate me. I'm still holding the door open for them. I used to say they'd come along after Truman was nominated. But they didn't come flocking to us the way I hoped." Baffled and hurt, Wallace nonetheless remained resolute. Once again, he proudly compared his third party to Gideon's Army, which in the end was reduced to three hundred men, after various members of the initial force had failed to pass muster. That his ranks, too, had thinned, Wallace declared, would not dishearten him. As one journalist observed, "In his inexplicable way, Wallace gloried in the fact. He said that that was the way he wanted it to be; that now, dispossessed of the faint-hearted, he and the others could go on to build the third party for the future." Even critics were taken by the pathos of such remarks.[22]

On the stump and over the airwaves, however, Wallace struck a different note. As the campaign wound down, his rhetoric became increasingly strident. Those working against him, he insisted, were not "just opponents," but "enemies." "Their real intention," he cried, "is to surrender this country—its resources and its people—our earnings and our children—to a chosen few who will march us either to slavery or to war—or both." "The men who are trying to run the world by dominating American foreign policy are the same kind of men who built up Germany for world conquest after World War I," he declared during a radio address in Fresno. "[They] have split Germany in order to create a new Nazi state in the heart of Europe." The anticommunist Germans opposing a Soviet takeover in Berlin, he asserted, were Nazis—"the same people, the same spirit." Speaking in Tacoma, Wallace claimed that the "bipartisan reactionaries" were replicating Hitler's anti-Comintern crusade. He compared Dewey and Truman to Nazi war criminals. At the Nuremberg trials, Wallace noted, the defendants claimed that they had not wanted war and were only trying to protect their country against a "Bolshevik menace." "Is it any less cynical or deceitful if these same things are said by Republicans and Democrats?" Wallace asked. "Will less people die under a false slogan if it is spoken in English rather than in German?"[23]

His extreme reaction to the Berlin crisis dramatically illustrated Wallace's conviction that conspiring Wall Street cartelists and fascist-minded militarists were directing U.S. policy. He accused the Truman administration of manufacturing yet another "phony war scare" and of then purposely avoiding a diplomatic settlement to whip up still more anti-Soviet hysteria. "The crisis atmosphere abroad is intended to numb you with fear," he told his supporters. "The bipartisans talk about a Berlin crisis . . . and the scare headlines hide from you what is really going on." The airlift itself, he asserted, was simply the latest sensationalistic "smoke screen" to obscure the efforts of monopolists to rebuild and rearm Nazi Germany. The profits of American munitions companies would soar, Wallace predicted, as German fascists were once again "turned loose" on the Soviet Union and the rest of Europe.[24]

When the Western powers submitted the matter of the Berlin blockade to the United Nations, Wallace only intensified his attacks. Though he had long called for a stronger UN, he now maintained that the Security Council was not the proper place to resolve such a dispute. Indeed, Wallace contended, Secretary of State Marshall was well aware of this, for his true objective was to destroy the UN by "using it as a forum for reckless attacks on Russia—a forum for incitement to war." Marshall, he asserted, was deliberately plotting "the expulsion of the Soviet Union from the United Nations." As an alternative to UN action Wallace proposed the creation of a "fact-finding commission of representative Americans" to look into "the pattern of recurrent war scares." Such an investigation, he said, "would uncover impartial evidence and show the relationship between these crises and the determination of great corporations which have infiltrated our government to continue fabulous war industry profits, high prices, and the militarization of America." When questioned by reporters, Wallace acknowledged that the Soviets might not allow his commission members to investigate in Russia or to circulate their final report there if it proved unfavorable to Moscow. Asked if he would accept its findings if it sustained the United States' position, he replied evasively, "I can't answer that now."[25]

In the meantime, Wallace called for the immediate resumption of direct U.S.-Soviet negotiations over Berlin. After pointing out that such talks had already proved fruitless, thus necessitating the referral to the

UN, journalists at a San Francisco press conference inquired what specific steps Wallace would take to ensure a more satisfactory outcome. Wallace responded with his now familiar refrain. "I would get the men in the State Department together and have them get hold of their opposite numbers in the Russian foreign office," he said. "Then I would have them go word by word into what differences lie between us. Many of our discords are [a] failure to get thoughts across the barrier of language. After that, I think it would be time for the heads of State to meet and find an agreement." Had not that approach already been tried, reporters wondered. How would he succeed where others had failed? "I am an optimist," Wallace told them.[26]

By mid-October, however, most commentators had concluded that Wallace was a Soviet apologist. "His language was shrill, angry, and utterly unconvincing," declared James Wechsler. "He echoed each line in the reckless Communist polemics. . . . He took left-wing gossip and elevated it to the plane of political oratory. . . . On his final Western trip he had reduced all the world's anxieties to the pattern of a political dime-novel. . . . Now, perhaps reflecting the desperation of the final hours, all variations from left-wing orthodoxy were stricken from the script. In the last 10,000 miles," Wechsler concluded, "Wallace's speeches had the uniformly ranting quality of a *Daily Worker* editorial." The candidate was the portrait of a man "wandering in a pink fog," observed the *Minneapolis Tribune*, "a man who gropes his confused and uncertain way through a cloudlike mass of unrealities. . . . To Wallace, the world and its woes may still be methodically reduced into the simple terms of Wall Street, American war profiteers, big business, and the hypocrisies of war-mongering Republicans and Democrats." "These outgivings," the *Los Angeles Times* suggested, "do not necessarily prove that Wallace is nutty. They may merely prove that he has been chased out on a limb by the facts . . . and does not know how to get back, except by denying that the facts exist."[27]

Others believed that Wallace was simply going through the motions— reading whatever was put in front of him without fully taking into account or even comprehending the gravity, and even the mendacity, of his allegations. Such behavior, some observers maintained, was not unprecedented for Wallace. Throughout his career, they noted, he had used language in a cavalier manner, making sweeping statements and provocative charges without offering supporting evidence or pausing to consider the ramifications of his words. When called on the matter, Wallace's usual response was to claim he had been misquoted or to downplay the significance of the comments in question by dismissing them as mere "political oratory." One contemporary account of his October campaign appearances draws a vivid portrait of the casual manner in which Wallace could deliver blistering criticisms. "Day by day," wrote Max Hall of the Associated Press, "Henry Wallace's campaign accusations have grown more explosive; reporters wonder how much further he will go in his bitter attacks on 'big business,' 'big brass' and 'Duman and Trewey.' But the blow-torch phrases of his recent speeches seem much more inflaming on paper than they do when Wallace reads them to an audience. He seldom raises his voice to put over a purple punch line. Many a sledge hammer sentence passes practically unnoticed. . . . Wallace puts on his glasses and starts reading the script. Solemnly, sometimes droningly, he plows on through his denunciations. . . . Then he finishes, he takes off his glasses, grins, nods, and waves again." Indeed, Wallace later tried to distance himself from his 1948 campaign addresses. "A very considerable number of speeches during that period were written by Lew," he recalled. "Frankly, I scarcely know what's in them to this day [1951]."[28]

Though some—including Wallace—then and later credited most of his inflammatory statements in campaign speeches to pro-Communist "ghostwriters," the same kinds of extreme statements also appear in his private correspondence. In early October, he wrote to a supporter that he found it "almost incredible" that "our own leaders should be hard at work rebuilding the Nazi world." In addition, copies of the formal public talks from this period, available in the Wallace Papers, contain edits in his own hand. Lew Frank, Wallace's principal speechwriter, later maintained that the candidate believed that many of the foreign policy positions set out in his addresses were "too mild" and that the "bipartisans" should be attacked even more sharply. Nonetheless, as Wechsler and others contended, the resemblance of Wallace's remarks to the Communist "line" in substance, argument, and even phrasing was too close to be entirely coincidental. Clearly his left-wing advisers were playing a significant role in shaping his thinking.[29]

Ultimately, it is impossible to explain with certainty how Wallace came to adopt particular points of view, but circumstantial evidence indicates that he uncritically accepted the Communist interpretation of events because it fleshed out in specific terms his own vague suspicion that evil men in the service of "Wall Street" were dictating U.S. foreign policy. Furthermore, the Communists' ability to present their case in simple, black-and-white terms and to express it with such deep-seated emotion and moral indignation appears to have appealed to Wallace, for he, too, was most comfortable discussing matters of policy in such highly charged and moralistic terms. Wallace's own lack of diplomatic experience and his limited knowledge of world affairs can also explain his willingness to believe (and repeat) everything his left-wing advisers told him. This ignorance was often painfully obvious when reporters confronted him with facts not recognized as such by the Communist Party, as in the case of the Czech coup and the Berlin crisis.[30]

Wallace's Christian utopianism also enters into the picture. Despite what appeared to be his early support for a "spheres of influence" settlement to ease U.S.-Soviet tensions, Wallace abhorred negotiated solutions based solely on power considerations. His stated conviction that nations should settle their differences according to the principles of the Sermon on the Mount was not mere rhetoric, but the bedrock of his entire philosophy of international relations. For Wallace, peace was the natural order of things and would prevail as long as morally upright men were in positions of power. Good men, he believed, could not have fundamental differences because they were all "children of God." In large part this explains why Wallace never offered a specific set of proposals or quid pro quos for negotiating with the Soviets. In his view, the details would work themselves out once honest "progressive" men—not Wall Street reactionaries—sat down and openly discussed their differences.

The weak link in this chain of logic, of course, was that Wallace could never provide any compelling evidence that Stalin thought along the same lines as he did, or that the Soviet leader's definition of a "just peace" was in any way compatible with his own. Rather than admit as much, Wallace took it on faith that Stalin was a "progressive." After all, he reasoned, as a Communist, Stalin did not put "property rights" first, as did the fascists and the reactionaries. Once the leaders of the U.S. government convinced the Soviet leader, through gestures of goodwill, that they, too, were "progressive," Wallace felt certain that Stalin would prove accommodating. Even before Wallace had launched his third party crusade, the distinguished columnist Walter Lippmann had noted that his utopian faith prevented Wallace from being an effective advocate for a plausible foreign policy. "His goodness is unworldly," declared Lippmann, "his heart is so detached from the realities that he has never learned to measure, as a statesman must, the relation of good and of evil in current affairs." Wallace had been "a good and faithful public servant," as long as he was "protected, led, guided, and disciplined," Lippmann observed. "But when he had to face the realities of our time directly, . . . the reality was too much for him."[31]

Others also discerned Wallace's inability to confront real-world problems. In one of the most penetrating contemporary analyses of the former vice president, David T. Bazelon argued that at the core of Wallace's being was an irreconcilable duality of "technical capacity" and "religious feeling." He was an "excellent technician"—"better with tools and with things," but when confronted with a nontechnical problem, Wallace relied on his spiritual instincts to bring him to a solution. In Bazelon's opinion, this often led him into murky confusion and flights of fancy. Wallace, he argued, was a *"non-functioning* moral symbol for the progressive struggle," but "in no sense a fighter for human betterment in a world of realities." Moreover, he often manifested an "almost calculated failure to discern the real factors of power," and, accordingly, only offered "purely rhetorical resolutions of problems." Bazelon, writing eight months before the founding of the New Party, concluded with an intriguing forecast: "It should not be too difficult to predict Wallace's role in a future progressive upsurge. As long as it is more Stalinist than socialist, and more religious than militant, he might well be at the head of it. But he would serve as a speechifying symbol of such a movement, rather than its actual leader."[32] In the final weeks of the campaign, Bazelon's assessment seemed remarkably prescient.

■ Halfway through the fall tour, Wallace's traveling party, and even the candidate himself, came to realize that the campaign desperately needed retooling. From Seattle, Lew Frank called New York to warn Baldwin and Abt—not for the first time—that the strategy of mass meetings had played itself out. He suggested that the party cancel all but the most important of Wallace's remaining public appearances. Instead, he proposed in several lengthy memos that the Progressives establish a "Peace Headquarters" at a Chicago radio station from which the candidate would broadcast his foreign policy views directly to the people—all day, every day until November 2. "The whole setting," he explained, "should be one of moral indignation, a demand for a return to principles and to the policies of FDR. It would be a call for a national crusade to regain principled polices." Incredibly, given the near unanimous popular approval of the dramatic Berlin airlift, Frank believed that the present situation provided the perfect rallying point for such a "peace offensive." He was certain that the people were anxious to express their opposition to the president's handling of the crisis. The Progressives, he contended, could mobilize this sentiment and thereby compel Truman to take the issue out of the hands of the UN and resume direct negotiations with the Soviets. Such a campaign, he predicted, would also secure "hundreds of thousands of Wallace votes."[33]

Though Frank correctly perceived that the party was in trouble, he did not discern that there was something more fundamentally wrong than merely the inability to get its message to the public. Like most Progressives, he remained confident that once "the people" were educated, they would finally see the light. "We've got the ammunition," he told Baldwin, "but we don't have the guns to fire it." In fact, precisely the opposite was true—Wallace had relentlessly asserted his "truths" to the voters, but they remained either indifferent or hostile to them. The more he campaigned, the more votes he lost. A Gallup poll released during the third week of October credited Wallace with 3.5 percent of the vote. He had had 5 percent in August; 6 percent in June; and 7 percent in January. More strikingly, he had the support of only 3.5 percent of CIO members—a constituency presumed to be well to the left of the general electorate. Public opinion polls showed not only Wallace's own numbers tumbling but also that Americans overwhelmingly opposed his positions on almost every major issue. Even more troubling from the Progressives' point of view, those voters best informed proved the staunchest supporters of Truman's foreign policies. The more a respondent knew about the Marshall Plan, for example, the more likely he or she was to approve of it. Notably, though Frank talked at great length in his memoranda about the threat of "clerical fascism" in Spain and the ominous rise of Charles de Gaulle in France, he not once sought to explain, or even to acknowledge, the role of the Soviet Union in contributing to the world crisis.[34] This ideological and ethical blind spot—not "red-baiting," strategic errors, or a failure to communicate effectively—accounted for the party's unpopularity. Yet paradoxically, any attempt to abandon its pro-Soviet orientation would have meant the dissolution of the Progressive Party, for this was the Communists' quid pro quo for continued support.

Some historians have echoed the Progressives' claim that Wallace "did not receive a fair and respectful hearing."[35] Yet simply because voters so overwhelmingly rejected the candidate and his message does not mean that they were not listening or were being kept from listening. Though it was difficult to challenge the anticommunist consensus of the early Cold War—particularly, it should be added, because there were perfectly rational reasons to be anticommunist during that period—it was not impossible. Wallace's Cold War critique failed to impress the reading public, which had easy access to the texts of his speeches and the platform of the Progressive Party, not because these men and women were obsessively anticommunist, but because the candidate's arguments were simplistic, unbalanced, and not carefully reasoned. Often, they were wrong on the facts and replete with false accusations. To be sure, if one strips away all the demagoguery and conspiratorial analysis, some cogent points emerge from Wallace's foreign policy speeches—the danger of American self-righteousness, the open-endedness of the Truman Doctrine, the failure to consider Soviet insecurities—but other prominent figures, most notably Walter Lippmann, offered similarly critical insights without all the distortion and disingenuousness that pro-Communist "researchers" and ghostwriters packed into the Progressive Party's public statements. It is therefore unpersuasive to attribute the Wallace movement's failure to "red-baiting" without carefully and critically examining what the candidate said and what tactics the party's leaders employed.

Though Baldwin and Abt ultimately rejected Frank's proposal, the campaign did shift gears during the final two weeks, not so much in strategy—the mass meetings continued—but in the tone of its message. Rather than persisting in his bludgeoning of the Truman administration, Wallace now claimed that the president had accepted his arguments and was running on the Progressive Party platform. In the last few days before the election, Wallace also advanced the theory that the Progressives had accomplished all they had set out to do. This hypothesis received its most dramatic articulation on October 26 at a climactic "get out the vote" rally in Madison Square Garden. "Our party . . . has become a beacon of hope to the common people of every nation of the world," Wallace declared. "Because of us, the fighter for liberty in Greece, the peasant in China, the Haganah in the trenches of the Negev, know that since there is hope in America, there is also hope for him. . . . Because of us," he continued, "the gallant patriots of Israel . . . have not been betrayed by Wall Street and its oil. . . . Because of us, the Bill of Rights was not murdered by those infamous agents of reaction, Mundt and Nixon. . . . Because of us . . . the Big Brass has halted in its attempt to saddle American youth with universal military training." "But above all," Wallace triumphantly concluded, "we have stopped the cold war in its tracks. We have delayed its progress. We have thrown it out of gear. . . . There shall be no war." Assessing these bold claims, the journalist Irwin Ross remarked, "Rarely have the fantasies of a doomed candidate been expressed with such abandon." On election day, the grim reality of the Progressives' failure would finally hit home for Wallace.[36]

CONCLUSION

The final election results proved a devastating blow to the Progressive Party and all those associated with it. The presidential ticket finished an embarrassing fourth behind the Dixiecrats, polling only 1.1 million votes, 2.37 percent of those cast. The narrowness of Wallace's appeal was equally striking. Thirty-seven percent of his nationwide total came from New York City. In California, his second strongest state, 53 percent of the votes came from Los Angeles County. Few had anticipated such a poor showing. The last preelection Roper survey had put Wallace at 3.6 percent, a figure the Progressives fiercely disputed, charging that the pollster had "suppressed" the real numbers because he knew there was a huge "hidden vote" for the third party.[1] The polls notwithstanding, on election eve, many Progressives remained convinced that Wallace would garner between 5 and 10 million votes.[2] Had the Republicans won as expected, there might have been some solace for the Progressives: perhaps the Democrats would have realized that they needed the support of the Wallace camp and adjusted their policies to facilitate a postelection alliance. Truman's victory, however, dramatically revealed the left's weakness and cast serious doubt on the future of any independent progressive movement. Clearly, the Democrats had little incentive to pursue such an alliance, and the left little to offer them. Even liberals who remained in the Truman camp found their position undermined as Democratic politicians came to see that the "threat" of the left had been illusory. Margaret Marshall of the *Nation* had seen this result coming long before election day. "Mr. Wallace," she wrote, "has lowered the prestige and splintered the force of liberal opinion; and in so far as he has identified liberal opinion with Communist opinion, he has made it tragically easy for his successful rival to ignore it and even to condemn it."[3]

Independent liberals emerged from the campaign significantly weakened, but the Communist Party was the biggest loser—though its leaders adamantly refused to acknowledge the obvious until years later.[4] The Party had thrown its entire weight behind the Wallace candidacy, jeopardizing its position in the labor movement and abruptly severing alliances with liberal political groups that had taken years to cultivate. Moreover, it had done so not in response to direct orders from Moscow. Rather, its own leadership's profound misreading both of the domestic mood and of the international situation had led it to misinterpret signals from the Soviets. Convinced that war and economic catastrophe were imminent, William Z. Foster had forced his comrades to embark on a suicidal course. Through its own intransigence and insistence on playing a "leading role" in the so-called antimonopoly coalition, the CP had so alienated pro-Wallace liberals that it lost the "cover" they had provided. "Standing alone, without the support of significant allies," Joseph Starobin observed, "the C.P. revealed a weakness which ten years of hard work had served to conceal. This weakness invited attack, and the attack contributed to further weakness." The Communist Party would endure relentless persecution in the years to come, but for all intents and purposes, its influence within American political life had already come to an end.[5]

So, too, had the political career of Henry Wallace. Some Progressives privately expressed relief and exhilaration at Truman's astonishing victory, but for Wallace, the president's triumph made his own dismal showing an even more difficult pill to swallow. He put on a brave face for the press and party workers, insisting he was "not in any way disappointed" with the results, but an angry and condescending telegram that he sent to Truman on election night revealed the depth of his bitterness. Failing to mention the president's victory, the statement called on Truman "to repudiate the bipartisan foreign policy, to remove the military from the civilian branch of government, and the bankers from the State Department." There was no word of congratulations. When aides suggested that this was an inappropriate omission and violated the spirit of good sportsmanship, Wallace retorted, "Under no circumstances will I congratulate that son of a bitch."[6]

In time, however, Wallace's views on the third party gambit changed. Though he never regretted launching what he called his "crusade for peace," he grew resentful at the Communists who had joined his campaign and assumed positions of influence. "My strong advocacy of peace with

Russia caused the Communist Party to make capital of my candidacy," he wrote in an article for *Life* magazine in 1956. "In their fanatical way, they ruined my campaign and destroyed the efforts of a great many truly patriotic Americans who worked very hard for the success of the Progressive Party." As early as 1949, Wallace had begun to distance himself from the Progressives. When Paul Robeson declared at a civil rights meeting that there should be no guarantee of free speech for "Trotskyites," Wallace asked that Robeson be removed as a party officer—a request that the executive board ignored. He also refused to involve himself in the controversy that resulted when violence broke out at a Robeson concert in Peekskill, New York, believing that the subsequent protests were fronted by the Communists. In 1950, Wallace made his final break with the Progressives when he refused to sign a statement blaming the United States for the Korean War. After rejecting what amounted to an endorsement of the Communist position on the war, Wallace officially resigned from the party he had founded—one of only two members of the 155-member national committee to do so, an indication of the degree to which the Progressive Party, while becoming less and less popular, had become more and more "front." Wallace also disagreed sharply with those who insisted that Communist infiltration of the Progressive Party during 1948 had been exaggerated. Indeed, an argument about the issue ended his friendship with Alfred and Martha Dodd Stern. In a somber conversation with Michael Straight in 1953, Wallace lamented the way things had turned out. "I blame Beanie for a lot," he told Straight.[7]

Wallace also changed his views on the liberals who had deserted Gideon's Army and on those potential soldiers who had never joined. In a testy exchange of letters with Curtis MacDougall, he made clear that he did not accept MacDougall's condemnation of the supposedly "weak willed" liberals who had abandoned the third party cause. "I disagree with you with regard to your criticism of the liberals who left the Progressive Party," Wallace wrote.

> There were millions of liberals who wanted to be associated with what we stood for in the Progressive Party but who did not want to be in the same Party with certain very loud-mouthed people who preached a doctrine utterly in line with the Communist Party at all times. While I did not realize it fully during the campaign, I began to realize it more and more after the campaign ended that it is impossible to have anything in the nature of a common front with the Communist Party. . . . My only regret is that I did not hit harder in this direction. Because I

did not, the liberals felt justified in leaving us. In retrospect I cannot criticize them for so doing.

Wallace eventually reconciled with Truman and many of the Democratic leaders he had denounced in 1948. At a Washington dinner party in 1962, he remarked to the former president, "You were right to fire me when you did." Though Wallace withdrew from public life after 1950, the issue of peace did remain foremost in his mind. Once the quintessential New Dealer, he voted twice for Dwight D. Eisenhower, convinced that the GOP nominee was more likely to keep the nation out of war.[8]

■ In the days and weeks after the election, Progressive Party officials, desperate to divert attention from the enormity of their defeat, gamely claimed credit for Truman's victory. Had Wallace and Taylor not forced the president to "move left," they asserted, he could never have won the support of the people. To some, such an argument had at least the ring of plausibility since many less partisan observers had also concluded that the president owed his reelection to the "fighting liberal" campaign he had waged down the stretch. Yet a closer look reveals that Truman's stated positions on the major domestic issues had changed little since his first message to Congress following Roosevelt's death. Though his rhetoric had grown increasingly heated, perhaps giving the impression that he was es-pousing a more "militant" program, it was difficult to point to any spe-cific issue, with the possible exception of civil rights, on which Truman had taken a more liberal position after Wallace's entry into the campaign. Moreover, the Progressive Party until the very last moment insisted that Truman had betrayed the New Deal. That he would suddenly reverse him-self due to the influence of a political movement that had proven itself so profoundly unpopular with the electorate was hardly convincing. As Jo-seph Starobin later maintained, had the Progressives voluntarily thrown their support behind Truman in August, they might have had a more le-gitimate claim to some credit for his come-from-behind victory. "Instead," Starobin noted, "they argued in November that they had a share of the victory because their audience had turned from them."[9]

One can make a more persuasive case that by siphoning off the Demo-cratic Party's relatively small pro-Soviet element, the Wallace candidacy allowed Truman to win back many disaffected Catholic and Eastern Eu-ropean voters who had grown disenchanted with the New Deal's "pinkish" tinge. Truman drew a record vote among Catholics, even outpolling Al Smith's numbers from 1928 in some areas. According to Samuel Lubell's post-election analysis, "this heavily Catholic turnout—perhaps the most astonishing single aspect of Truman's surprising victory—resulted largely from the return to the Democratic Party of supporters of Father Coughlin." In this instance, voters' perception of Truman as a "centrist," not a militant liberal, proved the draw. The liberals' failure to gain any traction for the most "advanced" items on their agenda during Truman's subsequent term suggests that the president's reelection did not signal a widespread popular desire for a shift to the left.[10]

The Progressives' presence in the race also prevented the Republicans from using the issue of communism against the Democrats, and indeed allowed Truman to bolster his own anticommunist credentials by attacking Wallace. Republican strategists acknowledged as much. The chairman of the Hamilton County Republican Committee in New York wrote to Thomas Dewey that in the absence of a third party, "all of the extreme left wingers, screwballs, etc., would have been in Truman's camp and he would have had a left-wing load to carry and explain." Dewey agreed. "There is a lot to what you say about the Wallace candidacy," he replied. "In many respects he helped the opposition more than he hurt them." "He would be missed in 1952," the historian William O'Neill has wryly observed.[11]

In yet another example of unintended consequences, rather than provoking a debate on foreign policy, Wallace's third party candidacy helped crystallize the Cold War consensus. Many liberals who held serious reservations about the president's conduct of international affairs but considered the Progressives' approach even more reckless found themselves in a difficult spot—"carefully threading their way between the Wallace wonderland and simple-minded Trumanism," as James Wechsler put it. Most tempered or suppressed altogether their concerns about certain aspects of the bipartisan foreign policy so as not to be identified with the third party and its Communist supporters. Those who opted to join the Progressive Party, including Rexford Tugwell and H. Stuart Hughes, found it impossible to engage their colleagues in a discussion of foreign policy that transcended the reflexive pro-Soviet cant of the Communist Party line. Ironically, they, too, found themselves limited to a choice of either suppressing their views or severing their ties with the Progressive Party. Ultimately, the Progressives—under the ideological policing of their Communist allies—reduced complex issues to slogans and epithets and thus contributed to the stifling of substantive and reasoned debate. This was not inadvertent. Adhering to the Zhdanov line that posited "two camps" and no middle ground, the Communists within the Wallace movement actively sought to simplify and polarize. So too did Wallace. Though never comfortable with the Communist presence in the Progressive Party, he did share the Communists' Manichaean worldview. Employing a populist argot that reduced difficult policy choices to the stark terms of a morality play—the "good" common people who wanted "peace" and the "bad" Wall Street interests who wanted "war"—Wallace contributed little to the debate on foreign policy and, arguably, did much to discredit dissent from the Truman policies he so abhorred. For their part, the Communists failed to hinder passage of the Marshall Plan and, through their relentlessly pro-Soviet rhetoric, convinced many Americans that the CPUSA was best seen as a "fifth column"—an image that would bode ill for the Communists in the difficult years to come.[12]

The Progressive Party's failure as an electoral coalition also marked a turning point in the history of the American left, for it demonstrated the bankruptcy of Popular Front liberalism. The ordeal of Gideon's Army exposed the intellectual shallowness of the Popular Front and, more precisely, the debilitating effects on an insurgent movement from the left when it had to accommodate itself to the agenda of the Communist Party. Had the Progressive Party not been so closely tied to the CPUSA, both in the public mind and in reality, its supporters might have been able to make a more compelling argument to voters that their party had honest differences with organized labor and the anticommunist liberals of ADA about how one defined "a good liberal" and what exactly "good liberals" stood for. Perhaps, in time, a new liberal party—or at least a new kind of liberalism— might have emerged, as Wallace had hoped. Yet the unstable nature of the liberal-Communist alliance that constituted the Progressive Party made this impossible. Beyond an abstract commitment to such universally desired objectives as "peace" and "abundance," the pro-Wallace liberals and pro-Soviet Communists had nothing in common politically—though it would appear that only the Communists recognized this at the time. The CPUSA's leaders dismissed Wallace's notion of "progressive capitalism" as a contradiction in terms. They had no interest in debating the relative merits of various social and economic reforms; they considered all such ameliorative measures to be "dangerous illusions." As far as the Communists were concerned, any form of liberalism or democratic socialism was no less an enemy than "monopoly capitalism." To those who formed and articulated the policies of the American Communist Party, the Popular Front was not a distinct or desired ideological position, but a strategic tactic. Since they could hardly agitate within the Progressive Party for their true political preference, Soviet-style communism, they preferred to avoid any substantive discussion of specific domestic policy matters lest their "politically immature" comrades—the rank and file of the CP—find merit in "reformist" arguments and be lured back into "Browderite revisionism."

Accordingly, to achieve their primary goal of mobilizing an organized opposition to the Truman administration's anti-Soviet policies, the Communist members of the Progressive Party relied more on emotional appeals than on logical arguments. Much like Wallace, though with less sincerity, they effectively employed populist rhetoric to cultivate the non-Communists' inchoate resentment into intense loathing for various abstract "enemies"—"Wall Street," "Big Business," "red-baiters," "bipartisan warmongers." This shared antipathy, more than any particular set of policy objectives, provided the "glue" that held the Progressive Party together. Such a strategy's shortcoming, however, was that the rank and file had to be kept in a constant state of emotional agitation to preserve an otherwise synthetic unity. On those occasions when the Communists' conjuring of outside "demons" failed to stir sufficient emotion to maintain unity—or when the non-Communists' anger turned on the Communists themselves—organizational chaos resulted, as happened in numerous states where a promising movement ultimately disintegrated into chaos and mutual recriminations.

More often, however, liberals simply grew weary of Communist dogmatism and deception. Rather than challenge the comrades on issues of policy or battle them for control of the local party organization, many quietly withdrew from active participation in the Wallace campaign; they did not want to engage in a fight that would make them appear to be "red-baiters." The vituperative tone the Communists brought to the Progressive Party campaign also alienated many would-be supporters who were seeking a thoughtful alternative to the two major parties. The Communists' preference for vilification, personal attacks, and, in many cases, complete disregard for the facts discredited the third party, even among those who found Wallace an attractive candidate. Likewise, the CP's insistence on operating secretly within the Progressive Party fueled resentment, cultivated an atmosphere of distrust and suspicion, and, to the Communists' great detriment, encouraged the public perception of the Party as a "conspiracy." In the final analysis, the Progressive Party could not become the politically influential, broad-based mass organization that both Wallace and the Communists had envisioned because the basis of their alliance was fragile and negative and their ultimate ends incompatible. Instead, the alliance ended up weakening both participants, and the brittle coalition crumbled. "Our whole history," one Connecticut Progressive aptly concluded, "was that of people leaving."[13]

NOTES

ABBREVIATIONS

ADA-M   Americans for Democratic Action Papers, Microfilm Edition
  CBP   Calvin Benham Baldwin Papers, University of Iowa, Iowa City
CIO-M   Congress of Industrial Organizations Executive Board Minutes,
        Microfilm Edition
 COHP   Columbia University Oral History Project, Microfilm Edition
HAW-M   Henry A. Wallace Papers, Microfilm Edition
 HDCP   Hollywood Democratic Committee Papers, Wisconsin State Historical
        Society, Madison
 HUAC   House Committee on Un-American Activities
  PPP   Progressive Party Papers, University of Iowa, Iowa City
  RTP   Rexford G. Tugwell Papers, Franklin D. Roosevelt Presidential Library,
        Hyde Park, N.Y.

PREFACE

1. Henry A. Wallace to Curtis MacDougall, August 21, 1952, Box 55, Folder 230, PPP.

2. Hamby, *Beyond the New Deal*; Zieger, *The CIO*; Delton, "Rethinking Post–World War II Anticommunism"; Arnesen, "Civil Rights and the Cold War at Home."

CHAPTER 1

1. The most thorough rendering of this interpretation appears in Americans for Democratic Action Publicity Department, "Henry A. Wallace: The First Three Months," 3–6, Series 3, Box 16, Folder 212, ADA Southeastern Pennsylvania Chapter Papers, Temple University, Philadelphia. See also Schlesinger, *The Vital Center*, 115–20.

2. MacDougall, *Gideon's Army*, 1:224–83.

3. Jacques Duclos, "A propos de la dissolution du P.C.A.," *Les Cahiers du Communisme*, n.s., no. 6 (April 1945), 21–38. An English translation that became the text of record for discussions among American Communists appeared in the *Daily Worker* on May 24, 1945.

4. On Browder's suspicions, see Starobin, *American Communism in Crisis*, 81–83, 271–72; and Ryan, *Earl Browder*, 246–49.

5. Klehr, Haynes, and Anderson, *The Soviet World of American Communism*, 91–106.

6. Most historians contend that until mid-1947 Stalin instructed both the French and Italian Communist Parties to adhere to an accommodationist position within their respective coalition governments. This entailed putting aside strident rhetoric about socialist revolution and emphasizing instead the need for "national unity." It is plausible, however, that the Soviets had become suspicious of the French and Italian parties' growing influence and, through the Duclos Letter, sought to remind them that accommodation was a short-term tactic that did not negate the fundamental struggle between the capitalist and socialist camps. For one version of this argument, see Ryan, *Earl Browder*, 249.

7. For this point, see Gaiduk, "Stalin: Three Approaches to One Phenomenon," 123–24. Gaiduk bases this assessment on his reading of *Bulletin* issues located in the Russian Center for the Preservation and Study of Documents of Contemporary History (RTsKhIDNI). Wohlforth, *The Elusive Balance*, 66–67, notes that internal Soviet documents written in 1946 were also far harsher in their assessment of the United States than public communications.

8. Klehr, Haynes, and Anderson, *The Soviet World of American Communism*, 100. For the view that the Duclos Letter amounted to a Soviet declaration of Cold War, see Schlesinger, "Origins of the Cold War," 43–44; and Jaffe, *The Rise and Fall of American Communism*, 209, 230.

9. Memorandum by Raymond E. Murphy, Special Assistant to the Director of European Affairs, "Possible Resurrection of Communist International, Resumption of Extreme Leftist Activities, Possible Effect on United States," June 2, 1945, in U.S. Department of State, *Foreign Relations of the United States: The Conference of Berlin, 1945*, 267–80; Joseph Grew to George F. Kennan, July 23, 1945, in U.S. Department of State, *Foreign Relations of the United States: Europe, 1945*, 5:872–73. Though exaggerating the degree to which the Duclos Letter heralded a new Communist strategy of "world revolution," Murphy's report did provide a fairly accurate analysis of how the American Communists would respond to what they perceived as a new "line." The White House, still committed at this point to preserving postwar cooperation with the Soviet Union, ignored Murphy's report. For background, see Morgan, *A Covert Life*, 146–49. For Browder's interpretation, see Browder, "How Stalin Ruined the American Communist Party," 45.

10. Moreover, scholars have even begun to question the extent to which Truman pursued a provocative, "get tough" policy during the first months of his administration. Wilson D. Miscamble, for example, finds far more evidence of attempts to conciliate the Soviets and to preserve the wartime alliance. He argues that Truman's occasional "outbursts" have been taken out of context and blown out of proportion. Miscamble, *From Roosevelt to Truman*, chaps. 3–5.

11. Wallace used the phrase "friendly, peaceful competition" to characterize his vision for U.S.-Soviet relations in his September 12, 1946, Madison Square Garden address. See Wallace, "The Path to Peace," 738–41.

12. Pechatnov, "Exercise in Frustration," 5. See also Pechatnov, "The Big Three after World War II"; Pechatnov, "'The Allies Are Pressing on You to Break Your Will . . .'"; and Haslam, *Russia's Cold War*, 31.

13. For a penetrating analysis of the change in line and its effects on the Party's leadership, see Starobin, *American Communism in Crisis*, 78–106.

14. Starobin, *American Communism in Crisis*, 122–25, 286. The top leadership was even hesitant to discuss intraparty disputes with Moscow. See Klehr, Haynes, and Anderson, *The Soviet World of American Communism*, 270.

15. Foster, *Problems of Organized Labor Today*, 18; Howe and Coser, *The American Communist Party*, 454; Levenstein, *Communism, Anti-Communism, and the CIO*, 209–11; Johanningsmeier, *Forging American Communism*, 316–17.

16. Boylan, *The New Deal Coalition and the Election of 1946*, 79. For this shift in focus on the part of Popular Front leftists in Southern California and in Minnesota, see respectively, Brownstein, *The Power and the Glitter*, 106–7; and Haynes, *Dubious Alliance*, 130–31. See also Warren, *Noble Abstractions*, 234–56.

17. Dalton Trumbo to Olivia de Havilland, June 24, 1946; Trumbo to Ernest Pascal, n.d. [June 1946]; de Havilland to Trumbo, June 27, 1946, Box 1, Folder 10 "Trumbo Correspondence (Jan. 1–Dec. 1946)," all in Dalton Trumbo Papers, State Historical Society of Wisconsin, Madison; *Los Angeles Examiner*, September 6, 1958, 1, 6; Vaughn, *Ronald Reagan in Hollywood*, 127–29.

18. For a useful summary of liberals' response to President Truman's foreign policy during 1945–46, see Hamby, *Beyond the New Deal*, 87–119. On the disproportionate influence that concealed Communists exercised within NCPAC and ICCASP, see Charney, *A Long Journey*, 175–76; Brownstein, *The Power and the Glitter*, 106–10; Ceplair and Englund, *The Inquisition in Hollywood*, 236–38.

19. Brownstein, *The Power and the Glitter*, 107.

20. Healey and Isserman, *California Red*, 103–4. See also Schwartz, *From West to East*, 394–95. Healey quotes Al Richmond, the editor of the *Daily People's World*, as expressing similar sentiments regarding Sparks. Healey replaced Sparks as the Los Angeles county chair in late 1948 when the CP, expecting that it would soon be outlawed, assigned him to organize a nationwide underground apparatus. During his remarkable career in the international Communist movement, Sparks operated under several pseudonyms and helped establish an autonomous industrial colony in Kuzbas, Siberia. For biographical information on Sparks, see "Finding Aid to the Nemmy Sparks Papers," at the Walter Reuther Library, Archives of Labor and Urban Affairs, Wayne State University, Detroit.

21. Hittelman quoted in Ceplair and Englund, *The Inquisition in Hollywood*, 237; and Healey and Isserman, *California Red*, 110. Eleanor (Bogigian) Hittelman (later Abewitz), who had been an activist in Upton Sinclair's End Poverty in California campaign, joined the party in the mid-1930s. For the Communists' "rechanneling of funds," see Jeanne Levey to Robert Bendiner, January 22, 1947, Box 13, Folder 218, Freda Kirchwey Papers, Schlesinger Library, Radcliffe College, Cambridge, Mass. Recounting for Bendiner her observations of a HICCASP-sponsored fund-raiser held in Hollywood shortly before the 1946 elections, Levey noted, "The rear end of the baby grand piano was piled high with stacks of checks and cash which looked like many thousands of dollars. A full report of the contributions was never made public nor how the monies were spent. The election was two days off and just how this late appeal could help the election of Democrats, I do not know. This is the manner in which the Communists have been working here and elsewhere."

22. Art Arthur to the Editor, *New Republic*, June 12, 1946, Reel 57, Series 3, Number 5, ADA-M; Minutes of Executive Council Meeting, February 8, 1946, Box 1, Folder 8;

Minutes of the Campaign Committee, February 13, 1946, Box 3, Folder 11; Minutes of HICCASP Membership Meeting, February 21, 1946, Box 1, Folder 12; Minutes of HICCASP Executive Board Meeting, May 14, 1946 and May 26, 1946, Box 1, Folder 8, all in HDCP; Carey McWilliams, "The Lesson of California," *Nation*, June 22, 1946, 743–44; McWilliams, *The Education of Carey McWilliams*, 121–22; *Los Angeles Times*, June 7, 1946, 1; *Time*, May 27, 1946, 24.

23. Boylan, *The New Deal Coalition and the Election of 1946*, 90; Memorandum, Emil Corwin to Alice Hunter, June 10, 1946, "Report of Primary Activities of Radio Division of HICCASP," Box 3, Folder 16, HDCP; Oliver Carlson, "Communists and CIO-PAC Beaten in California," *New Leader*, June 29, 1946, 6; Art Arthur to James Loeb, December 28, 1946, Reel 57, Series 3, Number 5, ADA-M; Henderson, "Earl Warren and California Politics," 263–70; Montgomery and Johnson, *One Step from the White House*, 60–63; California CIO Council, PAC Report to the Executive Board, July 14, 1946, 8–10, quoted in R. E. McCoy, "Labor in Politics," 117–18; *Daily People's World*, June 6, 1946, 1.

24. Starobin, *American Communism in Crisis*, 285; McWilliams, "The Lesson of California," 744; Carlson, "Communists and CIO-PAC Beaten in California," 6.

25. Brownstein, *The Power and the Glitter*, 108. For concerns about Communist manipulation within HICCASP, see Jeanne Levey to Robert Bendiner, January 27, 1947; Jeanne Levey to Freda Kirchwey, January 22, 1947; Bendiner to Levey, January 30, 1947, all in Box 13, Folder 218, Freda Kirchwey Papers.

26. Minutes of the Executive Council Meeting, HICCASP, July 3, 1946, July 10, 1946, and July 30, 1946; Minutes of the Executive Board Meeting, HICCASP, July 23, 1946 and August 6, 1946, Box 1, Folder 8, HDCP; James Roosevelt to Hannah Dorner, July 5, 1946; Roosevelt to Jo Davidson, July 9, 1946; Roosevelt to John Cromwell, July 27, 1946, all in Box 7, Folder 17, HDCP. For the full text of the rejected resolution, see Marjorie Allen to HICCASP Executive Council, n.d., Box 1, HDCP. Dunne quoted in Brownstein, *The Power and the Glitter*, 109.

27. William Z. Foster, "Leninism and Some Practical Problems of the Post-War Period," *Political Affairs* 25 (February 1946): 99–109; Foster, "On Building a People's Party," *Political Affairs* 26 (February 1947): 109–21; Dennis, *What America Faces*, 32; Isserman, *Which Side Were You On?*, 246. For Foster's estimation of the "war danger," see Foster, "American Imperialism, Leader of World Reaction" *Political Affairs* 25 (August 1946): 686–95.

28. On Stalin's thinking regarding the "war danger" and "imperialist contradictions," see Resis, *Stalin, the Politburo, and the Onset of the Cold War*, 6–17; and Wohlforth, *The Elusive Balance*, 66–71. For the official American reaction to Stalin's speech on February 9, see Gaddis, *The United States and the Origins of the Cold War, 1941–1947*, 299–303. On Dennis's reaction, see Starobin, *American Communism in Crisis*, 286.

29. George Blake Charney, "Lessons of the Congressional By-Election in N.Y.," *Political Affairs* 25 (April 1946): 362–70; Haynes and Klehr, *Venona*, 240; *New York Herald Tribune*, June 25, 1947, 21; Carter, "Pressure from the Left," 250–53; Shannon, *The Decline of American Communism*, 115–16; Charney, *A Long Journey*, 154.

30. Dennis, "Defeat the Imperialist Drive toward Fascism and War," *Political Affairs* 25 (September 1946): 778–809. This line differed little from Dennis's June 1945 summation of the Party's position. See Dennis, *America at the Crossroads*, 7–33.

31. Starobin, *American Communism in Crisis*, 128. This analysis also clarifies the unstable nature of the liberal-Communist alliance in what would become the Progressive Party.

32. Dennis, "Defeat the Imperialist Drive toward Fascism and War," 803–5; Dennis, "Concluding Remarks on the Plenum Discussion," *Political Affairs* 26 (January 1947): 11–13. For evidence of Communist efforts to carry out Dennis's instructions, see *The Party Builder*, an internal newsletter published by the Organization and Education Department of the Washington State Communist Party. In a spring 1947 issue, the editors reported that the party's Inter-professional Club was "concentrating mainly on building the PCA organization in Pierce County." Copy in Box 1, Mary and E. William Hopkinson Papers, University of Washington, Seattle.

33. Starobin, *American Communism in Crisis*, 141–43; Shannon, *The Decline of American Communism*, 116–18; Charney, *A Long Journey*, 173–75.

34. For a sympathetic account of Wallace's developing views on foreign policy, and particularly on U.S.-Soviet relations, between 1945 and 1947, see Walker, *Henry A. Wallace and American Foreign Policy*, 117–65. More critical is Hamby, "Henry A. Wallace, the Liberals, and Soviet-American Relations."

35. Blum, *The Price of Vision*, 499; Weinstein and Vassiliev, *The Haunted Wood*, 283–85. Gromov also went by the name "Anatoly Gorsky." On Edwin S. Smith, see Klehr, Haynes, and Firsov, *The Secret World of American Communism*, 99. Smith, a commissioner of the National Labor Relations Board in the 1930s, later became a registered agent for the Soviet Union.

36. MacDougall, *Gideon's Army*, 1:63; "Reminiscences of Henry A. Wallace," COHP, 4965.

37. Macdonald, *Henry Wallace*, 150. Macdonald, drawing on transcripts from the Mutual Broadcasting System, quotes Wallace's remarks made during the January 10, 1947, episode of *Meet the Press*. For an account of the speech's hostile reception and the substantial differences between the text that appeared in the newspapers and the version Wallace actually delivered at the Garden, see Schapsmeier and Schapsmeier, *Prophet in Politics*, 154–56.

38. *Daily Worker*, September 13, 1946, 6; September 15, 1946, 7; Charney, *A Long Journey*, 174. For an account of the *Worker*'s rapidly changing editorial line, see Schmidt, *Henry A. Wallace*, 22–24.

39. "Report from Washington: A Bulletin of Legislative News Issued by The Independent Citizens Committee of the Arts, Sciences, and Professions," Box 265, Folder 9, J. B. Matthews Papers, Duke University, Durham, N.C.; J. Edgar Hoover, Director, Federal Bureau of Investigation to Frederick B. Lyon, September 25, 1946, "Resignation of Secretary of Commerce Henry Wallace," Box 619, Folder 2, James F. Byrnes Papers, Clemson University, Clemson, S.C.; Straight, *After Long Silence*, 203–5. Collecting information from its informants within the CPUSA, the FBI kept close tabs on the pro-Communist left's embrace of Wallace. Hoover's report, cited above, details the efforts of the National Council of American-Soviet Friendship to "hold Wallace out as a new Roosevelt" and to emphasize a line of "war with Byrnes and peace with Wallace."

40. Frank Warren discusses Wallace's symbolic importance to liberals during World War II and their hopes that he would lead a revitalized progressive movement after the

war in *Noble Abstractions*, 70–89 and 243–44. For liberals' hope that the conclusion of World War II would precipitate a "democratic revolution," see, for example, Freda Kirchwey, "Out of the Ashes," *Nation*, April 7, 1945, 377. Bazelon, "The Faith of Henry Wallace," 309–19, and Wechsler, "The Liberal's Vote and '48," 216–25, contend that Wallace's appeal was primarily emotional rather than intellectual. "He *feels* so clearly," quoted in Schlesinger, *A Life in the Twentieth Century*, 416.

41. Klehr, Haynes, and Anderson, *The Soviet World of American Communism*, 257–71. The authors reprint two documents found in the Soviet archives that summarize the exchange of information. One is a report from Vronsky to Paniushkin detailing his meeting with Childs, and the other is a memo from Paniushkin to his superiors, Andrei Zhdanov and Alexsei Kuznetsov, offering his comments on Childs's questions.

42. Jaffe, "Notes on Wallace," Box 12, Folder 13, Philip Jaffe Papers, Emory University, Atlanta; Jaffe, *The Rise and Fall of American Communism*, 88–91; Starobin, *American Communism in Crisis*, 287–88. The Vronsky memo indicates that Childs had asked to see a member of the Central Committee, thus giving credibility to Jaffe's account of the meeting with Lozovsky. Jaffe also claimed that Childs met with Jacques Duclos in Paris and asked him to write another "letter" that might clear up the confusion within the CPUSA. Duclos declined, allegedly adding, "Look at what you did with the last one." Starobin, *American Communism in Crisis*, 288.

43. John Gates, "The 80th Congress and Perspectives for 1948," *Political Affairs* 26 (August 1947): 716–29; Dodd, *School of Darkness*, 202–3; Foster, "American Imperialism and the War Danger," *Political Affairs* 26 (August 1947): 675–87. See also Gates, *The Story of an American Communist*, 114–17. Gates notes that he "presented" the report, but he does not claim authorship.

44. Dennis, "Concluding Remarks on the Plenum Discussion," *Political Affairs* 26 (August 1947): 688–700. The text of Dennis's September 18 speech in Madison Square Garden appears in the *Sunday Worker*, September 28, 1947; Jack Stachel, "The Third Party Movement in the 1948 Elections," *Political Affairs* 26 (September 1947): 789.

45. Shannon, *The Decline of American Communism*, 133–34; *Daily Worker*, August 14, 1947, 6; August 16, 1947, 8; September 4, 1947, 3; September 6, 1947, 12; Howe and Coser, *The American Communist Party*, 464. Though the three Communist union leaders later denied having any conversation with Hollander concerning a third party, his account appears reliable given the overall CP strategy at the time. Starobin, *American Communism in Crisis*, 290, makes a compelling case that Hollander was telling the truth.

46. *Proceedings of the Second Biennial Convention of the National Union of Marine Cooks and Stewards*, 7, 125; *MCS Voice*, May 15, 1947, 6; May 29, 1947, 2; July 24, 1947, 6; August 21, 1947, 10; October 30, 1947, 3; *Daily People's World*, August 12, 1947, 1.

47. *Daily People's World*, May 20, 1948, 1, 3; C. B. Baldwin, "Report on Wallace Western Trip," June 3, 1947, Box 11, CBP; Henry A. Wallace, "Report from California," *New Republic*, June 9, 1947, 11–13; Moremen, "The Independent Progressive Party in California," 28.

48. Hale, "What Makes Wallace Run?," 245; Wechsler, "What Makes Wallace Run," 21.

49. Carey McWilliams, "California's Third-Party Donnybrook," *Nation*, April 24, 1948, 434; William R. Burke, "Report of the Fresno Conference to Launch Plans to

Nominate Henry Wallace for President on the Democratic Party Ticket," Reel 58, Series 3, Number 7, ADA-M; *Worker*, July 20, 1947, 3; *New York Times*, July 20, 1947, 16; *Daily People's World*, July 19, 1947, 1; July 21, 1947, 1, 3. Burke, the ADA executive secretary in Southern California, and two Steelworkers Union officials who attended the Fresno gathering estimated that 50 to 60 percent of the delegates were "CP people." Given their own political biases, they may have overstated the Communist presence, but other sources friendlier to the CP acknowledge that so-called left-wingers played a prominent role in the conference. See McWilliams, "California's Third-Party Donnybrook," 434, and Healey and Isserman, *California Red*, 108–10.

50. Carey McWilliams, "Wallace in the West," *Nation*, July 5, 1947, 7–8; James Loeb to Robert Clifton, July 24, 1947, Reel 57, Series 3, Number 5, ADA-M; *Sacramento Bee*, July 17, 1947, 1; Oliver Carlson, "Soviet Politics in California," *New Leader*, June 21, 1947, 5; Gallup, *The Gallup Poll*, 1:660, 655; MacDougall, *Gideon's Army*, 1:192; Healey and Isserman, *California Red*, 108.

51. *Sacramento Bee*, July 17, 1947, 24; *New York Times*, July 28, 1947, 7; *Daily Worker*, August 26, 1947, 7–8; Stevenson, *The Undiminished Man*, 71–72.

52. *MCS Voice*, August 7, 1948, 3; September 4, 1947, 1; *Daily People's World*, August 4, 1947, 1; August 23, 1947, 1, 3; August 24, 1947, 3; Call, "A Study in Group Support of the Independent Progressive Party of California," 26–33; Milla Logan to Vi Megrath, August 25, 1947, Reel 57, Series 3, Number 5, ADA-M; *Labor Action*, December 22, 1947, 2.

53. *Daily People's World*, August 25, 1947, 1, 3; August 26, 1947, 1, 3; *Los Angeles Times*, August 26, 1947, A4; Moremen, "The Independent Progressive Party," 28.

54. Starobin, *American Communism in Crisis*, 164, 288. Kenny described the meeting to Starobin during a 1967 interview; Johanningsmeier, *Forging American Communism*, 318–19.

55. *Daily People's World*, July 26, 1947, 1; August 4, 1947, 1; August 5, 1947, 6; August 6, 1947, 6; September 3, 1947, 1.

56. *New York Times*, October 6, 1947, 1; "Resolutions of the 9-Party Communist Conference," *Political Affairs* 26 (November 1947): 1051–56; A. A. Zhdanov, "The International Situation," *Political Affairs* 26 (December 1947): 1090–1111.

57. Klehr, Haynes, and Anderson, *The Soviet World of American Communism*, 271.

58. Starobin, *American Communism in Crisis*, 246.

59. DiBiago, "The Cominform as the Soviet Response to the Marshall Plan"; Pons, [new scholars hip] "Stalin, Togliatti, and the Origins of the Cold War in Europe." Pons concludes the formation of the Cominform was "more a sign of retreat than a shift toward the offensive" (ibid., 26). See also Zubok and Pleshakov, *Inside the Kremlin's Cold War*, 125–33. The Cominform met only three times and disbanded in 1956.

60. Starobin, *American Communism in Crisis*, 232, 170–71; Charney, *A Long Journey*, 186.

61. For the views of the more militant Communist union leaders, see Starobin, *American Communism in Crisis*, 159; and Charney, *A Long Journey*, 165–72. For Foster's reaction to the founding of the Cominform, see Starobin, 156–57, 171; Johanningsmeier, *Forging American Communism*, 320; and Gates, *The Story of an American Communist*, 116. Gates later emphasized that the formation of the Cominform, and particularly

Zhdanov's emphasis on the "united front from below," had been the "strongest influence on the decision of the CP to move for a third party." John Gates to Joseph Starobin, n.d. [1971], Box 10, Philip Jaffe Papers. On the rank and file's preference for a "left sectarian" line, see Charney, *A Long Journey*; Dodd, *School of Darkness*; Mitford, *A Fine Old Conflict*; and Meyer, *The Moulding of Communists*. But see especially Kraditor, *"Jimmy Higgins,"* a thorough and compelling analysis of the rank-and-file American Communist's worldview.

62. Lee, *Truman and Taft-Hartley*, 96–105; MacDougall, *Gideon's Army*, 1:178–79; Gallup, *The Gallup Poll*, 1:663; Barone, *Our Country*, 215; *New York Times*, July 21, 1947, 1. For the politics of Taft-Hartley and the significance of Truman's veto, see Plotke, *Building a Democratic Political Order*, 236–42; Zieger, *The CIO*, 275–76, 449; and Dubofsky, *The State and Labor in Modern America*, 203–8. On earlier support for a labor party within the United Auto Workers, see Emil Mazey to Local Union Presidents, Region 1 and 1A, April 30, 1947, Series 5, Box 38, "Emil Mazey" Folder, Walter P. Reuther Papers.

63. Foster, *The Union Politic*, 76–94; Kampelman, *The Communist Party vs. the CIO*, 110; Schatz, "Philip Murray," 249–54.

64. Carew, *Labour under the Marshall Plan*, 70–91; Lenburg, "The CIO and American Foreign Policy," 161–65; Foster, *The Union Politic*, 86–89; Kampelman, *The CIO vs. the Communist Party*, 107–9; Levenstein, *Communism, Anti-Communism, and the CIO*, 210–21; James Higgins, "How Long Can He Compromise?," *New Republic*, October 10, 1947, 12–15; *New York Times*, October 10, 1947, 17.

65. CIO, *Final Proceedings of the Ninth Constitutional Convention of the Congress of Industrial Organizations*, 290–91 (hereafter cited as *Proceedings*); *CIO News*, October 20, 1947; Preis, *Labor's Giant Step*, 339–40; Kempton, *Part of Our Time*, 75; James Higgins, "Murray and Marshall," *New Republic*, October 27, 1947, 9.

66. John Herling, "Two Conventions: AFL and CIO," *Labor and Nation*, November–December 1947, 14–16; CIO, *Proceedings*, 260–62; "Marshall and the CIO," *Newsweek*, October 27, 1947, 30, 32; CIO, "Transcript of Hearings before the Committee to Investigate Charges against the International Longshoremen's and Warehousemen's Union, Washington, DC, June 1950," 140 (hereafter cited as "ILWU Hearings"), Box 110, CIO Secretary-Treasurer Papers, Labor History Archives, Wayne State University, Detroit.

67. *Christian Science Monitor*, October 16, 1947, 18; Lenburg, "The CIO and American Foreign Policy," 167; CIO, *Proceedings*, 279–80.

68. CIO, *Proceedings*, 284–85.

69. Ibid., 283; *New York Times*, October 16, 1947, 3; *Labor Leader*, October 31, 1947, 1.

70. CIO, *Proceedings*, 291–92.

71. CIO, "ILWU Hearings," 66–67, 97–101; *Washington Post*, May 2, 1948, 1,2; Minutes of the Executive Board of the CIO, 1950, Reel 14, microfilm edition, 69–70. At this executive board meeting in 1950, Bryson claimed that he had never attended any such meeting, though most historians judge Quill's memory to be the more reliable.

72. *New York Herald Tribune*, November 16, 1947, 1; Starobin, *American Communism in Crisis*, 168–69. Reuther's use of anticommunism to facilitate his rise to power

within the UAW has occasioned a lively debate among labor historians. As a result, the significance of ideology as an issue in the UAW's factional fighting has been blown well out of proportion. Reuther's victories, as an earlier generation of commentators recognized, were based primarily on his program and on the opposition's shoddy wartime record, and not on his so-called red-baiting. For a summary of the literature and a useful corrective to the overemphasis on the Communist issue, see Goode, *Infighting in the UAW*. See also Howe and Coser, *The American Communist Party*, 458–59.

73. Philip Murray, "Memoranda on Meeting of CIO Vice Presidents, Thursday, April 22," Box 44, Philip Murray Papers, Catholic University, Washington, D.C.; CIO, "ILWU Hearings," 143, 66–67; Macdonald, "The Wallace Campaign," 180.

74. *Washington Post*, May 2, 1948, 1, 2; CIO, "ILWU Hearings," 67. Two other journalists, Edwin Lahey of the *Chicago Daily News* and Victor Reisel of the *New York Post*, also reported on these closed meetings. Their versions concur with Friendly's, whose story was the most detailed. See *Chicago Daily News*, May 17, 1948, and *New York Post*, May 7, 1948, clippings in Box 32A, Folder 7, PPP. Though historians accept Quill's general account, the exact chronology of events during late 1947 is still not entirely clear. In his testimony at the ILWU hearings in June 1950, and contrary to the above three newspaper stories, Quill insisted that Dennis and Thompson had demanded support for Wallace in October, not in December. Most scholars cite the December date, assuming that Quill had inadvertently juxtaposed two meetings when reconstructing events nearly three years after the fact. A memorandum in the Philip Murray papers (cited in note 73 above) reveals that Quill told the CIO president as early as April 1948 that the discussion of Wallace's candidacy had occurred in October, suggesting that Quill's recollections in 1950 were accurate. Other evidence, however, supports the case for December. During the November convention of the California State CIO Council, for example, Hugh Bryson spoke against a resolution calling for an outright endorsement of the IPP. Moremen, "The Independent Progressive Party in California," 80–84; California State CIO Council, *Proceedings of the Tenth Annual Convention, November 20–23, 1947*, 83–84, 89. Regardless of the exact dates, the picture to emerge is that of the top CPUSA leadership placing intense pressure on the party's "influentials," who tried to carry out instructions without immediately jeopardizing their positions in the labor movement.

75. John Gates to Joseph Starobin, n.d. [1971], Box 12, Folder 2, Philip Jaffe Papers.

CHAPTER 2

1. Straight, *After Long Silence*, 213; *Chicago Daily News*, May 23, 1947, 12; "Notes from an Interview with Harold Young, attorney, in Odessa, Texas, April 1953," Box 45, Folder 171, PPP. Straight discusses his relationship with the Cambridge spies in his memoir, but for a more candid account, see Haynes, Klehr, and Vassiliev, *Spies*, 245–52.

2. Straight, *After Long Silence*, 213–14.

3. Ibid., 217; Fraser, *Labor Will Rule*, 495–538, 566–72; Cochran, *Labor and Communism*, 232–35, 261–63. For Baldwin's influence on Wallace, see "The Reminiscences of Louis Bean," COHP, 259–61; Robertson, "Wallace and the New Dealers," 570–71; Schapsmeier and Schapsmeier, *Prophet in Politics*, 258. On Baldwin's New Deal

background, see "Calvin Benham Baldwin," *Current Biography* 4 (1943): 18–20; and Terkel, *Hard Times*, 254–62.

4. Clark Foreman to Edmonia Grant, October 6, 1947, Box 39, Folder 101, PPP; Remarks of Thomas Emerson, Meeting of the Executive Committee, PCA, December 15, 1947, Box 21, CBP; Marjorie Lansing to Curtis MacDougall, November 9, 1953, Box 58, Folder 248, PPP; Wallace, COHP, 5067–69. During the 1948 campaign, most political analysts assumed that Abt was a member of the Communist Party, though not until his eightieth birthday in 1984 did he reveal that he had been in the CP for fifty years. Abt with Myerson, *Advocate and Activist*, xvii–xviii.

5. Hale, "What Makes Wallace Run?," 246–47; Paul M. Sweezy to Michael Straight, August 22, 1947, Box 44, Folder 166A, PPP; Albert Deutsch to C. B. Baldwin, December 11, 1947, Box 21, CBP.

6. Remarks of Charlotte Carr and Helen Fuller, Meeting of the Executive Committee, PCA, December 15, 1947, Box 21, CBP; David Diamond to C. B. Baldwin, December 26, 1947; John P. Peters to C. B. Baldwin, December 20, 1947, Box 22, CBP.

7. Charney, *A Long Journey*, 174–76; "Editorial Comment: Outlook for 1948 and the Third Party," *Political Affairs* 27 (January 1948): 3–10; Jan DeGraaff to C. B. Baldwin, August 4, 1947, Box 22, CBP; James Imbrie to Henry A. Wallace, December 8, 1947, Box 45, Folder 174, PPP.

8. Schmidt, *Henry A. Wallace*, 34–35; MacDougall, *Gideon's Army*, 1:227; *New York Times*, December 5, 1947, 22; Henry A. Wallace, COHP, 5115.

9. Martha Dodd and Alfred K. Stern to Henry A. Wallace, December 12, 1947, Box 58, Folder 250; Lewis Frank to Curtis MacDougall, October 23, 1952, Box 58, Folder 260, both in PPP; MacDougall, *Gideon's Army*, 1:235; Marjorie Lansing to Curtis MacDougall, November 9, 1953, Box 58, Folder 248, PPP; Straight, *After Long Silence*, 217.

10. MacDougall, *Gideon's Army*, 1:231; "Wallace Is Pretty Harmless," *New Leader*, October 10, 1947, 16; *New York Post*, November 7, 1947, 6, December 4, 1947, 6; Bean, COHP, 258; Robert Bendiner, "Wallace: The Incomplete Angler," *Nation*, December 20, 1947, 668. Kingdon's many critics within the PCA charged that he feared that supporting the third party would hurt him financially or that he was manipulated by his allegedly ambitious wife, the actress Marcella Markham. Curtis MacDougall, a former PCA activist who apparently still held a grudge against Kingdon seventeen years after the 1948 election, uncritically repeats these and other unsubstantiated allegations in an ill-tempered account of the PCA chairman's split with the Wallace forces, the first of many indicators that scholars should use MacDougall's entire account with caution. MacDougall, *Gideon's Army*, 1:229–43.

11. MacDougall, *Gideon's Army*, 1:224, 231, 235–36; John Gates to Joseph Starobin, n.d. [1971], Box 10, Folder 2, Philip Jaffe Papers; author's telephone interview with Lillian Gates, September 3, 1996. Gates stated that her husband's identification of Baldwin as a CP member was "absolutely true." Baldwin, she said, was under party discipline, but, like many secret Communists, may not have carried a party card, since the discovery of his party membership would have compromised his political influence in liberal circles. Gates also confirmed that Baldwin reported to Albert Blumberg. John Abt acknowledged in his memoirs that Baldwin did have frequent meetings with

Eugene Dennis to discuss the third party, but he claimed that Baldwin was not a Communist. Abt with Myerson, *Advocate and Activist*, 165.

12. Starobin, *American Communism in Crisis*, 166.

13. Wallace, COHP, 5079, 5115, 5083.

14. Sullivan, "Interview with Lillian Baldwin," 1980, Box 2, Folder 2, Patricia Sullivan Research Interviews, Emory University, Atlanta. For Traugott's political background, see Klehr, Haynes, and Firsov, *The Secret World of American Communism*, 307–8. Wallace later attributed Baldwin's following of the Communist Party line to the influence of Abt and Traugott. He remembered Traugott as "quite an operator" who "seemed to be convinced that the Russian line was usually right." Wallace, COHP, 5069–70.

15. *Washington Star*, October 15, 1947, 1, 6; *Washington Post*, October 16, 1947, 4; Louis Azrael column, October 16, 1947, clipping in Box 23, PPP; Walker, *Henry A. Wallace and American Foreign Policy*, 179; *Louisville Courier-Journal*, November 22, 1947, 1; MacDougall, *Gideon's Army*, 1:229.

16. On this theme, see Haynes, *Red Scare or Red Menace?*, 17–36 and Ribuffo, *The Old Christian Right*, 185–96, Wheeler quoted on 193. For Kirchwey's remarks, see Kirchwey, "Curb the Fascist Press!," *Nation*, March 28, 1942, 357–58.

17. J. C. Rich, "How Independent Is Wallace?," *New Leader*, January 3, 1948, 4; *New York Times*, December 5, 1947, 2; Moss Hart to Progressive Citizens of America, October 22, 1947 [Letter of resignation from PCA], Box 23, CBP; "The Comintern's Challenge to Liberals," [ADA advertisement], clipping in Box 37, Folder 68, PPP; "The New 'Comintern,'" *Nation*, October 18, 1947, 398–99; Markowitz, *The Rise and Fall of the People's Century*, 249.

18. *PM*, December 12, 1947, 4; December 15, 1947, 8; Robert Bendiner, "Wallace: The Incomplete Angler," *Nation*, December 20, 1947, 668; Rich, "How Independent Is Wallace?," 4; Morris Rosenthal, COHP, 474.

19. MacDougall, *Gideon's Army*, 1:224–84; Culver and Hyde, *American Dreamer*, 438–70. Culver and Hyde's account of the 1948 campaign relies almost entirely on MacDougall's *Gideon's Army* and on other secondary sources that draw on MacDougall. More candid about the Communist involvement in the launching of the third party is an earlier team of Wallace biographers, Schapsmeier and Schapsmeier, *Prophet in Politics*, 162–96.

20. Harold D. Smith diary entry, February 14, 1942, quoted in Sirevåg, *American Hamlet*, 124; Fred W. Henshaw, COHP, 100; Samuel B. Bledsoe, COHP, 120–21; Doris Fleeson column, *Chicago Daily News*, January 5, 1948, clipping in Box 35, Folder 43, PPP; "Reports of Wallace Democrats in California," quoted in Walton, *Henry Wallace, Harry Truman, and the Cold War*, 167.

21. Morris S. Rosenthal, COHP, 445–54; Paul H. Appleby, COHP, 13–16; Samuel B. Bledsoe, COHP, 153, 160–63; Bernard L. Gladieux, COHP, 711; Sirevåg, *American Hamlet*, 100–104.

22. Hale, "What Makes Wallace Run?," 245, 247; Griffith, *Harry and Teddy*, 207–8; Bruce Bliven, COHP, 48; Bliven, *Five Million Words Later*, 269.

23. Lord, *The Wallaces of Iowa*, 453; Macdonald, *Henry Wallace*, 139, 23; Phillips, "That Baffling Personality, Mr. Wallace," 49; Shannon, *The Decline of American*

Communism, 144; "Third Parties," *Time*, August 9, 1948, 19; Hollander, *The Survival of the Adversary Culture*, 104.

24. *Daily Worker*, May 26, 1947; Markowitz, *Rise and Fall of the People's Century*, 271.

25. Shannon, *The Decline of American Communism*, 141; Howe and Coser, *The American Communist Party*, 470–71; Culver and Hyde, *American Dreamer*, 82; Stewart, "Wallace the Symbol," 8.

26. Shannon, *The Decline of American Communism*, 147, 392; Bliven, *Five Million Words Later*, 269.

27. Fahan, "What Makes Henry Run?," 54; Wallace, COHP, 5088–89; Schapsmeier and Schapsmeier, *Prophet in Politics*, 169.

28. Straight, *After Long Silence*, 219; Helen Gahagan Douglas to Henry A. Wallace, December 10, 1947, Box 45, Folder 174, PPP; Aubrey Williams to Henry A. Wallace, cited in Hasting, "Intraparty Struggle," 102; *PM*, January 21, 1947, 3; Markowitz, *The Rise and Fall of the People's Century*, 257–58.

29. Blum, *The Price of Vision*, 47–48.

30. Beanie Baldwin, "Memo to Henry A. Wallace on Presidential Announcement," December 2, 1947, Box 10, CBP; Manny Margolis, Harvard Students for Wallace to Dear Friends, December 15, 1947, Box 15, Folder 63, PPP; Lewis Frank, "Memo," November 26, 1947, Box 10, CBP; *Washington Post*, May 2, 1948, 1, 2.

31. Robert Kenny to Beanie Baldwin, December 3, 1947, Box 1, CBP; Kenny's reminiscences are in Starobin, *American Communism in Crisis*, 289.

32. MacDougall, *Gideon's Army*, 1:236–37, 240; *New York Post*, December 31, 1947, 24; Frank Kingdon, "Statement to Executive Committee of PCA," December 15, 1947, Box 45, Folder 174, PPP.

33. Remarks of Charlotte Carr, Thomas Emerson, and Helen Fuller, Meeting of the Executive Committee, PCA, December 15, 1947, Box 21, CBP; John P. Peters to C. B. Baldwin, Box 22, CBP; Straight, *After Long Silence*, 219; C. B. Baldwin to PCA Board member, December 18, 1947, Box 21, CBP; MacDougall, *Gideon's Army*, 1:235, 243; *New York Times*, December 16, 1947, 1, 35; *PM*, December 18, 1947, 13.

34. *PM*, December 18, 1947, 13; December 19, 1947, 2; January 7, 1948, 11; Bartley Crum to C. B. Baldwin, December 17, 1947; Albert Deutsch to C. B. Baldwin, December 17, 1947; J. Raymond Walsh to C. B. Baldwin, December 30, 1947, all in Box 22, CBP; J. Raymond Walsh, Transcript of radio broadcast, December 17, 1947, Box 21, CBP; MacDougall, *Gideon's Army*, 1:235, 242–43; J. W. Gitt to Albert Deutsch, January 7, 1948, Box 56, Folder 238, PPP.

35. MacDougall, *Gideon's Army*, 1:247; Starobin, *American Communism in Crisis*, 166, 289–90; Lewis Frank Jr. to Curtis MacDougall, October 23, 1952, Box 58, Folder 260; Alfred K. Stern to Curtis MacDougall, December 10, 1953, Box 55, Folder 230, both in PPP.

36. Weinstein and Vassiliev, *The Haunted Wood*, 68–69; MacDougall, *Gideon's Army*, 3:600. For a full account of the Sterns' lively careers in Soviet espionage, see Weinstein and Vassiliev, *The Haunted Wood*, 50–71, 118–24. For the Sterns' relationship with the Wallaces, which deteriorated precipitously after the election once Wallace realized the extent of Communist infiltration into his inner circle, see Fox, "'In Passion and in Hope,'" 255–81.

37. *New York Times*, December 19, 1947, 31; *Daily Worker*, December 19, 1947, 2, 10; *PM*, December 19, 1947, 2.

38. White and Maze, *Henry A. Wallace*, 257–58; *PM*, December 19, 1947, 2; *Labor Leader*, December 27, 1947, 4.

39. Wallace, COHP, 5082–83; Curtis MacDougall, Interview with Lew Frank, October 18, 1952, Box 49, Notebook 15, PPP.

40. "PCA's Quixotic Politics," *Nation*, December 27, 1947, 693; *PM*, December 18, 1947, 12; December 28, 1947, 2–4.

41. *PM*, December 28, 1947, 3; Parmet, *The Democrats*, 36–59; Goodman, "Hard to Digest," 64–68; Gallup, *The Gallup Poll*, 1:640, 660, 671, 702. Parmet's is one of the few studies to acknowledge the depth of white working-class resentment of the Democratic Party's "progressive" wing during the late 1940s, but see also Zeitz, *White Ethnic New York*.

42. Fenton, *In Your Opinion . . .*, 84; Gallup, *The Gallup Poll*, 1:682. By July 4, 1948, 69 percent of those polled believed the United States was being "too soft" in its policy toward the Soviet Union. "The Quarter's Polls," *Public Opinion Quarterly*, Fall 1948, 549.

43. Lewis Frank, "Memo," November 26, 1947, Box 10, CBP. In a Gallup poll taken July 4–9, 1947, 82 percent of those surveyed believed the Marshall Plan should continue without Russia. A poll taken May 23–28 and released on June 13, 1947 showed 74 percent favoring Universal Military Training and 21 percent opposed to it. Conservative isolationists likely accounted for much of this 21 percent. Gallup, *The Gallup Poll*, 1:663, 653–54.

44. *PM*, December 28, 1947, 3.

45. Richard Neuberger, "Curtain Raiser for '48," *Nation*, June 7, 1947, 682–83; *ADA World*, June 18, 1947, 3; *New York Times*, May 19, 1947, 1; *New York Times*, June 9, 1947, 1, 5; MacDougall, *Gideon's Army*, 1:184; Dubin, *United States Congressional Elections*, 567.

46. Andrew Biemiller, "Observations and Conclusions on Special Elections in Wisconsin and Pennsylvania," October 6, 1947, Box 75, "ADA - October 1947" Folder, Upholsterers International Union Papers, Temple University, Philadelphia; Jenkins, *The Cold War at Home*, 25–29; Foster, *The Union Politic*, 105–7.

47. Hale, "What Makes Wallace Run?," 247; Bean, COHP, 260; Wallace, COHP, 5088–90, 5118–20.

48. Karabell, *The Last Campaign*, 231; Wechsler, *The Age of Suspicion*, 221; Steel, *Walter Lippmann and the American Century*, 435; Norman Thomas, "The Broken Party System," *Progressive*, October 1948, 16; MacDougall, *Gideon's Army*, 1:236; Abels, *Out of the Jaws of Victory*, 111.

49. Wallace, "I Shall Run in 1948," 172–74.

50. *PM*, December 18, 1947, 12; *Chicago Sun*, January 1, 1948, 5; *Chicago Sun*, December 31, 1947, 3; *ADA World*, January 8, 1948, 1.

51. Abraham B. Held, "Will Wallace Swing Illinois to GOP?," *New Leader*, January 24, 1948, 7; *PM*, December 19, 1947, 2; C. B. Baldwin to [California Congressman] Chet Holifield, December 22, 1947, Box 2, CBP; Andrew Biemiller, "Notes on 1948 Elections, the 81st Congress, and a Third Party," Box 6, "Americans for Democratic Action" Folder, CIO Secretary-Treasurer Papers; *Chicago Sun*, January 21, 1948, 54.

52. Miller, *Plain Speaking*, 268; Clifford, *Counsel to the President*, 116–23, 224–25.

53. McHale quoted in Goulden, *The Best Years*, 350; *PM*, December 30, 1947, 5; Yarnell, *Democrats and Progressives*, 50–52; "Wallace's Four Year Plan," *Newsweek*, January 12, 1948, 18; Hamby, *Man of the People*, 453–55. For the Republicans' use of the Communist issue in the 1946 election, see Boylan, *The New Deal Coalition and the Election of 1946*, 135–40, 162–64.

54. *PM*, January 21, 1948, 3; A. F. Whitney to C. B. Baldwin, January 16, 1948, Box 22, CBP; *New York Times*, January 7, 1948, 3; Hamby, *Beyond the New Deal*, 216; *Labor Leader*, January 17, 1948, 1.

55. *New York Times*, December 19, 1947, 1; January 6, 1948, 1; January 8, 1948, 1, 14.

56. CIO, "Minutes of the Executive Board of the CIO," January 22–23, 1948, Reel 11, microfilm edition, 19–27, 114–29; CIO, "Transcript of Hearings before the Committee to Investigate Charges against the International Longshoremen's and Warehousemen's Union, Washington, DC, June 1950," 73–75, 104–17, Box 110, CIO Secretary-Treasurer Papers; Kampelman, *The Communist Party vs. the CIO*, 141–42.

57. During the ILWU hearings in 1950, Quill testified, "I questioned it [the Wallace candidacy] at the time, but I thought that running Wallace was a pressure campaign in order to get a better ticket at the Democratic convention, and that it was a straw in the wind that would be hauled back as soon as the Democrats would show some sign of loosening up on the ticket. To follow up the fears that I had of what the Communist Party were [*sic*] doing within the CIO, I discussed this new line with William Z. Foster, the National Chairman of the Communist Party, in the month of January, 1948. I expressed to him fears that this move will split the unions, and weaken our position locally and nationally against the employers. He said the Communist Party have [*sic*] decided that all the unions that it can influence within the CIO are to go down the line behind Wallace if it split the last union down the middle, but, he said, 'We have also decided to form a Third Federation of Labor in the United States carved out of the AF of L and the CIO in order to implement the Henry Wallace movement. . . .' I told Foster that day if he should do anything, any such thing, the Transport Workers Union would have nothing to do with the proposal." After speaking with the membership and Wallace, Quill continued, "my suspicions were becoming clearer. When I told Foster that he should count the Transport Workers out of any Third Federation of Labor he said the thing wasn't finalized yet, 'and we are not ready to go through with it, but that is our decision.'" CIO, "ILWU Hearings," 71–72, 120. Quill continued to support the third party through the early months of the campaign, telling reporters, "I'm still for Wallace if being for him will not split the CIO unions. If being for Wallace will split the CIO, the price is too great. I am a trade unionist first." By March 26, Quill determined that the Wallace candidacy was splitting the CIO and broke with both the third party and the Communists. Kampelman, *The Communist Party vs. The CIO*, 143–44. Some historians have noted that Quill's continuing support of Wallace seems to undercut his later testimony that he had opposed the third party since October 1947. Joseph Starobin notes, however, that "it is this very inconsistency in his behavior—strange to students who have no experience with Communism—which authenticates the Quill memorandum. He broke with the Party in a traumatic frame of mind after much soul searching and maneuvering." According to Starobin, his gradual estrangement from the party was

"entirely consistent with the behavior of dissidents within the Communist movement." Starobin, *American Communism in Crisis*, 293.

58. *PM*, January 23, 1948, 3; Gall, *Pursuing Justice*, 229–31.

59. *Daily Worker*, December 30, 1947, 6; January 12, 1948; *New York Herald Tribune*, December 31, 1947, 4.

60. MacDougall, *Gideon's Army*, 2:303–4. On October 5, 1944, Roosevelt had declared: "I have never sought and I do not welcome the support of any person or group committed to Communism or Fascism or any other foreign ideology which would undermine the American system of competitive enterprise and private property." When a reporter read this statement to Wallace at a press conference on January 17, Wallace responded, "I'll have to look up the record and find out what FDR really did." Quoted in MacDougall, *Gideon's Army*, 2:304.

61. Freda Kirchwey, "Wallace: Prophet or Politician?," *Nation*, January 10, 1948, 29; Eugene Lyons, "Wallace and the Communists," 136–37; Macdonald, "The Wallace Campaign," 179; *Washington Star*, January 5, 1948.

62. Joseph Starobin in the *Daily Worker*, January 2, 1948, 6; Charney, *A Long Journey*, 176. See also Paul Lyons, *Philadelphia Communists*, 148–54.

63. Wechsler, *The Age of Suspicion*, 218; Hale, "What Makes Wallace Run?," 248; Ray Matthews to the editor, February 2, 1948, Box 13, Folder 222, Freda Kirchwey Papers. These themes and phrases recur repeatedly in pro-Wallace letters. For a representative sampling, see *PM*, December 28, 1947, 25; January 8, 1948, 21; February 2, 1948, 32, and Box 13, Folders 200–222, Freda Kirchwey Papers, for letters to the *Nation*.

64. The themes and phrases in this paragraph appeared frequently in Wallace's weekly editorials in the *New Republic* and in his 1948 campaign speeches. Wallace first spoke of "political" versus "economic" democracy at a Soviet Friendship Rally in Madison Square Garden on November 8, 1942. In a 1946 *New Republic* editorial he declared, "We cannot hide the weaknesses in our democracy. If we take steps to overcome these weaknesses, then I believe the Russians, believing in the genuineness of our democracy, will move toward greater political freedom." For his preference for the "doctrines of Christ" over those of Machiavelli, see Wallace, "Thoughts at Christmas," *New Republic*, December 22, 1947, 12–13. For a helpful summary of Wallace's views on international affairs within the broader context of twentieth-century American liberalism, see Judis, *The Grand Illusion*, 46–73. See also Hamby, "Henry A. Wallace, the Liberals, and Soviet-American Relations," 153–69; and Wallace, *Statesmanship and Religion*, which offers revealing insights into the author's moralistic approach to international relations.

65. Stone and Grafton quoted in Stewart, "Wallace the Symbol," m-6; Rexford G. Tugwell, "Journal Entry, January 19, 1948," Box 35, RTP; Adams, "Wallace: Liberal or Star-Gazer," 52; Gael Sullivan, "Memo re: Wallace Situation," June 2, 1947, quoted in Yarnell, *Democrats and Progressives*, 22–23; James Loeb, "Report to the National Board Meeting of September 20, 1947," quoted in McAuliffe, *Crisis on the Left*, 38.

66. Margaret Marshall, "Notes by the Way," *Nation*, June 26, 1948, 719; *PM*, December 30, 1947, 10; *New York Herald Tribune*, December 31, 1947, 12.

67. MacDougall, *Gideon's Army*, 1:185–86; Phillips, "That Baffling Personality, Mr. Wallace," 46.

68. Eleanor Roosevelt, "My Day" clippings, Reel 106, Series 6, Number 3, ADA-M; *Washington Star*, January 19, 1948, 9; *ADA World*, January 8, 1948, 1, 3; Lash, *Eleanor*, 106.

69. *Socialist Call*, January 20, 1948, 8; *Washington Daily News*, January 16, 1948, 40; *Chicago Sun*, January 19, 1948, 5.

70. *Washington Star*, January 16, 1948, 6; January 17, 1948, 6; January 19, 1948, 3; Phillips, "That Baffling Personality, Mr. Wallace," 47; Curtis MacDougall, Interview with Ralph Shikes, Box 49, Notebook 11, PPP.

71. *Socialist Call*, January 20, 1948, 8; *Chicago Sun*, January 23, 1948, 6; *Chicago Sun*, January 19, 1948, 5.

72. Curtis MacDougall, "Notes from an Interview with Harold Young, attorney, in Odessa, Texas, April 1953," Box 45, Folder 171, PPP.

CHAPTER 3

1. *PM*, February 18, 1948, 15; *New York Herald Tribune*, February 19, 1948, 22.

2. *New York Times*, January 15, 1948, 15; January 20, 1948, 16; *PM*, January 22, 1948, 16.

3. *New York Times*, February 18, 1948, 17; Moscow, *Politics in the Empire State*, 110–19; Liberal Party Press Release, February 16, 1948; Liberal Party Press Release, February 17, 1948, both in Box 38, Folder 88, PPP; *PM*, February 12, 1948, 13; February 15, 1948, 12; Henry A. Wallace to Leo Isacson, January 28, 1948, Box 10, CBP.

4. *New York Herald Tribune*, February 20, 1948, 14; *Washington Post*, February 19, 1948, 2; *Transport Workers Union Bulletin*, January 1948, 2; *Daily Worker*, February 19, 1948, 2, 5; *New York Star*, October 29, 1948, 9. See also Isacson's obituary in the *New York Times*, September 25, 1996, 10-B.

5. *New York Times*, October 21, 1948, 24; "They Voted Against Us," *Time*, March 1, 1948, 13; *Labor Action*, March 1, 1948, 4; Michael Straight, "What Happened in the Bronx," *New Republic*, March 1, 1948, 7; Lubell, *The Future of American Politics*, 86–87.

6. Gus Tyler, "Memorandum on the Recent Election in the 24th Congressional District, Bronx, New York," Reel 106, Series 6, Number 5, ADA-M.

7. *New York World-Telegram*, February 14, 1948, 3; *Daily Worker*, February 3, 1948, 7. Some commentators had warned early on that Bronx Democrats were setting themselves up for a fall if they staked their reputations on Propper's performance in the Twenty-Fourth. The Flynn machine, they argued, was underestimating the ALP's ability to get out the vote in a special election. See Tom O'Connor and John K. Weiss in *PM*, January 15, 1948, 9; and "The Shape of Things," *Nation*, February 14, 1948, 171. After the election, the nationally known political columnist Arthur Krock made the same critique of boss Flynn's unwise decision to promote the election as a Wallace referendum. *New York Times*, February 19, 1948, 22.

8. *New York World Telegram*, February 10, 1948, 12; Tyler, "Memorandum on the Recent Election"; Straight, "What Happened in the Bronx," 7; *Socialist Call*, June 11, 1948, 6; *Daily Worker*, February 2, 1948, 6; February 3, 1948, 9; February 6, 1948, 5; *Labor Action*, March 1, 1948, 4; Schmidt, *Henry A. Wallace*, 69.

9. *New York World-Telegram*, February 2, 1948, 1; February 6, 1948, 3; February 12, 1948, 3.

10. *PM*, February 15, 1948, 12; *TWU Bulletin*, January 1948, 2; "Comments on Victory of Leo Isacson in New York" [New Party Internal Memo], February 24, 1948, Box 7, Folder 27, PPP.

11. Benson, *Harry S. Truman and the Founding of Israel*, 185; Cohen, *Truman and Israel*, 149–76; *Daily Worker*, February 11, 1948, 4, 7. In later years, historians hostile to Truman would likewise claim that the president had "deliberately and calculatingly" played politics with the Palestine issue in an attempt to win Jewish votes. See, most notably, Snetsinger, *Truman, the Jewish Vote, and the Creation of Israel*. Cohen and Benson, drawing on newly available and previously untapped primary sources in American and Israeli archives, conclude that domestic political considerations had little influence on the shaping of Truman's Palestine policy.

12. Straight, "What Happened in the Bronx," 7; *New York Times*, February 18, 1948, 17; February 19, 1948, 48.

13. *PM*, May 30, 1948, M7; *Socialist Call*, July 9, 1948, 2; *Labor Action*, June 14, 1948, 1, 4; "Wallace as Hypocrite on Israel," *New Leader*, June 26, 1948, 3.

14. For the change in the CPUSA line, see Alexander Bittelman, "New Tasks and Realignments in the Struggle for the Jewish State in Palestine," *Political Affairs* 27 (February 1948): 146–55. For the motivations behind Soviet policy toward Palestine during this period, see Ro'i, "Soviet-Israeli Relations, 1947–1954."

15. Charney, *A Long Journey*, 177.

16. For a contemporary report of growing anti-Semitism in the Soviet Union, see the former Moscow correspondent Drew Middleton's account in the *New York Times*, February 13, 1948, 13. See also Kostyrchenko, *Out of the Red Shadows*, esp. 79–101; and Mastny, *The Cold War and Soviet Insecurity*, 55–57. Mastny cites Stalin's January 1948 order for the staged murder of Shlomo Mikhoels, the president of the Anti-Fascist Jewish Committee, a front organization established to win over influential Jewish groups in the West to a more pro-Soviet position, as one of the early manifestations of this resurgent anti-Semitism.

17. *New York Times*, February 13, 1948, 3; *PM*, February 16, 1948, 10.

18. *Baltimore Sun*, February 15, 1948, 1, 2; *New York Times*, February 16, 1948, 1, 5; "Address by Henry A. Wallace before the Citizens Committee for Leo Isacson, February 15, 1948," Box 13, CBP.

19. *New York World-Telegram*, February 14, 1948, 3; February 17, 1948, 2; *New York Journal-American*, February 17, 1948, 1; Schaffer, *Vito Marcantonio*, 134; *PM*, February 18, 1948, 15–16.

20. "Lessons in Wallace Gain: Major-Party Weaknesses," *U.S. News and World Report*, February 27, 1948, 12; *Washington Post*, February 19, 1948, 2; "They Voted Against Us," 13.

21. *PM*, February 18, 1948, 15; February 19, 1948, 14; February 22, 1948, 31; Shannon, *The Decline of American Communism*, 157; Straight, "What Happened in the Bronx," 7; *Washington Post*, February 19, 1948, 1.

22. Tyler, "Memorandum on the Recent Election," 2; *Daily Worker*, February 20, 1948, 2, 10. On Isacson's relationship with the Communist Party, see "Fourth Report

from the FBI to President Truman," February 23, 1948, Harry S. Truman Papers: President's Secretary's Files reproduced in Merrill, *Documentary History of the Truman Presidency*, 129–31. See also Isacson's somewhat evasive responses to allegations of subservience to the CP line leveled by the Liberal party nominee Dean Alfange. *PM*, February 15, 1948, 18. In endorsing Isacson, the *PM* editor Max Lerner expressed uneasiness with the ALP candidate's "closeness" to the Communist machine but added that he did not think Isacson had "lost his independence." Given Isacson's behavior in subsequent years, this seems a fair assessment. In 1950, the ALP tentatively offered Isacson its gubernatorial nomination but withdrew it when he refused to accept the Communist line on the Korean War. *PM*, February 16, 1948, 10; *New York Times*, February 27, 1950, 2; August 3, 1948, 2; August 9, 1950, 1, 54.

23. *Washington Post*, February 18, 1948, 2; *New York World-Telegram*, February 20, 1948, 15, 16. Mrs. Roosevelt commented on the Bronx special election in her February 20 syndicated column, but see also Lash, *Eleanor*, 144–46.

24. *Washington Post*, February 29, 1948, 1B; Abels, *Out of the Jaws of Victory*, 25; *Washington Star*, February 19, 1948, 6; *Baltimore Sun*, February 24, 1948, 1.

25. Ferrell, *Truman in the White House*, 246; Truman to Bernard M. Baruch, February 18, 1948, quoted in Divine, *Foreign Policy and U.S. Presidential Elections, 1940–1948*, 174.

26. *New York Herald Tribune*, February 19, 1948, 2; *PM*, February 18, 1948, 15–16; *New York Times*, February 18, 1948, 17.

27. *Daily Worker*, February 20, 1948, 10; February 19, 1948, 9; author's telephone interview with Lillian Gates, September 3, 1996.

28. *New York World-Telegram*, February 20, 1948, 16; Straight, "What Happened in the Bronx," 7–8; Robert Bendiner, "Politics and People," *Nation*, February 28, 1948, 230; *New York Times*, February 18, 1948, 17; *Washington Star*, February 26, 1948, 15; *Chicago Daily News*, February 28, 1948, 6; Lewis, "Wallace Coup in the Bronx," 14. Propper promptly denied—to little effect—that he had ever represented a landlord in an eviction case.

29. Lubell, *Future of American Politics*, 87; Tyler, "Memorandum on the Recent Election," 3; *Chicago Defender*, March 20, 1948, 19.

30. Elmer Benson to Dear Friend, April 3, 1948, Box 31, Naomi Benson Papers, University of Washington, Seattle; *New York Times*, February 23, 1948, 15. For reports on the activities of newly founded Wallace organizations in the various states, see *Daily Worker*, February 17, 1948, 5; February 25, 1948, 5; *Detroit Free Press*, February 22, 1948, 1, 2; National Wallace-for-President Committee, "Facts on the Wallace Campaign," March 23, 1948, Box 15, Folder 62, PPP; *The Citizen* [A publication of the National Wallace-for-President Committee], April 1948.

31. *Worker*, February 29, 1948, 5; "Lessons in Wallace Gain," *New Republic*, March 1, 1948, 5; *New York Times*, February 20, 1948, 3; *Washington Star*, February 21, 1948, 9.

32. *San Francisco Chronicle*, February 19, 1948, 24; *Baltimore Sun*, February 19, 1948, 2; Stevenson, *The Undiminished Man*, 72; *PM*, February 2, 1948, 10; Moremen, "The Independent Progressive Party in California," 56–68; McWilliams, "California's Third-Party Donnybrook," 436; Robert Kenny, "My Forty Years in California Politics, 1922–1962," 356, Carton 13, Robert Kenny Papers, University of California, Berkeley.

33. Healey and Isserman, *California Red*, 109–10; Starobin, *American Communism in Crisis*, 164. On Communist participation in the IPP, see also Richmond, *A Long View from the Left*, 291–93; *Labor Action*, December 22, 1947, 2; January 5, 1948, 1; and Saposs, *Communism in American Politics*, 133–34.

34. Starobin, *American Communism in Crisis*, 164; Call, "A Study in Group Support of the Independent Progressive Party of California," 46–52; Testimony of William Don Waddilove, HUAC, *Investigation of Communist Activities in the Los Angeles, Calif. Area—Part 7*, 3660–3676; "The Independent Progressive Party: A Summary of its Foundation and Activity in San Diego County," 7–11, Box 266, Folder 8, J. B. Matthews Papers.

35. Moremen, "The Independent Progressive Party," 42–46; Testimony of Charles David Blodgett, HUAC, *Investigation of Communist Activities in the San Francisco Area—Part 3*, 3296–3305; Testimony of William Donald Ames, HUAC, *Investigation of Communist Activities in the San Francisco Area—Part 4*, 3403–08. On David Jenkins and the role of the California Labor School in the Wallace campaign, see Schwartz, *From West to East*, 380–82.

36. "The Independent Progressive Party: A Summary of its Foundation and Activity in San Diego County," 7–11, Box 266, Folder 8, J. B. Matthews Papers; Testimony of Lynn Ackerstein, HUAC, *Investigation of Communist Activities in the State of California—Part 11*, 7022–37. Ackerstein left the party in 1950; her testimony before HUAC offers a revealing glimpse of how the CP initially attracted and then repulsed many who were committed to progressive causes.

37. *Daily Worker*, February 24, 1948, 2, 10; *Washington Post*, February 24, 1948, 1, 2.

38. Crichton, "Idaho's Hot Potato," 21, 64; Gervasi, "Low Man on the Wallace Totem Pole," 16–17, 72–74; Neuberger, "Glen Taylor: Left-Wing Minstrel," 18–21; *Washington Post*, August 20, 1948, 20; Peterson, *Prophet without Honor*, 11–22; Schmidt, *Henry A. Wallace*, 56–60.

39. Peterson, *Prophet without Honor*, 23–34; Neuberger, "Cowboy on Our Side," *Nation*, August 24, 1946, 209–10.

40. *Congressional Record*, 80th Congress, 2nd Session, 94 (May 12, 1948), 5683; Peterson, *Prophet without Honor*, 94.

41. *Daily Worker*, December 15, 1947, 3; *PM*, January 7, 1948, 4; February 22, 1948, 12; *New York Star Magazine*, October 17, 1948, m11; Neuberger, "Glen Taylor," 265; Schmidt, *Henry A. Wallace*, 59–60. On Taylor's deliberations over whether to bolt the Democratic Party, see Peterson, *Prophet without Honor*, 99–103. Peterson accepts Taylor's contention that his decision to join Wallace was a matter of principle and conscience. Neuberger presents a more skeptical account, emphasizing Taylor's desire for national publicity. For Taylor's opposition to Truman's Cold War policies, see Peterson, *Prophet without Honor*, 78–95; and Pratt, "Senator Glen H. Taylor," 140–66. For Taylor's "genius," see *New York Post*, March 9, 1948, 12.

42. "Address by Walter Reuther, President UAW-CIO, to the First Annual Convention, Americans for Democratic Action, Sunday February 22, 1948," Reel 80, Series 4, Number 9, ADA-M; Reuther, "Against the Commissar and the Man on Horseback," 5; *Washington Post*, February 23, 1948, 1, 2. See also Reuther, "How to Beat the Communists," 11, 44–49.

43. *Baltimore Sun*, February 24, 1948, 12; James Loeb to Executive Committee, "Memorandum Re: Political Policy, March 16, 1948," Reel 33, Series 2, Number 62;

Minutes of the Executive Committee Meeting, March 18, 1948, Reel 80, Series 4, Number 6, both in ADA-M.

44. Loeb quoted in Hamby, *Man of the People*, 446. On the ADA-backed "Eisenhower boom," see Gillon, *Politics and Vision*, 44–47. For the liberals' assumption that the postwar period would herald a move toward the social democratic left in American politics, see Warren, *Noble Abstractions*, 246–56. For Truman's reaction to ADA's involvement in the Eisenhower boom, see Hamby, *Man of the People*, 447.

45. See, for example, McAuliffe, *Crisis on the Left*; Lipsitz, *Rainbow at Midnight*; Schrecker, *Many Are the Crimes*; Kleinman, *A World of Hope, a World of Fear*.

46. Delton, "Rethinking Post–World War II Anticommunism," 15; Plotke, *Building a Democratic Political Order*, 313, 322; Macdonald quoted in Schlesinger, *A Life in the Twentieth Century*, 459.

47. *New York Times*, February 23, 1948, 14; "Address by William Green, President, AFL to the First Annual Convention, Americans for Democratic Action, Sunday February 22, 1948," Reel 80, Series 4, Number 9, ADA-M; Titus and Nixon, "The 1948 Elections in California," 102; Moremen, "The Independent Progressive Party," 40–42; Leeds, "The AFL in the 1948 Elections," 207–18.

48. *New York Times*, February 11, 1948, 1.

49. Zieger, *The CIO*, 271–72; Altman, "CIO and Political Discipline," 28–29; Brophy, *A Miner's Life*, 289–90.

50. Moremen, "The Independent Progressive Party," 85–90.

51. *New York Times*, February 11, 1948, 1, 6; John Brophy to All Industrial Union Councils, March 8, 1948; Philip Murray to All Industrial Union Councils and CIO Regional Directors, January 27, 1948, both in Box 44, Philip Murray Papers. See also Jack Kroll to State and City PACs, CIO Regional Directors, PAC Representatives, January 30, 1948, Box 7, "CIO-PAC, 1945–1949," Jack Kroll Papers, Library of Congress, Washington, D.C. Kroll's letter to PAC employees echoed the instructions Brophy gave to the IUCs.

52. Healey and Isserman, *California Red*, 112–13; Greater New York CIO Council, "Statement of Policy Adopted by Executive Board Special Meeting, March 30, 1948," Box 44, Philip Murray Papers; MacDougall, *Gideon's Army*, 2:320; "The Reminiscences of John Brophy," COHP, 947–48; Brophy, *A Miner's Life*, 290; *San Francisco Chronicle*, February 27, 1948, 28; March 4, 1948, 7; March 6, 1948, 1, 8.

53. Brophy to Morris Zuzman, California Director, CIO Political Action Committee and Jerome Posner, Chairman, California National CIO Political Action Committee, April 7, 1948, Box 85, "Political Action Committee, 1948," CIO Secretary-Treasurer Papers.

54. *New York Times*, March 19, 1948, 46; *New York Herald Tribune*, March 17, 1948, 5; *New York Post*, March 5, 1948, 30; *San Francisco Chronicle*, March 6, 1948, 1, 8; March 16, 1948, 2; March 20, 1948, 1; *CIO News*, February 23, 1948, 2; March 8, 1948, 3.

55. Altman, "CIO and Political Discipline," 29.

CHAPTER 4

1. Henry A. Wallace, "Too Little, Too Late," *New Republic*, October 6, 1947, 12.
2. Schmidt, *Henry A. Wallace*, 73.

3. For the text of Wallace's Milwaukee address, see Wallace, "My Alternative for the Marshall Plan," *New Republic*, January 12, 1948, 13–14.

4. The full text of Wallace's statement appears in House Committee on Foreign Affairs, *United States Foreign Policy for a Post-War Recovery Program*, 1581–1603 (hereafter cited as *Hearings*).

5. For Wallace's early support of what he termed an "ever-normal granary," see Sirevåg, *The Eclipse of the New Deal and the Fall of Vice President Henry Wallace*, 380–81. Sirevåg notes that President Roosevelt rarely acknowledged Wallace's suggestions concerning postwar planning. Rather, FDR told Wallace that Congress should take the lead in such matters and, ironically, suggested he explain his ideas to Senator Truman.

6. On the internationalization of the Ruhr, see Leffler, *A Preponderance of Power*, 151–56. For changing liberal attitudes toward German reconstruction, see Wechsler, *The Age of Suspicion*, 190–98.

7. The full text of the question-and-answer portion of Wallace's testimony appears in *Hearings*, 1603–25.

8. *San Francisco Chronicle*, February 25, 1948, 14; Donald Harrington, "Hobson's Political Choice: Wallace and Liberalism," *New Leader*, May 8, 1948, 3.

9. *New York World-Telegram*, February 28, 1948, 8. On the failure of UNRRA, see Kessner, *Fiorello H. La Guardia*, 580–87. La Guardia replaced Herbert Lehman as Director General of UNRRA. He approached his position with many of the same ideals and assumptions that Wallace held but grew discouraged as public opinion balked at the United States contributing 72 percent of UNRRA's budget to supply hostile pro-Soviet governments.

10. Margaret Marshall, "Notes by the Way," *Nation*, June 26, 1948, 719; *PM*, January 2, 1948, 10.

11. Markowitz, *The Rise and Fall of the People's Century*, 249. See also Narinsky, "Soviet Foreign Policy and the Origins of the Cold War," 105–10; and Leffler, *The Struggle for Germany and the Origins of the Cold War*.

12. Macdonald, "The Wallace Campaign," 184; Wallace to Anita McCormick Blaine, April 2, 1948, Reel 47, Frame 710, HAW-M.

13. Macdonald, "The Wallace Campaign," 184–85; *Washington Post*, February 25, 1948, 12; *Hearings*, 1617–18. For confusion among Wallace supporters in the wake of his testimony, see T. O. Thackrey to Henry A. Wallace, February 24, 1948, Reel 44, Frame 475, HAW-M.

14. Warren, *Noble Abstractions*, 202.

15. For Wallace as a prescient devotee of "spheres of influence," see Walton, *Henry Wallace, Harry Truman, and the Cold War*. For Wallace's rejection of such a characterization of his views, see Judis, *Grand Illusion*, 68. Most scholars, regardless of their assessment of Wallace's views, have maintained that he was sketching a "spheres of influence" policy in the address at Madison Square Garden. In a persuasive, though largely overlooked analysis of the speech, Edward L. and Frederick H. Schapsmeier point out that Wallace was not condoning a "Russian sphere" but rather "coexistence as the first step toward ultimate world federation." Schapsmeier and Schapsmeier, *Prophet in Politics*, 153–56.

16. *New York Times*, August 1, 1948, section IV, 5; Claire Neifeind, "Europe and the Marshall Plan: Special Reports—Italy," *New Republic*, March 15, 1948, 13; Rice-Maximin, "The United States and the French Left, 1945–1949," 738–39. Recent scholarship on the Marshall Plan has not upheld either Wallace's or the Communists' allegations, emphasizing instead U.S. flexibility and European eagerness to cooperate with the Americans. See, for example, Young, *France, the Cold War and the Western Alliance, 1944–49*, 134–74; and Maier, "Alliance and Autonomy."

17. "Foreign Comment on Wallace," *Nation*, January 17, 1948, 74; "Henry Wallace's Decision," *New Statesman and Nation*, January 3, 1948, 2; "Wallace-Taft Axis," *Tribune*, January 2, 1948, 3; "Deserted Wallace," *Tribune*, January 9, 1948, 4; "The Myth of Henry Wallace: Stalin Pulls the Strings," *Tribune*, July 30, 1948, 2; *Manchester Guardian*, February 25, 1948, 4.

18. Jenny Lee to James Loeb, February 23, 1948, Reel 121, Series 7, Number 73, ADA-M; *ADA World*, March 31, 1948, 2; Ayer, "American Liberalism and British Socialism in a Cold War World, 1945–1951," 222–78. See also Jennie Lee to Henry A. Wallace, February 23, 1948, and Wallace to Lee, March 12, 1948, both on Reel 44, Frame 472, HAW-M.

19. Eleanor Roosevelt, "My Day," October 15, 1947, quoted in Berger, *Eleanor Roosevelt and American Foreign Policy*, 63–64.

20. Macdonald, "The Wallace Campaign," 183.

21. For the CPUSA's foreign aid proposal, see *PM*, November 10, 1947, 3. The research staff of Americans for Democratic Action circulated a memo calling attention to the "marked likeness" between the Communist and Wallace programs. See "Communist Sources of Wallace's Plan for European Recovery," January 8, 1948, Reel 106, Series 6, Number 3, ADA-M. On the Wallace "research group," including Ramsey, Perlo, Petran, and the wealthy Chicagoan Frederick Vanderbilt Field, see Markowitz, *The Rise and Fall of the People's Century*, 298; and Shannon, *The Decline of American Communism*, 159–61. On Perlo's involvement with the Soviet NKVD, see Haynes and Klehr, *Venona*, 116–27.

22. *Socialist Call*, February 6, 1948, 1; Thomas to Vandenberg, December 31, 1947, quoted in Pittman, "'Gideon's Army' and the Marshall Plan," 192.

23. "The Shape of Things," *Nation*, March 6, 1948, 261; Stephanson, "The United States," 34. For Kolko's critique, see in particular Joyce and Gabriel Kolko, *The Limits of Power*. Walton, *Henry Wallace, Harry Truman, and the Cold War* and Lader, "'. . . To Serve the World—Not to Dominate It,'" echo many of the Kolkos' views in their popularized versions of Cold War revisionism.

24. The motivations behind the Marshall Plan remain a controversial topic among scholars. Some historians, most prominently Melvyn Leffler, have argued that the Truman administration initiated the European Recovery Program primarily for strategic and national security reasons—"to prevent any potential adversary or coalition of adversaries from mobilizing the resources and economic-military potential of Europe for war-making purposes against the United States." Leffler, "The United States and the Strategic Dimensions of the Marshall Plan." Others, however, view the Marshall Plan as an American effort to export its "neo-capitalist ideology" to create a "global New Deal" based on "the politics of productivity." Like Wallace, though hardly in the same

conspiratorial terms, these "corporatist" historians emphasize the role of American business interests in influencing the formation of foreign policy. Unlike Wallace, who enthusiastically advocated just such a "global New Deal" strategy (and charged the Truman administration with allegedly abandoning this approach), these scholars are less sanguine about the transplanting of American economic ideology to other nations. See, for example, Hogan, *The Marshall Plan*.

25. Esposito, *America's Feeble Weapon*, esp. xxii; Romero, *The United States and the European Trade Union Movement, 1944–1951*; Milward, *The Reconstruction of Western Europe, 1945–1951*.

26. Lundestad, "Empire by Invitation?." Responding to an earlier generation of historians that criticized U.S. government and business leaders for allegedly imposing their priorities on unwilling Western Europeans, Lundestad and others have shown that European governments and their citizens shared many of the Americans' views, particularly their anti-Sovietism. In stark contrast to the Eastern Europeans' reaction to the introduction of Soviet influence in their countries, Western Europeans for the most part welcomed the Americans—and with good cause. Lundestad contrasts Washington's European Recovery Program with Moscow's Molotov Plan, under which the USSR extracted *from* its satellite states for its own recovery about the same $14 billion worth of goods that the United States supplied *to* its allies. See also Maier, "Alliance and Autonomy," as well as the essays by Georges-Henri Soutou on France (96–120) and Ilaria Poggiolini on Italy (121–43) in Reynolds, *The Origins of the Cold War in Europe*.

27. Even Wallace's colleagues at the *New Republic* repudiated his views on the Marshall Plan. See Michael Straight, "ERP: Aid to Peace . . . or Road to War?" *New Republic*, March 15, 1948, 11–12. See Maxfield, "The Progressive Party of 1948," 120–25, for an extended discussion of liberals' desertion of Wallace after his decision to oppose the Marshall Plan.

28. Kaplan, *The Short March*, 177–86. See also Lukes, "The Czech Road to Communism," 252–65; and Wettig, *Stalin and the Cold War in Europe*, 152–53.

29. Truman quoted in LaFeber, *America, Russia, and the Cold War*, 79; John D. Hickerson, quoted in Paterson, *On Every Front*, 82; U.S. State Department, *Bulletin* 18, March 7, 1948, 304.

30. Creswell, *A Question of Balance*, 11; "War Fears Grip Capital and Nation," *Newsweek*, March 22, 1948, 23–25. For the Truman Administration's response to the coup, see Leffler, *A Preponderance of Power*, 204–5. On the Finnish situation, see Devlin, "Finland in 1948."

31. Sterling, *The Masaryk Case*, 338–49, concludes that the Communists learned on March 9 that Masaryk intended to repudiate the new government, passed this information on to Moscow, and received orders hours later that he be murdered that night. In a recent re-examination of the case, Robin Bruce Lockhart reports that on March 8, 1948, his father, Sir Robert Bruce Lockhart, a longtime Masaryk associate, received a message from the foreign minister that he intended to flee Czechoslovakia. Others also confirmed that Masaryk had told them at the time that he was through with "the whole dirty business" of working with the Communists and had already begun to transfer money out of the country in preparation for his departure. "Alongside evidence of Jan's intention to escape," Lockhart writes, "stands a pile of medical

and other evidence—some admittedly circumstantial but totally damning—that he was murdered on instructions from Moscow." Lockhart's investigations led him to believe that a Moscow-trained NKVD Sudeten Czech, Major Augustin Sram, carried out the assassination. A few weeks after the foreign minister's death, Sram himself was murdered while, Lockhart notes, "virtually all those present at the Czernin Palace on the night of [Masaryk's] death 'disappeared' one way or another." This account generally supports Sterling's earlier findings. Lockhart, "Who Killed Jan Masaryk?," 5–7. Since no evidence from Czech or Soviet archives has yet emerged to confirm either hypothesis, the mystery remains unsolved.

32. *New York Times*, March 11, 1948, 1; *New York Post*, March 17, 1948, 22.

33. *Public Papers of the Presidents of the United States, Harry S. Truman: 1948*, 182–86; Divine, *Foreign Policy and U.S. Presidential Elections, 1940–1948*, 181–83. Some liberals took exception to the speech's emphasis on the military containment of communism to the detriment of what they considered the more "positive" approach of economic aid. See Hamby, *Beyond the New Deal*, 222.

34. Donovan, *Conflict and Crisis*, 360.

35. *Baltimore Sun*, February 28, 1948, 1, 2; "Speech by Henry A. Wallace, Minneapolis, Minnesota, February 27, 1948," and "Address of Henry A. Wallace at the Pennsylvania People's Convention, William Penn High School, York, Pennsylvania," Box 13, CBP.

36. Yergin, *Shattered Peace*, 346–50, 355–56; Leffler, *A Preponderance of Power*, 204–05. Yergin notes that at a top-secret briefing of the cabinet in November 1947, George Marshall predicted a Soviet crackdown on Czechoslovakia and characterized such a step as "a purely defensive move."

37. Kaplan, *The Short March*, vii; E. R. Gedye, "Behind the Struggle for Czechoslovakia," *Nation*, February 28, 1948, 230–32. On the domestic politics in Czechoslovakia that laid the groundwork for a Communist putsch, see Myant, *Socialism and Democracy in Czechoslovakia, 1945–1948*; and Abrams, *The Struggle for the Soul of the Nation*. Korbel, *The Communist Subversion of Czechoslovakia, 1938–1948*, discerns a more prominent Soviet role in the planning and carrying out of the coup, but it concurs that the Czech Communists' struggle for a monopoly of state power began in earnest before the cessation of hostilities in 1945. None of the scholarship on the 1948 Czech crisis claims that the democratic parties had any desire to oust the Communists from the National Front. In fact, the democratic leaders believed that the only way to avoid a Communist takeover was to preserve a National Front government that included the Communists.

38. Soutou, "France," 104, 97. Soutou concludes, "It is now generally recognized that the Truman administration had nothing to do with the departure of the communist ministers, even if it was quite happy with the outcome." Rice-Maximin, "The United States and the French Left," 734–35, notes that the French foreign minister, Georges Bidault, maintained that there was no need for the Americans to "force" the French government to expel the Communists from the cabinet since all the non-Communist ministers had reached the same viewpoint as Washington of their own accord. Hitchcock, *France Restored*, 225, observes that Bidault, though implacably hostile to the French Communist Party, actually resisted American interference in the constitution of the new government in 1947.

39. Brogi, *A Question of Self-Esteem*, 83, 109.

40. Reale, "The Founding of the Cominform," 259–68. For CPUSA claims that Washington had forced the removal of Communists from the French and Italian governments, see *Daily Worker*, December 10, 1947, 4.

41. Tigrid, "The Prague Coup of 1948," 414–19; Krátky, "Czechoslovakia, the Soviet Union, and the Marshall Plan"; Parrish, "The Turn toward Confrontation," 27–31. In his analysis of the Czechoslovak security sector, Karel Kaplan notes that the Soviets often operated within Czechoslovakia behind the backs of KSC politicians, fueling provocations without the knowledge of Gottwald and other top Communist officials. See Kaplan, *The Short March*, 143.

42. Ayer, "American Liberalism and British Socialism in a Cold War World," 292.

43. *Worker*, March 7, 1948; *Daily Worker*, February 26, 1948, 9. The American Communists nosily hailed the "people's victory" in Czechoslovakia. Accounts in the *Daily Worker* highlighted the "mass celebrations" that occurred in its wake and the dismissal of various "plotters" from public office. One dispatch noted with admiration the firings of a prison director and a doctor charged with "overfeeding collaborationist prisoners." *Daily Worker*, February 27, 1948, 3.

44. *Daily Worker*, March 1, 1948, 8.

45. *Daily Worker*, February 27, 1948, 3.

46. The *Daily Worker*'s first mention of Steinhardt's supposed coordination of a "rightist" plot appeared in Joseph Starobin's column on February 25. Foster confirmed Steinhardt's "treachery" in his own column two days later. This explanation of events in Czechoslovakia did not originate with the CPUSA, but it represented the official line determined in Moscow, as evidenced by its appearance in an article in the Soviet magazine, *New Times*, written by the Tass correspondent in Prague, V. Medov. *New Times*, ostensibly published by a Soviet trade union organization, was in fact put together under the auspices of the Soviet foreign minister, V. M. Molotov, who often wrote and edited the magazine's lead editorials. Medov, "The February Events in Czechoslovakia." For Molotov's involvement with *New Times*, see Parrish, "The Turn Toward Confrontation," 11.

47. *New York Times*, March 15, 1948, 1, 10; *Daily Worker*, March 12, 1948, 2; Wechsler, *The Age of Suspicion*, 223; *New York Post*, March 19, 1948, 28; *San Francisco Chronicle*, March 16, 1948, 20.

48. *San Francisco Chronicle*, March 18, 1948, 8. Compare Joseph Starobin's assessment in the *Daily Worker*: "It's very revealing that Mr. Steinhardt has just returned to Prague, and given a press conference, in which he's quoted as saying that he still hopes Czechoslovakia will come into the Marshall Plan. Now this is pretty crude diplomacy. It has only one meaning: that the United States would like the overthrow of the Communist leadership." *Daily Worker*, February 25, 1948, 8.

49. Macdonald, "The Wallace Campaign," 186; "The Shape of Things," *Nation*, March 27, 1948, 338; Wallace, "Where I Was Wrong," 7.

50. See, for example, Henry A. Wallace to Arthur Hays Sulzberger, March 24, 1948, Reel 44, Frames 654–55, HAW-M.

51. Aron quoted in Judt, *Postwar*, 217. For warnings to Wallace regarding the costs of his association with the Communists, see *Chicago Sun-Times*, March 1, 1948, 29; Bean,

COHP, 258–61; Donald R. Murphy [Editor of *Wallace's Farmer*] to Henry A. Wallace, March 29, 1948, Reel 44, Frame 677; Jonathan Daniels to Henry A. Wallace, March 30, 1948, Reel 44, Frame 684–85, both in HAW-M. Shannon, *The Decline of American Communism*, 162–63, and Fox, "'In Passion and in Hope,'" 269–70, offer some suggestive evidence regarding how concealed Communists gained Wallace's ear and won him over to the "party line" on Czechoslovakia. Wallace quoted in Abels, *Out of the Jaws of Victory*, 104.

52. Laski quoted in *Chicago Sun-Times*, April 19, 1948, 36. Some on the left, including Max Lerner, viewed Wallace as an American Laski, but the two men parted ways in their assessments of the Czech coup. Laski abandoned any hope for continuing Popular Front politics in Europe and adopted—albeit reluctantly—a more critical attitude toward the Soviet Union. For Laski's reaction to the coup, see Newman, *Harold Laski*, 304–5.

53. "The Shape of Things," *Nation*, February 28, 1948, 225; *PM*, March 3, 1948, 10; *New York Times*, February 29, 1948, 5E.

54. James Loeb to All ADA Chapters, March 22, 1948, Reel 80, Series 4, Number 6, ADA-M; *New York Times*, February 29, 1948, 10-E.

55. Schmidt, *Henry A. Wallace*, 73–74; Harrington, "Hobson's Political Choice," 14; Gillon, *The Democrats' Dilemma*, 24. Gillon notes that Mondale, though a Humphrey supporter, initially did not share his mentor's ardent anticommunism. His views changed in early 1948 after repeated unpleasant encounters with Communists active in Minnesota's Democratic-Farmer-Labor Party (DFL). On one occasion, a spokesperson for the DFL's pro-Communist faction, furious at Mondale's success in organizing a group of college students who opposed the Communist position, likened his efforts to those of the Hitler youth. Haynes, *Dubious Alliance*, 159. On liberal disillusionment with Wallace's response to the Czech coup, see also Julia C. Welden to Henry A. Wallace, March 19, 1948, Reel 44, Frames 638–39, HAW-M; "We Note . . . Letter to a Dissident Liberal," *Antioch Review*, March 1948, 121–22; and *PM*'s "Readers' Forum" on the question: "Is Czech Experience Final Proof That Communists Cannot Work With Other Parties in Democracies?" *PM*, March 14, 1948, 32.

56. "Text of Broadcast by Henry A. Wallace in Answer to President Truman's Message to Joint Session of Congress, March 18, 1948," Box 13, CBP; Henry A. Wallace, "Whipped-up Hysteria," *New Republic*, March 29, 1948, 10.

57. For this general theme, see Joyce and Gabriel Kolko, *Limits of Power*, esp. 397–98. Less ideologically insistent but equally skeptical of the authenticity of the war scare is Freeland, *The Truman Doctrine and the Origins of McCarthyism*, 274–87. See also Frank Kofsky, *Harry S. Truman and the War Scare of 1948*, 233–68. Though massively researched, Kofsky's work bases its case almost entirely on circumstantial evidence which could easily support less conspiratorial conclusions.

58. Leffler, *A Preponderance of Power*, 209–13. For further critiques of the "war scare" thesis, see also Woods and Jones, *Dawning of the Cold War*, 168–70; Ferrell, *Harry S. Truman*, 430–31, and Ferrell's review of Kofsky, in the *Journal of American History* 81 (December 1994): 1372.

59. About 3,000 Czechoslovaks had fled the country by May 1948. By mid-1950 the number had risen to 20,450, the overwhelming majority of whom were not leading

public figures but "common men and women." Myant, *Socialism and Democracy in Czechoslovakia*, 217.

60. Frank McNaughton to Don Bermingham, March 19. 1948, Box 15, "March 16–31, 1948," McNaughton Reports File, 1941–1949, Frank McNaughton Papers, Harry S Truman Library, Independence, Mo.

61. The Ambassador in the Soviet Union (Smith) to the Secretary of State, May 4, 1948, in *Foreign Relations of the United States: 1948, Eastern Europe; The Soviet Union*, 4:847–850, quotes on 850.

62. Ibid., 4:854–857, quote on 854; Smith, *My Three Years in Moscow*, 166; Walker, "'No More Cold War,'" 83; Walton, *Henry Wallace, Harry Truman, and the Cold War*, 217.

63. Wallace's open letter to Stalin is reprinted in Carlyle, *Documents on International Affairs, 1947–1948*, 160–63; Walton, *Henry Wallace, Harry Truman, and the Cold War*, 218.

64. *New York Times*, May 12, 1948, 14. Stalin's response is reprinted in Carlyle, *Documents on International Affairs, 1947–1948*, 163–64; *New York Times*, May 18, 1948, 4.

65. Walker, "'No More Cold War,'" 84, 87; *New York Times*, May 12, 1948, 8.

66. Walker, "'No More Cold War,'" 87–91; "The Stage of Put Up or Shut Up," *Newsweek*, May 31, 1948, 19. For a more recent interpretation of the Smith-Molotov exchange similar to Walker's, see Eisenberg, *Drawing the Line*, 404–7.

67. Department of State, *Bulletin* 18, June 6, 1948, 744–46; Miscamble, *George F. Kennan and the Making of American Foreign Policy*, 188–89; Divine, *Foreign Policy and U.S. Presidential Elections, 1940–1948*, 203.

68. Schmidt, *Henry A. Wallace*, 78; Freda Kirchwey, "Moves toward Peace," *Nation*, May 29, 1948, 593; Walker, "'No More Cold War,'" 90.

69. *Time*, May 31, 1948, 16. Press coverage and analysis of the Wallace-Stalin correspondence emphasized the view that the Soviets were trying to influence the U.S. presidential election. See, for example, Dorothy Thompson's column in the *Washington Star*, May 21, 1948.

70. Walker, "'No More Cold War,'" 87; Smith, *My Three Years in Moscow*, 158; Sulzberger, *A Long Row of Candles*, 427, 432. Sulzberger notes that Molotov expected Wallace to receive more than 6 million votes and to emerge as the leading contender for president in 1952. The Communist press in the Soviet Union and in Europe often featured positive coverage of the Progressive Party campaign, though this hardly helped Wallace win voters in the United States. See Saposs, *Communism in American Politics*, 180–181.

CHAPTER 5

1. *Chicago Sun-Times*, July 23, 1948, 3; *New York Times*, July 24, 1948, 6; *Philadelphia Inquirer*, July 24, 1948, 4; *Baltimore Afro-American*, July 31, 1948, 2; *San Francisco Chronicle*, July 24, 1948. 3. For Wallace's expectations regarding independent and Democratic liberals, see his remarks in the *New York Star*, July 25, 1948, 8, and in the *New York Post*, July 22, 1948, 4.

2. *Chicago Sun-Times*, July 29, 1948, 15. The CBS survey taken in early July showed that among voters aged twenty-one to thirty-four, Wallace's vote had dropped from 8.7 percent to 4.6 percent. Among union members, it had dropped from 12.8 percent to 6.2 percent. *New York Post*, July 22, 1948, 4, quotes the most recent Gallup poll and assesses the temper of Wallace activists.

3. *Chicago Defender*, July 24, 1948, 1; Mann, *The Walls of Jericho*, 15–16.

4. Allen Yarnell, *Democrats and Progressives*, 73–75; *Public Papers of the Presidents of the United States: Harry S. Truman, 1945–1953: 1948*, 422; MacDougall, *Gideon's Army*, 2:388.

5. For Gallup poll results, see *Philadelphia Bulletin*, July 21, 1948, 1; on factional disputes within the New Party at the state level, see Moremen, "The Independent Progressive Party in California," 110–11, for Nevada; Dwight Spencer to Curtis MacDougall, October 5, 1953, Box 37, Folder 55, PPP, for New Mexico and Colorado; and *Capital Times*, April 26, 1948, 1, 6, and Miles McMillin, "Memo on Peoples Progressive Party of Wisconsin," Reel 106, Series 6, Number 1, ADA-M, for Wisconsin. See also "The Shape of Things," *Nation*, July 24, 1948, 86.

6. Willis Hight to Rexford Tugwell, July 20, 1948, Box 24, CBP; *Denver Post*, August 1, 1948, 1, 2; *San Francisco Chronicle*, July 20, 1948, 18; J. W. Gitt to Henry A. Wallace, January 24, 1956, Reel 50, Number 344; HAW-M; Lee Fryer to Louis Adamic, July 10, 1948, Box 58, Folder 246, PPP; David Shannon interview with Earl Browder, November 1, 1956, Shannon Research Notes, State Historical Society of Wisconsin, Madison.

7. MacDougall, *Gideon's Army*, 2:426–27; David Shannon interview with Henry A. Wallace, November 10, 1956, Shannon Research Notes; Markowitz, *The Rise and Fall of the People's Century*, 298; Shannon interview with Browder, November 1, 1956, Shannon Research Notes; Henry A. Wallace to Curtis MacDougall, September 1, 1952, Box 55, Folder 230, PPP. Wallace later recalled the meeting with Adamic as taking place in September, though his 1948 correspondence indicates it occurred in June. See J. W. Gitt to Henry A. Wallace, July 3, 1948, Box 39, Folder 107, PPP.

8. Markowitz, *The Rise and Fall of the People's Century*, 276; *Philadelphia Bulletin*, July 30, 1948, 24.

9. See, for example, Marquis Childs, *New York Post*, July 1, 1948, 40; *Labor Action*, July 26, 1948, 1, 4; and Julio Alvarez Del Vayo, "Family Fight," *Nation*, July 10, 1948, 47. Like most of the Cominform's charges against Tito, the assertion that the Yugoslavs had subordinated the party to the "People's Front" was baseless. Indeed, Tito had been the first to criticize the Western European Communist parties for following such a strategy. As it happened, the most noteworthy long-term effect of the Stalin-Tito split on the CPUSA was an *intra*party witch hunt more so than a crackdown on liberal allies. See Swain, "The Cominform"; and Starobin, *American Communism in Crisis*, 191, 198.

10. Minutes of the Meeting of the Administrative Committee of the National Wallace for President Committee, June 28, 1948, Box 7, CBP; Memorandum on Convention Attendance from Luke Wilson to C. B. Baldwin, June 24, 1948," and Memorandum from Ralph E. Shikes to All State Wallace Committee Directors, July 16, 1948, Box 24, CBP; Memorandum from Ralph E. Shikes on Publicity on Convention Delegations, June 25, 1948, Box 12, Folder 49, PPP; *Philadelphia Inquirer*, July 26, 1948, 13. On the

Wallaceites' "peculiar sensitivity to color," see Norman Thomas's syndicated column in the *San Francisco Chronicle*, July 24, 1948, 3.

11. *Christian Science Monitor*, July 21, 1948, 11. On the timing of the indictments, over which Truman himself apparently had no influence, see Hamby, *Man of the People*, 454.

12. *Christian Science Monitor*, July 23, 1948, 3; *New York Herald-Tribune*, July 24, 1948, 8; *Philadelphia Bulletin*, July 24, 1948, 8; *Daily Worker*, July 23, 1948, 11. For Communists on the convention committees, see *San Francisco Chronicle*, July 23, 1948, 2; *Washington Star*, July 23, 1948, 7; Walter R. Storey, "Free Rides on the Wallace Merry-Go-Round," *New Leader*, July 31, 1948, 1, 14.

13. A press release with the excerpts Wallace read from the Polk letters is in Box 26 of the PPP. See also *New York Times*, July 24, 1948, 6.

14. *St. Louis Post-Dispatch*, July 24, 1948, 2; *New York Herald-Tribune*, July 24, 1948, 3.

15. *New York Times*, July 24, 1948, 6.

16. *Denver Post*, July 24, 1948, 8; Goulden, *Mencken's Last Campaign*, 87–88; MacDougall, *Gideon's Army*, 2:498. Swain, "Henry A. Wallace and the 'Guru Letters,'" details the long, complicated history of the controversy, which first arose during Wallace's campaign for the vice presidency in 1940. See also White and Maze, *Henry A. Wallace*, 271–74. White and Maze conclude that Wallace did write at least some of the "Guru letters" attributed to him. The reference to Sterne is courtesy of Alistair Cooke, who cited the quote in his account of the Wallace press conference. See Cooke, *Six Men*, 109.

17. *Philadelphia Bulletin*, July 23, 1948, 2; *St. Louis Post-Dispatch*, July 24, 1948, 2; *Socialist Call*, July 30, 1948, 2. See also *Denver Post*, July 24, 1948, 8; *Boston Globe*, July 23, 1948, 2.

18. *New York Herald-Tribune*, July 24, 1948, 3.

19. *Boston Globe*, July 23, 1948, 2; *Philadelphia Bulletin*, July 23, 1948, 2; *New York Times*, July 24, 1948, 6; *San Francisco Chronicle*, July 24, 1948, pp., 1, 3; *Denver Post*, July 24, 1948, 8.

20. *Washington Post*, July 26, 1948, 9.

21. Fleeson in the *Washington Star*, July 24, 1948, 7; Jackson, "Henry Wallace," 32; Ross, *The Loneliest Campaign*, 157. For the argument that an anticommunist press undermined the Progressive Party campaign, see Belfrage, *The American Inquisition*.

22. Rexford Tugwell to Dear Citizen, July 16, 1948, Reel 56, Series 2, Number 346, ADA-M; *The Citizen*, June-July, 1948, 1; MacDougall, *Gideon's Army*, 2:547.

23. *Philadelphia Inquirer*, July 20, 1948, 4, 17B; *New York Post*, July 21, 1948, 33; *Chicago Sun-Times*, July 23, 1948, 3; *Christian Science Monitor*, July 22, 1948, 3; *New York World-Telegram*, July 22, 1948, 6; *New York Times*, July 22, 1948, 2; *CIO News*, August 2, 1948, 2.

24. *Washington Star*, July 22, 1948, 1; *CIO News*, August 2, 1948, 2; Lerner in the *New York Star*, July 25, 1948, 17.

25. Cooke, *Six Men*, 104; *Washington Star*, July 22, 1948, 4.

26. *New York Post*, July 22, 1948, 4; *Philadelphia Inquirer*, July 23, 1948, 4; *Washington Post*, July 22, 1948, 6; Starobin, *American Communism in Crisis*, 296; Ryan, *Earl Browder*, 265.

27. MacDougall, *Gideon's Army*, 2:535; Abt with Myerson, *Advocate and Activist*, 148; James Wechsler to Charles Van Devander, May 7, 1948, Reel 121, Series 7, Number 73, ADA-M. In October, 1948, Pressman told a *New York Post* reporter, "I have not been and am not now a member of the Communist party." *New York Post*, October 18, 1948, 26. A year later, however, he testified before the House Committee on Un-American Activities that he had been a party member during 1934 and 1935. Pressman told the committee that he gave up his membership in 1935 but that his final and complete ideological break with communism had come "only recently." HUAC, *Hearings Regarding Communism in the United States Government—Part 2*, 2861–66.

28. Blum, *The Price of Vision*, 115.

29. John J. Abt to Marjorie Lansing, June 8, 1948; Abt to All State Directors, June 22, 1948, both in Box 44, Folder 166, PPP; Minutes of the Meeting of the Administrative Committee of the National Wallace for President Committee, June 12–13, 1948, Box 7, CBP; Outline for Proposed New Party Platform, Box 9, Folder 35; Lee Pressman to Paul Sweezy, July 14, 1948, Box 4, Folder 166, PPP; Brown, "The 1948 Progressive Campaign," 147–49.

30. Brown, "The 1948 Progressive Campaign," 140–41, 147. For background on Ramsey and Petran, see Shannon, *The Decline of American Communism*, 159–61; and Klehr, *The Heyday of American Communism* 77, 427.

31. "Draft of New Party Platform: Peace, Freedom, and Security" [The New York Draft], Box 44, Folder 166A, PPP. Compare to "Draft Platform of the CPUSA," *Worker*, May 30, 1948; Howe and Coser, *The American Communist Party*, 454–57.

32. Richard T. Watt, "Platform Draft"; Richard T. Watt to Paul Sweezy, July 7, 1948, both in Box 44, Folder 166A, PPP.

33. Paul M. Sweezy, "Platform Draft," Box 44, Folder 166A, PPP.

34. "Preamble—draft proposed by Buchanan;" Scott Buchanan to Rexford Tugwell, May 18, 1948, both in Box 44, Folder 166A, PPP.

35. Lee Pressman to Frederick L. Schuman, July 8, 1948, Box 4, Folder 21, PPP; Minutes of the National Wallace for President Committee, July 12, 1948, Box 7, CBP; Rexford G. Tugwell, Journal Entry, July 18, 1948, Box 35, RTP; Brown, "The 1948 Progressive Campaign," 152. Brown observed the advisory group meetings and all but one of the executive sessions of the platform committee. His dissertation provides a detailed account of the proceedings, all of which were closed to the public.

36. Brown, "The 1948 Progressive Campaign," 149–50; Tugwell, Journal Entry, July 18, 1948; Scott Buchanan to Curtis MacDougall, July 22, 1953, Box 44, Folder 166, PPP; Dennis, *The Third Party and the 1948 Elections*.

37. Brown, "The 1948 Progressive Campaign," 149.

38. Ibid., 120–22, 150–52; Daniel Bell, "Murray, Pressman and the Communists: A Conversation with Jim Carey Dated October 27, 1955," Box 4, Daniel Bell Collection, Tamiment Library, New York University, New York. On "monopoly's drive toward war," see, for example, Dennis, *The Third Party and the 1948 Elections*, 38; William Z. Foster, "The Struggle for Peace," *Political Affairs* 27 (September 1948): 775. The phrase also turned up frequently in the Progressive Party campaign literature produced at national headquarters, where Communists were a significant presence on the office staff.

39. Brown, "The 1948 Progressive Campaign," 146, 86; Tugwell, "Open Reply to Mr. Borgese," 81; MacDougall, *Gideon's Army*, 2:540–43; Brown, "The 1948 Progressive Campaign," 151; "Summary by Lee Pressman of Background of Draft Platform," July 20, 1948, Box 44, Folder 166, PPP.

40. Brown, "The 1948 Progressive Campaign," 153.

41. Ibid., 153–54. Tugwell assessed the Truman administration's foreign policy and summarized his own views in *A Chronicle of Jeopardy*.

42. Brown, "The 1948 Progressive Campaign," 154–55. On Communist tactics, see Seymour Freidin, "Totalitarian Echoes at Philadelphia," *New York Herald Tribune*, July 29, 1948, 20. See also Young, *Totalitarian Language*, 136–41, for an insightful analysis of Communists' use of the "two camps" thesis in their political discourse.

43. Brown, "The 1948 Progressive Campaign," 154–55.

44. Ibid., 154–56; MacDougall, *Gideon's Army*, 2:541–42.

45. Tugwell, "Open Reply to Mr. Borgese," 81; Brown, "The 1948 Progressive Campaign," 184, 158. See also Tugwell, "Journal Entry, July 26, 1948."

46. Brown, "The 1948 Progressive Campaign," 157–58. The emphasis is Brown's, and, presumably, Tugwell's. See also, Tugwell, "Open Reply to Mr. Borgese," 82–83.

47. Brown, "The 1948 Progressive Campaign," 153–56.

48. Ibid., 156–59; *New York Post*, July 22, 1948, 4. Popper, a concealed CP member, achieved notoriety as an attorney for the Hollywood Ten and later became the target of a congressional investigation. See HUAC, *Report 1135, Proceedings against Martin Popper*. During the course of the HUAC hearings, several witnesses testified that Popper belonged to a cell of Communist lawyers based in New York City. Popper took the Fifth Amendment when questioned about his association with the Communist Party and was convicted in 1961 on charges of contempt of Congress. *New York Times*, January 29, 1989, 36. See also Bosworth, *Anything Your Little Heart Desires*, 227, 374–78.

49. Brown, "The 1948 Progressive Campaign," 162–64. On Krzycki, see Binkowski, *Leo Krzycki and the Detroit Left*.

50. Brown, "The 1948 Progressive Campaign," 103, 128–31, 138–39; Norman Thomas in the *San Francisco Chronicle*, July 23, 1948, 2. Of the seventy-four members listed, Brown reports, only fifty-five attended the platform committee meetings.

51. For Tugwell's mood during the advisory group and platform committee meetings, see Tugwell, "Journal Entry, July 18, 1948"; MacDougall, *Gideon's Army*, 2:542–45; Ross, *The Loneliest Campaign*, 160; and Brown, "The 1948 Progressive Campaign," 158–59, 185–87. See also Tugwell, "Progressives and the Presidency," *Progressive*, April 1949, 5–7.

52. The CPUSA chairman William Z. Foster had recently journeyed to San Juan to whip up enthusiasm for the cause. In April, *Political Affairs*, the party's theoretical journal, featured an article by Foster's Puerto Rican counterpart calling for swift and total American withdrawal. See Cesar Andreu, "Fifty Years under American Imperialism," *Political Affairs* 27 (April 1948): 327–36. The demand for independence also appeared in the 1948 Communist Party platform. George Charney, a CP functionary in New York City who accompanied Foster on his trip to Puerto Rico, confirms in his memoirs that party propaganda intentionally presented a distorted view of the Puerto Rican situation. Charney, *A Long Journey*, 155–56.

53. Brown, "The 1948 Progressive Campaign," 180–86. See also Shannon, *The Decline of American Communism*, 168–69.

54. Brown, "The 1948 Progressive Campaign," 181–82.

55. Ibid., 182–86; *Labor Action*, August 2, 1948, 4.

56. Brown, "The 1948 Progressive Campaign," 184–85; *New York Star*, July 25, 1948, 17.

57. Tugwell, Journal Entry, July 26, 1948; Abels, *Out of the Jaws of Victory*, 116–17; David A. Shannon interview with Rexford Tugwell, April 17, 1956, Shannon Research Notes; Chicago *Daily News*, July 23, 1948, 1; Starobin, *American Communism in Crisis* 188–90; John Gates to Joseph Starobin, n.d. [1971], Box 10, Folder 2, Philip Jaffe Papers.

58. "Testimony of James Loeb, Jr., National Executive Secretary of Americans for Democratic Action," Reel 42, Series 2, Number 180, ADA-M. See also, *New York Post*, July 22, 1948, 5; *New York Times*, June 23, 1948, 1, 10; *Philadelphia Inquirer*, July 23, 1948, 1, 2; *Chicago Sun-Times*, July 23, 1948, 5, and July 24, 1948, 16.

59. *Daily Worker*, July 23, 1948, 3; James I. Loeb, "Notes, Comments, and Recollections on ADA," 19, Box 3, Folder 5, James I. Loeb Papers, Harry S Truman Presidential Library. For the complete text of Tugwell's statement, see "Press Release," New Party Founding Convention, Box 26, PPP.

60. *Philadelphia Inquirer*, July 23, 1948, 2; *ADA World*, August 7, 1948, 1, 3; *Washington Post*, July 23, 1948, 15; James Loeb, Jr. to Mrs. J. G. Schutte, July 27, 1948, and Loeb to Robert H. Ellis, August 4, 1948, both on Reel 17, Series 2, Number 1, ADA-M. Reports that Russian occupation troops in Germany were detaining and torturing German anticommunist leaders at the Buchenwald camp appeared in major American papers the week before the Progressive Party convention opened. See, for example, *Denver Post*, July 17, 1948, 4.

61. Loeb to Dr. John L. Childs, August 3, 1948, Reel 56, Series 1, Number 346, ADA-M.

62. *New York Times*, July 23, 1948, 10; *Newsweek*, August 2, 1948, 18; *Philadelphia Inquirer*, July 25, 1948, 5-B. Storey, "Free Rides on the Wallace Merry-Go-Round," 1.

63. For criticisms of Tugwell and references to Pressman's "running the show," see Cyrus Barnum to Curtis MacDougall, November 28, 1953, Box 37, Folder 62, PPP; and Genevieve Steefel to Elinor Gimbel, August 13, 1948, Box 1, Folder 3, Minnesota Progressive Party Papers, Library of Congress, Washington, D.C.

64. Loeb to Harry Girvetz, August 4, 1948, Reel 17, Series 2, Number 1, ADA-M.

65. Brown, "The 1948 Progressive Campaign," 164. For Taylor's address, see *PM*, February 24, 1948, 3–4. On the omission of the references to communism, see Schapsmeier and Schapsmeier, *Prophet in Politics*, 184. As far as the Communists were concerned, Taylor's remarks constituted "red-baiting" even in February. See *Daily Worker*, February 25, 1948, 10.

66. Brown, "The 1948 Progressive Campaign," 165–66. Ironically, Taylor repeated his statement on communism during his pre-convention press conference, apparently unaware that it now constituted "red-baiting." *New York Times*, July 23, 1948, 10.

67. Brown, "The 1948 Progressive Campaign," 166–68.

68. Ibid., 168–69; Frederick L. Schuman, "Notes on July 22–26, 1948," Box 4, Folder 21, PPP.

69. Brown, "The 1948 Progressive Campaign," 169–70; *Denver Post*, August 1, 1948, 1, 2.

70. Several authors sympathetic to Popular Front liberalism have also accepted un-critically—and, in some cases, echoed—the Communists' spurious cry of "red-baiter" to discredit those who rejected a political alliance with the CP or objected to its tactics. MacDougall's, *Gideon's Army* is particularly susceptible to this criticism. As a result, the author presents a distorted analysis of the Communists' influence within the Progressive Party and mischaracterizes the motives of the Progressives' liberal anticommunist critics.

71. *New York Times*, July 22, 1948, 1; *Washington Post*, July 22, 1948, 6; *Los Angeles Times*, July 22, 1948, 4; *Washington Post*, July 26, 1948, 7; Goldman, *Rendezvous with Destiny*, 421. For a contemporary analysis of progressives' tendency to minimize threats to individual liberty that came from the left, see Trilling, "The Repressive Impulse," 717–21. See also Ralph Matthews's column in the *Baltimore Afro-American*, July 31, 1948, 4, which takes issue with Edgar Brown's remarks and places them in the larger context of progressive intolerance.

72. William Z. Foster, "The Political Significance of Keynesism," *Political Affairs* 27 (January 1948): 43; Max Weiss, "Wallace's 'Toward World Peace,'" *Political Affairs* 27 (May 1948): 400–11. In the first seven months of 1948, all but one issue of *Political Affairs* contained at least one anti-Keynesian article.

73. Shannon, *The Decline of American Communism*, 153; *Labor Action*, July 26, 1948, 1, 4; Brown, "The 1948 Progressive Campaign," 178–79.

74. On Schuman, see O'Neill, *A Better World*, 27–30, 126–31. For Schuman on Byrnes, see Frederick L. Schuman, "The Devil and Jimmy Byrnes," *Soviet Russia Today*, December 1947, 7. For Schuman on Truman, see Schuman to Max Lerner, January 1, 1948, and January 18, 1948, both in Box 7, Folder 362, Max Lerner Papers, Yale University, New Haven, Conn.

75. Rexford Tugwell to Antonio Borgese, August 20, 1948, Box 35, RTP; Frederick L. Schuman to Tabitha Petran, May 17, 1948, Box 4, Folder 21, PPP. For similar sentiments, see Schuman to Lee Pressman, July 10, 1948, Box 4, Folder 21, PPP.

76. Schuman, "Proposed Preamble to platform section on PEACE," Box 4, Folder 21, PPP; Brown "The 1948 Progressive Campaign," 188–89.

77. Schuman, "Notes and Comments on Philadelphia, July 23–25, 1948: The Founding Convention of the Progressive Party"; Schuman, "Notes on July 22–26, 1948"; Schuman, "Proposed Preamble to platform section on PEACE," all in Box 4, Folder 21, PPP. See also MacDougall, *Gideon's Army*, 2:564–66; Henry A. Wallace, COHP, 5125–26; Henry A. Wallace, "Henry Wallace Tells of His Political Odyssey," 180–88; *New York Times*, July 26, 1948, 16; Storey, "Free Rides on the Wallace Merry-Go-Round," 14.

78. Schuman, "Notes on July 22–26, 1948;" MacDougall, *Gideon's Army*, 2:568.

79. *New York Times*, July 28, 1948, 2. For the charge that Communists "dictated" the Progressive Party platform, see especially Sumner Welles's column in the *New York Herald Tribune*, August 3, 1948, 19. William Henry Chamberlin, "The Wallace Communist Front," *New Leader*, October 2, 1948, 16.

80. See, for example, Lader, *Power on the Left*, 48–51; and Walton, *Henry Wallace, Harry Truman, and the Cold War*, 225–27. Most secondary accounts that discuss the 1948 Progressive Party platform draw almost exclusively from MacDougall's *Gideon's Army*, which denies that the Communists exercised any undue influence on the committee. Letters to MacDougall from committee members included in the Progressive Party Papers, however, paint quite a different picture, calling into question his interpretation.

81. Brown, "The 1948 Progressive Campaign," 207; "Third Parties," *Time*, August 2, 1948, 13.

CHAPTER 6

1. "A Note on the Delegates," Box 24, CBP; Helen Fuller, "For a Better World Right Now," *New Republic*, August 2, 1948, 12; *Boston Globe*, July 25, 1948, 18; Howard K. Smith, "The Wallace Party," *Nation*, August 7, 1948, 145; *New York Times*, July 23, 1948, 10; *Baltimore Afro-American*, July 31, 1948, 1B; August 7, 1948, 4; *Philadelphia Inquirer*, July 25, 1948, 3; *Berkshire Eagle*, July 29, 1948, 1, Clippings in Box 20, PPP. See also Frank, "1948," 36–37, 62–65.

2. For impressions of the delegates, see *Philadelphia Inquirer*, July 25, 1948, 3; *San Francisco Chronicle*, July 23, 1948, 2; *Chicago Sun-Times*, July 24, 1948, 2; *New York Post*, July 26, 1948, 28. Hester quoted in *Philadelphia Daily News*, July 24, 1948, 6.

3. *Christian Science Monitor*, July 23, 1948, 3; *Washington Post*, July 26, 1948, 9; Frederick L. Schuman, "Notes and Comments on Philadelphia," Box 4, Folder 21, PPP.

4. *New York Herald Tribune*, July 26, 1948, 14; "Touchstone," *Newsweek*, August 9, 1948, 42; *Washington Post*, July 26, 1948, 9; *Chicago Sun-Times*, July 28, 1948, 42; *Philadelphia Inquirer*, July 25, 1948, 3.

5. *Labor Action*, August 2, 1948, 4; *New York Post*, July 26, 1948, 4.

6. *Washington Star*, July 24, 1948, 2; *Chicago Sun-Times*, July 25, 1948, 5.

7. *New York Times*, July 24, 1948, 1, 6; *Manchester Guardian*, July 26, 1948, 6. Ironically, later in the summer, in the midst of a civil rights dispute in Iowa, members of the Communist-led Civil Rights Congress tagged Howard himself a "red-baiter" when he took a position unacceptable to them. See Horne, *Communist Front?*, 61.

8. "Text of Address by C. B. Baldwin, Campaign Manager for Henry Wallace at Opening Session of New Party Founding Convention, Friday night, July 23, 1948," Box 8, Folder 17, Sam Sweet Papers, Wayne State University, Walter Reuther Library of Labor and Urban Affairs, Detroit; *San Francisco Chronicle*, July 24, 1948, 3.

9. "Minutes of the Administrative Committee of the National Wallace for President Committee," June 12–13, 1948 and July 12, 1948, Box 7, CBP; MacDougall, *Gideon's Army*, 2:519–20. Brown, "The 1948 Progressive Campaign," 220–23, provides a revealing account of how the use of single lists of nominees aided the Communists and pro-Communists in securing their influence on the national committee. For example, he details how the left-wing leadership of the New York and Illinois delegations, while never technically violating democratic procedure, skillfully produced a list of politically "reliable" nominees without raising the suspicions of their non-Communist colleagues.

10. "Minutes of the First Meeting of the National Committee of the Progressive Party, July 25, 1948," J. B. Matthews Papers, Box 462, Folder 5, Duke University, Durham, N.C.; Brown, "The 1948 Progressive Campaign," 211–18. Markowitz, *The Rise and Fall of the People's Century*, 285–86. The Progressive Party and PCA constitutions were remarkably similar, both in structure and verbiage, to the 1945 constitution of the CPUSA. For a side-by-side comparison of these similarities, see Brown, "The 1948 Progressive Campaign," 214.

11. MacDougall, *Gideon's Army*, 2:521. For contemporary analyses of the pro-Soviet unionists' tactics and strategy regarding the Progressive Party, see *Labor Action*, August 30, 1948, 1; Peter Edson's column, "Core of Third Party Strength Are Left-wing Labor Leaders," August 3, 1948, clipping in Box 32A, Folder 7, PPP; and Victor Riesel, "Inside Labor," *New York Post*, August 3, 1948, 34 and August 9, 1948, 32. See also Dwight Spencer to Curtis MacDougall, October 5, 1953, Box 37, Folder 55, PPP; and Russ Nixon to C. B. Baldwin, June 25, 1948, Box 24, CBP.

12. Since the rules committee meetings were closed, reporters had no way of knowing the internal dynamics of this intraparty discord. As a result, most contemporary press accounts assumed that Marcantonio, who chaired the committee and presented its proposals to the convention, was behind the attempt to "pack" the national committee with pro-Communists from the functional divisions. See, for example, *New York Times*, July 25, 1948, 1, 37. For more accurate "inside" coverage of the dispute, see Fuller, "For a Better World Right Now," 12–13; and *Labor Action*, August 2, 1948, 1, 4. Brown, "The 1948 Progressive Campaign," 242–43, and Abt with Myerson, *Advocate and Activist*, 148–49, corroborate these sources. For the full text of Article 3, see "Rules of the Progressive Party," Box 25, CBP.

13. *New York Times*, July 25, 1948, 37; *Washington Star*, July 24, 1948, 2; *Labor Action*, August 2, 1948, 4; "Proceedings, National Founding Convention of the Progressive Party, Convention Hall and Shibe Park, Philadelphia, PA, July 23, 24, and 25, 1948," 118–23, Box 25, CBP, hereafter cited as "Proceedings"; Pedersen, *The Communist Party in Maryland*, 158, 161.

14. "Proceedings," 127–28.

15. Ibid., 123, 128–32.

16. Ibid., 132–36; *Labor Action*, August 2, 1948, 4; *Chicago Sun-Times*, August 6, 1948, 31; Brown, "The 1948 Progressive Campaign," 227; *Washington Post*, July 25, 1948, 1, 5; *Christian Science Monitor*, July 26, 1948, 1.

17. Brown, "The 1948 Progressive Campaign," 229–34. At the other extreme was North Dakota, whose sole representative cast all of the state's sixteen votes.

18. Brown, "The 1948 Progressive Campaign," 226–27. For suspicions, see "Some Questions on Philadelphia Convention," Box 1, Folder 3, Minnesota Progressive Party Papers, Library of Congress, Washington. For the text of the rule on roll calls, see "Official Program of the National Founding Convention of the New Party, Philadelphia, July 23–25, 1948," Box 7A, PPP.

19. Wechsler, "The Philadelphia Pay-Off," 9. On the delegates' lack of political sophistication, see Richard Strout in the *Christian Science Monitor*, July 26, 1948, 1; Norman Thomas in the *San Francisco Chronicle*, July 25, 1948, 2; H. L. Mencken in the

Baltimore Sun, July 25, 1948, and Alistair Cooke in the *Manchester Guardian*, July 26, 1948, 5. For Buchanan's comments, see *Labor Action*, August 2, 1948, 4.

20. *New York Times*, July 25, 1948, 36; *Chicago Daily News*, July 24, 1948, 3; Goulden, *Mencken's Last Campaign*, 81–82; *San Francisco Chronicle*, July 25, 1948, 2.

21. Most notable among those who questioned the sincerity of the cheers for Wallace were the columnists Joseph and Stewart Alsop. See *Philadelphia Bulletin*, July 24, 1948, 9. For less skeptical accounts, see *Washington Star*, July 24, 1948, 1, 2; *York [Pa.] Gazette and Daily*, July 27, 1948, 2, 6.

22. *Washington Star*, July 28, 1948, 13; "On Hybrid Americanism," *New Leader*, July 31, 1948, 1; *Manchester Guardian*, July 26, 1948, 5; the British journalist quoted in the *Chicago Defender*, July 31, 1948, 2. Rebecca West and Anne O'Hare McCormick also found the striking similarities to Nazi rallies unnerving. See *New York Herald Tribune*, July 26, 1948, 2; and *New York Times*, July 26, 1948, 16.

23. *Philadelphia Bulletin*, July 25, 1948, 1; *Philadelphia Inquirer*, July 25, 1948, 2; *Daily Worker*, July 23, 1948, 5; Goulden, *Mencken's Last Campaign*, 83.

24. "Text of Address by Vito Marcantonio, Saturday, July 24, 1948, Shibe Park, Philadelphia, Pa.," Box 26, PPP; MacDougall, *Gideon's Army*, 2:530.

25. "Text of Address by Paul Robeson, Saturday, July 24, 1948, Shibe Park, Philadelphia, Pa.," Box 26, PPP. *Philadelphia Bulletin*, July 25, 1948, 1; *Washington Post*, July 25, 1948, 3.

26. Ross, *The Loneliest Campaign*, 159, similarly questions the wisdom of placing Robeson and Marcantonio in the limelight. See also Doris Fleeson's column in the *Washington Star*, July 26, 1948, 13. For the delegates' concerns, see Barnum to MacDougall, November 28, 1953, Box 37, Folder 62, PPP; Curtis MacDougall, "Interview with Ralph Shikes," Box 49, Book 11, PPP. See also "Memorandum from Ralph E. Shikes on Publicity on Convention Delegations," June 25, 1948, Box 12, Folder 49, PPP; Marjorie Lansing to Curtis MacDougall, November 17, 1952, Box 56, Folder 236, PPP.

27. *Washington Star*, July 28, 1948, 13.

28. "Acceptance Speech by Senator Glen H. Taylor, Saturday, July 24, 1948, Shibe Park, Philadelphia, Pa.," Box 26, PPP.

29. On isolationist sentiment among the delegates, see *Philadelphia Bulletin*, July 22, 1948, 2; *Christian Science Monitor*, July 23, 1948, 3; *Philadelphia Inquirer*, July 23, 1948, 2; Goldman, *Rendezvous with Destiny*, 419–20.

30. Childs, "Year of Doubt," 8; *San Francisco Chronicle*, July 26, 1948, 2; "The Shape of Things," *Nation*, July 31, 1948), 113; Gallup, *The Gallup Poll*, 1:722.

31. *San Francisco Chronicle*, July 25, 1948, 1; *New York Times*, July 25, 1948, 1, 34.

32. Text of Wallace speech, as delivered, *New York Times*, July 25, 1948, 28.

33. *New York World-Telegram*, July 27, 1948, 17; *Philadelphia Bulletin*, July 30, 1948, 24; Roper cited in White, *Still Seeing Red*, 298.

34. *New York Times*, July 25, 1948, 34, notes the discrepancy between Wallace's prepared text and the version he delivered. See *Washington Post*, July 26, 1948, 8, for skepticism about Wallace's claims regarding Cold War casualties.

35. Lew Frank to Curtis MacDougall, May 15, 1954, Box 58, Folder 260, PPP; *Philadelphia Inquirer*, July 27, 1948, 17; *New York Times*, July 25, 1948, 34.

36. See, for example, *Washington Post*, July 25, 1948, 8; *Philadelphia Inquirer*, July 25, 1948, 8B; *Chicago Daily News*, July 27, 1948, 10.

37. U.S. Congress, House, Committee on Un-American Activities [hereafter HUAC], *Hearings Regarding Communist Methods of Infiltration (Entertainment—Part 1)*, 3869–70. Sloane also testified that he had written Charles Howard's keynote address.

38. *Philadelphia Bulletin*, July 28, 1948, 11. The market tended to confirm Page's views—stock prices had plummeted on July 15 when informed sources declared that the likelihood of war had gone from one in ten to one in four because of heightened tensions in Berlin. Divine, *Foreign Policy and United States Presidential Elections*, 222.

39. TRB, "Washington Wire," *New Republic*, August 9, 1948, 3; Melvyn Leffler, *A Preponderance of Power*, 220–21; Divine, *Foreign Policy and United States Presidential Elections*, 215; Wechsler, *The Age of Suspicion*, 233. For a well-documented refutation of Wallace's and Taylor's claim that Forrestal served the interests of Dillon, Read and the "oil lobby," see Hoopes and Brinkley, *Driven Patriot*, 398–99.

40. *New York Post*, August 4, 1948, 25; Cleater, *Letters from Baltimore*, 232.

41. *Detroit News*, July 26, 1948, 6; *Denver Post*, July 26, 1948, 7; Shannon, *Decline of American Communism*, 175; text of Tugwell's speech, Box 7A, Folder 30, PPP; *Chicago Sun-Times*, July 26, 1948, 5; Rexford G. Tugwell, "Journal Entry, July 26, 1948," Box 35, RTP.

42. *Labor Action*, August 2, 1948, 2; James Hayford to Curtis MacDougall, August 12, 1952, Box 32, Folder 5, PPP.

43. "Proceedings," 293.

44. *New York Times*, July 26, 1948, 16; *New York Star*, July 26, 1948, 4; Manchester, *Disturber of the Peace*, 309; Fecher, *The Diary of H. L. Mencken*, 455; *Washington Star*, July 26, 1948, 9.

45. This summary of the Vermont Resolution debate relies on the "Proceedings" of the Progressive Party convention, p318–31, Box 24, CBP. Some press accounts offer slightly different wording without altering the substance of the speakers' remarks. The full text of the debate can also be found in MacDougall, *Gideon's Army*, 2:572–76. For the crowd's response, see *New York Herald Tribune*, July 26, 1948, 1.

46. Gates to Starobin, n.d., Box 10, Folder 2, Philip Jaffe Collection. De Lacy is perhaps best known as the only delegate who did not vote for the Roosevelt-Wallace ticket at the 1940 Democratic Convention—a period when the CP line of the moment was anti-Roosevelt. On De Lacy, see Washington State Legislature, Joint Legislative Fact-Finding Committee on Un-American Activities, *Un-American Activities in Washington State, Report One*, 68; HUAC, *Hearings Regarding Communist Activities in the Pacific Northwest Area*, 5977; HUAC, *Hearings Regarding Communist Activities in the Dayton, Ohio Area*, 627–31.

47. On Genevieve Steefel, see Haynes, *Dubious Alliance*, 201–2. For the inconsistency on making insinuations against "wartime allies," see *New Leader*, July 31, 1948, 14.

48. *Philadelphia Inquirer*, July 27, 1948, 17; Ross, *The Loneliest Campaign*, 161; Akers's column appeared in the *Chicago Sun-Times*, July 28, 1948, 42; Schapsmeier and Schapsmeier, *Prophet in Politics*, 183; I. B. Smith to the Editor, *New York Post*, August 5, 1948, 20. For the reaction of the radio audience, see Schapsmeier and Schapsmeier, *Prophet in Politics*, 182–83; and Shannon, *Decline of American Communism*, 173.

These authors draw on their own memories of the radio coverage, as well as on the reactions of others. For similar sentiments, see also Henry Ransom to the Editor, *New York Star*, August 4, 1948, 13; Michael A. Turner to the Editor, *New York Star*, July 29, 1948, 13; and Samuel and Freda Sass to the Editor, *New Republic*, August 23, 1948, 29–30. All were Wallace supporters who abandoned the party after listening to the debate about foreign policy on the radio.

49. Wechsler, *The Age of Suspicion*, 232.

50. Fuller, "For A Better World Right Now," 11; Brown, "The 1948 Progressive Campaign," 194–95; Unknown to Unknown, August 3, 1948, Box 35, Folder 42, PPP. The greeting and signature have been cut from this letter. Schmidt, *Henry A. Wallace*, 195, quotes Ralph Shikes as saying that the Communists and fellow travelers did not oppose the Vermont Resolution because they believed it was harmless. Beanie Baldwin, too, later claimed that he would have supported the amendment had he been on the convention floor. In his memoirs, however, John Abt contradicts this view. "The Communist party opposed it," he wrote. "I was as sectarian and arrogant as the rest of the Party comrades . . . and also opposed the Vermont resolution." Abt with Myerson, *Advocate and Activist*, 149. George Charney corroborates Abt's account, citing the opposition the CP mustered to defeat the Vermont Resolution as an example of "our own pressures within the PP for an unequivocal stand in support of Soviet policy." Charney, *A Long Journey*, 179.

51. Hamilton, "A Pennsylvania Newspaper Publisher in 'Gideon's Army,'" 33; Brown, "The 1948 Progressive Campaign," 195; Hayford to MacDougall, August 12, 1952, PPP.

52. For a trenchant analysis of this brand of late 1940s progressivism, see O'Neill, *A Better World*, 142–60.

53. *Labor Action*, August 2, 1948, 4; "Proceedings," 343–44; *Detroit News*, July 26, 1948, 6; Wechsler, "The Philadelphia Pay-Off," 9–10.

54. "Proceedings," 355–58; Howe and Coser, *The American Communist Party*, 475–76; Wechsler, "The Philadelphia Payoff," 10; *Detroit News*, July 26, 1948, 6. Years later, John Roche added an interesting twist to this episode, claiming that he and a group of colleagues, all bitterly opposed to the Progressives, were actually behind the so-called Macedonian Resolution. They persuaded an unsuspecting delegate to appear before the open hearings of the platform committee and demand a resolution supporting "self-determination for the Macedonian people." With Rex Tugwell "dozing in the chair" and Lee Pressman, "the Stalinist sentinel," off to lunch, the resolution passed, to the delight of Roche and his friends, who knew full well that it was a "Titoist heresy." "What would Comrade Pressman do when he spotted it?," they asked each other mischievously. (According to Louis Adamic, Pressman spotted and deleted the apostasy at 3 A.M. Friday when he took over the platform committee after Tugwell had gone to bed.) Roche, "Sub Specie Aeternitatis," 1620–21.

55. Wechsler, *The Age of Suspicion*, 232. The outcome of this minor incident not only revealed the Progressives' obeisance to the Communists but also Moscow's hold on the CPUSA. Within the Communist world, the American party had long been known as being particularly sensitive to Moscow's cracking of the ideological whip, as the CPers' reaction to the Macedonian Resolution would indicate.

56. *Philadelphia Inquirer*, July 26, 1948, 2; MacDougall, *Gideon's Army*, 2:585–86; Shields, *Mr. Progressive*, 312.

CHAPTER 7

1. Frederick L. Schuman to C. B. Baldwin, July 28, 1948, Box 4, Folder 21, PPP; *Washington Star*, July 26, 1948, 3; *Washington Post*, July 26, 1948, 7; *Hickory [N.C.] Daily Record*, July 27, 1948, clipping in Box 33, Folder 9, PPP.

2. Fast, "Philadelphia Story," 1. See also L. Haize [Lee Hays], "Singing for Victory," *Worker Magazine*, August 15, 1948, 1, 10. For delegates' positive reactions to the convention, see Marian Mix to John M. Coe, July 29, 1948, Box 1, Folder 49, John M. Coe Papers, Emory University, Atlanta; Theodora and Elwyn to Naomi Benson, July 24, 1948, Box 31, Folder 22-4, Naomi Benson Papers, University of Washington, Seattle; Alan Lomax to Earl Robinson, August 3, 1948; Robinson to Lomax, September 9, 1948, both in Box 9, Folder 15, Earl Robinson Papers, University of Washington, Seattle.

3. *Washington Star*, July 28, 1948, 13.

4. For the disciplined responses of the delegates, see *Boston Herald*, July 25, 1948, clipping in Box 33, Folder 25, PPP.

5. *Denver Post*, July 27, 1948, 10; Lyons, *Philadelphia Communists*, 150.

6. Interview with Jerry Silverman of People's Songs, January 25, 1983, quoted in Lieberman, *"My Song Is My Weapon,"* 134; *Denver Post*, July 24, 1948, 10.

7. "The Report of C. B. Baldwin to the National Committee, September 10, 1948," Box 12, CBP; Fast, "Philadelphia Story," 1; *Daily Worker*, July 27, 1948, 8; "Address by Henry A. Wallace, State Directors Meeting, Philadelphia, PA, July 26, 1948," Box 24, CBP.

8. Wechsler, "The Philadelphia Pay-Off," 8–9; *Washington Star*, August 1, 1948, C-5.

9. *Philadelphia Inquirer*, July 27, 1948, 17; "The Shape of Things," *Nation*, July 31, 1948, 113.

10. Marjorie Lansing to Curtis MacDougall, November 17, 1952, Box 55, Folder 230, PPP. For a similar critique of Wallace's abdication of party leadership, see I. F. Stone, "What of the Communists in the Progressive Party?," in Stone, *The Truman Era*, 161–62.

11. *Amsterdam News*, August 7, 1948; Murray Klibanoff to the Editor, *New York Post*, August 22, 1948, 20; Henry Ransom to the Editor, *New York Star*, August 4, 1948, 13.

12. *Chicago Sun-Times*, July 30, 1948, 33; *Philadelphia Bulletin*, July 27, 1948, 17; James T. Farrell to Norman Thomas, July 28, 1948, Reel 17, 1708-12, Norman Thomas Papers, microfilm edition, Duke University, Durham, N.C.; *Labor Action*, August 30, 1948, 1.

13. John Williamson, "Only Militant, United Action Can Defeat the Drive against the Unions!," *Political Affairs* 27 (September 1948): 864; Shannon, *Decline of American Communism*, 176–77; Starobin *American Communism in Crisis*, 186. For a perceptive assessment of Foster's and other Communists' self-defeating utopianism throughout the late 1940s, see Charney, *A Long Journey*, 173–98. Gates, *The Story of an American Communist*, and Starobin, *American Communism in Crisis*, make similar observations and are sharply critical of Foster's leadership of the party during this period.

14. Starobin, *American Communism in Crisis*, 187–88.

15. Plotke, *Building a Democratic Political Order*, 328. Plotke notes that after 1945 the Communists explicitly abandoned the Popular Front, which they had never considered more than a technique allowing them to combine "tactical flexibility with doctrinal rigidity," even during the 1930s. See ibid., 320–28.

16. Starobin, *American Communism in Crisis*, 187.

17. *New York Post*, May 17, 1948, 6; *San Francisco Chronicle*, July 25, 1948, 3; *Washington Post*, September 1, 1948, 10.

18. Moremen, "The Independent Progressive Party in California," 121–22; *New Leader*, September 11, 1948, 14.

19. Moremen, "The Independent Progressive Party in California," 219–24; California Legislature, Senate, *Fifth Report on Un-American Activities in California, 1949*. On Tenney, see Scobie, "Jack B. Tenney and the 'Parasitic Menace'"; and Barrett, *The Tenney Committee*, 3–6, 35–46.

20. Moremen, "The Independent Progressive Party in California," 122–23; Fryer to Curtis MacDougall, March 1, 1953, Box 58, Folder 246, PPP; Call, "A Study in Group Support of the Independent Progressive Party of California," 85; Dunne, *Take Two*, 223.

21. *San Francisco Chronicle*, August 6, 1948, 10; August 8, 1948, 1, 9; August 9, 1948, 1; *Sacramento Bee*, August 9, 1948, 4; *Sacramento Union*, August 8, 1948, 11; Moremen, "The Independent Progressive Party in California," 129–31.

22. Moremen, "The Independent Progressive Party in Califrnia," 132.

23. "The Independent Progressive Party: A Summary of its Foundation and Activity in San Diego County," Box 266, Folder 8, J. B. Matthews Papers. For further reports on the Communist presence in the IPP, see the testimony of Ernistine Gatewood, HUAC, *Investigation of Communist Activities in the State of California—Part 10*, 4947, 4953; the testimony of Carol Bayme, HUAC, *Investigation of Communist Activities in the State of California—Part 9*, 4919; the testimony of Lynn Ackerstein, HUAC, *Investigation of Communist Activities in the State of California—Part 11*, 7022–37.

24. *Sacramento Bee*, August 9, 1948, 4; Moremen, "The Independent Progressive Party in California," 103, 133–34, 138–39; *San Francisco Chronicle*, August 15, 1948, 10; Starobin, *American Communism in Crisis*, 298.

25. *New York Times*, August 1, 1948, 42; Dwight Spencer to Curtis MacDougall, October 5, 1953, Box 37, Folder 55, PPP.

26. *Denver Post*, July 4, 1948, 1; July 6, 1948, 1; MacDougall, *Gideon's Army*, 3: 630–31, 773; Testimony of Charles David Blodgett, HUAC, *Investigation of Communist Activities in the San Francisco Area—Part 3*, 3305; William E. Leuchtenburg, "Wallace in the Rockies," *New Leader*, September 25, 1948, 5; *New York Times*, August 1, 1948, 42; *Denver Post*, August 4, 1948, 32.

27. William E. Leuchtenburg to Evelyn Dubrow, August 1, 1948, Reel 42, Series 2, Number 159, ADA-M. Lee Fryer to Curtis MacDougall, March 1, 1953, Box 58, Folder 246, PPP.

28. *Denver Post*, July 24, 1948, 1; August 1, 1948, 1, 2; Fryer to MacDougall, February 6, 1953, Box 58, Folder 246, PPP; Leuchtenburg, "Wallace in the Rockies," 5. For a similar account of factional strife in Washington State, see Naomi Benson, "Five Year Diary," July 6, September 8, 1948, Box 21, Naomi Benson Papers.

29. Alan MacNeil to Una Buxenbaum, September 10, 1948; Esther MacNeil to Helen MacMartin, September 28, 1948; Helen MacMartin to Curtis MacDougall, October 1, 1955, all in Box 58, Folder 255, PPP.

30. Chester Bowles to James Loeb, August 12, 1948, Reel 29, Series 2, Number 23, ADA-M.

31. Marjorie Lansing to Curtis MacDougall, November 17, 1952, Box 56, Folder 236, PPP; Frederick Schuman to Tabitha Petran, August 6, 1948, Box 4, Folder 21, PPP; *Baltimore Sun*, August 27, 1948, 2; Philbrick, *I Led Three Lives*.

32. Hughes, *Gentleman Rebel*, 195–209.

33. "Some Questions on the Philadelphia Convention," Box 2; Genevieve Steefel to Elinor Gimbel, August 13, 1948; and John Abt to Steefel, August 25, 1948, all in Box 1, Folder 3, Minnesota Progressive Party Papers, Library of Congress, Washington, D.C. See also Haynes, *Dubious Alliance*, 201–2.

34. Alfred G. Freeman et al. to Henry A. Wallace, August 6, 1948, Reel 45, Frames 259–60; and Henry A. Wallace to Alfred G. Freeman, August 17, 1948, Reel 45, Frames 332–33, HAW-M; Cyrus Barnum to Curtis MacDougall, November 28, 1948, Box 37, Folder 62, PPP; Henry A. Wallace to Alfred G. Freeman, August 14, 1948 [draft not sent], Reel 45, Frames 336–37, HAW-M.

35. Steefel to Gimbel, August 13, 1948, Box 1, Folder 3, Minnesota Progressive Party Papers.

36. Tugwell, "Progressives and the Presidency"; Shannon, *The Decline of American Communism*, 175; Rexford G. Tugwell to Rev. Sem. Ernest C. Fackler, April 29, 1964, Box 35, RTP; Dwight Macdonald, "The Wallace Campaign," 182.

37. *Baltimore Sun*, August 20, 1948, 1, 4; Rexford G. Tugwell, "Journal Entry, August 23, 1948," Box 35, RTP. In November, Tugwell voted for Truman. As a registered voter in Illinois, however, he did not have the opportunity to vote for Wallace, who was not on the ballot. "The Reminiscences of Rexford G. Tugwell," COHP, 15.

38. Rexford G. Tugwell, "Journal Entry, August 23, 1948," Box 35, RTP.

39. *Louisville Courier-Journal*, August 25, 1948, 1; *New York Herald Tribune*, August 25, 1948, 1, 8.

40. "How Do You Separate Them, Mr. Wallace?" *Nation*, September 4, 1948, 247.

41. *Washington Post*, August 30, 1948, 6. For a balanced discussion of Moscow's relationship with the Communist Parties of Europe during the late 1940s, see Spriano, *Stalin and the European Communists*.

42. Macdonald, "The Wallace Campaign," 183.

43. Norman Thomas to Rexford Tugwell, August 26, 1948, Reel 59, Socialist Party Papers, microfilm edition.

CHAPTER 8

1. Howe and Coser, *The American Communist Party*, 473; *Daily Californian*, May 10, 1948, 1; *Daily Tar Heel*, February 29, 1948, 1; *Daily People's World*, March 10, 1948, 2.

2. *New York Times*, July 23, 1948, 10.

3. "Wallace and Youth," *New Leader*, July 17, 1948, 3; Memorandum to Charles Van Devander from James Wechsler, May 7, 1948, Reel 121, Series 7, Number 73, ADA-M.

Wechsler had known Linfield since both men had been comrades in the Young Communist League at Columbia University. Linfield, according to Wechsler, had "always boasted openly that he was a party member."

4. MacDougall, *Gideon's Army*, 3:588; *Philadelphia Bulletin*, July 26, 1948, 2.

5. This account of the YPA convention is based on Steven Muller, "Draft Report on Wallace Youth Conclave," Reel 56, Series 2, Number 346, ADA-M; Philip H. Des Marais, "The 'Young Progressives' of America," *New Leader*, August 14, 1948, 5; *Washington Star*, July 26, 1948, 1, 3; and *Labor Action*, August 2, 1948, 4.

6. MacDougall, *Gideon's Army*, 3:591.

7. Muller, "Draft Report on the Wallace Youth Conclave"; *Labor Action*, August 2, 1948, 4.

8. MacDougall, *Gideon's Army*, 3:591–92.

9. *Washington Star*, July 26, 1948, 1; *Philadelphia Bulletin*, July 26, 1948, 2.

10. *Denver Post*, July 26, 1948, 7; *New York Herald Tribune*, July 26, 1948, 2.

11. *Philadelphia Bulletin*, July 26, 1948, 2.

12. Muller, "Draft Report on the Wallace Youth Conclave"; Des Marais, "The 'Young Progressives' of America," 5.

13. Schmidt, *Henry A. Wallace*, 119; Howe and Coser, *The American Communist Party*, 476; Jane Wilder, Executive Secretary, SDA to SDA National Board and SDA Chapters and Organizing Committees, "Founding Convention of Young Progressives of America," Reel 126, Series 8, Number 51, ADA-M. For the political background of the leading YPAers, see Des Marais, "The 'Young Progressives' of America"; and *Labor Action*, August 2, 1948, 4.

14. *New York World-Telegram*, July 29, 1948, 17; Eleanor Roosevelt to M. Mortimer, August 6, 1948, quoted in Berger, *A New Deal for the World*, 65; *New York World-Telegram*, August 23, 1948, 5; August 27, 1948, 15. For Mrs. Roosevelt's disillusioning experience with Communist duplicity in the American Youth Congress, see Cohen, *When the Old Left Was Young*, 301–4; 413–14.

15. C. B. Baldwin to State PP Directors, "Young Volunteers for Wallace," September 14, 1948; "Organizational Manual: Young Progressives for Wallace;" *The Young Progressive*, September 1948, both in Box 8, Folder 32, PPP; "Hey! You're Blocking Traffic! But Don't Step Aside," YPA recruiting pamphlet, Box 31, Naomi Benson Papers; Alice Nelson to Curtis MacDougall, January 19, 1953, Box 38, Folder 90, PPP; *Roosevelt Torch*, October 10, 1948, 1; Rivlin, *Fire on the Prairie*, 45–46. On the YPA's efforts to desegregate public tennis courts in Baltimore, see *New York Times*, July 12, 1948, 3. For YPA's bungled attempt at fighting discrimination at the University of Wisconsin's Campus Soda Grill, see *Madison [Wisc.] Capital-Times*, September 28, 1948, 1, 6.

16. For Thompson's column, *Denver Post*, August 4, 1948, 11; for YPA response, *The Young Progressive*, September 1948, 2.

17. *New York Star*, July 25, 1948, 8; Schmidt, *Henry A. Wallace*, 119. For the conservative political mood on campus, see Phillips, "Why They Join the Wallace Crusade," 26–28. In contrast, some scholars have argued that the late 1940s "promised to be a hospitable time for campus radicalism." See Isserman, *If I Had a Hammer*, 58.

18. *Pittsburgh Press*, March 2, 1948, 1, 2. For similar incidents, see MacDougall, *Gideon's Army*, 2:402–3.

19. Ellis, *The Dark Side of the Left*, 276. Though he does not discuss the Progressive Party per se, Ellis's perceptive study of the illiberal tendencies of what he calls "radical egalitarian" movements offers valuable insight into the forces that drove many young Wallace supporters. See especially, 271–79.

20. Vincent Sheean, "The Wallace Youth: A Communication," *New Republic*, November 1, 1948, 19; Morris H. Rubin, "State of the Nation," *Progressive*, March 1948, 30–31; Kempton, *Part of Our Time*, 159.

21. *Louisville [Ky.] Courier-Journal*, August 27, 1948, 7; Harvard Committee for Wallace, "Students for Wallace," January 30, 1948, Box 14, Folder 57, PPP.

22. *The Young Progressive*, September 1948; Phillips, "Why They Join the Wallace Crusade," 12. For a revealing discussion of Wallace's appeal to young liberals, see McGovern, *Grassroots*, 43–45. McGovern, who would himself run for the presidency in 1972, supported Wallace in 1948. He and his wife attended the Progressive Party convention as delegates from Illinois. In later years, McGovern recounted that the rejection of the Vermont Resolution had soured him on the third party and that he had voted for Truman.

23. *New York Herald Tribune*, August 25, 1948, 8; August 27, 1948, 11; *PM*, February 26, 1948, 3; March 4, 1948, 9; Students for Democratic Action, National Office, "Memo to All SDA Chapters and Organizing Committees re: the Fall of Czechoslovakia," March 1948; Jane Wilder to Robert Bendiner, September 1, 1948, both on Reel 126, Series 8, Number 51, ADA-M.

24. "The Quarter's Polls," *Public Opinion Quarterly* (Fall 1948): 555.

25. Sidney Lens, *Unrepentant Radical*, 157; Sidney Lens to "Bill," June 15, 1948, Box 22, Folder 4, Sidney Lens Papers, Chicago Historical Society, Chicago; Isserman, *If I Had a Hammer*, 148. By March 1949, YPA membership at the University of California, Berkeley, had fallen from six hundred to one hundred; at Brooklyn College it had declined from five hundred to one hundred. Most campuses saw similar drop-offs. See Falk, "American Student Movement: A Survey," 90.

26. *Philadelphia Inquirer*, July 24, 1948, 4. For a complete listing of the membership of the National Labor Committee for Wallace and Taylor, see Box 9, Folder 21, Len De Caux Papers, Wayne State University, Detroit. On Nixon's background, see Wechsler, *The Age of Suspicion*, 193–98.

27. "Agenda: National Labor Committee for Wallace and Taylor Meeting," July 23, 1948, Box 8, Folder 12, Sam Sweet Papers; *Philadelphia Bulletin*, July 23, 1948, 2; *Denver Post*, July 24, 1948, 8; *Worker*, July 25, 1948, 3, 14; *The Score*, August 9, 1948, 2–3; Russ Nixon, "Report on Organization: National Labor Committee for Wallace and Taylor," Box 9, Folder 21, Len De Caux Papers; "Statement of National Labor Committee for Wallace and Taylor, July 23, 1948," Box 8, Folder 17, Sam Sweet Papers. *The Score*, a four-page newsletter published bimonthly by the National Labor Committee of the Progressive Party, provides the most complete coverage of labor's activities on behalf of the Wallace campaign. For a full run of *The Score*, see Box 8, Folder 34, PPP.

28. Freeman, *In Transit*, 294–96; *TWU Bulletin*, August-September, 1948, 3, 12, 16; *CIO News*, August 2, 1948, 3; *New York Times*, September 9, 1948, 18; Michael J. Quill to Luigi Longo, April 16, 1948, Reel 2, Series 1, Number 75, Earl Browder Papers, microfilm edition, University of North Carolina, Chapel Hill, Chapel Hill, N.C.; Alex

Lichtenstein, "'Scientific Unionism' and the 'Negro Question,'" 74; Quill, *Mike Quill, Himself,* 195.

29. *New York Times,* September 2, 1948, 17; September 6, 1948, 1, 2; September 7, 1948, 1, 16; *The Score,* September 13, 1948, 1.

30. Filippelli and McColloch, *Cold War in the Working Class,* 233, 118; Schatz, *The Electrical Workers,* 211; Johnson, "Organized Labor's Postwar Red Scare," 33–34; Milton Edelman, "The Labor Vote in '48: An Analysis," *Nation,* October 23, 1948, 465; *New York Times,* September 11, 1948, 3.

31. Testimony of Leothar "Oakie" Wornstaff, HUAC, *Investigation of Communist Activities in the Dayton, Ohio Area—Part 1,* 6844–55.

32. Lubell, *The Future of American Politics,* 210–11. See also Jenkins, *Cold War at Home,* 26–27. Local 1102 in St. Louis proved an exception to the rule, however. Though many UE members had no use for Wallace or for the Progressive Party, they stood by their pro-Soviet leaders despite political differences. Johnson, "Organized Labor's Postwar Red Scare," 33–35.

33. Stein, "The Ins and Outs of the CIO," 62. Gallup surveyed CIO members on October 9, 1948. A poll taken shortly before the Progressive Party convention showed Wallace's support among all union members at 7 percent. Gallup, *The Gallup Poll,* 1:763, 751.

34. Horowitz, *"Negro and White, Unite and Fight!,"* 198–201; Halpern, *Down on the Killing Floor,* 231–34; Richter, *Labor's Struggles,* 114–18; Abraham B. Held, "The CIO Packers' Convention," *New Leader,* July 10, 1948, 3.

35. *CIO News,* August 2, 1948, 8; *New York Post,* July 26, 1948, 10; Preis, *Labor's Giant Step,* 359. For Curran and the NMU's defection from the pro-Soviet camp, see Levenstein, *Communism, Anticommunism, and the CIO,* 253–58. For evidence of some Wallace support among the NMU rank and file, see Lannon, *Second String Red,* 120–22; and De Caux, *Labor Radical,* 496–500.

36. "Cold War on the Waterfront," *New Republic,* September 20, 1948, 5–6; Cochran, *Labor and Communism,* 304; Starobin, *American Communism in Crisis,* 295; MacDougall, *Gideon's Army,* 2:320.

37. On the IUCs' overall failure to cultivate pro-Wallace sentiment among the CIO membership, see Levenstein, *Communism, Anticommunism, and the CIO,* 225–27; and Zieger, *The CIO,* 272–74.

38. *CIO News,* August 16, 1948, 2; MacDougall, *Gideon's Army,* 3:617; Haynes, *Dubious Alliance,* 188; *Madison [Wisc.] Capital-Times,* August 2, 1948, 1, 6; *San Francisco Chronicle,* August 4, 1948, 1.

39. *Labor Action,* April 5, 1948, 2; Adolph Germer Diary, April 27, 28, 29, 30, 1948, Box 25, Adolph Germer Papers, State Historical Society of Wisconsin, Madison; *Detroit News,* June 17, 1948, clipping in Box 19, Folder 29, Adolph Germer Papers; Cary, "Adolph Germer," 169–71.

40. Persky, "Walter Reuther, the UAW-CIO, and Third Party Politics," 197–202; Cary, "Adolph Germer," 171–73; Adolph Germer Diary, September 2, 3, 4, 1948, Box 25, Adolph Germer Papers; *Detroit News,* September 2, 1948, 53; September 4, 1948, 1; September 5, 1948, 1; September 6, 1948, 31; *Labor Action,* September 13, 1948, 1, 4. For a version of the Wayne County IUC dispute sympathetic to the pro-Soviet position,

see Philip M. Connelly, "A Report on the Detroit and New York CIO Councils," October 8, 1948, 1–4, Box 19, CIO Western Region (California), 1948–1952, Adolph Germer Papers. Connelly, a member of the Communist Party, was the secretary of the Los Angeles IUC. See also *Worker* (Michigan edition), August 8, 1948, 14.

41. Foster, *The Union Politic*, 84; Persky, "Walter Reuther," 199–200, 203–4; Lichtenstein, *The Most Dangerous Man in Detroit*, 310; *Detroit News*, February 29, 1948.

42. Kampelman, *The Communist Party vs. the CIO*, 112–19; Haynes, *Dubious Alliance*, 158–60, 181–82, 206–7.

43. Moremen, "The Independent Progressive Party in California," 84–97; William S. Lawrence to Elmer Benson, March 2, 1948, Box 7, CBP.

44. The notion that pro-Soviet unions were inherently more "democratic" than those led by anticommunists was, for a time, conventional wisdom among some labor historians, many of whom accepted Communist claims at face value. Sympathetic to Popular Front politics and contemptuous of anticommunism in any form, they tended to emphasize the undemocratic practices of anticommunist union officials without subjecting pro-Soviet leaders to the same degree of scrutiny. See, for example, Prickett, "Some Aspects of the Communist Controversy in the CIO." Recently, however, a closer examination of the Communists' conduct in the unions they controlled has revealed a more complex picture. Though some pro-Soviet unions, such as the United Electrical Workers in the late 1940s, were fairly democratic, others were not—particularly those in which resistance to CP leadership was negligible. Pluralism of forces, not pro-Soviet leadership, was the primary factor in accounting for the level of union democracy. For an early expression of this argument, see Cochran, *Labor and Communism*, 379–80.

45. *Labor Action*, September 13, 1948, 1. For the pro-Soviet faction's support for stronger national CIO authority during World War II, particularly in the enforcement of the no-strike pledge, see Howe and Coser, *The American Communist Party*, 408–19. For further evidence of pro-Soviet union leaders' use of desperate tactics to retain power, see Lichtenstein, "'Scientific Unionism,'" 77.

46. On the relationship between the Marshall Plan and the American labor movement, see William Z. Foster, "Organized Labor and the Marshall Plan," *Political Affairs* 27 (February 1948): 99–109; and Foster, "Danger Ahead for Organized Labor," 24–34. For the most compelling explanations of the Communist labor leaders' motivations for supporting the third party, see Charney, *A Long Journey*, 164–71, 176–78, 186–88; Healey and Isserman, *California Red*, 107–13; Starobin, *American Communism in Crisis*, 177–80; and Howe and Coser, *The American Communist Party*, 454–74. Gilbert J. Gall also offers an informative analysis of the factors that led Lee Pressman to break with Philip Murray and to join the third party. Gall, *Pursuing Justice*, 192–236. Charney, Starobin, and Howe and Coser emphasize the requirements of international Communism and the CIO Communists' ideological affinity for the Soviet Union, while Healey and Gall stress the Communists' concern with the advance of "reaction" in American politics.

47. Weinstein, "The Grand Illusion." Labor historians have frequently noted the ideological distance between the rank and file and the Communist leadership of the pro-Soviet trade unions. See, for example, the various essays in Rosswurm, *The CIO's Left-Led Unions*. This gap accounted in part for the leadership's failure to mobilize

members behind Wallace's third party. Freeman, *In Transit*, 300–1, comments on the similar inability of TWU Communists to instill in their members "a larger political vision to which they were willing to subordinate parochial interests."

48. Record, *The Negro and the Communist Party*, 277.

49. Nelson, Barrett, and Ruck, *Steve Nelson*, 289; *New York Times*, February 2, 1948, 11; Schmidt, *Henry A. Wallace*, 160–61. The $9,000 figure represents funds given by international unions to the Progressive Party's national campaign office and does not take into account individual members' donations or monies spent by local unions in support of Wallace. Even these contributions may not have demonstrated a spontaneous outpouring for Wallace among the rank and file. The Communist-led Fur and Leather Workers reported more than $21,000 in "voluntary" donations from its rank and file, but fur manufacturers presented extensive evidence to congressional investigators that union officials had employed coercion to secure these funds. For the Communists' own assessment of the disappointing performance of its "labor influentials" in the "Left-progressive" unions, see John Williamson, "Only Militant, United Action Can Defeat the Drive Against the Unions!" *Political Affairs* 27 (September 1948): 857–79.

50. Howe and Coser, *The American Communist Party*, Kampelman, *The Communist Party vs. the CIO*, and Saposs, *Communism in American Unions*, offer representative accounts of those critical of the CIO Communists, while Keeran, *The Communist Party and the Auto Workers Unions*, Honey, *Southern Labor and Black Civil Rights*, and Filippelli and McColloch, *Cold War in the Working Class*, are more admiring. But see also Lisa Kannenberg's review of Filippelli and McColloch in *International Labor and Working Class History* 50 (Fall 1996): 231–33. Kannenberg notes that the authors fail to explain adequately why the UE leadership backed Wallace when, as they themselves acknowledge, doing so was clearly not in the union's best interests.

51. Cochran, *Labor and Communism*, 303.

52. On pockets of support for Wallace, see Halpern, *Down on the Killing Floor*, 244–45; Robert Korstad, "Daybreak of Freedom," 340–59; De Caux, *Labor Radical*, 498–99.

53. Lee Fryer to Curtis MacDougall, February 6, 1953, Box 58, Folder 246, PPP; Hugh Bryson to MacDougall, March 4, 1953, Box 58, Folder 246, PPP; MacDougall, *Gideon's Army*, 3:612–13.

54. On the Wallace labor rally, see *Denver Post*, July 24, 1948, 8; *New York World-Telegram*, July 26, 1948, 6; *New York Post*, August 9, 1948, 32. For the YPA convention, see *Daily Worker*, July 27, 1948, 2.

55. See, for example, *Daily Worker*, July 27, 1948, 7; July 28, 1948, 8; August 17, 1948 8; *Worker* (Pennsylvania edition), August 1, 1948, 1A; *Worker* (Calumet edition), August 8, 1948, 2. "Look at Murray . . . ," Campaign leaflet, Box 32A, Folder 7, PPP.

56. Gall, *Pursuing Justice*, 282; "Speech by Henry A. Wallace at Bridgeport, Connecticut Saturday August 21, 1948," Box 13, CBP; *New York Post*, August 23, 1948, 32; Wechsler, "My Ten Months with Wallace," *Progressive*, November 1948, 7.

57. CIO, "Minutes of the Executive Board of the CIO," August 31–September 2, 1948, Reel 12, CIO-M, 134–38.

58. Ibid., 209–10. For anti-Wallace sentiment in the locals, see "Minutes," Reel 12, CIO-M, 223, 252–58, 266–70.

59. "Minutes," Reel 12, CIO-M, 222.

60. Ibid., 123, 129–30. Henderson, a concealed Communist, had also served as a secret member of the Central Committee of the CPUSA. Klehr and Haynes, "Communists and the CIO," 443.

61. "Minutes," Reel 12, CIO-M, 135, 156, 140, 152.

62. Ibid., 194–99, 205–8.

63. Ibid., 213–22.

64. Ibid., 226–27, 239.

65. Ibid., 155. Murray reiterated his position publicly at a CIO-PAC rally in Hershey, Pennsylvania, the following weekend, sharply condemning the Communists for their shifts of position "wholly contingent on the Party Line from Moscow." *CIO News*, September 6, 1948, 10.

66. For a summary of the Progressive position, see C. B. Baldwin's statement to the CIO leadership released the day before the executive board meeting, reprinted in the *Daily Worker*, August 31, 1948, 2.

67. *New York Times*, August 6, 1948, 1.

68. Haynes and Klehr, *Venona*, 15. See also Moynihan, *Secrecy*, 70–74.

69. *New York Times*, August 9, 1948, 4; *Daily Worker*, August 9, 1948, 2, 11.

70. "A Tradition the Spy Scares Cannot Wipe Out," *Worker*, August 22, 1948, 6–7, 10.

71. Gall, *Pursuing Justice*, 282. Pressman's statement to the FBI was undoubtedly self-serving, but his comments on Abt's and Witt's concerns ring true. Evidence now available indicates that both men had been more deeply involved in the underground activities of the AAA's "Ware group" than had Pressman, particularly in the period after Pressman left Washington and returned to his private law practice in New York. The committee also subpoenaed Victor Perlo, another concealed Communist working for the Progressive Party in Washington. Haynes and Klehr chronicle Perlo's extensive involvement in Soviet espionage in *Venona*, 116–27.

72. *New York Times*, August 21, 1948, 1, 3; August 13, 1948, 2.

73. Haynes and Klehr, *Venona*, 62–65, 116–28; Weinstein and Vassiliev, *The Haunted Wood*, 232–35; Haynes, Klehr, and Vassiliev, *Spies*, 425–28. The decrypted Venona cables do not mention Nathan Witt, but documents in the Soviet archives confirm that he, too, was a concealed member of the Communist Party. There remains some controversy regarding the significance and proper interpretation of the Venona transcripts, but the evidence is incontrovertible that Abt and Kramer passed information to individuals working for Soviet intelligence. In his autobiography published before the release of the Venona transcripts, Abt denied any participation in espionage but did acknowledge that as a member of the Ware group, he had passed inside information to officials of the CPUSA. Abt with Myerson, *Advocate and Activist*, 39–46. Regarding Kramer, Weinstein and Vassiliev have uncovered documents that indicate the Soviets valued him as an agent but expressed disappointment at the quality of the information he provided and at his reluctance to deliver written reports on U.S. policy matters during the early months of the Truman administration.

74. HUAC, *Hearings Regarding Communist Espionage in the United States Government*, 623; Abt with Myerson, *Advocate and Activist*, 150.

75. Laurence Duggan, who some alleged was Wallace's choice for secretary of state, also came under suspicion in December 1948. Though both men denied Bentley's allegations under oath, the Venona transcripts and declassified NKVD documents provide compelling evidence that White and Duggan were Soviet agents. Haynes and Klehr, *Venona*, 138–45, 201–4; Weinstein and Vassiliev, *The Haunted Wood*, 1–21. At the time, Wallace was not alone in dismissing HUAC's charges against the two men. Eleanor Roosevelt and the well-known journalists Drew Pearson and Edward R. Murrow also vouched for White's and Duggan's loyalty.

76. *Sacramento Union*, August 9, 1948, 1.

77. Gallup, *The Gallup Poll*, 1:756–57. See also the syndicated columnist David Lawrence's analysis of these polling numbers in the *Detroit News*, September 7, 1948, 14.

78. Abt with Myerson, *Advocate and Activist*, 150, 167.

79. "Speech by Henry A. Wallace at Bridgeport, Connecticut Saturday August 21, 1948," Box 13, CBP; Henry A. Wallace to Glen H. Taylor, April 18, 1956, Reel 51, Frames 57–59, HAW-M.

80. *New York Times*, August 8, 1948, 1, 48; August 13, 1948, 1, 3; August 15, 1948, Section 4, 1; Vladimir Zenzinov, "The Kasenkina 'Kidnapping,'" *New Leader*, August 28, 1948, 1, 12. The Kasenkina story received extensive coverage in the nation's newspapers. Two other teachers, Mikhail Ivanovitch and Klaudia Samarin, also sought refuge at Reed Farm the same week, but they were not "rescued." Molotov's statement protested their "kidnapping" as well. Tass, the Russian news agency, reported that Kasenkina fell accidentally from the building and was taken "by force" to a hospital by "American intelligence agents in the guise of American police." *New York Times*, August 15, 1948, 3.

81. *New York Times*, August 14, 1948, 1, 3; August 26, 1948, 1; *San Francisco Chronicle*, August 15, 1948, 6; William Henry Chamberlin, "The Testimony of Kosenkina," *New Leader*, August 21, 1948, 16.

82. The *Daily Worker* dutifully reported the Soviet version of the Kasenkina "kidnapping" from beginning to end. On August 13 it was the only New York paper not to run the news of her leap from the consulate on the front page. For representative stories on "White Guard" conspiracies, see *Daily Worker*, August 10, 1948, 9; August 11, 1948, 2, 11; August 15, 1948, 2; August 23, 1948, 1, 9, 11.

83. *San Francisco Chronicle*, August 15, 1948, 6; *New York Times*, August 21, 1948, 1, 2; August 22, 1948, 1; "A Leap to Freedom," *New Leader*, August 21, 1948, 16.

84. *New York World-Telegram*, August 17, 1948, 17; Carruthers, *Cold War Captives*, 3; *Berkshire [Pittsfield, Mass.] Evening Eagle*, August 20, 1948, 14. On the athletes' defections, see *New York Times*, August 16, 1948, 1, 3; August 17, 1948, 1. Though the Kasenkina story captivated the public at the time, it received almost no attention from historians until the appearance of Carruthers's book. See its first chapter for her detailed account and analysis.

85. *New York Post*, August 25, 1948, 30.

86. *Louisville Courier-Journal*, August 25, 1948, 1. In contrast to his public remarks, Wallace privately expressed support for the U.S. offer of asylum to Kasenkina.

87. *New York Herald Tribune*, August 29, 1948, 5-B; *Daily Worker*, September 3, 1948, 10.

CHAPTER 9

1. *Chicago Daily News*, November 19, 1965, 6. The reporter, Edwin A. Lahey, accompanied Wallace through the South. He wrote on the occasion of Wallace's death in 1965.

2. For representative summaries of this argument, see Clark Foreman to Frank Porter Graham, February 13, 1948, Box 35, Folder 88 "1948," Frank Porter Graham Papers, University of North Carolina, Chapel Hill, N.C.; and Henry A. Wallace, "Violence and Hope in the South," *New Republic*, December 8, 1947, 14–16.

3. Clark Foreman to Members of the Board, Southern Conference for Human Welfare and Southern Conference Educational Fund, May 17, 1948, Box 35, Folder 88 "1948," Frank Porter Graham Papers. John Moreno Coe to Marjorie Haynes, June 10, 1948, Box 1, Folder 47, John Moreno Coe Papers. On John Coe, see Brown, "Pensacola Progressive," 1–26.

4. See Korstad and Lichtenstein, "Opportunities Found and Lost"; Bartley, *The New South*, 38–72, 455–60; Goldfield, "The Failure of Operation Dixie"; and Hall, "The Long Civil Rights Movement and the Political Uses of the Past."

5. Alan Draper, *Conflict of Interests*, 13; Norrell, "Labor at the Ballot Box," 234. Draper also finds unpersuasive case studies of left-led unions that claim CIO officials ignored effective alternative strategies for organizing the region. In "The New Southern Labor History Revisited," he offers compelling evidence that left-wing interracial organizing strategies had little to do with Mine Mill's success in Birmingham, thus undercutting the argument of those who cite Mine Mill as an example of an alternative approach to organizing that could have produced a more progressive South if applied on a broad scale. For a similar critique of Robert Korstad's work on the Food, Tobacco, Agricultural, and Allied Workers, see Stein, "The Ins and Outs of the CIO."

6. *Baltimore Afro-American*, September 4, 1948, 2; *Charlotte Observer*, August 30, 1948, 2.

7. *Baltimore Sun*, August 27, 1948, 2; August 30, 1948, 2; *New York Star*, August 30, 1948, 6.

8. *New York Herald Tribune*, August 30, 1948, 2.

9. *Asheville Citizen*, August 30, 1948, 2.

10. *Baltimore Sun*, August 31, 1948, 17; *New York Times*, August 30, 1948, 11.

11. Henry Wallace, "Report on the South," *New Republic*, July 14, 1947, 14; MacDougall, *Gideon's Army*, 3:707.

12. *Durham Herald*, August 22, 1948, 4. See also Mary Price to Beanie Baldwin, March 3, 1948, Box 45, Folder 173, PPP, in which Price predicts that the Progressives could win North Carolina in November.

13. The Committee for North Carolina of the SCHW provided the organizational backbone for the Progressive Party in the state. Michael Ross, an organizer for the furniture workers union, ran for Congress on the Progressive Party ticket. Louis Austin,

the African American publisher of the Durham-based *Carolina Times*, helped organize the state party and served on its executive board. For further background on the evolution of the campaign in North Carolina, see Box 2, Folders 12–13, Junius Scales Papers, University of North Carolina, Chapel Hill, N.C.

14. *Tar Heel Progressive*, vol. 1, no. 1, 1. For coverage of the student rally, see *Daily Tar Heel*, February 29, 1948, 1.

15. *Greensboro Daily News*, August 4, 1948, 1. Progressive Party of North Carolina, "Analysis of Election Results," Box 45, Folder 173, PPP.

16. Palmer Weber interview with Curtis MacDougall, n.d., Box 49, Notebook 11, PPP.

17. *Greensboro Daily News*, August 3, 1948, 6.

18. "Proposed Trip for Henry Wallace in Eleven Southern States and Missouri," Box 11, CBP; "Reports on State Activities in Wallace Campaign" and "State Directors Reports—Chicago Conference, April 10, 1948," Box 7, CBP.

19. Patricia Sullivan, "Interview with Junius Scales," 1979, Box 2, Patricia Sullivan Research Interviews, Emory University, Atlanta. Lillian Gates, a Communist active in the Progressive Party in New York City, recalled that the party instructed the many young Communists assigned to do campaign work for the Progressives in the South to keep their party membership secret. Author's telephone conversation with Lillian Gates, September 6, 1996.

20. Sullivan, "Gideon's Southern Soldiers," 262; MacDougall, *Gideon's Army*, 3:732.

21. Sullivan, "Gideon's Southern Soldiers," 267; Sullivan, "Interview with Junius Scales"; MacDougall, *Gideon's Army*, 3:680, 592–93.

22. Schmidt, *Henry A. Wallace*, 137; Sullivan, "Gideon's Southern Soldiers," 262–64.

23. Progressive Party of North Carolina, "Analysis of Election Results." In the *Durham Herald*, August 6, 1948, 4-B, Mary Price estimated that blacks accounted for about half of the petition signatures. Likewise, election returns confirmed that what little support Progressives received in North Carolina came primarily from African Americans. See *Durham Herald*, November 3, 1948, 3; *Winston-Salem Journal*, November 3, 1948, 2.

24. Cannon, "The Organization and Growth of Black Political Participation in Durham, North Carolina," 62–64. The Durham Committee on Negro Affairs was especially effective in mobilizing the black electorate, which generally voted in a bloc for candidates the committee endorsed.

25. *Charlotte News*, August 26, 1948, 2. Though the NAACP's national leadership and most of the organization's state and local officials opposed the Wallace candidacy as impractical and self-defeating, several individual members gave the campaign their personal support, including a handful who ran for office on the Progressive Party ticket. See Sullivan, *Days of Hope*, 251; Pitre, *In Struggle against Jim Crow*, 75–78.

26. *Durham Labor Journal*, September 3, 1948, 4; *Raleigh News and Observer*, September 1, 1948, 11.

27. *Winston-Salem Journal*, May 30, 1948, 1B.

28. HUAC, *Hearings Regarding Communist Espionage in the United States Government*, 529–30, 687–89, 726, 729–30, 741, 755; Haynes and Klehr, *Venona*, 99–106; Haynes, Klehr, and Vassiliev, *Spies*, 173–77; *Daily Worker*, August 3, 1948, 11; *Greensboro Daily News*, August 9, 1948, 1. For press skepticism, see *Greensboro Daily News*, August 3, 1948, 6.

29. See, for example, "Interview with Virginia Foster Durr," March 15, 1975, Southern Oral History Project, University of North Carolina, Chapel Hill, in which Durr states repeatedly that those who rejected her Popular Front–style liberalism did so because they feared being "red-baited." For a critique of this tendency in the historiography, see Barkin, "Operation Dixie"; and Arnesen, "Civil Rights and the Cold War at Home."

30. *Daily Worker*, August 3, 1948, 11; *Winston-Salem Journal*, August 1, 1948, 1. Price's remarks also quoted in *Greensboro Daily News*, August 9, 1948, 1.

31. *Greensboro Daily News*, August 3, 1948, 6; August 2, 1948, 4.

32. *Raleigh News and Observer*, August 28, 1948; *Durham Herald*, August 28, 1948, 1; *Durham Sun*, August 28, 1948, 2; *High Point Enterprise*, August 29, 1948, 4-A; Clark Foreman interview with Curtis MacDougall, September 8, 1952, Box 49, Notebook 11, PPP.

33. Patton, "The Popular Front Alternative"; Progressive Party of North Carolina, "Analysis of Election Results."

34. "Henry Wallace Will Be Guest of Local Negro," *Durham Herald*, August 28, 1948, 1, 4; "Negro to Be Wallace Host," *Raleigh News and Observer*, August 28, 1948, 1. Both papers were considered "liberal" by southern standards of the time, further evidence of how deeply engrained Jim Crow was in the South of 1948—and an indication of the isolation Progressives experienced when trying to alter the racial status quo.

35. *Durham Sun*, August 28, 1948, 4; *New York Herald Tribune*, August 30, 1948, 2; *Durham Sun*, August 31, 1948, 4.

36. Editorials in the *Charlotte Observer*, September 1, 1948, 6; *New York Post*, September 1, 1948, 29; *Atlanta Constitution*, September 1, 1948, 10; and *Raleigh News and Observer*, September 11, 1948, 4, attributed the Progressives' confrontational tactics in the South to the Communist influence in the party. Price, who helped set the tone, was a party member, but one must take such an interpretation with a grain of salt. The southern press was hostile to *any* opponent of segregation and eager to attribute any challenge to this system to "outsiders" and "Communists." In later years, however, Wallace himself came to believe that the Communists had deliberately resorted to such tactics to undermine the broader message he wished to convey. Lew Frank to Curtis MacDougall, April 19, 1953, Box 58, Folder 260, PPP.

37. This and the succeeding paragraphs draw on accounts from the following newspapers: *Charlotte Observer*, *Durham Herald*, *Durham Sun*, *New York Times*, *New York Post*, *New York Star*, *New York Herald Tribune*, and *Washington Post*, all August 30, 1948; *Raleigh News and Observer*, September 2, 1948; *Baltimore Afro-American* and *Pittsburgh Courier*, both September 4, 1948. Robert Bendiner, "Dixie's Fourth Party," *Nation*, February 14, 1948, 174.

38. *Baltimore Afro-American*, September 4, 1948, 1. Several reporters had commented on the absence of any direct racial conflicts during the Wallace tour. Newbold Noyes, the correspondent for the *Washington Star*, observed repeatedly the incongruous scene of white men shouting "nigger lover" at the candidate while rubbing shoulders with black men in the audience. *Washington Star*, September 2, 1948, 1, 5.

39. *New York Times*, August 30, 1948, 11; *New York Herald Tribune*, August 30, 1948, 2.

40. Violence following the meeting was not reported in the local press, though southern newspapers were notoriously biased in their reporting of racial violence. Yet northern-based journalists also did not report any incidents of violence. The *New York Herald Tribune*, for example, noted that "both factions dispersed in an orderly and apparently good-humored fashion." For an account that describes further incidents of harassment, see Scales and Nickson, *Cause at Heart*, 196.

41. *Washington Star*, August 30, 1948, 5.

42. *New York Times*, September 1, 1948, 22. See also *New York Post*, September 1, 1948, 29; *New York World-Telegram*, August 31, 1948, 18; *Los Angeles Times*, September 1, 1948, 4.

43. *Durham Herald*, September 1, 1948, 4; *Raleigh News and Observer*, September 2, 1948, 2; *Durham Sun*, August 30, 1948, 4; August 31, 1948, 4; Patricia Sullivan, "Interview with John Popham," November 24, 1979, Box 2, Patricia Sullivan Research Interviews.

44. Sullivan, "Interview with Junius Scales," 1979, Box 2, Patricia Sullivan Research Interviews. *Durham Sun*, August 31, 1948, 4; *Winston-Salem Journal*, September 2, 1948, 13. See also Clark Foreman interview with Curtis MacDougall, September 8, 1952, Box 49, Notebook 11, PPP.

45. Henry A. Wallace, "Violence and Hope in the South," 15.

46. *Charlotte Observer*, August 31, 1948, 2; *New York Post*, September 1, 1948, 5.

47. *Greensboro Daily News*, August 31, 1948, 3.

48. For an insightful analysis of white liberals' response to southern racism, see Kellogg, "Northern Liberals and Black America." In examining the complex links between race and economic status, some scholars have argued that racism often manifested itself as a central element of working-class consciousness. See, for example, Roediger, *The Wages of Whiteness*, which examines nineteenth-century workers. See also Gerstle, "Working-Class Racism," for comments on workers in the 1930s and 1940s.

49. *Durham Sun*, August 31, 1948, 4.

50. *High Point Enterprise*, August 31, 1948, 1; *Raleigh News and Observer*, September 1, 1948, 2.

51. The next two paragraphs draw on reports from the following newspapers: *Burlington Daily Times-News*, *Durham Sun*, *Twin City Sentinel* (Winston-Salem, N.C), all August 30, 1948; *Greensboro Daily News*, *High Point Enterprise*, *Charlotte News*, *Charlotte Observer*, *Knoxville News-Sentinel*, *New York Herald Tribune*, *New York Times*, *Washington Post*, *Louisville Courier-Journal*, all August 31, 1948; *New York Post*, September 1, 1948. Also see Sullivan, "Interview with John Popham."

52. Almost unanimously, the press corps agreed that the experience in Burlington was the most harrowing of the trip. See *Raleigh News and Observer*, September 2, 1948, 1, Sullivan, "Interview with John Popham"; and Sullivan, "Interview with James Wechsler."

53. *Charlotte Observer*, August 31, 1948, 2; *High Point Enterprise*, August 31, 1948, 1.

54. *Greensboro Daily News*, August 31, 1948, 1B.

55. *New York Herald Tribune*, August 31, 1948, 2. In its inimitable fashion, the *Daily Worker* reported from Greensboro that "Southern audiences are greeting Henry Wallace with friendly warmth." *Daily Worker*, August 31, 1948, 1.

56. *High Point Enterprise*, August 31, 1948, 4.

57. *Twin City Sentinel*, August 30, 1948, 1, and August 31, 1948, 11.

58. For endorsements by the FTA international and Local 22, see *Winston-Salem Journal*, January 19, 1948, 1, and January 24, 1948, 3.

59. Local 22 officials also conducted a successful drive to register black voters in Winston-Salem, raising the total from three hundred to three thousand in two years. Ladd, *Negro Political Leadership in the South*, 58–61. For a discussion of FTA's political activities in Winston-Salem and the election of 1947, see Korstad, "Daybreak of Freedom," chap. 7, and Scales and Nickson, *Cause at Heart*, 202–8. Scales expresses more skepticism about Communist influence and tactics in FTA Local 22 than does Korstad.

60. Korstad, "Daybreak of Freedom," 340, 351, 359. Korstad blames postwar anticommunism as embodied in the Taft-Hartley Act for FTA's decline while downplaying white racism as a contributing factor. For a different view, see Draper, *Conflict of Interests*, 12–13.

61. *Salisbury [N.C.] Post*, August 31, 1948, 1.

62. *Durham Herald*, August 31, 1948, 1.

63. Korstad, "Black and White Together," 89. Wallace received 698 votes in Forsyth County, which includes the city of Winston-Salem. For final county results, see Heard and Strong, *Southern Primaries and Elections*, 104.

64. *Winston-Salem Journal*, October 30, 1948, 6; Korstad, "Daybreak of Freedom," 368.

65. *Charlotte Observer*, September 1, 1948, 1, 2.

66. *Charlotte News*, August 31, 1948, 1.

67. *Twin City Sentinel*, August 31, 1948, 1.

68. *New York Herald Tribune*, September 1, 1948, 11. Southern Progressives frequently complained that the national office did them more harm than good. See Sullivan, "Interview with Junius Scales" and "Interview with Palmer Weber"; "Interview with Virginia Foster Durr," March 15, 1975, Southern Oral History Project.

69. *New York Herald Tribune*, September 1, 1948, 11.

70. *New York Times*, September 1, 1948, 13; MacDougall, *Gideon's Army*, 3:717; Mary Frederickson, "Interview with Mary Price Adamson," Southern Oral History Project; *New York Herald Tribune*, September 1, 1948, p1, 11; *Asheville Citizen*, September 1, 1948, 1, 5.

71. *Raleigh News and Observer*, September 2, 1948, 2.

72. *New York Post*, September 1, 1948, 5.

73. *New York Post*, September 1, 1948, 5; Wechsler, *The Age of Suspicion*, 226; Sullivan, "Interview with James Wechsler." Wechsler recalled being told on the train that "tomorrow may be the day it all blows up."

74. *Chicago Daily News*, September 1, 1948, 1; *Washington Star*, September 1, 1948, 4.

75. *Washington Post*, September 2, 1948, 9; *Knoxville News-Sentinel*, September 2, 1948, 11; *Winston-Salem Journal*, September 2, 1948, 1; *Washington Post*, September 2, 1948, 9.

76. *Jackson [Miss.] Daily News*, September 6, 1948, 4.

77. *Chicago Daily News*, September 4, 1948, 5; Sullivan, "Gideon's Southern Soldiers," 330. For Gadsden's antilabor tradition and its later emergence as a solid union town, see Martin, "Southern Labor Relations in Transition."

78. *New York Herald Tribune*, September 2, 1948, 8; MacDougall, *Gideon's Army*, 3:721.

79. A series of church and home bombings in black neighborhoods from 1947 to 1949 had earned the city the nickname "Bombingham." Between March and May 1948 alone, two homes were bombed and police shot and killed six blacks, physically assaulted several NAACP members, and allegedly beat local black businessmen. On June 10, more than a hundred Klansmen demonstrated at a Girl Scout camp that was training black women to become scout leaders. When African American community spokespersons protested the violence in a formal petition, Bull Connor dismissed their initiative as part of a communist plot. See Corley, "The Quest for Racial Harmony," 47–50, quote on 50; Reed, *Simple Decency and Common Sense*, 152; Nunnelley, *Bull Connor*, 3, 36.

80. Reporting on Wallace's trek through Alabama, Robert Ruark recalled Connor's quote of ten years earlier. See *Knoxville News-Sentinel*, September 1, 1948, 12. The inaugural gathering of the SCHW also produced another memorable episode. First lady Eleanor Roosevelt, who arrived late at one of the meetings, did not notice that the crowd was racially divided and took her seat on the "colored" side of the auditorium. When asked to move—or so it has come to be told—she placed her chair in the center aisle straddling the chalk line separating the races. John Egerton claims, however, that this story has been so embellished with each retelling that the resulting depiction of a "boldly rebellious" first lady defiantly confronting the Birmingham authorities is actually more myth than reality. Egerton, *Speak Now against the Day*, 193–94. Still, the commissioner's behavior forced Southern Conference members to confront segregation more directly than they initially may have intended, marking the first of many times in his long career that Connor would strengthen the resolve of those he sought to discredit.

81. Robert J. Norrell, "Labor at the Ballot Box," 223–24, 233.

82. Adams, *James A. Dombrowski*, 167. On Connor's 1945 campaign, see Nunnelley, *Bull Connor*, 26–29.

83. Nunnelley, *Bull Connor*, 32–33. For the activities of the SNYC and its close connection to the Communist Party, see Kelley, *Hammer and Hoe*, 200–226; and Record, *Race and Radicalism*, 97–100, 148–51. Louis Burnham, an African American Communist from New York City, served as the SNYC's executive director as well as as the co-director of the Progressive Party's southern campaign.

84. *New York Times*, May 2, 1948, 1, 37; May 3, 1948, 1, 12; Nunnelley, *Bull Connor*, 34.

85. Nunnelley, *Bull Connor*, 32–33.

86. *Knoxville News-Sentinel*, September 1, 1948, 12.

87. *Durham Sun*, August 31, 1948, 2; *New York Times*, September 2, 1948, 15; *New York Herald Tribune*, September 2, 1948, 8.

88. *Washington Star*, September 2, 1948, 5; *New York Times*, September 2, 1948, 15.

89. "Broadcast of Henry A. Wallace," Birmingham, Alabama, September 1, 1948, Box 1, Folder 5, Lew Frank Papers, University of Iowa, Iowa City.

90. MacDougall, *Gideon's Army*, 3:723; Palmer Weber to Thurgood Marshall, September 11, 1948, Part 16, Board of Directors' Correspondence, Series B, Reel 23–864, NAACP Papers, microfilm edition, Duke University, Durham, N.C.; *Washington Post*, September 5, 1948, 1B.

91. *Worker*, Southern edition, September 12, 1948, 1.

92. On Folsom's admiration for Wallace and his criticisms of the Truman administration, see Sims, *The Little Man's Big Friend*, 94–100; Barnard, *Dixiecrats and Democrats*, 96, 101–7; and Grafton and Permaloff, *Big Mules and Branchheads*, 110–13.

93. Representative of this trend in liberal opinion is A. G. Mezerik's series on the South, "Dixie in Black and White," which appeared in the *Nation* during the spring and summer of 1947. See Mezerik, "Dixie in Black and White III: Big Jim of Alabama," *Nation*, April 19, 1947, 449. In a January 1948 follow-up report, Mezerik still maintained that "the ordinary white people of the South may turn out to be ahead of the old-line liberals." Mezerik, "Dixie Inventory," *Nation*, January 10, 1948, 42. Similarly, the *New Republic* reported in March 1948 that many believed Folsom was "the catalyst of a new upsurge of Southern liberalism quite outside the Democratic Party leadership." Even Folsom's denunciation of the Truman civil rights proposals on grounds of states' rights did not discourage the editors. "For all the ambiguity of his present stand on white supremacy," they wrote, "his friends believe he may some day take a liberal position on Negro rights in the South." "Big Jim," *New Republic*, March 15, 1948, 7.

94. Sims, *The Big Man's Little Friend*, 96–99; Barnard, *Dixiecrat and Democrats*, 106; "Five States Heard From," *New Republic*, May 17, 1948, 9; Sullivan, "Gideon's Southern Soldiers," 327–28.

95. See, for example, Thomas Sancton, "Slowly Crumbling Levies," *New Republic*, March 8, 1948, 18–21; Thomas Sancton, "White Supremacy—Crisis or Plot? I," *Nation*, July 24, 1948, 94–98; and Thomas Sancton, "White Supremacy—Crisis or Plot? II," *Nation*, July 31, 1948, 125–28. Sancton believed the Dixiecrat revolt had little to do with race. Rather, it represented a conspiracy of political and corporate interests who exploited racial prejudice to consolidate their own power. See also Joseph E. Finley, "A Yankee Looks at the Dixie Revolt," *Nation*, July 3, 1948, 17–18.

96. Lillian Smith, "Pay Day in Georgia," *Nation*, February 1, 1947, 118–19. Examining an earlier period of the state's history, another student of Alabama politics has written: "The ideals of the ante-bellum South were the ideals of the southern citizenry. Students who insist upon attributing the evil of the region to a ruling class—who, in effect, absolve the populace from blame in the creation of its society—are often attempting to close their eyes to a fact which they do not wish to believe: that democracy contains no intrinsic tendency towards producing good. Democracy as a form of government is merely a mirror of men." J. Mills Thornton III, *Politics and Power in a Slave Society: Alabama, 1800–1860* (Baton Rouge: Louisiana State University Press, 1978), 4. This admonition seems equally appropriate for those analyzing political behavior in the 1940s.

97. Minchin, *What Do We Need a Union For?*, 37–44; Nelson, "'CIO Meant One Thing for the Whites and Another Thing for Us,'" 113–45; Alex Lichtenstein, "'Scientific Unionism,'" 59–85; Norrell, "Caste in Steel"; Draper, "The New Southern Labor History Revisited."

98. See Roediger, *Wages of Whiteness*, 9–11; and Nelson, "Class, Race and Democracy in the CIO." In his study of Mississippi during the Jim Crow era, Neil R. McMillen argues that the ideology of white supremacy was not merely a tool used for maintaining social control or for obscuring more fundamental conflicts, but an "ideal" with its own logic and legitimacy. McMillen, *Dark Journey*.

99. *Chicago Daily News*, September 2, 1948, 3, and September 4, 1948, 5. At its September meeting in Atlanta, the executive committee of the Southern Regional Council, a liberal organization that worked for better race relations in the South, also compared the current situation in Dixie to that of the 1850s: "Today the old issue is back, in a new guise, and we are performing in the same old way." Sosna, *In Search of the Silent South*, 162.

100. *Washington Post*, September 5, 1948, 1B, 5B.

101. Barnard, *Dixiecrats and Democrats*, 96; *Chicago Daily News*, September 2, 1948, 16; Bazelon, "The Faith of Henry Wallace," 317.

102. Wallace's speech quoted from the *New Orleans Times-Picayune*, September 3, 1948, 21, and the *Jackson [Miss.] Advocate*, September 11, 1948, 1.

103. Many liberals shared Wallace's view that federal money used to develop southern industry would diminish racial tensions by bringing prosperity to all. See Newberry, "Without Urgency or Ardor," 149–54. In fact, pervasive job discrimination continued even as southern industry prospered. The result, Samuel Lubell observed in 1951, was the marginalization of black labor and the reinforcement of white supremacy. Lubell, *The Future of American Politics*, 118–20.

104. Both contemporary and historical studies of CIO activity in the South offer evidence for this. See, for example, Roper, "The CIO Organizing Committee in Mississippi"; and Draper, "The New Southern Labor History Revisited." Draper cites Alabama's Tennessee Coal, Iron, and Railroad Corporation as an example of a northern-owned corporation whose recognition of NLRB authority may have made the difference in Mine Mill's successful effort to organize Birmingham workers. Agreements reached between the parent company—in this case, U.S. Steel—and union internationals often benefited southern workers who stood little chance of negotiating such deals without outside assistance. To be sure, not all union contracts provided equal benefits for northern and southern workers, a major bone of contention between labor and management during this period, but the issue was more complex than "good" southern owners versus "bad" northern investors. See also Flynt, "The New Deal and Southern Labor," 76–80.

105. *Jackson [Miss.] Advocate*, September 11, 1948, 4. See Wallace, *Toward World Peace*, 114–15. See also Weiler, "Statesmanship, Religion, and the General Welfare," 183–87.

106. For a sampling of editorial criticism of Wallace's economic proposals for the South, see *Baltimore Sun*, August 30, 1948, 17; *New York Times*, August 31, 1948, 22; *New York Herald Tribune*, September 1, 1948, 20; *Arkansas Gazette*, September 2, 1948, 4.

107. On this theme, see two perceptive dissertations, largely neglected by Wallace scholars: King, "The Rhetoric of Henry Agard Wallace," 214–16; and Weiler, "Statesmanship, Religion, and the General Welfare," 183–87.

108. George N. Peek, with Samuel Crowther, "In and Out: Laying the Foundation for Regimentation," *Saturday Evening Post*, May 23, 1936, 108.

109. For the effect of postwar prosperity in bringing about the demise of the "politics of subsistence and crisis" associated with the Depression and war years, see Boylan, *The New Deal Coalition and the Election of 1946*, chaps. 9 and 10. For the declining effectiveness of populist arguments in the postwar South, see Lubell, "The Future of the Negro Voter in the United States," 407–17.

110. Minchin, 59, 60; *Louisville Courier-Journal*, August 26, 1948, 6, and August 27, 1948, 7. Minchin's exhaustive research in the Operation Dixie records effectively challenges earlier studies that have attributed the CIO's failure at Cannon to company intimidation. Carlton, "Paternalism and Southern Textile Labor," likewise argues that historians have overemphasized employer "repression" in trying to explain the failure of unionization in the southern textile industry. See also Wright, "The Aftermath of the General Textile Strike," for further evidence that wages and conditions at Piedmont mills improved substantially during the late 1940s.

111. MacDougall, *Gideon's Army*, 3:724; Lawson, *Black Ballots*, 134; Matthews and Prothro, *Negroes and the New Southern Politics*, 148.

112. See MacDougall, *Gideon's Army*, 3:733; and Dwight Spencer to Curtis MacDougall, October 5, 1953, Box 37, Folder 55, PPP. Contrast the formidable risks southern blacks were willing to take in joining the CIO, an organization that they believed offered both the opportunity for economic advancement and a chance to receive equal treatment with whites. See Honey, *Southern Labor and Black Civil Rights*, and Korstad, *Civil Rights Unionism*.

113. *Nashville Tennessean*, September 5, 1948, 2-A.

114. *Washington Star*, September 5, 1948, 1, 8; *New York Post*, September 5, 1948, 21; *Chicago Daily News*, September 3, 1948, 10; *New York Herald Tribune*, September 5, 1948, 20.

115. *Chicago Daily News*, September 4, 1948, 5; *New York Star*, September 9, 1948, 10; Palmer Weber to Curtis MacDougall, July 3, [1955?], Box 58, Folder 250, PPP; Murphy, "Henry Wallace," 315; *Nashville Banner*, September 13, 1948, 6; Progressive Party of North Carolina, "Report on the Meeting of Candidates and Staff," Junius Scales Papers.

116. *New York Times*, September 5, 1948, 4.

117. Wallace wrote admiringly of the Old Testament prophets and clearly saw them as role models for contemporary reformers. See, in particular, Wallace, *Statesmanship and Religion*, especially 18–38. See also Schlesinger, *The Age of Roosevelt*, 30–31. Schlesinger notes that in political discussions, Wallace cited the views of the prophets "as he might those of elder liberal statesmen with whom he lunched the day before."

118. *Washington Star*, September 5, 1948, 8; "Wallace in the South," *Nation*, September 11, 1948, 277; Wechsler, "My Ten Months with Wallace," 5; Wechsler, *The Age of Suspicion*, 227.

119. Kellogg, "Northern Liberals and Black America," 337–44; Sosna, *In Search of the Silent South*, 140–65.

120. Kellogg, "Civil Rights Consciousness in the 1940s," 18–41. See also Southern, *Gunnar Myrdal and Black-White Relations*, 101–26.

121. See, for example, Korstad and Lichtenstein, "Opportunities Found and Lost"; and Bartley, *The New South, 1945-1980.* Arnesen, "Civil Rights and the Cold War at Home," challenges this line of reasoning, which he believes has become the "consensus" view in the historiography of the long civil rights movement.

122. For the inspirational effect of Wallace's southern tour, see Sullivan, "Proud Days," 94–98; Gallup, *The Gallup Poll,* 1:722–23, 747–48.

123. "Wallace's Southern Tour," *Crisis,* October 1948, 297.

124. Moon, *Balance of Power,* 204; Sitkoff, "Harry Truman and the Election of 1948," 608; Progressive Party News Release, October 4, 1948, Box 32, Folder 1, PPP; *Norfolk Journal and Guide,* March 20, 1948.

125. Record, *The Negro and the Communist Party,* 279–83; Murphy, "Henry Wallace," 299, 315–16. The National Wallace-for-President Committee churned out an avalanche of printed materials aimed at African American voters. See, for example, "The Old Parties TALK 'Civil Rights' . . . BUT ACT JIM-CROW," *These Fifteen Million,* a four-page newspaper detailing Progressive Party activity in the black community, and various other materials in Box 9, Folder 38, PPP.

126. *New York Star,* August 30, 1948, 11; MacDougall, *Gideon's Army,* 3:653; Barnard, *Outside the Magic Circle,* 201.

127. *Durham Herald,* November 3, 1948, 1. For further evidence of Progressives' confidence in winning a significant portion of the black vote, see John Coe to Louis Touby, November 11, 1948, Box 1, Folder 56, John Moreno Coe Papers; Hack Gleichman to Barney Conal, [May?] 1948, Box 9, Folder 104, Southern Conference for Human Welfare Records, Tuskegee University Archives, Tuskegee, Ala.

128. MacDougall, *Gideon's Army,* 3:679, 731; Williams, "The People's Progressive Party of Georgia," 229. For a similar argument, see Moon, *Balance of Power,* 190–204.

129. MacDougall, *Gideon's Army,* 3:680; Lubell, *The Future of American Politics,* 209; Egerton, *Speak Now against the Day,* 497; Henry L. Moon, "The Negro in Politics," *New Republic,* October 18, 1948, 9–10.

130. Ira De A. Reid, "Walden the Democrat," *New Republic,* October 18, 1948, 14. Reid observed that "not one [Negro Democrat in the South] has gone on the political record as favoring the elimination of segregation." In their study of the Congress of Racial Equality (CORE), August Meier and Elliott Rudwick recount that in CORE's early days, many local affiliates wished to employ direct action tactics to achieve their goals. Much like the Progressive Party, however, CORE leaders found that without deep roots in the black community, their group could not command the widespread support needed to make such tactics effective. Meier and Rudwick, *CORE,* 61–65.

131. *Chicago Defender,* September 11, 1948, 1.

132. On the amalgam of anticommunism and race during the Wallace campaign in the South, see Sullivan, "Interview with Junius Scales," 1979, Box 2, Patricia Sullivan Research Interviews. For a broader overview, see Woods, *Black Struggle, Red Scare.*

133. *Washington Post,* September 5, 1948, 5B. "The placards and the yells from the crowds always struck two notes," Edward Folliard reported, "'Nigger lover' and 'Go back to Russia.'" Various other press accounts echoed Folliard's observation.

134. See "Interview with Virginia Foster Durr," March 15, 1975, Southern Oral History Project; Clark Foreman interview with Curtis MacDougall, September 8,

1952, Box 49, Notebook 11, PPP. The history of the NAACP also demonstrates that anticommunism had a more complicated effect on racially progressive organizations than some scholars allow. The NAACP, August Meier and John H. Bracey note, repeatedly faced charges of being "Communist-inspired, -led, and -dominated" yet "employed the threat posed by the Cold War and the influence of the Soviet Union among nonwhite peoples of the world to press its own agenda." "In fact," they conclude, "as an organization, the NAACP entered its most prosperous period during the heyday of the Cold War." Meier and Bracey, "The NAACP as a Reform Movement, 1909–1965," 22.

135. Fredrickson, "Red, Black, and White," 35; Minchin, *What Do We Need a Union For?*, 45; John Dos Passos, *State of the Nation* (Boston: Houghton Mifflin, 1943), 82.

136. George Brown Tindall, "Mythology: A New Frontier in Southern History," in Tindall, *The Ethnic Southerners*, 23.

137. *Washington Post*, September 5, 1948, 5B. See also *New York Herald Tribune*, September 5, 1948, 20.

138. Nelson "Organized Labor and the Struggle for Black Equality." For a bitter critique of what he perceived as white southern Progressives' paternalistic attitude toward black party workers, see James Baldwin, "Journey to Atlanta," *New Leader*, October 9, 1948, 8–9. Marvin Caplan also notes that the Progressive Party leadership in Richmond displayed similar attitudes. The head of the local party, a white New York transplant whom Caplan assumed to be a Communist, annoyed many Richmond party members with his repeated condescending references to "the little people." Caplan, *Farther Along*, 84–86.

139. Even into the 1960s, Samuel Lubell has noted, the majority of white southern workers were segregationists. They joined Citizen Councils, not the CIO. Lubell, *White and Black*, 69.

CHAPTER 10

1. *New York Times*, September 11, 1948, 5; *Daily Worker*, September 13, 1948, 3, 11.

2. Wallace, "Tell the People Who We Are," 743–45.

3. The drafts in Wallace's hand are in Box 1, Folder 5, Lew Frank Jr. Papers, University of Iowa, Iowa City. See also Curtis MacDougall, Interview with Lew Frank, October 18, 1952, Box 49, Notebook 15, PPP.

4. *St. Louis Post-Dispatch*, September 11, 1948, 2; MacDougall, *Gideon's Army*, 3:804.

5. *New York Post*, September 12, 1948, 4.

6. *New York Times*, September 7, 1948, 1, 16; September 8, 1948, 1, 25; Saposs, *Communism in American Politics*, 137–40; Matles quoted in Lader, *Power on the Left*, 42.

7. *New York Star*, August 25, 1948, 13.

8. C. B. Baldwin to State Directors, "Urgent Request for Information on Congressional Candidates," August 25, 1948, Box 10, Folder 43, PPP; Americans for Democratic Action Publicity Department, "Henry A. Wallace: The First Three Months," Series 3, Box 16, Folder 212, ADA Southeastern Pennsylvania Chapter Papers, Temple University, Philadelphia; *CIO News*, September 6, 1948, 3; Textile Workers Union of America,

"Third Party: Red Ally of Reaction," Pamphlet Collection, Duke University, Durham, N.C.; *Washington Star*, September 6, 1948, 1.

9. Brown, "The 1948 Progressive Campaign," chap. 6. Brown conducted a close analysis of several congressional races around the country and found no evidence that the Progressives were engaged in a nationwide strategy to elect "reactionary" candidates. See also Schmidt, *Henry A. Wallace*, 225–29.

10. Healey and Isserman, *California Red*, 111; *Sacramento Union*, August 9, 1948, 2. Though Progressives later claimed that despite filing candidates against Helen Gahagan Douglas and other liberal Democrats in California, they never had any intention of actively opposing them, the contemporary record suggests otherwise. During his May 1948 visit to Los Angeles, Wallace campaigned for Douglas's IPP opponent, Sidney Moore, and told reporters, "If Helen Gahagan Douglas becomes a war-monger, we'll do everything we can to put Moore across." *New York Star*, May 25, 1948, 4.

11. *New York Post*, August 22, 1948, 38; *Labor Action*, October 11, 1948, 1, 2; Haynes, *Dubious Alliance*, 209–10; Kampelman, *The Communist Party vs. the CIO*, 136–37; Jenkins, *The Cold War at Home*, 59, 107–9; *CIO News*, September 6, 1948, 3.

12. C. B. Baldwin, "Remarks to Businessmen for Wallace, Hotel Commodore, September 21, 1948," Box 12, CBP; *Daily Worker*, August 31, 1948, 2. On Douglas's relationship with the IPP, see Scobie, *Center Stage*, 217–19.

13. "Excerpts from H. A. Wallace Speech; Commodore Hotel, September 21, 1948," Box 58, Folder 260, PPP; *New York Times*, September 22, 1948, 1, 18; Progressive Party News Release, Box 42, Folder 128, PPP; "New Party's New Policy," *Nation*, October 2, 1948, 359.

14. *Minneapolis Tribune*, October 1, 1948, 1; October 3, 1948, 1; Haynes, *Dubious Alliance*, 209–10; *Labor Action*, October 11, 1948, 1, 2; "Analysis of Progressive Party Congressional Candidacies," Box 16, Folder 71, PPP; "Statement by C. B. Baldwin on the Role of the Progressive Party in Congressional Races," September 30, 1948, Box 12, CBP.

15. *Labor Action*, October 11, 1948, 2. For an example of opposition to "capitulation" on the issue of foreign policy among rank-and-file Progressives, see Frederick O. Miller to Henry A. Wallace, October 5, 1948, Box 1, John Moreno Coe Papers.

16. "The Skids under Wallace," *Newsweek*, October 18, 1948, 335–36; Moremen, "The Independent Progressive Party in California," 216–17, 242; *San Francisco Chronicle*, October 5, 1948, 14.

17. Americans for Democratic Action Publicity Department, "Henry A. Wallace: The Last Seven Months of His Presidential Campaign," Box 42, Folder 128, PPP; Bell, *The End of Ideology*, 292–98. See also Mark Sullivan's column, "Meaning of Candidate Withdrawals," *Washington Post*, October 9, 1948, 9.

18. *New York Times*, October 10, 1948, E-10; *Minneapolis Tribune*, October 3, 1948, 4; *Louisville Courier-Journal*, August 28, 1948, 4.

19. *New York Times*, October 3, 1948, 45; *Los Angeles Times*, October 3, 1948, 1, 16; October 4, 1948, 2; *San Francisco Chronicle*, October 4, 1948, 1; October 5, 1948, 14; *Daily People's World*, October 4, 1948, 1.

20. Dalton Trumbo to Albert Maltz, [c. late 1961 or early 1962] quoted in Manfull, *Additional Dialogue*, 560.

21. *Chicago Sun-Times*, September 29, 1948, 5. On the Missouri Progressive Party, see MacDougall, *Gideon's Army*, 3:805–7. MacDougall acknowledges that several

"extreme left-wingers" had risen to positions of leadership in the state party and that there was "constant friction" within the organization.

22. Ross, *The Loneliest Campaign*, 229; *Chicago Sun-Times*, September 29, 1948, 5; Wechsler, "My Ten Months with Wallace," 8.

23. *San Francisco Chronicle*, October 8, 1948, 2; Radio Address by Henry A. Wallace, Station KMJ, Fresno, California, October 4, 1948, Box 46, Folder 177, PPP; *San Francisco Chronicle*, October 10, 1948, 11.

24. Address of Henry A. Wallace, Newark, N.J., October 24, 1948, Box 21, Folder 80, PPP; *New York Star*, October 10, 1948, 6. For similar remarks, see the coverage of Wallace's speeches in *New York Times*, September 21, 1948, and October 3, 1948.

25. C. B. Baldwin, "U.N. Crisis," Press statement, September 28, 1948, Box 46, Folder 177, PPP; *New York Star*, September 30, 1948, 6; *Minneapolis Tribune*, October 1, 1948, 6; Lewis Corey, "What Is Henry Wallace?—Part 2. Imperialism and 'War-Mongering,'" *New Leader*, October 9, 1948, 4; Abels, *Out of the Jaws of Victory*, 212.

26. *San Francisco Chronicle*, October 7, 1948, 3.

27. Wechsler, "My Ten Months with Wallace," 8; *Minneapolis Tribune*, October 1, 1948, 6; *Los Angeles Times*, September 29, 1948, 4.

28. Clipping from *Middletown [Ohio] Journal*, October 15, 1948, Box 33, Folder 10, PPP; Henry A. Wallace, COHP, 5077-78.

29. Henry A. Wallace to E. Jasinski, October 7, 1948, quoted in Walker, *Henry A. Wallace and American Foreign Policy*, 197; Markowitz, *The Rise and Fall of the People's Century*, 302.

30. On Wallace's lack of expertise in foreign policy, see Schapsmeier and Schapsmeier, *Prophet in Politics*, 195-96; and Judis, *The Grand Illusion*, 46-73.

31. *New York Herald Tribune*, April 15, 1947, 27.

32. Bazelon, "The Faith of Henry Wallace," 319.

33. MacDougall, *Gideon's Army*, 3:767-68; Frank's memoranda to Baldwin are in Box 33, Folder 10, PPP. See also Progressive Party, "Minutes of the Executive Committee," October 2, 1948, Box 9, Folder 35, PPP.

34. Memo, Lew Frank to Beanie Baldwin, October 1948, Box 33, Folder 10, PPP. For Wallace's decline in the polls, see Americans for Democratic Action Publicity Department, "Henry A. Wallace," 29-30; Milton Edelman, "The Labor Vote in '48: An Analysis," *Nation*, October 23, 1948, 465. For polls demonstrating public support for the Marshall Plan, see Gallup, *The Gallup Poll*, 1:661, 678, 683-84, 692; and "War Fears Grip Capital and Nation," *Newsweek*, March 22, 1948, 23-25.

35. Walker, *Henry A. Wallace and American Foreign Policy*, 201. See also White and Maze, *Henry A. Wallace*; and Culver and Hyde, *American Dreamer*.

36. MacDougall, *Gideon's Army*, 3:825; *New York Times*, October 27, 1948, 1, 17; Ross, *The Loneliest Campaign*, 230.

CONCLUSION

1. http://uselectionatlas.org/RESULTS/national.php?year=1948, (accessed August 1, 2011); Shannon, *The Decline of American Communism*, 180-81; "Facts on the Wallace

Campaign," October 13, 1948, Box 15, Folder 62, PPP; *National Guardian*, September 1948, 1.

2. See, for example, Jaffe, *The Rise and Fall of American Communism*, 121. Jaffe notes that in left-wing circles, it was generally believed that Wallace would get between 5 and 10 million votes. At an election-night gathering he attended, Jaffe predicted that Wallace would not receive more than 1.25 million votes. His host thereupon agreed that if Jaffe proved correct, he would accept all of his previous arguments about the inadvisability of a third party. After the final totals were in, Jaffe noted, "the result for me personally was that not a single person who had been at that gathering, including my host and friend, ever spoke to me again."

3. Margaret Marshall, "Notes by the Way," *Nation*, June 26, 1948, 720.

4. Not until 1953 did the CP own up to the disastrous course it had taken in 1947–48. Even then, the leadership did not accept responsibility, blaming instead "strong sectarian tendencies" within the party's ranks. National Committee, CPUSA, "Resolution on the Situation Growing out of the Presidential Elections (Final Text)," *Political Affairs* 32 (July 1953): 12.

5. Starobin, *American Communism in Crisis*, 190.

6. *New York Times*, December 7, 1948, 7; MacDougall, *Gideon's Army*, 3:882–83.

7. Wallace, "Henry Wallace Tells of His Political Odyssey," 183; Curtis MacDougall, interview with Lew Frank, October 18, 1952, Box 49, Notebook 15, PPP; Wallace, "Henry Wallace Tells: Where I Stand . . . And Where I Stood," 4; Fox, "'In Passion and in Hope,'" 278–81; Straight, *After Long Silence*, 222–23.

8. Henry A. Wallace to Curtis MacDougall, September 1, 1952, Box 55, Folder 230, PPP; *Newsweek*, November 29, 1965, 33; Wallace, "Political Odyssey," 184; *Chicago Sun-Times*, December 2, 1955, 18.

9. C. B. Baldwin, "Report to the Meeting of the National Committee," November 13, 1948, Box 27, CBP; *New York Times*, November 14, 1948, 43; November 21, 1948, E7. For Truman's consistency, see Hamby, "The Democratic Moment," 269–73; and Spalding, *The First Cold Warrior*, 132–34; Starobin, *American Communism in Crisis*, 190.

10. Lubell, *The Future of American Politics*, rev. ed., 224.

11. Donovan, *Conflict and Crisis*, 415; O'Neill, *American High*, 97.

12. Wechsler, "The Liberal's Vote and '48," 222.

13. MacDougall, *Gideon's Army*, 3:628.

BIBLIOGRAPHY

MANUSCRIPTS

Atlanta, Georgia
    Atlanta University Center, Robert W. Woodruff Library
        Southern Conference for Human Welfare Papers
    Emory University, Robert W. Woodruff Library
        John Moreno Coe Papers
        Theodore Draper Files
        Philip J. Jaffe Papers
        Patricia Sullivan Research Interviews
          ✓Mairi Fraser Foreman
          John Popham
          Junius Scales
          ✓Lillian Baldwin
          James A. Wechsler
Berkeley, California
    University of California, Berkeley, Bancroft Library
        Robert W. Kenny Papers
Boston, Massachusetts
    John F. Kennedy Library
        Arthur M. Schlesinger Jr. Papers
Cambridge, Massachusetts
    Radcliffe College, Schlesinger Library
        ✓Freda Kirchwey Papers
Chapel Hill, North Carolina
    University of North Carolina, Davis Library
        Americans for Democratic Action Papers, Microfilm Edition
        Earl Browder Papers, Microfilm Edition
    University of North Carolina, Southern Historical Collection
        Kenneth Douty, "The Southern Conference for Human Welfare: A Report"
        Frank Porter Graham Papers
        Junius Scales Papers
        Southern Oral History Project Interviews
          ✓Mary Price Adamson
          ✓Virginia Durr
          Clark Foreman
          John Popham

Chicago, Illinois
   Chicago Historical Society
      Ernest DeMaio Papers
      Independent Voters of Illinois Papers
      Sidney Lens Papers
   Clemson, South Carolina
   Clemson University, Strom Thurmond Institute
      James F. Byrnes Papers
Detroit, Michigan
   Wayne State University, Walter P. Reuther Library of Labor and Urban Affairs
      Congress of Industrial Organizations Secretary-Treasurer Papers
      Len De Caux Papers
      Michigan AFL–CIO, Series I: Michigan CIO President, 1943–1954 Papers
      Michigan AFL–CIO, Series II: Michigan CIO Secretary-Treasurer, 1944–1954
         Papers
      Walter P. Reuther Papers
      Nemmy Sparks Papers
      Sam Sweet Papers
      United Auto Workers Political Activities Vertical File
Durham, North Carolina
   Duke University, Perkins Library
      Columbia Oral History Program, Microfilm Edition
         Paul H. Appleby
         Louis Bean
         Samuel B. Bledsoe
         Bruce Bliven
         John Brophy
         Marquis Childs
         Julius Emspak
         Bernard L. Gladieux
         Fred W. Henshaw
         James LeCron
         Lee Pressman
         Morris Rosenthal
         Rexford G. Tugwell
         Henry A. Wallace
      J. B. Matthews Papers
      National Association for the Advancement of Colored
         People Papers, Microfilm Edition
      Socialist Party Papers, Microfilm Edition
      Textile Workers Union of America, "Third Party: Red
         Ally of Reaction," Pamphlet Collection
      Norman Thomas Papers, Microfilm Edition
Hyde Park, New York
   Franklin D. Roosevelt Presidential Library

Gardner Jackson Papers

Rexford Guy Tugwell Papers

Independence, Missouri

Harry S. Truman Presidential Library

Clark Clifford Papers

James I. Loeb Papers

Frank McNaughton Papers

Iowa City, Iowa

University of Iowa, Main Library

Calvin Benham Baldwin Papers

Lewis Frank Jr. Papers

Progressive Party Papers

Los Angeles, California

University of California, Los Angeles, Young Research Library

Independent Progressive Party Papers

Madison, Wisconsin

State Historical Society of Wisconsin

Robert Bendiner Papers

Adolph Germer Papers

Hollywood Democratic Committee (HICCASP) Papers

Liston M. Oak Papers

David A. Shannon Research Notes

Dalton Trumbo Papers

James A. Wechsler Papers

New Brunswick, New Jersey

Rutgers University, Alexander Library

American Labor Party Papers

New Haven, Connecticut

Yale University, Sterling Library

Max Lerner Papers

Dwight Macdonald Papers

New York, New York

New York Public Library

Vito Marcantonio Papers

New York University, Tamiment Institute

Daniel Bell Collection

Sam Darcy Papers

Max Shachtman Papers

Transport Union of America Papers

Philadelphia, Pennsylvania

Temple University, Urban Archives

Americans for Democratic Action, Southeastern Pennsylvania Chapter Papers

John F. Lewis Papers

Upholsterers International Union Papers

Raleigh, North Carolina

North Carolina State University, D. H. Hill Library
    Congress of Industrial Organizations Executive Board
        Minutes, Microfilm Edition
    Henry A. Wallace Papers, Microfilm Edition
Seattle, Washington
    University of Washington, Allen Library
      ✓Naomi Benson Papers
      Hugh De Lacy Papers
      Fair Taylor Ekroth Papers
      ✓Mary and E. William Hopkinson Papers
      Thomas Lynch Vertical File
      Thomas C. Rabbitt Papers
      Earl Robinson Papers
Stanford, California
    Hoover Institution Archives
      National Republic Records
    Stanford University, Green Library
      Bruce Bliven Papers
Tuskegee, Alabama
    Tuskegee University Archives
      Southern Conference for Human Welfare Records
Washington, D.C.
    Catholic University, Mullen Library
      Philip Murray Papers
      John Brophy Papers
    Library of Congress, Manuscript Division
      Joseph and Stewart Alsop Papers
      Jo Davidson Papers
      Jack Kroll Papers
      Minnesota Progressive Party Papers
      Joseph Rauh Papers
      ✓Martha Dodd Stern Papers

INTERVIEWS

Bendiner, Robert. Interview with author, May 12, 1996.
Brudney, Juliette. Telephone interview with author, June 27, 1996.
Gates, Lillian. Telephone interview with author, September 3, 1996.
Ross, Irwin. Interview with author, May 13, 1996.
Schlesinger, Arthur M., Jr. Interview with author, November 23, 1994.
Starobin, Norma. Telephone interview with author, November 27, 1996.
Wechsler, Nancy. Interview with author, May 13, 1996.

ADA World
Akron (Ohio) Journal
Arkansas Gazette
Asheville (N.C.) Citizen
Atlanta Constitution
Baltimore Afro-American
Baltimore Sun
Berkshire (Mass.) Eagle
Birmingham (Ala.) News
Boston Globe
Boston Herald
Burlington (N.C.) Daily
    Times-News
CIO News
Carolina Times
Charlotte News
Charlotte Observer
Chicago Daily News
Chicago Defender
Chicago Sun-Times
Chicago Tribune
Christian Science
    Monitor
Citizen (National
    Wallace-for-President
    Committee)
Daily Californian
    (Berkeley)
Daily People's World (San
    Francisco)
Daily Worker (New York
    City)
Daily Tar Heel (Chapel
    Hill, N.C.)
Denver Post
Detroit Free Press
Detroit News
Durham (N.C.) Herald
Durham (N.C.) Labor
    Journal
Durham (N.C.) Sun
Greensboro (N.C.) Daily
    News

Greenville (Ohio)
    Advocate
Hickory (N.C.) Daily
    Record
High Point (N.C.)
    Enterprise
Jackson (Miss.) Advocate
Jackson (Miss.)
    Clarion-Ledger
Jackson (Miss.) Daily
    News
Knoxville (Tenn.)
    News-Sentinel
Labor Action
Labor and Nation
Labor Leader
Los Angeles Daily News
Los Angeles Times
Louisville (Ky.)
    Courier-Journal
Madison (Wisc.)
    Capital-Times
Manchester Guardian
    (U.K.)
Marine Cooks and
    Stewards Voice
Memphis Commercial
    Appeal
Minneapolis Tribune
Nashville Banner
Nashville Tennessean
Nation
National Guardian
New Leader
New Orleans
    Times-Picayune
New Republic
New York Daily Mirror
New York Daily News
New York Herald Tribune
New York
    Journal-America
New York Post

New York Star
New York Sun
New York Times
New York World-Telegram
Newsweek
Philadelphia Bulletin
Philadelphia Daily News
Philadelphia Inquirer
Pittsburgh Courier
Pittsburgh Press
Pittsfield (Mass.) Evening
    Eagle
PM (New York City)
Political Affairs
Progressive Citizen
Public Opinion Quarterly
Raleigh News and
    Observer
Sacramento Bee
Sacramento Union
Salisbury (N.C.) Post
San Francisco Chronicle
The Score
Socialist Call
St. Louis Post-Dispatch
Time
Times (London)
Transport Workers Union
    Bulletin
Twin City Sentinel
    (Winston-Salem, N.C.)
U.S. News and World
    Report
Washington Daily News
Washington Post
Washington Star
Washington Times-Herald
Winston-Salem (N.C.)
    Journal
Worker (New York)
York (Pa.) Gazette and
    Daily
The Young Progressive

Abels, Jules. *Out of the Jaws of Victory*. New York: Henry Holt, 1959.

Abt, John J., with Michael Myerson. *Advocate and Activist: Memoirs of an American Communist Lawyer*. Urbana: University of Illinois Press, 1993.

Adams, Frank T. *James A. Dombrowski: An American Heretic, 1897–1983*. Knoxville: University of Tennessee Press, 1992.

Alpern, Sara. *Freda Kirchwey: A Woman of "The Nation."* Cambridge: Harvard University Press, 1987.

Barone, Michael. *Our Country: The Shaping of America from Roosevelt to Reagan*. New York: Free Press, 1990.

Barrett, James R. *William Z. Foster and the Tragedy of American Radicalism*. Urbana: University of Illinois Press, 1999.

Barrett, Edward L., Jr. *The Tenney Committee: Legislative Investigation of Subversive Activities in California*. Ithaca: Cornell University Press, 1951.

Bartley, Numan V. *The New South 1945–1980*. Baton Rouge: Louisiana State University Press, 1995.

Belfrage, Cedric. *The American Inquisition, 1945–1960*. New York: Bobbs-Merrill, 1973.

Bell, Daniel. *The End of Ideology: On the Exhaustion of Political Ideas in the Fifties*. Rev. ed. New York: Free Press, 1962.

Bell, Jonathan. *The Liberal State on Trial: The Cold War and American Politics in the Truman Years*. New York: Columbia University Press, 2004.

Benson, Michael T. *Harry S. Truman and the Founding of Israel*. Westport, Conn.: Praeger, 1997.

Bentley, Elizabeth. *Out of Bondage: The Story of Elizabeth Bentley*. New York: Devin-Adair, 1951; reprint, New York: Ballantine Books, 1988.

Bentley, Eric, ed. *Thirty Years of Treason: Excerpts from Hearings before the House Committee on Un-American Activities, 1938–1968*. New York: Viking Press, 1971.

Berger, Jason. *A New Deal for the World: Eleanor Roosevelt and American Foreign Policy*. New York: Columbia University Press, 1981.

Berman, William C. *The Politics of Civil Rights in the Truman Administration*. Columbus: Ohio State University Press, 1970.

Bernard, William D. *Dixiecrats and Democrats: Alabama Politics 1942–1950*. University: University of Alabama Press, 1974.

Bernstein, Barton J., ed. *Politics and Policies of the Truman Administration*. Chicago: Quadrangle Books, 1970.

Binkowski, Don. *Leo Krzycki and the Detroit Left*. Bloomington, Ind.: Exlibris, 2002.

Black, Allida M. *Casting Her Own Shadow: Eleanor Roosevelt and the Shaping of Postwar Liberalism*. New York: Columbia University Press, 1996.

Bliven, Bruce. *Five Million Words Later: An Autobiography*. New York: John Day, 1970.

Blum, John M., ed. *The Price of Vision: The Diary of Henry A. Wallace, 1942–1946*. Boston: Houghton Mifflin, 1973.

Bohlen, Charles E. *Witness to History, 1929–1969*. New York: W. W. Norton, 1973.

Bosworth, Patricia. *Anything Your Little Heart Desires: An American Family Story*. New York: Simon and Schuster, 1997.

Boylan, James R. *The New Deal Coalition and the Election of 1946*. New York: Garland Publishing, 1981.

Brock, Clifton. *Americans for Democratic Action: Its Role In National Politics*. Washington: Public Affairs Press, 1962.

Brogi, Alessandro. *A Question of Self-Esteem: The United States and the Cold War Choices in France and Italy, 1944–1958*. Westport, Conn.: Praeger, 2002.

Brophy, John. *A Miner's Life*. Madison: University of Wisconsin Press, 1964.

Brownstein, Ronald. *The Power and the Glitter: The Hollywood-Washington Connection*. New York: Pantheon Books, 1990.

Budenz, Louis Francis. *Men without Faces: The Communist Conspiracy in the U.S.A.* New York: Harper, 1950.

Byrnes, James F. *Speaking Frankly*. New York: Harper, 1947.

Camp, Helen C. *Iron in Her Soul: Elizabeth Gurley Flynn and the American Left*. Pullman: Washington State University Press, 1995.

Caplan, Marvin. *Farther Along: A Civil Rights Memoir*. Baton Rouge: Louisiana State University Press, 1999.

Carew, Anthony. *Labour under the Marshall Plan: The Politics of Productivity and the Marketing of Management Science*. Detroit: Wayne State University Press, 1987.

Carlyle, Margaret, ed. *Documents on International Affairs, 1947–1948*. New York: Oxford University Press, 1952.

Carruthers, Susan L. *Cold War Captives: Imprisonment, Escape, and Brainwashing*. Berkeley: University of California Press, 2009.

Caute, David. *The Fellow-Travellers: Intellectual Friends of Communism*. Rev. ed. New Haven: Yale University Press, 1988.

Ceplair, Larry, and Steven Englund. *The Inquisition in Hollywood: Politics in the Film Community, 1930–1960*. Garden City, N.Y.: Anchor Press/Doubleday, 1980.

Charney, George. *A Long Journey*. Chicago: Quadrangle Books, 1968.

Clayton, Obie, Jr., ed. *An American Dilemma Revisited: Race Relations in a Changing World*. New York: Russell Sage Foundation, 1996.

Cleater, Philip E., ed. *Letters from Baltimore: The Mencken-Cleater Correspondence*. East Brunswick, N.J.: Associated University Presses, 1982.

Clifford, Clark, with Richard Holbrooke. *Counsel to the President: A Memoir*. New York: Random House, 1991.

Cobb, James C., and Michael V. Namorato, eds. *The New Deal and the South*. Jackson: University of Mississippi Press, 1984.

Cochran, Bert. *Labor and Communism: The Conflict That Shaped American Unions*. Princeton: Princeton University Press, 1977.

Cohen, Michael J. *Truman and Israel*. Berkeley: University of California Press, 1990.

Cohen, Robert. *When the Old Left Was Young: Student Radicals and America's First Mass Student Movement, 1929–1941*. New York: Oxford University Press, 1993.

Congress of Industrial Organizations. *Final Proceedings of the Ninth Constitutional Convention of the Congress of Industrial Organizations*. Washington: Congress of Industrial Organizations, 1947.

Cooke, Alistair. *Six Men*. New York: Alfred. A. Knopf, 1977.

Cormier, Frank, and William Eaton. *Reuther*. Englewood Cliffs, N.J.: Prentice-Hall, 1970.

Cottrell, Robert C. *Izzy: A Biography of I. F. Stone*. New Brunswick: Rutgers University Press, 1992.

Creswell, Michael. *A Question of Balance: How France and the United States Created Cold War Europe*. Cambridge: Harvard University Press, 2006.

Crossman, Richard, ed. *The God That Failed*. New York: Harper and Row, 1950.

Culver, John C., and John Hyde. *American Dreamer: The Life and Times of Henry A. Wallace*. New York: W. W. Norton, 2000.

Dalfiume, Richard M. *Desegregation of the U.S. Armed Forces: Fighting on Two Fronts, 1939–1953*. Columbia: University of Missouri Press, 1969.

Dallek, Robert. *The Lost Peace: Leadership in a Time of Horror and Hope, 1945–1953*. New York: Harper Collins, 2010.

Daniels, Jonathan. *The Man of Independence*. Philadelphia: J. B. Lippincott, 1950.

De Caux, Len. *Labor Radical: From the Wobblies to CIO*. Boston: Beacon Press, 1970.

Delton, Jennifer A. *Making Minnesota Liberal: Civil Rights and the Transformation of the Democratic Party*. Minneapolis: University of Minnesota Press, 2002.

Denning, Michael. *The Cultural Front: The Laboring of American Culture in the Twentieth Century*. London: Verso, 1996.

Dennis, Eugene. *America at the Crossroads: Postwar Problems and Communist Policy*. New York: New Century Publishers, 1945.

———. *The Third Party and the 1948 Elections*. New York: New Century Publishers, 1948.

———. *What America Faces*. New York: New Century Publishers, 1946.

Dennis, Peggy. *The Autobiography of an American Communist: A Personal View of a Political Life*. Westport, Conn.: Lawrence Hill, 1977.

Diggins, John Patrick. *The Rise and Fall of the American Left*. New York: W. W. Norton, 1992.

———. *Ronald Reagan: Fate, Freedom, and the Making of History*. New York: W. W. Norton, 2007.

Divine, Robert A. *Foreign Policy and U.S. Presidential Elections, 1940–1948*. New York: New Viewpoints, 1974.

Djilas, Milovan. *Conversations with Stalin*. Translated by Michael B. Petrovich. New York: Harcourt, Brace and World, 1962.

Dodd, Bella V. *School of Darkness*. New York: P. J. Kenedy, 1954.

Donaldson, Gary A. *Truman Defeats Dewey*. Lexington: University Press of Kentucky, 1999.

Donovan, Robert J. *Conflict and Crisis: The Presidency of Harry S Truman, 1945–1948*. New York: W. W. Norton, 1977.

Draper, Alan. *Conflict of Interests: Organized Labor and the Civil Rights Movement in the South, 1954–1968*. Ithaca: ILR Press, 1994.

Draper, Theodore. *A Present of Things Past: Selected Essays*. New York: Hill and Wang, 1990.

Duberman, Martin Bauml. *Paul Robeson: A Biography*. New York: Alfred A. Knopf, 1988.

Dubin, Michael J., ed., *United States Congressional Elections, 1788–1997: The Official Results*. Jefferson, N.C.: McFarland, 1998.

Dubofsky, Melvyn. *The State and Labor in Modern America*. Chapel Hill: University of North Carolina Press, 1994.

Dunne, Philip. *Take Two: A Life in Movies and Politics*. Rev. ed. New York: Limelight Editions, 1992.

Durr, Virginia Foster. *Outside the Magic Circle: The Autobiography of Virginia Foster Durr*. Edited by Hollinger F. Barnard. University: University of Alabama Press, 1986.

Egerton, John. *Speak Now against the Day: The Generation before the Civil Rights Movement in the South*. New York: Alfred A. Knopf, 1994.

Ehrman, John. *The Rise of Neoconservatism: Intellectuals and Foreign Affairs, 1945–1994*. New Haven: Yale University Press, 1995.

Eisenberg, Carolyn. *Drawing the Line: The American Decision to Divide Germany, 1944–1949*. New York: Cambridge University Press, 1996.

Ekirch, Arthur A., Jr. *The Decline of American Liberalism*. New York: Longmans, Green, 1955.

Ellis, Richard J. *The Dark Side of the Left: Illiberal Egalitarianism in America*. Lawrence: University Press of Kansas, 1998.

Ernst, Morris L., and David Loth. *The People Know Best: The Ballots vs. the Polls*. Washington: Public Affairs Press, 1949.

Esposito, Chiarella. *America's Feeble Weapon: Funding the Marshall Plan in France and Italy, 1948–1950*. Westport, Conn.: Greenwood Press, 1994.

Fairclough, Adam. *Race and Democracy: The Civil Rights Struggle in Louisiana, 1915–1972*. Athens: University of Georgia Press, 1995.

Fariello, Griffin, ed. *Red Scare: Memories of the American Inquisition; An Oral History*. New York: W. W. Norton, 1995.

Fast, Howard. *The Naked God: The Writer and the Communist Party*. New York: Praeger, 1957.

Fecher, Charles A., ed. *The Diary of H. L. Mencken*. New York: Alfred A. Knopf, 1989.

Fenton, John M. *In Your Opinion . . . .* Boston: Little, Brown, 1960.

Ferrell, Robert H. *Choosing Truman: The 1944 Democratic Convention*. Columbia: University of Missouri Press, 1994.

———. *Harry S. Truman: A Life*. Columbia: University of Missouri Press, 1994.

———, ed. *Truman in the White House: The Dairy of Eben Ayers*. Columbia: University of Missouri Press, 1991.

Field, Bruce E. *Harvest of Dissent: The National Farmers Union and the Early Cold War*. Lawrence: University Press of Kansas, 1998.

Field, Frederick Vanderbilt. *From Right to Left: An Autobiography*. Westport, Conn.: Lawrence Hill, 1983.

Filippelli, Ronald L., and Mark D. McColloch. *Cold War in the Working Class: The Rise and Decline of the United Electrical Workers*. Albany: State University of New York Press, 1995.

Flynn, Edward J. *You're the Boss*. New York: Viking Press, 1947.

Forrestal, James. *The Forrestal Diaries*. Edited by Walter Millis with Eugene S. Duffield. New York: Viking Press, 1951.

Foster, James Caldwell. *The Union Politic: The CIO Political Action Committee*. Columbia: University of Missouri Press, 1975.

Foster, William Z. *Problems of Organized Labor Today*. New York: New Century Publishers, 1946.

Fraser, Steven. *Labor Will Rule: Sidney Hillman and the Rise of American Labor*. New York: Free Press, 1991.

Freeland, Richard M. *The Truman Doctrine and the Origins of McCarthyism*. New York: Alfred A. Knopf, 1975.

Freeman, Joshua B. *In Transit: The Transport Workers Union in New York City, 1933-1966*. New York: Oxford University Press, 1989.

Friedman, Mickey. *A Red Family: Junius, Gladys, and Barbara Scales*. Urbana: University of Illinois Press, 2009.

Gaddis, John Lewis. *The Cold War: A New History*. New York: Penguin, 2005.

———. *The United States and the Origins of the Cold War, 1941-1947*. New York: Columbia University Press, 1972.

———. *We Now Know: Rethinking Cold War History*. New York: Oxford University Press, 1997.

Gall, Gilbert J. *Pursuing Justice: Lee Pressman, the New Deal, and the CIO*. Albany: State University of New York Press, 1999.

Gallup, George H., ed. *The Gallup Poll: Public Opinion, 1935-1971*, 4 vols. New York: Random House, 1972.

Gardner, Michael R. *Harry Truman and Civil Rights*. Carbondale: Southern Illinois University Press, 2002.

Garson, Robert A. *The Democratic Party and the Politics of Sectionalism, 1941-1948*. Baton Rouge: Louisiana State University Press, 1974.

Gates, John. *The Story of an American Communist*. New York: Thomas Nelson, 1958.

Gieske, Millard L. *Minnesota Farmer-Laborism: The Third Party Alternative*. Minneapolis: University of Minnesota Press, 1979.

Gillon, Steven M. *The Democrats' Dilemma: Walter F. Mondale and the Liberal Legacy*. New York: Columbia University Press, 1992.

———. *Politics and Vision: The ADA and American Liberalism, 1947-1985*. New York: Oxford University Press, 1987.

Glazer, Nathan. *The Social Basis of American Communism*. New York: Harcourt, Brace and World, 1961.

Gleason, Abbott. *Totalitarianism: The Inner History of the Cold War*. New York: Oxford University Press, 1995.

Goldman, Eric. *Rendezvous with Destiny: A History of Modern American Reform*. New York: Alfred A. Knopf, 1966.

Goode, Bill. *Infighting in the UAW: The 1946 Election and the Ascendancy of Walter Reuther*. Westport, Conn.: Greenwood Press, 1994.

Goodman, Walter. *The Committee: The Extraordinary Career of the House Committee on Un-American Activities*. New York: Farrar, Straus and Giroux, 1968.

Gornick, Vivian. *The Romance of American Communism*. New York: Basic Books, 1977.

Goulden, Joseph C. *The Best Years, 1945–1950*. New York: Atheneum, 1976.

———, ed. *Mencken's Last Campaign: H. L. Mencken on the 1948 Election*. Washington: New Republic Book Company, 1976.

Grafton, Carl, and Anne Permaloff. *Big Mules and Branchheads: James E. Folsom and Political Power in Alabama*. Athens: University of Georgia Press, 1985.

Griffith, Robert, and Athan Theoharis, eds. *The Specter: Original Essays on the Cold War and the Origins of McCarthyism*. New York: New Viewpoints, 1974.

Griffith, Thomas. *Harry and Teddy: The Turbulent Friendship of Press Lord Henry R. Luce and His Favorite Reporter, Theodore H. White*. New York: Random House, 1995.

Gullan, Harold I. *The Upset That Wasn't: Harry S. Truman and the Crucial Election of 1948*. Chicago: Ivan R. Dee, 1998.

Hahn, Werner G. *Postwar Soviet Politics: The Fall of Zhdanov and the Defeat of Moderation, 1946–1953*. Ithaca: Cornell University Press, 1982.

Halpern, Martin. *UAW Politics in the Cold War Era*. Albany: State University of New York Press, 1988.

Halpern, Rick. *Down on the Killing Floor: Black and White Workers in Chicago's Packinghouses, 1904–1954*. Urbana: University of Illinois Press, 1997.

Hamby, Alonzo L. *Beyond the New Deal: Harry S. Truman and American Liberalism*. New York: Columbia University Press, 1973.

———. *Man of the People: A Life of Harry S. Truman*. New York: Oxford University Press, 1995.

Hammond, Thomas T., ed. *The Anatomy of Communist Takeovers*. New Haven: Yale University Press, 1975.

———, ed. *Witnesses to the Origins of the Cold War*. Seattle: University of Washington Press, 1982.

Harbutt, Fraser J. *The Iron Curtain: Churchill, America, and the Origins of the Cold War*. New York: Oxford University Press, 1986.

Haslam, Jonathan. *Russia's Cold War: From the October Revolution to the Fall of the Wall*. New Haven: Yale University Press, 2011.

Haynes, John Earl. *Dubious Alliance: The Making of Minnesota's DFL Party*. Minneapolis: University of Minnesota Press, 1984.

———. *Red Scare or Red Menace? American Communism and Anticommunism in the Cold War Era*. Chicago: Ivan R. Dee, 1996.

Haynes, John Earl, and Harvey Klehr. *Early Cold War Spies: The Espionage Trials That Shaped American Politics*. New York: Cambridge University Press, 2006.

———. *Venona: Decoding Soviet Espionage in America*. New Haven: Yale University Press, 1999.

Haynes, John Earl, Harvey Klehr, and Alexander Vassiliev. *Spies: The Rise and Fall of the KGB in America*. New Haven: Yale University Press, 2009.

Healey, Dorothy Ray, and Maurice Isserman. *California Red: A Life in the American Communist Party*. Urbana: University of Illinois Press, 1993.

Heard, Alexander, and Donald S. Strong. *Southern Primaries and Elections*. University: University of Alabama Press, 1950.

Hitchcock, William I. *France Restored: Cold War Diplomacy and the Quest for Leadership in Europe, 1944–1954*. Chapel Hill: University of North Carolina Press, 1998.

Hofstadter, Richard. *The Paranoid Style in American Politics and Other Essays*. New York: Alfred A. Knopf, 1965.

Hogan, Michael J. *The Marshall Plan: America, Britain, and the Reconstruction of Western Europe, 1947–1952*. New York: Cambridge University Press, 1987.

Hollander, Paul. *Political Pilgrims: Travels of Western Intellectuals to the Soviet Union, China, and Cuba*. New York: Oxford University Press, 1981.

———. *The Survival of the Adversary Culture: Social Criticism and Political Escapism in American Society*. New Brunswick, N.J.: Transaction Publishers, 1988.

Honey, Michael K. *Southern Labor and Black Civil Rights: Organizing Memphis Workers*. Urbana: University of Illinois Press, 1993.

Hoopes, Townsend, and Douglas Brinkley. *Driven Patriot: The Life and Times of James Forrestal*. New York: Alfred A. Knopf, 1992.

Horne, Gerald. *Black and Red: W. E. B. Du Bois and the Afro-American Response to the Cold War, 1944–1962*. Albany: State University of New York Press, 1986.

———. *Communist Front? The Civil Rights Congress, 1946–1956*. Rutherford, N.J.: Fairleigh Dickinson University Press, 1988.

Horowitz, Roger. *"Negro and White, Unite and Fight!": A Social History of Industrial Unionism in Meatpacking, 1930–1990*. Urbana: University of Illinois Press, 1997.

Howe, Irving, and B. J. Widick. *The U.A.W. and Walter Reuther*. New York: Random House, 1949.

Howe, Irving, and Lewis Coser. *The American Communist Party: A Critical History*. Rev. ed. New York: Praeger, 1962.

Hughes, H. Stuart. *Gentleman Rebel: The Memoirs of H. Stuart Hughes*. New York: Ticknor and Fields, 1990.

Huthmacher, J. Joseph. *Senator Robert F. Wagner and the Rise of Urban Liberalism*. New York: Atheneum Books, 1968.

Isserman, Maurice. *If I Had a Hammer . . . The Death of the Old Left and the Birth of the New*. New York: Basic Books, 1987.

———. *Which Side Were You On? The American Communist Party during the Second World War*. Middletown, Conn.: Wesleyan University Press, 1982.

Jackson, Walter. *Gunnar Myrdal and America's Conscience: Social Engineering and Racial Liberalism, 1938–1987*. Chapel Hill: University of North Carolina Press, 1990.

Jacobs, Paul. *Is Curly Jewish? A Political Self-Portrait Illuminating Three Turbulent Decades of Social Revolt, 1935–1965*. New York: Atheneum Books, 1965.

Jaffe, Philip J. *The Rise and Fall of American Communism*. New York: Horizon Press, 1975.

Jenkins, Philip. *Cold War at Home: The Red Scare in Pennsylvania, 1945–1960*. Chapel Hill: University of North Carolina Press, 1999.

Jensen, Vernon H. *Nonferrous Metals Industry Unionism, 1932–1954: A Story of Leadership Controversy*. Ithaca: Cornell University Press, 1954.

Johanningsmeier, Edward P. *Forging American Communism: The Life of William Z. Foster*. Princeton: Princeton University Press, 1994.

Johnpoll, Bernard K. *Pacifist's Progress: Norman Thomas and the Decline of American Socialism*. Chicago: Quadrangle Books, 1970.

Judis, John. *Grand Illusion: Critics and Champions of the American Century*. New York: Farrar, Straus and Giroux, 1992.

Judt, Tony. *Postwar: A History of Europe since 1945*. New York: Penguin, 2005.

Kampelman, Max. *The Communist Party vs. the CIO: A Study in Power Politics*. New York: Praeger, 1957.

Kaplan, Karel. *The Short March: The Communist Takeover in Czechoslovakia, 1945–1948*. New York: St. Martin's Press, 1987.

Karabell, Zachary. *The Last Campaign: How Harry Truman Won the 1948 Election*. New York: Alfred A. Knopf, 2000.

Kazin, Michael. *American Dreamers: How the Left Changed a Nation*. New York: Alfred A. Knopf, 2011.

———. *The Populist Persuasion: An American History*. New York: Basic Books, 1995.

Keeran, Roger. *The Communist Party and the Auto Workers Unions*. Bloomington: University of Indiana Press, 1980.

Kelley, Robin D. G. *Hammer and Hoe: Alabama Communists during the Great Depression*. Chapel Hill: University of North Carolina Press, 1990.

Kempton, Murray. *Part of Our Time: Some Monuments and Ruins of the Thirties*. New York: Dell Publishing, 1955.

———. *Rebellions, Perversities, and Main Events*. New York: Times Books, 1994.

Kennan, George F. *American Diplomacy, 1900–1950*. Chicago: University of Chicago Press, 1951.

Kessner, Thomas. *Fiorello H. La Guardia and the Making of Modern New York*. New York: Penguin, 1989.

Key, V. O. *Southern Politics in State and Nation*. New York: Alfred A. Knopf, 1949.

Kimmage, Michael. *The Conservative Turn: Lionel Trilling, Whittaker Chambers, and the Lessons of Anti-Communism*. Cambridge: Harvard University Press, 2009.

Kirkendall, Richard S., ed. *The Harry S. Truman Encyclopedia*. Boston: G. K. Hall, 1989.

Klehr, Harvey. *Communist Cadre: The Social Background of the American Communist Party Elite*. Stanford, Calif.: Hoover Institution Press, 1978.

———. *The Heyday of American Communism: The Depression Decade*. New York: Basic Books, 1984.

Klehr, Harvey, and John Earl Haynes. *The American Communist Movement: Storming Heaven Itself*. New York: Twayne Publishers, 1992.

Klehr, Harvey, John Earl Haynes, and Kyrill M. Anderson. *The Soviet World of American Communism*. New Haven: Yale University Press, 1998.

Klehr, Harvey, John Earl Haynes, and Fridrikh Igorevich Firsov. *The Secret World of American Communism*. New Haven: Yale University Press, 1995.

Kleinman, Mark L. *A World of Hope, a World of Fear: Henry A. Wallace, Reinhold Niebuhr, and American Liberalism*. Columbus: Ohio State University Press, 2000.

Kofsky, Frank. *Harry S. Truman and the War Scare of 1948: A Successful Campaign to Deceive the Nation.* New York: St. Martin's Press, 1993.

Kolko, Gabriel, and Joyce Kolko. *The Limits of Power: The World and the United States Foreign Policy, 1945–1954.* New York: Harper and Row, 1972.

Korbel, Josef. *The Communist Subversion of Czechoslovakia, 1938–1948.* Princeton: Princeton University Press, 1959.

Korstad, Robert. *Civil Rights Unionism: Tobacco Workers and the Struggle for Democracy in the Mid-Twentieth-Century South.* Chapel Hill: University of North Carolina Press, 2003.

Kostyrchenko, Gennadi. *Out of the Red Shadows: Anti-Semitism in Stalin's Russia.* Amherst, N.Y.: Prometheus Books, 1995.

Kovrig, Bennett. *Of Walls and Bridges: The United States and Eastern Europe.* New York: New York University Press, 1991.

Kraditor, Aileen S. *"Jimmy Higgins": The Mental World of the American Rank-and-File Communist, 1930–1958.* New York: Greenwood Press, 1988.

Krock, Arthur. *Memoirs: Sixty Years on the Firing Line.* New York: Funk and Wagnalls, 1968.

Kurth, Peter. *American Cassandra: The Life of Dorothy Thompson.* Boston: Little, Brown, 1990.

Kutulas, Judy. *The Long War: The Intellectual People's Front and Anti-Stalinism, 1930–1940.* Durham: Duke University Press, 1995.

Lacey, Michael J., ed. *The Truman Presidency.* New York: Cambridge University Press, 1989.

Ladd, Everett Carll, Jr. *Negro Political Leadership in the South.* Ithaca: Cornell University Press, 1966.

Lader, Lawrence. *Power on the Left: American Radical Movements since 1946.* New York: W. W. Norton, 1979.

LaFeber, Walter. *America, Russia, and the Cold War, 1945–2006.* 10th ed. New York: McGraw-Hill, 2008.

LaGumina, Salvatore J. *Vito Marcantonio: The People's Politician.* Dubuque, Iowa: Kendall/Hunt Publishing, 1969.

Lakoff, Sanford. *Max Lerner: Pilgrim in the Promised Land.* Chicago: University of Chicago Press, 1998.

Lannon, Albert Vetere. *Second String Red: The Life of Al Lannon, American Communist.* Lanham, Md.: Lexington Books, 1999.

Lasch, Christopher. *The Agony of the American Left.* New York: Alfred A. Knopf, 1969.

Lash, Joseph P. *Eleanor: The Years Alone.* New York: W. W. Norton, 1972.

Latham, Earl. *The Communist Controversy in Washington: From the New Deal to McCarthy.* Cambridge: Harvard University Press, 1966.

Lawson, Steven. *Black Ballots: Voting Rights in the South, 1944–1969.* New York: Columbia University Press, 1976.

Leab, Daniel J. *I Was a Communist for the FBI: The Unhappy Life and Times of Matt Cvetic.* University Park: Pennsylvania State University Press, 2000.

Lee, R. Alton. *Truman and Taft-Hartley: A Question of Mandate.* Lexington: University of Kentucky Press, 1966.

Leffler, Melvyn P. *For the Soul of Mankind: The United States, the Soviet Union, and the Cold War*. New York: Hill and Wang, 2007.

———. *A Preponderance of Power: National Security, the Truman Administration, and the Cold War*. Stanford: Stanford University Press, 1992.

———. *The Struggle for Germany and the Origins of the Cold War*. Occasional Paper No. 16. Washington: German Historical Institute, 1996.

Leffler, Melvyn P., and Odd Arne Westad. *Origins*. Vol. 1 of *The Cambridge History of the Cold War*. New York: Cambridge University Press, 2010.

Lens, Sidney. *Left, Right, and Center: Conflicting Forces in America*. Hinsdale, Ill.: Henry Regnery, 1949.

———. *Unrepentant Radical: An American Activist's Account of Five Turbulent Decades*. Boston: Beacon Press, 1980.

Lerner, Max. *Actions and Passions: Notes on the Multiple Revolution of Our Time*. New York: Simon and Schuster, 1949.

———. *Wounded Titans: American Presidents and the Perils of Power*. New York: Arcade Publishing, 1996.

Leuchtenburg, William E. *In the Shadow of FDR: From Harry Truman to Barack Obama*. 4th ed. Ithaca: Cornell University Press, 2009.

Levenstein, Harvey A. *Communism, Anti-Communism, and the CIO*. Westport, Conn.: Greenwood Press, 1981.

Levering, Ralph, Vladimir O. Pechatnov, Verena Botzenhart-Viehe, and C. Earl Edmondson. *Debating the Origins of the Cold War*. Lanham, Md.: Rowman and Littlefield, 2002.

Lewi, Guenter. *The Cause That Failed: Communism in American Political Life*. New York: Oxford University Press, 1990.

Lewis, George. *The White South and the Red Menace: Segregationists, Anticommunism, and Massive Resistance, 1945–1965*. Gainesville: University Press of Florida, 2004.

Lichtenstein, Nelson. *Labor's War at Home: The CIO in World War II*. New York: Cambridge University Press, 1982.

———. *The Most Dangerous Man in Detroit: Walter Reuther and the Fate of American Labor*. New York: Basic Books, 1995.

Lieberman, Robbie. *"My Song Is My Weapon": People's Songs, American Communism, and the Politics of Culture, 1930–1950*. Urbana: University of Illinois Press, 1989.

Liebowich, Louis. *The Press and the Origins of the Cold War, 1944–1947*. New York: Praeger, 1988.

Lipsitz, George. *Rainbow at Midnight: Labor and Culture in the 1940s*. Urbana: University of Illinois Press, 1994.

Lord, Russell. *The Wallaces of Iowa*. Boston: Houghton Mifflin, 1947.

Lubell, Samuel. *The Future of American Politics*. Garden City, N.Y.: Doubleday, 1951.

———. *The Future of American Politics*, Rev. ed. Garden City, N.Y.: Doubleday, 1956.

———. *White and Black: Test of a Nation*. New York: Harper and Row, 1964.

Lyons, Eugene. *The Red Decade*. New York: Bobbs-Merrill, 1941.

Lyons, Paul. *Philadelphia Communists, 1936–1956*. Philadelphia: Temple University Press, 1982.

Macdonald, Dwight. *Henry A. Wallace: The Man and the Myth*. New York: Vanguard Press, 1948.

MacDougall, Curtis D. *Gideon's Army* 3 vols. New York: Marzani and Munsell, 1965.

MacKay, Kenneth C. *The Progressive Movement of 1924*. New York: Columbia University Press, 1947.

MacShane, Denis. *International Labour and the Origins of the Cold War*. New York: Oxford University Press, 1992.

Maddox, Robert James. *From War to Cold War: The Education of Harry Truman*. Boulder, Colo.: Westview Press, 1988.

Manchester, William. *Disturber of the Peace: The Life of H. L. Mencken*. Amherst: University of Massachusetts Press, 1986.

Manfull, Helen, ed. *Additional Dialogue: Letters of Dalton Trumbo, 1942–1962*. New York: M. Evans, 1970.

Mann, Robert. *The Walls of Jericho: Lyndon Johnson, Hubert Humphrey, Richard Russell, and the Civil Rights Struggle*. New York: Harcourt, Brace, 1996.

Markowitz, Norman D. *The Rise and Fall of the People's Century: Henry A. Wallace and American Liberalism, 1941–1948*. New York: Free Press, 1973.

Marshall, F. Ray. *Labor in the South*. Cambridge: Harvard University Press, 1967.

Martin, John Fredrick. *Civil Rights and the Crisis of Liberalism: The Democratic Party, 1945–1976*. Boulder, Colo.: Westview Press, 1979.

Marton, Kati. *The Polk Conspiracy: Murder and Cover-up in the Case of CBS News Correspondent George Polk*. New York: Farrar, Straus and Giroux, 1990.

Mastny, Vojtech. *The Cold War and Soviet Insecurity: The Stalin Years*. New York: Oxford University Press, 1996.

———. *Russia's Road to the Cold War*. New York: Columbia University Press, 1979.

Matles, James J., and James Higgins. *Them and Us: Struggles of a Rank and File Union*. Englewood Cliffs, N.J.: Prentice-Hall, 1974.

Matthews, Donald R., and James W. Prothro. *Negroes and the New Southern Politics*. New York: Harcourt, Brace and World, 1966.

Mattson, Kevin. *When America Was Great: The Fighting Faith of Liberalism in Postwar America*. New York: Routledge, 2004.

May, Gary. *Un-American Activities: The Trials of William Remington*. New York: Oxford University Press, 1994.

McAuliffe, Mary Sperling. *Crisis on the Left: Cold War Politics and American Liberals, 1947–1954*. Amherst: University of Massachusetts Press, 1978.

McClure, Arthur F. *The Truman Administration and the Problems of Postwar Labor, 1945–1948*. Rutherford, N.J.: Farleigh Dickinson University Press, 1969.

McCoy, Donald R. *The Presidency of Harry S. Truman*. Lawrence: University Press of Kansas, 1984.

McCoy, Donald R., and Richard T. Ruetten. *Quest and Response: Minority Rights and the Truman Administration*. Lawrence: University Press of Kansas, 1973.

McCullough, David. *Truman*. New York: Simon and Schuster, 1992.

McDonald, David J. *Union Man*. New York: E. P. Dutton, 1969.

McDougall, Walter A. *Promised Land, Crusader State: The American Encounter with the World since 1776*. Boston: Houghton Mifflin, 1997.

McGovern, George. *Grassroots: The Autobiography of George McGovern*. New York: Random House, 1977.

McMillen, Neil R. *Dark Journey: Black Mississippians in the Age of Jim Crow*. Urbana: University of Illinois Press, 1989.

McWilliams, Carey. *The Education of Carey McWilliams*. New York: Simon and Schuster, 1978.

Meier, August, and Elliott Rudwick. *CORE: A Study in the Civil Rights Movement, 1942-1968*. New York: Oxford University Press, 1973.

Merrill, Dennis K., ed. *Documentary History of the Truman Presidency*. Vol. 14. Bethesda, Md.: University Publications of America, 1995.

Merry, Robert W. *Taking on the World: Joseph and Stewart Alsop, Guardians of the American Century*. New York: Viking Press, 1996.

Messer, Robert L. *The End of an Alliance: James F. Byrnes, Roosevelt, Truman, and the Origins of the Cold War*. Chapel Hill: University of North Carolina Press, 1982.

Meyer, Frank S. *The Moulding of Communists: The Training of the Communist Cadre*. New York: Harcourt, Brace and Company, 1961.

Meyer, Gerald. *Vito Marcantonio: Radical Politician, 1902-1954*. Albany: State University of New York Press, 1989.

Milkman, Paul. *"PM": A New Deal in Journalism, 1940-1948*. New Brunswick: Rutgers University Press, 1997.

Miller, Merle. *Plain Speaking: An Oral Biography of Harry S. Truman*. New York: G. P. Putnam, 1974.

Miles, Jonathan. *The Dangerous Otto Katz: The Many Lives of a Soviet Spy*. New York: Bloomsbury, 2010.

Milward, Alan. *The Reconstruction of Western Europe, 1945-1951*. Berkeley: University of California Press, 1984.

Minchin, Timothy J. *What Do We Need a Union For? The TWUA in the South, 1945-1955*. Chapel Hill: University of North Carolina Press, 1997.

Miscamble, Wilson D. *From Roosevelt to Truman: Potsdam, Hiroshima, and the Cold War*. New York: Cambridge University Press, 2007.

———. *George F. Kennan and the Making of American Foreign Policy, 1947-1950*. Princeton: Princeton University Press, 1992.

Mitchell, Franklin D. *Harry S. Truman and the News Media: Contentious Relations, Belated Respect*. Columbia: University of Missouri Press, 1998.

Mitford, Jessica. *A Fine Old Conflict*. New York: Alfred A. Knopf, 1977.

Montgomery, Gayle B., and James W. Johnson. *One Step from the White House: The Rise and Fall of Senator William F. Knowland*. Berkeley: University of California Press, 1998.

Moon, Henry Lee. *Balance of Power: The Negro Vote*. Garden City, N.Y.: Doubleday, 1948.

Morgan, Ted. *A Covert Life: Jay Lovestone, Communist, Anti-Communist, and Spymaster*. New York: Random House, 1999.

———. *Reds: McCarthyism in Twentieth-Century America*. New York: Random House, 2003.

Morrison, Dennis. *Henry A. Wallace: Up, Down, and Out in the Democratic Party.* Waterbury, Conn.: Emancipation Press, 1995.

Moscow, Warren. *Politics in the Empire State.* New York: Alfred A. Knopf, 1948.

Moynihan, Daniel Patrick. *Secrecy: The American Experience.* New Haven: Yale University Press, 1998.

Myant, M. R. *Socialism and Democracy in Czechoslovakia, 1945–1948.* New York: Cambridge University Press, 1981.

Naimark, Norman M. *The Russians in Germany: A History of the Soviet Zone of Occupation, 1945–1949.* Cambridge: Harvard University Press, 1995.

Namorato, Michael V. *Rexford G. Tugwell: A Biography.* New York: Praeger, 1988.

Nelson, Bruce, ed. *U.S. Labor Relations, 1945–1989: Accommodation and Conflict.* New York: Garland Publishing, 1990.

Nelson, Steve, James R. Barrett, and Rob Ruck. *Steve Nelson: American Radical.* Pittsburgh: University of Pittsburgh Press, 1981.

Newman, Michael. *Harold Laski: A Political Biography.* Houndmills, Basingstoke (U.K.): Macmillan Press, 1993.

Niebuhr, Reinhold. *The Children of Light and the Children of Darkness.* New York: Charles Scribner's Sons, 1944.

Ninkovich, Frank A. *The Diplomacy of Ideas: U.S. Foreign Policy and Cultural Relations, 1938–1950.* New York: Cambridge University Press, 1981.

Nolan, William A. *Communism versus the Negro.* Chicago: Henry Regnery, 1951.

Nunnelley, William A. *Bull Connor.* Tuscaloosa: University of Alabama Press, 1991.

Nye, Russel B. *Midwestern Progressive Politics: A Historical Study of Its Origins and Development, 1870–1958.* Lansing: Michigan State University Press, 1959.

Olmsted, Kathryn S. *Red Spy Queen: A Biography of Elizabeth Bentley.* Chapel Hill: University of North Carolina Press, 2002.

O'Neill, William L. *American High: The Years of Confidence, 1945–1960.* New York: Free Press, 1986.

———. *A Better World: The Great Schism; Stalinism and the American Intellectuals.* New York: Simon and Schuster, 1982.

Painter, Nell Irvin. *The Narrative of Hosea Hudson: His Life as a Negro Communist in the South.* Cambridge: Harvard University Press, 1979.

Parmet, Herbert S. *The Democrats: The Years after FDR.* New York: Macmillan, 1976.

Paterson, Thomas G. *On Every Front: The Making and Unmaking of the Cold War* Rev. ed. New York: W. W. Norton, 1992.

———, ed. *Cold War Critics: Alternatives to American Foreign Policy in the Truman Years.* Chicago: Quadrangle Books, 1971.

Payne, Charles M. *I've Got the Light of Freedom: The Organizing Tradition and the Mississippi Freedom Struggle.* Berkeley: University of California Press, 1995.

Pederson, Vernon L. *The Communist Party in Maryland, 1919–1957.* Urbana: University of Illinois Press, 2001.

Pells, Richard H. *The Liberal Mind in a Conservative Age: American Intellectuals in the 1940s and 1950s.* New York: Harper and Row, 1985.

Peterson, F. Ross. *Prophet without Honor: Glen H. Taylor and the Fight for American Liberalism.* Lexington: University Press of Kentucky, 1974.

Philbrick, Herbert. *I Led Three Lives*. New York: Harper and Row, 1952.

Phillips, Cabell. *The Truman Presidency: The History of a Triumphant Succession*. New York: Macmillan, 1966.

Pietrusza, David. *1948: Harry Truman's Improbable Victory and the Year That Transformed America*. New York: Union Square Press, 2011.

Pisani, Sallie. *The CIA and the Marshall Plan*. Lawrence: University Press of Kansas, 1991.

Pitre, Merline. *In Struggle against Jim Crow: Lulu B. White and the NAACP, 1900–1957*. College Station: Texas A&M University Press, 1999.

Plotke, David. *Building a Democratic Political Order: Reshaping American Liberalism in the 1930s and 1940s*. New York: Cambridge University Press, 1996.

Plummer, Brenda Gayle. *Rising Wind: Black Americans and U.S. Foreign Policy, 1935–1960*. Chapel Hill: University of North Carolina Press, 1996.

Pollard, Robert A. *Economic Security and the Origins of the Cold War, 1945–1950*. New York: Columbia University Press, 1985.

Porter, Kirk H., and Donald Bruce Johnson, eds. *National Party Platforms, 1840–1956*. Urbana: University of Illinois Press, 1956.

Powers, Richard Gid. *Not without Honor: The History of American Anticommunism*. New York: Free Press, 1995.

Preis, Art. *Labor's Giant Step: Twenty Years of the CIO*. Rev. ed. New York: Pathfinder Press, 1972.

Proceedings of the Second Biennial Convention of the National Union of Marine Cooks and Stewards, CIO, May 5, 6, 7, 8, 9, 1947. San Francisco: National Union of Marine Cooks and Stewards, 1947.

Public Papers of the Presidents of the United States: Harry S. Truman. 9 vols. Washington: Government Printing Office, 1961–66.

Quill, Shirley. *Mike Quill, Himself: A Memoir*. Greenwich, Conn.: Devin-Adair, 1985.

Radosh, Ronald. *Commies: A Journey through the Old Left, the New Left, and the Leftover Left*. San Francisco: Encounter Books, 2001.

———. *Divided They Fell: The Demise of the Democratic Party, 1964–1996*. New York: Free Press, 1996.

Radosh, Ronald, and Allis Radosh. *Red Star over Hollywood: The Film Colony's Long Romance with the Left*. San Francisco: Encounter Books, 2005.

Reagan, Ronald, with Richard G. Hubler. *Where's the Rest of Me? The Autobiography of Ronald Reagan*. New York: Duell, Sloan, and Pearce, 1965.

Record, Wilson. *The Negro and the Communist Party*. Chapel Hill: University of North Carolina Press, 1951.

———. *Race and Radicalism: The NAACP and the Communist Party in Conflict*. Ithaca: Cornell University Press, 1964.

Redding, Jack. *Inside the Democratic Party*. Indianapolis: Bobbs-Merrill, 1958.

Reed, Linda. *Simple Decency and Common Sense: The Southern Conference Movement, 1938–1963*. Bloomington: Indiana University Press, 1991.

Resis, Albert. *Stalin, the Politburo, and the Onset of the Cold War*. Pittsburgh: University of Pittsburgh Center for Russian and Eastern European Studies, 1988.

Reynolds, David, ed. *The Origins of the Cold War in Europe: International Perspectives*. New Haven: Yale University Press, 1994.

Ribuffo, Leo. *The Old Christian Right: The Protestant Far Right from the Great Depression to the Cold War*. Philadelphia: Temple University Press, 1983.

Richmond, Al. *A Long View from the Left: Memoirs of an American Revolutionary*. Boston: Houghton Mifflin, 1973.

Richter, Irving. *Labor's Struggles, 1945–1950: A Participant's View*. New York: Cambridge University Press, 1994.

Rivlin, Gary. *Fire on the Prairie: Chicago's Harold Washington and the Politics of Race*. New York: Henry Holt, 1992.

Ro'i, Yaacov. *Soviet Decision-Making in Practice: The USSR and Israel, 1947–1954*. New Brunswick, N.J.: Transaction Books, 1980.

Roberts, Geoffrey. *Stalin's Wars: From World War to Cold War, 1919–1953*. New Haven: Yale University Press, 2006.

Robertson, David. *Sly and Able: A Political Biography of James F. Byrnes*. New York: W. W. Norton, 1994.

Roediger, David. *The Wages of Whiteness: Race and the Making of the American Working Class*. New York: Verso, 1991.

Romero, Federico. *The United States and the European Trade Union Movement, 1944–1951*. Translated by Harvey Fergusson II. Chapel Hill: University of North Carolina Press, 1992.

Roper, Elmo. *You and Your Leaders: Their Actions and Your Reactions, 1936–1956*. New York: William Morrow, 1957.

Ross, Irwin. *The Loneliest Campaign: The Truman Victory of 1948*. New York: New American Library, 1968.

Rosswurm, Steven. *The FBI and the Catholic Church, 1935–1952*. Amherst: University of Massachusetts Press, 2009.

———, ed. *The CIO's Left-Led Unions*. New Brunswick: Rutgers University Press, 1992.

Runyon, John H., Jennefer Verdini, and Sally S. Runyon, eds. *Source Book of American Presidential Campaign and Election Statistics, 1948–1968*. New York: Frederick Ungar, 1971.

Ryan, James G. *Earl Browder: The Failure of American Communism*. Rev. ed. Tuscaloosa: University of Alabama Press, 2005.

Sakmyster, Thomas. *Red Conspirator: J. Peters and the American Communist Underground*. Urbana: University of Illinois Press, 2011.

Salmond, John. *Miss Lucy of the CIO: The Life and Times of Lucy Randolph Mason, 1882–1959*. Athens: University of Georgia Press, 1988.

———. *A Southern Rebel: The Life and Times of Aubrey Williams 1890–1965*. Chapel Hill: University of North Carolina Press, 1983.

Salter, J. T., ed. *Public Men In and Out of Office*. Chapel Hill: University of North Carolina Press, 1946.

Saposs, David J. *Communism in American Politics*. Washington: Public Affairs Press, 1960.

———. *Communism in American Unions*. New York: McGraw-Hill, 1959.

Savage, Sean J. *Truman and the Democratic Party*. Lexington: University Press of Kentucky, 1997.

Scales, Junius, and Richard Nickson. *Cause at Heart: A Former Communist Remembers*. Athens: University of Georgia Press, 1987.

Schaffer, Alan. *Vito Marcantonio: Radical in Congress*. Syracuse, N.Y.: Syracuse University Press, 1966.

Schapsmeier, Edward L., and Frederick H. Schapsmeier. *Henry A. Wallace of Iowa: The Agrarian Years, 1910–1940*. Ames: Iowa State University Press, 1968.

———. *Prophet in Politics: Henry A. Wallace and the War Years, 1940–1965*. Ames: Iowa State University Press, 1970.

Schatz, Ronald W. *The Electrical Workers: A History of Labor at General Electric and Westinghouse, 1923–60*. Urbana: University of Illinois Press, 1983.

Schlesinger, Arthur M., Jr. *The Age of Roosevelt: The Coming of the New Deal*. Boston: Houghton Mifflin, 1958.

———. *A Life in the Twentieth Century: Innocent Beginnings, 1917–1950*. Boston: Houghton Mifflin, 2000.

———. *The Vital Center: The Politics of Freedom*. Boston: Houghton Mifflin, 1949.

Schmidt, Karl M. *Henry A. Wallace: Quixotic Crusade 1948*. Syracuse, N.Y.: Syracuse University Press, 1960.

Schrecker, Ellen. *Many Are the Crimes: McCarthyism in America*. Boston: Little, Brown, 1998.

Schuman, Frederick L. *Soviet Politics at Home and Abroad*. New York: Alfred A. Knopf, 1946.

Schwartz, Stephen. *From West to East: California and the Making of the American Mind*. New York: Free Press, 1998.

Scobie, Ingrid Winther. *Center Stage: Helen Gahagan Douglas, A Life*. New York: Oxford University Press, 1992.

Seaton, Douglas P. *Catholics and Radicals: The Association of Catholic Trade Unionists and the American Labor Movement from Depression to Cold War*. Lewisburg, Penn.: Bucknell University Press, 1981.

Seidler, Murray B. *Norman Thomas: Respectable Rebel*. Syracuse, N.Y.: Syracuse University Press, 1961.

Selcraig, James Truett. *The Red Scare in the Midwest, 1945–1955: A State and Local Study*. Ann Arbor, Mich.: UMI Research Press, 1982.

Shannon, David A. *The Decline of American Communism: A History of the Communist Party of the United States since 1945*. New York: Harcourt, Brace, 1959.

Sherrill, Robert. *Gothic Politics in the Deep South: Stars of the New Confederacy*. New York: Grossman Publishers, 1968.

Shields, James. *Mr. Progressive: A Biography of Elmer Austin Benson*. Minneapolis: T. S. Denison, 1971.

Shlaim, Avi. *The United States and the Berlin Blockade, 1948–1949*. Berkeley: University of California Press, 1983.

Sims, George E. *The Little Man's Big Friend: James E. Folsom in Alabama Politics, 1946–1958*. Tuscaloosa: University of Alabama Press, 1985.

Sirevåg, Torbjørn. *American Hamlet: Henry A. Wallace and the Presidency, 1935–1948*. Oslo: University of Oslo, 1969.

———. *The Eclipse of the New Deal and the Fall of Vice President Henry Wallace*. New York: Garland Publishing, 1985.

Sirgiovanni, George. *An Undercurrent of Suspicion: Anti-Communism in America during World War II*. New Brunswick, N.J.: Transaction Publishers, 1990.

Smith, Richard Norton. *Thomas E. Dewey and His Times*. New York: Simon and Schuster, 1982.

Smith, Walter Bedell. *My Three Years in Moscow*. Philadelphia: J. B. Lippincott, 1950.

Snetsinger, John. *Truman, the Jewish Vote, and the Creation of Israel*. Stanford, Calif.: Hoover Institution Press, 1974.

Sosna, Morton. *In Search of the Silent South: Southern Liberals and the Race Issue*. New York: Columbia University Press, 1977.

Southern, David W. *Gunnar Myrdal and Black-White Relations: The Use and Abuse of An American Dilemma, 1944–1969*. Baton Rouge: Louisiana State University Press, 1987.

Spalding, Elizabeth Edwards. *The First Cold Warrior: Harry Truman, Containment, and the Remaking of Liberal Internationalism*. Lexington: University Press of Kentucky, 2006.

Spriano, Paolo. *Stalin and the European Communists*. London: Verso, 1985.

Starobin, Joseph R. *American Communism in Crisis: 1943–1957*. Cambridge: Harvard University Press, 1972.

Stedman, Susan W., and Murray S. Stedman. *Discontent at the Polls*. New York: Columbia University Press, 1950.

Steel, Ronald. *Walter Lippmann and the American Century*. Boston: Little, Brown, 1980.

Steinberg, Alfred. *The Man from Missouri: The Life and Times of Harry S. Truman*. New York: G. P. Putnam's Sons, 1962.

Stephan-Norris, Judith, and Maurice Zeitlin. *Left Out: Reds and America's Industrial Unions*. New York: Cambridge University Press, 2003.

———. *Talking Union*. Urbana: University of Illinois Press, 1996.

Sterling, Claire. *The Masaryk Case*. New York: Harper and Row, 1969.

Stevenson, Janet. *The Undiminished Man: A Political Biography of Robert Walker Kenny*. Novato, Calif.: Chandler and Sharp Publishers, 1980.

Stone, I. F. *The Truman Era, 1945–1952: A Nonconformist History of Our Times*. Boston: Little, Brown, 1953.

Stouffer. Samuel A. *Communism, Conformity, and Civil Liberties: A Cross-section of the Nation Speaks Its Mind*. New York: Doubleday, 1955.

Straight, Michael. *After Long Silence*. New York: W. W. Norton, 1983.

Sullivan, Patricia. *Days of Hope: Race and Democracy in the New Deal Era*. Chapel Hill: University of North Carolina Press, 1996.

Sulzberger, C. L. *A Long Row of Candles: Memoirs and Diaries, 1934–1954*. New York: Macmillan, 1969.

Sumner, Gregory D. *Dwight Macdonald and the Politics Circle: The Challenge of Cosmopolitan Democracy.* Ithaca: Cornell University Press, 1996.

Swanberg, W. A. *Norman Thomas: The Last Idealist.* New York: Charles Scribner's Sons, 1976.

Taubman, William. *Stalin's American Policy: From Entente to Détente to Cold War.* New York: W. W. Norton, 1982.

Taylor, Glen H. *How It Was with Me.* Secaucus, N.J.: Lyle Stuart, 1979.

Taylor, Gregory S. *The History of the North Carolina Communist Party.* Columbia: University of South Carolina Press, 2009.

Terkel, Studs. *Hard Times: An Oral History of the Great Depression.* New York: Pantheon Books, 1986.

Theoharis, Athan. *Seeds of Repression: Harry S. Truman and the Origins of McCarthyism.* Chicago: Quadrangle Books, 1971.

Tindall, George Brown, ed. *The Ethnic Southerners.* Baton Rouge: Louisiana State University Press, 1976.

Tuck, Jim. *The Liberal Civil War: Fraternity and Fratricide on the Left.* Lanham, Md.: University Press of America, 1998.

Tugwell, Rexford Guy. *A Chronicle of Jeopardy: 1945–1955.* Chicago: University of Chicago Press, 1955.

Ulam, Adam. *The Communists: The Story of Power and Lost Illusions, 1948–1991.* New York: Charles Scribner's Sons, 1992.

———. *The Rivals: America and Russia since World War II.* New York: Viking Press, 1971.

Ullmann, Walter. *The United States in Prague, 1943–1948.* Boulder, Colo.: Eastern European Quarterly, 1978.

Vandenberg, Arthur H. *The Private Papers of Senator Vandenberg.* Edited by Arthur H. Vandenberg Jr. Boston: Houghton Mifflin, 1952.

Varsori, Antonio, and Elena Calandri, eds. *The Failure of Peace in Europe, 1943–1948.* New York: Palgrave, 2002.

Vaughn, Stephen. *Ronald Reagan in Hollywood: Movies and Politics.* New York: Cambridge University Press, 1994.

Walker, J. Samuel. *Henry A. Wallace and American Foreign Policy.* Westport, Conn.: Greenwood Press, 1976.

Wall, Irwin. *The United States and the Making of Postwar France, 1945–1954.* New York: Cambridge University Press, 1991.

Wallace, Henry A. *Statesmanship and Religion.* New York: Roundtable Press, 1934.

———. *Toward World Peace.* New York: Reynal and Hitchcock, 1948.

Walton, Richard J. *Henry Wallace, Harry Truman, and the Cold War.* New York: Viking Press, 1976.

Warren, Frank A., III. *Liberals and Communism: The "Red Decade" Revisited.* Bloomington: University of Indiana Press, 1966.

———. *Noble Abstractions: American Liberal Intellectuals and World War II.* Columbus: Ohio State University Press, 1999.

Wechsler, James A. *The Age of Suspicion.* New York: Random House, 1953.

Weinstein, Allen. *Perjury: The Hiss-Chambers Case*. Rev. ed. New York: Random House, 1997.

Weinstein, Allen, and Alexander Vassiliev. *The Haunted Wood: Soviet Espionage in America, the Stalin Era*. New York: Random House, 1999.

Weinstein, James. *Ambiguous Legacy: The Left in American Politics*. New York: New Viewpoints, 1975.

———. *The Long Detour: The History and Future of the American Left*. Boulder, Colo.: Westview Press, 2003.

Westad, Odd Arne, Sven Holtsmark, and Iver B. Neumann, eds. *The Soviet Union in Eastern Europe, 1945–1989*. New York: St. Martin's Press, 1994.

Wettig, Gerhard. *Stalin and the Cold War in Europe: The Emergence and Development of East-West Conflict, 1939–1953*. Lanham, Md.: Rowman and Littlefield, 2008.

White, Graham, and John Maze. *Henry A. Wallace: His Search for a New World Order*. Chapel Hill: University of North Carolina Press, 1995.

White, John Kenneth. *Still Seeing Red: How the Cold War Shapes the New American Politics*. Boulder, Colo.: Westview Press, 1997.

Whittemore, L. H. *The Man Who Ran the Subways: The Story of Mike Quill*. New York: Holt, Rinehart, and Winston, 1968.

Wittner, Lawrence S. *Rebels against War: The American Peace Movement, 1933–1983*. Philadelphia: Temple University Press, 1984.

Wohlforth, William Curti. *The Elusive Balance: Power and Perceptions during the Cold War*. Ithaca: Cornell University Press, 1993.

Woods, Jeff. *Black Struggle, Red Scare: Segregation and Anti-Communism in the South, 1948–1968*. Baton Rouge: Louisiana State University Press, 2004.

Woods, Randall B., and Howard Jones. *The Dawning of the Cold War: The United States' Quest for Order*. Athens: University of Georgia Press, 1991.

Wreszin, Michael. *A Rebel in Defense of Tradition: The Life and Politics of Dwight Macdonald*. New York: Basic Books, 1994.

———, ed. *A Moral Temper: The Letters of Dwight Macdonald*. Chicago: Ivan R. Dee, 2001.

Yarnell, Allen. *Democrats and Progressives: The 1948 Presidential Election as a Test of Postwar Liberalism*. Berkeley: University of California Press, 1974.

Ybarra, Michael J. *Washington Gone Crazy: Senator Pat McCarran and the Great American Communist Hunt*. Hanover, N.H.: Steerforth Press, 2004.

Yergin, Daniel. *Shattered Peace: The Origins of the Cold War*. Rev. ed. New York: Penguin, 1990.

Young, John W. *France, the Cold War, and the Western Alliance, 1944–49: French Foreign Policy and Post-war Europe*. New York: St. Martin's Press, 1990.

Young, John Wesley. *Totalitarian Language: Orwell's Newspeak and Its Nazi and Communist Antecedents*. Charlottesville: University Press of Virginia, 1991.

Zeman, Zbynek, with Antonin Klimek. *The Life of Edvard Beneš 1884–1948: Czechoslovakia in Peace and War*. Oxford: Clarendon Press, 1997.

Zieger, Robert H. *The CIO, 1935–1955*. Chapel Hill: University of North Carolina Press, 1995.

————. *For Jobs and Freedom: Race and Labor in America since 1865.* Lexington: University Press of Kentucky, 2007.

————, ed. *Southern Labor in Transition, 1940-1995.* Knoxville: University of Tennessee Press, 1997.

Zeitz, Joshua. *White Ethnic New York: Jews, Catholics, and the Shaping of Postwar Politics.* Chapel Hill: University of North Carolina Press, 2007.

Zubok, Vladislav M. *A Failed Empire: The Soviet Union in the Cold War from Stalin to Gorbachev.* Chapel Hill: University of North Carolina Press, 2007.

Zubok, Vladislav, and Constantine Pleshakov. *Inside the Kremlin's Cold War: From Stalin to Khrushchev.* Cambridge: Harvard University Press, 1996.

ARTICLES

Adams, Mildred. "Wallace: Liberal or Star Gazer." *New York Times Magazine,* September 15, 1946, 18, 50–52.

Adler, Les K., and Thomas G. Paterson. "Red Fascism: The Merger of Nazi Germany and Soviet Russia in the American Image of Totalitarianism, 1930s-1950s." *American Historical Review* 75 (April 1970): 1046–64.

Alsop, Joseph, and Stewart Alsop. "Tragedy of Liberalism." *Life,* May 20, 1946, 68–76.

Altman, Jack. "CIO and Political Discipline." *Labor and Nation,* May-June 1948, 28–29.

Angoff, Charles. "Wallace's Communist-Front Party." *American Mercury,* October 1948, 413–21.

Arnesen, Eric. "Civil Rights and the Cold War at Home: Postwar Activism, Anticommunism, and the Decline of the Left." *American Communist History* 11 (April 2012): 5–44.

————. "Class Matters, Race Matters." *Radical History Review* 60 (Fall 1994): 230–35.

————. "The Final Conflict? On the Scholarship of Civil Rights, the Left, and the Cold War." *American Communist History* 11 (April 2012): 63–80.

————. "No 'Graver Danger': Black Anticommunism, the Communist Party, and the Race Question." *Labor: Studies in Working-Class History of the Americas* 3 (Winter 2006): 13–52.

Baldwin, C. B. "Wallace's Campaign Manager Replies to Gardner Jackson." *Atlantic Monthly,* August 1948, 16–19.

Barkin, Solomon. "Operation Dixie: Two Points of View." *Labor History* 31 (June 1990): 378–85.

Bartley, Numan V. "The Southern Conference and the Shaping of Post–World War II Southern Politics." In *Developing Dixie: Modernization in a Traditional Society,* edited by Winfred B. Moore Jr. et al., 179–97. New York: Greenwood Press, 1988.

Bazelon, David T. "The Faith of Henry Wallace: The Populist Tradition in the Atomic Age." *Commentary,* April 1947, 309–19.

Beichman, Arnold. "The Wallace Case." *National Review,* August 1, 1994, 52–54.

Bendiner, Robert. "Civil Liberties and the Communists: Checking Subversion without Harm to Democratic Rights." *Commentary,* May 1948, 423–31.

Berg, Manfred. "Black Civil Rights and Liberal Anticommunism: The NAACP in the Early Cold War." *Journal of American History* 94 (June 2007): 75–96.

Bernstein, Barton J. "Henry A. Wallace and the Agony of American Liberalism." *Peace and Change* 2 (Fall 1974): 62–67.

Billington, Monroe. "Civil Rights, President Truman and the South." *Journal of Negro History* 58 (April 1973): 127–39.

Bixler, Paul. "Henry Wallace and His Followers." *Antioch Review*, September 1948, 368–76.

———. "Letter to a Dissident Liberal." *Antioch Review*, March 1948, 121–24.

Browder, Earl. "How Stalin Ruined the American Communist Party." *Harper's*, March 1960, 45–51.

Brown, Sarah Hart. "Pensacola Progressive: John Moreno Coe and the Campaign of 1948." *Florida Historical Quarterly* 68 (July 1989): 1–26.

Budenz, Louis. "How the Reds Snatched Away Henry Wallace." *Collier's*, September 18, 1948, 14–15, 76–77.

Carlton, David L. "Paternalism and Southern Textile Labor: A Historiographical Review." In *Race, Class, and Community in Southern Labor History*, edited by Gary M. Fink, and Merl E. Reed, 17–26. Tuscaloosa: University of Alabama Press, 1994.

Carlton, David L., and Peter A. Coclanis. "Another 'Great Migration': From Region to Race in Southern Liberalism, 1938–1945." *Southern Cultures* 3 (Winter 1997): 37–62.

Chamberlin, William Henry. "Ten Fallacies of Fellow-Travelers." *American Mercury*, September 1948, 345–50.

Childs, Marquis. "Year of Doubt." *Yale Review* 38 (September 1948): 1–10.

Cohen, Elliot E. "Citizen's Victory: Defeat of the 'Common Man.'" *Commentary*, December 1948, 511–20.

Coser, Lewis, and Irving Howe. "Authoritarians of the 'Left.'" *Dissent*, Winter 1955, 40–50.

Crichton, Kyle. "Idaho's Hot Potato." *Collier's*, June 30, 1945, 21, 64.

Davies, E. Powell. "I Saw Democracy Murdered in Prague." *Progressive*, April 1948, 9–10.

Delton, Jennifer A. "Rethinking Post–World War II Anticommunism," *Journal of the Historical Society*, 10 (March 2010): 1–41.

Devlin, Kevin. "Finland in 1948: The Lesson of a Crisis." In *The Anatomy of Communist Takeovers*, edited by Thomas T. Hammond, 433–47. New Haven: Yale University Press, 1975.

DiBiago, Anna. "The Cominform as the Soviet Response to the Marshall Plan." In *The Failure of Peace in Europe, 1943–1948*, edited by Antonio Varsori and Elena Calandri, 297–305. New York: Palgrave, 2002.

Divine, Robert A. "The Cold War and the Election of 1948." *Journal of American History* 59 (June 1972): 90–110.

Donaldson, Gary A. "Who Wrote the Clifford Memo? The Origins of Campaign Strategy in the Truman Administration." *Presidential Studies Quarterly* 23 (Fall 1993): 747–54.

Draper, Alan. "The New Southern Labor History Revisited: The Success of the Mine, Mill and Smelter Workers Union in Birmingham, 1934–1938." *Journal of Southern History* 62 (February 1996): 87–108.

Draper, Theodore. "The Life of the Party." *New York Review of Books*, January 13, 1994, 45–51.

———. "The Popular Front Revisited." *New York Review of Books*, May 30, 1985, 44–50.

Du Bois, W. E. B. "From McKinley to Wallace." *Masses and Mainstream*, August 1948, 3–13.

Durr, Kenneth. "When Southern Politics Came North: The Roots of White Working-Class Conservatism in Baltimore, 1946–1964." *Labor History* 37 (Summer 1996): 309–31.

Engel, Benjamin. "Innocent Abroad: 1948 Model." Review of *From the Heart of Europe*, by F. O. Matthiessen. *Commentary*, November 1948, 493–94.

Fahan, R. "What Makes Henry Run? Wallace's Social and Political Role." *New International*, February 1948, 54–57.

Falk, Julius. "American Student Movement: A Survey." *New International*, March 1949, 84–91.

Fast, Howard. "Philadelphia Story." *Uncensored*, August 1948, 1.

Ferrell, Robert H. "The Last Hurrah." *Wilson Quarterly* 12 (Spring 1988): 66–82.

———. Review of *Harry S. Truman and the War Scare of 1948*, by Frank Kofsky. *Journal of American History* 81 (December 1994): 1372.

Feuer, Lewis S. "The Fellow-Travellers." *Survey*, Spring-Summer 1974, 206–10.

Filippov, M. "The Progressive Citizens of America." *New Times*, January 1, 1948, 10–12.

Finlay, Mark R. "Dashed Expectations: The Iowa Progressive Party and the 1948 Election." *Annals of Iowa* 49 (Summer 1988): 329–48.

Flynt, J. Wayne. "The New Deal and Southern Labor." In *The New Deal and the South*, edited by James C. Cobb and Michael V. Namorato, 63–95. Jackson: University Press of Mississippi, 1984.

Foreman, Clark H. "The Decade of Hope." *Phylon*, Summer 1951, 137–50.

Foster, William Z. "Danger Ahead for Organized Labor." *Masses and Mainstream*, July 1948, 24–34.

Frank, Reuven. "1948: Live . . . From Philadelphia . . . It's the National Conventions." *New York Times Magazine*, April 17, 1988, 36–37, 62–65.

Franklin, Julian. "Why I Broke with the Communists." *Harper's*, May 1947, 413–18.

Fredrickson, George M. "Red, Black, and White." *New York Review of Books*, June 8, 1995, 33–39.

Gaddis, John Lewis. "On Moral Equivalency and Cold War History." *Ethics and International Affairs* 10 (1996): 131–48.

———. "The Tragedy of Cold War History." *Diplomatic History* 17 (Winter 1993): 1–16.

Gaiduk, Ilya. "Stalin: Three Approaches to One Phenomenon." *Diplomatic History* 23 (Winter 1999): 115–25.

Gall, Gilbert J. "A Note on Lee Pressman and the FBI." *Labor History* 32 (Fall 1991): 551–61.

Gerstle, Gary. "Race and the Myth of the Liberal Consensus." *Journal of American History* 82 (September 1995): 579–86.

——. "Working-Class Racism: Broaden the Focus." *International Labor and Working-Class History* 44 (Fall 1993): 33–40.

Gervasi, Frank. "Low Man on the Wallace Poll." *Collier's*, May 8, 1948, 16–17, 72–74.

Goldfield, Michael. "The Failure of Operation Dixie: A Critical Turning Point in American Political Development." In *Race, Class, and Community in Southern Labor History*, edited by Gary M. Fink, and Merl E. Reed, 166–89. Tuscaloosa: University of Alabama Press, 1994.

——. "Race and the CIO: The Possibilities for Racial Egalitarianism during the 1930s and 1940s." *International Labor and Working-Class History* 44 (Fall 1993): 1–32.

Goodman, Walter. "Hard to Digest: Is There More Truth About Communism in the *Reader's Digest* or the *Nation*?" *Harper's*, June 1982, 64–68.

Grayson, A. G. "North Carolina and Harry Truman, 1944–1948." *Journal of American Studies* 9, no. 3 (1975): 283–300.

Green, James. "Fighting on Two Fronts: Working Class Militancy in the 1940s." *Radical America* 9 (July-August 1975): 7–47.

Grossman, Atina. "A Question of Silence: The Rape of German Women by Occupation Soldiers." *October* 72 (Spring 1995): 43–63.

Hale, William Harlan. "What Makes Wallace Run?" *Harper's*, March 1948, 241–48.

Hall, Jacqueline Dowd. "The Long Civil Rights Movement and the Political Uses of the Past." *Journal of American History* 91 (March 2005): 1233–63.

Halpern, Rick. "Organized Labour, Black Workers, and the Twentieth-Century South: The Emerging Revision." *Social History* 19 (October 1994): 359–83.

Hamby, Alonzo L. "The Democratic Moment: FDR to LBJ." In *Democrats and the American Idea: A Bicentennial Appraisal*, edited by Peter B. Kovler, 247–84. Washington: Center for National Policy Press, 1992.

——. "Henry A. Wallace, the Liberals, and Soviet-American Relations." *Review of Politics* 30 (April 1968): 153–69.

——. "The Liberals, Truman, and FDR as Symbol and Myth." *Journal of American History* 56 (March 1970): 859–67.

——. "The Vital Center, the Fair Deal, and the Quest for a Liberal Political Economy." *American Historical Review* 77 (June 1972): 653–78.

Hamilton, Mary A. "A Pennsylvania Newspaper Publisher in 'Gideon's Army': J. W. Gitt, Henry Wallace, and the Progressive Party of 1948." *Pennsylvania History* 61 (January 1994): 18–44.

Hartwell, Dickson. "The Abundant Mr. Wallace." *Collier's*, September 20, 1947, 24–25, 111–13.

Haynes, John Earl. "The New History of the Communist Party in State Politics: The Implications for Mainstream Political Theory." *Labor History* 27 (Fall 1986): 549–63.

Heale, M. J. "Red Scare Politics: California's Campaign against Un-American Activities, 1940–1970." *Journal of American Studies* 20 (April 1986): 5–32.

Heaps, David. "Union Participation in Foreign Aid Programs." *Industrial and Labor Relations Review* 9 (October 1955): 100–8.

Hill, Herbert. "The Problem of Race in American Labor History." *Reviews in American History* 24 (June 1996): 189–208.

Holmes, John Haynes. "Midget Minds in the Atomic Age." *Progressive*, September 1948, 21–23.

Holt, Thomas C. "Racism and the Working Class." *International Labor and Working-Class History* 45 (Spring 1994): 86–95.

Honey, Michael. "Operation Dixie: Labor and Civil Rights in the Postwar South." *Mississippi Quarterly* 45 (Fall 1992): 439–52.

———. "The Popular Front in the American South: The View from Memphis." *International Labor and Working-Class History* 30 (Fall 1986): 44–58.

Hook, Sidney. "The Fellow-Traveler: A Study in Psychology." *New York Times Magazine*, April 17, 1949, 9, 20–23.

———. "Why Democracy Is Better." *Commentary*, March 1948, 195–204.

Howe, Irving. "The Sentimental Fellow-Traveling of F. O. Matthiessen." *Partisan Review* 15 (October 1948): 1125–29.

Humphrey, Hubert H. "A Reply to Rex Tugwell." *Progressive*, April 1949, 7–9.

———. "What's Wrong with the Democrats?" *Progressive*, April 1948, 5–8.

Isserman, Maurice. "The 1956 Generation: An Alternative Approach to the History of American Communism." *Radical America* 14 (March-April 1980): 43–51.

Jackson, Gardner. "Henry Wallace: A Divided Mind." *Atlantic Monthly*, August 1948, 27–33.

James, Harold, and Marzenna James. "The Origins of the Cold War: Some New Documents." *Historical Journal* 37 (September 1994): 615–22.

Johnson, Ronald W. "Organized Labor's Postwar Red Scare: The UE in St. Louis." *North Dakota Quarterly* 48 (Winter 1980): 28–39.

Kazin, Michael. "The Agony and Romance of the American Left." *American Historical Review* 100 (December 1995): 1488–1512.

Kelley, John L. "An Insurgent in the Truman Cabinet: Henry A. Wallace's Effort to Redirect Foreign Policy." *Missouri Historical Review* 77 (October 1982): 64–93.

Kellogg, Peter J. "The Americans for Democratic Action and Civil Rights in 1948: Conscience in Politics or Politics in Conscience?" *Midwest Quarterly* 20 (October 1978): 49–63.

———. "Civil Rights Consciousness in the 1940s." *Historian* 42 (November 1979): 18–41.

Kennedy, Randall. "'Keep the Nigger Down!': The Age of Segregation in Mississippi." *Reconstruction* 1 (1991): 115–23.

Kirkendall, Richard S. "Commentary on the Thought of Henry A. Wallace." *Agricultural History* 41 (April 1967): 139–42.

———. "Election of 1948." In *History of American Presidential Elections, 1789–1968*, vol. 4, edited by Arthur M. Schlesinger Jr. and Fred Israel, 3099–3211. New York: Chelsea House, 1971.

Klehr, Harvey, and John Earl Haynes. "The Comintern's Open Secrets." *American Spectator*, December 1992, 34–43.

———. "Communists and the CIO: From the Soviet Archives." *Labor History* 35 (Summer 1994): 442–46.

Knoll, Irwin. "How the Left Was Lost." *Progressive*, October 1994, 46–48.

Korstad, Karl. "Black and White Together: Organizing in the South with the Food, Tobacco, Agricultural and Allied Workers Union (FTA-CIO), 1946-1952." In *The CIO's Left-Led Unions*, edited by Steve Rosswurm, 69–94. New Brunswick: Rutgers University Press, 1992.

Korstad, Robert. "The Possibilities for Racial Egalitarianism: Context Matters." *International Labor and Working-Class History* 44 (Fall 1993): 41–44.

Korstad, Robert, and Nelson Lichtenstein. "Opportunities Found and Lost: Labor, Radicals, and the Early Civil Rights Movement." *Journal of American History* 75 (December 1988): 786–811.

Krátky, Karel. "Czechoslovakia, the Soviet Union, and the Marshall Plan." In *The Soviet Union in Eastern Europe, 1945-1989*, edited by Odd Arne Westad et al., 9–25. New York: St. Martin's Press, 1994.

Lader, Lawrence. "'. . . To Serve the World, Not to Dominate It.'" *American Heritage* 28 (December 1976): 42–51.

Lasch, Christopher. "The Politics of Nostalgia: Losing History in the Mists of Ideology." *Harper's*, November 1984, 65–70.

Lasky, Victor. "Who Runs Wallace?" *Plain Talk*, June 1948, 1–13.

Leeds, Morton H. "The AFL in the 1948 Elections." *Social Research* 17 (June 1950): 207–18.

Leffler, Melvyn P. "Inside Enemy Archives: The Cold War Reopened." *Foreign Affairs* 75 (July-August, 1996): 120–35.

———. "The United States and the Strategic Dimensions of the Marshall Plan." *Diplomatic History* 12 (Summer 1988): 277–306.

Lerner, Max. "The Outlook for a Party Realignment." *Virginia Quarterly Review* 25 (Spring 1949): 179–93.

Leuchtenburg, William E. "An Echo Not a Choice." *Book Week*, March 27, 1966, 5, 12.

Lewis, Walter K. "Wallace Coup in the Bronx." *Plain Talk*, May 1948, 43–45.

"Liberal Anti-Communism Revisited: A Symposium." *Commentary*, September 1967, 312–79.

Lichtenstein, Alex. "Putting Labor's House in Order: The Transport Workers Union and Labor Anti-Communism in Miami during the 1940s." *Labor History* 39 (February 1998): 7–24.

———. "'Scientific Unionism' and the 'Negro Question': Communists and the Transport Workers Union in Miami, 1944-1949." In *Southern Labor in Transition, 1940-1995*, edited by Robert H. Zieger, 58–85. Knoxville: University of Tennessee Press, 1997.

Lichtenstein, Nelson. "The Communist Experience in American Trade Unions." *Industrial Relations* 19 (Spring 1980): 119–39.

Lockhart, Robin Bruce. "Who Killed Jan Masaryk?" *History Today* 42 (September 1992): 5–7.

Lubell, Samuel. "The Future of the Negro Voter in the United States." *Journal of Negro History* 26 (Summer 1957): 407–17.

———. "Who Really Elected Truman." *Saturday Evening Post*, January 22, 1949, 15–17, 54–64.

Lukes, Igor. "The Czech Road to Communism." In *The Establishment of Communist Regimes in Eastern Europe, 1944–1949*, edited by Norman Naimark and Leonid Gibianskii, 243–65. Boulder, Colo.: Westview Press, 1997.

Lundestad, Geir. "Empire by Invitation? The United States and Western Europe, 1945–1952." In *The Cold War in Europe: Era of a Divided Continent*, edited by Charles S. Maier, 143–65. New York: Markus Wiener Publishing, 1991.

Luža, Radomir V. "February 1948 and the Czechoslovak Road to Socialism." *East Central Europe* 4, no. 1 (1977): 44–55.

Lyons, Eugene. "Wallace and the Communists." *American Mercury*, August 1947, 133–40.

Macdonald, Douglas J. "Communist Bloc Expansion in the Early Cold War: Challenging Realism, Refuting Revisionism." *International Security* 20 (Winter 1995–96): 152–88.

Macdonald, Dwight. "The Wallace Campaign: An Autopsy." *Politics* 5 (Summer 1948): 179–88.

Maier, Charles S. "Alliance and Autonomy: European Identity and U.S. Foreign Policy Objectives in the Truman Years." In *The Truman Presidency*, edited by Michael J. Lacey, 273–98. New York: Cambridge University Press, 1989.

Martin, Charles H. "The Rise and Fall of Popular Front Liberalism in the South: The Southern Conference for Human Welfare, 1938–1948." In *Perspectives on the American South*, vol. 3, edited by James C. Cobb and Charles R. Wilson, 119–44. New York: Gordon and Breach Science Publishers, 1985.

———. "Southern Labor Relations in Transition: Gadsden, Alabama, 1930–1943." *Journal of Southern History* 67 (November 1981): 545–68.

Medov, V. "The February Events in Czechoslovakia." *New Times*, March 3, 1948, 3–10.

Meier, August, and John H. Bracey Jr. "The NAACP as a Reform Movement, 1909–1965: 'To Reach the Conscience of America.'" *Journal of Southern History* 59 (February 1993): 3–30.

Miller, James E. "Taking Off the Gloves: The United States and the Italian Elections of 1948." *Diplomatic History* 7 (Winter 1983): 35–55.

Milward, Alan S. "Was the Marshall Plan Necessary?" *Diplomatic History* 13 (Spring 1989): 231–53.

Minor, Steven Merritt. "Revelations, Secrets, Gossip, and Lies: Sifting Warily through the Soviet Archives." *New York Times Book Review*, May 14, 1995, 19–21.

Mitau, G. Theodore. "The Democratic-Farmer-Labor Party Schism of 1948." *Minnesota History* 34 (Spring 1955): 187–94.

Moley, Raymond. "Corn-Fed Proletarian: Henry A. Wallace." In *27 Masters of Politics in a Personal Perspective*. New York: Funk and Wagnalls Company, 1949.

Murphy, George B., Jr. "Henry Wallace." *Crisis*, October 1948, 315–16.

Murray, Philip. "If We Pull Together." *American Magazine*, June 1948, 21, 133–36.

Muste, A. J. "A Vote for Wallace Will Be a Vote for the Communists." *Fellowship*, July 1948, 7–9.

"The Myth of Henry Wallace: Stalin Pulls the Strings." *Tribune*, July 30, 1948, 2.

Narinsky, Mikhail. "Soviet Foreign Policy and the Origins of the Cold War." In *Soviet Foreign Policy, 1917–1991: A Retrospective*, edited by Gabriel Gorodetsky, 105–10. London: Frank Cass, 1994.

Nelson, Bruce. "'CIO Meant One Thing for the Whites and Another Thing for Us': Steelworkers and Civil Rights, 1936–1974." In *Southern Labor in Transition, 1940–1995*, edited by Robert H. Zieger, 113–45. Knoxville: University of Tennessee Press, 1997.

———. "Class, Race, and Democracy in the CIO: The 'New' Labor History Meets the 'Wages of Whiteness.'" *International Review of Social History* 41 (December 1996): 351–74.

———. "The 'Lords of the Docks' Reconsidered: Race Relations among West Coast Longshoremen, 1933–61." In *Waterfront Workers: New Perspectives on Race and Class*, edited by Calvin Winslow, 155–92. Urbana: University of Illinois Press, 1998.

———. "Organized Labor and the Struggle for Black Equality in Mobile during World War II." *Journal of American History* 80 (December 1993): 952–88.

———. "Working-Class Agency and Racial Inequality." *International Review of Social History* 41 (December 1996): 407–20.

Neuberger, Richard L. "Glen Taylor: Crooner on the Left." *American Mercury*, September 1948, 263–72.

———. "Glen Taylor: Left-Wing Minstrel." *Progressive*, April 1948, 18–21.

Norrell, Robert J. "Caste in Steel: Jim Crow Careers in Birmingham, Alabama." *Journal of American History* 73 (December 1986): 669–95.

———. "Labor at the Ballot Box: Alabama Politics from the New Deal to the Dixiecrat Movement." *Journal of Southern History* 57 (May 1991): 201–34.

Oshinsky, David M. "Soldiers for Stalin." *Reviews in American History* 17 (December 1989): 608–12.

Painter, Nell Irvin. "Hosea Hudson and the Progressive Party in Birmingham." In *Perspectives on the American South*, vol. 1, edited by Merle Black and John Shelton Reed, 119–41. New York: Gordon and Breach Science Publishers, 1981.

Parrish, Scott D. "The Turn toward Confrontation: The Soviet Reaction to the Marshall Plan, 1947." Working Paper No. 9 in *Cold War International History Project*. Washington: Woodrow Wilson International Center for Scholars, 1994.

Patterson, James T. "The Enemy Within." *Atlantic Monthly*, October 1998, 106–16.

Patton, Randall L. "The CIO and the Search for a 'Silent South.'" *Maryland Historian* 19 (Fall/Winter 1988): 1–14.

———. "The Popular Front Alternative: Clark H. Foreman and the Southern Conference for Human Welfare, 1938–1948." In *Georgia in Black and White: Explorations in the Race Relations of a Southern State, 1865–1950*, edited by John C. Inscoe, 225–45. Athens: University of Georgia Press, 1994.

Pechatnov, Vladimir O. "'The Allies Are Pressing on You to Break Your Will . . .': Foreign Policy Correspondence between Stalin and Molotov and Other Politburo Members, September 1945– December 1946." Working Paper No. 26 in *Cold War International History Project*. Washington: Woodrow Wilson International Center for Scholars, 1999.

———. "The Big Three After World War II: New Documents on Soviet Thinking about Post War Relations with the United States and Great Britain." Working Paper No. 13 in *Cold War International History Project*. Washington: Woodrow Wilson International Center for Scholars, 1995.

———. "Exercise in Frustration: Soviet Foreign Propaganda in the Early Cold War, 1945–1947." *Cold War History* 1 (January 2001): 1–27.

Peterson, F. Ross. "Fighting the Drive toward War: Glen H. Taylor, the 1948 Progressives, and the Draft." *Pacific Northwest Quarterly* 61 (January 1970): 41–45.

———. "Protest Songs for Peace and Freedom: People's Songs and the 1948 Progressives." *Rocky Mountain Social Sciences Journal* 9 (January 1972): 1–10.

Phillips, Cabell. "That Baffling Personality, Mr. Wallace." *New York Times Magazine*, February 8, 1948, 14, 44–49.

———. "Why They Join the Wallace Crusade." *New York Times Magazine*, May 23, 1948, 12, 24–30.

Phillips, William. "The Politics of Desperation." *Partisan Review* 15 (April 1948): 449–55.

Pittman, Von V., Jr. "'Gideon's Army and the Marshall Plan: An Example of Consensus." *Research Studies* 43 (September 1975): 189–92.

Poggiolini, Ilaria. "Italy." In *The Origins of the Cold War in Europe: International Perspectives*, edited by David Reynolds, 96–120. New Haven: Yale University Press, 1994.

Pons, Silvio. "Stalin, Togliatti, and the Origins of the Cold War in Europe." *Journal of Cold War Studies* 3 (Spring 2001): 3–27.

Pratt, William C. "The Farmers Union and the 1948 Henry Wallace Campaign." *Annals of Iowa* 49 (Summer 1988): 349–70.

———. "Glen H. Taylor: Public Image and Reality." *Pacific Northwest Quarterly* 60 (January 1969): 10–16.

———. "Senator Glen H. Taylor: Questioning American Unilateralism." In *Cold War Critics: Alternatives to American Foreign Policy in the Truman Years*, edited by Thomas G. Paterson, 146–66. Chicago: Quadrangle Books, 1971.

Prickett, James R. "Some Aspects of the Communist Controversy in the CIO." *Science and Society* 33 (Summer-Fall 1969): 299–321.

Raack, R. C. "Stalin Plans His Post-war Germany." *Journal of Contemporary History* 28 (January 1993): 53–73.

Rahv, Philip. "Disillusionment and Partial Answers." *Partisan Review* 15 (May 1948): 519–29.

Reale, Eugenio. "The Founding of the Cominform." In *The Comintern: Historical Highlights*, edited by Milorad M. Drachkovitch and Branko Lazitch, 253–68. New York: Praeger, 1966.

Reuther, Walter P. "Against the Commissar and the Man on Horseback." *Labor and Nation*, May-June 1948, 5–11.

———. "How to Beat the Communists." *Collier's*, February 28, 1948, 11, 44–49.

Rice, Charles Owen. "Confessions of an Anti-Communist." *Labor History* 30 (Summer 1989): 449–62.

Rice-Maximin, Edward. "The United States and the French Left, 1945–1949: The View from the State Department." *Journal of Contemporary History* 19 (October 1984): 729–47.

Ribuffo, Leo. "The Complexity of American Communism." In *Right, Center, Left: Essays in American History.* New Brunswick: Rutgers University Press, 1992.

Roberts, Geoffrey. "Moscow and the Marshall Plan: Politics, Ideology, and the Onset of the Cold War, 1947." *Europe-Asia Studies* 46 (August 1994): 1371–86.

Robertson, Nathan. "Wallace and the New Dealers." *American Mercury,* May 1948, 567–71.

Roche, John P. "Sub Specie Aeternitatis." *National Review,* December 24, 1982, 1620–21.

Rodell, Fred. "Henry Wallace: His Talk and Act Don't Mix." Review of *Toward World Peace,* by Henry A. Wallace. *Progressive,* March 1948, 33.

Ro'i, Yaacov. "Soviet-Israeli Relations, 1947–1954." In *The USSR and the Middle East,* edited by Michael Confino and Shimon Shamir, 123–46. New York: John Wiley, 1973.

Rosen, Jerold A. "Henry A. Wallace and American Liberal Politics, 1941–1948." *Annals of Iowa* 44 (Fall 1978): 462–74.

Schatz, Ronald. "Philip Murray and the Subordination of the Industrial Unions to the United States Government." In *Labor Leaders in America,* edited by Melvyn Dubofsky and Warren Van Tine, 234–57. Urbana: University of Illinois Press, 1987.

Schlesinger, Arthur M., Jr. "The American Communist Party." *Life,* July 29, 1946, 84–96.

——. "Origins of the Cold War." *Foreign Affairs* 46 (October 1967): 22–52.

Scobie, Ingrid Winther. "Jack B. Tenney and the 'Parasitic Menace': Anti-Communist Legislation in California, 1940–1949." *Pacific Historical Review* 43 (May 1974): 188–211.

Shannon, David A. "Neither Progressive nor a Party." *New Leader,* April 3, 1961, 23–24.

Sheean, Vincent. "Why I Will Not Vote for Wallace." *Saturday Evening Post,* September 18, 1948, 23, 153–55.

Shogan, Robert. "1948 Election." *American Heritage* 19 (June 1968): 22–31, 104–11.

Sirevåg, Torbjørn. "The Dilemma of the American Left in the Cold War Years: The Case of Henry A. Wallace." In *Americana Norvegica: Norwegian Contributions to American Studies,* vol. 4, edited by Brita Seyersted, 399–421. Oslo: Universitets Foralaget, 1973.

Sitkoff, Harvard. "Harry Truman and the Election of 1948: The Coming of Age of Civil Rights in American Politics." *Journal of Southern History* 37 (November 1971): 597–616.

Southern, David W. "*An American Dilemma* Revisited: Myrdalism and White Southern Liberals." *South Atlantic Quarterly* 75 (Spring 1976): 183–97.

Soutou, Georges-Henri. "France." In *The Origins of the Cold War in Europe: International Perspectives,* edited by David Reynolds, 96–120. New Haven: Yale University Press, 1994.

Staritz, Dietrich. "The SED, Stalin, and the German Question: Interests and Decision-Making in the Light of New Sources." *German History* 10 (October 1992): 274–89.

Stein, Judith. "The Ins and Outs of the CIO." *International Labor and Working-Class History* 44 (Fall 1993): 53–63.

———. "Why American Historians Embrace the 'Long Civil Rights Movement.'" *American Communist History* 11 (April 2012): 55–58.

Stephanson, Anders. "The United States." In *The Origins of the Cold War in Europe: International Perspectives*, edited by David Reynolds, 23–52. New Haven: Yale University Press, 1994.

Stevenson, Marshall F., Jr. "Beyond Theoretical Models: The Limited Possibilities of Racial Egalitarianism." *International Labor and Working-Class History* 44 (Fall 1993): 45–52.

Stewart, Kenneth. "Wallace the Symbol." *PM Picture News*, November 9, 1947, 6–9.

Sugrue, Thomas J. "Crabgrass-Roots Politics: Race, Rights, and the Reaction against Liberalism in the Urban North, 1940–1964." *Journal of American History* 82 (September 1995): 551–78.

———. "Reassessing the History of Cold War America." *Prospects* 20 (1995): 493–509.

———. "Segmented Work, Race-Conscious Workers: Structure, Agency and Division in the CIO Era." *International Review of Social History* 41 (December 1996): 389–406.

Sullivan, Patricia A. "Proud Days: Henry Wallace's Campaign for the Presidency." *Southern Exposure* 12 (February 1984): 94–98.

Swain, Bruce. "Henry A. Wallace and the 'Guru Letters': A Case of Successful Stonewalling." *Mid-America* 69 (January 1987): 5–19.

Swain, Geoffrey. "The Cominform: Tito's International?" *Historical Journal* 35 (September 1992): 641–63.

Thomas, Brian. "The Cold War and Henry Wallace." *Listener*, September 15, 1966, 377–78.

Thompson, Dorothy. "How I Was Duped by a Communist." *Saturday Evening Post*, April 16, 1949, 19, 73–85.

Tigrid, Pavel. "The Prague Coup of 1948: The Elegant Takeover." In *The Anatomy of Communist Takeovers*, edited by Thomas T. Hammond, 414–19. New Haven: Yale University Press, 1975.

Titus, Charles H., and Charles R. Nixon. "The 1948 Elections in California." *Western Political Quarterly* 2 (March 1949): 97–102.

Trilling, Lionel. "The Repressive Impulse." *Partisan Review* 15 (June 1948): 717–21.

Tugwell, Rexford G. "Open Reply to Mr. Borgese." *Common Cause*, October 1948, 81–84.

———. "Progressives and the Presidency." *Progressive*, April 1949, 5–7.

Van Auken, Cecelia. "The Negro Press in the 1948 Presidential Election." *Journalism Quarterly* 26 (December 1949): 431–35.

Walker, J. Samuel. "'No More Cold War': American Foreign Policy and the 1948 Soviet Peace Offensive." *Diplomatic History* 5 (Winter 1981): 75–91.

Wallace, Henry A. "Henry Wallace Tells of His Political Odyssey." *Life*, May 14, 1956, 174–90.

——. "Henry Wallace Tells: Where I Stand . . . And Where I Stood." *New Leader*, August 26, 1950, 2–4.

——. "How I'd Stop the March of Stalin." *Coronet*, November 1950, 103–08.

——. "I Shall Run in 1948." *Vital Speeches of the Day*, January 1, 1948, 172–74.

——. "The Path to Peace." *Vital Speeches of the Day*, October 1, 1946, 738–41.

——. "Tell the People Who We Are," *Vital Speeches of the Day*, October 1, 1948, 743–45.

——. "Where I Was Wrong." *This Week*, September 7, 1952, 7, 39, 46.

"Wallace's Southern Tour." *Crisis*, October 1948, 297.

Waltzer, Kenneth. "The New History of American Communism." *Reviews in American History* 11 (June 1983): 259–67.

Ward, Paul W. "Wallace the Great Hesitator." *Nation*, May 8, 1935, 535–38.

Wechsler, James A. "Did Truman Scuttle Liberalism? The Progressives' Complaint and the Administration's Record." *Commentary*, March 1947, 222–27.

——. "The Liberal's Vote and 1948: What Price Third Party?" *Commentary*, September 1947, 216–25.

——. "My Ten Months with Wallace." *Progressive*, November 1948, 4–8.

——. "The Philadelphia Pay-Off." *Progressive*, August 1948, 8–10.

——. "What Makes Wallace Run." *Progressive*, February 1948, 19–21.

Weinberg, Jules. "Priests, Workers, and Communists: What Happened in a New York Transit Workers Union." *Harper's*, November 1948, 49–56.

Weinstein, James. "The Grand Illusion." Review of *Them and Us*, by James Matles and James Higgins. *Socialist Revolution* 5 (June 1975): 87–103.

Williams, Samuel W. "People's Progressive Party of Georgia." *Phylon*, Fall 1949, 226–30.

Wilson, Veronica A. "Elizabeth Bentley and Cold War Representation: Some Masks Not Dropped." *Intelligence and National Security* 14 (Summer 1999): 49–69.

Wright, Annette C. "The Aftermath of the General Textile Strike: Managers and the Workplace at Burlington Mills." *Journal of Southern History* 60 (February 1994): 82–112.

Zieger, Robert H. "Déjà Vu All Over Again." *American Communist History* 11 (April 2012): 59–62.

——. "Labor-Liberalism Lost." *Labor History* 37 (Summer 1996): 352–57.

——. "The Popular Front Rides Again." In *Political Power and Social Theory: A Research Annual*, vol. 4, edited by Maurice Zeitlin and Howard Kimeldorf, 297–302. Greenwich, Conn.: JAI Press, 1984.

DISSERTATIONS AND THESES

Ayer, Douglas Richard. "American Liberalism and British Socialism in a Cold War World, 1945–1951." Ph.D. diss., Stanford University, 1983.

Brown, John Cotton. "The 1948 Progressive Campaign: A Scientific Approach." Ph.D. diss., University of Chicago, 1949.

Call, Kenneth L. "A Study in Group Support of the Independent Progressive Party of California, 1947–48." M.A. thesis, University of Redlands, 1955.

Cannon, Robert. "The Organization and Growth of Black Political Participation in Durham, North Carolina, 1933–1958." Ph.D. diss., University of North Carolina, Chapel Hill, 1975.

Carter, Robert F. "Pressure from the Left: The American Labor Party, 1936–1954." Ph.D. diss., Syracuse University, 1965.

Cary, Lorin Lee. "Adolph Germer: From Labor Activist to Labor Professional." Ph.D. diss., University of Wisconsin, 1968.

Corley, Robert Gaines. "The Quest for Racial Harmony: Race Relations in Birmingham, Alabama, 1947–1963." Ph.D. diss. University of Virginia, 1979.

Fox, John Francis, Jr. "'In Passion and in Hope': The Pilgrimage of an American Radical, Martha Dodd Stern and Family, 1933–1990." Ph.D. diss., University of New Hampshire, 2001.

Gallagher, Steven. "Walking the Tightrope": Americans for Democratic Action in the South, 1947–1963." Ph.D. diss., University of Florida, 2008.

Hasting, Ann Celeste. "Intraparty Struggle: Harry S. Truman, 1945–1948." Ph.D. diss., St. Louis University, 1971.

Henderson, Lloyd Ray. "Earl Warren and California Politics." Ph.D. diss., University of California, Berkeley, 1965.

Hinchey, Mary Hedge. "The Frustration of the New Deal Revival, 1944–1946." Ph.D. diss., University of Missouri, 1965.

Kellogg, Peter J. "Northern Liberals and Black America: A History of White Attitudes, 1936–1952." Ph.D. diss., Northwestern University, 1971.

King, Robert G. "The Rhetoric of Henry Agard Wallace." Ph.D. diss., Columbia University, 1964.

Korstad, Robert Rogers. "'Daybreak of Freedom': Tobacco Workers and the CIO, Winston-Salem, North Carolina, 1943–1950." Ph.D. diss., University of North Carolina, Chapel Hill, 1987.

Lenburg, LeRoy J. "The CIO and American Foreign Policy, 1935–1955." Ph.D. diss., Pennsylvania State University, 1973.

Maxfield, Charles Robert, Jr. "The Progressive Party of 1948: A Crisis for Liberals as Seen in Basic Left-Wing Publications." M.A. thesis, Wayne State University, 1966.

McCoy, Robert Edwin. "Labor in Politics: The CIO-PAC in California, 1938–1948." M.A. thesis, Stanford University, 1949.

Moremen, Merrill Raymond. "The Independent Progressive Party in California, 1948." M.A. thesis, Stanford University, 1950.

Newberry, Anthony Lake. "Without Urgency or Ardor: The South's Middle-of-the-road Liberals and Civil Rights, 1945–1960." Ph.D. diss, Ohio University, 1982.

Persky, Marvin. "Walter Reuther, the UAW-CIO, and Third Party Politics." Ph.D. diss., Michigan State University, 1974.

Roper, Eugene A., Jr. "The CIO Organizing Committee in Mississippi: June, 1946–January, 1949." M.A. thesis, University of Mississippi, 1949.

Sullivan, Patricia A. "Gideon's Southern Soldiers." Ph.D. diss., Emory University, 1983.

Waltzer, Kenneth. "The American Labor Party: Third Party Politics in New Deal–Cold War New York, 1936–1954." Ph.D. diss., Harvard University, 1977.

Weiler, Richard M. "Statesmanship, Religion, and the General Welfare: The Rhetoric of Henry A. Wallace." Ph.D. diss., University of Pittsburgh, 1979.

GOVERNMENT DOCUMENTS

California Legislature. Senate. *Fifth Report on Un-American Activities in California, 1949.* Sacramento: Senate of the State of California, 1949.

U.S. Congress. House. Committee on Foreign Affairs. *Hearings Regarding United States Foreign Policy for a Post-war Recovery Program.* 80th Cong., 2nd. sess., 1948. Washington: Government Printing Office, 1948.

U.S. Congress. House. Committee on Un-American Activities. *Hearings Regarding Communist Espionage in the United States Government.* 80th Cong., 2nd sess., 1948. Washington: Government Printing Office, 1948.

——. *Hearings Regarding Communism in the United States Government, Part 2.* 81st Cong., 2nd sess., 1949. Washington: Government Printing Office, 1949.

——. *Hearings Regarding Communist Activities in the Dayton, Ohio Area.* 83rd Cong., 2nd sess., 1954. Washington: Government Printing Office, 1954.

——. *Hearings Regarding Communist Activities in the Los Angeles, Calif. Area— Part 7.* 84th Cong., 2nd sess., 1954. Washington: Government Printing Office, 1954.

——. *Hearings Regarding Communist Activities in the San Francisco Area— Part 3.* 83rd Cong., 1st sess., 1954. Washington: Government Printing Office, 1954.

——. *Hearings Regarding Communist Activities in the San Francisco Area— Part 4.* 83rd Cong., 1st sess., 1954. Washington: Government Printing Office, 1954.

——. *Hearings Regarding Communist Activities in the Pacific Northwest Area.* 83rd Cong., 2nd sess., 1954. Washington: Government Printing Office, 1954.

——. *Hearings Regarding Communist Activities in the State of California—Part 9.* 83rd Cong., 2nd sess., 1954. Washington: Government Printing Office, 1954.

——. *Hearings Regarding Communist Activities in the State of California—Part 10.* 83rd Cong., 2nd sess., 1954. Washington: Government Printing Office, 1954.

——. *Hearings Regarding Communist Activities in the State of California—Part 11.* 83rd Cong., 2nd sess., 1954. Washington: Government Printing Office, 1954.

——. *Hearings Regarding Communist Methods of Infiltration (Entertainment— Part 1).* 83rd Cong., 2nd sess., 1954. Washington: Government Printing Office, 1954.

——. *Report 1135: Proceedings against Martin Popper.* 86th Cong., 1st sess., 1959. Washington: Government Printing Office, 1959.

U.S. Department of State. *1948: Eastern Europe; the Soviet Union.* Vol. 4 of *Foreign Relations of the United States.* Washington: Government Printing Office, 1948.

U.S. Department of State. *The Conference of Berlin, 1945.* Vol. 1 of *Foreign Relations of the United States.* Washington: Government Printing Office, 1945.

U.S. Department of State. *Europe, 1945.* Vol. 5 of *Foreign Relations of the United States.* Washington: Government Printing Office, 1945.

Washington State Legislature. Joint Legislative Fact-Finding Committee on Un-American Activities. *Un-American Activities in Washington State, Report One.* Olympia: Senate of the State of Washington, 1948.

Washington State Legislature. Joint Legislative Fact-Finding Committee on Un-American Activities. *Un-American Activities in Washington State, Report Two.* Olympia: Senate of the State of Washington, 1948.

ACKNOWLEDGMENTS

I have received much assistance in the writing of this book, and it is a pleasure finally to acknowledge those who have helped me along the way. Numerous archivists at scores of repositories around the United States facilitated the research process. I am particularly grateful to the Special Collections staff at the University of Iowa, who saw to my every need and slyly pointed out that one of the copying machines was not deducting money from the pay cards. Several individuals, many of them now deceased, shared their memories of the 1948 campaign with me: Daniel Aaron, Robert Bendiner, Lillian Gates, Irwin Ross, Arthur M. Schlesinger Jr., George B. Tindall, Theodore F. Watts, and Nancy Wechsler. Norma Starobin, while searching for a recipe for gazpacho soup, came across her late husband's notes taken at Communist Party meetings during the late 1940s, and kindly allowed me to consult them. Harvey Klehr directed me to several important documents in the Philip Jaffe Papers at Emory University. Peter Filene, Michael Hunt, and Roger Lotchin at the University of North Carolina at Chapel Hill provided detailed feedback that significantly improved the manuscript. So, too, did John Earl Haynes, the Twentieth-Century Librarian at the Library of Congress. At various points during the revision process, John Broesamle, Alonzo Hamby, Donal O'Sullivan, Ronald Radosh, and W. J. Rorabaugh shared insights from their own work that helped me to sharpen my arguments.

On the financial side, a Mellon Foundation research fellowship, a Doris G. Quinn fellowship, and two George E. Mowry research grants defrayed travel expenses and gave me an extended and uninterrupted period that I could devote entirely to research and writing. Several summer stipends and research grants from the College of Social and Behavioral Sciences at California State University, Northridge, assisted me in the later stages of this project.

I am sure there are many people who thought this book would never be finished. I count myself among them. Chuck Grench, my able and patient editor at the University of North Carolina Press, also comes to mind. More than anyone, I thank him for remaining committed to this project. I shudder to think how many times he must have been tempted to cut me loose. Paul Betz shepherded the manuscript through the various stages of production, and Petra Dreiser proved a careful and meticulous copyeditor. William L. O'Neill and Robert H. Zieger offered wise criticisms and unwarranted compliments in their reviews for UNC Press. I took both in the spirit they were offered and hope the final product demonstrates how much I valued their close reading of my work.

When this project began, I was a Philadelphian, late of Georgetown, improbably masquerading as a Tar Heel. As it ends, I am a transplanted easterner who, equally improbably, has come to love LA. My identity has transformed in more ways than one, however. Arriving at California State University, Northridge, I saw myself as a "scholar-teacher." After only a short time interacting with CSUN students, I realized that I was far happier being a "teacher-scholar." This shift in priorities accounts in part for why it took so long to get this book to press, but it was a trade-off I was happy to make. I thank my students for their attention, engagement, and hard work. The hours I've spent with them in and out of the classroom have been among the most reward-ing in my professional life. If you are a former student of mine now reading this, yes, I do remember you; yes, I'd love to hear from you; and, yes, you really should buy this book. In particular, I want to acknowledge one student, Mason Palmer, who gave the manuscript a thorough read and caught several errors I had somehow overlooked. Regrettably, Mason did not live to see this book in print, but I will not soon forget his biting wit, delightful irreverence, and all the laughs we shared during hikes through Will Rogers State Park.

During my time at CSUN, Provost Harry Hellenbrand, Dean Stella Theodoulou, and my chairs—Charles Macune, Tom Maddux, and Richard Horowitz—have offered en-couragement, wry remarks aplenty, and financial support, even when funds were tight. Indeed, publication of this book was made possible, in part, by a generous subvention from the College of Social and Behavioral Sciences and the Office of the Provost. My colleagues in the History Department, past and present, have made the sixth floor of Si-erra Tower a most welcoming and congenial place to work. Shiva Bajpai taught me that I must "celebrate my limitations." Ron Davis imparted shrewd advice and reminded me how important it is to laugh at the world's absurdities. Joyce Broussard helped me keep things in perspective and every so often suggested that I might want to get some sleep. Merry Ovnick overwhelmed me with her generosity and kindness. Steve Bourque, Patricia Juarez-Dappe, and Miriam Neirick provided humor and moral sup-port throughout the long revision process. Jim Sefton, in his inimitable way, insisted that I "do things right" and, equally important, told me to avoid doing things that were "profoundly stupid." Two of my favorite people, Sue Mueller and Kelly Winkleblack-Shea, looked after me and, when necessary, covered my tracks.

Serious eye troubles have made the final stages of this process particularly challeng-ing in a number of ways. Dr. Farzin Avaz saved my vision—first in one eye, and then in the other. In fact, as I have told him, he saved my life, or at least my life as I wanted to live it. How does one say "thank you" for that? As a first installment of payback, this book is co-dedicated to him. Luckily, Kaiser-Permanente is making all the other payments. As I slowly recovered, a legion of colleagues, students, former students, and friends have looked in on me, provided books on tape, sent warm words of encouragement, and never hesitated to laugh when they saw me bump into things. I thank them all. For their unfailing support—both emotional and logistical—throughout an extremely difficult period of time, I am profoundly grateful to Karen Abramowitz, James Adams, Kathleen Addison, Laura Arrowsmith, Julia Bricklin, John Broesamle, Andrea Cohen, Karen Drohan, Erik Greenberg, Samantha Jones, Matthew Lucas, Tom Maddux, Art Nelson, Merry Ovnick, Anne Robison, Jeremiah Sladeck, Neil Thompson, and Nan Ya-mane. I especially thank Jeff Kaja, my colleague and, for a time, designated chauffeur. His unique blend of mordant humor, foreboding pessimism, and, to be fair, occasional kindness sustained me as I groped my way to the finish line. I'm not yet sure how I'm going to repay him, but I am certain that he has kept a careful account of what is owed.

This book is co-dedicated to William E. Leuchtenburg, who has been behind me and my work since day one. His encouragement, enthusiasm, and good humor kept me going even through the rough patches. Scores of other scholars whom he has mentored can attest to Professor Leuchtenburg's exceptional editorial skills and magisterial knowledge of twentieth-century U.S. history; but it has been his intellectual integrity and common decency as a person that I have come to admire most. At a time when the phrase "role model" is tossed around far too casually, William E. Leuchtenburg, in his scholarship, in his teaching, and in his commitment to civility and the free exchange of ideas, has long been the genuine article. In my professional life, I am who I am because of his influence, example, and support.

Most of my friends and relatives have no idea what this book is about, let alone why I would have spent so much time on it, and that's perfectly all right. I like living a life that has various compartments and was quite content not to have Henry Wallace occupying all of them. Nonetheless, I appreciate the lodging, food, conversation, and fun that so many offered throughout the years as I passed through town on a "research trip." Two, however, were not so lucky: Rob Giuntoli, my roommate in Chapel Hill who had to live with Wallace for four years, and, as a result, knows far more about the Progressive Party than any gynecological oncologist really should; and Kevin Mundy, who patiently endured my ramblings about the 1948 election when we weren't discussing the decidedly uneven performance of the Phillies lineup. Thanks, guys. I'm sure having your names appear in the acknowledgments more than makes up for Henry's intrusion into your lives.

Finally, from across the country, my parents, Thomas and Anne Marie Devine, have closely followed the evolution of this project. Before that, they closely followed the evolution of me, which, I'm given to understand, was far more challenging. I really don't have the words to thank them for all that they have done for me or to express all that they have meant to me, but I trust they know how grateful I am.

INDEX

Brotherhood of Sleeping Car Porters, 61–62

Browder, Earl, xiii, 3–7, 13, 126, 239

Browderism, 6, 7, 13, 14, 125, 186, 213, 218, 292

Brown, Earl, 184

Brown, Edgar G., 150

Brown, John Cotton, 137, 139–42, 175

Browning, Alfred, 44

Brownstein, Ronald, 12

Bryan, William Jennings, 47, 171

Bryson, Hugh, 21, 23, 32, 84, 161–62, 220

Buchanan, Frank, 273

Buchanan, Scott, 134–35, 137, 152, 162–64

Bulletin of the Information Bureau of the CCVKP(b): Issues of Foreign Policy, 4–5, 294 (n.7)

Burnham, Louis, 260–61, 346 (n. 83)

Byrnes, James F., 151

Cadden, Joseph, 205

Cambridge spies, 35

Cameron, Angus, 192

Cannon, Charles, 258

Carey, James, 134, 137

Cassidy, Jack, 211

Chamberlin, William Henry, 154, 230

Chambers, Whittaker, 146, 226

Charney, George, 14, 17, 26, 76

Chatham, Thurmond, 238

Chiakulas, Charles, 209–10

Childs, Marquis, 167

Childs, Morris, 18–19, 298 (n. 42)

Churchill, Winston, 6, 218

Cochran, Bert, 219

Coe, John M., 148, 234

Colmer, William M., 99

Cominform (Information Bureau of the Communist Parties), 25–27, 35, 41, 110–11, 130, 139, 177, 299 (n. 59)

Communist Party of the United States (CPUSA): in California, 10–11, 23–25, 83–84, 187–90; and CIO, 27–33, 63, 84, 93–94, 160–61, 211–26, 247–48, 273, 337 (nn. 44, 47); influence at Progressive Party convention, 127–28, 154–55, 159–67, 170–71, 173–78, 184–85, 195–96, 326 (n. 80), 330 (n. 50); and Leo Isacson campaign, 74, 79–81; loss of influence after 1948, 287; and 1948 coup in Czechoslovakia, 111–14, 317 (nn. 43, 46); and origins of Progressive Party, xiii, 2–3, 14, 16–19, 26–27, 32–33, 40, 48–49; and Palestine partition, 74–76; Popular Front strategy of, xii–xiii, 6–8, 25, 141, 143, 186, 291–92, 332 (n. 15); post-Duclos line of, xii, 6–20 passim, 25, 34, 37, 65, 126–27, 134, 137, 185–86, 216, 219, 297 (n. 32); rejects Wallace's "progressive capitalism," 151, 186, 258, 291; response to Wallace's candidacy, 63–64; in South, 237–38, 241, 247, 259, 266–67; and Soviet Union, xiii, 1–2, 13, 18–19, 26, 217–18, 330 (n. 55)

Communist Political Association (CPA), 3–4, 6. *See also* Communist Party of the United States

Congress of Industrial Organizations (CIO), 8, 14, 21, 133–34, 137, 160–61, 275, 284; August 1948 Executive Board meeting, 221–26; 1947 National Convention, 29–31, 62; opposes Progressive Party, 28–33, 54, 62–63, 90–92, 200, 211–21; in South, 234–35, 238–39, 247–48, 250–51, 255, 257–58, 266–68, 272–73, 348 (n. 104), 349 (n. 110)

CIO Industrial Union Councils (IUCs), 14, 21, 84, 91–94, 133, 214–17

CIO Political Action Committee (CIO-PAC), 10–11, 36, 38, 214, 239, 248

Congress of Racial Equality (CORE), 350 (n. 130)

Connelly, Philip, 11

Connor, Theophilus Eugene ("Bull"), 251–52

62–63, 91–93, 160, 210–11, 213–16, 218, 273; speaks at August 1948 CIO Executive Board meeting, 221–26

amendment, 173–77, 330 (n. 50);
defeat of, 286–92; defections from,
186–99 passim, 271, 276–78; fall
campaign, 270–71, 276–78, 283–85;
and HUAC hearings, 227–29,
239; National Convention, 123,
126–27, 156–79; in North Carolina,
235–49, 341 (n. 13); platform of,
131–55 passim, 172–79; withdrawal of
congressional candidates, 272–76
Propper, Karl, 72, 74–81
Public opinion polls, 23, 39, 55–56,
121–22, 124–26, 168–69, 209, 212,
228, 262, 284, 286, 305 (nn. 42, 43),
320 (n. 2), 336 (n. 33)

Quill, Michael, 31–33, 62–63, 75, 211–12,
220, 224, 301 (n. 74), 306 (n. 57)

Rabin, Benjamin J., 72
Rainey, Joseph H., 165
Ramsey, David, 105, 134
Randolph, A. Philip, 61, 211
Rankin, John, 228, 270
Rauh, Joseph, 124
Rayburn, Sam, 118
Redding, Jack, 80
Reece, B. Carroll, 59
Reed Farm, 229–30
Reston, James, 120
Reuther, Walter P., 30, 32, 62, 87–88,
214, 221, 300 (n. 72)
Richards, James P., 98
Robeson, Paul, 69, 75, 153, 166–67, 288
Rogers, Will, Jr., 10–11
Rohrer, Charles, 142
Romero, Frederico, 107
Roosevelt, Eleanor, 48, 68–69, 75, 77, 80,
104, 205, 346 (n. 80)
Roosevelt, Franklin D., x–xi, 8, 15–17,
22, 30, 44, 46, 63, 68, 84–85, 93–94,
168, 184, 186, 198, 212, 222, 226, 265,
283, 307 (n. 60)
Roosevelt, James, 9, 12
Ross, Irwin, 131, 175, 285

Rothstein, Ida, 84
Ruark, Robert, 230, 250
Rubin, Morris, 207
Russia. *See* Soviet Union
Ryan, James, 133

Sage, Samuel, 215
Savage, Charles, 56–57
Savage, Gus, 206
Scales, Junius, 237
Schapsmeier, Edward and Frederick, 175,
313 (n. 15)
Schmidt, Karl M., 96, 206
Schuman, Frederick L., 151–54, 157, 175,
180, 192
Scott, Lawrence, 210
Seeger, Pete, 165, 242
Segure, Rose, 190
Shachtman, Max, 185
Shannon, David A., 46, 126, 151
Sheean, Vincent, 207
Sherbell, Kenneth, 54
Shikes, Ralph, 127, 166
Sinclair, Upton, 187
Sloane, Allan E., 170–71
Smith, Alfred E., 289
Smith, Edwin S., 17, 297 (n. 35)
Smith, Harold, 44
Smith, Jessica, 37
Smith, Lawrence H., 99
Smith, L. G., 245
Smith, Lillian, 254
Smith, Walter Bedell, 119–20, 122
Smith-Molotov Exchange, 118–22
Socialist Party, xi
Sorokin, Valentin, 53
Southern Conference for Human Welfare
(SCHW), 236, 241, 251–52, 261, 346
(n. 80)
Southern Negro Youth Congress (SNYC),
251–52
Soviet Union: and Kasenkina affair,
229–31; position on Progressive
Party, 18–19, 33, 53, 122, 319 (n. 70);
post–World War II foreign policy,

5–6, 8, 13, 26, 97, 138–39, 324 (n. 60)

Sparks, Nemmy, 9–10, 24–25, 84, 295 (n. 20)

Sperling, Milton, 9

Stachel, Jack, 20, 218

Stalin, Josef, ix–x, xiii, 5, 13, 17, 23, 26, 62, 67–68, 88, 96, 101, 151, 177, 282, 294 (n. 6); exchange of letters with Wallace, 119–22

Starobin, Joseph, 14–15, 26, 64, 83, 113, 174, 182, 185–86, 287, 289

States Rights Democratic Party. *See* Dixiecrats

Stearns, Arthur F., 155

Steefel, Genevieve, 174, 194–95

Steel, Johannes, 14, 73

Stein, Leonard, 162

Steinhardt, Laurence, 112–13, 317 (n. 46)

Stephanson, Anders, 106

Stern, Alfred K., 52–53, 288

Stern, Martha Dodd, 53, 288

Stewart, Kenneth, 97

Stokes, Thomas L., 157

Stone, I. F., 66, 100, 271

Storch, Philip, 57

Stover, Fred, 164

Straight, Michael, 35–37, 39, 45, 47, 70, 288

Students for a Democratic Society (SDA), 204–5

Sullivan, Gael, 67

Sweezy, Paul, 134–35, 137

Taft, Robert A., 25, 43, 56, 59, 78

Taft-Hartley Act, 28, 56, 134, 222, 225, 247

Taylor, Dora, 85

Taylor, Glen H., 159, 197, 203, 229, 289; campaign stop in Alabama, 251–52; foreign policy views of, 84–87, 153, 167; joins Progressive Party ticket, 84–85, 87, 148; at Progressive Party convention, 123, 128, 131, 164, 167–68, 183

Taylor, Paul, 189

Tenney, B. Jack, 187–88

Tenney Committee (California), 187–89

Textile Workers Union of America (TWUA), 30

Thomas, Cedric, 142, 148–49

Thomas, Norman, xi, 58, 105, 157, 167, 185, 198

Thompson, Dorothy, 130, 164, 181, 206

Thompson, Robert, 31–33, 81

Thurmond, J. Strom, 242, 265

Tindall, George B., 267

Tito, Josip Broz, 8, 126, 130, 177–78, 197–98, 320 (n. 9)

Tolstoy, Alexandria, 229

Toward World Peace, 70

Townsend, Francis E., 132

Townsend, Willard, 82

Transport Workers Union of America (TWU), 31, 33, 62, 211–12, 224

Traugott, Lillian, 41, 303 (n. 14)

Troy, Smith, 56

Truman, Harry S, ix–x, 16–18, 21–23, 28–30, 35, 39, 44, 56, 61–62, 67–68, 71, 74, 86, 92, 120–21, 123, 146, 151–52, 166, 168, 211–12, 215, 217–18, 223–25, 231–32, 238, 248–49, 270–71, 278, 289; and civil rights, 124–25, 254, 262–66, 287–88; CPUSA criticism of, 7–8; and HUAC hearings, 226, 228; and Palestine partition, 75–78, 309 (n. 11); response to 1948 coup in Czechoslovakia, 108–9; on Wallace's candidacy, 60–61, 80, 116; and "war scare" of March 1948, 116–18

Truman Doctrine, xiii–xiv, 5, 23, 57, 81, 110, 138, 274–75

Trumbo, Dalton, 9, 277

Tugwell, Rexford G., 66, 198–99; and drafting of Progressive Party platform, 131–48 passim, 152, 172, 178; and Puerto Rican independence, 144–46; withdraws from Progressive Party, 195–96, 232, 290, 333 (n. 37)

Turpin, Sally, 181

United Auto Workers (UAW), 20, 30, 32, 62, 211, 214

United Electrical Workers (UE), 31, 162, 211, 218, 271, 273

United Nations, 68–69, 96, 101, 279–80; and Palestine partition, 75–76

United Nations Relief and Recovery Administration (UNRRA), 97–98, 100–101, 119, 131, 313 (n. 9)

United Office and Professional Workers Association, 202

United Packinghouse Workers of America (UPWA), 213

United Retail, Wholesale, and Department Store Employees, 93

United Steelworkers of America (USWA), 210–11, 220

Universal Military Training (UMT), 56, 109, 131, 209

Valentine, Anthony, 238

Vandenberg, Arthur, 105

Vassiliev, Alexander, 53

Venona (National Security Agency project), xiii, 14, 226–27, 239

Vronsky, B., 18–19

Walker, Christine, 202–4

Walker, J. Samuel, 120–21

Wallace, Henry A.: attacks Truman Administration, x, xiv, 5, 15–18, 41, 65–66, 116–18, 168, 221, 231–32, 274–75, 278–79; CPUSA recruits, as third party candidate, 32–33, 35–40, 48–49, 54; decides to run as third party candidate, 41, 49, 57–59; and drafting of Progressive Party platform, 133–34, 145–46, 153; as editor of the *New Republic*, 18, 35–36, 40, 44–45, 70; European officials criticize, 102–4; and "Guru letters," ix, 129–30, 321 (n. 16); and HUAC hearings, 227–29; and Madison Square Garden address (1946), 17–18, 48, 102; and organized labor, 54, 94, 212, 221, 270–71; and Palestine partition, 75–78; passive role in Progressive Party campaign, 183–84, 280–81; press criticism of, 62–64, 99–105, 128–31, 170–72, 181–83, 197–98, 241–42, 257, 280, 282–83; at Progressive Party convention, 123, 128–31, 159, 164, 168–72, 180; reacts to 1948 election results, 287; relies heavily on advisors, 43–44, 114; southern tour, ix–x, xiv, 233–35, 242–56, 259–60; at YPA convention, 203–4

—views of: on Communists, 37, 45–47, 63, 126, 128–29, 194–95, 197, 231, 287–89, 343 (n. 36); on economic policy, 151, 253, 256–58, 313 (n. 5); on segregation, xiii–xiv, 124–25, 240–41, 243–44, 253, 255, 260–62, 269–70; on U.S.-Soviet relations, xiii–xiv, 58–59, 66–68, 95, 130–31, 168–70, 279–82, 284–85, 307 (n. 64), 313 (n. 15)

Wallace, Ilo, 53

Walsh, J. Raymond, 51–52

Wanamaker, Sam, 165, 168

Warren, Earl, 11

Warren, Frank A., 102

Washington, Harold, 206

Watt, Richard T., 135

Weber, Palmer, 236, 250, 252, 259–60

Wechsler, James A., 58, 113, 133, 163, 171, 175, 178, 183, 249, 261, 280–81, 290

Weinstein, Allen, 53

Weinstein, James, 218

Weir, Ernest T., 105

Welsh, William, 209

West, Rebecca, 128, 130

Wheeler, Burton K., 42

White, Harry Dexter, 228–29, 340 (n. 75)

White, Theodore, 45

Whitney, A. F., 28, 48, 61

Wholesale and Warehouse Workers Union, 54